Microsoft® 365 Modern Desktop Administrator Guide to
Exam MD-100: Windows® 10

BYRON WRIGHT
LEON PLESNIARSKI

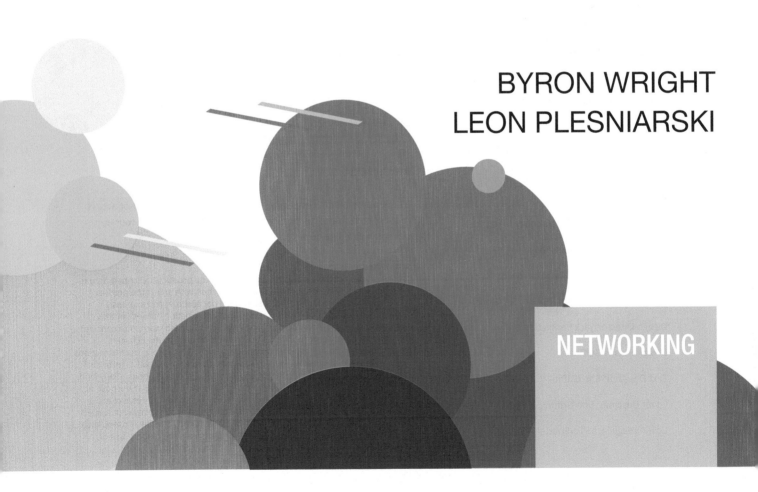

NETWORKING

 CENGAGE

Australia • Brazil • Canada • Mexico • Singapore • United Kingdom • United States

Microsoft® 365 Modern Desktop Administrator Guide to Exam MD-100: Windows® 10
Byron Wright and Leon Plesniarski

SVP, Higher Education Product Management: Erin Joyner

VP, Product Management: Thais Alencar

Product Team Manager: Kristin McNary

Product Manager: Danielle Klahr

Product Assistant: Tom Benedetto

Director, Learning Design: Rebecca von Gillern

Senior Manager, Learning Design: Leigh Hefferon

Learning Designer: Natalie Onderdonk

Vice President, Marketing – Science, Technology, & Math: Jason Sakos

Senior Marketing Director: Michele McTighe

Product Specialist: Mackenzie Paine

Director, Content Creation: Juliet Steiner

Senior Manager, Content Creation: Patty Stephan

Content Manager: Christina Nyren

Director, Digital Production Services: Krista Kellman

Digital Delivery Lead: Jim Vaughey

Technical Editor: Danielle Shaw

Developmental Editor: Lyn Markowicz

Production Service/Composition: SPi Global

Design Director: Jack Pendleton

Designer: Erin Griffin

Text Designer: Erin Griffin

Cover Designer: Erin Griffin

Cover image(s): sollia/ShutterStock.com

For product information and technology assistance, contact us at
**Cengage Customer & Sales Support, 1-800-354-9706
or support.cengage.com.**

For permission to use material from this text or product, submit all requests online at **www.cengage.com/permissions.**

Library of Congress Control Number: 2020922799

ISBN: 978-0-357-50175-7

Cengage
200 Pier 4 Boulevard
Boston, MA 02210
USA

Cengage is a leading provider of customized learning solutions with employees residing in nearly 40 different countries and sales in more than 125 countries around the world. Find your local representative at: **www.cengage.com.**

To learn more about Cengage platforms and services, register or access your online learning solution, or purchase materials for your course, visit **www.cengage.com.**

Notice to the Reader
Publisher does not warrant or guarantee any of the products described herein or perform any independent analysis in connection with any of the product information contained herein. Publisher does not assume, and expressly disclaims, any obligation to obtain and include information other than that provided to it by the manufacturer. The reader is expressly warned to consider and adopt all safety precautions that might be indicated by the activities described herein and to avoid all potential hazards. By following the instructions contained herein, the reader willingly assumes all risks in connection with such instructions. The publisher makes no representations or warranties of any kind, including but not limited to, the warranties of fitness for particular purpose or merchantability, nor are any such representations implied with respect to the material set forth herein, and the publisher takes no responsibility with respect to such material. The publisher shall not be liable for any special, consequential, or exemplary damages resulting, in whole or part, from the readers' use of, or reliance upon, this material.

Printed at CLDPC, USA, 02-24

BRIEF CONTENTS

INTRODUCTION XI

MODULE 1
Introduction to Windows 10 1

MODULE 2
Using the System Utilities 25

MODULE 3
User Management 67

MODULE 4
Networking 101

MODULE 5
Managing Disks and File Systems 163

MODULE 6
Windows 10 Security Features 213

MODULE 7
User Productivity Tools 261

MODULE 8
Windows 10 Application Support 297

MODULE 9
Performance Tuning and System Recovery 321

MODULE 10
Enterprise Computing 359

MODULE 11
Managing Enterprise Clients 385

MODULE 12
Automating Windows 10 Deployment 415

APPENDIX A
Microsoft Windows Exam MD-100 Objectives 449

APPENDIX B
Preparing for Certification Exams 453

GLOSSARY **454**

INDEX **468**

BRIEF CONTENTS

INTRODUCTION xi

MODULE 1
Introduction to Windows 10 1

MODULE 2
Using the System Utilities 25

MODULE 3
User Management 67

MODULE 4
Networking 101

MODULE 5
Managing Disks and File Systems 163

MODULE 6
Windows 10 Security Features 213

MODULE 7
User Productivity Tools 281

MODULE 8
Windows 10 Application Support 327

MODULE 9
Performance Tuning and System Recovery 371

MODULE 10
Enterprise Computing 399

MODULE 11
Managing Enterprise Clients 383

MODULE 12
Automating Windows 10 Deployment 415

APPENDIX A-4
Microsoft Windows Exam MD-100 Objectives 449

APPENDIX B
Preparing for Certification Exams 452

GLOSSARY 454

INDEX 456

TABLE OF CONTENTS

INTRODUCTION   XI

MODULE 1

INTRODUCTION TO WINDOWS 10   1

Understanding Operating Systems   1
- Operating System Architecture   2
- Windows 10 Extras   2
- Alternative Operating Systems   3

Windows 10 Editions   3
- Windows 10 Home   3
- Windows 10 Pro   4
- Windows 10 Pro for Workstations   4
- Windows 10 Enterprise   4
- Windows 10 Enterprise LTSC   5
- Windows 10 Education Editions   5
- Windows 10 N & KN Editions   5
- 32-Bit Versions   6

Installing Windows 10   6
- Hardware Requirements   6
- DVD Boot Installation   7
- Upgrading to Windows 10   9
- Edition Upgrades   9

Licensing Windows 10   10

Activating Windows 10   10
- OEM and FPP License Activation   10
- Volume License Activation   11
- Troubleshooting MAK Activation   12
- Troubleshooting KMS Activation   12
- Troubleshooting Active Directory-Based Activation   13

Using Windows 10   14
- Lock Screen   14
- Start Menu   15
- Search Interface   16
- Taskbar   16
- Notification Area   17
- Advanced Window Management   18

Windows 10 Networking Models   19
- Workgroup Model   20
- Domain Model   20
- Azure AD Join   21

SUMMARY   22

KEY TERMS   22

REVIEW QUESTIONS   22

CASE PROJECTS   24

MODULE 2

USING THE SYSTEM UTILITIES   25

Settings Overview   25

Administrative Tools   29
- Microsoft Management Console   31
- Computer Management   32
- Services   33

Command-Line Administration Tools   36
- Command Prompt   36
- Windows PowerShell   37

Display   41
- Display Settings   41
- Visual Effects   43
- Desktop Backgrounds   44
- Screen Savers   44
- Multiple Monitors   45

Managing Optional Features   46

Hardware Management   48
- Device Drivers   48
- Device Driver Compatibility   49
- Device Manager   49
- Device Driver Signing   51
- Hardware Component Installation   52

Power Management   53
- ACPI States   54
- Modern Standby   54
- Legacy Power Management   55
- Power Plans   55
- Fast Startup   57
- Power Button Options   57
- Troubleshooting Power Management   58

Task Scheduler   60

SUMMARY   63

KEY TERMS   64

REVIEW QUESTIONS   64

CASE PROJECTS   66

MODULE 3

USER MANAGEMENT   67

User Accounts   67
- Sign-In Methods   68
- Naming Conventions   72

Default User Accounts 72
Default Groups 74
Creating and Managing User Accounts 75
Accounts 76
User Accounts Applet 78
Local Users and Groups MMC Snap-In 79
Command-Line User Management 83
Managing User Profiles 84
The Default Profile 85
Mandatory Profiles 86
Roaming Profiles 86
Folder Redirection 87
The Public Profile 87
Start Menu and Taskbar Customization 88
Advanced Authentication Methods 90
Picture Password 90
Windows Hello PIN 90
Windows Hello Biometric Authentication 91
Windows Hello for Business 92
Security Key 92
Dynamic Lock 93
Smart Cards 93
Network Integration 94
Peer-to-Peer Networks 94
Domain-Based Networks 95
Cached Credentials 95
Azure AD Join 96
SUMMARY 97
KEY TERMS 97
REVIEW QUESTIONS 98
CASE PROJECTS 99

MODULE 4

NETWORKING 101

Networking Overview 101
Network and Internet Settings 102
Network and Sharing Center 102
Remembered Networks 103
Connections 106
IP VERSION 4 109
IPv4 Addresses 109
Subnet Masks 110
Default Gateways 112
DNS 112
WINS 112

Methods for Configuring IPv4 113
Essential Networking Tools 116
Troubleshooting IPv4 120
IP VERSION 6 123
IPv6 Address Notation 123
IPv6 Address Types 123
Methods for Configuring IPv6 125
Troubleshooting IPv6 Settings 128
INTERNET CONNECTIVITY 129
Single-Computer Internet Connectivity 129
Shared Internet Connectivity 130
WIRELESS NETWORKING 134
Creating a Wireless Connection 135
Managing Wireless Connections 137
Troubleshooting Wireless Connections 140
WINDOWS DEFENDER FIREWALL 143
Basic Firewall Configuration 144
Advanced Firewall Configuration 146
SUMMARY 158
KEY TERMS 158
REVIEW QUESTIONS 159
CASE PROJECTS 161

MODULE 5

MANAGING DISKS AND FILE SYSTEMS 163

DISK TECHNOLOGY 164
Internal Disk 164
External Disk 164
Virtual Hard Disk (VHD) 164
Multiple Disks as One Logical Disk 164
DISK PARTITION STYLES 165
DISK TYPES 165
Basic Disks 165
Dynamic Disks 165
Storage Spaces 166
DISK MANAGEMENT TOOLS 167
Disk Management Console 167
DiskPart 167
Storage Cmdlets in Windows PowerShell 169
MANAGING PHYSICAL DISKS 170
Adding a New Drive 170
Moving Drives 171
VIRTUAL DISK MANAGEMENT TASKS 171

Creating VHDs   172
Attaching and Detaching VHDs   173

MANAGING STORAGE SPACES   174

Creating an Initial Storage Pool
and Storage Space   174
Maintaining Storage Pools and Storage
Spaces   176
Configuring Storage Spaces Fault Tolerance   177

FILE SYSTEMS   178

File Allocation Table (FAT)   178
New Technology File System (NTFS)   179
Resilient File System (ReFS)   183
Universal Disk Format (UDF)   184

FILE SYSTEM TASKS   184

Changing Drive Letters   184
Converting File Systems   184

FILE AND FOLDER ATTRIBUTES   185

Managing Attributes   187
Copying and Moving Compressed Files   188

FILE AND FOLDER PERMISSIONS   188

Default Folder Permissions   188
Basic NTFS Permissions   190
Advanced NTFS Permissions   190
Permission Scope   190
Permission Inheritance   192
Effective Permissions   193
Ownership   193
Permission Changes when Content Is
Copied or Moved   194
Permission Strategy Considerations   195

FILE SHARING   196

Sharing Individual Files   196
Sharing the Public Folder   197
Creating and Managing Shared Folders   198
Monitoring Shared Folders   205

SUMMARY   207

KEY TERMS   208

REVIEW QUESTIONS   208

CASE PROJECTS   210

MODULE 6

WINDOWS 10 SECURITY FEATURES 213

Windows 10 Security Policies   213

Account Policies   214
Local Policies   216
AppLocker   217
Software Restriction Policies   223

Other Security Policies   223

Auditing   224

User Account Control   228

Application Manifest   228
UAC Configuration   228

Malware Protection   231

Virus and Threat Protection   232
App & Browser Control   237
Device Security   238

Data Security   239

Encryption Algorithms   240
Encrypting File System   242
BitLocker Drive Encryption   246

Windows Update   251

Servicing Branches   252
Controlling Windows Updates   252
Removing Windows Updates   255
Updating Microsoft Store Apps   256

SUMMARY   257

KEY TERMS   258

REVIEW QUESTIONS   258

CASE PROJECTS   260

MODULE 7

USER PRODUCTIVITY TOOLS   261

File Explorer   261

Ribbon Tabs   262
Libraries   263
Search   264

OneDrive   267

OneDrive Client   267
OneDrive Web Interface   268
Managing Files   270
Sharing Files and Folders   270
Managing Synchronization   270
Controlling Network Utilization   270
Personal Vault   271
OneDrive for Business   271

Printing   273

Printing Scenarios   273
Printer Drivers   274
Printer Management Tools   277
Printer Configuration   281

Browsers   285

Microsoft Edge   285
Security Zones   287

Group Policy Settings for Microsoft Edge   288
IE Mode   289

Accessories and Shortcuts   291

Text Editing   292
Graphics Editing   293

SUMMARY   **294**

KEY TERMS   **294**

REVIEW QUESTIONS   **294**

CASE PROJECTS   **296**

MODULE 8

WINDOWS 10 APPLICATION SUPPORT   297

Application Environments   297

Windows API   298
.NET Framework   299
Universal Windows Platform   299
Legacy Applications   300

The Registry   300

Registry Structure   300
Registry Editing Tools   302

Installing Apps   305

Automating MSI Installation   305
UWP Apps   307
MSIX Deployment   309
Windows 10 in S Mode   310
Microsoft 365 Apps Click-to-Run Deployment   310

App Compatibility   311

Compatibility Settings for Executables   311
Windows ADK Tools   312
Desktop Analytics   314
Client Hyper-V   314
Virtual Desktop Infrastructure and
    RemoteApp   314
App-V   315

Remote Desktop Services   315

RemoteApp   315
Accessing Virtual Desktops and RemoteApp   316
Windows Virtual Desktop   317

SUMMARY   **318**

KEY TERMS   **318**

REVIEW QUESTIONS   **318**

CASE PROJECTS   **320**

MODULE 9

PERFORMANCE TUNING AND SYSTEM RECOVERY   321

Performance Tuning Overview   321

Establishing a Baseline   322
Recognizing Bottlenecks   322
Tuning Performance   324

Performance Monitoring Tools   324

Task Manager   324
Resource Monitor   327
Performance Monitor   329

Performance Options   335

Controlling Application Startup   336

Tools for Managing Application Startup   336
Startup Methods Used by Applications   338

Troubleshooting Windows 10 Errors   339

Steps Recorder   339
Reliability Monitor   340
Event Viewer   341

Local File Recovery and Backup   344

Configuring File History   345
Configuring Backup and Restore (Windows 7)   347
Restoring Previous Versions of Files
    and Folders   347

System Recovery   349

Reset this PC   350
Windows Recovery Environment   351
Restore Points   353
Recovery Drive   355

SUMMARY   **355**

KEY TERMS   **356**

REVIEW QUESTIONS   **356**

CASE PROJECTS   **357**

MODULE 10

ENTERPRISE COMPUTING   359

Active Directory   359

Active Directory Structure   360
Active Directory Partitions   363
Active Directory Sites and Replication   363
Active Directory and DNS   363
Joining a Domain   364

Time Synchronization   366
Offline Domain Join   366

Group Policy   367

Group Policy Inheritance   368
Group Policy Preferences   369
Multiple Local Policies   371
Controlling Device Installation   372

Enterprise Management Tools   374

Windows Server Update Services   374
Microsoft Endpoint Configuration Manager   376
Microsoft BitLocker Administration
    and Monitoring   376

Enterprise File Services   377

Distributed File System   377
BranchCache   378

Microsoft Cloud Services   379

Azure AD   380
Azure AD Join   380
Microsoft Intune   381

SUMMARY   381

KEY TERMS   382

REVIEW QUESTIONS   382

CASE PROJECTS   383

MODULE 11

MANAGING ENTERPRISE CLIENTS   385

Troubleshooting and Managing
Enterprise Clients   385

Remote Desktop   386
Remote Assistance   391
Quick Assist   393
MMC Snap-Ins   394
Registry Editor   396
Windows PowerShell Remoting   397

Managing Profiles for Roaming Users   398

Mapped Drive Letters   398
Folder Redirection   399
Credential Roaming   399
User Experience Virtualization   399
Profile Synchronization with Microsoft
    Account or Azure AD   400

Using a VPN for Remote Access   400

Configuring VPN Clients   401
VPN Protocols   401
Creating a VPN Connection   403

Automated VPN Deployment   404
Authentication Protocols   406
Network Settings   407
Always On VPN   408
DirectAccess   409

Synchronizing Data for Mobile Clients   409

OneDrive   410
Offline Files   410
Work Folders   411

SUMMARY   412

KEY TERMS   412

REVIEW QUESTIONS   413

CASE PROJECTS   414

MODULE 12

AUTOMATING WINDOWS 10
DEPLOYMENT   415

Windows 10 Installation Methods   415

OEM Installation   416
Removable Media Installation   416
Distribution Share Installation   416
Image-Based Installation   416

Windows 10 Installation Types   417

Upgrade Installations   417
Clean Installations   417
Migrating User Settings and Files   418

Windows 10 Assessment and
Deployment Kit   418

Windows PE   420

Unattended Installation   422

Configuration Passes   422
Answer File Names and Locations   424
Windows System Image Manager   424

Preparing Windows 10 for Imaging   429

Configuration Passes for Image-Based
    Installation   430
Sysprep System Cleanup Actions   430
Sysprep Limitations   431
Sysprep Command-Line Options   431

Using DISM for Imaging   433

Image File Formats   433
Windows PE Boot Media Creation   434
Capturing and Applying WIM Images   435
Capturing and Applying FFU Images   437
Image Maintenance   438

Provisioning	439
Enterprise Deployment Tools	442
User State Migration Tool	442
Windows Deployment Services	443
Microsoft Deployment Toolkit	444
Windows AutoPilot	445
SUMMARY	**446**
KEY TERMS	**446**
REVIEW QUESTIONS	**447**
CASE PROJECTS	**448**

APPENDIX A

MICROSOFT WINDOWS EXAM MD-100 OBJECTIVES   **449**

APPENDIX B

PREPARING FOR CERTIFICATION EXAMS   **453**

GLOSSARY	**454**
INDEX	**468**

INTRODUCTION

Welcome to *Microsoft® 365 Modern Desktop Administrator Guide to Exam MD-100: Windows® 10*. This book offers you real-world examples, interactive activities, and many hands-on activities that reinforce key concepts and prepare you for a career in network administration using Microsoft Windows 10. This book also features troubleshooting tips for solutions to common problems that you will encounter in the realm of Windows 10 administration.

This book offers in-depth study of all the functions and features of installing, configuring, and maintaining Windows 10 as a client operating system. Throughout the book, we provide detailed hands-on activities that let you experience firsthand the processes involved in Windows 10 configuration and management. We then provide pointed Review Questions to reinforce the concepts introduced in each chapter and help you prepare for the Microsoft certification exam. Finally, to put a real-world slant on the concepts introduced in each chapter, we provide Case Projects to prepare you for situations that must be managed in a live networking environment.

CERTIFICATION

Microsoft® 365 Modern Desktop Administrator Guide to Exam MD-100: Windows® 10 is intended for people starting a career in desktop support or system administration. It can also be used by experienced system administrators who want a more in-depth understanding of Windows 10. To best understand the material in this book, you should have a background in basic computer concepts and have worked with applications in a Windows environment.

The Microsoft 365 Certified: Modern Desktop Administrator Associate certification allows technology professionals to prove their expertise in configuring and managing Windows 10. To obtain this certification, you must pass the MD-100: Windows 10 and MD-101: Managing Modern Desktops exams. This book prepares you to take the MD-100: Windows 10 exam and introduces many concepts in the MD-101 exam. After completing this book, you will not only be prepared for the certification exam, you will also be prepared to implement and maintain Windows 10 in a business environment.

New to This Edition

This entire book has been reviewed and updated to ensure that it covers the objectives in the MD-100: Windows 10 exam. Information about new technologies introduced in recent feature updates has been added and obsolete features have been removed.

New activities, review questions, and case projects have been created to reinforce the concepts and techniques presented in each module and to help you apply these concepts to real-world scenarios.

MODULE OUTLINE

The topics covered in the 12 modules of this book are comprehensive and organized as explained in the following descriptions.

Module 1, Introduction to Windows 10, outlines the role of an operating system and the editions of Windows 10. You learn how to perform a basic installation of Windows 10 and the options available for activation. The Windows 10 user interface and networking models are explained.

Module 2, Using the System Utilities, examines the tools used to manage Windows 10. This includes graphical tools, such as Computer Management, the command prompt, and Windows PowerShell. These are used to configure hardware components, power management, display settings, scheduled tasks, and optional features.

Module 3, User Management, covers the creation and management of user accounts for Windows 10. Multiple Windows 10 authentication methods are discussed along with user profiles. Integration with Windows networks and Azure AD are explained.

Module 4, Networking, provides comprehensive coverage of networking connectivity in Windows 10. This module discusses IP version 4 and IP version 6, Internet connectivity, wireless networking, and Windows Defender Firewall.

Module 5, Managing Disks and File Systems, explores disk technologies and partition styles. Basic disks, dynamic disks, virtual hard disks, and Storage Spaces are discussed, including the tools to manage them. File permissions and file sharing are also discussed.

Module 6, Windows 10 Security Features, explores a wide variety of security settings in Windows 10, including the local security policy, auditing, User Account Control, and malware protection. Data security features, such as Encrypting File System and BitLocker, are also covered. Finally, managing Windows Updates is covered.

Module 7, User Productivity Tools, identifies features to manage files and printing. File management with File Explorer and OneDrive are both covered. Installation and management of printers by using various methods is explored. Finally, browsers in Windows 10 are covered along with accessories and keyboard shortcuts.

Module 8, Windows 10 Application Support, examines the application types that can run in Windows 10, the installation types for each, and app compatibility solutions. The registry and Remote Desktop Services also are covered.

Module 9, Performance Tuning and System Recovery, details how to use tools such as Performance Monitor, Resource Monitor, and Task Manager to identify and resolve performance problems. Tools for data backup and recovery are also discussed. Finally, the various tools for system recovery, such as PC reset, Windows Recovery Environment, and restore points, are explained.

Module 10, Enterprise Computing, describes and demonstrates management features that are required in larger organizations. An overview of Active Directory concepts is presented, followed by an explanation of how Group Policy can be used to manage many computers. Enterprise management tools, such as Windows Server Update Services and enterprise file services, are discussed. Finally, cloud services for management, including Azure AD and Microsoft Intune, are described.

Module 11, Managing Enterprise Clients, explains Windows 10 configuration options that are used in large organizations to simplify management and provide remote access to resources. Methods for remotely connecting to Windows 10 for management and troubleshooting are described. Centralization of profile data is discussed to support roaming users. For mobile users, virtual private network configuration and data synchronization are explored.

Module 12, Automating Windows 10 Deployment, provides coverage of how large organizations use tools to automate the deployment of Windows 10. The discussion of options includes using the Windows 10 Assessment and Deployment Kit to create unattended answer files, imaging, and provisioning. Enterprise tools discussed include the User State Migration Tool, Windows Deployment Services, the Microsoft Deployment Toolkit, and Windows AutoPilot.

Appendix A, Exam MD-100: Windows 10 Objectives, maps each exam objective to the module and section where you can find information on that objective.

Appendix B, Preparing for Certification Exams, provides strategies and additional resources for studying for the MD-100: Windows 10 exam.

FEATURES AND APPROACH

Microsoft® 365 Modern Desktop Administrator Guide to Exam MD-100: Windows® 10 differs from other networking books in its unique hands-on approach and its orientation to real-world situations and problem solving. To help you see how Microsoft Windows 10 concepts and techniques are applied in real-world organizations, this book incorporates the following features:

Module Objectives—Each module begins with a detailed list of the concepts to be mastered. This list gives you a quick reference to the module's contents and is a useful study aid.

Activities—Activities are incorporated throughout the text, giving you practice in setting up, managing, and troubleshooting a network system. The activities give you a strong foundation for carrying out network administration tasks in the real world. Because of the book's progressive nature, completing the activities in each module is essential before moving on to the end-of-module materials and subsequent modules.

Summaries—Each module's text is followed by a summary of the concepts introduced in that module. These summaries provide a helpful way to recap and revisit the ideas covered in each module.

Key Terms—All terms introduced with boldfaced text are gathered together in the Key Terms list at the end of the module. This provides you with a method of checking your understanding of all the terms introduced.

Review Questions—The end-of-module assessment begins with a set of Review Questions that reinforce the ideas introduced in each module. Answering these questions correctly will ensure that you have mastered the important concepts.

Case Projects—Finally, each module closes with a section that proposes certain situations. You are asked to evaluate the situations and decide upon the course of action to be taken to remedy the problems described. This valuable tool will help you sharpen your decision-making and troubleshooting skills, which are important aspects of network administration.

TEXT AND GRAPHIC CONVENTIONS

Additional information has been added to this book to help you better understand what's being discussed in the module. Visual graphics throughout the text alert you to these additional materials. The visual graphics used in this book are described as follows:

NOTE

Notes, which appear in the margins, present additional helpful material related to the subject being discussed.

 TIP   Tips offer extra information on resources, how to attack problems, and time-saving shortcuts.

 **CAUTION**   The Caution icon identifies important information about potential mistakes or hazards.

INSTRUCTOR MATERIALS

Everything you need for your course in one place. This collection of book-specific lecture and class tools is available online. Please visit **login.cengage.com** and log in to access instructor-specific resources on the Instructor Companion Site, which includes the Guide to Teaching Online; Instructor Manual; Solutions to the review questions in the textbook and Live Virtual Machine Labs; Test Bank files; PowerPoint Presentations; and Syllabus.

- **Guide to Teaching Online.** The Guide to Teaching Online includes two main parts. Part 1 offers general technological and pedagogical considerations and resources, and Part 2 provides discipline-specific suggestions for teaching when you can't be physically present with students.
- **Electronic Instructor Manual.** The Instructor Manual that accompanies this textbook includes the following items: additional instructional material to assist in class preparation, including suggestions for lecture topics, additional projects, and class discussion topics.
- **Solutions Manuals.** The instructor resources include solutions to all end-of-module material, including review questions and case projects. The Live Virtual Machine Labs Solutions include examples of correct screen shots and answers to the inline questions found within the labs.
- **Test Banks with Cengage Testing Powered by Cognero.** This flexible, online system allows you to do the following:
  - Author, edit, and manage test bank content from multiple Cengage solutions.
  - Create multiple test versions in an instant.
  - Deliver tests from your LMS, your classroom, or wherever you want.
- **PowerPoint Presentations.** This book comes with a set of Microsoft PowerPoint slides for each module. These slides are meant to be used as a teaching aid for classroom presentations, to be made available to students on the network for module review, or to be printed for classroom distribution. Instructors are also at liberty to add their own slides for other topics introduced.
- **Syllabus.** The sample syllabus provides an example of a template for setting up your course.

MindTap

MindTap for *Microsoft® 365 Modern Desktop Administrator Guide to Exam MD-100: Windows® 10* is a personalized, fully online digital learning platform of content, assignments, and services that engages students and encourages them to think critically, while allowing you to easily set your course through simple customization options.

MindTap is designed to help students master the skills they need in today's workforce. Research shows employers need critical thinkers, troubleshooters, and creative problem solvers to stay relevant in our fast-paced, technology-driven world. MindTap helps you achieve this with assignments and activities that provide hands-on practice, real-life relevance, and certification test prep. Students are guided through assignments that help them master basic knowledge and understanding before moving on to more challenging problems.

All MindTap activities and assignments are tied to defined learning objectives. Readings support course objectives, while Networking for Life activities encourage learners to read articles, listen to podcasts, or watch videos to stay current with what is happening in the field of IT and networking. You can use these activities to help build student interest in the field of networking, as well as lifelong learning habits.

Reflection activities encourage self-reflection and open sharing among students to help improve their retention and understanding of the material. Visualize Videos help explain and illustrate difficult information technology concepts.

The Live Virtual Machine Labs provide hands-on practice and give students an opportunity to troubleshoot, explore, and try different, real-life solutions in a secure, private sandbox environment.

Test Prep questions in the ATP app allow students to quiz themselves on specific exam domains, and the pre- and post-course assessments measure exactly how much they have learned. CNOW quizzes provide test questions in the style of the MD-100: Windows 10 certification exam and help you measure how well learners mastered the material after completing each MindTap module.

MindTap is designed around learning objectives and provides the analytics and reporting to easily see where the class stands in terms of progress, engagement, and completion rates.

Students can access eBook content in the MindTap Reader, which offers highlighting, note-taking, search, and audio, as well as mobile access. Learn more at **www.cengage.com/mindtap/**.

BEFORE YOU BEGIN

Almost all the activities in this book can be completed by using a single computer running Windows 10. For the computer running Windows 10, you can use a physical computer or a virtual machine, whichever is the most convenient; however, some special considerations include the following:

- Module 10, Enterprise Computing, requires a second computer to act as a server to complete activities. This server is running Windows Server 2019, and instructions for installation are provided in Module 10.
- Module 11, Managing Enterprise Clients, has some activities that assume the Windows 10 computer has been joined to the domain created in Module 10.

Software

All activities that require specific software to be downloaded provide links within the lab. It is beneficial, however, to download some of the larger pieces of software ahead of time and make them available for students. Installation steps for the software are provided in the appropriate activities. The software recommended for download ahead of time is:

- Windows 10 Enterprise Edition (Trial)—https://www.microsoft.com/en-us/evalcenter/evaluate-windows-10-enterprise
- Windows 10 Assessment and Deployment Toolkit—https://docs.microsoft.com/windows-hardware/get-started/adk-install
- Windows PE add-on for the ADK—https://docs.microsoft.com/windows-hardware/get-started/adk-install
- Windows Server 2019 Evaluation—https://www.microsoft.com/en-us/evalcenter/evaluate-windows-server

Classroom Setup: Notes for Instructors

Although this course can be performed on physical computers, it is significantly easier to manage if you use virtual machines. Some of the activities performed in the course are destructive to the local operation system configuration or applications. This makes it undesirable for students to use a physical computer. Students could use Client Hyper-V in Windows 10 (or other virtualization software) to create and manage their own virtual machines, or virtual machines could be hosted on a server.

Activities from Modules 10 and 11 require Windows Server in a separate virtual machine. The ideal scenario is for students to have their own virtual machine for running Windows Server 2019 and joining their own domain. To avoid naming conflicts, you will need to provide students with a unique naming system for domains and unique IP addresses for the servers. These requirements are noted in the appropriate activities.

It is assumed that the client computers are using a dynamic IP address and that there is connectivity to the Internet. Some activities require students to access the Internet. This is a requirement when accessing cloud-based resources, such as a Microsoft account and OneDrive.

ACKNOWLEDGMENTS

We would like to thank the entire team that we have worked with at Cengage Learning. As on previous projects, you help us take what we know and turn it into an excellent book that can help people improve within the IT industry.

In particular, we would like to thank Lyn Markowicz, whose suggestions invariably led to improved readability and clarity. We would also like to thank Danielle Shaw, who painstakingly reviewed every step in every activity to verify the accuracy of the steps. A special thanks to Julie Boyles, Jason Carman, and Jeffrey Riley, the peer reviewers who evaluated the first draft of our modules and provided feedback on them. Your insights were a valuable contribution to the book.

Byron would like to thank his family—Tracey, Samantha, and Michelle—for enduring endless discussion about Windows 10 at all times of the day. He'd also like thank his parents for indulging his curiosity about computers that led to a rewarding career in the computing industry.

Leon would like to thank his loving wife, Angela, and his boys, Tyler, Terry, Andrew, Nathaniel, and Matthew, for sharing their family time with all the people who will use this book as part of their greater education.

ABOUT THE AUTHORS

Byron Wright (@ByronWrightGeek) is a consultant who works with organizations to design and deploy solutions based on Microsoft technologies, such as Microsoft 365, Windows Server, Windows 10, Active Directory, Azure AD, and Exchange Server. He has authored and co-authored several books about Microsoft Technologies for Cengage Learning. Byron also teaches information systems courses for the Asper School of Business at the University of Manitoba. Microsoft recognized Byron's contributions to the technology community with an MVP award for Exchange Server and Office 365 from 2012 to 2015.

Leon Plesniarski is a cloud solutions architect who has been building with Microsoft Products since 1984. Leon graduated as a Computer and Electrical Engineer, applying his skills to a wide range of technical jobs, consulting, and certified technical training. He currently works as a consultant for Broadview Networks to analyze client requirements and provide practical solutions for their needs. His passion for helping others to learn and enjoy the type of work he has come to love has motivated him to contribute to this and other books. Leon's mantra remains "always learn, always improve yourself."

INTRODUCTION TO WINDOWS 10

After reading this module and completing the exercises, you will be able to:

1. Describe the role of an operating system
2. Select an appropriate edition of Windows 10
3. Install Windows 10
4. Select an appropriate activation method for Windows 10
5. Understand the Windows 10 user interface
6. Identify network models available for Windows 10

For business computing, Windows is the most popular client operating system and Windows 10 is the latest version. Windows 10 is popular because it is widely supported by business applications. Microsoft also provides well-understood tools that information technology (IT) departments can use to deploy Windows 10 and control Windows 10 configuration.

In this module, you begin by learning the core functionality that Windows 10 provides for applications and hardware management. Then you learn about the multiple editions of Windows 10 that are available to ensure that you can select the most fitting edition for a given scenario. Performing an attended installation of Windows 10, including activation, also is discussed. Finally, you learn about the network models available for Windows 10 that control who can sign in.

UNDERSTANDING OPERATING SYSTEMS

At home, you use computers for gaming, accessing websites, and running productivity software such as Microsoft Word. You also use computers to communicate with friends and family using email and messaging applications such as Skype. At work, you use computers for similar purposes but also include line-of-business applications and other specialized software.

The common need among home users and business users is running applications. **Applications** are programs used to accomplish tasks, and the purpose of computing is to complete those tasks. When you select an **operating system** for computing, you first identify the applications you want to run and then identify the operating system requirement for those applications.

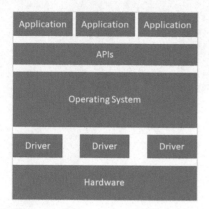

Figure 1-1 Operating system architecture

One of the reasons that Windows 10 is popular is the wide availability of applications. Windows operating systems have a long history of providing developers with features that simplify application development. Consequently, many home and business applications were created only for Windows.

Operating System Architecture

Computer hardware (i.e., the physical components of a computer), an operating system, and applications all work together as shown in Figure 1-1. Applications are written to communicate with a specific operating system. The operating system is responsible for communicating with hardware. This simplifies application development because the developers don't need to be aware of specific hardware details.

A computer requires an operating system to function because you need to have software that understands how to use computer hardware. The processor, memory, hard drive, graphics card, and other components have the potential to perform tasks, but they must be instructed what to do.

Many hardware manufacturers and types of hardware exist. It is impossible for any operating system to understand all of them, so operating systems use a modular approach that loads small pieces of software called hardware drivers. **Hardware drivers** provide the functionality required for the operating system to work with specific types of hardware. Almost all hardware manufacturers create hardware drivers for Windows 10.

To support application developers, an operating system provides **application programmer interfaces (APIs)**. Application developers use APIs to perform common functions like opening and writing to a file. Even functionality like the Save as dialog box is provided by the operating system. An API is generally provided as part of a programming framework such as the .NET Framework provided with Windows 10. Application developers select a consistent framework to use for development.

In general, an application written for one operating system will not run on another operating system because each operating system uses different APIs. That is why it's important to identify applications you need, and the operating system requirements for those applications, before selecting an operating system.

Windows 10 Extras

While application availability is one reason for the popularity of Windows 10, much of the extra functionality is also useful. For end users, Windows 10 includes an intuitive and familiar graphical interface for using applications and managing files. Many simple but useful applications are included in Windows 10, such as:

- Notepad
- Calculator
- Microsoft Edge (browser)
- Remote Desktop Connection
- Snip & Sketch

For IT departments, manageability is a key concern for operating systems. Windows 10 includes tools for centralized management with no extra costs. Many additional tools that you can purchase for enhanced management also are available.

Some of the management features included in Windows 10 are:

- Automatic updates: Updates are provided by Microsoft for free and are automatically deployed to Windows 10.
- Integration with Active Directory: **Active Directory** is a centralized database that contains information about users and computers. By using Active Directory, administrators can control authentication to Windows 10 clients without manually configuring user accounts on each one.
- Group Policy: The settings available in **Group Policy** allow administrators to configure thousands of operating system settings in Windows 10. These policies can be deployed quickly to thousands of computers for consistent configuration of all computers in a department or across the entire organization.

Alternative Operating Systems

Windows 10 is not the only operating systems available. Most organizations have a mix of operating systems in use for different purposes. For example, Windows 10 is not available on smartphones.

Some alternative operating systems include the following:

- MacOS is a desktop operating system for Apple computers that is popular with businesses for graphic design tasks. It is also popular with home users because it is easy to use.
- Linux is an open source operating system for desktops that is preferred by some IT professionals; however, it is generally too difficult for an average computer user to configure and has limited applications.
- Android is a mobile operating system that is used by many smartphones and tablets.
- iOS is a mobile operating system for Apple iPhones.
- iPadOS is a mobile operating system for Apple iPad tablets.

WINDOWS 10 EDITIONS

Not all Windows 10 users have the same requirements for an operating system. For example, home users do not typically need their computer to integrate with Active Directory for authentication. To address the needs of each user segment, Microsoft has created multiple editions of Windows 10. Each edition is designed to meet the needs of a unique group of users and has unique features.

The five market segments with unique editions of Windows 10 are:

- Home
- Small business
- Small business power users
- Enterprise
- Education

 TIP   If you need an updated list of features in the varying editions of Windows 10, Wikipedia provides a well-maintained list at https://en.wikipedia.org/wiki/Windows_10_editions.

Windows 10 Home

Windows 10 Home edition is the baseline edition of Windows 10 that is oriented to home users. This edition of Windows 10 includes all the core functionality required to run Windows applications. When you buy a PC with Windows 10 from a retail store, this is the edition of Windows 10 that is most likely included.

The following are some of the features in Windows 10 Home:

- Support for 1 physical processor and up to 128 GB of memory
- Run Windows applications
- Customizable Start menu
- Cortana voice assistant
- Microsoft Edge browser
- Windows Hello biometric authentication
- Device encryption
- Tablet mode
- Windows Update
- Local user accounts
- Local Group Policy
- Windows Defender Antivirus

- Windows Defender Firewall
- Windows Defender Exploit Protection (partial features)
- Microsoft Store

Windows 10 Pro

Business environments have management requirements that home users don't have. The IT department needs to be able to centrally control authentication to desktop computers, access to resources and applications, deployment of applications, and security settings. None of these is possible with Windows 10 Home. **Windows 10 Pro** adds these features that businesses require.

Some of the features added in Windows 10 Pro are:

- Support for 2 physical processors and up to 2 TB of memory
- Domain join to Active Directory for centralized authentication
- Azure Active Directory (Azure AD) join for centralized management and authentication
- Group Policy from Active Directory for centralized management
- Windows Hello for Business with PIN authentication
- Remote Desktop for remote access
- Client Hyper-V to create virtual machines
- BitLocker drive encryption
- Windows Defender Credential Guard
- Windows Defender System Guard
- Windows Autopilot for deployment
- Windows Update for Business with additional controls
- Microsoft Store for Business with organization-specific customization

Windows 10 Pro for Workstations

For power users with high speed processing requirements, Microsoft has introduced **Windows 10 Pro for Workstations**. This edition of Windows 10 has support for higher end hardware that might be used for processing large amounts of data performing data analysis or engineering works.

Features added in Windows 10 Pro for Workstations include:

- Support for 4 physical processors and up to 6 TB of memory
- ReFS file system to support larger volumes and files
- Persistent memory using nonvolatile memory for high-performance local file access
- SMB Direct for high-performance network file access

Windows 10 Enterprise

For larger organizations with advanced security and management needs, Microsoft produces **Windows 10 Enterprise** edition. This edition of Windows 10 provides the fullest feature set.

Features added in Windows 10 Enterprise include:

- Windows Defender Application Guard to isolate untrusted websites from enterprise data
- Windows Defender Application Control and Applocker to control which applications are allowed to run
- Desktop Analytics to analyze upgrade readiness and compliance
- Branchcache
- **Windows 10 Enterprise Long Term Servicing Channel (LTSC)** for specialized software
- Cloud activation
- Manage Microsoft Store access, the Start menu, Taskbar, and Cortana settings
- Windows Virtual Desktop use rights
- Microsoft Application Virtualization (App-V) for easier application distribution
- Microsoft User Environment Virtualization (UE-V) for simplified user roaming among computers

Windows 10 Enterprise LTSC

Microsoft releases feature updates of Windows 10 twice per year, and each feature update is supported for 18 months. A feature update can enable and remove features from Windows 10. During the 18-month period, updates are provided for a feature update. For example, if a feature update is released in March of 2020 then updates are provided until September 2021. The intent is that you will install a new feature update before support ends.

 TIP Some older documentation refers to Windows 10 Enterprise LTSC as Windows 10 Enterprise Long Term Servicing Branch (LTSB).

In some scenarios where certification is required for a specific combination of hardware and software, performing updates every two years might not be possible. For example, consider a computer that controls specialized medical equipment, such as an MRI. The hardware and software vendor might consider it too much of a burden to recertify on a regular basis. The Windows 10 Enterprise LTSC is designed for these scenarios, and each release is supported for 10 years. A new version of Windows 10 LTSC is released every 2–3 years.

Windows 10 Enterprise LTSC has removed some features from Windows 10 Enterprise to minimize change requirements. Some of the functionality removed includes:

- The Microsoft Store
- Modern apps (a newer development method for applications)
- Microsoft Edge

Below is a list of items to remember about using Windows 10 Enterprise LTSC:

- Most applications are not tested or supported on Windows 10 Enterprise LTSC.
- The .NET Framework required for many applications will not be updated to the latest versions.
- The latest hardware advances will not be supported, and you might be limited using older hardware.

 **CAUTION** Do not use Windows 10 Enterprise LTSC as a standard desktop operating system to avoid applying updates to Windows 10 or to disable the Microsoft Store. Instead develop a deployment and update process that works for your organization.

Windows 10 Education Editions

Schools are a unique market because, unlike business environments, computers are typically shared by students, and it is not desirable for students to configure those computers. Microsoft makes two versions of Windows available specifically for schools:

- **Windows 10 Pro Education** has the same feature set as Windows 10 Pro.
- **Windows 10 Education** has the same feature set as Windows 10 Enterprise.

Both education editions of Windows 10 disable the display of Windows 10 tips, "fun facts," and Microsoft Store suggestions by default. If you turn on Microsoft Store suggestions, then only Microsoft apps are displayed. This is the primary technical difference between the education editions and the editions on which they are based.

 TIP Before version 1703, Windows 10 Pro Education and Windows 10 Education disabled Cortana by default. That is no longer the case.

Windows 10 N & KN Editions

Microsoft makes variants of Windows 10 editions available specifically for the European and South Korean markets. European versions are denoted with an N and South Korean versions are denoted with KN. Neither the N nor KN variants include Windows Media Player or other multimedia software; however, users with these variants can download the Media Feature Pack from Microsoft, which includes the removed functionality. These variants exist due to legal requirements in Europe and South Korea.

32-Bit Versions

Windows 10 is available in both 32-bit and 64-bit versions. For example, there is a 32-bit version of Windows 10 Pro and a 64-bit version of Windows 10 Pro. Older computers (prior to 2010) had processors that were capable only of 32-bit processing. All newer computers support 64-bit processing, which you might see referred to as x64 architecture.

A 32-bit processor can address only 4 GB of memory. When you use this 32-bit version of Windows 10 with a 64-bit processor, the same 4 GB limit applies. The 32-bit version of Windows 10 can use only 4 GB of memory regardless of how much physical memory is installed in the computer.

Many applications are still written as 32-bit applications that can run on 32-bit or 64-bit versions of Windows 10. Some applications that are written as 64-bit applications, however, cannot run on the 32-bit version of Windows 10. To use 64-bit applications, you need to have the 64-bit version of Windows 10.

 TIP For best application compatibility and performance, you should always use a 64-bit version of Windows 10 unless you have a specific requirement to use a 32-bit version.

The main reason to run a 32-bit version of Windows 10 is to support legacy software or hardware drivers. Some legacy software is 16-bit software that can't run on a 64-bit version of Windows 10. A 32-bit version of Windows 10 can run 16-bit software.

Some examples of 16-bit software are:

- A driver for specialized hardware, such as lab equipment
- An older business-critical application that was not updated by the vendor
- A custom-developed application with no ongoing support

INSTALLING WINDOWS 10

Most computers are purchased with Windows 10 already installed by the manufacturer. As a home user, you just turn on the computer, wait for a small setup routine to run, and then start using it. In a business environment, however, it is quite common for the Windows 10 operating system installed by the manufacturer to be removed and a different version installed.

Hardware Requirements

The minimum hardware requirements for Windows 10 that Microsoft provides are sufficient to install Windows 10, but they do not provide a satisfactory user experience. The minimum requirements are listed in Table 1-1 below.

Table 1-1   Minimum Hardware Requirements for Windows 10

System Component	Recommendation
CPU	32- or 64-bit processor, 1 GHz or faster
System RAM	1 GB for 32-bit, 2 GB for 64-bit CPU
Disk space	16 GB for 32-bit, 32 GB for 64-bit editions
Video card drivers	DirectX 9 graphical processor and WDDM 1.0 (or higher)

The minimum RAM (random access memory) identified by Microsoft is inadequate for day-to-day use of Windows 10. At minimum, you should have 4 GB of memory for reasonable performance; if you are purchasing new computers, strongly consider getting 8 GB of memory to ensure that you can run multiple applications simultaneously without impacting performance. It's not uncommon for a browser with a few tabs open to consume over 1 GB of memory.

The disk space required for the operating system files is not an accurate representation of the disk space required in the computer. Additional disk space is consumed by data files, applications, and temporary files. Some users might be able to function with 120 GB hard drives, but 240 GB or larger is preferred.

 TIP Using an SSD (solid-state drive) instead of a spinning disk has a dramatic impact on system performance. If you're buying new systems, opt for an SSD drive.

DVD Boot Installation

The simplest method for installing Windows 10 is a DVD boot installation. To perform a DVD boot installation, you need to have the Windows 10 installation files on DVD and configure your computer to boot from DVD. When you start your computer with the DVD inserted, the computer starts the installation of Windows 10 from the DVD.

The DVD boot installation method is the least suitable method for a large volume of computers. It requires you to visit each computer with a DVD and to leave the DVD in the computer during the installation process. This method is suitable for small organizations that only occasionally install Windows 10. Other installation methods are covered later in Module 12 Automating Windows 10 Deployment.

With a DVD boot installation, the degree of customization performed is low because it includes only the drivers and components included on the Windows 10 installation DVD. It does not include additional applications or updates; however, you can add drivers during installation by using removable media, such as USB storage.

To speed up a DVD boot installation, you can put the installation files on faster media, such as USB storage. The USB interface on modern computers with an external disk drive or flash storage is much faster than a DVD drive.

Activity 1-1: Installing Windows 10

Time Required: 30 to 60 minutes
Objective: Install Windows 10
Description: You have just received a new copy of Windows 10. You are considering deploying Windows 10 for your organization. To sell the management team on implementing Windows 10, you need to install the system and provide a demonstration of the new features. In this activity, you install Windows 10 (a new install, not an upgrade) on your computer.

1. Ensure that your computer is configured to boot from DVD. The boot configuration of your computer is configured in the BIOS or UEFI firmware settings of your computer. Refer to the documentation specific to the computer to determine the steps to complete this requirement. Many newer computers will boot from the DVD drive automatically if no operating system is installed on the system's hard drive.
2. Place your Windows 10 DVD in the DVD drive of your computer.
3. Restart your computer.
4. If directed by the startup screen, press any key to boot from DVD. This message may appear only if the hard drive has an existing bootable partition or if the computer's boot sequence is configured to allow it.
5. In the Windows Setup window, confirm that the installation language, time and currency format, and keyboard layout are correct and then click **Next**.
6. Click **Install now** and then wait for setup to start.
7. On the Applicable notices and license terms page, select the **I accept the license terms** check box and then click **Next**.
8. On the Which type of installation do you want screen, click **Custom: Install Windows only (advanced)**. This is required to perform a new installation.
9. On the Where do you want to install Windows screen, if necessary, install additional disk drivers as described by your instructor.

10. If any existing partitions appear, delete each partition using the following steps:
    a. Click the partition to select it.
    b. Click **Delete**.
    c. Click **OK** to confirm that you understand that all data on the partition will be deleted.
11. Examine the number in the Free space column. Exercises in other modules require at least 30 GB of space to remain unallocated.
12. Click **Drive 0 Unallocated Space** and then click **New**.
13. In the **Size** text box, enter a value that is no less than 50000 and that leaves at least 30000 MB of disk space unallocated and then click **Apply**.
14. In the warning window, click **OK** to acknowledge that additional partitions may be created. Windows 10 automatically creates several partitions to support recovery and advanced boot options.
15. Click **Drive 0 Partition 4** to select it and then click **Format**.
16. In the warning window, click **OK** to confirm that all data on the partition will be lost when it is formatted. No data is on this partition at this time.
17. If necessary, click **Drive 0 Partition 4** to select it and then click **Next**. Windows now copies system files to the hard drive, reboots, performs additional configuration tasks, reboots one or more times, and then asks for user input again. This portion of the installation can take up to 30 minutes but may be faster depending on your hardware. When your computer reboots, do not press a key to start from the DVD.
18. On the Let's start with region screen, select your region and then click **Yes**.
19. On the Is this the right keyboard layout screen, select the correct keyboard layout and then click **Yes**.
20. On the Want to add a second keyboard layout screen, click **Skip**.
21. On the Sign in with Microsoft screen, in the lower left corner, select **Domain join instead**.
22. On the Who's going to use this PC screen, in the Name box, type **User*x***, where x is a number assigned to you by your instructor.
23. On the Create a super memorable password screen, in the Password box, type **password** and then click **Next**.

NOTE 1

If you choose a more secure password than "password" be sure to document it so that you don't forget it.

24. On the Confirm your password screen, in the Confirm password box, type **password** and then click **Next**.
25. On the Create security questions for this account screen, in the Security question (1 of 3) box, select a security question.
26. In the Your answer box, type an answer and then click **Next.**
27. Repeat Steps 25 and 26 twice to complete answers for questions 2 and 3.
28. On the Do more across devices with activity history screen, click **Yes**.
29. On the Get help from your digital assistant screen, click **Accept**.
30. On the Choose privacy settings for your device screen, click **Accept**.
31. Wait for a minute or two while your user profile is created.
32. Right-click the Start button and select **Windows PowerShell (Admin)**.
33. In the User Account Control window, click **Yes** to allow this app to make changes to your computer.
34. At the Windows PowerShell prompt, type **hostname** and then press **Enter**. Note that the name of the computer is listed as the output of the command, and that the name has been automatically generated during the operating system's installation.
35. Type **Get-ComputerInfo** and then press **Enter**. This returns a large amount of information about your computer in addition to the computer name.
36. Type **shutdown /s /t 5** and then press **Enter**. This causes the computer to exit all running applications and shut down the computer in 5 seconds. Note that the computer can be shut down from the Start menu, but this command-line technique is commonly used by administrators who are remotely managing a user's computer.

Upgrading to Windows 10

If you have computers running a previous version of Windows, they can be upgraded to Windows 10. During the installation of Windows 10, you need to select the option Upgrade: Install Windows and keep files, settings, and applications, as shown in Figure 1-2. When you perform an upgrade, user data and applications are retained; however, if an application is not compatible with Windows 10 it won't be functional after the upgrade. In rare cases, the upgrade process will identify an incompatible application.

NOTE 2

You can view a complete list of Windows 10 upgrade paths at https://docs.microsoft.com/en-us/windows/deployment/upgrade/windows-10-upgrade-paths.

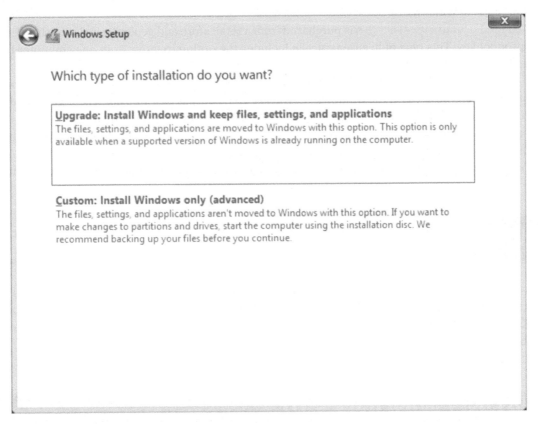

Figure 1-2   The Windows 10 setup screen

Not all previous versions of Windows can be upgraded to Windows 10. You can upgrade Windows 7 SP1 or Windows 8.1 to Windows 10. It is not possible to upgrade Windows 8.0 to Windows 10.

You should consider the restrictions on which editions of Windows 10 you might purchase when upgrading. In general, you should be upgrading to an equivalent or better edition of Windows 10. For example, you can upgrade Windows 7 Pro to Windows 10 Pro, but you cannot upgrade Windows 7 Pro to Windows 10 Home.

NOTE 3

You can view a complete list of Windows 10 edition upgrade paths at https://docs.microsoft.com/en-us/windows/deployment/upgrade/windows-10-edition-upgrades.

Edition Upgrades

You can upgrade the edition of Windows 10 without doing an installation from DVD. To upgrade from a lower version of Windows 10 to a higher version of Windows 10, you can enter the new product key. For example, you can upgrade from Windows 10 Home to Windows 10 Pro by entering the Windows 10 Pro product key. This is useful if you've purchased a computer with Windows 10 Home included but need the features of Windows 10 Pro to join the domain in the office.

LICENSING WINDOWS 10

Multiple methods for purchasing Windows 10 licenses are available to you. You can select the type of licensing that you want based on pricing and ease of implementation. A general overview of licensing is provided below, but Microsoft licensing is a complex subject; you should verify all licensing details before you purchase your own license(s).

When you purchase a new computer that includes Windows 10, the license for Windows 10 is an original equipment manufacturer (OEM) license. This type of license is tied to the physical device and cannot be reused if you purchase a new computer. OEM product keys are stored in the firmware of your computer and are automatically detected if you reinstall Windows 10.

A full packaged product (FPP) license is purchased from a retail store and generally includes the media for installation and a product key. This type of license typically includes the option to move from one computer to another. In part because the license is transferrable, it costs more than OEM licensing.

Volume licensing is a license agreement that organizations purchase to obtain software directly from Microsoft. When you purchase volume licenses for Windows 10, you are given access to a website where you can download the software you have licensed. That same website also has the product keys for your software.

You get additional benefits when you purchase volume licensing. For example, Windows 10 volume licensing includes imaging rights for easier installation that are not included with OEM licenses. Microsoft also provides an option to purchase software assurance with volume licensing, which provides new version rights and other benefits.

 **CAUTION** Volume licensing for Windows 10 is upgrade licensing from OEM versions. You cannot use volume licensing on a computer without an OEM license.

Cloud licensing is available to upgrade computers from Windows 10 Pro to Windows 10 Enterprise. You can purchase a cloud-based subscription for Windows 10 Enterprise alone; it also is included in larger packages, such as Microsoft 365. This type of licensing is enabled by signing in to Microsoft Azure AD, where a license has been assigned, rather than by using a product key.

ACTIVATING WINDOWS 10

Product activation is a process put in place by Microsoft to reduce piracy. If an installation of Windows 10 is not activated, some operating system features are disabled. At a minimum, some personalization features are disabled. At this writing, no other functionality is impaired, but older Microsoft operating systems have also forced a shutdown every 60 minutes for a nonactivated system.

Product activation requires very little additional work on the part of a computer user and significantly reduces piracy. It is now designed to inform a user that an unscrupulous retailer is selling illegitimate copies of Windows 10 rather than to punish the user.

OEM and FPP License Activation

For OEM and FPP licenses, activation usually happens automatically over the Internet after installation. You can view activation status for Windows 10 on the Activation screen in Update & Security. Figure 1-3 shows the Activation screen for a computer that has already been activated. You can also view the edition of Windows 10 and change the product key.

 TIP If activation can't be completed via the Internet, you can use phone-based activation; however, this option should be avoided when possible because it is time-consuming.

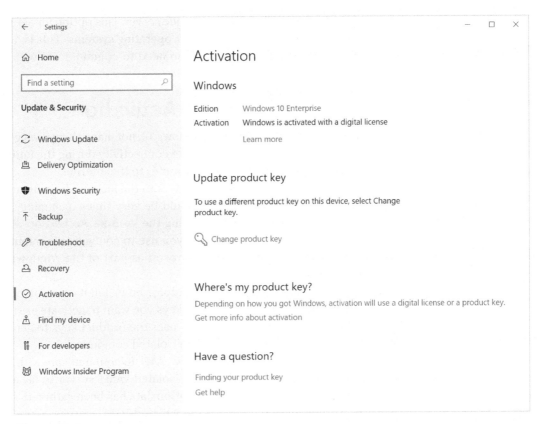

Figure 1-3   Activation information

When Windows 10 is activated, the product key used during installation is associated with the specific computer that is performing the activation. Information about the hardware in the computer is used to generate a unique identifier that is sent as part of the activation process. No personal information is sent as part of the process.

If you perform significant hardware changes to your computer, you may be forced to reactivate Windows 10, because Windows 10 assumes that it is installed on a new computer. Reactivation is not forced for simple upgrades such as an additional hard drive or additional RAM; however, installing a new motherboard typically requires reactivation.

In practice, at the time of this writing, Microsoft has been allowing two automatic product activations for FPP license keys before requiring users to call the Activation Center. This is useful when moving your copy of Windows 10 to a new computer. If you do need to call the Activation Center, Microsoft confirms your license information and the reason for an additional installation before issuing you an activation code.

Volume License Activation

In larger organizations, managing license keys separately for each computer would be time consuming. Volume licensing simplifies the management of license keys and provides multiple options for activation, which are listed below:

- **Multiple Activation Key (MAK)**—This type of product key functions the same as an OEM or retail product key that can be activated over the Internet or by phone. A MAK, however, can be used on a specific number of computers rather than just once. This simplifies key management for midsized organizations.
- **Key Management Service (KMS)**—This type of product key requires you to install KMS on a computer to act as a central point for product registration on your internal network. Product keys are installed on the KMS server and activated by having the KMS server communicate with the Internet. Computers activate by communicating with the KMS server on the internal network. This scenario simplifies key management in very large organizations. It also allows activation to occur in scenarios where the client computer is not able to directly perform activation due to firewalls.
- **Active Directory-based activation**—If computers will contact an Active Directory domain at least every 180 days, you can implement Active Directory-based activation. Computers activate by communicating with

NOTE 4

For an in-depth reference on volume activation, see Troubleshooting Windows Volume Activation at https://docs.microsoft.com/en-us/windows-server/get-started/activation-troubleshooting-guide.

NOTE 5

For detailed steps about using VAMT for proxy activation, see Scenario 2: Proxy Activation at https://docs.microsoft.com/en-us/windows/deployment/volume-activation/scenario-proxy-activation-vamt.

Active Directory rather than a specific server. This option for activation was introduced for Windows 8 or newer operating systems. This is an improvement over KMS because there is no need to communicate with a specific server.

Troubleshooting MAK Activation

When you use MAK product keys for Windows 10, not many things can go wrong. The most common problem is a lack of Internet connectivity during the initial activation attempt. To resolve this, connect the computer to the Internet.

If it is not possible to connect computers to the Internet for activation, you can use phone-based activation, but that would be very time-consuming. Instead, you should configure proxy activation by using the **Volume Activation Management Tool (VAMT)**. VAMT is also the tool that you use to configure a computer as a KMS host. You can download VAMT from Microsoft as part of the Windows Automated Deployment Toolkit (Windows ADT).

When you use VAMT for proxy activation, you install it on a computer that has access to the Internet. Then, the product keys you want to activate are installed into VAMT and the isolated computers. VAMT uses the product keys to generate activation information that is distributed to the isolated computers.

If the isolated environment can't allow VAMT to communicate with the Internet, then you can export information from an isolated VAMT server to file and import it to a VAMT server that does have Internet access for activation. When activation data has been gathered, it is exported from the Internet connected VAMT server as a file and imported on the isolated VAMT server. You can move the exported file between the isolated VAMT server and Internet-connected VAMT server by using removable media or a network file copy.

Activation with a MAK can also fail when the maximum number of activations for a key is reached. This can occur when you are using the same MAK to install Windows on a new set of computers. For example, you might have purchased 50 licenses of Windows 10 Pro and used the MAK with 50 activations for a set of computers two years ago. When you purchase 25 new computers and use the same MAK, it exceeds your activation limit even though you are within your license terms because you are retiring 25 older computers. In such a case, call the Activation Center and inform them of what you are doing; they will increase the number of activations for the MAK.

Troubleshooting KMS Activation

KMS activation simplifies product key management on computers, but is fairly complex to set up and configure. You need to set up a KMS server in your organization and add the license keys to that KMS server. Clients automatically connect to the KMS server for activation and you can view the number of activations on the KMS server.

>  **CAUTION** If you have an older KMS server already implemented, you might need to update it to support Windows 10 clients.

To use KMS activation, the client computers being activated need to be configured with a **generic volume license key (GVLK)**. The GVLK for an edition of Windows 10 is not unique to your organization. If a computer is not activating, ensure that you have entered the correct GVLK.

> **TIP** You can obtain the GVLKs for all Windows editions at https://docs.microsoft.com/en-us/windows-server/get-started/kmsclientkeys.

A KMS server has minimum activation thresholds that must be met before clients can be activated. For Windows 10, the minimum activation threshold is 25. This means that no instances of Windows 10 are activated until 25 instances have attempted to activate on the KMS server. You can verify the number of activation attempts on the KMS server.

When you install the KMS server, it creates a service (SRV) record in the domain name system (DNS). This SRV record contains the name of the KMS server for clients to contact. For example, if your domain is giganticlife.com then an SRV record of _vlmcs._tcp.giganticlife.com is created. That SRV record points to the KMS server. When troubleshooting, you should verify that the SRV record is present and that the client computer can connect to the KMS server.

 **CAUTION** In a multidomain environment you need to configure the DNSDomainPublishList registry key on the KMS server to ensure that the SRV record is created in all domains.

A KMS activation is valid for 180 days. If a computer is going to be disconnected from the KMS server for more than 180 days, you should use MAK for activation instead. For example, if you have computers for external sales staff that do not visit the office regularly, then use MAK instead of KMS activation.

 TIP When troubleshooting activation, you can use the command **slmgr /dlv** to view detailed licensing information.

Troubleshooting Active Directory-Based Activation

Active Directory-based activation is like KMS activation but is not reliant on a KMS server. Instead, all of the information is stored in Active Directory as activation objects, which is a more reliable source than a single KMS server. Active Directory-based activation also does not have minimum activation thresholds. The first client can be activated using Active Directory-based activation.

Because so much less configuration is required in Active Directory-based activation, much less troubleshooting is necessary. The steps for troubleshooting are to confirm the following:

- Windows 10 has a GVLK installed
- Windows 10 is joined to Active Directory where Active Directory-based activation is configured
- Windows 10 can properly authenticate to Active Directory
- Windows 10 has authenticated to Active Directory within the last 180 days
- The KMS key for Windows 10 was installed for Active Directory-based activation

Activity 1-2: Viewing Activation Information

Time Required: 5 minutes
Objective: View Windows 10 activation information.
Description: You have recently installed Windows 10 and want to verify that it was activated properly. This is useful for troubleshooting activation issues.

1. If necessary, start your computer and sign in.
2. Click the **Start** button and then click **Settings**.
3. In the Settings window, select **Update & Security**.
4. In the left pane, select **Activation** and read the activation information.
5. Close the Settings window.
6. Right-click the Start button and then click **Windows PowerShell (Admin)**.
7. In the User Account Control window, click **Yes**.
8. At the Windows PowerShell prompt, type **slmgr /dlv** and press **Enter**.
9. In the Windows Script Host window, read the licensing information and then click **OK**.
10. At the Windows PowerShell prompt, type **slmgr** and then press **Enter**. This shows all the available parameters for running slmgr.
11. In the Windows Script Host window, read the options and then click **OK**.

12. Repeat Step 11 four times to read all five screens of information.

13. At the Windows PowerShell prompt, type **Get-CimInstance -ClassName SoftwareLicensingProduct** and then press **Enter**.

14. Read the licensing information and then close the Windows PowerShell prompt.

USING WINDOWS 10

The Windows 10 user interface is similar to previous versions of Windows and quite intuitive to use. For anyone who has used previous version of Windows, the interface is similar and familiar.

Lock Screen

The Windows 10 lock screen is displayed when the computer first starts, as shown in Figure 1-4. The lock screen is a security and display layer that initiates access to the local device running Windows 10. Previous versions of Windows presented a screen asking the user to press **Ctrl+Alt+Delete** to initiate the sign-in process. Given that Windows 10 is used with a larger range of devices, the lock screen was changed to a format that is similar to what you would see on a smartphone. Useful information can be displayed on the lock screen, such as weather, battery charge indicator, date and time, Windows Store information, Cortana, and other customizable details that would be safe for anyone to see. By default, the picture displayed on this screen is updated every few days by Microsoft. The icons on the screen provide additional information when you move the pointer over them.

You can trigger the lock screen to remove itself by performing an action like clicking a mouse button, pressing a key, or touching a touch-sensitive screen. After one of these actions occur, the sign-in screen replaces the lock screen and allows the user to sign in, as shown in Figure 1-5. If multiple local accounts are detected, a list of accounts appears

Figure 1-4   The Windows 10 lock screen

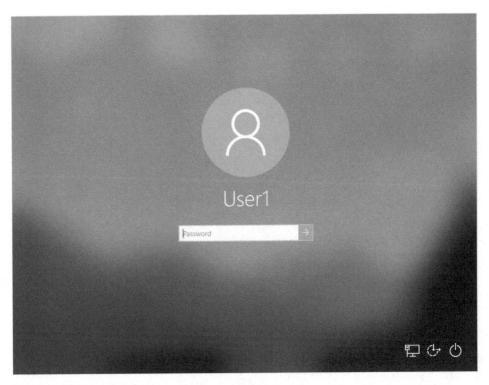

Figure 1-5   The Windows 10 sign-in screen

in the lower-left corner and you can click to select the one you want to sign in as. The lower-right corner of the screen contains icons for network connectivity, accessibility settings, and shutdown.

Start Menu

Many people were disappointed when the **Start menu** was removed in Windows 8. The same Start menu that was popular in Windows 7 returns to Windows 10 with an updated look. Clicking the Start button displays the Start menu, as shown in Figure 1-6.

When you browse the Start menu, three columns of information are displayed. The left-hand column displays small icons to identify the currently signed-in user and to access documents, pictures, system settings, and power controls. A description of each small icon can be seen by hovering the pointer over the icon. If desired, this column can be expanded by clicking the menu icon at the top of the column.

The middle column contains a list of applications, with the user's most frequently used applications at the top, and a sorted list of installed applications below that. When new applications are installed, they appear in this area. Folders in this column are used to organization applications. To view the applications, you need to expand the folder.

The right-hand column is an area that you can customize to contain your most commonly used apps in the order that you prefer. For example, you could put the Microsoft Office apps here along with your preferred browser. When you install applications, they sometimes automatically place an icon here, but you can remove it.

 TIP   Centralized management of the Start menu layout for computers in an organization is possible with Windows 10 Pro, Windows 10 Enterprise, and Windows 10 Education. For detailed information about how to customize the Start menu layout, visit https://blogs.technet.microsoft.com/deploymentguys/2016/03/07/windows-10-start-layout-customization/.

Some of the applications in the Start menu have Live Tiles. Live Tiles allow applications to provide quick summary information without the need to run the application. For example, a weather application can display the temperature in the icon. Some people prefer that the icons remain static so that they are more easily identifiable, and this feature can be disabled.

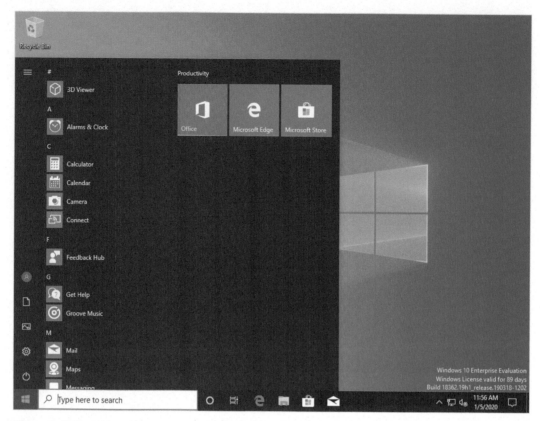

Figure 1-6   Start menu

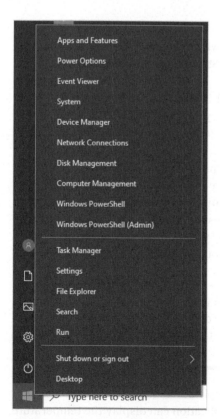

Figure 1-7   Shortcut menu for
administrative tools

Windows 10 uses jump lists to identify content recently opened by an application or common tasks for that application. To view the jump list for an application, right-click it. For example, if you right-click the icon for Microsoft Word, you will see a list of documents recently opened by using Word. Similarly, right-clicking a browser application will display a list of frequently visited websites.

For administrators, right-clicking the Start button displays a shortcut menu of commonly used administrative tools, as shown in Figure 1-7. This is a fast and easy to remember way to access these tools.

Search Interface

A Search box appears next to the Start button, as shown in Figure 1-8. Typing text in the Search box allows you to find content on the local computer, the Internet, and the Microsoft Store. This provides a single point you can use to search for documents, windows settings, websites, and applications.

Taskbar

The **taskbar** is a horizontal bar located at the bottom of the screen by default, as shown in Figure 1-9. On the left side of the taskbar are the Start button and search tool. On the right side of the taskbar is the notification area. In the middle of the taskbar is an area containing icons to start applications and icons that identify running applications.

The taskbar has some application icons by default. You can customize these to match your own work habits. The applications here by default are Cortana, Task View, Microsoft Edge, File Explorer, the Microsoft Store, and Mail.

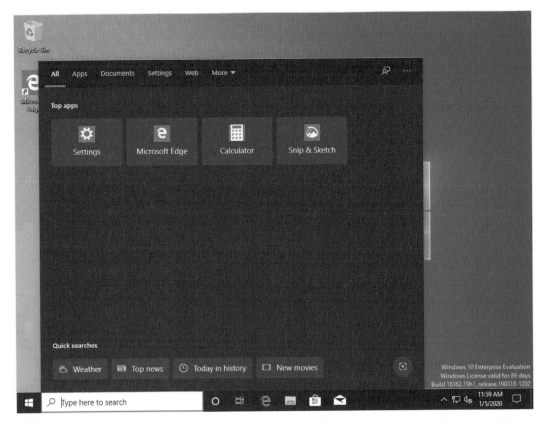

Figure 1-8   Search tool

Start menu   Search box   taskbar   notification area

Figure 1-9   Taskbar

Many people remove the Microsoft Store and Mail icons to make room for more running applications. You can also select applications that you want easily available and pin them to the taskbar.

When multiple windows are open, the screen can get cluttered and windows might overlap one another. To better organize open windows, an icon is placed on the taskbar that represents the running application.

Hovering the pointer over an icon for a running program (indicated by a colored bar beneath the icon) displays a preview of each window the application has open above the taskbar button. Hovering the pointer over a preview window previews only that window on the desktop. This is known as the Peek feature because a user can conveniently peek at an active window without having to fully switch to it. If the pointer is moved away from the preview window without selecting it, the desktop reverts to the way it was before the preview. If the user clicks a preview window, that window becomes the active window.

Notification Area

In previous versions of Windows, the notification area could easily get cluttered with notifications and icons from multiple applications and the operating system. The notification area has been simplified by default to display the clock and icons for volume, network connectivity, and Action Center notifications. Additional icons may be displayed for touch screen controls, battery power, and stylus utilities, depending on the hardware capabilities of the device running Windows 10.

The Action Center lists important notifications from the operating system to the user in one place. You should periodically check this area to see if there are new notifications of problems or solutions that Windows 10 has discovered.

Other applications can add icons to the notification area, but they are not displayed automatically. The extra icons are viewed by clicking the up arrow icon at the left-hand side of the notification area, which opens a window containing other notification icons that may be active. You can configure settings to control which icons are displayed in the notification area.

Activity 1-3: Configuring the Windows 10 User Interface

Time Required: 5 minutes

Objective: Configure the Windows 10 user interface.

Description: You have recently installed Windows 10. You are configuring the user interface to gain more experience with the available options. This will help you understand the options available to end users in your organization when you need to help them.

1. If necessary, start your computer and sign in.
2. Click **Start**, right-click **Calculator**, and then click **Pin to Start**.
3. In the Search box, type **notepad**.
4. In the details pane, below **Notepad**, click **Pin to Start**.
5. Click **Start** and verify that both Calculator and Notepad are on the Start menu.
6. Click **Start** to close the Start menu.
7. On the taskbar, right-click the **Mail** icon and then click **Unpin from taskbar**.
8. On the taskbar, right-click the **Microsoft Store** icon and then click **Unpin from taskbar**.
9. On the taskbar, right-click an open area, expand **Search**, and click **Show search icon**. This frees up a great deal of space on the taskbar when the screen resolution is low.
10. On the taskbar, right-click an open area, point to Cortana on the shortcut menu, and then click **Show Cortana button** on the submenu. This removes the Cortana icon from the taskbar.
11. On the taskbar, in the notifications area, click the up arrow to display the status of background applications.
12. On the taskbar, click the Action Center icon on the far right. Because your computer is a brand-new installation, there might be no new notifications to view.
13. Click the Action Center icon again to close the Action Center.
14. On the taskbar, right-click an open area and then click **Taskbar settings**.
15. In the Settings window, read the available settings.
16. Click the Start tab in the left pane and read the available settings.
17. Close the Settings window.

Advanced Window Management

Windows 10 includes features that make it easier to manage open windows and arrange them. These features are useful when you have multiple applications running.

The Snap feature allows you to quickly resize windows by clicking the title bar of the window and dragging it to the top, sides, or middle of the screen. If the window is dragged to the top of the screen, the application is maximized to use the whole screen. If the window is dragged to the right or left side of the screen, window is resized to fill half the screen on that side. Note that windows resizing doesn't take effect until you let go of the mouse button after dragging the window.

The Shake feature minimizes all other windows except for one you are interested in. To shake a window, you click the title bar and move (shake) the mouse rapidly from side to side. All other windows automatically minimize. Repeating the shake restores all other windows to their original size and location.

The Task View feature has a dedicated taskbar icon next to the Search box at the lower-left side of the screen. Clicking the Task View icon changes the display to show an ordered preview of all application windows that are currently open. Clicking a window's preview image brings that window forward to become the active window.

Clicking the Task View icon also allows you to access a new feature called Virtual Desktop. Virtual Desktop allows you to create multiple desktops that can host different open windows. The windows visible on a desktop are specific to that virtual desktop. You could decide to have one virtual desktop to show only business-related applications and perhaps another to show only personal applications. Using the Task View control, you can toggle between virtual desktops as required and avoid a confusing mix of windows on a single desktop.

Activity 1-4: Performing Advanced Window Management

Time Required: 10 minutes
Objective: Perform advanced window management for applications.
Description: You have recently installed Windows 10 and want to learn about advanced windows management. You will use this knowledge to help the end users in your organization to use their computers more efficiently.

1. If necessary, start your computer and sign in.
2. Click **Start** and then click **Notepad**.
3. Click **Start** and then click **Calculator**.
4. In the Calculator window, click the title bar and drag it until the pointer is at the far right of the screen. When you release the mouse button, Calculator is sized to use the right side of the screen.
5. On the left side of the screen, click **Notepad**. When you snap a window to the right or left side, you are given the option to select a second window for the other side. This configuration is very useful for wide monitors when you want to work on two applications at the same time.
6. In the Notepad window, click the title bar and drag it down until the window reverts to its original size.
7. In the Notepad window, click the title bar and shake it back and forth rapidly. This minimizes the Calculator window.
8. In the Notepad window, click the title bar and shake it back and forth rapidly. This restores the Calculator window to its previous state.
9. In the Notepad window, click the title bar and drag it to the top of the screen. This maximizes the window to use the whole screen.
10. On the taskbar, hover the pointer over Calculator to display a preview of content in the Calculator window.
11. On the taskbar, click the **Task View** icon. Notice that you can see both Notepad and Calculator listed.
12. Click **Calculator** to make Calculator the active window.
13. On the taskbar, click the **Task View** icon and then click **New desktop**. Task View now shows Desktop 1 and Desktop 2.
14. Click **Desktop 2**. This desktop copies all the configuration for Desktop 1 but does not include the running applications.
15. On the desktop, right-click the Microsoft Edge shortcut and click **Delete**.
16. On the taskbar, click **Microsoft Edge**.
17. On the taskbar, click the **Task View** icon and click **Desktop 1**.
18. Close Calculator and Notepad. Notice that the Microsoft Edge shortcut deleted from Desktop 2 is also deleted from Desktop 1.
19. On the taskbar, click the **Task View** icon and click **Desktop 2**.
20. Close the Microsoft Edge window.
21. On the taskbar, click the **Task View** icon.
22. In Task View, hover the pointer over **Desktop 2** and click the **X** to remove it.
23. Press **Esc** to view the desktop again.

WINDOWS 10 NETWORKING MODELS

Networks connect multiple computers to share data and resources. A network model details a logical framework for sharing, securing, and managing data and resources across that network. Just as different versions of Windows 10 are available to meet the differing needs of customers, different network models also are available to connect computers. Some networking models support more computers and offer greater administrative control. Other models try to simplify the framework for simpler and smaller environments.

Workgroup Model

By default, when you install Windows 10, it is configured as a member of a workgroup. A **workgroup** is a loosely knit collection of peer computers on a network where no computer has control over or plays a superior role to any other computer. The peers can share resources with one another over the network. This can be useful for a small number of computers in a typical home or small business network.

When you browse the network, you see the workgroup name, and if you expand the workgroup, you'll see computers that are members of that workgroup. Each computer is identified by its name and address on the network. The workgroup itself is identified by an assigned name. The default workgroup name is WORKGROUP.

A computer can be a member of only one workgroup at a time. More than one workgroup can coexist on the same network. Being a member of a workgroup helps you find shared resources such as files and printers on the peer computers, but it does not restrict you from accessing resources located outside the workgroup of which your computer is a member.

In low-security environments where resources can be shared with all users, the workgroup model is fairly easy to manage. For example, you can share a printer attached to your computer with everyone. If you have varying security requirements for access to different sets of data, however, a workgroup is very difficult to manage.

The workgroup model relies on local user accounts that you create on each computer running Windows 10. No mechanism exists to create a user account that has access to resources on all computers.

Managing access to resources in a workgroup can quickly become difficult. For example, if you want to share files on your computer with Jeff, then you need to create a local user account with a password on your computer for Jeff. Then when Jeff attempts to access the shared files from his computer, he is prompted for the username and password you created. This means that Jeff might have a unique username and password for each computer on which he accesses resources.

You can try to simplify access to resources in a workgroup by creating user accounts on each computer with the same username and password. That works in the short term, but as soon as Jeff changes the password for the account on his own computer, the passwords are out of sync.

Microsoft recommends that workgroups should not be used for more than 10 to 20 computers. Sharing resources from computers running Windows 10 has a practical limit. All Windows 10 editions are limited to support a maximum of 20 simultaneous connections. For example, a shared folder can be accessed from only 20 other computers at the same time.

 **CAUTION**   Windows 10 can be configured to use a Microsoft account for authentication. This works well for authenticating locally but not for assigning access to shared resources.

Domain Model

A domain model is a client/server strategy that simplifies management of its members. A **domain** is a collection of computers and users that are identified by a common security database. The database is stored on one or more dedicated servers called domain controllers (DCs). Computers that are part of the domain can reference the domain database and read the user and computer accounts contained within. Member computers can access shared resources on other computers from the same domain, using the security information referenced by the DC to control access.

The major differences between the workgroup and domain models are how the members are managed and the limits to sharing resources. A computer running Windows 10 can be used as a server in a domain, but the connection limits mentioned in the workgroup model still apply. Server-class operating systems, such as Windows Server 2019, can theoretically have an unlimited number of clients access a shared resource simultaneously. The practical limit with centralized servers is determined by overall performance and licensing.

Domain networking is typically employed in business environments, so not all editions of Windows 10 have support for it. Windows 10 Pro, Education, and Enterprise editions support joining a domain networking system.

When a server shares a resource, it can define permissions to access the resource based on the domain user and computer names stored on the DC. If a new user is added to the domain, each domain computer can directly reference the new domain user name by verifying it with the domain controller. Likewise, if a domain user account needs to be removed, it has to be removed only from the domain database on the domain controller and not each domain member computer.

A computer can be a member of a workgroup or a domain, but not both at the same time. A computer cannot be a member of more than one domain at the same time. The computer and the domain must be identified by unique names.

Access to shared resources in other domains and workgroups is still allowed, but the user has to authenticate to those remote systems. For example, if a computer is a member of a workgroup and accessing resources in a domain, the user would be prompted to provide a user ID and password for the domain.

More than one domain can coexist on a network, with the domain defining a security boundary. Changes made to the security or configuration of a domain usually only impact domain members. It is possible, however, for different domains to trust one another to allow shared access among domains. The limits of how domains trust one another depend on the type of domain in use.

The Microsoft implementation of a central database that stores domain information is Active Directory. Active Directory has a central database of user and computer accounts and centralized tools to manage them. The domain database is stored on dedicated DC servers. All DCs are capable of updating the database and replicating those changes to the other DCs in the domain. This is commonly referred to as multimaster replication.

Active Directory systems use a naming strategy based on Domain Name System (DNS) technology. Active Directory domain names are in the same format as Internet names, such as microsoft.com. This was done to better support the TCP/IP network protocols that link networks around the globe today.

From an administrator's perspective, another advantage of Active Directory is the ability to manage the user and computer environment of its members. The administrator can use Group Policy to configure items such as installed applications, security settings, environment settings, and limits. The Group Policy settings are stored as part of the Active Directory database and are visible to all members of the Active Directory domain. The Active Directory administrator can define specific criteria that control to which computers or users the settings apply.

Windows 10 can be a client of a domain, but it can never be a DC. To create an Active Directory domain, you must purchase and install a Windows Server operating system that supports Active Directory on a dedicated computer (which can be a physical or virtual system). Likewise, domain Group Policy settings apply only if the Windows 10 computer is a member of the domain.

Azure AD Join

Azure AD is a directory service hosted by Microsoft as a cloud-based service via the Internet. A company can create a tenant in Azure AD that can be used to manage Windows 10 devices.

You can use **Azure AD join** to register a Windows 10 device with Azure AD to enable centralized management of that device by the company's administrators. Once registered, an Azure AD joined device can be given access to organizational applications and resources whether the Windows 10 device is owned by the corporation or the individual.

The traditional Active Directory domain model is still used with corporate computers, on-premises, with limited domain management functionality outside the corporate private network from the Internet. The traditional domain join can still provide the best on-premises managed experience for devices that are capable of domain joining.

Azure AD join is suitable for devices that cannot join a domain and in environments where users can best be managed from the cloud with **Mobile Device Management (MDM)** solutions, such as Microsoft Intune, instead of traditional domain management tools like Group Policy. As organizations move their business to the cloud and reduce on-premises infrastructure, Azure AD becomes key in several areas.

User accounts created in Azure AD can be used to sign in to a computer running Windows 10 that is Azure AD joined. This allows administrators to centrally control user accounts for authentication even if the computer is outside the office. As long as the computer has Internet access, the computer can be Azure AD joined.

With the configuration capabilities linked to Azure AD join, end users can configure a brand-new device out of the box without help from an administrator. Everything is configured ahead of time and automatically applied when the user signs in.

Azure AD joined devices are not typically used for sharing data like computers in a workgroup are. Instead, using Azure AD join is appropriate for the small business environment that uses cloud services for collaboration. The services available in Office 365 are one example of a set of cloud services that can be used for collaboration.

SUMMARY

- The main purpose for using a computer is completing tasks by using applications. Applications are written for specific operating systems. It is the operating system that manages the computer hardware. In addition to managing hardware, Windows 10 also includes some small but useful applications.
- Multiple editions of Windows 10 are available. Each edition has different features; you need to select the correct edition for your scenario. Windows 10 Pro and Windows 10 Enterprise are the two editions more commonly used for business.
- The minimum hardware requirements provided by Microsoft for Windows 10 installation are not realistic for day-to-day use. If you are installing Windows 10 or upgrading, ensure your computer systems have adequate hardware for reasonable performance.
- When you upgrade from a previous version of Windows to Windows 10, you need to ensure that it is a valid upgrade path. In general, you can upgrade to the same edition or a higher-level edition. Windows 8 cannot be upgraded to Windows 10.
- Windows 10 can be licensed by using an OEM license, an FPP license, volume licenses, or cloud licenses. Consider factors such as whether you need to move licenses to new hardware when you select licensing.
- You can activate Windows 10 via the Internet, by using a KMS server, or by using Active Directory-based activation. Only volume licensing can use a KMS server or Active Directory-based activation.
- The Windows 10 user interface is similar to previous version of Windows. The user interface includes a Start menu and taskbar. The taskbar includes a search area and a notifications area. Some advanced window management options are available, such as virtual desktops and snap.
- For networking and sharing resources, Windows 10 can use the workgroup model, the domain model, and Azure AD join. The domain model is used by most businesses. The workgroup model and Azure AD join are used by small organizations or in situations where joining a domain is not practical.

Key Terms

Action Center
Active Directory
Active Directory-based activation
application programmer interfaces (APIs)
applications
Azure AD
Azure AD join
cloud licensing
computer hardware
domain
DVD boot installation
full packaged product (FPP) license
generic volume license key (GVLK)

Group Policy
hardware drivers
Key Management Service (KMS)
Mobile Device Management (MDM)
Multiple Activation Key (MAK)
notification area
operating system
original equipment manufacturer (OEM) license
product activation
Start menu
Task View
taskbar
Virtual Desktop

Volume Activation Management Tool (VAMT)
volume licensing
Windows 10 Education
Windows 10 Enterprise
Windows 10 Enterprise Long Term Servicing Channel (LTSC)
Windows 10 Home
Windows 10 Pro
Windows 10 Pro Education
Windows 10 Pro for Workstations
workgroup
x64 architecture

Review Questions

1. A friend has asked you which version of Windows 10 should be purchased to start a new home-based business. Your friend needs only one computer for now and requires support for Windows Store applications needed to manage the business. Your friend is not very experienced with computers and has asked for easy-to-use features. Which version of Windows 10 do you recommend?

   a. Windows 10 Education
   b. Windows 10 Home

    c. Windows 10 Pro

    d. Windows 10 Enterprise

2. The new browser included with Windows 10 is called _____.

    a. Charlie

    b. Virtual Desktop

    c. Cortana

    d. Microsoft Edge

    e. Windows Hello

3. You are considering purchasing an inexpensive computer from a friend that has a 32-bit CPU and 8 GB of RAM. You install Windows 10 Home, 32-bit edition, but you can't see the full amount of RAM. What is wrong?

    a. The CPU does not support hyperthreading.

    b. You need to install a 64-bit version of Windows 10.

    c. The CPU does not support multiple cores.

    d. You must install Windows 10 Pro.

    e. Windows 10, 32-bit editions cannot support more than 4 GB of RAM.

4. Your workstation is running Windows 10 Pro, and you decide to share a folder on your computer. Twenty-two people in your office are trying to connect to that folder at the same time over the network. The first 20 people can connect, but the other two cannot. To fix this, you could _____.

    a. buy a computer, software, and licenses to run Windows Server 2016

    b. restart your computer

    c. make sure the network card is using WDF device drivers

    d. none of the above

5. Which of the following is an advantage of domain networking?

    a. no central security database

    b. included in every version of Windows 10

    c. centralized security management

    d. support for up to 25 simultaneous shared connections

6. A new company will have 40 workstations in one building sharing a single network. All users must be able to share files and printers with one another. Access to shared information must be secure and simple to administer. The best technology for this system is _____.

    a. workgroups

    b. Windows Peer-to-Peer Networking

    c. people to people

    d. domain networking

7. Application windows can be docked to the sides and corners of the screen using a feature called

    _____.

    a. Snap

    b. Shake

    c. Virtual Desktop

    d. Peek

    e. Docker

8. An administrator of a manufacturing company would like to manage corporate computers with Group Policy. The administrator is reviewing a purchase request for 20 new computers from the business owners. Which version of Windows 10 should the administrator consider for installation on the new computers? (Select two.)

    a. Windows 10 Home

    b. Windows 10 Pro

    c. Windows 10 Education

    d. Windows 10 Enterprise

    e. Windows 10 Ultimate

9. You are installing a computer to run a nuclear reactor management system. The software lists Windows 10 as a requirement. To ensure that future feature updates do not impact the stability of the software, you should consider what type of Windows 10 installation?

    a. Windows 10 Pro

    b. Windows 10 Enterprise

    c. Windows 10 Core

    d. Windows 10 Enterprise LTSC

10. Which of the following is a disadvantage of workgroup computing?

    a. Requires one or more expensive servers

    b. Supports an unlimited number of workstations

    c. No centralized security management

    d. Simple to set up initially

11. What type of software does Windows 10 require to manage a new type of hardware?

    a. Hardware driver

    b. Hardware shim

    c. Plug and play software

    d. Resource configuration driver

    e. API

12. Which editions of Windows 10 have support for 6 TB of memory? (Select two.)

    a. Windows 10 Enterprise

    b. Windows 10 Home

    c. Windows 10 Pro

    d. Windows 10 Pro for Workstations

    e. Windows 10 Pro Education

13. Which type of license cannot be moved from one physical computer to another?
   a. OEM
   b. FPP
   c. MAK
   d. KMS
   e. Volume licensing

14. A volume license for Windows 10 is an upgrade from an OEM edition of Windows 10. True or False?
   a. True
   b. False

15. Which of the following are valid upgrade paths? (Select 3)
   a. Windows 7 Home to Windows 10 Pro
   b. Windows 8 Enterprise to Windows 10 Enterprise
   c. Windows 7 Enterprise to Windows 10 Pro
   d. Windows 8.1 Pro to Windows 10 Enterprise
   e. Windows 8.1 Pro to Windows 10 Pro

16. You can use cloud licensing for which specific scenario?
   a. New installations of Windows 10 Enterprise
   b. Upgrading from Windows 10 Pro to Windows 10 Enterprise
   c. Upgrading Windows 8.1 Pro to Windows 10 Enterprise
   d. New installations of Windows 10 Pro

17. Which type of license has the product key embedded in firmware?
   a. OEM
   b. FPP
   c. MAK
   d. KMS
   e. Volume licensing

18. Active Directory-based activation is more reliable than KMS. True or False?
   a. True
   b. False

19. What is the minimum activation threshold when using KMS with Windows 10?
   a. 5
   b. 10
   c. 15
   d. 20
   e. 25

20. To use KMS or Active Directory-based activation, you need to configure all Windows 10 computers with the same key. True or False?
   a. True
   b. False

Case Projects

Case Project 1-1: Designing a Small Network

Master Motors is an automobile dealership and repair shop with 18 computers running Windows 8.1 Home. Their main dealership management software is installed on one person's computer and shared with other users. Their software vendor has told them that they need to host the application on a server if they have more than 20 computers.

You are a representative from a managed services provider (MSP) that needs to design a solution for Master Motors that includes an upgrade to Windows 10. Which networking model will you suggest? Which edition of Windows 10 will you suggest?

Case Project 1-2: Upgrading to Windows 10

Gigantic Life Insurance has 4,000 users spread over five locations in North America. They have called you as a consultant to discuss different options for deploying Windows 10 to the desktops in their organization.

Most of the existing desktop computers are a mix of Windows 7 Pro and Windows 8.1 Pro, but one office is running Windows 8 Enterprise. They have System Center Configuration Manager to control the deployment process automatically. They want to begin distributing applications by using App-V.

Can you identify any issues that need to be resolved before the project begins? Which edition of Windows 10 should they use? Which type of activation should they use?

USING THE SYSTEM UTILITIES

After reading this module and completing the exercises, you will be able to:

1. Understand and use Settings to configure Windows 10
2. Understand the Administrative Tools
3. Use command-line administration tools
4. Configure displays
5. Manage Windows 10 optional features
6. Manage hardware components
7. Understand and configure power management
8. Use Task Scheduler

Windows 10 includes a wide range of system utilities in Settings and in Administrative Tools. A thorough knowledge of these utilities can help you manage, tune, and improve your system. Some of the more advanced tools are Microsoft Management Console (MMC) snap-ins. A snap-in is the standardized format for creating system management utilities in Windows.

This module provides an overview of Settings and Administrative Tools, along with a description of the MMC. In-depth coverage also is provided of how to manage hardware components, configure power management, configure the display, and use Task Scheduler.

SETTINGS OVERVIEW

Most of the configuration options for Windows 10 can be accessed through Settings, shown in Figure 2-1. The settings are organized into categories to make it easier to find the specific settings you are looking for. To access Settings, click the Start button and then click Settings on the Start menu.

The categories within Settings are:

- *System*—These are general settings for configuring Windows 10 functions. This category includes settings for display, sound, notifications, power, storage, tablet mode, multitasking, clipboard, and Remote Desktop.
- *Devices*—This category includes settings for Bluetooth, printers, scanners, mouse, typing, Windows Ink, AutoPlay, and USB.

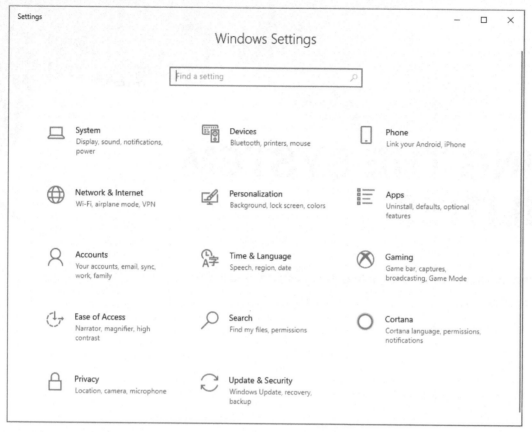

Figure 2-1   Windows 10 Settings window

- *Phone*—These are settings for the My Phone feature that lets you link an iPhone or Android device to your computer. You can use My Phone to access photos and text messages on your phone. You can also use your computer to send text messages and make phone calls through your phone.
- *Network & Internet*—This category includes settings for connectivity, which includes network status, network connections, virtual private networks (VPNs), data usage, and proxy configuration.
- *Personalization*—This category has settings to configure the look and feel of Windows 10. These settings include desktop background, colors, the lock screen, themes, fonts, the Start menu, and taskbar.
- *Apps*—This category includes settings for managing applications. You can add or remove applications and Windows 10 optional features. You can also configure default applications for content types and which applications run at startup.
- *Accounts*—This category allows you to configure authentication to Windows 10. This includes creating and managing local user accounts.
- *Time & Language*—This category has settings for the date and time, regional formats, language, and speech recognition.
- *Gaming*—This category has settings for the game bar, capturing gameplay, broadcasting gameplay, Game Mode, and Xbox Networking with Xbox Live services.
- *Ease of Access*—The category contains settings that can make it easier for people with visual or physical challenges to use Windows 10. You can configure options such as high contrast display colors and enable Narrator to read text on the screen.
- *Search*—This category contains settings that let you customize Windows search results from the Internet and your local computer. This includes settings to customize which local files are indexed and included in search results.

- *Cortana*—This category contains settings to customize when Cortana can be used and to which of your data Cortana has access.
- *Privacy*—This category has settings that control which data Windows 10 can capture on your computer and submit to web services. For example, you can disable diagnostic and usage data from being submitted to Microsoft. This category also includes settings to control which applications can access data and devices on your computer, such as location, camera, microphone, documents, and calendar.
- *Update & Security*—This category has a wide range of settings for Windows Update, backup, troubleshooting, recovery, activation, find my device, and the Windows Insider program.

> **(!) CAUTION**   Many of the configuration options in Settings are controlled by toggle switches. Changing a toggle switch between Off and On takes effect immediately; no option to cancel or undo is available.

If you don't know which category a setting is in, then search for it instead of browsing. Searching for a setting is much faster than browsing through multiple categories. After you search for it, you'll be able to see which category it's in.

In Windows 7 and earlier versions of Windows, **Control Panel** was used to access configuration settings. Control Panel, shown in Figure 2-2, is still available in Windows 10. Most configuration options can be accessed through Settings, but some are still accessible only through Control Panel. In some cases, a configuration option can be accessed through both Settings and Control Panel. Newer configuration options are available only in Settings.

NOTE 1

Options in Settings can vary depending on the hardware present in a computer running Windows 10. You might see some inconsistency among the computers you use.

Figure 2-2   Control Panel window

Activity 2-1: Exploring Settings

Time Required: 10 minutes

Objective: Review the available settings

Description: In Windows 10, Settings is where most of the user-level configuration options are accessed. You should be familiar with these settings so that you understand what options are available. In this activity, you browse through Settings to identify the available options.

1. If necessary, start your computer and sign in.
2. Click the **Start** button and then click **Settings**.
3. If necessary, expand the Settings windows so that all categories are visible and then click **System**.
4. Read the settings on the Display screen. If necessary, scroll down to view them all.
5. Click **Focus assist** in the left pane and read the default settings.
6. Click **Multitasking** in the left pane and read the default settings.
7. Scroll down in the left pane and then click **About**. Read the information that is displayed about your computer. Information about your computer is located here, such as processor type and speed, memory, and computer name.
8. Click **Home** in the left pane and then click **Devices**.
9. Click **AutoPlay** in the left pane and review the default settings.
10. Click **Home** in the left pane and then click **Apps**.
11. In Apps & features, read the list of installed apps.
12. Click **Default apps** in the left pane and read the default settings.
13. Click **Home** in the left pane and then click **Time & Language**.
14. In the Date & time screen, read the default settings.
15. Click **Region** in the left pane and read the default settings.
16. Click **Language** in the left pane and review the option to install an additional language.
17. Click **Home** in the left pane and then click **Privacy**.
18. In the General screen, review the default settings.
19. Click **Diagnostics & feedback** in the left pane and read the default settings.
20. Scroll down in the left pane, click **Microphone**, and read the default settings.
21. Take time to review any other categories that interest you and then close the Settings window.

Activity 2-2: Using Ease of Access Features

Time Required: 10 minutes

Objective: Explore the Ease of Access features in Windows 10

Description: Your organization has several people with visual and hearing challenges. You need to explore the Ease of Access features in Windows 10 to ensure that you understand how best to support them.

1. If necessary, start your computer and sign in.
2. Click the **Start** button and then click **Settings**.
3. In Settings, click **Ease of Access** and read the Display settings.
4. Click **Cursor & pointer** in the left pane and read the available settings.
5. Click **Magnifier** in the left pane and then click the **Turn on Magnifier** toggle to change the setting to **On**.
6. Move the pointer to the edges of the screen to change the portion of the screen that is visible.
7. In the Magnifier window, click **Views** on the toolbar and then click **Lens**.
8. Move the pointer around to change the area that is magnified.
9. Close the Magnifier window.

10. Click **Color filters** in the left pane and then click the **Turn on color filters** toggle to change the setting to **On**. This feature is useful if the user is color-blind.
11. Scroll down until you can see the color wheel, and then click **Red-green (green weak, deuteranopia)**.
12. Click **Blue-yellow (tritanopia)** and notice that the color wheel changes.
13. Scroll up and then click the **Turn on color filters** toggle to change the setting to **Off**.
14. Click **High contrast** in the left pane, and then click the **Turn on high contrast** toggle to change the setting to **On**.
15. In the Choose a theme box in the right pane, select **High Contrast #1**.
16. Click the **Turn on high contrast** toggle to change the setting to **Off**.
17. Scroll down in the left pane, click **Keyboard**, and read the available settings.
18. Click the **Use the On-Screen Keyboard** toggle to change the setting to **On**. This can be useful for someone with limited hand movement who is unable to use a regular keyboard.
19. Close the On-Screen Keyboard window.
20. Close the Settings window.

ADMINISTRATIVE TOOLS

Windows 10 includes a collection of system configuration utilities that are grouped in a category called Administrative Tools and found in System and Security in Control Panel. Most of the tools in this category use the Microsoft Management Console (MMC). The MMC is a framework that simplifies the development of administrative tools. The Administrative Tools are shown in Figure 2-3. Brief descriptions of these tools follow; later modules offer more detailed coverage.

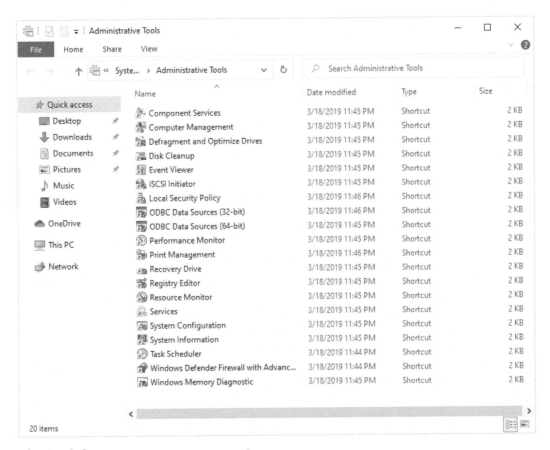

Figure 2-3   Administrative Tools window

Component Services is used to configure settings for some apps. It includes settings for COM, DCOM, and Distributed Transaction Coordinator. Typically, these settings are modified only if you receive instructions from an application developer or as part of a troubleshooting document.

Computer Management is a tool that allows you to manage multiple parts of Windows 10, such as local users and disks. You can use this tool instead of opening multiple other tools.

The Administrative Tools in Windows 10 include disk management tools. The Defragment and Optimize Drives tool moves file blocks around on the disk to make individual files contiguous and faster to access. It is seldom required to perform this task manually because defragmentation is performed once per week automatically. The Disk Cleanup tool helps you identify unneeded files that can be removed.

Event Viewer is used to view messages from apps or Windows 10. These messages are useful for troubleshooting errors. When you find an error, you can search the Internet for a solution if the fix is not obvious.

The iSCSI protocol allows computers to communicate with external storage over standard Ethernet networks. External storage devices that support iSCSI are known as iSCSI targets. The computers that access iSCSI targets are iSCSI initiators. The iSCSI Initiator tool lets you configure Windows 10 to communicate with iSCSI targets and use the iSCSI targets as external disks over the network. The iSCSI protocol is used only in corporate environments and mostly on servers rather than workstations.

The Local Security Policy tool allows you to edit a wide variety of security settings on the local computer. Some of the settings include password policies, account lockout policies, auditing policies, user rights assignment, and software restriction policies. When Group Policies are used in a corporate environment, the Group Policy settings configured centrally by the administrator override the settings configured locally with this tool.

Open Database Connectivity (ODBC) is a standard mechanism for allowing applications to access databases. Applications written to use ODBC can communicate with any supported database, such as Microsoft SQL Server, Microsoft Access, or Oracle databases. A network administrator must then configure an ODBC data source to communicate with the proper database. This isolates the application from the database, makes application development easier, and provides greater flexibility when choosing a database. Windows 10 includes separate tools for configuring ODBC connections for 32-bit apps and 64-bit apps.

Performance Monitor is used to monitor and troubleshoot performance issues in Windows 10. It includes the capability to monitor many system resources, including the processor, disk, memory, and the network. Performance Monitor can log resource status over time and generate reports.

Print Management is a tool for monitoring and managing printers. In a single view, you can monitor and manage local and network printers.

Recovery Drive is a tool that you can use to create media for installing Windows 10. Because most computers do not ship with a Windows 10 installation DVD, this is important if you want to reinstall Windows 10.

Registry Editor allows you to edit data in the Windows 10 registry. The registry is a centralized database of settings for Windows 10 and for applications. This tool is used for advanced troubleshooting and when instructed by help documentation.

Resource Monitor is a tool that provides detailed information about the processes running on your computer. You can use it to view the processor utilization, memory utilization, network utilization, and disk activity of individual processes. It is like a more advanced version of Task Manager.

Services allows you to configure Windows 10 services. You can also start and stop services if required for troubleshooting. This functionality is also available in Computer Management.

System Configuration gives you access to boot configuration, service startup, startup applications, and system tools. The General tab, shown in Figure 2-4, lets you select the type of startup you want to perform. The Boot tab lets you configure boot options, such as Safe Mode. The Services tab lets you enable or disable services. The Startup tab provides a link to Task Manager where you can disable any of the applications that Windows 10 is starting automatically. The Tools tab gives you easy access to a variety of system tools, such as the Registry Editor.

System Information provides detailed information about Windows 10 configuration for hardware and software. You can view information such as hardware resources, device configuration, device drivers, services, and running tasks.

Task Scheduler lets you create system maintenance tasks that are performed on a regular schedule or when system events occur. Windows 10 uses Task Scheduler to perform many background maintenance tasks. You can also create your own tasks.

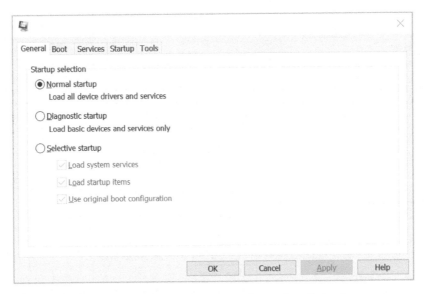

Figure 2-4   General tab in System Configuration dialog box

Windows Defender Firewall with Advanced Security is an advanced editor for configuring Windows Firewall. It allows you to configure advanced settings for Windows Firewall that are not available through the Windows Firewall applet in Control Panel or Settings. In addition, Windows Defender Firewall with Advanced Security can configure IPSec settings. IPSec is a protocol used to encrypt data communication over the network.

The **Windows Memory Diagnostics Tool** is used to perform tests on the physical memory of a computer running Windows 10. The physical memory of a computer cannot be tested when Windows 10 is running because the memory diagnostics tool needs access to test all the memory, including the memory used by Windows 10. So, when you choose to use the Windows Memory Diagnostics Tool, your computer reboots to run the tool without Windows 10 in memory.

Microsoft Management Console

The MMC is a graphical interface shell that provides a structured environment to build management utilities. The MMC provides basic functionality, such as menus, so that management utility developers do not have to create it themselves. This also provides a consistent user interface for all management utilities, which makes network administrators more productive.

Network administrators use MMC consoles with **MMC snap-ins** to perform management tasks. Each MMC console can host one or more snap-ins. A snap-in is a component that adds control mechanisms to the MMC console for a specific service or object. For example, the Disk Management snap-in is used to manage hard disks. Snap-ins typically are capable of multiple functions. For example, the Disk Management snap-in can partition and format hard disks.

An MMC console, shown in Figure 2-5, is composed of a console menu bar, console tree, details pane, and an Actions pane. The contents of the Action and View menus in the console menu bar change based on the snap-in that is active in the console. The console menu bar also contains a mini-icon toolbar of shortcuts to common tasks in the Action and View menus. The console tree is the left pane of the console and displays the snap-ins that are loaded into the console. The details pane is the middle pane of the console and displays the details of the item selected in the console tree. The Actions pane on the right is used to provide easy access to the options in the Action menu. For example, in Figure 2-5, Event Viewer is selected, and the Actions pane shows the options available at that node.

Figure 2-5 shows the pre-built Computer Management administrative tool that includes several snap-ins. You also can create a customized MMC console by adding the snap-ins you want to a single console and then saving the console as an .msc file. Because you can share .msc files among users and computers, administrators can be more productive.

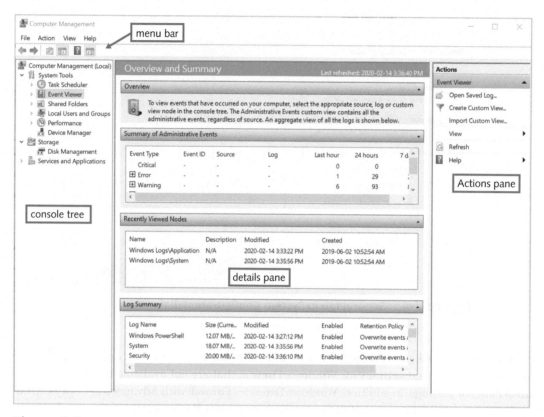

Figure 2-5   Computer Management MMC console

Computer Management

Computer Management is an MMC console that serves as a common troubleshooting and administrative interface for several snap-ins. The Computer Management console is divided into three sections: System Tools, Storage, and Services and Applications.

The System Tools section contains:

- *Task Scheduler*—This provides a way to schedule programs to run at a specified time or when an event occurs.
- *Event Viewer*—This is another way to access the same information as is found in the Event Viewer administrative tool.
- *Shared Folders*—This is a way to view the shared folders on the local system. The Shares folder lets you see all shares, including hidden shares, the path of each share, and the number of clients connected to each share. The Sessions folder lets you view which users are connected to the local system over the network, how many files they have open, and the computer they are using. The Open Files folder lets you see which files are open and which user has them open.
- *Local Users and Groups*—This is a way to access similar information as Accounts in Settings; however, this option is more advanced and provides additional options.
- *Performance*—This is another way to access the same information as is available in the Performance Monitor administrative tool.
- *Device Manager*—This provides a way to view and modify the configuration of hardware devices in your computer.

The Storage section contains:

- *Disk Management*—This is used to manage hard disks. You can partition and format hard disks.

The Services and Applications section contains:

- *Services*—This is used to enable, configure, and disable Windows 10 services.
- *WMI Control*—This provides a way to back up and restore, control security, and specify a default namespace for Windows Management Instrumentation (WMI). WMI is used to perform remote monitoring and management of Windows.

 TIP You can also open Computer Management by pressing **Win+X** and selecting Computer Management.

Activity 2-3: Using Computer Management

Time Required: 5 minutes

Objective: Use the Computer Management MMC Console

Description: The Computer Management MMC console is one of the most commonly used administrative tools. It has several useful snap-ins, such as Event Viewer, Disk Management, and Services. In this activity, you open Computer Management using two different methods.

1. If necessary, start your computer and sign in.
2. Click the **Start** button, type **Control Panel** in the Search box, and then click **Control Panel**.
3. Click **System and Security** and then click **Administrative Tools** in the right pane.
4. Double-click **Computer Management** in the left pane. Notice that a number of options to manage Windows 10 using this single MMC console are listed.
5. In the left pane, expand **Services and Applications** and click **Services**. This is the same information you can see in the Services tool that is available in Administrative Tools.
6. Close Computer Management.
7. Close the Administrative Tools window and close the System and Security window.
8. Right-click the **Start** button and then click **Computer Management**. This is another way to start Computer Management.
9. Close Computer Management.

Services

A **service** is a program that runs in the background without user interaction. Services typically perform tasks for other software applications or perform housekeeping tasks for Windows 10. For example, the DHCP Client service is responsible for communicating on the network to get a network address that allows Windows 10 to access servers and the Internet. Windows Defender Firewall also runs as a service.

The **Services** administrative tool is used to manage Windows 10 services. The details pane of Services has a standard view and an extended view that can be selected from tabs at the bottom of the console. The extended view, shown in Figure 2-6, displays the description of the selected service at the left side of the details pane and includes shortcuts for starting, stopping, and restarting the selected service.

Both views show the following service information:

- *Name*—Each service is given a name to identify it. You can modify the name of a service, but it is not recommended. If you call a vendor for support, the vendor will expect services to be using standard names.

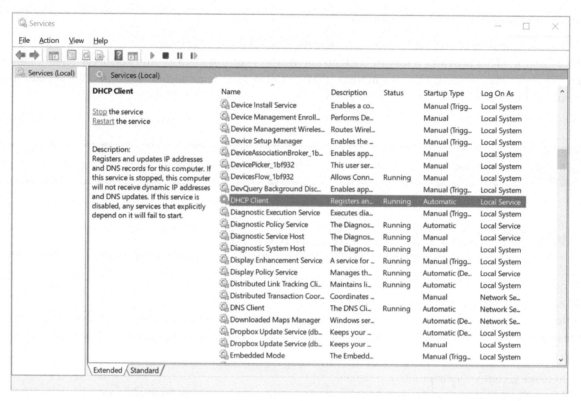

Figure 2-6   Services window

- *Description*—The description of a service provides information about what tasks the service performs. Descriptions for Windows services are provided by Microsoft, while descriptions for other services are provided by the vendor.
- *Status*—The status of a service indicates whether it is started or stopped. In rare cases, a service may have a status of starting or stopping if the service is experiencing problems during startup or shutdown.
- *Startup Type*—Services with an Automatic startup type are started when Windows 10 boots. Services with an Automatic (Delayed Start) startup type are started several minutes after Windows 10 boots. Services with a Manual startup type must be started manually by a user or by another application. Services with a Disabled startup type cannot be started.
- *Log On As*—Each service logs on to (or signs in to) Windows to determine its permissions to perform tasks such as file manipulation. Services can log on as the Local System account, which has full access to Windows 10, or a specific user account. Most Windows 10 services log on as Local System. However, logging on as a specific user account is more secure. Some Windows 10 services log on as Network Service or Local Service. Both of these accounts are more limited than Local System.

When you view the properties of a service, you can see additional information about it. You can also modify characteristics of the service. The Properties dialog box of a service, shown in Figure 2-7, includes the following tabs:

- *General*—Displays the service name, description, path to executable, and start parameters. In addition, it includes buttons to start, stop, pause, and resume the service. Stopping and starting a service is often performed when the service has experienced an error. Pausing and restarting a service is typically done when testing service functionality.
- *Log On*—Allows you to specify the account name used by a service to log on to perform its tasks.
- *Recovery*—Allows you to specify which action is taken after first, second, and subsequent failures. The actions include taking no action, restarting the services, running a program, and restarting the computer.
- *Dependencies*—Shows you which other services require this service to be running before they can start. In addition, this tab shows you the other services that must be running for this service to start.

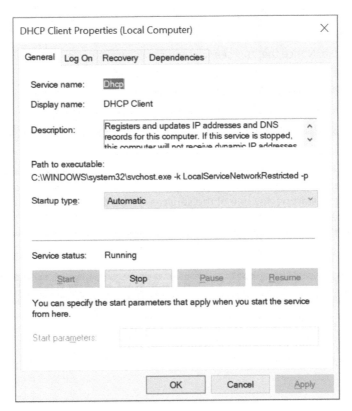

Figure 2-7   Properties of a service dialog box

Activity 2-4: Managing Services

Time Required: 10 minutes

Objective: Manage Windows 10 services by using the Services tool

Description: Windows 10 has a number of services that run in the background performing system tasks. As part of a trouble-shooting process, you often need to verify the status of services and occasionally stop or start services. In this activity, you manage services by using the Services MMC snap-in.

1. If necessary, start your computer and sign in.
2. Click the **Start** button, type **Services**, and then click **Services**.
3. If necessary, scroll to and then click **Bluetooth Support Service**. The extended view in the Services snap-in shows a description of the service at the left side of the window. This description can also be viewed when you are looking at the properties of a service.
4. Click the **Standard** tab at the bottom of the window. This view removes the service description and makes it easier to see information about the services.
5. Scroll down, right-click **Network Connection Broker**, and then click **Restart** on the shortcut menu. When you restart a service, you are given a list of other services that depend on it and are notified that the dependent services will also be restarted.
6. In the Restart Other Services window, click **Yes**. This stops and starts the service and the dependent services. It is occasionally necessary to stop and start a service if it is not functioning properly.
7. Double-click **Network Connection Broker**. The General tab in the Properties dialog box shows most of the same information that was visible in the summary of services you have already been viewing. Notice that this tab shows the executable file that runs as a service.
8. Click the **Log On** tab. If a service is configured to run as a particular user account to limit its permissions, then the credentials are entered here.

9. Click the **Recovery** tab. This tab contains settings for the actions to be taken if this service fails one or more times. Notice that this service is automatically restarted after each failure.

10. Click the **Dependencies** tab. Notice that this service requires several services to run properly, and one service depends on it.

11. Click **Cancel** and then close the Services window.

 **CAUTION** When you restart a service with dependencies, sometimes the process fails due to delays stopping or starting any one of the services. When this happens, you need to manually verify that all services were restarted.

COMMAND-LINE ADMINISTRATION TOOLS

A command-line interface (CLI) is a text-based interface that requires you to type in all the commands. Older operating systems such as MS-DOS had only a command line interface, and all the utilities and management was done with a keyboard. Even though Windows 10 has a graphical interface, you still have the option to do much management from a command-line.

Command Prompt

The first Windows operating systems included a command prompt for command-line administration. Windows 10 still includes a command prompt, shown in Figure 2-8, for you to run command-line tools and applications. You're unlikely to find command-line applications anymore, but plenty of useful command-line tools are included in Windows 10.

You'll see many command-line tools throughout this book, but here are a few examples:

- Ping.exe for testing network connectivity
- Ipconfig.exe to view network configuration settings
- Netsh.exe to modify network configuration settings
- Dism.exe to configure features and packages in Windows 10

```
Command Prompt                                              —   □   ×
Microsoft Windows [Version 10.0.18363.535]
(c) 2019 Microsoft Corporation. All rights reserved.

C:\Users\User1>ipconfig

Windows IP Configuration


Ethernet adapter Ethernet:

   Connection-specific DNS Suffix  . :
   Link-local IPv6 Address . . . . . : fe80::7453:59c3:eb60:cde5%3
   IPv4 Address. . . . . . . . . . . : 192.168.1.118
   Subnet Mask . . . . . . . . . . . : 255.255.255.0
   Default Gateway . . . . . . . . . : 192.168.1.1

C:\Users\User1>
```

Figure 2-8 Command Prompt window

In addition to running executable files designed for command-line use, you might also see batch files. A batch file is a text file with the .bat extension. Inside the text file, each line is one command. Batch files are not commonly used in Windows 10 anymore, but you might see them in some environments for logon scripts or other automated tasks.

When you are learning to use command-line utilities, one difficulty is identifying the available options. Fortunately, most command-line utilities are self-documenting and include help information. To get help information for most command line utilities, use the /? switch.

Activity 2-5: Using a Command Prompt

Time Required: 10 minutes

Objective: Use a command prompt to run utilities

Description: Windows 10 includes a command prompt for administration. In this activity, you learn how to open a command prompt and run command-line utilities.

1. If necessary, start your computer and sign in.
2. Click the **Start** button and then type **cmd**. Notice that you have the option to run the command prompt as administrator. This is required to perform some administrative actions.
3. Click **Command Prompt** in the left pane.
4. At the command prompt, type **ipconfig.exe** and then press **Enter**. This command displays network configuration information.
5. Type **ipconfig** and then press **Enter**. Notice that you can run the command without specifying .exe. However, it is running the same file both times.
6. Type **ipconfig /?** and then press **Enter**.
7. Scroll through the help information for ipconfig and read it.
8. Type **dir** and then press **Enter**. This shows the folders and files in the current directory. Notice that ipconfig.exe is not in the current directory.
9. Type **echo %path%** and press **Enter**. This displays the value of the path environment variable. All these locations are searched for executable files when you attempt to run them.
10. Type **dir.exe** and then press **Enter**. This fails because the dir command is built into the command prompt and not an executable file.
11. Type **dir /?** and then press **Enter**. This displays the help information for the dir command.
12. Close the command prompt window.

Windows PowerShell

Windows PowerShell is a newer command-line interface, shown in Figure 2-9, for performing system configuration in Windows 10. First introduced in Windows Vista, Windows PowerShell has become an essential administrative tool. You can perform many configuration tasks by using Windows PowerShell, but the real usefulness for Windows PowerShell is scripting. Windows PowerShell scripts are an effective replacement for batch scripts and Visual Basic scripts. Most people find it significantly easier to work with Windows PowerShell than batch scripts or Visual Basic scripts.

Each version of Windows PowerShell adds additional capabilities for managing Windows. Some of the actions you can perform with Windows PowerShell are:

- Manage services
- Manage processes
- Manage networking
- Edit the registry
- Manipulate files and folders
- Retrieve event log events

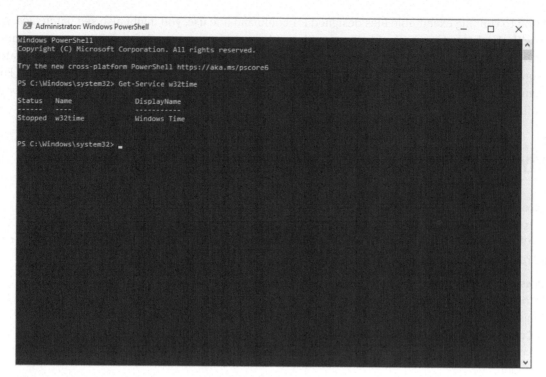

Figure 2-9   Windows PowerShell prompt

The individual commands in Windows PowerShell are cmdlets (pronounced command-lets). Each **cmdlet** is a verb-noun format. The verb describes what you want to do, and the noun describes what you want to do it to. For example, Start-Service is used to start a service. Some of the common verbs are: Get, Set, Remove, Start, and Stop.

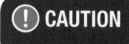 **CAUTION**   Microsoft has released PowerShell Core as a cross-platform solution for command-line administration; however, it does not support some of the cmdlets that are available in Windows PowerShell.

Most cmdlets have parameters that are used to provide instructions to the cmdlet. The parameters of a cmdlet are similar to using switches to modify the actions of an executable. A dash is used at the beginning of all parameter names, for example, "Start-Service -Name W32Time".

You can learn to use cmdlets in several ways, such as:

- *Do a search for examples*—If you are trying to accomplish a specific task, search for that task plus the word PowerShell. Many people have well-written blog postings and sample scripts.
- *Do an Internet search for the cmdlet*—If you execute an Internet search for a specific cmdlet, the Microsoft help information for that cmdlet is usually at the top of the results list. That help information includes a description of all the available parameters and examples.
- *Use the Get-Help cmdlet*—The Get-Help cmdlet provides a description of parameters and examples for a cmdlet. Use the -Full parameter to get all of the available information. For example, "Get-Help Get-Service -Full" shows all of the available help for the Get-Service cmdlet.

 TIP   Use tab completion when you are typing in cmdlets and parameters. When you are typing, press Tab and the name of the cmdlet or parameter will be autocompleted for you. If multiple matches for what you have typed are listed, pressing Tab multiple times cycles through them. Using autocomplete makes entering commands faster and increases accuracy.

Objects and Properties

When you use a Get-* cmdlet to retrieve a list of items such as services or processes, the items retrieved are objects that you can examine and manipulate. Objects have properties that can be examined and modified. For example, when you use Get-Service to retrieve a list of services that are running, each service returned is an object that has properties. Properties for a service include elements such as Status, Name, and StartType.

When you query a list of objects, you can pipe those objects to another cmdlet for further processing. To pipe objects between cmdlets, you use the pipe symbol (|), which is a vertical line. The following example queries a list of services and then pipes the objects to the Sort-Object cmdlet to sort based on the value in the status property:

Get-Service | Sort-Object Status

To view all information about an object type, you use the Get-Member cmdlet. This cmdlet accepts an object as input and then displays all of the properties in that object type. Get-Member also displays methods that can be used to manipulate that object type. The following example shows all of the properties and methods available for services:

Get-Service | Get-Member

Formatting Output

Each cmdlet has a default output format that identifies which properties are displayed in list format or table format. Typically, a cmdlet displays only a subset of properties on the screen. If you need to see the value of other properties, you can modify the output to display specific properties. The two common display formats are:

- *List*—Displays each property as a separate line and each object is listed consecutively. This format allows you to see more detail about objects. Pipe output to Format-List to display output in a list format.
- *Table*—Displays object properties in a table format in which each object is a row and each property is a column. This makes object information easily readable if you want to display a limited amount of information on the screen. Pipe output to Format-Table to display output in a table format.

Windows PowerShell Scripts

Windows PowerShell scripts are text files saved with the .ps1 file extension. Although it is possible to create PowerShell scripts by using a simple text editor, such as Notepad, you should use a more advanced editor, such as the Windows PowerShell Integrated Scripting Environment (ISE). **Windows PowerShell ISE**, shown in Figure 2-10, provides color coding of the script as you type it to help you identify when syntax errors are entered. It also includes debugging functionality. Windows PowerShell ISE is included in Windows 10.

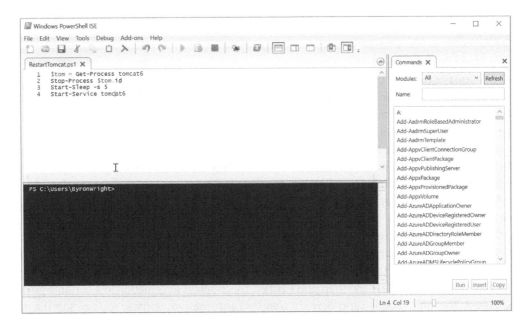

Figure 2-10   Windows PowerShell ISE window

TIP Windows PowerShell ISE is no longer in active development. Consider using the free Visual Studio Code editor from Microsoft instead. To create and edit Windows PowerShell scripts with Visual Studio Code, you need to download and install the PowerShell extension for Visual Studio Code. For more information see https://docs.microsoft.com/en-us/powershell/scripting/components/vscode/using-vscode.

Windows 10 includes an execution policy setting that controls which Windows PowerShell scripts can be run. The valid settings are:

- *AllSigned*—All scripts must be digitally signed by a trusted publisher.
- *RemoteSigned*—All scripts downloaded from the Internet must be signed by a trusted publisher.
- *Restricted*—No scripts can be run. This is the default for Windows 10.
- *Unrestricted*—Any script can be run.
- *Bypass*—All scripts can be run and no warnings will be issued.

Windows PowerShell vs. Command Prompt

You can use Windows PowerShell as a unified solution for command-line administration. Almost all utilities that you can run at a command prompt also work properly at a Windows PowerShell prompt. This means that you can choose the utilities and commands that you are most comfortable with when working at a Windows PowerShell prompt. For example, you can use cmdlets for most tasks, but continue using ipconfig.exe to view network configuration.

 TIP Most problems running command-line utilities in a Windows PowerShell prompt are caused by characters that are valid at a command prompt but are reserved in Windows PowerShell. For example, the - character used by some utilities to specify options is reserved in Windows PowerShell to indicate a parameter. The { } characters used with bcdedit.exe are also reserved characters in Windows PowerShell.

Activity 2-6: Using Windows PowerShell

Time Required: 10 minutes
Objective: Use Windows PowerShell to display information about Windows 10
Description: Windows 10 includes many PowerShell cmdlets for viewing information and configuring Windows 10. In this activity, you query information and format it.

1. If necessary, start your computer and sign in.
2. Right-click the **Start** button and then click **Windows PowerShell (Admin)** on the shortcut menu.
3. In the User Account Control window, click **Yes**.
4. At the Windows PowerShell prompt, type **Get-Service** and then press **Enter**. This displays all services with the default view showing Status, Name, and DisplayName.
5. Type **Get-Service | Sort-Object Status** and then press **Enter**. This command sends the list of services to the Sort-Object cmdlet which sorts the services based on the value of the Status property.
6. Type **Get-Service -Name w32time** and then press **Enter**. This gets information for just one service.
7. Type **Get-Service w32time | Format-List** and then press **Enter**. This displays the information for the service in a list format.
8. Type **Get-Service w32time | Format-List *** and then press **Enter**. This displays all properties in a list format.
9. Type **Get-Service w32time | Format-Table Name,DisplayName,Status,StartType** and then press **Enter**. This displays specific properties in a table format.
10. Type **Get-Process | Out-GridView** and then press **Enter**. This displays information in a sortable grid view similar to a spreadsheet. The information in grid view is a snapshot and does not update. You can sort the data by clicking the column names.

11. Close the Get-Process | Out-GridView window.
12. At the Windows PowerShell Prompt, type **Get-Command *-Service** and then press **Enter**. This displays all the cmdlets you can use to manage services.
13. Type **Get-Help Restart-Service** and then press **Enter**.
14. Type **y** and then press **Enter** to update the help content from the Internet. Wait for a few minutes while the help updates.
15. Read the help information that is displayed for Restart-Service. This is only the summary information.
16. Type **Get-Help Restart-Service -Full** and then press **Enter**.
17. Scroll up and down to read the full help for the Restart-Service cmdlet. This information now includes detailed information about the parameters and examples.
18. Type **Get-ExecutionPolicy** and then press **Enter**. By default, running Windows PowerShell scripts is not allowed.
19. Type **Set-ExecutionPolicy RemoteSigned** and then press **Enter**. This allows you to run any Windows PowerShell scripts that you create but not unsigned scripts from the Internet.
20. Type **y** and then press **Enter** to confirm making the change.
21. Close the Windows PowerShell prompt window.

 TIP When you want to repeat a command in a Windows PowerShell prompt, you can press the up arrow on the keyboard to display the previous command.

DISPLAY

As a system administrator, your main concern for displays is the display drivers that are required for Windows 10. Windows 10 requires a display driver that supports the Windows Display Driver Model (WDDM) and DirectX 9. This is approximately the same video requirements that were in place for Windows 7 and should be met by all more recent video cards. With the correct driver installed, you can ensure that the display is configured to match the needs of your users.

Display Settings

The Display settings, shown in Figure 2-11, allow you to modify commonly configured display settings. You can change the size of text and applications if you have a very high-resolution screen and want to make items appear larger. You can change the orientation of monitors to be landscape or portrait to match the physical orientation of the monitor. The night light option allows you to change the screen colors away from the blue spectrum at night.

The display resolution is the number of pixels that your display can show. A pixel is a single dot on the screen. The resolution is expressed as the number of horizontal pixels by the number of vertical pixels. For example, a resolution of 1366 × 768 means that there are 1366 pixels across the screen and 768 pixels up and down the screen. The common high definition (HD) resolution is 1920 × 1080. If you get a 4K monitor, the resolution is 3840 × 2160.

The optimal display resolution varies depending on the display you are using and your video card. In general, monitors should be used at their native resolution. If you set your screen resolution at less than the native resolution, the display appears fuzzy.

Modern monitors are Plug and Play, and Windows 10 queries the optimal display resolution for the monitor. The optimal display resolution is selected by default and marked as recommended.

The display settings vary depending on your computer hardware. For example, the Play HDR games and apps option appears only when supported by the video card and the display.

The Advanced display settings option allows you to view detailed configuration options for each display, including the resolution, refresh rate, and color configuration. You can also open the display adapter properties shown in Figure 2-12. On the Adapter tab, you can configure the screen resolution and color depth being used by selecting a mode. The Monitor tab allows you to set the refresh rate for the monitor. You can set a color profile on the Color Management tab to optimize colors for a particular display or purpose.

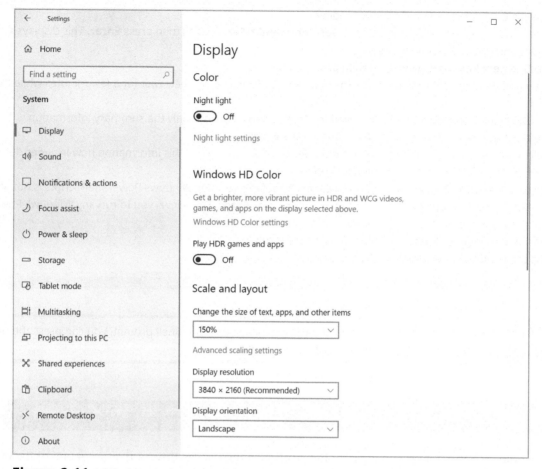

Figure 2-11   Display settings

Figure 2-12   Display adapter properties

Activity 2-7: Configuring Display Settings

Time Required: 10 minutes

Objective: Configure the screen resolution and color depth for your computer

Description: Windows 10 automatically selects display settings based on the display device that is connected to your computer during installation. You might want to modify the display settings, however, to suit your own preferences. In this activity, you change the display settings and view the results.

1. If necessary, start your computer and sign in.
2. Right-click the desktop and then click **Display settings** on the shortcut menu.
3. In the Settings window, in the Scale and layout area, take note of the existing setting in the Change the size of text, apps, and other items box. On most computers this value will be 100%, but high resolution displays might be using a larger value, such as 300%.
4. In the Change the size of text, apps, and other items list, select **125%**. Notice that all text on the screen changed size. This is useful on high resolution displays or small screens.
5. In the Change the size of text, apps, and other items list, select the original value you took note of in Step 3.
6. Click **Advanced scaling settings** in the right pane.
7. Read the advanced scaling settings and then click the back arrow.
8. Read the value in the Display resolution box and take note of it.
9. Click the Display resolution box, select **800 × 600**, and click **Keep changes**. If you are using a physical computer, everything appears larger when the screen resolution gets smaller. If you are using a virtual machine, the virtual machine viewing window might become smaller instead of the graphics becoming larger.
10. Click **Advanced display settings**. Notice that the screen resolution listed is what you configured.
11. Click **Display adapter properties for Display 1**. If you do not see the adapter Properties window, it might be located behind the Settings window.
12. In the adapter Properties window, click the **List All Modes** button. This displays all of the screen resolution, color depth, and refresh rate combinations that your display and video card are capable of providing.
13. Select the mode with a display resolution that matches what you noted in Step 8 and then click **OK**.
14. Click the **Monitor** tab. This tab shows you what type of monitor is installed and allows you to configure the screen refresh rate.
15. Click **OK** and then click **Keep changes** to keep the new settings.
16. Close the Settings window.

Visual Effects

The performance options for Windows 10 includes visual effects that can be enabled or disabled, as shown in Figure 2-13. In most cases, you should use the Let Windows choose what's best for my computer option. When this option is selected, Windows enables and disables specific options based on the performance capabilities of your computer.

Because the visual effects seldom need to be configured, they are not directly accessible in Settings. To access the visual effects:

1. Click the **Start** button, type **control**, and then click **Control Panel**.
2. In Control Panel, click **System and Security** and then click **System** in the right pane.
3. In the System window, click **Advanced system settings** in the left pane.
4. In the System Properties dialog box, on the Advanced tab, in the Performance area, click **Settings**.

Figure 2-13   Visual effects settings

Desktop Backgrounds

Personalizing the desktop background is one of the most common actions users want to perform when receiving a new computer. Some corporate environments dictate that a standard desktop background must be used. Standardizing the desktop background has no effect on the performance of a computer; however, a standardized background can be used to display information, such as contact information for the help desk.

Windows 10 comes with a number of desktop backgrounds from which you can choose. Most people, however, want to use their own pictures for a desktop background. This is the computer equivalent of putting a picture on your desk. When you use your own image for a desktop background, it can be in any common picture format such as bitmap (.bmp), Joint Picture Experts Group (.jpeg, .jpg), Graphics Interchange Format (.gif), or Portable Network Graphics (.png) format.

When you select a desktop background, you must also select how the graphic is laid out on the page. You can choose to stretch the picture to the size of the screen, center the picture on the screen, or tile the picture. Stretching the picture distorts the image if the original graphic is not the same proportion as the screen. Centering the picture ensures that the image is not distorted but may leave blank spaces around the picture. Tiling the picture repeats the image if the size of the picture is less than the screen resolution.

You have the option to configure a slideshow for your background. You can define how often the pictures are changed and use the Shuffle option to randomize how they are displayed.

Screen Savers

At one point in time, screen savers were used to prevent screen burn-in, sometimes called ghosting or etching. Screen burn-in occurred in monitors that displayed the exact same image for an extended period of time. After screen burn-in occurs, a ghosted image appears on the screen. Screen savers were meant to combat screen burn-in by constantly changing the information displayed on the screen.

Screen savers are no longer required to prevent screen burn-in. Modern displays are much less susceptible to screen burn-in than older devices. In addition, power-saving features in modern computers turn off displays quite quickly, often in the same time frame you would configure a screen saver to turn on.

Screen savers are now a security mechanism for locking a computer. By default, no screen saver is configured in Windows 10 and the screen does not lock. To increase security, you should enable the On resume, display logon screen option, shown in Figure 2-14. After you enable this option, you can define how many minutes of inactivity are required before the screen saver starts. If no screen saver is selected, the screen is blanked instead. When you resume using the computer, you are forced to sign in again. This ensures that if you leave your computer unattended, no one can access your work.

 TIP   To ensure consistent application, many organizations use Group Policy to configure screen lock settings on all computers.

Multiple Monitors

Windows 10 supports **multiple monitors** attached to a single computer. When you use multiple monitors, there are three configuration options; each option is useful in different scenarios:

- *PC only*—On a laptop computer with an external display connected, this option allows you to display only on the laptop display and leave the external display blank. This is useful when a laptop is connected to a projector for a presentation, but you want to do some work before the presentation that is not displayed on the projector.

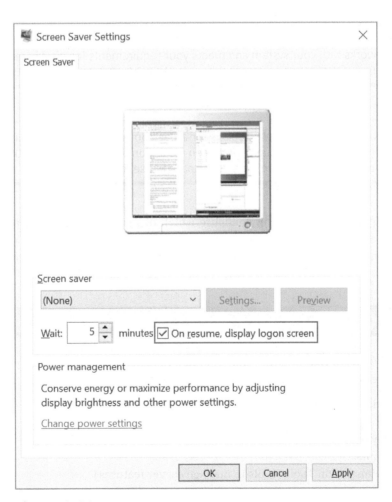

Figure 2-14   Screen saver settings

- *Duplicate*—The default option for multiple monitors is to mirror the desktop on both displays. This is most useful when one display is a projector and you are performing a presentation or demonstration.
- *Extended*—When the desktop is extended onto the second display, you have additional screen space to perform your work. You can move windows back and forth between the two displays and even stretch windows across both monitors. This makes it easier to use multiple applications at the same time. For example, a system administrator can perform remote desktop operations on one display while reading documentation on the other display. Microsoft PowerPoint automatically uses this option when available to display presentation notes on the local display and slides on the external display.
- *Second screen only*—When you are running a laptop on batteries, it is useful to turn off the LCD panel display and use only an external projector during presentations and demonstrations. This can also be useful when connecting a laptop or tablet to a larger monitor.

 TIP You can connect more than two displays to a computer if you have a need and purchase the necessary hardware.

The hardware requirements for multiple monitors vary depending on whether your computer is a laptop computer or a desktop computer. Some desktop computers include multiple connectors for displays or support the installation of multiple video cards. Laptop computers may include a connector for external displays, but it is more common to require an external adapter. You can purchase external video adapters that will work with desktop computers and laptop computers.

 CAUTION When purchasing an external video adapter, make sure that you purchase an adapter that works with your system and meets your requirements for display resolution and refresh rate. External adapters can connect by using USB 2.0, USB 3.0, USB-C, or DisplayPort connectors.

TIP Instead of purchasing multiple displays for a desktop computer, consider using a 4K television with HDMI connectivity. This produces the screen resolution of four HD (1920 × 1080) monitors with a single connection, which provides ample screen space to use multiple applications at the same time.

When you have multiple displays, you can configure which display is primary. The primary display is the one that displays the taskbar and Start button. Both displays are shown in Display settings. You can configure whether the taskbar is displayed on additional monitors and which apps are listed on the taskbar of the secondary monitor.

MANAGING OPTIONAL FEATURES

Windows 10 has optional features that provide additional functionality, which is not always required. Because these features are not part of the Windows 10 core functionality, they can be added or removed. Some of the features are:

- Language-based handwriting and speech recognition
- Internet Explorer 11
- Windows Media Player
- Language specific fonts
- Remote Server Administration Tools (tools to manage server features)
- Hyper-V
- Internet Information Services (IIS)

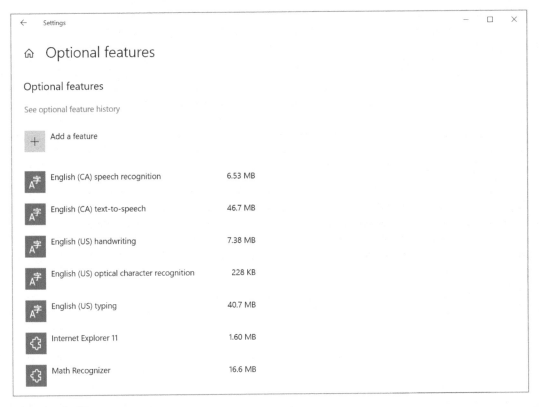

Figure 2-15   Optional features

Some optional features can be viewed in Settings in Apps & features, as shown in Figure 2-15. These optional features are primarily applications for users and user interface features.

A different set of optional features is accessible by using the Turn Windows features on or off option in Control Panel, dism.exe, or the Enable-WindowsOptionalFeature and Disable-WindowsOptionalFeature cmdlets. This set of features tends to be more technical and is likely to be used only by system administrators.

Activity 2-8: Managing Windows Optional Features

Time Required: 10 minutes
Objective: Manage Windows optional features
Description: Optional features in Windows 10 can be enabled or disabled depending on your requirements. For example, if you need to use server management tools from your computer running Windows 10, you can enable Remote Server Administration Tools. In this activity, you will manage optional features in Windows 10.

1. If necessary, start your computer and sign in.
2. Click the **Start** button and then click **Settings**.
3. In the Settings window, click **Apps** and then click **Optional features** in the Apps & Features area on the Apps and features screen.
4. Review the list of optional features that are already installed and then click **Add a feature**.
5. Scroll down and read the list of optional features available for installation and then close the Settings window.
6. Click the **Start** button, type **control**, and then click **Control Panel**.
7. In Control Panel, click **Programs** and then click **Turn Windows features on or off** in the Programs & Features area in the right pane.
8. In the Windows Features dialog box, scroll up and down to read the list of available features, and then click **Cancel**.

9. Close Control Panel.
10. Right-click the **Start** button and then click **Windows PowerShell (Admin)** on the shortcut menu.
11. At the User Account Control prompt, click **Yes**.
12. At the Windows PowerShell prompt, type **Get-WindowsOptionalFeature -Online** and then press **Enter**. This queries the status of all optional features.
13. Scroll through the list of optional features and read them. This list includes many optional features not available in Settings.
14. Type **Get-WindowsOptionalFeature -Online | Where-Object State -eq Enabled** and then press **Enter**. This generates a list of optional features that are enabled.
15. Type **Get-WindowsOptionalFeature -Online -FeatureName TelnetClient** and then press **Enter**.
16. Type **telnet.exe** and then press **Enter**. This fails because the telnet client is not enabled.
17. Type **Enable-WindowsOptionalFeature -Online -FeatureName TelnetClient** and then press **Enter**.
18. Type **telnet.exe** and then press **Enter**. This telnet client starts because it has been enabled.
19. Type **quit** and then press **Enter**. This exits the telnet client.
20. Type **dism.exe /online /get-features** and then press **Enter**. This provides the same information as the Get-WindowsOptionsFeature cmdlet.
21. Type **dism.exe /online /get-featureinfo:telnetclient** and then press **Enter**.
22. Type **dism.exe /online /disable-feature:telnetclient** and then press **Enter**. This removes the TelnetClient feature.

HARDWARE MANAGEMENT

Managing and maintaining computer hardware is a task performed regularly by network administrators. Windows 10 supports a wide variety of internal and external hardware components with which you should be familiar. Internal hardware components include network cards, video cards, and hard disk drives. External components are typically peripheral devices, such as a mouse, printer, or USB drive.

Windows 10 requires device drivers to manage and communicate with hardware components. Device drivers are written specifically for a particular type and model of component. For example, a GeForce GTX 1650 video card driver is different than a Radeon RX 570 video card driver.

NOTE 2

The Windows 10 Update Assistant can be downloaded from https://www.microsoft.com/en-us/software-download/windows10.

Microsoft does not provide a list of hardware that is compatible with Windows 10. In most cases, hardware that functioned properly in Windows 7 or newer works with Windows 10. If your computer is running Windows 7 SP1 or Windows 8.1, you can use the Windows 10 Update Assistant to verify compatibility.

To manage hardware in Windows 10, you should understand:

- Device drivers
- Device driver compatibility
- Device Manager
- Device driver signing
- Procedures for adding new hardware components

Device Drivers

Hardware devices, such as modems, network adapter cards, and video cards, are manufactured by a wide variety of vendors. The capabilities and functions of these devices vary depending on the model and manufacturer.

Device drivers act as intermediaries between a hardware component and an operating system, such as Windows 10. A device driver contains the instructions on how to use the full capabilities of a device properly. After they are installed, device drivers load automatically as part of the boot process each time Windows 10 is started.

In some cases, a device driver not specifically designed for a hardware component may allow that component to function. For example, the Microsoft Basic Display Adapter driver works with almost all video cards. If an incorrect device driver works, it is because the basic functionality of a class of hardware devices, such as video cards, is similar. Installing the wrong device driver for a hardware component, however, results in poor performance and does not let you use the advanced features of a device. Using the incorrect device driver for a hardware component may also make Windows 10 unstable.

Vendors regularly release updated device drivers to improve performance, add features, or fix flaws. It is a best practice to use the latest device drivers that are available from the manufacturer's website. When a device is not working properly, installing the latest device driver should be one of the first troubleshooting steps.

 TIP   Some device drivers are distributed by Windows Update as optional updates.

Device Driver Compatibility

Some device drivers designed for previous versions of Windows do not work properly with Windows 10. The driver incompatibility is due to changes that make Windows 10 more stable and secure. If a driver does not function properly in Windows 10, you must get an updated driver from the device manufacturer.

Some potential device driver compatibility issues are:

- A 32-bit version of Windows 10 requires 32-bit drivers, and a 64-bit version of Windows 10 requires 64-bit drivers.
- All driver files referenced in an .inf file must be part of the driver installation package. The .inf file for a driver describes the files that need to be installed. In some previous versions of Windows, including all files in the driver package was preferred, but not enforced. This might cause the installation of some drivers to fail.
- Installers cannot display a user interface during installation. Some older device drivers display a user interface during installation to request configuration information. You must obtain an updated device driver from the manufacturer that does not present a user interface during installation.
- All 64-bit drivers that run in kernel mode must be digitally signed by Microsoft. This means that manufacturers must submit kernel mode drivers to Microsoft for testing and approval. Previous versions of Windows allowed kernel mode drivers to be digitally signed by the manufacturer. Kernel mode drivers have unrestricted access to the computer.
- Windows 10 uses the NDIS 6.x interface for network devices. Old network cards with an NDIS 5.x driver that was compatible with Windows XP are not supported.
- Kernel mode printer drivers cannot be used in Windows 10. Replace kernel-mode printer drivers with newer, user-mode drivers from the printer manufacturer. This affects a very small number of printer drivers. Affected printer drivers are typically specialized devices used in manufacturing environments, such as bar code printers.

Device Manager

Device Manager is the primary tool for managing device drivers. The main purpose of Device Manager is to allow you to view and modify hardware device properties. Some of the tasks that can be performed with Device Manager are:

- Determining whether installed hardware is functioning correctly
- Viewing and changing hardware resource settings
- Determining and changing the drivers used by a device
- Enabling, disabling, and uninstalling devices
- Configuring advanced settings for devices
- Viewing and printing summary information about installed devices

After installing Windows 10, you should use Device Manager to confirm that all devices are working properly. You should also use Device Manager to confirm that a new component is working after installation. A hardware component that is not functioning correctly is displayed with a yellow exclamation mark. A hardware component that has been manually disabled is displayed with a down arrow, as shown in Figure 2-16.

If a hardware component is not functioning properly, you should install an updated driver for it. You can install an updated device driver from the Driver tab in the Device Properties dialog box, shown in Figure 2-17. To access the properties for a device, right-click the device and click Properties. You can also install an updated device driver by using the Hardware Update Wizard that is accessible by right-clicking the device.

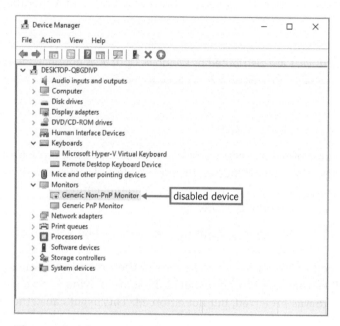

Figure 2-16   Device Manager window

Figure 2-17   Properties of a device, Driver tab

Although vendors perform extensive testing, occasionally an updated device driver causes problems. You can roll back a device driver to the previous version when an updated device driver causes problems.

 TIP   Device Manager is a stand-alone tool and also is included in Computer Management.

Activity 2-9: Using Device Manager

Time Required: 10 minutes

Objective: Use Device Manager to configure hardware components and device drivers

Description: Device Manager is an administrative tool that can configure hardware components and device drivers. You can use it to install updated drivers and disable devices that are not functioning properly. In this activity, you view the status of the network card in your computer.

1. If necessary, start your computer and sign in.
2. Right-click the **Start** button and then click **Device Manager** on the shortcut menu. If some devices are listed with a yellow question mark, it means that no device driver is loaded for those devices.
3. Expand **Network adapters** and then double-click your network card to display the Properties dialog box (the name of the network card will vary depending on your hardware). The General tab gives general information about your network card, including its status.
4. Click the **Advanced** tab. The contents of the Advanced tab vary depending on the model of network card. The properties are defined by the device driver.
5. Click the **Driver** tab. This shows information about the device driver, including date, version number, and publisher. You can also update drivers here.
6. Click **Driver Details**. This displays the files that are used as part of the device driver.
7. Click **OK** in the Driver File Details dialog box and then click the **Details** tab. You can select and view the value of all the device driver properties on this tab.
8. Click the **Property** arrow and browse through the list of properties that you can view.
9. Click the **Events** tab. This tab displays information about actions taken by the device, such as loading or starting the device driver.
10. If present, click the **Resources** tab. You can view and modify the resources used by a device on this tab. This tab might not be available if your Windows 10 installation is virtualized.
11. If present, click the **Power Management** tab. You can use this tab to control how the network adapter interacts with power management. This tab might not be available if your Windows 10 installation is virtualized.
12. Click **Cancel**.
13. Close the Device Manager window.

Device Driver Signing

Windows 10 uses file signatures on system files to ensure system stability. Device drivers can also be signed. Device driver signing ensures that a driver for a specific hardware component has been verified by Microsoft to be from a known software publisher (meaning it is authentic). Device driver signing also ensures that the device driver has not been modified in any way since it was signed (meaning it has integrity). Viruses are unable to spread by using device drivers because digital signing shows an infected device driver as corrupted.

If you attempt to install an unsigned device driver in Windows 10, one of the following messages will appear:

- *Windows can't verify the publisher of this driver software*—This message appears when no digital signature is present, or the digital signature cannot be verified as valid. You should install an unsigned driver only if you are confident it is from a legitimate source.

- *This driver software has been altered*—This message appears if the device driver has been altered since the developer added the digital signature. In most cases, this message indicates that the original device driver has been infected by a malicious program and it should not be installed.
- *Windows cannot install this driver software*—This message appears only on the 64-bit versions of Windows 10. The 64-bit versions of Windows 10 do not allow unsigned device drivers to be installed by default. For testing purposes, however, you can disable the check for driver signing by using bcdedit.exe or in the Windows 10 advanced startup settings.

You can verify that existing drivers and system files are signed by running the File Signature Verification utility (sigverif.exe). The file name, location, modification date, and version number are returned for each unsigned file. You can then investigate whether signed versions of these files are available. It is best practice to use only signed device drivers.

 **CAUTION**   A signed device driver does not indicate that Microsoft has performed stability or quality testing.

Hardware Component Installation

When hardware components are installed in a computer, they are assigned resource settings that allow them to access the system processor and memory in different ways. Devices for modern computers and operating systems, such as Windows 10, support Plug and Play, which automatically assigns resources to devices. Universal Serial Bus (USB) devices are also Plug and Play. Only settings for legacy ports, such as parallel ports and serial ports might require manual configuration of resources in Windows 10.

To install a Plug and Play device:

1. Install or attach the new hardware component.
2. Windows 10 automatically detects the new device.
3. A device driver is loaded automatically if Windows 10 contains an appropriate device driver.
4. If Windows 10 does not contain an appropriate device driver, you are prompted to provide one.

Some USB devices require you to install the driver before attaching the USB device the first time. This is required to ensure that Windows 10 does not attempt to load an incompatible driver before the correct driver is available. Read the instructions that come with the device to be sure.

 TIP   Windows 10 might not contain the latest device driver for your hardware component. You can update the device driver after installation.

To simplify the location of device drivers, you can make them available to computers by staging the drivers in the driver store or by providing a location to search. Windows 10 contains a driver store with a large set of device drivers included on the Windows 10 installation media. You can add new drivers to the driver store by using the pnputil.exe command. By adding a device driver to the driver store, you ensure that Windows 10 is able to find and install the driver when the matching hardware is attached. For example, you could stage the driver for a new USB printer on all Windows 10 computers. Then, when that printer is attached to any Windows 10 computer in the office, the appropriate driver is automatically loaded without asking the user to locate the appropriate driver.

You can also store drivers in a centralized network location. If you store drivers in a network location, you need to modify a registry key on the Windows 10 computers to configure the computers to search in that location when looking for drivers. Edit the following registry key: HKLM\Software\Microsoft\Windows\CurrentVersion\DevicePath.

TIP You should use an automated tool to update this registry key on all of the computers to simplify deployment.

POWER MANAGEMENT

Power management is becoming a major concern for corporate and personal computer owners alike. Hardware manufacturers have started to address this concern by focusing on reduced power consumption in their new products. Minimizing power usage is driven by both cost and environmental factors.

The basic settings for power management are shown in Figure 2-18. These settings let you control when the display is turned off and when your computer goes into sleep mode. If you have a device with a battery, such as a laptop computer, you can set the display and sleep timing independently for when on battery power and when plugged in. If the device does not have a battery, then the when on battery power options are not displayed.

Windows 10 relies on power management capabilities in computer hardware to perform power management. Computers must meet the specifications of the **Advanced Configuration and Power Interface (ACPI)** standard to be managed by Windows 10. All current computers meet this standard but can implement varying options.

The ACPI standard defines power states for global power management and individual devices. Power states define which devices are drawing power in the system. Depending on the power plan you have configured, power states can be implemented at different times.

 TIP Organizations using Active Directory can centrally control power management by using Group Policy.

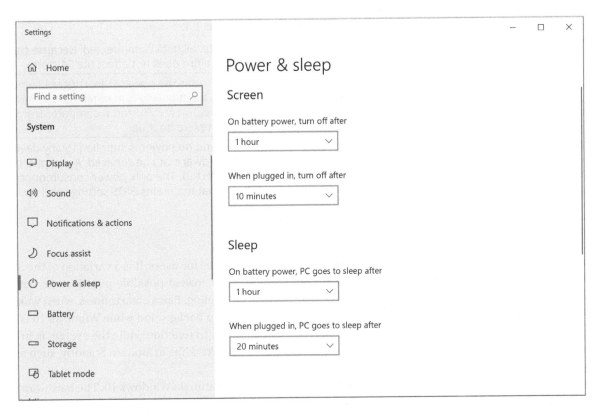

Figure 2-18 Power & sleep settings

ACPI States

The ACPI standard defines several global power management states; however, not all states are used by Windows 10. Table 2-1 lists the ACPI power states used by Windows 10.

Table 2-1 ACPI Power States Used by Windows 10

Power state	Description
S0 (or G0) Working	The **S0 state** is the fully functioning computer. While in this state, individual devices, such as the processor and hard disks, can be in varying power states. For example, the spinning of a hard disk can be stopped after a few minutes of inactivity to reduce power usage.
	For faster recovery from sleep mode, some hardware manufacturers support **Modern Standby** in the S0 state. Modern Standby maximizes power savings while still providing an instant on experience. Systems capable of using Modern Standby do not use the typical S3 state for sleep.
S3 Sleep	The **S3 state** is also known as suspend to RAM. In this state, all system devices are powered down except the RAM. The RAM retains the state of all running applications. Returning from S3 to S0 requires only that the hardware be reinitialized.
	If power is lost while the computer is in the S3 state, all data from memory is lost. This is equivalent to losing power while the computer is running.
	ACPI also defines sleep states S1 and S2, but they are less commonly implemented by hardware manufacturers. They also stop processing data but provide slightly less power saving.
S4 Hibernate	The **S4 state** is also known as suspend to disk. In this state, the contents of RAM are saved to disk and all devices including RAM are powered off. During restart, the contents of RAM are loaded from disk rather than booting the operating system. When a computer system has a large amount of RAM, restarting from the S4 state can take a long period of time. For example, a computer with 2 GB of RAM needs to load 2 GB of data from disk during startup from the S4 state. This state is commonly known as **hibernate**.
	If power is lost while the computer is in the S4 state, all data is unaffected. Because the contents of memory are stored on disk, a power failure does not affect the S4 state.
S5 (or G2) Soft Off	In this state, the operating system is not running. This is the power state triggered when the operating system is shut down. Minimal hardware functionality is maintained, such as the ability to start booting the computer by using Wake-on-LAN. To start a computer from this state, the operating system must go through a complete boot up.
G3 Mechanical Off	In this state, the operating system is not running and no power is supplied to any devices in the computer. This is the only state in which hardware can be serviced. A computer that is in the G3 state can be unplugged and not be affected. The only power consumption for a computer in the G3 state is from a small battery that maintains BIOS settings and the clock.

Modern Standby

Modern Standby is the power saving option that provides the best experience for users. It is a variation of the S0 power state that minimizes power usage by putting hardware devices into their lowest possible power state, but leaving processes running. For users, Modern Standby provides an "instant-on" feeling, like a smartphone, when waking up.

This allows applications, such as an email client, to retrieve data in the background while Windows 10 is in Modern Standby. Also, other applications, such as media players, can continue to function while the system is in Modern Standby. Finally, Windows 10 can also complete scheduled maintenance tasks while in Modern Standby, such as installing updates.

Most newer computer hardware supports using the Modern Standby feature in Windows 10. The hardware support for Modern Standby varies, but if your computer supports Modern Standby it is usually enabled by default. If you want to enable legacy power management, the firmware might contain an option to do so, but the name of that option will vary depending on the computer manufacturer.

Using Modern Standby is automatically configured during installation of Windows 10 if the hardware supports it. If you want to switch back to legacy power management, you'll need to reinstall Windows 10 after configuring the appropriate firmware setting.

On battery-backed systems such as a laptop or tablet, the risk of data loss in Modern Standby is minimal because hibernation will be triggered when the battery gets low. For desktop computers using Modern Standby, there is a risk of data loss if a power interruption occurs while the computer is sleeping. Modern Standby does not save the system state or data. To mitigate the risk of data loss, you should connect computers to an uninterruptible power supply (UPS) or enable hibernation after a specified period of time. By default, hibernation is disabled when using Modern Authentication.

Legacy Power Management

For computer systems that do not support Modern Sleep, the S3 power state is used. In this power state, all processing is stopped. Applications cannot obtain data and Windows does not perform updates; however, the system can be woken up by events such as the use of Wake-on-LAN functionality where a special data packet is sent on the network to trigger a wake up.

Windows 10 also implements a hybrid sleep mode. **Hybrid sleep** saves the contents of memory to disk when entering the S3 state. This effectively means the computer is in the S3 state but prepared for the S4 state. Hybrid sleep is available depending on the hardware capabilities of the computer. When available, it is enabled by default.

Hybrid sleep provides the following advantages:

- If power is lost in the S3 state, the computer can recover from the S4 state on reboot. No data is lost when a power outage occurs in the S3 state.
- Hybrid sleep eliminates the requirement to leave sleep mode to enter hibernation.

Away Mode can be used to maximize power savings on computers running Windows 10 that need to maintain background processes, such as media sharing. Away Mode provides functionality similar to Modern Standby. Away Mode is implemented entirely in software and does not require hardware support. Computers in Away Mode are still in the S0 state. However, the computer looks and sounds like it is off. Away Mode maximizes device-level power savings while continuing to work in the background if required.

After Away Mode is enabled, it replaces Standby requests. For example, if shutdown normally puts the computer in the S3 state, it now puts the computer in Away Mode instead. You configure Away Mode in the Multimedia settings of a power plan. Configure the When sharing media option to Allow the computer to enter Away Mode.

Power Plans

Windows 10 uses **power plans** to control how your computer implements power management. As many as four default power plans are provided, as shown in Figure 2-19. The plans available by default vary depending on the hardware capabilities of your computer. A computer that supports Modern Hybrid shows only the Balanced power plan by default. Some hardware manufacturers, such as Dell, include their own additional power management plan as part of the default operating system configuration.

The basic settings for a power plan are the same display blanking (i.e., going blank) and sleep timing that you can configure in Settings, but you can configure more advanced granular settings. Some of the advanced settings you can configure are:

- How long the hard disk is idle before turning it off
- Power saving mode for wireless network adapters
- Minimum processor state (as percentage of clock rate)
- Maximum processor state (as percentage of clock rate)

 TIP   When you edit the display blanking and sleep timing in Settings, you are editing the values for the currently selected power plan.

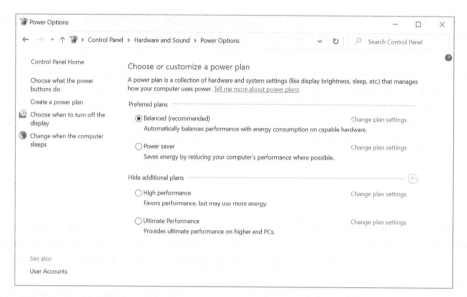

Figure 2-19   Power plans

Activity 2-10: Configuring a Power Plan

Time Required: 5 minutes

Objective: Configure a power plan to reduce power consumption

Description: Windows 10 includes default power plans to maximize performance, maximize power savings, and provide balanced power savings and performance. In most environments, the Balanced plan is the most appropriate because maximum performance is not required. In this activity, you configure a power plan.

1. If necessary, start your computer and sign in.
2. Click the **Start** button and then click **Settings**.
3. Click **System** and then click **Power & sleep** in the left pane. The options available here are very limited. If your system is virtualized, you might see only the option to control when the screen will be turned off.
4. Click **Additional power settings** in the Related Settings area in the right pane.
5. If available, click **Change settings that are currently unavailable**. This is required to allow you to select a power plan.
6. In the Power Options window, under Preferred plans, click **Power saver**. This changes the current power plan.
7. Next to the Power saver plan, click **Change plan settings**. Notice that when using the Power saver plan, the display turns off after 5 minutes. The content displayed here will vary depending on whether your computer is ACPI compliant. An ACPI-compliant computer will also have a setting for when the computer goes to sleep.
8. Click **Change advanced power settings**. This allows you to see more detailed information about the power plans.
9. Read the setting for turning off a hard disk. This setting is relevant for only spinning (magnetic) disks and not for SSD drives.
10. Expand **Processor power management** and expand **Minimum Processor State**. The minimum processor state is 5%. A virtualized version of Windows 10 might not have this setting.
11. Expand **System cooling policy**. This controls whether the system will use fans to cool the processor. When set to Passive instead of Active, the processor speed is slowed to prevent heat buildup instead of using fans. This can result in a significant performance decrease.
12. Expand **Maximum processor state**. The maximum processor state is 100%. You could reduce the maximum processor state to reduce battery utilization, but it will also decrease system performance.
13. Close all open windows and dialog boxes.

TIP   If you forget what changes you have made when editing a power plan, you can click the Restore plan defaults button.

Fast Startup

Windows 10 makes shutting down and restarting your computer faster with **Fast Startup**. When you shut down a Windows 10 computer with Fast Startup enabled, it signs out all the user accounts, closes all applications, and hibernates Windows 10. When you turn your computer back on again, it resumes from hibernation rather than performing a complete startup. Fast Startup is enabled by default.

The benefit of Fast Startup is faster startup times after performing a shutdown. This means, however, that your computer never completely shuts down the operating system, and if any part of the operating system becomes unstable, a shutdown and start won't fix it. Instead, you need to do a restart. A restart always completely unloads Windows 10 and starts it again.

When Windows 10 is in hibernation mode, the contents of memory are stored in C:\hiberfil.sys. This file can be several GB in size. This can be a concern on computers with small hard disks and little free space.

Power Button Options

On a computer running Windows 10, you can define what happens when the power button is pressed, when the sleep button is pressed, or when the lid on a laptop computer is closed. Also, if a device has a battery, you can define different settings for On battery and Plugged in, as shown in Figure 2-20. The options for each action vary depending on your system capabilities, but can include Do nothing, Sleep, Hibernate, Shut down, and Turn off the display.

The default settings for the power button, sleep button, and lid closing vary depending on whether Modern Sleep is supported. When Modern Sleep is supported, all options are configured to trigger sleep mode. When Modern Sleep is not supported, the power button triggers a shut down.

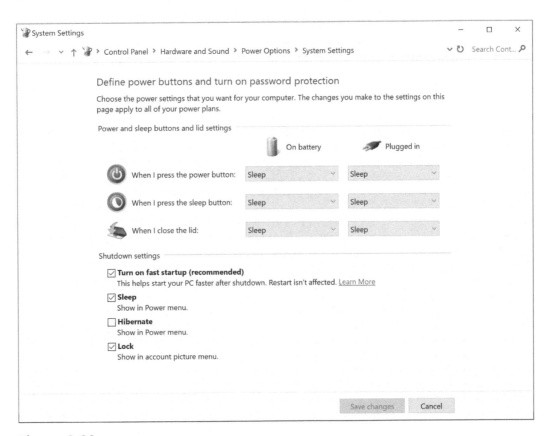

Figure 2-20   Power button options

You also have these options to configure Windows 10 shutdown settings:

- *Turn on fast startup (recommended)*—Fast startup is enabled by default and should be left enabled for best startup performance.
- *Sleep*—Leave this option on to display Sleep as an option for users in the Power menu.
- *Hibernate*—Turn this option on to display Hibernate as an option for users in the Power menu.
- *Lock*—Leave this option enabled to allow users to lock their screen from the account picture menu.

Troubleshooting Power Management

When you get a new batch of computers for your organization, one problem you might run into is expected power management settings not being available. For example, you might have only the Balanced power management plan available by default. Or, you might not have the ability to enable hybrid sleep. Both issues occur when Windows 10 is configured to use Modern Sleep. You need to understand whether your new computers support Modern Sleep and the ramifications of that for power management.

To identify whether a computer is using Modern Sleep you can use **powercfg.exe**. When you run powercfg.exe /a, as shown in Figure 2-21, if Modern Sleep is supported then Standby (S0 Low Power Idle) Network Disconnected will be listed as available. The state Standby (S0 Low Power Idle) Network Connected might also be listed as available depending on the capabilities of your hardware.

If Windows 10 is not turning off the display, going into sleep mode, or hibernating when expected, the first thing you should do is verify the power management settings. For example, if you expect the display to turn off after 10 minutes of idle time, make sure that setting is in the power plan.

Sometimes applications running in the background prevent Windows 10 power management from behaving as expected. You can run powercfg.exe /requests to identify applications that are making power management requests. If you identify the application, the best option is to either reconfigure or remove that application. If that's not possible, you can use the /requestsoverride option of powercfg.exe to block that process from making power management requests.

It is also possible that a hardware device is waking up Windows 10. You can run powercfg.exe /lastwake to identify the source of the last wake event. You can verify which hardware devices in your computer are allowed to wake the system by running powercfg.exe /devicequery -wake_armed.

If your computer supports Modern Sleep, but you find the battery is draining too quickly while sleeping, then you should configure the power plan to initiate hibernation after a period of time. For example, you could initiate

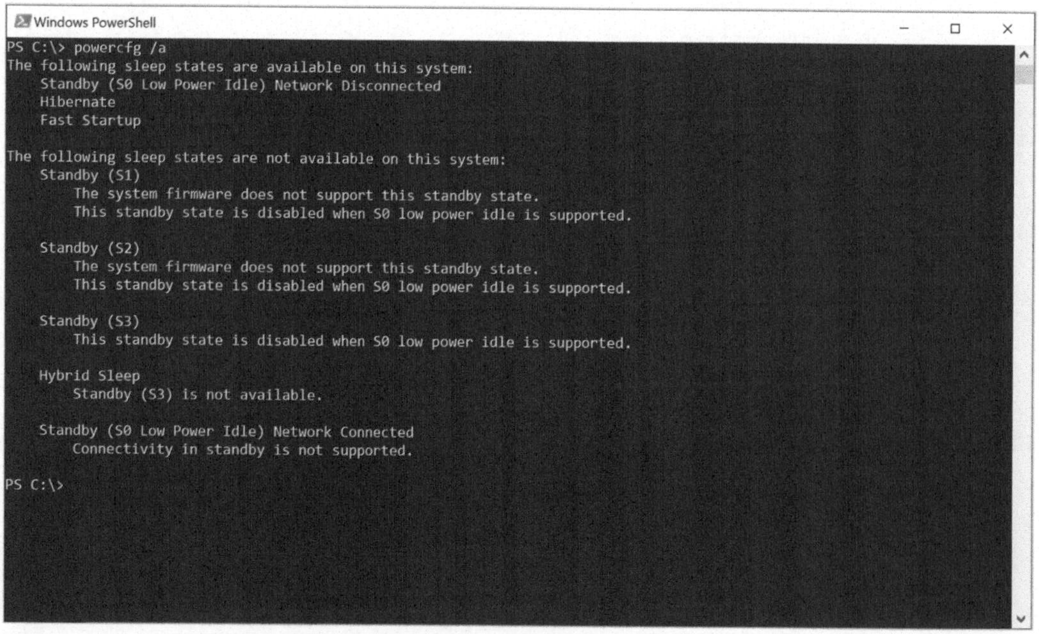

Figure 2-21   Powercfg.exe showing available sleep states

hibernation after 4 hours of sleep. This would provide you with the advantages of Modern Sleep during the workday but extend battery life by hibernating overnight.

You can also configure hibernation in a power plan if you are concerned about data loss for non-battery powered computers running Windows 10. When hibernation is initiated, all contents in memory are written to disk, including unsaved application data. If a power loss event occurs after hibernation, then no data is lost.

Powercfg.exe can also be used to manage power plans and generate reports. Table 2-2 shows some useful options not mentioned above.

Table 2-2   Powercfg.exe Options

Option	Description
/List	Lists all power plans.
/Query	Displays the settings in a power plan.
/DuplicateScheme	Copies the settings from an existing power plan to a new one.
/SetActive	Sets the power plan that is active.
/Energy	Analyzes the computer for common energy usage and battery problems. Results are stored in a report named energy-report.html in the current directory.
/BatteryReport	Creates a report named battery-report.html, which shows battery usage and charging information.
/SleepStudy	Creates a report named sleepstudy-report.html, which shows time spent in the various power states and the transitions between them. The /SystemPowerReport options generates the same report.
/SystemSleepDiagnostics	Creates a report named system-sleep-diagnostics.html, which shows user not present intervals and analysis of when the computer did not go to sleep when you might have expected it to go to sleep.

 TIP   Windows 10 does not include Windows PowerShell cmdlets for managing power plans or settings. Powercfg.exe is the command-line tool for managing power settings.

Activity 2-11: Using the Powercfg.exe Command

Time Required: 15 minutes
Objective: View the options available when using powercfg.exe
Description: When you are troubleshooting issues with power management, the powercfg.exe utility can be very useful. This tool allows you to generate reports and perform configuration that is not easily available in any other way. In this activity, you will use the powercfg.exe command to generate reports and view configuration information.

1. If necessary, start your computer and sign in.
2. Right-click the **Start** button and then click **Windows PowerShell (Admin)** on the shortcut menu. Starting the Windows PowerShell prompt with administrative permissions is necessary for some powercfg.exe functionality.
3. In the User Account Control window, click **Yes**.
4. At the Windows PowerShell prompt, type **powercfg.exe /?** and then press **Enter**.
5. Scroll through the list of powercfg.exe options and read the descriptions.
6. Type **powercfg.exe /AvailableSleepStates** and then press **Enter**.
7. Read the sleep states supported by your computer. If your computer is virtualized, it is expected that no sleep states are available.
8. Type **powercfg.exe /List** and then press **Enter**. This output refers to each power plan as a power scheme. An asterisk is used to indicate that the Power saver power plan is the currently selected plan.

9. Type **powercfg.exe /Query 381b4222-f694-41f0-9685-ff5bb260df2e** and then press **Enter**. This displays the settings for the Balanced power plan. The default power plans have a known and consistent GUID for all Windows 10 installations.

10. Scroll through the list of settings for the Balanced power plan and read them.

11. Type **powercfg.exe /SetActive 381b4222-f694-41f0-9685-ff5bb260df2e** and then press **Enter**.

12. Type **powercfg.exe /List** and then press **Enter**. Verify that the Balanced power plan is now the active power plan.

13. Type **powercfg.exe /Energy** and then press **Enter**.

14. When the report is generated (this might take a few moments), type **energy-report.html** and then press **Enter**. This opens the file in Microsoft Edge.

15. Review the content in the Power Efficiency Diagnostics Report and then close Microsoft Edge. If your computer is virtualized, it will contain only limited information.

16. Type **powercfg.exe /SleepStudy** and then press **Enter**.

17. Type **sleepstudy-report.html** and then press **Enter**. This opens the file in Microsoft Edge.

18. Review the content in the System Power Report and then close Microsoft Edge. If your computer is virtualized, it will contain only limited information.

19. Close the Windows PowerShell prompt window.

TASK SCHEDULER

Network administrators seldom have enough time to visit workstations and perform preventive maintenance. In most cases, the only time a network administrator sees a workstation is after it is already having problems.

Task Scheduler, shown in Figure 2-22, allows you to be proactive about computer maintenance. You can schedule a task to run at a particular time or after a particular event. For example, you could trigger disk maintenance to be performed each day at noon, when the network users are typically having lunch. If the computer is in standby, it

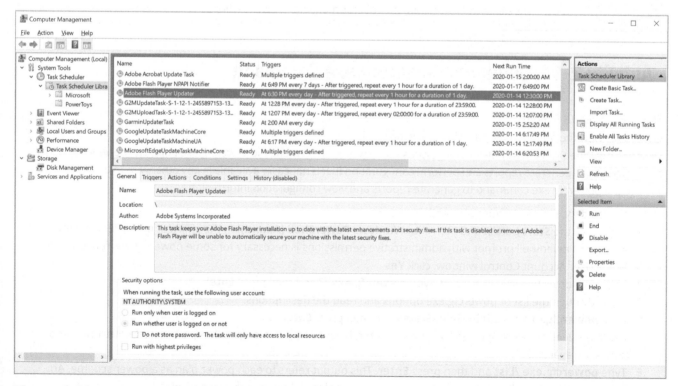

Figure 2-22   Task Scheduler

wakes up, performs the scheduled task, and then goes back into standby. Many Windows maintenance tasks are now performed automatically by the Task Scheduler instead of relying on services to remain running.

Tasks can be configured to run interactively or in the background. When a task runs interactively, it creates a window that users can interact with and see. For users to interact with a task, the task needs to run within the user's own security context. When you create an interactive task for your own computer as a single user, you can specify your account. If you are creating a task for all users on a computer, then use a generic credential such as NT Authority\Interactive. To create an interactive task, select the Run only when user is logged on option.

Most scheduled tasks run as background processes that do not require a user to be signed in. This option is preferred because it prevents users from closing a window that is performing maintenance. For a task that runs in the background, however, you need to specify a user account to define the permissions used when the task is run. To configure a task that runs as a background process, select the Run whether user is logged on or not option.

You can provide a local user account or a domain user account with the necessary permissions to run a background task. When you provide a user account, you are prompted to provide a password for the user account, and those credentials are stored locally on the computer in Credential Manager. A domain user account is required when the scheduled task needs to access network resources.

When you select the Do not store password option, the local permissions of the account are used, but the task does not have access to any network resources. Selecting this option triggers the use of Service for User (S4U), which is a specific authentication feature for domain-based networks. This feature is not available for local accounts. If you choose to store the password, the password is secured in Credential Manager.

You can also specify built-in accounts that do not use passwords:

- *NT AUTHORITY\SYSTEM*—This account provides full access to the local computer. Any scheduled task using this account can perform any action on the local computer.
- *NT AUTHORITY\LOCAL SERVICE*—This account has user access equivalent to the local Users group. This account only has access to the local computer.
- *NT AUTHORITY\NETWORK SERVICE*—In a domain environment, this account has permissions equal to the computer account in the domain. This account can access resources over the network.

Some features of Task Scheduler are:

- The Task Scheduler in Windows 10 allows all users to create scheduled tasks. Security is not compromised because users cannot schedule a task to run using permissions higher than their own.
- The Task Scheduler Summary shows the status of previously run and currently active tasks. In addition, each task has a History tab that allows you to view detailed information about that particular task. By default, however, history for tasks is disabled. To enable history for all tasks, click Enable All Tasks History.
- You can schedule a task to run at a specific scheduled time; however, many additional triggers exist, including at sign-in, at startup, on idle, on an event, on registration, on Terminal Server session connect, on Terminal Server session disconnect, on workstation lock, and on workstation unlock. If multiple triggers are specified, all triggers must be activated to run the task.
- You can include multiple actions in a single task. When multiple actions are specified, they are completed in order. This allows you to complete an entire process that has multiple actions that must be performed in a specific order. Each action can run a program, send an email, or send a message via pop-up window. The options to send an email or display a pop-up message have been deprecated and you should avoid using them. Instead, run a program or script to accomplish the same task.
- Conditions include power states and network conditions. Power states let you specify that certain tasks are run only when the computer is or is not in a sleep state. Network conditions let you specify that the task should be run only if certain network connections are available.
- Other settings are available to control how tasks behave when they start or fail. For example, you can configure a task to restart every few minutes if it fails. You can also control whether the task can be run manually regardless of the triggers and conditions that are in place.

Activity 2-12: Using Task Scheduler

Time Required: 5 minutes

Objective: Use Task Scheduler to view a task

Description: The Task Scheduler is used extensively by Windows 10 to run background processes. In this activity, you view a scheduled task that defragments your computer hard disk.

1. If necessary, start your computer and sign in.
2. Right-click the **Start** button and then click **Computer Management** on the shortcut menu.
3. In the left pane, click **Task Scheduler**. This displays the Task Scheduler Summary in the middle pane, which shows the status of currently running tasks and previously run tasks. As well, all tasks scheduled to run in the future are listed under active tasks.
4. In the Actions pane, click **Enable All Tasks History**. The history is useful information to have when you are troubleshooting whether a task has been running properly.
5. In the left pane, expand Task Scheduler, expand Task Scheduler Library, expand Microsoft, expand Windows, and then click **Defrag**. You can see in the left pane that many categories of tasks have been created for system maintenance. ScheduledDefrag is one task.
6. In the middle pane, click the **Triggers** tab. You can see that the ScheduledDefrag task does not have a schedule. This is because the task is triggered by automatic maintenance.
7. Click the **Actions** tab. You can see that this task runs the defrag.exe program.
8. Click the **Conditions** tab. You can see that this task runs only if the computer is on AC power. If the computer switches to battery power, the task stops.
9. Click the **Settings** tab. You can see that if the computer is turned off when the task is configured to run, the task starts as soon as possible after the computer is turned on.
10. Click the **History** tab. This shows you all the event log entries for this task, including when it started, when it completed, and if any errors occurred.
11. Close the Computer Management window.

Activity 2-13: Creating a Scheduled Task

Time Required: 10 minutes

Objective: Use Task Scheduler to create a task

Description: As a system administrator, you might want to add your own scheduled tasks to Windows 10 to perform maintenance. In this activity, you create a scheduled task that runs a Windows PowerShell script to delete temporary files that are no longer needed for an application.

1. If necessary, start your computer and sign in.
2. Right-click the **Start** button and then click **Windows PowerShell** on the shortcut menu.
3. At the Windows PowerShell prompt, type **md C:\Scripts** and then press **Enter**. This creates a new folder that you will use to hold scripts.
4. Type **md C:\AppTemp** and then press **Enter**. This is the folder that will hold the application temporary files that need to be deleted.
5. Type **"unneeded log file" | Set-Content C:\AppTemp\LogFile.txt** and then press **Enter**. This creates LogFile.txt that will be deleted by the script.
6. Type **Get-ChildItem C:\AppTemp** and press then **Enter**. Get-ChildItem is the Windows PowerShell equivalent of the dir command. Verify that LogFile.txt is present as expected.
7. Type **"Get-ChildItem C:\AppTemp | Remove-Item" | Set-Content C:\Scripts\CleanTemp.ps1** and then press **Enter**. This creates the script that will delete the temporary files.

8. Type **Get-Content C:\Scripts\CleanTemp.ps1** and then press **Enter**. Verify the contents of the script were typed correctly. If the script contents are incorrect, repeat Step 7.
9. Right-click the **Start** button and then click **Computer Management** on the shortcut menu.
10. In Computer Management, expand **Task Scheduler** and then click **Task Scheduler Library**.
11. In the Actions pane, click **Create Basic Task**.
12. In the Create Basic Task Wizard window, in the Name box, type **Clean Application Temp Files** and then click **Next**.
13. On the Task Trigger screen, select **Weekly** and then click **Next**.
14. On the Weekly screen, in the Start box, enter a time of **11:00:00 PM**.
15. Select **Sunday** and then click **Next**.
16. On the Action screen, if necessary, click select **Start a program** and then click **Next**.
17. On the Start a Program screen, in the Program/script box, type **powershell.exe**.
18. In the Add arguments box, type **-File C:\Scripts\CleanTemp.ps1** and then click **Next**.
19. Click **Finish**.
20. Read the security options for your new task. It will run only when you are signed in.
21. Double-click **Clean Application Temp Files**.
22. In the Clean Application Temp Files Properties (Local Computer) dialog box, click **Change User or Group**.
23. In the Select User or Group dialog box, in the Enter the object name to select box, type **System**, click **Check Names**, and then click **OK**.
24. In the Clean Application Temp Files Properties (Local Computer) dialog box, click **OK**.
25. Right-click **Clean Application Temp Files** and then click **Run**.
26. Click the **History** tab and verify that the task ran successfully. Note that successful execution of the task does not mean that it performed the action we wanted it to. In this context, it means only that powershell.exe was successfully started.
27. At the Windows PowerShell prompt, type **Get-ChildItem C:\AppTemp** and then press **Enter**. This command generates no output, because running the task removed the file in this folder.
28. Close all open windows.

NOTE 3

To successfully run the task in this activity, execution of Windows PowerShell scripts needs to be enabled. Enabling Windows PowerShell script execution was done in Activity 2-6 Using Windows PowerShell.

SUMMARY

- Settings provides access to change the more commonly manipulated settings in Windows 10. For more advanced settings, Control Panel is still used.
- Administrative Tools is a collection of system maintenance utilities. All of the administrative tools are MMC consoles. Two of the more commonly used administrative tools are Computer Management and Services.
- You can use either a command prompt or Windows PowerShell to perform command-line administration of Windows 10. Windows PowerShell provides a much better scripting environment. To allow scripts to run, you need to set the execution policy.
- Windows 10 uses device drivers to properly communicate with various hardware components in a computer. Most device drivers designed for Windows 7 and newer versions of Windows are compatible with Windows 10.
- Device Manager is the MMC snap-in that is used to manage device drivers and hardware components. You can use Device Manager to update drivers, roll back to previous driver versions, or view the resources a hardware component is using.

- Power Management in Windows 10 reduces power utilization by allowing the computer to go to sleep or hibernate when not in use. Fast Startup uses hibernation to speed up the boot process. Power plans are used to define how power management is implemented for various devices.
- The display on a Windows 10 computer can be customized by controlling the display resolution, color depth, and refresh rate. The optimal configuration for display settings varies depending on the display device. Desktop backgrounds let you display a picture on your desktop. Screen savers are used to implement security. You can implement multiple displays to enhance productivity.
- Task Scheduler has been enhanced with security improvements for credentials, improved logging, and expanded triggers for starting tasks. Multiple actions are allowed per task, and additional conditions can be required for a task to run.
- Windows PowerShell is a command-line interface for managing Windows 10. Many cmdlets are included, and Get-Help can be used to find out more information about a cmdlet. Use the Windows PowerShell ISE for creating and editing PowerShell scripts.

Key Terms

Administrative Tools	File Signature Verification utility	S0 state
Advanced Configuration and Power Interface (ACPI)	hibernate	S3 state
	hybrid sleep	S4 state
Away Mode	Microsoft Management Console (MMC)	service
cmdlet		Services
Computer Management	MMC snap-ins	Settings
Control Panel	Modern Standby	System Configuration
device driver signing	multiple monitors	System Information
device drivers	Open Database Connectivity (ODBC)	Task Scheduler
Device Manager		Windows Memory Diagnostics Tool
display resolution	Performance Monitor	Windows PowerShell
driver store	pixel	Windows PowerShell ISE
Event Viewer	power plans	
Fast Startup	powercfg.exe	

Review Questions

1. Which of the following accurately describe the administrative tools available in Control Panel? (Choose all that apply.)
   a. Most are MMCs.
   b. You can schedule tasks.
   c. You can change the screen resolution.
   d. You can change power options.
   e. You can manage device drivers.

2. Which Settings category allows you to control whether apps can access your location?
   a. System
   b. Devices
   c. Network & Internet
   d. Accounts
   e. Privacy

3. A(n) _____ is a type of Windows application that runs in the background without user intervention.

4. Which of the following is used by apps to connect to databases?
   a. DB sources
   b. ODBC
   c. SQL
   d. RPC
   e. local ports

5. Which of the following are found in Administrative Tools? (Choose all that apply.)
   a. Event Viewer
   b. Windows Memory Diagnostic
   c. Computer Management
   d. Installed Programs
   e. Task Scheduler

6. You can build a customized MMC console by adding _____ to the console.

7. Which snap-ins are available in Computer Management? (Choose all that apply.)
   a. Task Scheduler
   b. Folder Options
   c. Services
   d. Security Configuration Management
   e. Device Manager

8. Which tasks can you accomplish using the Services administrative tool? (Choose all that apply.)
   a. Stop a service.
   b. Configure a service to start automatically.
   c. Configure the credentials for a service.
   d. Schedule the time when a service will start.
   e. Configure the dependencies for a service.

9. A(n) _____ is software used to manage communication between hardware components and Windows 10.

10. To find a list of hardware components certified to run on Windows 10, you should consult the Hardware Compatibility List. True or False?
    a. True
    b. False

11. Which tasks can you perform in Device Manager? (Choose all that apply.)
    a. Determine which devices do not have a driver loaded.
    b. Disable devices.
    c. Install new hardware.
    d. View hardware resource configuration.
    e. Roll back a device driver.

12. You can use the Get-Member cmdlet to view the properties available for an object. True or False?
    a. True
    b. False

13. With a signed device driver, which of the following can Windows 10 do? (Choose all that apply.)
    a. Determine if a driver has been modified.
    b. Determine if a driver has been adequately tested.
    c. Determine if the publisher is valid.
    d. Determine if the driver is 32-bit or 64-bit.
    e. Automatically download updates.

14. Hybrid sleep is a combination of which ACPI power states? (Choose two.)

    a. S0
    b. S3
    c. S4
    d. S5
    e. G3

15. Modern Standby puts the computer in which ACPI power state?
    a. S0
    b. S3
    c. S4
    d. S5
    e. G3

16. Which requirements must be met for display adapters in Windows 10? (Choose all that apply.)
    a. minimum 256 MB of RAM on the video card
    b. support for WDDM
    c. support for DirectX 9
    d. do not use Windows 10 Starter Edition
    e. computer is certified as "Designed for Windows 10"

17. The primary purpose of a screen saver is to prevent screen burn-in. True or False?
    a. True
    b. False

18. Which multiple monitor display mode should you select when you are using each monitor for different tasks?
    a. PC only
    b. Office workspace
    c. Duplicate
    d. Extended
    e. Second screen only

19. Which tool can you use to create reports about power management?
    a. Device Manager
    b. Powerrpt.exe
    c. Create-PowerReport
    d. System Information
    e. Powercfg.exe

20. When you view optional features in Settings, dism, and Get-WindowsOptionalFeature, they all show the same list of optional features. True or False?
    a. True
    b. False

Case Projects

Case Project 2-1: Mobile Users

All the salespeople in Hyperactive Media Sales use laptops so that they can take their applications and data on the road to client sites. One of the salespeople, Bob, has a docking station so that his laptop easily connects to a printer and external monitor when he is in the office. What should you do to ensure that Windows 10 uses the proper device drivers when Bob is in and out of the office?

Case Project 2-2: Saving Money by Using Power Management

Gigantic Life Insurance is always looking for ways to save money. This month, the saving theme at the managers meeting was power consumption. The operations manager has proposed changing some of the fluorescent lighting to LED lighting. As the IT manager, what can you propose for Windows 10 computers?

Case Project 2-3: Tiny Text

Superduper Lightspeed Computers sells laptop computers with 4K displays. One of their customers called to complain that the text on his display is too small. He is very upset that he is unable to easily read text on the display. What might you be able to do to fix the small text?

Case Project 2-4: Accessibility Options

Over the last few months, Sanjay, the accountant for Buddy's Machine Shop has had problems reading his computer display but has been too embarrassed to tell anyone. Today, he finally lets you know about his problem and asked if you can do anything to help him. He is using Windows 10 on his computer. What can you suggest?

Case Project 2-5: Managing Device Drivers

One Windows 10 computer in the engineering department of Way North University has been experiencing network connectivity problems. This computer is a different brand and model than all the other computers because it was purchased directly by a professor as part of a research project. As a result, you are not sure whether the problem is hardware or software. You were able to test that the network cabling is functioning properly. What can you suggest for solving this problem?

USER MANAGEMENT

After reading this module and completing the exercises, you will be able to:

1. Describe local user accounts and groups
2. Create and manage user accounts
3. Manage user profiles
4. Configure advanced authentication methods
5. Describe Windows 10 integration with networks

User accounts are the most basic level of Windows 10 security. Authenticating to Windows 10 as an individual user account is the basis for all other Windows 10 security mechanisms. In this module, you learn about local user accounts and groups, including how to create and manage user accounts. Each user has customized settings, such as desktop and program configuration data, stored in a user profile.

Windows 10 includes advanced authentication methods, such as picture password, PIN, and biometrics. It is important to understand how these newer authentication methods can be used to increase security. In addition, the creation of user accounts for different network environments is important for efficiently controlling security.

USER ACCOUNTS

User accounts are required for individuals to sign in to Windows 10 and use resources on the computer. Each **user account** has attributes that describe the user and control access. Some user account attributes are:

- Name
- Password
- Group membership
- Profile location

When a Windows 10 computer is not part of an Active Directory domain, you can sign in by using a **local user account** or a **Microsoft account**. Both types of accounts function similarly on a Windows 10 computer. The main difference between them is where the account credentials (user name and password) are stored. A local user account exists only on the one local Windows 10 computer and cannot be used to sign in to other computers. A Microsoft account is stored online by Microsoft and can be added to multiple Windows 10 computers and mobile devices.

Using a Microsoft account to sign in has several advantages:

- *Single set of credentials across devices*—If you configure multiple computers and mobile devices to use the same Microsoft account for authentication, you need to remember only one account name and one password for authentication. When you change the password for the Microsoft account, it automatically takes effect for all devices.

- *Password reset capability*—If you are authenticating with a Microsoft account, you can reset the password on the Microsoft account by using an alternate email account you've provided, a mobile phone number, or by answering security questions. A local user account has fewer options for password reset.
- *Synchronization of some profile information*—A Microsoft account includes cloud storage that can be used to synchronize some settings among devices running Windows 10. You can synchronize settings such as the theme, stored passwords, language preferences, and ease of access settings.
- *Integration with family settings*—For home computers, Microsoft accounts integrate with family settings to control web browsing and track computer usage.
- *Integration with other Microsoft apps*—A Microsoft account can be used for multiple Microsoft apps, such as OneDrive, Skype, or Xbox Live. When you use your Microsoft account to authenticate on Windows 10, those same credentials can automatically be used to access the Microsoft apps that use a Microsoft account. For example, when you authenticate using a Microsoft account in Windows 10, you automatically are authenticated to the OneDrive storage for that account.

Local user accounts are stored in the **Security Accounts Manager (SAM) database** of Windows 10. When you sign in as a local user, the user name and password in the SAM database are used to verify your credentials.

If you use a Microsoft account to sign in to Windows 10, a local user account is created in the SAM database that is linked to the Microsoft account. Your credentials, however, are verified with Microsoft over the Internet. If your computer is disconnected from the Internet, you can still sign in by using a Microsoft account because the credentials are cached locally in Windows 10 when you authenticate. Changing the password for the Microsoft account does not affect the cached credentials. The new password is used only when the computer running Windows 10 is reconnected to the Internet.

If the computer is part of an Active Directory domain, and the user signs in using a domain user account, the SAM database is not used. Windows 10 sends domain user credentials to a server configured as a domain controller for verification.

To facilitate assigning permissions to resources, all user accounts have a **security identifier (SID)**. For example, when a user is assigned permissions to access a folder, the SID is written to the folder access control list, not the user account name. Using a SID for security ensures that accounts can be renamed without losing security information. The SID for each user account is a guaranteed unique identifier (GUID), such as S-1-5-21-1561371318-2357482352-4200497431-1002. When you work with user accounts and assigning permissions to resources, Windows 10 automatically translates the user name to a SID for you.

To fully comprehend user accounts, you should understand the following:

- Sign-in methods
- Naming conventions
- Default user accounts
- Default groups

Sign-In Methods

Users must sign in to Windows 10 before they can access resources and interact with the system. Windows 10 supports several sign-in methods; which method you choose depends on your requirements as network administrator, user needs, and whether the computer is a member of a domain.

Windows Sign-In Screen

For computers that are not joined to a domain, the Windows sign-in screen shown in Figure 3-1 displays a list of local user accounts that you can select from for authentication. For domain-joined computers, only the most recently used account is listed. The SAM database typically has only a few user accounts, so a graphical sign-in screen that displays each local user account is reasonable. In a domain-based environment with hundreds or thousands of accounts, it would not be possible to display an icon for each user account.

On the Windows sign-in screen, each user is represented by an icon and name. The name is the name of the user account. The icon is selected when the user account is created, but it can be changed at any time.

Secure Sign-In

Secure sign-in increases security on your computer by forcing you to press Ctrl+Alt+Delete before signing in. This protects your computer from malware that might attempt to steal your password by imitating the Windows sign-in screen.

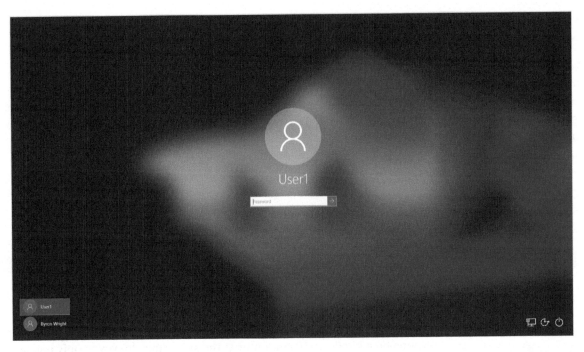

Figure 3-1 Windows 10 sign-in screen

The key sequence Ctrl+Alt+Delete is filtered by Windows operating systems, including Windows 10. The key sequence is captured by the operating system and not passed to applications. A virus or spyware never sees that you pressed Ctrl+Alt+Delete; therefore, if you press this key combination and a sign-in window appears, it is the legitimate Windows sign-in screen. Secure sign-in can be enabled on the Advanced tab of the advanced User Accounts applet, shown in Figure 3-2.

Figure 3-2 Enable secure sign-in

Activity 3-1: Implementing Secure Sign-In

Time Required: 5 minutes

Objective: Implement secure sign-in for all users

Description: Secure sign-in makes Windows 10 more secure by ensuring that no malicious software running in Windows 10 is creating a false sign-in screen and capturing user names and passwords. In this activity, you implement secure sign-in, which forces users to press Ctrl+Alt+Delete before signing in.

1. If necessary, start your computer and sign in.
2. Click the **Start** button, type **netplwiz**, and then press **Enter**.
3. Click the **Advanced** tab.
4. Select the **Require users to press Ctrl+Alt+Delete** check box and then click **OK**.
5. Sign out. Notice that the screen indicates that you must press Ctrl+Alt+Delete to sign in.

NOTE 1

Some virtualization software used remote desktop to connect to remote systems and won't enforce using Ctrl+Alt+Del. For Hyper-V, ensure that you disable Enhanced Session on the View menu to experience the standard desktop sign-in.

Fast User Switching

Fast user switching allows multiple users to have applications running in the background on a Windows 10 computer at the same time; however, only one user can be actively using the computer at a time. For example, User1 signs in to Windows 10 and starts creating a document in Word. User1 then locks the computer before leaving for lunch with the Word document still open. User2 comes to the computer during lunch, signs in to check email, and then signs out. After lunch, User1 returns, signs in, and continues to compose the Word document. Fast user switching allows this to happen. Without fast user switching, User1 would have been signed out automatically when User2 signed in and any unsaved work in the Word document would have been lost.

In environments where multiple users share the same computer, fast user switching is a very important feature. This is extremely useful in lab environments and for computers at a front reception desk in an office environment.

Automatic Sign-In

In some environments, it is desirable for the computer to automatically sign in as a specific user each time it is started. This is appropriate for libraries and other public locations where users are not assigned their own sign-in credentials. The term kiosk is sometimes used to refer to an environment where automatic sign-in is desired. A kiosk is a computer in a public space that is dedicated for a single purpose.

Automatic sign-in is configured on the Users tab of the User Accounts applet, shown in Figure 3-3. When you deselect the Users must enter a user name and password to use this computer check box and then click OK, you are prompted for the credentials to be used for the automatic sign-in. From this point forward, Windows 10 automatically signs in using the credentials you specified.

When you need to do system maintenance on a computer with automatic sign-in enabled, you must stop the automatic sign-in from occurring. Holding down the Shift key during the boot process stops the automatic sign-in from occurring. Then you can sign in with your own credentials to perform the maintenance tasks. Alternatively, you can sign out after the user is automatically signed in to access the Windows sign-in screen.

Assigned Access

Assigned access is an advanced sign-in option for configuring Windows 10 as a kiosk. This option can be used when a company has Windows 10 tablets being used for filling in surveys or when a public access computer is being used to search a catalog.

When you enable assigned access, you select (or create) a local user account and a Windows Store app, as shown in Figure 3-4. At that point, the selected user account is limited to using that one app when signed in. Many normal functions, such as exiting the application, are not possible.

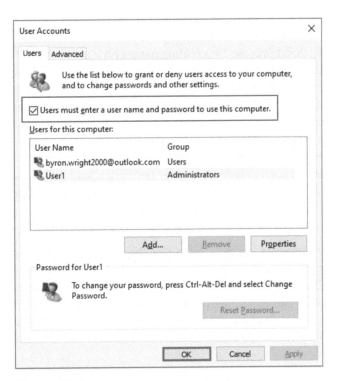

Figure 3-3   Enable automatic sign-in

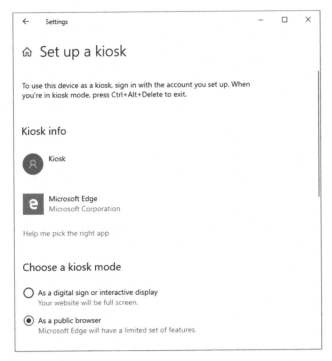

Figure 3-4   Assigned access

If you select Microsoft Edge as the application, you are given specific configuration options for the kiosk. If you choose the As a digital sign or interactive display option, then Edge is forced to full screen and displays a URL that you specify. If you choose the As a public browser option, you can specify a home page and an idle timeout to restart the browser to clear private data.

NOTE 2

For more kiosk configuration options, see Configure kiosks and digital signs on Windows desktop editions at https://docs .microsoft.com/en-us/windows/ configuration/kiosk-methods.

Naming Conventions

A naming convention is a standardized process for creating names on a network or stand-alone computer. Corporate environments establish naming conventions for user accounts, computers, folders, shared folders, printers, and servers. Names should be descriptive enough that anyone can figure out what the resource is. For example, computer names are often the same as their asset tracking number (inventory tracking number) or include the name of the person who uses the computer most often.

Using a naming convention for small networks might seem unnecessary, but even small networks benefit from resources with meaningful names. For example, in a small network with two servers named "Files" and "Email," it is easy to guess what resources are on each server. In another network where the two servers are named "Sleepy" and "Dopey," users have no logical way to know what resources are on each server. If your network grows, you will be happy you implemented a naming convention early in the process.

Some common naming conventions for user names are:

- *First name*—In small environments, there is little risk that two users will have the same first name. This approach is easy for users to remember.
- *First name and last initial*—This naming convention helps ensure that user sign-in names are not duplicated. In small and mid-sized environments, if two users have the same first name, they are unlikely to have the same last initial.
- *First initial and last name*—Many large environments use this naming convention or a variation of it. Last names are more likely to be unique than first names, so this convention reduces the risk of duplicate user sign-in names.
- *First name.last name*—This naming convention is becoming more popular because many organizations like to also use it for email addresses. This has an even lower chance of duplicates than other conventions.

No matter which naming convention you select, you must have a plan to address duplicate user sign-in names. For example, Byron Wright and Blair Wright might be in the same organization. If your naming convention is first initial and last name, both users will have the same user sign-in name of "bwright." To fix this, you could add a numeral to the end of the second user account created, to make the user sign-in name "bwright2." You could also use two letters of the first name, in which case the user sign-in names would be "bywright" and "blwright."

When creating new local users, you must be aware of the restrictions imposed by Windows 10 on the user name, such as the following:

- *User names must be unique*—No two users can have the same sign-in name because the sign-in name is used by the computer to identify the user and verify the password associated with it during sign-in.
- *User names must be 20 characters or fewer*—This restriction is typically not a problem because no users want to type a sign-in name of more than 20 characters.
- *User names are not case sensitive*—You cannot change the case of letters to create unique user sign-in names; Windows 10 reads BWright and bwright as the same name. Helpfully, this means that users do not need to be concerned about case when they type in their user name. Passwords, however, are case sensitive.
- *User names cannot contain invalid characters*—Windows 10 uses some characters for special functions, so they cannot be used in user sign-in names. The following characters are invalid:
  /\ { } : ; | = , + * ? < >

Default User Accounts

Each Windows 10 computer has an **Administrator** account and a **Guest** account that are created during installation. The Administrator and Guest accounts are called built-in accounts because they are created on every Windows 10 computer. They also have unique characteristics. In addition, a user-specified **initial account** is created during installation. The initial account is not a built-in account.

Administrator

The Administrator account is the most powerful local user account possible. This account has unlimited access and unrestricted privileges to every aspect of Windows. The Administrator account can manage all security settings, other users, groups, the operating system, printers, shares, and storage devices. Because of these far-reaching privileges, the Administrator account must be protected from misuse.

The Administrator account has the following characteristics:

- It is not visible on the sign-in screen.
- It has a blank password by default.
- It cannot be deleted.
- It cannot be locked out due to incorrect sign-in attempts.
- It cannot be removed from the local Administrators group.
- It can be disabled.
- It can be renamed.

To protect the Administrator account from misuse, it is disabled by default in Windows 10; however, the Administrator account is automatically enabled when you enter Safe Mode so that you can use it for troubleshooting. Safe Mode is a boot option you can use when troubleshooting Windows 10.

 TIP Because the Administrator account is available only in Safe Mode, it is typically used only for troubleshooting or as an account of last resort when signing in.

Because the password for the Administrator account is blank by default, this password should be changed immediately after installation. This prevents users from starting in Safe Mode and signing in as Administrator. If users sign in as Administrator, they can perform any system action, such as adding software, deleting files, creating a new account with administrative privileges, or increasing the privileges of an existing account.

 TIP Windows 10 restricts accounts with blank passwords to console access only. This means that no one can sign in over the network using an account with a blank password, including the Administrator account.

The Administrator account is unique because it is considered an account of last resort for signing in and troubleshooting; therefore, the Administrator account cannot be deleted or locked out after too many incorrect sign-in attempts. The Administrator account also cannot be removed from the local Administrators group because the local Administrators group is where the Administrator account derives most of its privileges.

Guest

The Guest account is one of the least privileged user accounts in Windows. This account has extremely limited access to resources and computer activities and is intended for occasional use by low-security users. For example, a company might have a computer in the lobby with Internet access for customers. The customers would sign in as a guest. The Guest account has no capability to change the computer settings.

The Guest account has the following characteristics:

- It cannot be deleted.
- It can be locked out.
- It is disabled by default.
- It has a blank password by default.
- It can be renamed.
- It is a member of the Guests group by default.
- It is a member of the Everyone group.

Most organizations have no need for a Guest account. To ensure that the Guest account is not accidentally assigned privileges that are used by anonymous users, the Guest account is disabled by default. This way, even if privileges are assigned to the Guest account by accident, no one can sign in as the Guest account and use those privileges.

The Guest account derives all its privileges from being a member of the Guests group and the Everyone group. Both these groups have very limited privileges. The Guests group is explicitly created for assigning permissions to Guest users. The Everyone group encompasses all users who have signed in, including the Guest account. Windows security has evolved so that the Everyone group has very limited privileges. Most privileges formerly assigned to the Everyone group are now assigned to the Authenticated Users group. Authenticated Users includes all users who have signed in except for the Guest account.

 **CAUTION**   If you enable the Guest account, the Everyone group includes anonymous users. This allows you to give users access to resources on a computer over the network without requiring a valid user name or password.

Initial Account

During installation, you are prompted for the information required to create a user. The user created from that information is given administrative privileges. Having administrative privileges means that the initial account created during installation is capable of performing all the same tasks as the Administrator account. The initial account can be used to configure Windows 10, including creating other user accounts.

Differences between the Administrator account and the initial account include the following:

- The initial account is visible on the sign-in screen.
- The initial account does not have a blank password by default.
- The initial account can be deleted.
- The initial account can be locked out due to incorrect sign-in attempts.
- The initial account can be removed from the Administrators group.

Other Accounts

Windows 10 creates multiple local accounts that it uses for background processes, such as Windows Defender Application Guard. These accounts are disabled by default to ensure that they don't create a security risk. Little or no documentation about these accounts exist, and you should not modify them. These accounts are:

- DefaultAccount
- WDAGUtilityAccount

Default Groups

Groups are used to simplify the process of assigning security rights and permissions. When users are members of a group, they have access to all the resources that the group has been given permissions to access. It is easier to assign permissions to a group and make five users a member of that group than to assign permissions directly to five users, particularly if the permissions change.

Windows has a number of **built-in local groups** that exist by default and cannot be deleted. These groups are assigned rights and permissions to Windows 10. Like local user accounts, local groups are stored in the SAM database and can be assigned permissions only to resources on the local computer.

The Windows 10 built-in groups are:

- *Access Control Assistance Operators*—Members of this group can access authorization attributes and permissions for resources on this computer remotely. This group contains no default members.
- *Administrators*—Members of this group have full access to the computer. The local Administrator account is always a member of this group. The initial account created during installation is also a member of this group by default. If the computer has joined a domain, the Domain Admins group is a member of this group. Making Domain Admins a member of the local Administrators group provides centralized control of domain computers through a single sign in.
- *Backup Operators*—Members of this group can back up and restore all files and folders on the computer; however, the ability to read and modify files is still controlled by file system security. Backup operators cannot automatically read and modify files; they must be assigned the necessary file permissions. By default, this group has no members.
- *Cryptographic Operators*—Members of this group are able to perform cryptographic operations. Only members of this group are able to modify encryption settings for IPSec in Windows Firewall when configured in Common Criteria mode. Common Criteria is a standard for security.
- *Device Owners*—Members of this group can change system-wide settings.

- *Distributed COM Users*—Members of this group are able to run and activate Distributed COM objects on the computer. This group is relevant only when using DCOM applications, which is relatively rare.
- *Event Log Readers*—Members of this group have the ability to read event logs on the local computer. You can add members to this group if you want them to be able to review the event logs for errors but not have the ability to erase the logs.
- *Guests*—Members of this group have the same access to the system as members of the Users group. Members are able to sign in and save files but are not able to change system settings or install programs. The exception to this is the Guest account, which has additional restrictions.
- *Hyper-V Administrators*—Members of this group can manage all aspects of Hyper-V on this computer.
- IIS_IUSRS—This group is used to configure security for Internet Information Services (IIS). Only the system account NT AUTHORITY\IUSR is a member by default. The rights and permissions assigned to this group are applied to all IIS users who are not authenticated.
- *Network Configuration Operators*—Members can configure network components and change IP address information. This group is useful if you need to delegate the ability to change IP address configuration to other users, but do not want to give those users full administrative rights. By default, this group has no members.
- *Performance Log Users*—Members of this group are able to monitor performance counters and access performance logs on the computer. This group has no members by default. In a domain environment, domain users and groups can be added to this group to perform remote monitoring.
- *Performance Monitor Users*—Members of this group are able to monitor performance counters on the computer but cannot access performance logs. This group has no members by default. In a domain environment, domain users and groups can be added to this group to perform remote monitoring.
- *Power Users*—Members of this group have almost all administrative permissions. It was common in previous versions of Windows to use this group for all users to ensure that they could make changes to their systems. In Windows 10, this group has been deprecated, and Microsoft recommends using it only when necessary to support legacy applications that do not run when a user has lower privileges.
- *Remote Desktop Users*—Members of this group can sign in remotely by using Remote Desktop. This group has no members by default.
- *Remote Management Users*—Members of this group can query and configure Windows Management Instrumentation (WMI) objects over the network.
- *Replicator*—This group is used by special user accounts to perform file replication between computers. This group has no members by default.
- *System Managed Accounts Group*—Members of this group are managed by Windows 10 and should not be manually modified.
- *Users*—Members can operate the computer and save files but cannot install programs, modify user accounts, share resources, or alter system settings. All user accounts created on the system are a member of this group by default. In addition, the system accounts NT AUTHORITY\Authenticated Users and NT AUTHORITY\INTERACTIVE are members of the group. In a domain environment, the Domain Users group is also a member.

CREATING AND MANAGING USER ACCOUNTS

Creating a user account can be done from Settings, Control Panel, or the **Local Users and Groups MMC snap-in**. You also can create and manage users with command-line tools and Windows PowerShell cmdlets. The process varies depending on which tool is used, but the options are similar in each tool.

A **standard user account** derives its privileges from being a member of the local Users group. As a member of the local Users group, a user account can use software but not install or remove software. A standard user also is not able to change computer settings that affect other users or delete operating system files. Effectively, a standard user cannot compromise the security or stability of Windows 10.

Some older software requires administrative rights to run properly. In this case, User Account Control prompts the user for the password of a user with administrative rights. To avoid being prompted for a password, you might want to make the user an administrative user.

An **administrator account** derives its privileges from being a member of the local Administrators group. Administrator accounts have complete access to the system. An administrator can make changes that compromise the stability and security of Windows 10, such as installing software, changing file system security, and updating device drivers.

In Windows 10, most actions that are triggered by an administrator do not result in a prompt from User Account Control; however, changes triggered by software do result in a prompt from User Account Control. This ensures that changes are not made by malicious software.

Accounts

From the Accounts settings, you manage your own user account and create additional user accounts. For your own account, you can switch authentication between a local account and a Microsoft account. When you switch between these options, your account settings remain the same and no data is lost. You merely are changing the process used to sign in.

You add other users from the Family & other users screen, shown in Figure 3-5. The wizard for adding new accounts starts by asking how the user will sign in. If you indicate that you don't have sign-in information for the user (the user's Microsoft account), you are prompted to create a Microsoft account for the user. If you don't want to use a Microsoft account for authentication, you can choose the Add a user without a Microsoft account option to create a local user account instead.

 TIP   Users should not create a new Microsoft account for authenticating to Windows 10 if they already have one. Using the same Microsoft account for multiple services makes authentication simpler for users.

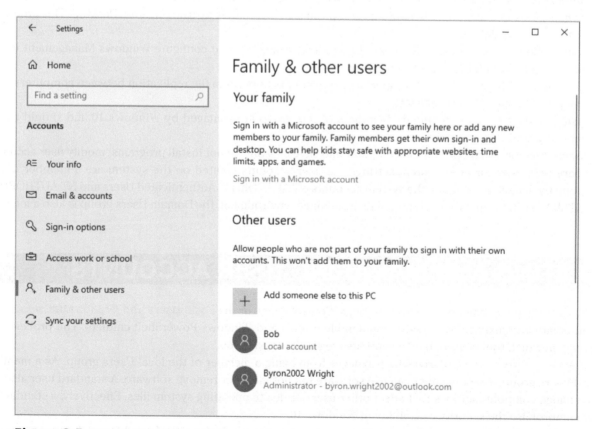

Figure 3-5   Family & other users screen

Activity 3-2: Creating a Local User Account in Settings

Time Required: 10 minutes

Objective: Create a local user account

Description: Local user accounts are required to sign in to Windows 10. The Accounts window in Settings provides a simplified way to create accounts. In this activity, you create one user account that authenticates locally.

1. If necessary, start your computer and sign in.
2. Click the **Start** button and then click **Settings**.
3. In the Settings window, click **Accounts** and then click **Family & other users**.
4. In the Other users area, click **Add someone else to this PC**.
5. On the How will this person sign in screen, click **I don't have this person's sign-in information**.
6. On the Create account screen, click **Add a user without a Microsoft account**.
7. On the Create an account for this PC screen, enter the following information and then click **Next**:
   - User name: **Bob**
   - Password: **password**
   - Security question 1: **What was your first pet's name?**
   - Your answer: **Fido**
   - Security question 2: **What was your childhood nickname?**
   - Your answer: **Fido**
   - Security question 3: **What's the first name of your oldest cousin?**
   - Your answer: **Fido**
8. Sign out as User*x* and sign in again as Bob. Notice that it takes a few minutes to build Bob's profile during the first sign-in.
9. On the Choose privacy settings for your device screen, click **Accept**.
10. Click the **Start** button, click **Settings**, and then click **Accounts**. Notice that the Family & other users option is not available because Bob is a standard user instead of an administrator.
11. Sign out as Bob.

Activity 3-3: Creating a Microsoft Account in Settings

Time Required: 10 minutes

Objective: Create a Microsoft account for signing in

Description: Microsoft accounts are an optional method for signing in to Windows 10. The Accounts window in Settings provides the option to create a new Microsoft account. In this activity, you create a user account that authenticates by using a Microsoft account.

1. If necessary, start your computer and sign in.
2. Click the **Start** button and then click **Settings**.
3. In the Settings window, click **Accounts** and then click **Family & other users**.
4. Click **Add someone else to this PC**.
5. On the How will this person sign in screen, click **I don't have this person's sign-in information**.
6. On the Create account screen, in the First name box, type your first name.
7. In the Last name box, type your last name.
8. Click **Get a new email address**.
9. In the New email box, type **yourfirstname.yourlastname@outlook.com**, substituting your first name and last name in the email address and then click **Next**. If the email address is not available, try different combinations until an address is available.

10. In the Create password box, type a password that you will remember and then click **Next**. Use a strong password because the Microsoft account you are creating is accessible on the Internet.
11. On the What's your name screen, enter your name and then click **Next**.
12. On the What's your birth date screen, select the correct country, enter your birth date, and then click **Next**.
13. Read the list of users on the Family & other users screen. Notice that the new account has been added to the list of users.
14. Click the new account and then click **Change account type**.
15. In the Change account type window, in the Account type box, select **Administrator** and then click **OK**.
16. Sign out as User*x* and sign in with the new Microsoft account.
17. When prompted to set up a PIN, close the window. (Signing in with a PIN is covered later in this module.)
18. On the Back up your files with OneDrive screen, click **Next**.
19. On the Choose privacy settings for your device screen, click **Accept**.
20. Click the **Start** button, click **Settings**, and then click **Accounts**. Notice that the Family & other users option is available because the Microsoft account is recognized as an administrator instead of a standard user.
21. Sign out of your Microsoft account.

User Accounts Applet

In older versions of Windows, the preferred interface for creating and managing user accounts was the User Accounts applet in Control Panel. The User Accounts applet in Control Panel, shown in Figure 3-6, is still available in Windows 10 but has less functionality. For example, you cannot create a new user account in the User Accounts applet.

The administrative options with a shield beside them in the applet are restricted to administrative users. If a standard user tries to perform these tasks, the user is prompted to provide the credentials of an administrator account.

Administrative options for user accounts include the following:

- *Change your account name*—Allows administrators to change the account name of a user.
- *Change your account type*—Allows administrators to change the user account from one type of account to another. For example, you can change a standard user to an administrative user.
- *Manage another account*—Allows administrators to select a different account to manage.
- *Change User Account Control settings*—Allows administrators to modify when prompts from User Account Control (UAC) are presented.

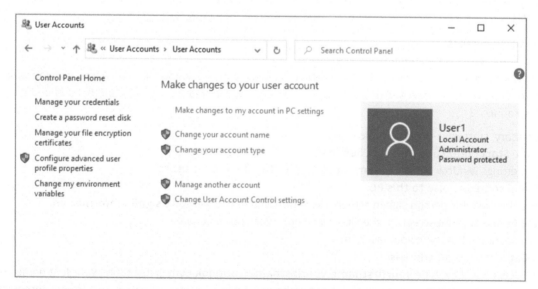

Figure 3-6 User Accounts applet in Control Panel

Additional available tasks include:

- *Manage your credentials*—This option opens the window for configuring Credential Manager. Credential Manager allows users to add, remove, and edit network locations with stored credentials. Network locations can include websites, FTP sites, and servers. Storing credentials avoids having to type in the credentials each time a resource is accessed. If your password for the resource changes, you need to edit the network location to change the password. In domain-based networks, this is not required to access domain resources.
- *Create a password reset disk*—This option creates a password reset disk. If users forget their password, the disk allows them to reset their password to a new password. Once created, a password reset disk does not need to be updated when the user password is changed. The password reset information is stored on a USB drive. This is less likely to be used now that Windows 10 has added security questions as an option for resetting passwords.
- *Manage your file encryption certificates*—This option allows users to manage the certificates used to support Encrypting File System (EFS). EFS encrypts specific files that are stored on the hard drive. Within this wizard, you can select or create a file encryption certificate, back up the certificate, configure EFS to use a smart card, and update a previously encrypted file to a new certificate.
- *Configure advanced user profile properties*—This option opens the dialog box that allows you to manage user profiles. For example, you can configure a roaming user profile. This option is seldom used.
- *Change my environment variables*—This option allows you to configure the environment variables for your computer that define characteristics such as the location of temporary files. This option seldom is used.

Activity 3-4: Using the User Accounts Applet

Time Required: 10 minutes

Objective: Manage a local user account by using the User Accounts applet in Control Panel

Description: You can use the User Accounts applet in Control Panel to manage existing user accounts. In this activity, you change a local user account to an administrator from a standard account.

1. If necessary, start your computer and then sign in.
2. Click the **Start** button, type **control**, and then click **Control Panel**.
3. In the Control Panel window, click **User Accounts**.
4. In the User Accounts window, click **User Accounts**.
5. In the User Accounts window, click **Manage another account**.
6. In the Choose the user you would like to change box, click **Bob**.
7. Read the options you have for managing the account and then click **Change the account type**.
8. In the Change Account Type window, click **Administrator** and then click **Change Account Type**.
9. Close the Change an Account window.

Local Users and Groups MMC Snap-In

The Local Users and Groups MMC snap-in allows you to create and manage both user accounts and groups. The fastest way to access this snap-in is through the Computer Management Administrative Tool. The Users node contains all the users, and the Groups node contains all the groups, as shown in Figure 3-7.

The general user tasks you can perform are:

- Create a new user.
- Delete a user.
- Rename a user.
- Set a user password.

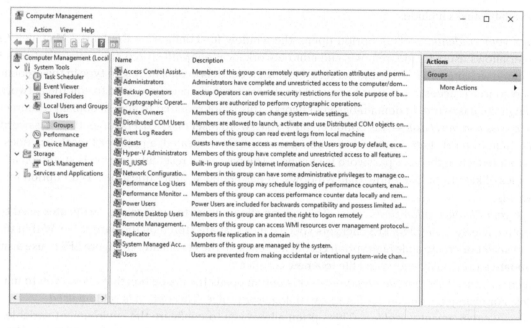

Figure 3-7   Local Users and Groups in Computer Management

 TIP   Setting a user password is relevant only for local user accounts. Accounts that are authenticated by using a Microsoft Account do not use a local password even though the option to reset the user's password appears in the interface.

Other user options can be configured in the properties of the user account. The General tab, shown in Figure 3-8, lets you view and configure the following:

- *Account name*—This information is displayed at the top of the tab but cannot be changed on this tab. To change the account name, you must right-click the user account and then select Rename.
- *Full name*—This is the full name of the person using the account. This can be changed.

Figure 3-8   User Properties, General tab

- *Description*—This is an optional text box that can be used to describe the purpose or use of the account.
- *User must change password at next logon*—This option forces users to change their password the next time they log on (sign in). Forcing a password change is common in corporate environments after a temporary password has been assigned.
- *User cannot change password*—This option prevents users from changing their passwords. Preventing a password change is often done for user accounts that are used as credentials for multiple services, such as scheduling system maintenance tasks. A password change would need to be updated on all services, and this ensures that it does not happen accidentally.
- *Password never expires*—This option exempts the user from the account policy that defines the maximum lifetime of a password. Preventing password expiration is useful for accounts that are used as credentials for services, such as scheduled tasks.
- *Account is disabled*—This option locks the account to prevent anyone from signing in and using the account; however, the account is retained and can be enabled again at any time. An account often is disabled when a user is away for an extended period of time. Disabling an account is also often done as an intermediary step before the account is deleted when a user leaves the organization.
- *Account is locked out*—This option is selected when Windows 10 locks out an account because of too many incorrect sign-in attempts. When an account is locked, no one can sign in by using the account. To unlock the account and allow the user to sign in again, deselect this option.

The Member Of tab, shown in Figure 3-9, lists the groups of which the user account is a member. Any rights and permissions assigned to these groups are also given to the user account. You can add and remove the user account from groups on this tab. Be aware that changes in group membership do not take effect until the user has signed out and signed in again. This is because the security token that contains group memberships and is used to access resources is generated during sign-in.

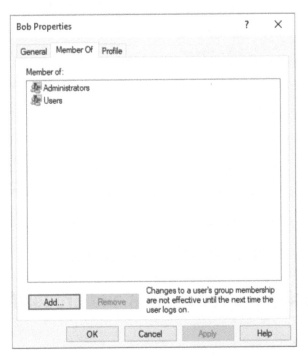

Figure 3-9   User Properties, Member Of tab

The Profile tab typically is not used on stand-alone computers or workgroup members. Similar information is available for user accounts in a domain. It is much more common for these properties to be set in a domain.

This tab can be used to define the following:

- The location of a roaming user profile
- A logon script
- A home folder

The profile path specifies the location of the profile for this user. By default, profiles are stored in C:\Users\%USERNAME%, where %USERNAME% is a variable representing the name of the user account. If you specify a network location for the profile, the profile becomes a roaming user profile.

The logon script box defines a script that is run each time during sign-in. This script can be located on the local computer or another workgroup member. The logon script is typically a batch (.bat) file or VBScript (.vbs) file that is used to configure the computer with mapped drive letters for accessing network shares.

 TIP You can use Windows PowerShell scripts for log on scripts. To specify a Windows PowerShell script, you need to use Group Policy instead of the user properties.

The home folder defines a default location for saving files. If a network location is used as a home folder, a mapped drive letter is created that points to the network location. The default location for saving files is defined by the application being used. Some applications use the home folder, while others use the Documents folder. If you do not define a home folder, it resolves to the user's profile folder, for example, C:\Users\User1.

When you view the properties of a group, there is only a single tab, as shown in Figure 3-10. The General tab provides a description of the group and a list of the group members. You can add and remove users from the group here.

Figure 3-10   Group Properties

Activity 3-5: Using the Local Users and Groups MMC Snap-In

Time Required: 10 minutes

Objective: Manage users and groups by using the Local Users and Groups MMC snap-in

Description: The Local Users and Groups MMC snap-in is the only management tool for creating and managing groups. You can also use it for creating and managing users. The user management options in the Local Users and Groups MMC snap-in are more detailed than Accounts settings. In this activity, you create a new user, create a new group, and place the new user in the new group.

1. If necessary, start your computer and sign in.
2. Right-click the **Start** button and then click **Computer Management**.
3. In the left pane, expand Local Users and Groups and then click **Users**. Notice the users who are listed here: Administrator, Bob, DefaultAccount, Guest, WDAGUtilityAccount, User*x*, and your Microsoft account.

4. Double-click **Bob**.

5. In the Bob Properties dialog box, on the General tab, in the Full name box, type **Robert Smith** and read the other available options.

6. Click the **Member Of** tab and read the list of groups that Bob is a member of, and then click **Cancel**.

7. In Computer Management, right-click **Users** and then click **New User**.

8. In the User name box, type **Jacob**.

9. In the Full name box, type **Jacob Smith**.

10. In the Password and Confirm password boxes, type **password**. Notice that, by default, the User must change password at next logon check box is selected.

11. Click **Create** and then click **Close**.

12. In the left pane, click **Groups**. Notice all the built-in groups that exist by default.

13. Double-click **Administrators** and read the list of group members. Notice that any user account configured as an administrator account is a member of this group.

14. In the Administrator Properties dialog box, click **Cancel**.

15. Right-click **Groups** and then click **New Group**.

16. In the New Group dialog box, in the Group name box, type **TestGroup**.

17. Click the **Add** button.

18. In the Select Users dialog box, in the Enter the object names to select box, type **Jacob**, click **Check Names**, and then click OK.

19. Click **Create** and then click **Close**.

20. In the left pane, click **Users**.

21. Right-click **Jacob** and then click **Properties**.

22. Click the **Member Of** tab. Notice that Jacob is a member of TestGroup and Users.

23. Click **Cancel** and then close the Computer Management window.

24. Switch the user to **Jacob Smith**. Notice that you are given a message indicating that the password must be changed.

25. Click **OK**.

26. In the New password and Confirm password boxes, type **password2** and then press **Enter**.

27. Click **OK** and wait for the new profile to be created.

28. On the Choose privacy settings for your device screen, click **Accept**.

29. Sign out as Jacob.

Command-Line User Management

Most management of local users is done with graphical utilities because they are easier to use; however, you do have the option to use command-line tools for local user administration. Table 3-1 lists Windows PowerShell cmdlets that you can use to manage local users.

Table 3-1   Windows PowerShell cmdlets for Local User Management

Cmdlet	Description
New-LocalUser	Creates new local users.
Remove-LocalUser	Deletes local users.
Get-LocalUser	Retrieves information about local users.
Set-LocalUser	Modifies local users.
Rename-LocalUser	Renames local users.
Disable-LocalUser	Disable local users that are enabled.
Enable-LocalUser	Enables local users that are disabled.

TIP   The net.exe command-line tool can create, configure, and delete local users. For more information run **net user /?** at a command prompt.

Activity 3-6: Performing Command-Line User Management

Time Required: 10 minutes

Objective: Manage users and groups by using command-line tools

Description: Most of the time you will perform user management tasks using graphical utilities. Sometimes, however, when you are querying information it is faster to use command-line tools. In this activity, you perform user management tasks by using command-line tools.

1. If necessary, start your computer and sign in.
2. Right-click the **Start** button and then click **Windows PowerShell (Admin)**.
3. In the User Account Control dialog box, click **Yes**.
4. At the Windows PowerShell prompt, type **net user** and then press **Enter**.
5. At the Windows PowerShell prompt, type **net user /?** and then press **Enter**.
6. At the Windows PowerShell prompt, type **net user Jacob** and then press **Enter**.
7. At the Windows PowerShell prompt, type **Get-LocalUser** and then press **Enter**.
8. At the Windows PowerShell prompt, type **Get-LocalUser | Where Enabled -eq $true** and then press **Enter**.
9. At the Windows PowerShell prompt, type **Get-LocalUser Jacob** and then press **Enter**.
10. At the Windows PowerShell prompt, type **Get-LocalUser Jacob | Format-List** and then press **Enter**.
11. At the Windows PowerShell prompt, type **Set-LocalUser Jacob -Description "Test User Account"** and then press **Enter**.
12. At the Windows PowerShell prompt, type **Disable-LocalUser Jacob** and then press **Enter**.
13. At the Windows PowerShell prompt, type **Get-LocalUser Jacob | Format-List** and then press **Enter**. Notice that the describe text is present and the account is not enabled.
14. Close the Windows PowerShell prompt window.

MANAGING USER PROFILES

A user profile is a collection of desktop and environment configurations for a specific user or group of users. By default, each user has a separate profile stored in C:\Users. Many of the folders in the profile are not visible by default in File Explorer because they are marked as hidden or system files. You can change the view settings in File Explorer to make all of the folders visible.

A profile contains the following folders and information:

- *3D Objects*—The default save location for the Paint 3D application.
- *AppData*—A hidden folder containing user-specific information for applications, such as configuration settings.
- *Application Data*—A hidden shortcut to AppData for backward compatibility with Windows 2000 and Windows XP applications.
- *Contacts*—A folder to hold contacts and their properties. Contact properties include addresses, phone numbers, email addresses, and digital certificates. Contacts can be used by various applications, but the most common are email applications.
- *Cookies*—A hidden shortcut to the storage location for Internet Explorer cookies. This shortcut is for backward compatibility with previous versions of Internet Explorer. Microsoft Edge uses a location in the AppData folder for cookies.

- *Desktop*—A folder that contains all the shortcuts and files on the user desktop.
- *Documents*—A folder that is typically the default location for saving documents.
- *Downloads*—A folder that is used to store files and programs downloaded from the Internet.
- *Favorites*—A folder that holds Internet Explorer favorites. Microsoft Edge uses a location in the AppData folder for favorites.
- *Links*—A folder in Windows 8 that contained links that were displayed as Favorites in File Explorer. This folder is not used by File Explorer in Windows 10.
- *Local Settings*—A hidden shortcut that is included for backward compatibility with Windows 2000 and Windows XP applications.
- *Music*—A folder for storing music files.
- *My Documents*—A hidden shortcut that is included for backward compatibility with Windows 2000 and Windows XP applications.
- *NetHood*—A hidden shortcut to a location storing user-specific network information, such as drive mappings. This is included for backward compatibility.
- *OneDrive*—A folder that is synchronized with cloud storage in Microsoft OneDrive. All Microsoft accounts are allocated storage space online in OneDrive.
- *Pictures*—A folder for storing picture files. It appears as My Pictures in Windows Explorer.
- *PrintHood*—A hidden shortcut to a location storing user-specific printing information, such as network printers. This is included for backward compatibility.
- *Recent*—A hidden shortcut to a location storing shortcuts to recently used documents. This is included for backward compatibility.
- *Saved Games*—A folder for storing saved games that are in progress.
- *Searches*—A folder that stores saved search queries so that they can easily be accessed again.
- *SendTo*—A hidden shortcut to the location storing shortcuts that appear in the Send To menu when right-clicking a data file. This is included for backward compatibility.
- *Start Menu*—A hidden shortcut to the location storing the shortcuts and folders that appear in the Start menu. This is included for backward compatibility.
- *Templates*—A hidden shortcut to the location storing application templates, such as Word document templates. This is included for backward compatibility.
- *Videos*—A folder for storing videos.
- *Ntuser.dat*—A file that stores user-specific registry information.
- *Ntuser.dat.log*x—A file that tracks changes in Ntuser.dat. This file is used to recover Ntuser.dat if the system shuts down unexpectedly.
- *Ntuser.dat{guid}.tm.blf*—A temporary file used for controlling registry changes.
- *Ntuser.ini*—A file that controls which portions of a profile are not to be copied up to a server when roaming profiles are enabled.

In most cases, you never need to customize profiles. You can allow users to modify their own profiles as desired; however, options are available that you can use to standardize and modify profiles, such as mandatory profiles, that might be useful in specific scenarios.

The Default Profile

The **default profile** is used when new user profiles are created. When a new user signs in for the first time, Windows 10 copies the default user profile to create a profile for the new user. The folder structure in the default profile is the same as a user profile; however, the folders are empty by default.

In older versions of Windows, such as Windows XP, you created a consistent environment for users by configuring the default profile on each computer to be the same. In a more modern computer network, it is rare to manually configure the default profile. Instead, you should use centralized management tools such as Group Policy to enforce consistent settings on computers.

Although you can see user profiles in the file system, you cannot copy them using File Explorer. If you copy a profile using File Explorer, the security permissions are incorrect, and the user will experience several errors. If you want to configure the default profile, the only supported method is by using Sysprep.

 **CAUTION** Modifying the Start menu layout within the default profile is not supported.

To configure the default profile:

1. If desired, create a new local user with administrative privileges to allow for creation of a blank user profile. Domain users are not supported.
2. Sign in as the designated local user with administrative privileges.
3. Modify the user's profile as desired and delete all other user profiles. You must delete the other profiles to ensure that the correct user profile is copied.
4. Create an answer file with the CopyProfile parameter set to true.
5. Run Sysprep with the /generalize option and specify the location of the answer file.
6. Image the computer and deploy the image. When the image is started after deployment, the default user profile is created from the profile of the local user account used in the preceding steps.

 TIP In many online blog postings, users complain about inconsistent functionality of CopyProfile with Windows 10. Instead of configuring a default profile, use Group Policy to provide consistent user settings. Default profile settings are copied only when the profile is first created, whereas Group Policy settings can be changed at any time after deployment.

Mandatory Profiles

A **mandatory profile** is a profile that cannot be modified. Users can make changes to their desktop settings while they are signed in, but the changes are not saved. This means that if a configuration problem occurs, all the user needs to do is sign out and sign back in to get pristine settings again.

You can implement mandatory profiles for a single user that is causing problems or for a group of users. Most often, a single consistent desktop is implemented for a group of users. Most mandatory profiles are implemented as roaming user profiles.

To change a profile to a mandatory profile, you rename the file Ntuser.dat to Ntuser.man. After this change is made, user modifications to the profile are not saved.

 **CAUTION** If you implement mandatory profiles, you need to ensure that users are aware that any files that they save to their Desktop or Documents folders are lost when they sign out.

Roaming Profiles

A **roaming profile** is stored in a network location rather than on the local hard drive. The main benefit of roaming profiles is that settings move with a user from computer to computer on the network. Typically, roaming profiles are used in large corporations where users move among different computers each day, such as a call center.

When roaming user profiles are in place, users have a consistent work environment regardless of which computer they sign in at. This means that any customization application settings and configuration files move with the user between computers.

To configure a roaming profile, you must edit the user account to point the profile directory at a network location. You then copy the existing user profile up to the network location.

Each time a user signs in, the roaming profile is copied to the local computer. If a user signs in and cannot contact the server with the roaming profile, the local copy of the profile is used.

Many administrators prefer not to implement roaming user profiles for the following reasons:

- *Slow sign-in and sign-out*—If users store large files in their user profile, sign-in and sign-out are slow. The slowness is caused because the user profile is copied over the network each time the user signs in and signs out.

- *Corrupted profiles*—Although not as common as with older versions of Windows, roaming user profiles can become corrupted. When a profile is corrupted, users are signed in with a temporary profile and do not have access to their normal settings. Intervention by an administrator is required to remove the corrupted profile.

Folder Redirection

Most organizations that want the ability to roam among computers implement folder redirection. **Folder redirection** lets you specify a network location for specific profile folders as an alternative to storing the data on the local client. Because the folders are redirected rather than copied, the speed of signing in or signing out is not impacted. To users, the redirected folders appear and function the same as if the folder were stored locally.

You can combine folder redirection with roaming profiles to mitigate the shortcomings of roaming profiles. Redirecting folders avoids the slow sign-in and sign-out process that can occur with large files. Profile corruption is also minimized because the sign-out process is faster and access to the registry is more likely to be terminated properly during sign-out.

You can manually redirect some folders, such as Documents, as shown in Figure 3-11. In most cases, however, folder redirection is implemented by using Group Policy.

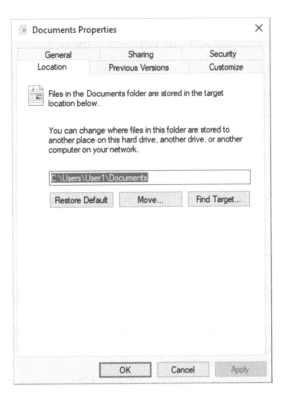

Figure 3-11   Folder redirection for Documents

The Public Profile

The **public profile** is different from other profiles because it is not a complete profile and it is not assigned exclusively to a user. The public profile does not include an Ntuser.dat file and consequently does not include any registry settings. The public profile is a series of folders. The content of these folders is merged into the profiles of other users when they sign in. For example, shortcuts or files placed in the Public Desktop Folder appear on the desktop of each user. Some applications place a shortcut in the Public Desktop folder as part of installation to make it available to all users. Only users with administrative permission can modify the contents of the Public profile.

The public profile includes the following folders:

- *Libraries*—Libraries stored here do not appear in user profiles but are available to all users in File Explorer.
- *Public Account Pictures*—Pictures selected by users for display with their user accounts are stored here.
- *Public Desktop*—Files and shortcuts stored here appear on the desktop of each user.
- *Public Documents*—Files stored here appear in the Documents library of each user.
- *Public Downloads*—Files stored here do not appear in profiles, but the files in it are available to all users.
- *Public Music*—Files stored here appear in the Music library of each user.
- *Public Pictures*—Files stored here appear in the Pictures library of each user.
- *Public Videos*—Files stored here appear in the Videos folder of each user.

Activity 3-7: Modifying the Public Profile

Time Required: 5 minutes

Objective: Modify the public profile and see how it affects users

Description: The public profile is merged into the profile of all users. Adding content to the public profile means that the content is available to all users. In this activity, you place a file in the Public Documents folder, which makes it available to all users.

1. If necessary, start your computer and sign in.
2. On the taskbar, click **File Explorer**.
3. In the left pane, expand **This PC**, expand **Local Disk (C:)**, expand **Users**, expand **Public**, and then click **Public Documents**.
4. In the right pane, right-click an open area, point to **New**, and then click **Shortcut**.
5. In the Type the location of the item box, type **C:\Windows\notepad.exe** and then click **Next**.
6. In the Type a name for this shortcut box, type **Notepad** and then click **Finish**.
7. Right-click the **Notepad** shortcut and then click **Cut**.
8. In the File Explorer address bar, type **C:\Users\Public\Desktop** and then press **Enter**.
9. Right-click an empty area and then click **Paste**. Notice that even an administrative user is prompted for permission to copy files here.
10. Click **Continue**. Notice that a shortcut to Notepad now is on your desktop.
11. Double-click the **Notepad** shortcut on your desktop to test it.
12. Exit Notepad.
13. Close the File Explorer window.

START MENU AND TASKBAR CUSTOMIZATION

In Windows 7, the Start menu was a collection of folders and shortcuts to applications. You could modify the Start menu by creating folders and shortcuts. In Windows 10, you cannot manually create folders and shortcuts in the Start menu. Instead, for your own profile, you can add and remove programs from the Start menu by right-clicking the program and pinning it to the Start menu. You can also create your own groups in the Start menu to organize items.

You can use Group Policy to customize the Start screen. The layout of the Start menu is defined by an XML file that you create. The XML file is stored in a central location, and the Group Policy directs computers to the XML file. You can apply a full Start layout, which users cannot modify, or a partial Start layout, in which the specified groups cannot be modified but other groups can.

By default, the exported XML file is configured to apply the full StartLayout. To apply a partial Start layout, you need to modify the <DefaultLayoutOverride> element as <DefaultLayoutOverride LayoutCustomizationRestrictionType="OnlySpecifiedGroups">.

NOTE 3

For detailed information about customizing the Start layout, see Customize and export Start layout at https://docs.microsoft.com/en-us/windows/configuration/customize-and-export-start-layout.

You also need to edit the XML file to include only the groups and tiles that you want to be locked because those are merged with the existing Start menu.

You can also customize the Start menu by using Windows Imaging and Configuration Designer (ICD). Windows ICD can create provisioning packages that configure a customized Start layout.

 **CAUTION** You cannot use Group Policy or provisioning packages to customize the Start menu layout or taskbar for Windows 10 Home.

Activity 3-8: Customizing the Start Layout

Time Required: 10 minutes

Objective: Modify the Start layout and see how it affects users

Description: You can customize the Start menu for Windows 10 Enterprise and Windows 10 Education editions. In this activity, you customize the Start menu and then export it so that it can be used on other computers. You also test applying the Start layout by using a local Group Policy.

1. If necessary, start your computer and sign in.
2. Click the **Start** button, type **Paint**, right-click **Paint**, and then click **Pin to Start**.
3. Click the **Start** button, move the pointer above the Paint tile until Name group appears, and then click **Name group**.
4. Type **Tools** and then press **Enter**.
5. Close the Start menu, click the **Start** button, type **Computer**, right-click **Computer Management**, and then click **Pin to Start**.
6. Click the **Start** button and then drag **Computer Management** to the Tools group.
7. Click the **Start** button, type **PowerShell**, right-click **Windows PowerShell**, and then click **Pin to Start**.
8. Click the **Start** button and then drag **Windows PowerShell** to the Tools group.
9. Click **Windows PowerShell**.
10. At the Windows PowerShell prompt, type **md C:\Start** and then press **Enter**.
11. Type **Export-StartLayout -Path C:\Start\Start.xml** and then press **Enter**.
12. Type **notepad.exe C:\Start\Start.xml** and then press **Enter**.
13. Review the contents of the file. Notice that two groups are named Productivity and Tools. Read the information for the programs in each group.
14. Exit Notepad and close the Windows PowerShell window.
15. Click the **Start** button, type **mmc**, and then click **mmc**.
16. In the User Account Control dialog box, click **Yes**.
17. In the Console1 window, click **File** on the menu bar and then click **Add/Remove Snap-in**.
18. In the Add or Remove Snap-ins window, click **Group Policy Object Editor**, click **Add**, click **Finish**, and then click **OK**.
19. In the Console1 window, in the left pane, navigate to **\Local Computer Policy\User Configuration\ Administrative Templates\Start Menu and Taskbar**.
20. In the right pane, right-click **Start Layout** and then click **Edit**.
21. In the Start Layout window, click **Enabled**.
22. In the Start Layout File box, type **C:\Start\Start.xml** and then click **OK**.
23. Leave the Console1 window open.
24. Switch users and then sign in as Bob.
25. Click the **Start** button and verify that the Tools group appears.
26. Sign out as Bob and then sign in as User$x$.
27. In the Console1 window, double-click **Start Layout**, click **Not Configured**, and then click **OK**.
28. Close all open windows. Do not save settings if prompted.

TIP   After disabling the customized Start layout, user profiles with the customized layout will retain it, but users can now modify it.

NOTE 4

For detailed examples of customizing the taskbar, see Configure Windows 10 taskbar at https://docs.microsoft.com/en-us/windows/configuration/configure-windows-10-taskbar.

You deploy a customized taskbar layout by using the same XML file that you use for customizing the Start layout. You need to add more XML elements for the taskbar apps you want to configure. No option to export the XML is available, but Microsoft does provide detailed examples on their website. You can configure the XML file to include only taskbar configuration information, which leaves the Start menu unmodified.

When you configure the taskbar, you can add apps to the existing default configuration or remove defaults and include only the apps you specify. This is controlled by the <CustomTaskBarLayoutCollection> tag. By default, the apps you specify merge with the existing default configuration. If you want to replace existing apps, you need to modify the tag as <CustomTaskBarLayoutCollectionPinListPlacement="Replace">.

ADVANCED AUTHENTICATION METHODS

Windows 10 includes advanced authentication methods to make using your computer more convenient and more secure. PIN or picture password authentication allows you to sign in with unique information other than your user name and password. Biometric authentication allows you to sign in based on facial recognition, fingerprints, or iris scanning.

When you use a user name and password to authenticate to Windows 10, a risk exists that the user name and password could be stolen. They can be stolen by someone looking or recording over your shoulder when you sign in. They can also be stolen by keylogging malware installed on your computer. After your credentials are stolen, an unauthorized person can use your credentials to get access to all your resources. Advanced authentication methods avoid this problem because you no longer type in your user name and password.

Multifactor authentication increases security by requiring you to have something in addition to a user name and password. The advanced authentication methods add multifactor authentication because they are unique to the device on which you are authenticating. For example, if you enable PIN-based authentication, the PIN you select is different for each device. If someone steals your PIN, that person also needs your device for that information to be useful. In the case of biometric authentication, the something that must be provided is you.

Picture Password

After **picture password authentication** is configured, to sign in, you perform gestures on a picture that you have selected. To configure picture password authentication, you need to select a picture and then provide gestures on that picture. The gestures are typically going to be tracing out significant features on the picture, but they can be any gesture that you like.

When you configure picture password authentication, it is unique for each computer or device. Knowing your gestures and picture are useful only if someone also gets physical access to your device. Malware is unable to capture and use this information.

Windows Hello PIN

Configuring **PIN authentication** provides similar benefits to picture password authentication. When you configure PIN (personal identification number) authentication, you provide a unique PIN for authenticating instead of your user name and password. As with picture password authentication, this PIN is unique to a specific computer. Knowing the PIN is useful only if someone also gets physical access to your device.

Activity 3-9: Configuring PIN Authentication

Time Required: 10 minutes

Objective: Configure PIN authentication for a user

Description: PIN authentication enhances security in Windows 10 by avoiding reuse of a user name and password. In this activity, you enable and test PIN authentication for a user.

1. If necessary, start your computer and sign in.
2. Click the **Start** button and then click **Settings**.
3. In the Settings window, click **Accounts** and then click **Sign-in options**.
4. On the Sign-in options screen, click **Windows Hello PIN** and then click **Add**.
5. In the First verify your account password dialog box, type **password** (or your password) and then click **OK**.
6. In the Set up a PIN dialog box, in the New PIN and Confirm PIN boxes, type **982377** and then click **OK**.
7. Sign out and then sign back in by using your PIN.
8. Click the **Start** button and then click **Settings**.
9. In the Settings window, click **Accounts** and then click **Sign-in options**.
10. Click **Windows Hello PIN** and then click **Remove**.
11. Read the message about removing the PIN and then click **Remove**.
12. In the First, verify your account password dialog box, type **password** (or your password) and then click **OK**.
13. Close all open windows.

Windows Hello Biometric Authentication

Biometric authentication has long been available for Microsoft operating systems. Many mobile computers include fingerprint readers that were compatible with earlier versions of Windows. As new versions of Windows were released, Microsoft enhanced the operating system support for biometric authentication. This made it easier for manufacturers of biometric readers to develop drivers because the operating system provided specific support for the process. In Windows 10, **Windows Hello** is the infrastructure that supports passwordless authentication, including biometric authentication.

Windows Hello supports the following biometric authentication methods:

- *Fingerprint*—To authenticate with a fingerprint, you place your finger on a fingerprint reader (or swipe, depending on the type of reader).
- *Facial recognition*—To authenticate with facial recognition, you place your face in front of the camera. This can happen immediately when you sit down in front of your computer.

To make biometric authentication more secure, Windows Hello requires biometric readers to have advanced functionality to ensure accurate authentication. For example, cameras for facial recognition need to have infrared support (which prevents someone from using a picture of you to sign in). Consequently, most biometric readers available before the release of Windows 10 are not compatible with Windows Hello. If you want to use biometric authentication, verify that any new biometric readers are compatible with Windows Hello.

Before you enable biometric authentication, you need to configure PIN authentication. PIN authentication is used as a backup authentication method if biometric authentication fails.

When biometric authentication is enabled, you need to provide your biometric information during configuration. Windows Hello, however, does not store a picture of your fingerprint, face, or iris. Instead, Windows Hello stores information about the unique pattern that your biometric information provides. This ensures that data from Windows Hello cannot be used to re-create your biometric information.

You can tell whether your computer has the necessary hardware to support biometric authentication from the Sign-in options screen shown in Figure 3-12. If your computer lacks the necessary hardware, the sign-in option will indicate "This option is currently unavailable" like is shown for Windows Hello Face. A supported fingerprint reader is available on the computer.

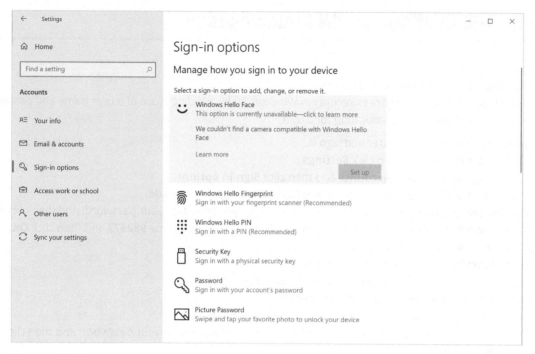

Figure 3-12   Sign-in options screen

Windows Hello is designed for stand-alone devices, and no synchronization of credentials between devices is supported. So, if you have two laptops and change your Microsoft account password on one of them, you will need to enter the new Microsoft account password manually on the second system before you can authenticate. Effectively, Windows Hello is encrypting a locally stored copy of the credentials. When you sign in by using Windows Hello, it unlocks the stored credentials.

Windows Hello for Business

Windows Hello for Business is a more advanced authentication system that builds on the infrastructure provided by Windows Hello. Its purpose is still to allow users to sign in by using a PIN or biometric authentication, but more advanced techniques are used for a high level of security and better user experience. In particular, changing your user password does not require manually entering the new password is multiple devices, because passwords are not used for authentication.

NOTE 5

For an overview video of how Windows Hello for Business Works, see How Windows Hello for Business works at https:// docs.microsoft.com/en-us/ windows/security/identity-protection/hello-for-business/ hello-how-it-works.

To use Windows Hello for Business, the computer running Windows 10 must be joined to a domain, Azure AD joined, or registered with Azure AD. Each identity provider that supports Windows Hello for Business identifies you by using a unique certificate with a public key and private key. The identity provider retains the public key while Windows 10 retains the private key. Access to the private key in Windows 10 is secured by Windows Hello. When you access an identity provider, Windows Hello authenticates you and then uses the private key to verify your identity with the identity provider holding the corresponding public key.

If your computer has a trusted platform module (TPM), the private key for the certificate is stored in the TPM. If no TPM is present, the private key is stored and secured by software. A TPM is a chip on the motherboard of a computer that is used to store encryption keys and certificates. Not all computers have a TPM.

Security Key

A **security key** is a hardware device (usually USB connected) that is used to uniquely identify you. Having possession of that security key allows you to sign in to websites, such as Office 365. You can take the security key with you to multiple devices, and your ability to authenticate to websites travels with the security key. You can also use a security key to sign into Windows 10.

Security key support for signing in to web-based applications is not a Microsoft-specific protocol. It is based on standards from the FIDO Alliance which are supported by the major browsers.

Simply plugging in the security key is not enough to allow authentication. You need to also provide a PIN or biometric information to unlock the security key. Many security keys include a fingerprint reader as part of the device.

 TIP You can use a security key to enable fingerprint-based authentication on computers that don't have a fingerprint scanner.

Dynamic Lock

You can use **dynamic lock** to increase security on computers that have Bluetooth functionality. When you leave a computer unattended, you should remember to lock the screen if you don't sign out. If you don't lock the screen, the computer could be used by an unauthorized person until the screen saver starts (assuming you've enabled the option to require unlock after the screen saver starts).

Dynamic lock triggers your computer to lock when a specified Bluetooth device that is paired with your computer is out of range. Most of the time a mobile phone will be used for dynamic lock, but you could use other devices like a Fitbit that is Bluetooth enabled. When you forget to lock the screen and leave to grab a coffee, your computer will lock when your Bluetooth device and computer can no longer communicate.

 **CAUTION** Because the signal strength of Bluetooth devices can vary, it's not possible to predict the exact distance that will trigger dynamic lock.

Smart Cards

You can use smart cards as another form of multifactor authentication in Windows 10. A **smart card** contains a certificate that is used for authentication in much the same way as Microsoft Passport; however, smart card authentication is applicable only to signing in to Windows and not additional resources, such as websites.

To use smart cards for authentication, each computer must have a smart card reader. You also need to install and configure a certification authority to issue the certificates that are stored on the smart cards. The cost of hardware and relatively high complexity of smart cards has prevented most organizations from implementing smart cards even though they have been supported since Windows 2000.

When users sign in by using a smart card, they first need to put the smart card in the smart card reader. Then, the user is prompted to enter a PIN that is associated with the smart card. The PIN is required to access the certificate on the smart card.

Windows 8 and newer versions of Windows also have the ability to use virtual smart cards. A **virtual smart card** stores the certificate in the TPM of the computer instead of on a physical smart card; however, like a physical smart card, the user needs to enter a PIN to use the virtual smart card.

When a virtual smart card is present in a computer, it functions like a smart card that is permanently attached to the computer. To authenticate by using the smart card at the sign-in screen, you need to select the correct sign-in option and then provide the PIN.

Virtual smart cards can be created by using the same certificate infrastructure that you would use for physical smart cards; however, you can also use the Tpmvscmgr.exe command-line tool. To use Tpmvscmgr.exe, you must have administrative rights on the computer.

 **CAUTION** Smart card sign-in can be used only on domain-based networks and local user accounts.

NETWORK INTEGRATION

Additional considerations must be taken into account when you place Windows 10 on a network and want to interact with other network users. User sign-in and authorization is very different in a networked environment. A networked environment requires you to understand the configuration of the local computer and other networked computers. You need to understand both peer-to-peer and domain-based network types. You should also understand Azure AD and how cached credentials work in Windows 10.

Peer-to-Peer Networks

A **peer-to-peer network** (or workgroup) consists of multiple Windows computers that share information. No computer on the network serves as a central authoritative source of user information. Each computer maintains a separate list of users and groups in its own SAM database. Figure 3-13 shows a peer-to-peer network.

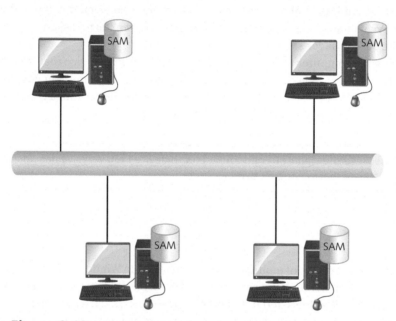

Figure 3-13   Peer-to-peer network

This type of network is most commonly implemented in homes and small offices. Windows 10 has a limit of 20 concurrent connections, which makes it impractical for sharing files and printers in larger environments.

In a peer-to-peer network, when you access shared folders or printers on a remote computer, you must authenticate as a user that exists on the remote computer. In most cases, it is preferred that the remote computer has a user account with the exact same name and password as the local machine. This allows **pass-through authentication** to occur. Pass-through authentication occurs when Windows attempts to authenticate to a remote resource by using the local Windows credentials to sign in to the remote computer. This requires a user account with the same user name and password to exist on the remote computer.

Pass-through authentication is the simplest authentication method for users. Managing the user accounts and passwords on each computer is difficult. No automated mechanism exists to synchronize user accounts and passwords among computers in a peer-to-peer network. As a consequence, security management for peer-to-peer networks is progressively more difficult as the number of computers expands.

Newer authentication methods, such as Windows Hello, PIN, picture password, and Microsoft accounts, do not work with pass-through authentication because you are no longer using a local password to authenticate and you cannot synchronize the alternate credentials.

TIP   You might see some older documentation that describes using Homegroups to simplify resource sharing in workgroups; however, this feature was removed from Windows 10 in the March 2018 feature update. Explore using cloud services, such as OneDrive, to simplify file sharing for workgroups.

Domain-Based Networks

User accounts for a **domain-based network** are much easier to manage than user accounts for a peer-to-peer network. A central server called a domain controller is responsible for maintaining user accounts and computer accounts. All computers in the domain share the user accounts on the domain controller. So, user accounts need to be created only once, and no concerns about synchronizing passwords among multiple accounts should arise. Figure 3-14 shows a domain-based network.

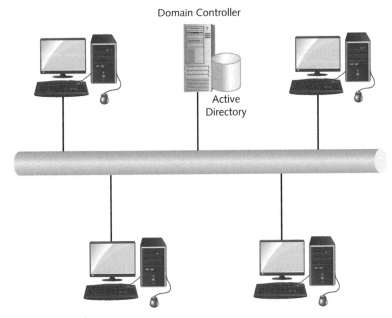

Figure 3-14   Domain-based network

To participate in a domain, Windows 10 computers are joined to the domain. The joining process creates a computer account for the Windows 10 computer and integrates Windows 10 security with the domain. Any existing local user accounts continue to exist and can still be used for local authentication.

Security is integrated with the domain in the following ways:

- Windows 10 trusts domain controllers in the domain to perform authentication.
- The Domain Admins group in the domain becomes a member of the local Administrators group to allow centralized administration by the domain administrators.
- The Domain Users group becomes a member of the local Users group to allow all users in the domain to sign in to Windows 10.

Some organizations prefer not to allow all domain users to sign in to any domain-joined computer. After the computer is joined to the domain, you can remove Domain Users from the local Users group and add only the specific domain user accounts that you want to allow. You could allow only members of a specific department or a single user.

Cached Credentials

When you use Windows 10 and sign in to a domain, your authentication credentials are automatically cached in Windows 10. This **cached credentials** capability is important for mobile computers that are not always connected to the domain. After credentials are cached locally, you can sign in to a computer using a domain user account, even when the domain cannot be contacted. For example, users with mobile devices can sign in with their domain account when on the road at a client site or at home.

By default, the credentials of the last 10 users to sign in are cached. If required, however, you can increase this up to 50 users, or disable cached credentials entirely. You might want to disable cached credentials because there are known methods for decrypting cached credentials if you are able to sign in as an administrator of the local computer.

 TIP   Cached credentials can be disabled by using Group Policy to configure the Interactive logon: number of previous logons to cache (in case domain controller is not available) setting to a value of 0.

Cached credentials are also used when you select to sign in with a Microsoft account in non-domain networks. Cached credentials for Microsoft accounts ensure that you can sign in when your computer does not have access to the Internet. The Group Policy setting that disables cached domain credentials does not affect caching of a Microsoft account.

Azure AD Join

Some smaller organizations are starting to use Microsoft cloud services as their core business applications. When user accounts are created for Microsoft cloud services like Office 365, the user account is created in Azure AD. Azure AD is the Microsoft cloud service for identity management.

The role of Azure AD for cloud services is similar to Active Directory in on-premises environments. Recall that you can use Azure AD join to connect computers running Windows 10 to Azure AD and allow users to sign in by using Azure AD accounts. This means that users can authenticate to their desktop computer by using the same account that they use for Microsoft cloud services.

 TIP A computer running Windows 10 can be joined to Azure AD during initial setup or after initial configuration. For detailed information about how to perform an Azure AD join, see Join your work device to your organization's network at https://docs.microsoft.com/en-us/azure/active-directory/user-help/user-help-join-device-on-network.

When you join Windows 10 to Azure AD, the user performing the join process is made a member of the local Administrators group. To support management by the organization, Azure AD global administrators and Azure AD device administrators are also made members of the local Administrators group. No other Azure AD user accounts are automatically given permission to use an Azure AD joined device; however, you can manually add more Azure AD users in the Accounts settings, as shown in Figure 3-15. In the figure, additional Azure AD users can be added in the Work or school users area. Local users and Microsoft accounts are managed in the Other users area.

 TIP It is possible to have a hybrid deployment where Windows 10 devices are joined to both Active Directory and Azure AD. Hybrid Azure AD join allows single sign-on to on-premises and cloud-based resources.

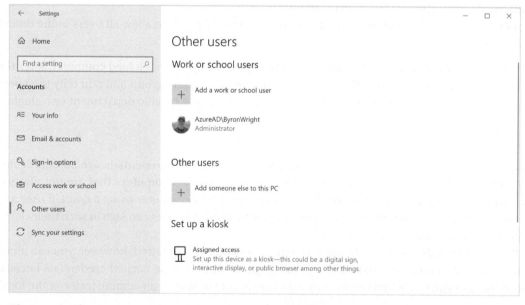

Figure 3-15 Other users screen when Azure AD joined

SUMMARY

- User accounts are required for users to sign in to Windows 10 and use resources on that computer. Local user accounts are stored in the SAM database of each computer. You can authenticate by using local credentials or a Microsoft account.
- Windows 10 sign-in security can be enhanced by enabling secure sign-in. When secure sign-in is enabled you need to press Ctrl+Alt+Delete to sign in.
- Fast user switching allows multiple users to be signed in to a computer at the same time.
- For kiosk computers, you can configure automatic sign-in and assigned access. Both features simplify using a kiosk computer.
- Three default accounts are created upon installation of Windows 10: Administrator, Guest, and the initial user account. The Administrator account does not have a password but is disabled to be used only in Safe Mode. The initial user account is configured as an administrator.
- Groups help to simplify management by organizing users. Many built-in groups are created by default. The Administrators group and the Users group are the more commonly used.
- User accounts can be created from Settings, Control Panel, or the User and Groups MMC snap-in. The Accounts settings provide access to the current functions, such as Microsoft accounts that older tools do not recognize. The User Accounts applet in Control Panel can still be used for managing users, but it is not preferred. The Local Users and Groups MMC snap-in allows you to manage users and groups. Command-line tools for user management also are available.
- User profiles store user-specific settings. Profiles contain a number of folders and an Ntuser.dat file. New profiles are based on the default profile and are created the first time a user signs in. The default location for user profiles is C:\Users.
- You can modify profiles to make them mandatory or roaming. Mandatory profiles cannot be modified by users. Roaming profiles move with users when they sign in to different computers. Folder redirection is generally preferred to roaming user profiles. Information in the public profile is applied to all users.
- You can modify the Start menu and taskbar layout by using an XML file defined in Group Policy. You can also use Windows ICD to create a provisioning package that modifies the Start menu and taskbar layout.
- Windows 10 includes advanced authentication methods to increase security by tying authentication to a specific device. Picture password and PIN authentication can be implemented without any special hardware. Biometric authentication requires hardware devices that meet the strict requirements of Windows Hello. A security key can be used to authenticate to Windows 10 and web-based applications. You can use smart cards and virtual smart cards in a domain environment.
- In a peer-to-peer network, each computer authenticates users by using the local SAM database. User accounts and passwords are not synchronized between computers automatically.
- In a domain-based network, user authentication is controlled centrally by a domain controller. Credentials are cached at first sign-in, which ensures users can sign in even if a domain controller cannot be contacted.
- Joining computers running Windows 10 to Azure AD lets you use Azure AD as a central identity store for authentication to Windows 10. This functions in a manner similar to joining Windows 10 to an on-premises Active Directory domain.

Key Terms

Administrator
administrator account
assigned access
biometric authentication
built-in local groups
cached credentials
default profile
domain-based network
dynamic lock

fast user switching
folder redirection
Guest
initial account
kiosk
local user account
Local Users and Groups MMC
   snap-in
mandatory profile

Microsoft account
Ntuser.dat
pass-through authentication
peer-to-peer network
picture password authentication
PIN authentication
public profile
roaming profile
secure sign-in

Security Accounts Manager (SAM) database

security identifier (SID)

security key

smart card

standard user account

user account

User Accounts applet

user profile

virtual smart card

Windows Hello

Windows Hello for Business

Review Questions

1. Local user accounts are stored in the SAM database. True or False?

2. Each user account is assigned a(n) _____ to ensure that security is kept intact if the account is renamed.

3. How do you reset the password for a Microsoft account?
   a. A local administrator can reset the password in the User Accounts applet in Control Panel.
   b. The user needs to reset the password on the Microsoft website for Microsoft accounts.
   c. Use a password reset disk.
   d. A local administrator can reset the password in Accounts settings.
   e. A local administrator can reset the password by using the Local Users and Groups MMC snap-in.

4. Which sign-in method requires users to press Ctrl+Alt+Delete before signing in?
   a. assigned access
   b. secure sign-in
   c. fast user switching
   d. automatic sign-in

5. Which sign-in method allows multiple users to have applications running on the computer at the same time?
   a. assigned access
   b. secure sign-in
   c. fast user switching
   d. automatic sign-in

6. Which characters are not allowed in user account names? (Choose all that apply.)
   a. \
   b. 1
   c. $
   d. *
   e. !

7. Because user names are case sensitive, you can use capitalization to ensure that they are unique. True or False?

8. Which characteristics apply to the Administrator account? (Choose all that apply.)

a. It has a blank password by default.
b. It cannot be deleted.
c. It cannot be renamed.
d. It is visible on the sign-in screen.
e. It can be locked out.

9. Which security feature can you enable to lock computers that are left unattended?
   a. security key
   b. dynamic lock
   c. secure sign-in
   d. fast user switching
   e. Windows Hello

10. Because the initial user account created during installation is a member of the Administrators group, it has all the characteristics of the Administrator account. True or False?

11. Standard users are members of which built-in local group?
    a. Administrators
    b. Guests
    c. Remote Desktop Users
    d. Users

12. Which user management tool is required to assign a logon script to a user?
    a. User Accounts in Control Panel
    b. Local Users and Groups MMC snap-in
    c. Advanced User Accounts applet
    d. Advanced Users and Groups MMC snap-in

13. Which file in a profile contains user-specific registry settings?
    a. AppData
    b. Ntuser.dat
    c. Ntuser.man
    d. System.dat
    e. Local Settings

14. Which profile is copied to create a profile for new user accounts?
    a. Default User
    b. Public
    c. Blank
    d. Default
    e. New

15. A roaming profile is located on a network server. True or False?

16. Which profile is merged into each user profile when the user is signed in?
   a. Default User
   b. Public
   c. Blank
   d. Default
   e. New

17. After you set a PIN for an Azure AD account on your laptop, that PIN can be used only on your laptop. True or False?

18. Which authentication method requires the computer to be joined to either a domain or Azure AD?
   a. Microsoft account
   b. domain account
   c. Windows Hello
   d. Windows Hello for Business
   e. security key

19. In a domain-based network, each server authenticates users by using the SAM database. True or False?

20. The _____ group becomes a member of the Administrators local group when a Windows 10 computer joins a domain.

Case Projects

Case Project 3-1: Network Integration

You are an IT manager at Gigantic Life Insurance. You have a new desktop support person starting today whose experience is limited to supporting peer-to-peer networks. What do you need to tell him about how Windows 10 integrates into a domain-based network?

Case Project 3-2: Public Use Computer

Buddy's Machine Shop has a lounge for customers to wait in while their parts are being retrieved. Because customers sometimes arrive a little early, they might have to wait up to an hour for their parts to be ready. Buddy has decided that it would be nice to give waiting customers Internet access. Describe how you would configure Windows 10 for public use.

Case Project 3-3: Secure Authentication Methods

At the most recent staff meeting of Hyperactive Media Sales, the general manager gave you instructions to make the laptops used by the salespeople as secure as possible. You have decided to implement a new advanced sign-in process for the users. How will you explain to the general manager how using new authentication methods makes the laptops more secure?

Case Project 3-4: Managing Desktop Settings

You are the system administrator for Precision Accounting Services, which employs 20 accountants and 25 accounting assistants. The accounting assistants sit at different computers each day in a shared workspace. You want to give them a consistent desktop experience no matter which computer they sign in to. How can you do this? Does it matter if the computers are joined to a domain or in a workgroup?

NETWORKING

After reading this module and completing the exercises, you will be able to:

1. Understand Windows 10 network components
2. Describe and configure Internet Protocol version 4
3. Describe and configure Internet Protocol version 6
4. Connect Windows 10 to the Internet
5. Describe and configure wireless networking
6. Configure Windows Defender Firewall

The vast majority of computers are networked today. Many homes and businesses have multiple computers that are used to share files and access the Internet. In this module's context, we examine how computers are linked to allow them to share data with other computers in an interactive way. People use applications on the computer to interact with other people and services to be productive, exchange information, and develop social connections. That can also be called networking in a human context, but networking in this module describes how to configure Windows 10 for computer-to-computer networking. Configuring those settings correctly will subsequently enable people's access to information and services beyond the individual computer.

In this module, you learn how to configure networking in Windows 10, including both IPv4 and IPv6 protocols. Supported Internet connectivity technologies and sharing Internet connectivity are discussed. You learn about configuring connectivity to wireless networks, including managing wireless connections in Windows 10. You also learn to secure network connectivity by using Windows Defender Firewall.

NETWORKING OVERVIEW

Windows 10 includes the basic components of networking, such as clients, services, protocols, and network drivers; however, additional features have been added and evolved over time as computing needs have changed. The basic components of Windows 10 that support networking are as follows:

- Network and Internet Settings
- Network and Sharing Center
- Remembered Networks
- Connections

Network and Internet Settings

Network and Internet Settings is the preferred way to manage the configuration of the network to which you are currently connected. The areas of Network and Internet Settings, as shown in Figure 4-1, are:

- *Network Status*—This area shows summary information for the network to which you are connected. It displays the network , the type of network it is (e.g., public/private), the type of access you have (e.g., wired/wireless), and the specific connection (i.e., network interface) used to access the network.
- *Advanced network settings*—This area shows links to advanced configuration and troubleshooting tools.
- *Network and Internet settings categories*—This area selects subsections of network and Internet settings, including overall status, settings by network technology (e.g., ethernet, Wi-Fi, Dial-up), as well as airplane mode and proxy settings.

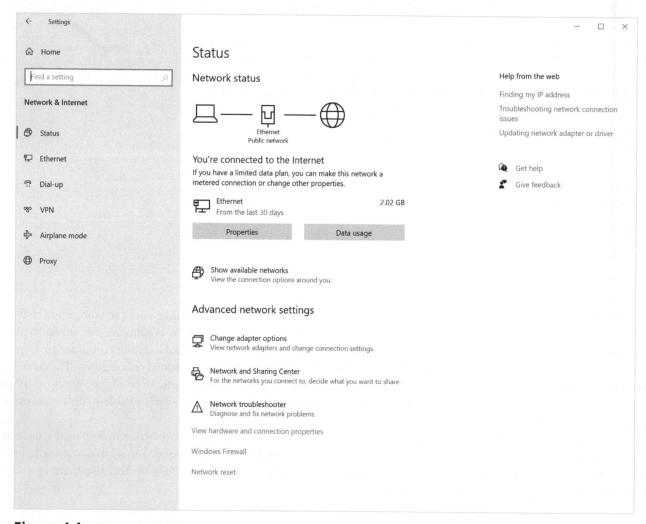

Figure 4-1   Network and Internet Settings

Network and Sharing Center

Network and Sharing Center is a Control Panel tool that provides similar functionality to the Network and Internet Settings for Windows 10. Earlier Windows operating systems relied on the Network and Sharing Center as the primary interface for network configurations. The areas of Network and Sharing Center, as shown in Figure 4-2, are:

- *View your active networks*—This area shows summary information for the network to which you are connected. It displays the network you are connected to, the type of network it is, the type of access you have, and the connection being used to access the network.
- *Change your networking settings*—This area displays links to common configuration and troubleshooting wizards.

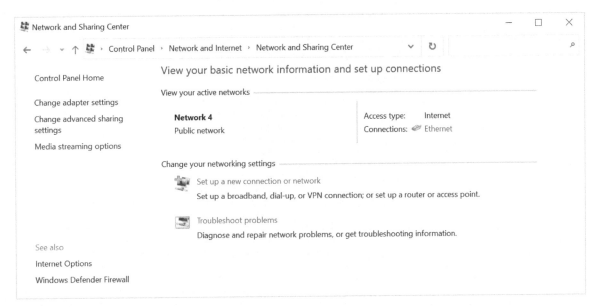

Figure 4-2   Network and Sharing Center

Remembered Networks

In early versions of Windows, the operating system was simply aware of a network card being physically connected (or not connected) to a network. Windows 10 has been enhanced to be network location aware. When you move a computer from one network to another, Windows 10 is aware that it is connected to a different network. Windows 10 keeps track of enough network properties to profile the network to which it is connected. If the network is disconnected and reconnected later, Windows 10 may recognize the network from a list of stored network profiles and associate certain properties with that network profile, such as its assigned network location type.

Network location awareness allows you to configure the security settings for each location differently. For example, for the network in your office, you might allow your computer to be discoverable by other computers on the network because you trust that network. When you are traveling on the road and using public networks in hotels and airports, however, you might want to restrict your computer's capability to be discoverable. The configuration settings for each remembered network are saved so that you do not need to reconfigure your computer as you move from one frequently used network location to another. Each remembered network is assigned a network name and an associated location type.

 TIP The service called Network Location Awareness is set to automatically start when the computer is started and is responsible for collecting and storing information for the network, as well as notifying programs when this information is modified. If the service is stopped, remembered network connections' configuration information might be unavailable.

Network Name

When you first connect to a network, the network is given a name to uniquely identify it as a remembered network to Windows 10. Wireless networks are named after the broadcast ID of the wireless access point. For example, connecting to the wireless network at work could create a network profile called Corp-Private. For Ethernet networks, the new network is assigned the prefix "Network" followed by a sequence number of the next available network number in the network profile history. For example, plugging into a new wired network at a hotel could create a network profile named Network 5.

Location Types

Each remembered network location is assigned a location type. When you first connect to a network, Windows 10 prompts you if your computer should be visible, or discoverable, to other computers on the network, as shown in Figure 4-3. Depending on how you respond, different security settings are applied. Components that are configured

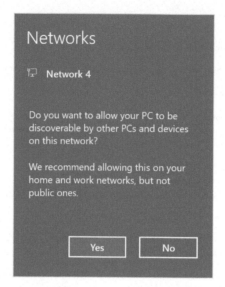

Figure 4-3   Confirming if you want your computer discoverable on a new network

include **Windows Defender Firewall** and **network discovery**. Previous editions of Windows differentiated between home and work locations, but Windows 10 simplifies the location list to locations that are trusted for computer discovery and those that are not.

The location types are:

- *Private network*—The **private network** category is used when the computer is connected as part of a peer-to-peer network in a trusted location. Typically, this is used at home or at work for peer-to-peer networking. The computer is able to access other network computers, and you are able to share files and printers on your computer.
- *Public network*—**Public network** is the default location type for a new network and is used when the computer is connected in an untrusted public location, such as an airport. In a public location, you cannot be sure of who else is using the network. Other network computers have limited or no visibility to your computer on the network.

    Your computer can connect to publicly available network resources, but you are not able to share files and printers on your computer. Connections to your computer that are initiated from other computers on the public network are blocked by default.

>  **CAUTION**   The level of visibility mentioned here is based on what shared files and printers are visible from your computer, but that does not hide your network connection and its traffic on the network.

- *Domain network*—The **domain network** category is used in corporate environments when your computer is part of a domain network. When Windows 10 can communicate with a domain controller, the network connection is automatically placed in this location category. You cannot manually place a computer in this category. The computer settings for computers on a domain network are determined by Group Policy settings configured by the network administrator.

Network Discovery

One of the network characteristics you can configure is network discovery. Network discovery provides you with an easy way to control how your computer views other computers on the network and advertises its presence on the network. Network discovery settings can be reviewed or modified by selecting the Change advanced sharing settings link in the Network and Sharing Center, as seen previously in Figure 4-2. This displays the Advanced sharing settings screen where for each type of network location, you can adjust the network discovery behavior of that type of location, as shown in Figure 4-4.

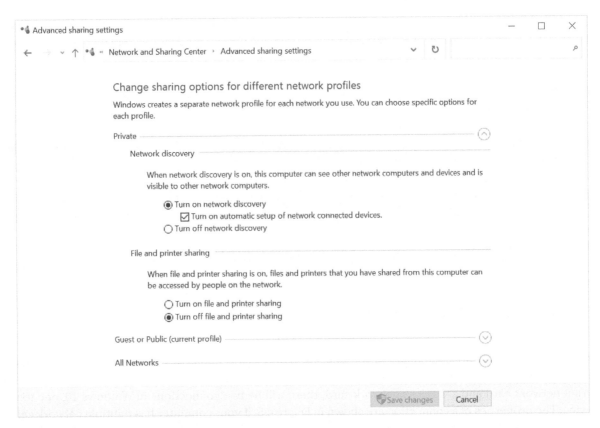

Figure 4-4   Advanced sharing settings, network discovery

The options for network discovery are:

- *Turn on network discovery*—You can see and access other computers and devices on the network. Other computers can also see your computer on the network and access shared resources. This is the default configuration when the network is in the Private location type.
- *Turn off network discovery*—You cannot see or access other computers and devices on the network. Other computers also cannot see your computer on the network or access shared resources. This is the default configuration for networks in the Public location type.

Activity 4-1: Exploring Network & Internet Settings

Time Required: 5 minutes

Objective: Become familiar with the options that are available in Network & Internet Settings

Description: Network & Internet Settings provides you with an overview of the network configuration on your computer. In this activity, you explore a few of the options available to you.

1. If necessary, start your computer and sign in.
2. Right-click the **Start** button and then click **Settings**.
3. Click **Network & Internet**. If not already selected, click **Status** in the left navigation pane to display the overall network status for your computer.
4. In the Status page's subsection titled Network Status, review the network connection listed there and note if it is a public or private network.
5. Below the connection status, click the connection's **Properties** button (which may be a link called Change connection properties in earlier Windows 10 editions). Click that to bring up the remembered connection's settings.

6. Scroll to the bottom of that window if necessary to observe the Properties section. Much of the same information is visible by running the ipconfig /all command from a command prompt window, but note that the user does not have to perform those extra steps because the settings summary view includes the detail. Note that key information such as DHCP enabled, Physical Address, IPv4 Address, IPv4 DNS servers, and Link-local IPv6 address are displayed.

7. Click the back arrow in the upper-left corner of the connection's settings window to return to the main Network & Internet settings. The highlighted subsection below Network & Internet has changed from Status to the subsection that matches that network connection's type (typically one of these: Ethernet, Wi-Fi, Dial-Up, Cellular). Click **Status** in the left navigation pane to return to the status page.

8. At the bottom of the Status page's subsection Advanced network settings (which may be called Change your network settings in earlier Windows 10 editions), click **Network troubleshooter**.

9. If no problems were found (none is expected in the lab environment), note the message that troubleshooting couldn't identify the problem. Click **Close**.

10. Close all open windows.

Connections

Connections in Windows 10 are fundamentally the same as in previous versions of Windows. For each network device installed in your computer, a connection is created to manage that network device. For example, if your computer has an Ethernet network card and a wireless network card, there will be two connections in Windows 10, one to manage each device. The properties of a connection are shown in Figure 4-5. If your computer has multiple network cards, you will see an additional Sharing tab when viewing connection properties.

Connections are composed of the following:

- Clients and services
- Protocols
- Network drivers

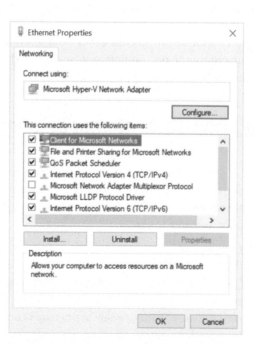

Figure 4-5 Network and Sharing Center, network connection properties

Clients and Services

Clients and services are the applications that use the network to communicate. A client allows you to connect to a particular service running on a remote computer. A service allows your computer to accept connections from and provide resources to a remote computer.

As shown in Figure 4-5, the clients and services included with Windows 10 are as follows:

- *Client for Microsoft Networks*—**Client for Microsoft Networks** allows Windows 10 to access shared files and printers on other Windows computers.
- *File and Printer Sharing for Microsoft Networks*—**File and Printer Sharing for Microsoft Networks** allows Windows 10 to share files and printers with other Windows computers.
- *QoS Packet Scheduler*—This service controls the flow of network traffic in Windows 10. It is responsible for optimizing network communication by controlling the **Quality of Service (QoS)**. Corporate environments can use QoS policies to give certain network content types higher priority within Windows 10. For private networks, QoS incorporates features to ensure that audio and video streams get higher network priority than data streams, which are more tolerant of network delays.

> **NOTE 1**
>
> All three client and service components in Windows 10 are installed by default.

Both the Client for Microsoft Networks and File and Printer Sharing for Microsoft Networks use the **Server Message Block (SMB)** protocol. Early versions of Windows included additional clients for accessing third-party server types, such as Novell NetWare networks. These third-party clients have been removed from Windows 10 but can be installed if you have a client installation disk from the other vendor.

Protocols

A network **protocol** is a set of rules for communicating across the network. For example, they define how much data can be sent and the format of the data as it crosses the network. Windows 10 includes several protocols for network communication.

- *Internet Protocol Version 4 (TCP/IPv4)*— **Internet Protocol Version 4 (TCP/IPv4)** is the standard protocol used on corporate networks and the Internet. This protocol is installed by default and cannot be removed; however, it can be disabled.
- *Internet Protocol Version 6 (TCP/IPv6)*— **Internet Protocol Version 6 (TCP/IPv6)** is an updated version of TCP/IPv4 with a larger address space and additional features. Windows 10 uses this protocol for some peer-to-peer networking applications. This protocol is installed by default and cannot be removed. However, it can be disabled.
- *Link-Layer Topology Discovery Mapper I/O Driver*—The Link-Layer Topology Discovery Mapper I/O Driver protocol is responsible for discovering network devices on the network, such as computers and routers. It is also responsible for determining the network speed.
- *Link-Layer Topology Discovery Responder*—The Link-Layer Topology Discovery Responder protocol is responsible for responding to discovery requests from other computers.
- *Microsoft LLDP Protocol Driver*—This protocol is used by network devices to advertise their identity, capabilities, and neighbors on a local network.

> **NOTE 2**
>
> Detailed information about TCP/IP v4 and v6 is found later in this module.

Network Drivers

A **network driver** is responsible for enabling communication between Windows 10 and the network device(s) in your computer. Each make and model of network device requires a driver specifically developed for that device, just as each printer requires a printer driver specific to that make and model of printer.

Windows 10 includes network drivers for network devices from a wide variety of manufacturers. If the network driver for your network device is not included with Windows 10, however, you can obtain the driver from the manufacturer's website.

 **CAUTION** Windows will automatically look for and install network adapter drivers when it detects an unconfigured network adapter. If that doesn't work and you need to manually install a driver, you will need to know the PC manufacturer name along with the associated model name or number. Some manufacturers will additionally require you to know the network adapter's manufacturer name and its own associated model name or number to select the correct driver.

Activity 4-2: Viewing a Network Connection

Time Required: 5 minutes

Objective: View the properties and status of a network connection

Description: To configure Windows 10 for network connectivity, you need to understand the components of a network connection and how to view their status. In this activity, you view the status and properties of a network connection using the older Control Panel interface.

1. If necessary, start your computer and sign in.
2. Click the **Start** button, in the search box type **control panel**, and then press **Enter**.
3. Click **Network and Internet** and then click **Network and Sharing Center.**
4. Below the View your active networks subheading, and to the right of Connections, click the named network connection. The name of the network connection will be different on different computers but will likely be called Ethernet. This shows the current connection status.
5. Click the **Details...** button. Note that this will display the network connection's configuration details, even if they were assigned automatically. Note that the list of details is like the connection properties listed when you browsed network connection details via Settings in Activity 4-1, but some of the miscellaneous properties listed are different between the two apps. As legacy control mechanisms like Control Panel are phased out, the Settings app's functionality will expand and be the preferred control mechanism for network connections.
6. Click **Close** to close the Network Connection Details dialog box.
7. Click the **Properties** button in the network status dialog box. This displays all of the clients, services, and protocols that are installed as part of that network connection.
8. Click the **Configure** button. This allows you to modify the configuration of the network adapter or an associated network adapter driver.
9. Click the **Advanced** tab. This tab allows you to configure many settings for your network adapter. The options available here vary depending on the adapter; however, all adapters allow you to in some way configure the connection speed and duplex. These are important settings to ensure proper connectivity when connecting to some network switches in the event that **autonegotiation** fails.
10. Click the **Driver** tab. This tab lets you view driver details, update the driver, roll back the driver to a previous version, disable the device, and uninstall the device, as well as optionally uninstall the driver.

 **CAUTION** If you uninstall the driver without a backup copy of the driver to install and Windows cannot install its own version of the driver, you will need to download the correct driver from the manufacturer's website, likely using a different PC that has a working network connection.

11. Click the **Details** tab. This allows you to browse through additional information about the driver, such as its version and the company that provided the driver, its installation date, and a driver description among other details.
12. Click the **Events** tab. This shows you a history of driver events that may assist with troubleshooting in the event of a problem.
13. Close all open dialog boxes and windows.

IP VERSION 4

TCP/IP is the most popular networking protocol to allow two computers to communicate in the world today. Although Windows 10 has the capability to use multiple protocols, only TCP/IP is included with Windows 10 for network communication, such as file sharing or accessing the Internet. IP version 4, also known as IPv4, is a standard first deployed in 1983. It defines how to specify and decipher the address of a computer that sent a piece of TCP/IP data, and the address of the computer that will receive it. The IPv4 addressing scheme works whether the computers are right next to each other or if they are located on opposite sides of the globe.

IPv4 Addresses

Each computer must have a unique IP address to communicate on a local area network. If any two computers on the same network have the same IP address, it is impossible for information to be correctly delivered to them.

IPv4 addresses are actually a binary number, 32 bits (binary digits) wide. Each bit can have the value 1 or 0. Computers work with bits and bytes, but people seldom do. IPv4 addresses are most commonly displayed in dotted decimal notation to make it easier for humans to work with the 32-bit address. In this format, an IP address is displayed as four decimal numbers, each decimal number representing an octet, separated by periods. An example of an IP address written in dotted decimal notation is 192.168.5.66. In this example, 192 is the first octet, 168 is the second, 5 is the third, and 66 is the fourth and last octet. Each octet represents the decimal number equivalent of the 8 binary bits in that portion of the 32-bit address. An octet value can range between 0 and 255.

The value of the first octet determines the general class of an IPv4 address, as shown in Table 4-1.

Table 4-1   IPv4 Address Classes

First Octet Value Range	Corresponding Class
0 to 127	A
128 to 191	B
192 to 223	C
224 to 239	D
240 to 255	E

Special cases and considerations that are in the IPv4 class-based system include:

- If the first octet is zero, the remaining octets identify local machines on the same network as the computer sending data. The special IPv4 address 0.0.0.0 is used in routing logic to represent "all other computers."
- A first octet value of 127 identifies a destination that is local to the computer sending data. The address in this range that is commonly seen is 127.0.0.1, or the loopback address.

 TIP Data sent to the loopback address returns to the computer that sent it and does not appear on the actual network. This is useful for troubleshooting, which is covered later in this module.

- A first octet identifying a Class D address represents a multicast address. Computers that belong to the same multicast group have the same multicast address assigned to them. Data sent to that multicast address attempts to deliver copies of the data to all multicast members with the same address. This is useful for application services that run on servers within the network but the client doesn't know their exact address to reach them, only the multicast address assigned to the service with which it is trying to connect. Class D addresses are not used to identify a single host computer with a unique IPv4 address.
- A first octet identifying a Class E address is reserved for future use and special purposes. Class E addresses are not used to identify a single host computer with a unique IPv4 address.

TIP   The special IPv4 address 255.255.255.255 is used as a broadcast address that represents the destination "all computers in this network." Data sent to this broadcast address cannot leave the local network through a router.

Several ranges of IP addresses are reserved for internal private network use and cannot be routed on the Internet; however, they can be routed internally on corporate networks. A proxy server or Network Address Translation (NAT) must be used to provide Internet access to computers using these addresses. Table 4-2 shows the network addresses that are reserved for internal networks.

Table 4-2   Addresses for Internal Networks

IP Address Range	Network (in CIDR Notation)
192.168.0.0.–192.168.255.255	192.168.0.0/16
172.16.0.0–172.31.255.255	172.16.0.0/12
10.0.0.0–10.255.255.255	10.0.0.0/8

Subnet Masks

An IP address is composed of two parts: a network ID followed by a host ID. Using the concept of a postal address for comparison, the network ID is similar to a street name and the host ID is similar to a house number. When a packet of information is being delivered on a corporate network, the network ID is used to get the packet to the proper area of the network through routers and the host ID is used to deliver the packet to the correct computer connected to a router responsible for its network ID. The total number of binary bits used to define a network ID plus the host ID must equal 32 bits exactly in order to fit in an IPv4 address. The number of bits used to specify the network ID can be variable, anywhere from 0 to 31 of the first bits in the 32-bit address. The host ID uses the bits left over that the network ID does not use. A network architect will decide where the split should happen based upon their design of the network, which is an advanced skill. The split is not arbitrary, so in addition to specifying an IPv4 address for a computer, you must identify where that computer will split its address into a network ID and a host ID.

A subnet mask is another 32-bit address used to define which part of an IP address is the network ID and which part of the IP address is the host ID. If the subnet mask is configured incorrectly, Windows 10 might not be able to communicate with computers on other parts of the network.

The subnet mask is specified separately from the IP address itself. For discussion's sake, consider this example of a subnet mask value in binary form (blank spaces inserted for readability):

Subnet mask = 1111 1111 1111 1111 1111 1111 0000 0000

The subnet mask's bits set to 1 identify what part of an assigned IPv4 address belongs to the network ID. The bits set to 0 in a subnet mask identify what part of an address belongs to the host ID. In this example, this would be interpreted by a computer as the first 24 bits of the IPv4 address identify the computer's network ID; the last 8 bits of the IPv4 address identify the computer's host ID.

For convenience, the dotted decimal notation is used to enter the subnet mask value into the IP settings of a network interface. Using dotted decimal notation, the preceding subnet mask binary value would be entered as 255.255.255.0.

The subnet mask octet value of 255 indicates that the corresponding IPv4 address octet belongs to the network ID. The subnet mask octet value of 0 indicates that the corresponding IPv4 address octet belongs to the host ID. For example, consider the following breakdown of an IPv4 address into its network and host ID components given a subnet mask:

IPv4 address = 192.168.4.1 with subnet mask = 255.255.255.0
Network ID = 192.168.4.0
Host ID = 0.0.0.1

If two computers have the same network ID in their respective assigned IPv4 address, they should be able to directly communicate on the same local network through a common device, such as a network switch. If the network ID is not the same, routers must receive the data from one computer and pass it to the destination network for delivery to the target computer. For example, consider the following three IPv4 addresses and a given subnet mask:

IPv4 address A = 172.16.4.254
IPv4 address B = 192.168.4.254
IPv4 address C = 172.16.4.1
Subnet mask for all three computers = 255.255.0.0

If these three IP addresses are assigned to three different computers on the same local network, and all three computers have the same subnet mask assigned, then each computer would analyze their network ID portion as:

Network ID portion of address A = 172.16.0.0
Network ID portion of address B = 192.168.0.0
Network ID portion of address C = 172.16.0.0

Address A and C have the same network ID; therefore, address C is considered directly reachable from address A. Those two computers will try to send data directly over the local network to each other. However, the computer assigned address A considers address B to be reachable only through a router because their network IDs do not match.

The computers assigned address A and B (and B and C) would not realize that they are on the same local network even though you know you put them on the same physical network. A router would need to be present and configured to relay data by routing traffic between the two network IDs. For example, a computer with address A trying to send to a computer with address B would send a packet to the router, the router would confirm it knew the path to send the packet to address B, then the router would send the packet to the computer with address B. That adds delays in communications, equipment cost, and administrative complexity—but it would work. In advanced networking scenarios, this may even be a required design for other reasons such as network segmentation and rule-based traffic controls, device categorization, and business requirements to name a few justifications. If setting up a router was not realistic and not required, and you just want all three computers to talk to each other, then you could fix the problem by changing address B to an IP address that shares the same network ID as address A and C.

Documenting subnet mask values with dotted decimal values is not the only way to write a subnet mask value using a shorthand notation. Another way to specify a subnet mask is to write the IPv4 address followed by a slash and a number that identifies the number of contiguous binary ones on the left-hand side of the subnet mask. For example, consider this subnet mask expressed in binary and dotted decimal notation:

Subnet mask (binary) = 1111 1111 1111 1111 0000 0000 0000 0000
Subnet mask (dotted decimal) = 255.255.0.0

In the case of the preceding example, there are 16 ones in the subnet mask value; therefore, the IP address and subnet mask value can be written as *IPaddress*/16. If this subnet mask was applied to the IP address 172.16.34.1, it would be written as 172.16.34.1/16. This notation is commonly referred to as classless interdomain routing (CIDR) notation and is becoming more popular than the older dotted decimal notation.

Default subnet mask values were originally defined by the class of the IPv4 address, as shown in Table 4-3.

NOTE 3

Analyzing subnet mask octet values other than 255 and 0 is an advanced TCP/IP design topic. See this link for more subnetting information: https://support.microsoft.com/en-us/help/164015/understanding-tcp-ip-addressing-and-subnetting-basics.

Table 4-3   Class-Based Default Subnet Mask Values

Class	Default Subnet Mask Value	Default Subnet Mask Value (in CIDR Notation)
A	255.0.0.0	/8
B	255.255.0.0	/16
C	255.255.255.0	/24

Default Gateways

The Internet and corporate networks are large networks that are composed of many smaller networks. Routers control the movement of packets through the networks. An individual computer is capable of delivering packets on the local network, but not to remote networks. To deliver packets to a remote network, the packet must be delivered to a router. The router sends the packet on toward its final destination.

A computer's **default gateway** is a router on the local network that is used to deliver packets to remote networks. The default gateway is identified in the computer's IP settings by entering the IP address assigned to the router's local network connection.

 TIP   If a Windows 10 computer has multiple network interfaces configured, each with its own IPv4 settings, only one interface is typically configured with a default gateway setting to identify to where to send network traffic to communicate with computers beyond the local network.

NOTE 4

Windows includes the route command-line tool to manage and view the routing table; for example, you can view the table with the route print command.

If the default gateway is configured incorrectly, the computer cannot communicate outside the local network. This means Internet connectivity is not possible and the computer will likely not have access to all resources within a corporate routed environment.

Windows 10 stores the default gateway setting internally as part of a larger table, called the **routing table**. The routing table can be useful in advanced scenarios where the computer must track where to send data for multiple network interfaces with multiple gateways defined.

DNS

Domain Name System (DNS) is a part of TCP/IP and is essential to communicate on a TCP/IP network. The most common use for DNS is to resolve (i.e., translate) host names to IP addresses. When you access a website, you access a location, such as www.microsoft.com. This is a **fully qualified domain name (FQDN)**, which is a name useful to humans. Computers cannot connect to a service on the Internet directly using just the name. Instead, they convert the host name to an IP address and then access the service using the IP address.

DNS serves other functions beyond converting the name of a website to an IP address. In a corporate network, DNS is also required for Windows 10 computers in an Active Directory domain-based network to find domain services, controllers, and sign in.

Given how essential the DNS function can be to a workstation, you can specify a primary and secondary DNS server address for any network connection. To avoid operational problems, it must be clear how Windows 10 will use multiple DNS server entries if they are defined. When a program asks Windows 10 to translate a host name to an IP address, it picks the IP of one of the DNS servers and sends it a DNS query. There is no guarantee that the primary DNS server will always be the server queried first, but typically it is checked first.

When the computer receives a response from a DNS server telling it an answer has been found, or a response that no matching information is available, Windows 10 considers the DNS server active and functional. It is only when the DNS server fails to respond at all that Windows 10 sends the request to one of the other defined DNS servers. A response that a name couldn't be translated into an IP address is still a valid response and the other DNS servers will not be queried for an answer to the same question.

Windows 10 also provides a text file called hosts in the folder C:\Windows\System32\drivers\etc\ that maps IP addresses to host names. Entries in the hosts file take precedence over data retrieved from DNS servers. Custom data can be entered into the hosts file to override DNS server data; however, this is a local file and can be difficult to remotely administer.

WINS

Windows Internet Naming Service (WINS) is a legacy technology used to resolve **NetBIOS** names to IP addresses. In addition, it stores information about services such as domain controllers. WINS is primarily used for backward compatibility with older NetBIOS-based networks. NetBIOS names can be used to access network services, such as file shares. Windows 10 is capable of using WINS but uses DNS as its primary name-resolution mechanism. IPv6 does not support using WINS.

Methods for Configuring IPv4

Windows 10 supports configuring IPv4 settings with static configuration, automatic assignment, and IPv4 configuration commands.

Static Configuration

All IP configuration information can be manually entered on each Windows 10 computer, but this approach is not very efficient. With each manual entry, the risk of a typographical error arises. In addition, if the IP configuration changes, visiting each computer to modify the configuration can be an enormous task. Manually entering IP configuration information is called static configuration and can be done from Settings or from the Control Panel using different interfaces. Figure 4-6 shows TCP/IP version 4 configured with a static IP address using the Network and Internet Control Panel application. Figure 4-7 shows an IPv4 static address and settings being applied with the Network and Internet settings.

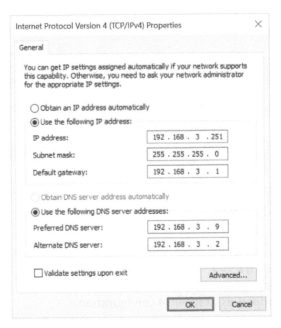

Figure 4-6   Network and Sharing Center, network connection IPv4 properties, static IPv4 configuration

Automatic Assignment

Automatic IPv4 configuration is usually preferred and accomplished with Dynamic Host Configuration Protocol (DHCP) servers, which support an automated mechanism used to assign IP addresses, subnet masks, default gateways, DNS servers, WINS servers, and other IP configuration information to network devices. Automating this process avoids the problem of information being entered incorrectly. If a change needs to be made to the IP address information, you modify the configuration of the DHCP server. The DHCP server can be configured with a range of IP addresses to hand out, specific exclusions to never hand out, or specific reservations that are given out to DHCP client computers with specified MAC addresses. Obtaining IP configuration information automatically is called dynamic configuration.

If Windows 10 is configured to use dynamic IP configuration and is unable to contact a DHCP server, the default action is to use an Automatic Private IP Addressing (APIPA) address. These addresses are on the 169.254.0.0/16 network.

APIPA is designed as a solution for very small networks with no Internet connectivity requirements. When two computers generate APIPA addresses, they are able to communicate with each other because they are considered to be on the same local network (i.e., 169.254.0.0), with a randomly generated unique host address in the last two octets. Unfortunately, APIPA addresses have little benefit in most scenarios because no default gateway is configured and no

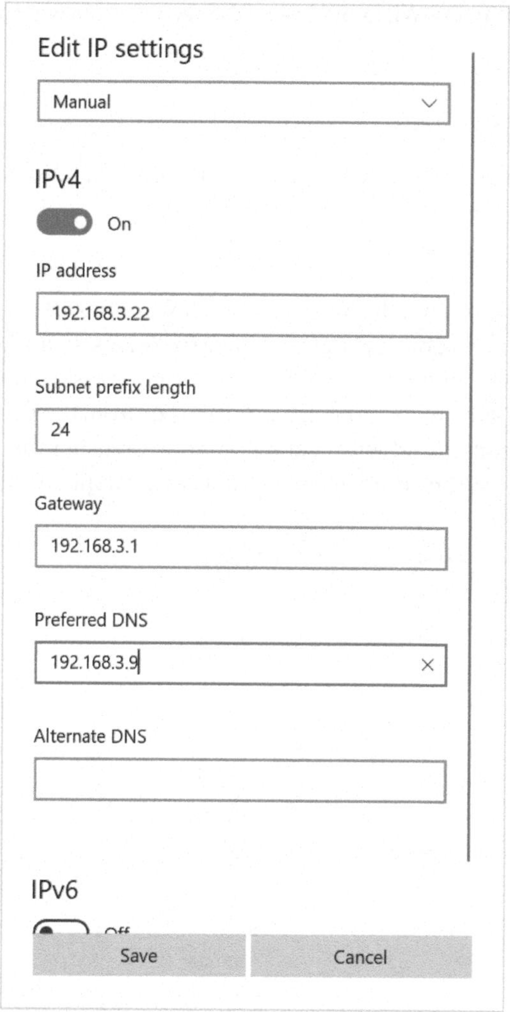

Edit IP settings

| Manual | ∨ |

IPv4

⬤◯ On

IP address

192.168.3.22

Subnet prefix length

24

Gateway

192.168.3.1

Preferred DNS

192.168.3.9   ✕

Alternate DNS

IPv6

◯ Off

| Save | Cancel |

Figure 4-7 Network and Internet
settings, network connection IPv4
properties, static IPv4 configuration

DNS server is assigned. This means that the computers cannot access the Internet. Consequently, a computer using an APIPA address is usually just a sign that the computer could not contact a DHCP server.

When a network connection is set to obtain its IP address automatically, Windows 10 also allows you to configure a static set of alternate IP configuration options from the Network and Internet control panel application. If a DHCP server cannot be contacted, the alternate IP configuration is used instead of APIPA but only if the alternate IP configuration is defined ahead of time. One advantage to specifying the alternate IP configuration is that a gateway can be specified, which APIPA does not allow. Figure 4-8 shows the Alternate Configuration tab for Internet Protocol Version 4.

IPv4 Configuration Commands

The administrator may optionally decide to use the netsh command-line tool or Set-NetIPAddress PowerShell cmdlet to assign a static IP address to a network interface. For example, netsh interface ipv4 set address name="Ethernet3" source=static address= 72.16.12.35 mask=255.255.0.0 gateway=172.16.0.1 tells the Network Shell utility to switch to the interface context and set the IPv4 address detail for the interface referenced with the name Ethernet3. The netsh utility has an interactive mode where these settings can be applied sequentially using its built-in menu system; however, netsh is commonly used by running one long command with the required command-line parameters. Some settings might require running the netsh command more than once. For example, the previous netsh command set the IP address, subnet mask, and default gateway, but the command netsh interface ipv4 set dnsservers name="Ethernet3" source=dhcp is required to set the network interface Ethernet3 to obtain DNS server addresses from DHCP as a subsequent step.

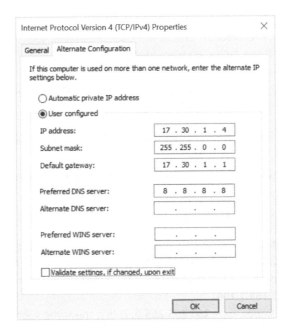

Figure 4-8 Network and Sharing Center, network connection IPv4 alternate configuration

Activity 4-3: Viewing and Configuring IPv4

Time Required: 10 minutes

Objective: View and configure IPv4 settings

Description: When you are troubleshooting network connectivity, it is essential that you understand how to view the existing IPv4 configuration to evaluate whether it is a problem. Basic IPv4 settings can be changed using the Settings app; however, the advanced settings are still accessed from the legacy Control Panel interface. In this activity, you view and configure IPv4 settings using the Settings app and the graphical interface from Control Panel.

NOTE 5

To avoid disrupting communications, the changes you are making in this activity are not saved and you will be asked to cancel your changes.

1. If necessary, start your computer and sign in.
2. Right-click the **Start** button and then click **Settings**.
3. Click **Network & Internet**. If not already selected, click **Status** in the left navigation pane to display the overall network status for your computer.
4. In the Status page's subsection titled Network status, below the connection status, click the connection's **Properties** button (which may be a link called Change connection properties in earlier Windows 10 editions) to display the connection's settings.
5. In the connection's settings, locate a heading called IP settings and then click **Edit**.
6. In the Edit IP settings window that opens, you should see Automatic (DHCP) is the current selection. Note that if you have already worked through later modules and their activities, you may already have your connection setting set to Manual. Click the arrow and then click **Manual**.
7. Options to turn on and configure an IPv4 address and an IPv6 address will be displayed. Click to turn on IPv4, if it is not already on.
8. In the IP address box, type **192.168.1.100**.
9. In the Subnet prefix length box, type **24**. Note that you are specifying the subnet mask using a CIDR value and not a dotted decimal notation in this case.

10. In the Gateway box, type **192.168.1.1**.
11. In the Preferred DNS box, type **192.168.1.5**.
12. Note that no advanced IPv4 settings option appears in this window.
13. Click **Cancel**. If you saved these settings, the network interface would change to a static IP address. Because you do not want to disrupt activities in later modules, you will not save your changes and will leave the adapter configuration as Automatic (DHCP).
14. Exit the Settings app.
15. Click the **Start** button, in the search box type **control panel**, and then press **Enter**.
16. Click **Network and Internet** and then click **Network and Sharing Center**.
17. Below the View your active networks heading, and to the right of Connections, click the named network connection. The name of the network connection will be different on different computers but will likely be called Ethernet.
18. Click the **Properties** button.
19. Click to highlight **Internet Protocol Version 4 (TCP/IPv4)** and then click **Properties**. This shows you the basic configuration of IPv4. By default, an IP address and DNS server address are obtained automatically through DHCP.
20. Click **Use the following IP address**. This allows you to enter in a static IPv4 configuration.
21. In the IP address box, type **192.168.1.100**.
22. If necessary, in the Subnet mask box, type **255.255.255.0**. This is the same subnet mask you entered earlier in this activity, but this time you are specifying dotted decimal notation instead of CIDR notation.
23. In the Default gateway box, type **192.168.1.1**.
24. If necessary, click **Use the following DNS server addresses**.
25. In the Preferred DNS server box, type **192.168.1.5**.
26. Click the **Advanced** button. In the Advanced TCP/IP Settings, you can configure additional options. On the IP Settings tab, you can configure multiple IP addresses and default gateways for the network connection.
27. Click the **DNS** tab. This tab allows you to control how DNS lookups are performed and whether this computer attempts to register its name with the DNS servers by using dynamic DNS.
28. Click the **WINS** tab. This tab allows you to configure how WINS lookups are performed. Some networks prefer to disable NetBIOS over TCP/IP to reduce network broadcasts; however, some legacy applications require NetBIOS, so test your applications before disabling NetBIOS over TCP/IP.
29. Click **Cancel** to close the Advanced TCP/IP Settings dialog box.
30. Click **Cancel** to close the Internet Protocol Version 4 (TCP/IPv4) Properties dialog box without saving any changes. If you saved these settings, the network interface would change to a static IP address. Because you do not want to disrupt activities in later modules, you will not save your changes and will leave the adapter configuration as automatic.
31. Click **Cancel** to close the Ethernet Properties dialog box.
32. Click **Close** to close the Ethernet Status dialog box.
33. Close all open windows.

Essential Networking Tools

Several key utilities or PowerShell cmdlets can be used to configure and diagnose IP settings. Some of these utilities make low-level changes to the TCP/IP functionality. Some of these changes will be denied unless the utility or command is run from an administrator elevated prompt. Table 4-4 shows some of the common IP configuration and troubleshooting utilities.

Ipconfig

The **ipconfig** command by itself displays basic TCP/IP settings of all active network connections at a command prompt. Several command-line options make the command versatile in troubleshooting TCP/IP settings, as well. Table 4-5 shows some of the most useful.

Table 4-4   Common Command-Line IP Troubleshooting Utilities

Utility	Description
hostname	Displays the host name of the computer on which it is run. The **hostname** utility is useful when you are at a computer and do not know the computer name.
ipconfig	Shows the current IPv4 and IPv6 configuration. You can also display some DNS information.
ping	Verifies connectivity to a destination by sending an ICMP request packet.
tracert	Provides similar information as the ping command but shows response times for every router on the path to the destination. Note that the routers consider ICMP requests low priority, which can provide unreliable latency information.
pathping	Provides similar information as **tracert**; however, **pathping** sends 100 ICMP requests per router in an attempt to identify packet loss.
route	Displays and modifies information in the local routing table.
netstat	Displays statistics and information about network connections.
nbtstat	Displays information about legacy NetBIOS over TCP/IP. **Nbtstat** can display the NetBIOS names known to the computer and purge the cache.
getmac	Displays MAC addresses associated with network adapters. Use getmac /v to obtain a more detailed output that includes the adapter name in addition to the adapter identifier. Use getmac /s HostIP /u userid /p password to obtain MAC addresses from a remote system.
arp	Displays and modifies the contents of the address resolution protocol (ARP) table, which maps IP addresses to MAC addresses. Use arp -a or arp -g to display the contents of the ARP table. Uses arp -d HostIP to delete an entry from the ARP table.
netsh	Modifies network configuration. Most of this functionality is now replicated in Windows PowerShell cmdlets.
nslookup	Queries DNS records directly from a DNS server. This is used to verify whether DNS records on various servers are configured correctly.

Table 4-5   Common Ipconfig Options for Troubleshooting TCP/IP

Command	Description
ipconfig /all	Displays all TCP/IP configuration settings in verbose detail. This includes DNS servers, the default gateway, and DHCP server (if applicable).
ipconfig /release	Removes dynamically assigned IP addresses from network connections. This disables TCP/IP operations on those interfaces.
ipconfig /renew	Attempts to renew IP addresses for all network connections that are configured to obtain an IP address automatically. If the renewal of a network connection's current IP address is refused by the DHCP server, the IP address is lost and a new IP address must be assigned by the DHCP server.
ipconfig /registerdns	Forces Windows 10 to register its name and IP address with the DNS server defined on a network interface's properties. This process is performed at startup. So, it is typically done manually only if the IP address has recently changed.
ipconfig /displaydns	Displays all cached DNS lookup data, including negative acknowledgements that a name was not found using DNS.
ipconfig /flushdns	Deletes the cached DNS lookup data, including wrong results or negative acknowledgements that may have been corrected at the DNS server since they were first cached. Useful if you don't want to wait for the cached data to naturally expire based on the response's **time to live (TTL)**.

Ping

The **ping** command confirms basic IP connectivity between the computer that it is run on and a specified target host. The ping command tests the capability of network data to reach a target and return; it does not confirm that applications on the target computer are operating properly. The target host may be identified with an IP address or DNS name. The ping utility sends out a special type of packet called an ICMP request packet. The computer that receives this packet may reply with a response ICMP packet. The ping utility measures the total time it takes for the request to get to the destination and response packet to get back to the computer running the ping command. This latency time is measured in milliseconds (ms).

Table 4-6 shows some useful command-line switches for the ping command.

NOTE 6

Some network devices and firewall software, such as Windows Defender Firewall, may actively block ping ICMP traffic even though the network connection is perfectly healthy.

Table 4-6   Common Ping Options for Troubleshooting

Command	Description
ping -t	Continues pinging indefinitely
ping -a	Forces a reverse DNS lookup to identify the FQDN associated with an IP address
ping -n	Specifies the number of requests to send
ping -4	Forces use of IPv4
ping -6	Forces use of IPv6

Netstat

The **netstat** command can display different types of TCP/IP statistics for active software and connections. Many options are available that can be reviewed by typing netstat /? at the command line. Several common netstat command-line options used in troubleshooting network connections are shown in Table 4-7.

Table 4-7   Common Netstat Options for Network Troubleshooting

Command	Description
netstat -a	Displays all connections including active and listening ports waiting for a connection
netstat -e	Displays statistics about total data sent and received
netstat -r	Displays the routing table
netstat -b	Displays the name of a program responsible for a connection or listening for one
netstat -o	For each active or waiting connection, displays the process ID of the process that owns the connection

The netstat command is useful for documenting the network activity and connections at a moment in time. You can view the information on screen, but it is often easier to view if you direct the output to file.

Nslookup

The **nslookup** command can be used at the command prompt to look up a DNS entry from a specific DNS server, or it can provide an interactive text-based console for advanced DNS queries.

Nslookup is a powerful tool because it can query a DNS server directly, even if it is a different one than the network settings on a local computer are using right now. The debug feature allows the administrator to deeply diagnose what data can be returned to the Windows 10 client and why. Nslookup can be used to contrast answers from external Internet DNS servers and from local DNS servers that might be customized to serve LAN clients and Active Directory users and computers. Third-party web-based DNS lookup tools can be pretty, but they are limited in how deeply they can analyze responses from DNS servers, and they don't report on internal DNS servers. Using nslookup can be an essential pro-level troubleshooting tool.

To fully appreciate the utility, the administrator must have knowledge of the type of records a DNS server includes, such as:

- *A*—Maps a host name to an IPv4 address
- *AAAA*—Maps a host name to an IPv6 address
- *PTR*—Maps an IPv4 or IPv6 address to a host name
- *MX*—Identifies the mail server(s) responsible for managing email for a domain
- *NS*—Identifies the DNS servers that authoritatively hold custom DNS data for a domain
- *TXT*—Text records associated with a domain that can be used for a variety of reasons, for example: vouch for domain ownership, implement Sender Policy Framework (SPF) to vouch for servers sending email on behalf of the domain, DomainKeys Identified Email (DKIM) to publish public SSL certificate records used to validate signed email messages and headers

NOTE 7

To review nslookup commands, start nslookup in interactive mode by entering nslookup on the command line and then pressing Enter. At the nslookup interactive prompt, >, type help.

PowerShell Cmdlets for Networking

Table 4-8 shows some of the common IP configuration and troubleshooting PowerShell cmdlets.

Table 4-8   PowerShell IP Configuration and Troubleshooting Cmdlets

PowerShell Cmdlet	Description
Clear-DnsClientCache	Deletes all contents from the DNS client cache, similar to ipconfig /flushdns.
Get-DnsClientCache	Retrieves the contents of the DNS client cache, similar to ipconfig /displaydns.
Get-NetAdapter	Gets the basic network adapter properties.
Get-NetIPAddress	Gets IP address configuration, similar to ipconfig.
Get-NetIPConfiguration	Gets network configuration including network profile name, IP addresses, gateway address, and DNS servers; similar to ipconfig.
Get-NetIPv4Configuration	Gets global IPv4 settings, such as ICMP settings, default hop limit, neighbor cache limit, and the multicast configuration. Note that these are global IPv4 protocol settings and not IP address information.
Get-NetIPv6Configuration	Gets global IPv6 settings, such as ICMP settings, default hop limit, neighbor cache limit, values for temporary addresses, and the multicast configuration. Note that these are global IPv6 protocol settings and not IP address information.
Get-NetRoute	Gets routing table information, similar to the route command-line utility.
Get-NetTCPConnection	Gets current TCP/IP network connections including local and remote IP addresses, ports and connection state; similar to the netstat command-line utility.
New-NetIPAddress	Creates and configures an IP address.
Remove-NetIPAddress	Removes an IP address and its configuration.
Resolve-DnsName	Perform a DNS query for a specified name, similar to nslookup command-line utility.
Set-NetIPAddress	Modifies the configuration of an existing IP address.
Set-NetIPv4Configuration	Sets global IPv4 settings, such as ICMP settings, default hop limit, neighbor cache limit, and the multicast configuration. Note that these are global IPv4 protocol settings and not IP address information.
Set-NetIPv6Configuration	Sets global IPv6 settings, such as ICMP settings, default hop limit, neighbor cache limit, values for temporary addresses, and the multicast configuration. Note that these are global IPv6 protocol settings and not IP address information.
Test-NetConnection	Display diagnostic information for a connection, supports ping test, TCP test, route tracing, route selection diagnostics, similar to ping and tracert command-line utilities.

Troubleshooting IPv4

To successfully troubleshoot IPv4-based communications, the technician should follow an incremental process that has proven successful in most situations. IPv4 has been in use for a very long time. Many problems actually have simple causes, such as a connection being in the wrong state or a feature turned off unexpectedly.

A common approach is to perform the following in order:

1. Confirm current settings.

2. Validate IPv4 connectivity.

3. Verify DNS name resolution.

4. Verify data connections.

Confirm Current Settings

The existing IPv4 settings should be confirmed. Assumptions about what settings are active lead to incorrect trouble-shooting progress. The ipconfig and netsh utilities can display the current settings from the command line; for example, netsh interface ipv4 show config will show all network interface IPv4 settings. The PowerShell cmdlets Get-NetIPAd-dress and Get-NetIPConfiguration can also display the current IP address settings. If the IPv4 address looks valid, it is possible that the default route (i.e., gateway) or routing table is incorrect. The default route can be displayed with the ipconfig or route command, or the Get-NetRoute and Get-NetIPConfiguration cmdlets. If all settings appear correct, the computer's connectivity with those settings must be validated.

Validate IPv4 Connectivity

If all settings appear correct, the ping utility (or Test-NetConnection cmdlet) can be used to confirm that the computer can ping its own loopback address. If the command is successful, the TCP/IP IPv4 protocol is functional on the computer.

The ping command can be used to ping a local host, such as the default gateway. If the local default gateway can be pinged, connectivity to the local network and the default gateway are validated in one attempt.

If the router can be pinged, attempt to ping a remote host using its IPv4 address. If this fails, confirm the path the traffic is taking with either the pathping or tracert commands.

Verify DNS Name Resolution

If IPv4 communications to remote hosts work when the raw IP address is specified in a command, but not by name, a DNS issue likely exists. The nslookup utility or Resolve-DnsName cmdlet can be used to query DNS servers directly and confirm the lookup is working as expected.

Confirm the correct DNS servers are specified on network settings manually or automatically through DHCP with the ipconfig utility or the Get-NetIPConfiguration cmdlet. If the wrong servers were entered, that should be corrected first. While troubleshooting, if there are multiple DNS servers specified, consider simplifying the list to just one server that you expect has the correct data.

The DNS resolver caches data, and that data may contain obsolete data or invalid responses. The DNS data being cached can be displayed with ipconfig /displaydns or the Get-DnsClientCache cmdlet to confirm that expected answers are being correctly obtained by the Windows computer from either the local Hosts file or the DNS server(s). If the problem was with DNS data and it has been corrected, the cache data can be purged with ipconfig /flushdns or the Clear-DnsClientCache cmdlet to provide a clean start to name resolution.

The DNS cached data tells you what answer the workstation received, but not from which DNS server, and not if the data the DNS server is holding is correct.

A common but subtle mistake is configuring a domain-joined workstation with an ISP's DNS server in addition to a corporate domain DNS server. When the workstation tries to look up DNS data to find corporate domain servers, it may ask the ISP's DNS server where they are located instead of the domain DNS server. You can specify a preferred order for Windows 10 to query DNS servers, but you cannot restrict Windows 10 from using both interchangeably. The ISP DNS server sends back a valid response—the domain servers' DNS data (e.g., where to find domain-specific Kerberos, global catalog, and LDAP services) does not exist in its database—and the client caches the response as a valid lookup result saying those services were not found. As a result, domain operations are disrupted and fail to oper-ate correctly on the workstation. When the workstation is restarted by the user, it might go back to working with the correct domain DNS server. The workstation user might report intermittent overall failures and annoyance as a result.

Verify Data Connections

If basic IP communications and name resolution appear healthy, the problem might be a result of data filtering by a firewall restriction or corruption. Any computer or device between the local client and the destination might be filtering data connections, disallowing them entirely. Windows 10 has a firewall component built in to filter inbound and outbound data connections, which is covered later in this module.

Many server-based data services listen on a specific data port. The Transmission Control Protocol (TCP) portion of TCP/IP allows an application to identify itself with a specific port value. The IP address identifies the computer itself; the TCP port identifies the listening application on that computer. Many third-party tools report the status of TCP ports for a given remote IP address. Windows 10 can report active port connections on the computer using the netstat command or the Get-NetTCPConnection cmdlet.

A crude test to check for connectivity to remote servers is to use the telnet application on the local computer to attempt a connection to a remote active TCP port. The telnet utility is available for installation as part of Windows, but it is not installed by default. It can be installed by opening Control Panel, Programs, Programs and Features, and selecting the task Turn Windows features on or off. The telnet client can then be selected and installed.

The telnet program provides an interactive interface that normally connects to a telnet server on its default TCP port number. A different port number can be specified on the command line, one that is used by a service other than telnet. For example, the mail server protocol for the Simple Mail Transfer Protocol (SMTP) is port 25. The telnet command telnet mail.example.com 25 opens an interactive session with the mail server, identified by the name mail.example.com, which is listening for connections on TCP port 25. If the data connection is allowed, the mail server greeting should be displayed. If it is, this confirms some level of data connectivity is allowed.

Additional filtering or data corruption may happen after the initial TCP connection to give the impression of a data communication problem. To see the full network conversation between two computers, a utility that can capture the network conversation would have to be employed. Microsoft had previously created two such utilities called Message Analyzer and Network Monitor. These were not included by default with Windows 10 but used to be available as a free download. Both utilities have been retired, and Microsoft has not continued development of a similar network traffic capture tool. You may still find that someone has a download of the older free tools, but remember that they are no longer patched or developed. Network Monitor itself has been deprecated before Windows 10 and should definitely not be used with Windows 10.

Installing a full network monitoring tool isn't always practical or desirable. Consider that Windows 7 introduced the capability to record network traffic using a network capture feature built into the operating system with the netsh utility (e.g., netsh trace). Windows 10 version 1809 also introduced a new packet-level monitoring tool called Packet Monitor (pktmon.exe) that runs from the command line and allows you to observe data in real-time or log data to a human readable or encoded data file (e.g., a data file with the .etl file extension) that can be opened in a tool like Message Analyzer.

NOTE 8

A popular open source alternative to a legacy tool like Message Analyzer is Wireshark, which is also supported by the Packet Monitor utility starting with Windows 10 version 2004. To learn more about Wireshark, see https://wireshark.org.

Activity 4-4: Using Ipconfig, Netsh, and PowerShell to View Basic IPv4 Data

Time Required: 15 minutes

Objective: Use ipconfig, netsh, and PowerShell to view and configure IPv4

Description: Windows 10 includes ipconfig, netsh, and PowerShell cmdlets to view and configure IPv4 information at the command line. These utilities and cmdlets can also be used for scripting. Ipconfig is used to view IPv4 configuration or release and renew IP configuration from a DHCP server. Netsh can be used to configure IPv4. PowerShell allows you to run cmdlets that can display and configure details using an object-based approach. In this activity, you use ipconfig and netsh to view and configure IPv4. Several PowerShell cmdlets are used to show IPv4 configuration details, test connectivity with ping/ICMP tests, and view resulting DNS cached data.

1. If necessary, start your computer and sign in.
2. Click the **Start** button, in the search box type **cmd**, right-click **Command Prompt**, and then click **Run as administrator** on the shortcut menu.
3. If you are prompted by a User Account Control window, click **Yes**.

4. At the command prompt, type **ipconfig** and then press **Enter**. This command displays a summary of your IPv4 and IPv6 information.

5. Type **ipconfig /all** and then press **Enter**. This command displays more detailed IP configuration information.

6. Note that if you have completed later modules that have reset your network connection address to static instead of assigned automatically and you are repeating this activity, then skip this step and the next. Type **ipconfig / release** and then press **Enter**. This command releases the DHCP address on your computer. Notice that no IPv4 address is listed in the results.

7. Type **ipconfig /renew** and then press **Enter**. This command renews a DHCP address on your computer or obtains a new one. Notice that the newly acquired IPv4 address is displayed. Note that the IPv4 address may be the same as the adapter had assigned previously. DHCP server implementations support the option of the client identifying the previous IP it had and asking for it again if it is still available.

8. Type **netsh** and then press **Enter**. Netsh can be used in an interactive mode where you navigate through menu levels to view information.

9. Type **interface** and then press **Enter**. This command changes to the interface context, where you can get more information about network interface configuration.

10. Type **ipv4** and then press **Enter**. This command changes to the IPv4 context, where you can get more information about IPv4 configuration.

11. Type **show** and then press **Enter**. This command displays a list of the information that can be displayed.

12. Type **show addresses** and then press **Enter**. This command shows the IPv4 addresses that are used by this computer.

13. Type **set address** and then press **Enter**. This command shows help information on how to configure an IP address for DHCP or as static. If a command is missing required information, the help screen for that command is automatically output.

14. Type **..** and then press **Enter**. This will change the interactive context level back one level.

15. Type **?** and then press **Enter**. This will display a long list of commands inherited from the netsh context in general, commands available in the current netsh context, and sub-contexts you can drill into.

16. Type **exit** and then press **Enter**. This will exit the netsh interactive mode.

17. Type the command **netsh interface ipv4 show addresses** and then press **Enter**. This noninteractive use of netsh will return the same result as the interactive commands you entered earlier.

18. Close the command prompt and all other open windows.

19. Right-click the **Start** button and then click **Windows PowerShell**.

20. In the Windows PowerShell window that opens, type **Get-NetIPConfiguration** and then press **Enter**. Note the IPv4Address listed for any reported interfaces.

21. Type **Resolve-DnsName -Name localhost** and then press **Enter**. Note the two loopback addresses that are reported in the results, one an IPv4 address and one an IPv6 address.

22. Type **Test-NetConnection 127.0.0.1 -traceroute** and then press **Enter**. Note the reported value of PingSucceeded.

23. To clear the DNS cache, type **ipconfig /flushdns** and then press **Enter**. This is not a PowerShell command but can be safely executed in a PowerShell window. This is not true for all legacy command-line utilities. Typically, PowerShell cmdlets can do the equivalent operation in a PowerShell script or window.

24. Type **Clear-DnsClientCache** and then press **Enter**. This is the equivalent of the previous ipconfig /flushdns command.

25. Type **Test-NetConenction www.novell.com** and then press **Enter**. This will both ping the site www.novell.com and populate the DNS cache with data that resolves the name www.novell.com with its DNS equivalent data. Note that if you do not have Internet connectivity, this command will fail.

26. Type **Get-DnsClientCache -Entry "www.novell.com"** and then press **Enter**. If you have Internet connectivity, this will display the DNS client cache entry for only the name www.novell.com, unlike ipconfig /displaydns, which will display the entire DNS client cache.

27. Type **Get-DnsClientCache -Entry "www.nothere.com"** and then press **Enter**. Note that PowerShell can report data that is not found with what appears as alarming red text when it really is just reporting only that it could not find a match.

28. Close the Windows PowerShell window.

IP VERSION 6

IPv6 is the replacement for IPv4. The creators of IPv4 could not have anticipated the expansion of the Internet and, as a result, IPv4 has some serious shortcomings when used for global networking. IPv6 addresses these shortcomings.

Improvements found in IPv6 include:

- Increased address space
- Hierarchical routing to reduce the load on Internet backbone routers
- Simpler configuration through automatic address management
- Inclusion of encryption services for data security
- Quality of service
- Capability to add and extend new features

IPv6 Address Notation

The address space for IPv4 on the Internet has essentially been depleted; IPv6 has a significantly larger address space. IPv6 addresses are 128 bits long, while IPv4 addresses are only 32 bits long. IPv6 provides many more addresses than are available in IPv4.

IPv6 has many more addresses than would normally be required for computing devices, but it is designed for ease of use rather than efficiency of allocation. Many of these addresses will probably never be assigned to a host. In fact, only one-eighth of the total address space is allocated for Internet-accessible addresses.

IPv6 addresses are represented in hexadecimal for convenience, where each hexadecimal value actually represents the equivalent 4-bit binary value. Hexadecimal values are grouped into four-digit segments separated by colons for readability. The total address length is a maximum of 32 hexadecimal digits. An example of an IPv6 address is 222D:10B5:3355:00F3:8234:0000:32AC:099C.

At times, you will see shorter IPv6 addresses than the previous example, and there are some formatting rules to help understand why. To simplify the expression of IPv6 addresses, any group of four hexadecimal digits can drop leading zeros, leaving at least one digit visible. The IPv6 address in the previous example can be simplified to 222D:10B5:3355:F3:8234:0:32AC:99C.

When an IPv6 address contains a long set of zeros, the zeros can be compressed to a double colon — :: — to signify that the data is all zeros in that part of the IPv6 address. For example, the multicast address FF02:0:0:0:0:0:112A:CC87 could be shortened to FF02::112A:CC87. This type of zero compression can be used only once per address. In general, it doesn't matter if the compression is done on the right or left side of the address; what really matters is that it can be done only once.

IPv6 Address Types

The format of an IPv6 address is more complex than an IPv4 address. Depending on the purpose of the IPv6 address, analyzing the different parts of the address changes. Unlike IPv4 with its network and host ID with a subnet mask, IPv6 can be much more complicated and variable. The full decomposition of different address types is an advanced topic beyond the scope of this book. The numbers on the left side of a written IPv6 address provide a clue as to what type of address it is, which is covered in this module.

IPv6 uses the CIDR notation of adding a slash and a number after the slash to the end of the IPv6 address. That number indicates the number of bits on the left side of the written address that makes up the network portion of the address. This network portion of the address is referred to in general as the **address prefix**. For example, 10F0:0:0:6501::/64 is a possible IPv6 prefix. The address prefix contains information that helps devices, such as routers, decide how to move data among networks and the links between those networks.

It is important to recognize that IPv6 is a young standard and it is still evolving. Some of the format information current today may change over time.

Knowing the type of address helps to set expectations of how data can be delivered to an interface. The designers of IPv6 knew that the end point for delivery could be a physical device such as a network card, a wireless device, or some program that is receiving data and acting as an end point for IPv6 data. The end point for IPv6 data delivery is called an interface. A single computer is typically called a node, which is capable of running multiple interfaces. Each interface can have one or more IPv6 addresses assigned to it. Recognizing the address type by its address prefix (see Table 4-9) is a required skill to analyze IPv6 addresses assigned to an interface.

Table 4-9   Common IPv6 Address Prefixes

IPv6 Address Type	Address Prefix
Link-local unicast	FE80::/64
Global unicast	2000::/3
Unique local unicast	FC00::/7
Site-local unicast (deprecated)	FEC0::/10
Multicast	FF00::/8

Link-Local Unicast

A **unicast** address defines a delivery destination that identifies a specific single interface. Data sent to or from link-local unicast addresses is not allowed to pass through IPv6-aware routers. A link-local unicast address is automatically assigned to any active interface on the computer by Windows 10. A link-local address allows computers in a local network to communicate with one another without requiring the use of a router. In IPv4, this same link-local behavior is provided by Automatic Private IP Addressing (APIPA), which generates IP addresses in the range 169.254.0.0 to 169.254.255.255.

The address prefix of a link-local address in IPv6 is FE80::/64. The last 64 bits of the address are randomly generated by Windows 10 as the host ID. An example of a link-local unicast address is FE80::F9:1435:305E:DFF2.

A computer can have more than one link-local address if it has multiple network interfaces. The address prefix for each link-local address on that computer is exactly the same. When the computer is sending to a link-local address, the routing table cannot tell which interface to use to send data to a destination link-local address. If this causes a problem, the link-local address can be extended with a zone ID.

Each network interface in Windows 10 is assigned a network interface ID, otherwise known as a zone ID. The zone ID can be used to identify what network interface is used to send the data. The syntax to specify a zone ID is IPAddress*%ZoneID*, where IPAddress is the destination link-local address and ZoneID is the interface ID of the network interface.

To see the current identifier for each network interface, open a command window and issue the ipconfig command or netsh interface ipv6 show interface command. The output of the netsh command lists a column titled Idx (shown later in Figure 4-9), which identifies the interface ID for each interface listed. The ipconfig output lists it at the end of each link-local address displayed below each connection.

 TIP   If a command such as ping fe80::613a:325f:5e1b:d9b4 returns the error result "Destination host unreachable" or "PING: transmit failed. General failure," it may be due to the command using the wrong interface to send the ping request. As an example, consider that the netsh command was issued to display the interface IDs and the correct interface to use was determined to be 15 on that computer. The ping command could be modified to include it as ping fe80::613a:325f:5e1b:d9b4%15.

Global Unicast

A global address can be routed as a public address on the Internet through routers and networks. Global unicast IPv6 addresses are usually assigned by an ISP or public registration authority.

Note that a global unicast address can be generally identified with the address prefix 2000::/3. Even though that is the current block of IPv6 addresses being handed out to public end points, this may change in the future. Large portions of the IPv6 address space are still unused. An example of a global unicast address is: 2001:0:4137:9E76:F9:14 35:304E:DFF2.

Unique Local Unicast

The unique local unicast address type is intended for local communications within a private site. These addresses are similar in function to IPv4 internal private addresses (refer to Table 4-2) in that they are not intended to be directly routable over the Internet.

The unique local address type allows an administrator to identify a site and route internally within that private site. Routers that connect to the global Internet will drop data with this address type if it is sent directly out to the Internet. Note that a unique local unicast address can be generally identified with the address prefix FC00::/7.

Multicast

An IPv6 **multicast** address serves the same purpose as an IPv4 multicast address. One or more computers can be assigned a multicast address that identifies them as members of the same group of computers. When data is sent to a multicast address, all computers with an interface that belongs to that multicast group will receive a copy of the data.

The address prefix of a multicast address is FF00::/8. Managing multicast addresses is not a typical administration task for Windows 10, so these settings are not reviewed in detail here.

Special Addresses

Two special addresses exist in IPv6: the loopback address and the unspecified address. The loopback address in IPv6 is specified as 0:0:0:0:0:0:0:1, otherwise written as ::1 or ::1/128. This is similar in function to the IPv4 loopback address 127.0.0.1. The loopback address is assigned only to a virtual interface, never to a physical one. Any data sent to the loopback address for a computer will deliver in software back to the computer that sent it. The data will not be sent out on the physical network; the entire process will happen in software using the virtual interface only.

The unspecified address is 0:0:0:0:0:0:0:0, otherwise written as :: or ::/128. The unspecified address is never assigned to a computer. It indicates the absence of an address. This can be observed when an IPv6 address is unspecified in a configuration window or when a computer is sending an IPv6 packet, but it doesn't have a source address yet (i.e., it hasn't learned its address yet).

IPv6 Tunneling through IPv4

When IPv6 was still new, mechanisms like 6to4, Teredo, and Intra Site Automatic Tunneling Address Protocol (ISATAP) were included as part of Windows to carry IPv6 data over the existing IPv4 public networks. Best-practice advice is to not use these transition technologies as they are deprecated and disabled by default as Windows 10 evolves. Where possible, always use native IPv6 support instead.

Methods for Configuring IPv6

A computer running Windows 10 automatically configures its network interfaces with a link-local address. These can be displayed by entering the ipconfig command at the command line, as shown in Figure 4-9. The link-local addresses allow the computer to interact with other computers on the local network but not through a router to other networks.

To configure IPv6, you can use:

- Static configuration
- Automatic configuration
- IPv6 Configuration Commands

NOTE 9

Some references will mention a site-local unicast prefix as FEC0::/10 as an alternative to unique local unicast; however, these types of addresses were considered flawed in their design and application and therefore officially deprecated. See https://tools.ietf.org/html/rfc3879 for further details.

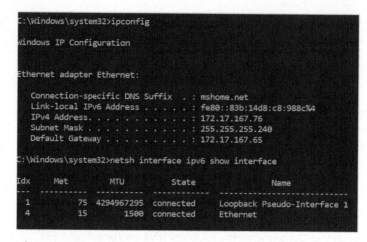

```
C:\Windows\system32>ipconfig

Windows IP Configuration

Ethernet adapter Ethernet:

   Connection-specific DNS Suffix   . : mshome.net
   Link-local IPv6 Address . . . . . : fe80::83b:14d8:c8:988c%4
   IPv4 Address. . . . . . . . . . . : 172.17.167.76
   Subnet Mask . . . . . . . . . . . : 255.255.255.240
   Default Gateway . . . . . . . . . : 172.17.167.65

C:\Windows\system32>netsh interface ipv6 show interface

Idx     Met         MTU          State                Name
---  ----------  ----------  ------------  ---------------------------
  1          75  4294967295   connected    Loopback Pseudo-Interface 1
  4          15        1500   connected    Ethernet
```

Figure 4-9   Netsh and ipconfig output displaying interface index ID

Static Configuration

A network connection's properties include settings for IPv6. By default, the properties are configured to obtain an IPv6 address automatically, as shown in Figure 4-10. It is not common to configure an IPv6 address statically. To configure a static address, a network interface's IPv6 properties must be reconfigured to use a specific IPv6 address with a specified subnet prefix length, as shown in Figure 4-11.

The Advanced button in the IPv6 Properties window allows the interface to be assigned one or more default gateways, multiple IPs, and custom DNS settings. IPv6 does not implement NetBIOS over TCP/IP, so there are no WINS configuration options.

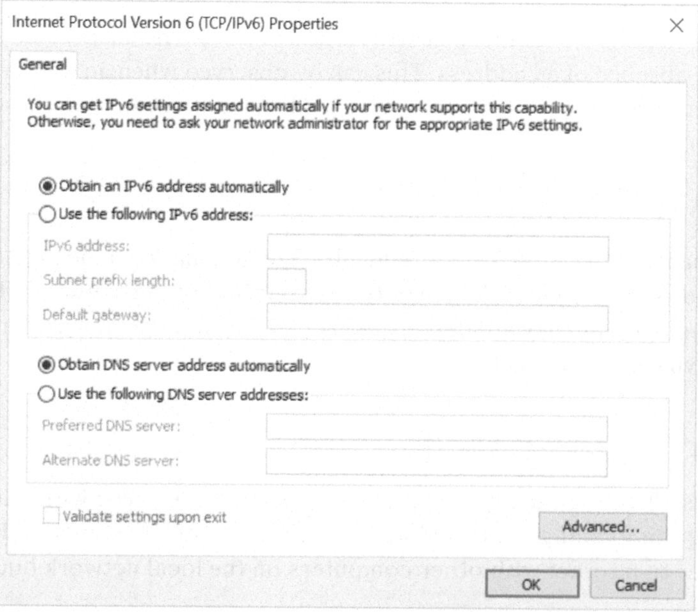

Figure 4-10   Network and Sharing Center, network connection IPv6 automatic connection properties

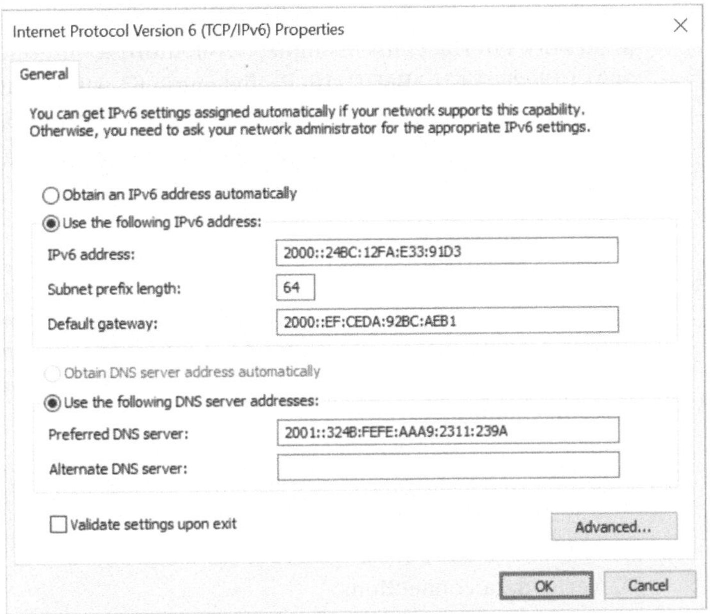

Internet Protocol Version 6 (TCP/IPv6) Properties   ✕

General

You can get IPv6 settings assigned automatically if your network supports this capability.
Otherwise, you need to ask your network administrator for the appropriate IPv6 settings.

○ Obtain an IPv6 address automatically
◉ Use the following IPv6 address:

IPv6 address: 2000::24BC:12FA:E33:91D3
Subnet prefix length: 64
Default gateway: 2000::EF:CEDA:92BC:AEB1

○ Obtain DNS server address automatically
◉ Use the following DNS server addresses:
Preferred DNS server: 2001::324B:FEFE:AAA9:2311:239A
Alternate DNS server:

☐ Validate settings upon exit   Advanced...

                                                  OK   Cancel

Figure 4-11   Network and Sharing Center, network
connection IPv6 properties, static IPv6 configuration

Automatic Configuration

Automatic configuration can be done in two ways: stateful and stateless. **Stateful automatic address configuration** involves one or more devices that track the state of the client in internal data tables. Traditional IPv4 address allocation through DHCP is an example of stateful address allocation. IPv6 can also obtain an address from an IPv6 DHCP server (DHCPv6) if one is configured on the local network. Windows Server 2008 or later can support IPv6 configuration as a DHCP server, but earlier versions of Windows Server cannot. A compatible IPv6 DHCP relay can also be used with IPv6 addressing to enable a client to interact with a DHCPv6 server on a different network.

In stateful address allocation, the DHCPv6 server tracks details about the client while it is operational with a leased address assigned by that DHCP server. This can restrict the mobility of a client, as it has to coordinate its address assignment with servers and other devices while it moves from one network to another. The client and DHCP server present a DHCP Unique Identifier (DUID) to identify themselves when exchanging DHCPv6 messages. The clients DHCPv6 DUID can be seen by issuing the ipconfig /all command at a command prompt.

Stateless automatic address configuration empowers the client to collect as many settings as possible from the network around it and have it create its own IPv6 address. The subnet address in use on a local network is advertised by an IPv6-aware router as the subnet ID. The client generates a random interface ID and combines it with the subnet ID to create its own IPv6 address. Configuration options, such as DNS server settings, are collected from DHCP servers or the router connected to the local network. If no router is connected, the interface can automatically configure only a link-local address. The advantage to stateless configuration is that less equipment and configuration effort is required to set up the IPv6 address for a network.

In small networks, even settings such as the DNS server settings may not be required. Windows 10 can resolve local client names using the **Link-Local Multicast Name Resolution (LLMNR)** protocol and related supporting services. This allows a computer to query the names of other computers on the local network using IPv4 and IPv6 without relying on NetBIOS, WINS, or DNS name resolution. This can minimize the requirement to have name configuration servers defined ahead of time and configured for clients.

IPv6 Configuration Commands

Script commands using netsh can be used to configure IPv6 settings on the computer. The netsh command is powerful and can be used to configure a variety of network settings; for example, netsh interface ipv6 add address "Ethernet4" 2001:EB8::8:801:20C4:2 will add the specified IPv6 address to the interface called Ethernet4.

NOTE 10

If the network adapter does not already have an IPv6 address, then you would use the New-NetIPAddress cmdlet instead of Set-NetIPAddress.

PowerShell cmdlets like Set-NetIPAddress can also change the IPv6 settings for a network interface, for example, Set-IPAddress -InterfaceAlias Ethernet -IPAddress 2001:CCE:2025:61fC:B65:C216 -PrefixLength 64 will update the IPv6 address already assigned to the network interface identified with the alias Ethernet.

Changes to a network interface's settings may take multiple commands to completely configure the interface.

Troubleshooting IPv6 Settings

NOTE 11

The PowerShell cmdlet Set-NetIPv6Protocol is designed to change global IPv6 parameters and not IPv6 address settings on a network interface.

Because IPv6 addressing is new and there are new details of how to configure it, many people assume that troubleshooting is different. The overall troubleshooting methodology is similar to IPv4 troubleshooting with the following notable considerations in each troubleshooting stage:

1. Confirm current settings.
2. Validate IPv6 connectivity.
3. Verify DNS name resolution.
4. Verify data connections.

Confirm Current Settings

The existing IPv6 settings should be confirmed due to the default nature of IPv6 clients attempting to autoconfigure themselves. By default, Windows favors IPv6 global unicast addresses over IPv4 addresses, but this can be updated in the registry by an Administrator, either directly or using Group Policy.

 **CAUTION** Some administrators are tempted to disable IPv6 because it is new and unfamiliar; however, some Windows 10 components are designed to use only IPv6 and may not function correctly if the disabling occurs.

Validate IPv6 Connectivity

If all settings appear correct, the ping utility can be used to confirm that the computer can ping its own loopback address by issuing the ping ::1 command or the Test-NetConnection ::1 PowerShell command. If either command is successful, the TCP/IP IPv6 protocol is functional on the computer.

The computer keeps track of which computers it communicated with recently, and some of that information can be out of date. The IPv4 system uses an ARP table to keep track of network devices to which it last connected. IPv6 uses a neighbor and destination cache to essentially do that, as well.

The neighbor and destination cache can be viewed and managed with the netsh utility or the Get-NetNeighbor/Set-NetNeighbor PowerShell cmdlets. The neighbor cache lists known computers on the same local network as the client computer. The destination cache lists the next IPv6 address the computer should send data to, to reach a particular destination.

If either the neighbor or destination cache data is in doubt, they can be cleared with the netsh utility or the Remove-NetNeighbor cmdlet. For example, the PowerShell command Remove-NetNeighbor -State Unreachable will remove all neighbor cache entries that are unreachable.

Verify DNS Name Resolution

Different types of records are registered with the DNS server depending on the IP data the client is registering. An IPv4 address and host name are stored in the DNS server using an A record. The A record maps the name of the computer to its IP address. An IPv6 address and host name are stored in the DNS server using an AAAA record. The AAAA record maps the name of the computer to its IPv6 address.

A DNS server may be configured to map the IP address back to the name of the computer using PTR records, but this is not commonly implemented for IPv6. IPv4 addresses are stored in a DNS server data table called in-addr.arpa. IPv6 also uses a PTR record to match an IPv6 address to a name, but it uses a data table called ip6.arpa.

DNS servers may resolve a name to either an IPv4 address or an IPv6 address. There is no guarantee the DNS server will respond with IPv4 or IPv6 data in all cases. A computer may have a valid IPv4 A record stored in DNS but no IPv6

AAAA record. To restrict troubleshooting to IPv6 addresses, the ping command can be forced to only use IPv6 addresses by issuing the ping -6 *TargetName* command, where *TargetName* is the target name of the remote computer. If the DNS server cannot provide an answer that is a valid IPv6 address, the command reports that the host name could not be found.

Verify Data Connections

Using the telnet application is a common tool for administrators to test application connectivity. The telnet utility does not guarantee it will use IPv6 to connect to a remote service unless the target address is specified as an IPv6 address. Carefully consider that specifying a target DNS host name to connect to does not guarantee that an IPv6 address will be used instead of an IPv4 address. This is true for any application you use to test data connections over the network.

INTERNET CONNECTIVITY

Today, almost every computer is configured to communicate on the Internet; however, depending on your needs, how your computer connects to the Internet will vary. The way you connect to the Internet will also vary depending on whether a single computer or multiple computers are using an Internet connection.

Single-Computer Internet Connectivity

Many homes have one or more computers sharing the Internet. How a computer is configured to connect to the Internet depends on the type of Internet connection you have.

For some Internet connection types, the IP address provided to you is usually a fully routable IP address on the Internet. This means that anyone on the Internet can connect to and communicate with your computer. In those cases, it is important to enable Windows Defender Firewall to protect your computer.

NOTE 12

Detailed information about Windows Defender Firewall is provided later in this module.

Cable

Almost all cable companies offer high-speed Internet connectivity as an option to their subscribers. In most cases, this is the simplest way to connect to the Internet.

When you subscribe to an Internet connection with your cable provider, you will be supplied with a cable modem that connects to the same cable that you hook up to your TV. The cable modem is responsible for converting signals from a format that travels properly over the cable provider network to standard Ethernet in your home using either a wired or wireless connection to your computer.

By default, Windows 10 networking is configured to use DHCP to obtain IP configuration information. When you connect your computer to the cable modem, the cable provider's DHCP server provides IP configuration information to Windows 10. Moments after you plug in an Ethernet cable to the cable modem or connect to its WiFi access point, you should be able to access the Internet.

DSL

Digital subscriber line (DSL) is a high-speed Internet connection over telephone lines. This type of Internet connectivity is often as fast as cable but can be slightly more difficult to configure.

When you subscribe to DSL, you are supplied with a DSL modem that connects to a phone line. The DSL modem is responsible for converting signals from a format that travels properly over the phone system to standard Ethernet in your home. The DSL modem is commonly combined with a router/firewall appliance in one physical box. You connect an Ethernet cable from your computer to the DSL modem or connect to its WiFi access point to connect to the Internet.

DSL connections usually use **Point-to-Point Protocol over Ethernet (PPPoE)** to secure connections. Your DSL provider supplies you with a PPPoE user name and password to connect to the network. In a home situation, the installer can program this information into the DSL modem for you. Only after you are authenticated by using PPPoE will you be able to obtain IP configuration information from the DSL provider and connect to the Internet.

If the DSL provider has supplied only a DSL modem, and it does not have a router/firewall supplied with it, Windows 10 has built-in support to connect directly via PPPoE. You can connect to a network requiring PPPoE by creating a broadband connection from the Network and Sharing Center. The options in a broadband connection are similar to a dial-up connection.

Dial-Up

Although progressively becoming much less common, some people still access the Internet using a dial-up connection over a phone line by using a modem. Although this is a much slower way to access the Internet, it is suitable when are no other options are available. Windows 10 includes support for dial-up connections.

Cellular

Wireless wide area networks (WWANs) are fully supported by Windows 10 using cellular data network devices that connect through broadband cell towers and Wi-Fi hotspots for Internet data transfer. Those cellular data network devices can be built into the Windows 10 device, plugged in as an add-on device via USB, or a wired/wireless attached device, such as a smartphone. These devices have a Subscriber Identity Module commonly referred to as a SIM card or eSIM in them to identify the user to the cellular data network, enabling connectivity to the Internet.

Several requirements must be met in order for this option to work. The provider of the broadband service must enable this option for the portable device, typically for an extra fee. Most broadband vendors refer to this feature as "tethering" the computer to the mobile device. The mobile device must also be configured to recognize that this feature is active. The advantage of this technology is that broadband support for mobile devices is now widespread. The disadvantage is that the data plan contract to pay for the bandwidth used by the mobile device while it operates in this mode can be expensive. Windows 10 works with this type of connection fully aware that it is a WWAN service. Windows 10 includes options to control potentially expensive cellular usage, such as data roaming, using cellular instead of Wi-Fi for data, controlling which apps can use your cellular data, setting and managing a SIM PIN, and setting a data limit (i.e., metering).

Shared Internet Connectivity

It is possible for multiple computers to share a single Internet connection. This is not commonly done for dial-up connections, but is quite common for cable modem and DSL Internet connections. For multiple computers on your network to share a single Internet connection, a mechanism must be in place to share the single IP address given to you by your ISP. The two most common mechanisms for sharing an IP address are a router or Internet Connection Sharing (ICS).

Router Connection Sharing

Multiple computers can share an Internet connection with a dedicated router appliance. The router is assigned an IP address from the ISP to connect to the public Internet. Computers on the router's internal network are assigned private IP addresses that are not routable on the Internet. The computers on the internal network use the router as their default gateway, sending Internet-bound traffic to the router for delivery.

The hardware routers sold in retail stores, cable modems, and DSL modems are also simple firewalls that perform Network Address Translation (NAT). NAT is the process that allows multiple computers to effectively share the single IP address assigned by the ISP.

Mobile Hotspot

If a Windows 10 computer has a wireless network adapter or Bluetooth adapter, it can be configured to act as a local hotspot that shares the computer's Internet connection with other computers or devices over either one of those interfaces. The Mobile hotspot settings are found in the Network and Internet Settings, which include the settings shown in Figure 4-12.

NOTE 13

Customize your mobile hotspot settings before turning on the Share my Internet connection with other devices option.

Your mobile hotspot is shared using a selected local Wi-Fi or Bluetooth network interface and is given a name you can edit to identify it to others. The feature is protected with a simple password you manage as part of the mobile hotspot settings.

This feature is not designed to support large groups of users; rather, it's designed to share with a few devices only (maximum of 8) as a convenience. To use it, the nearby computers or devices can open their Wi-Fi settings, find your network name, select it and enter the password that you share with them to connect.

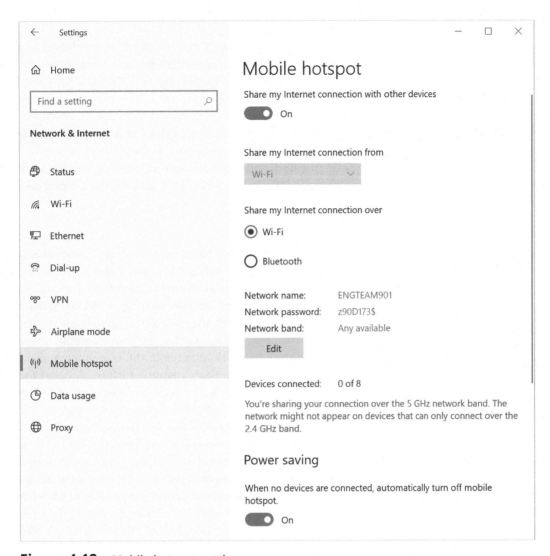

Figure 4-12   Mobile hotspot settings

Internet Connection Sharing

Internet Connection Sharing (ICS) is an older technology that allows a Windows 10 computer with multiple network interfaces to act as an Internet router for other local computers. The ICS computer is called the host computer. To use ICS, the host computer must have an Internet connection (public interface) plus one additional network connection (private interface). The public interface obtains an IP address from your ISP or router. The private interface uses a private IP address to communicate with other computers with which you are sharing the Internet connection.

Using ICS to share an Ethernet based connection was popular when it was first introduced with Windows 98, but that is not a common use for it today. ICS is managed by the Internet Connection Sharing service, which requires you to set the service's startup type to Automatic as well as configure the ICS settings manually.

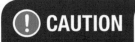 **CAUTION**   It is not recommended that you use ICS manually, as the service is set by default to shut down after four minutes if no traffic passes through it and not restart automatically. Use a router or modern mobile hotspot technology instead of ICS.

Some Windows network features, such as wireless hosted networks (discussed later in this module), depend on using ICS in a custom fashion, but they will manage the service independently.

Wireless Ad Hoc

Many standards are written by organizations such as the **Institute of Electrical and Electronics Engineers (IEEE)** to guide the manufacturers of wireless network products and help make them functional and compatible with one another. The IEEE standard most commonly used for popular wireless networking products is IEEE **802.11**. The 802.11 is a collection of continuously evolving standards, so you will notice that different 802.11 specifications will add descriptive labels or letters to identify specific sections of the overall standard.

Wireless Ad Hoc is based on the IEEE 802.11 ad hoc network standard to share wireless and was introduced with Windows Vista.

The use of wireless ad hoc networking is deprecated, and since the introduction of Windows 8.1, Microsoft's recommendation has been to use Wi-Fi Direct (covered later in this module) or some other current wireless sharing technology instead.

NOTE 14

Wi-Fi Direct and the IEEE 802.11 Wi-Fi ad hoc network standard are not the same thing. Wi-Fi Direct has features, such as improved security and support for WPA2 encryption, where traditional Windows versions of Wi-Fi ad hoc networking support only weak WEP encryption.

Wireless Hosted Network

Wireless Hosted network was introduced with Windows 7 as another option to turn your Windows PC into a wireless hotspot you can share with others. The feature relies on legacy components, such as Internet Connection Sharing (ICS), to enable **personal area network (PAN)** and Internet sharing scenarios. When it is enabled, one or more virtual wireless network adapters are created automatically to represent and manage a software access point for other wireless clients to connect to.

The physical wireless network adapter in the computer must have a driver that supports being used as a wireless hosted interface. Support for this feature has faded from some manufacturers as newer wireless hotspot technologies have become popular. If a Windows 10 computer was upgraded from an older operating system, say Windows 7, it is likely that the wireless network driver was retained after the upgrade and still supports this feature. If you decided to do a clean install of Windows 10 onto the same hardware, the newly installed wireless network driver may have dropped support. To determine if the current wireless network interface driver supports hosted networking, open a command prompt and run the netsh wlan show drivers command and look for the Hosted network supported value, as shown in Figure 4-13.

If the driver does not support hosted networks, you could try installing an older version of the wireless network card driver; however, you would be rolling back to an older driver that could limit the use of newer Windows 10 networking features and introduce instability.

If the driver does support hosted networks, you could configure the virtual access point by opening an administrative command prompt and run netsh to define basic settings like the advertised SSID and a passphrase, for example, netsh wlan set hostednetwork mode=allow ssid=myLocalPan key=9849897bw. You would continue to manage this virtual access point using netsh commands; for example, you could start that access point with the netsh wlan start hosted network command and stop it with netsh wlan stop hosted network.

Wi-Fi Direct

Wi-Fi Direct is a peer-to-peer wireless connection technology that allows devices certified for use with Wi-Fi Direct to securely discover, connect, and transfer information among one another. Wi-Fi Direct is a specification developed by the Wi-Fi Alliance. Wi-Fi Direct devices do not need to connect to a traditional Wi-Fi access point first or use existing Wi-Fi ad hoc mechanisms. Similar to other wireless sharing solutions, this feature will create Microsoft Wi-Fi Direct Virtual Adapters to support shared access.

 TIP   A command like ipconfig /all will show the presence of the Microsoft Wi-Fi Direct Virtual Adapters in the command's output, but you will not see the adapter in Device Manger. You can optionally turn on the display of hidden devices in Device Manager from its View menu, showing the hidden adapters in the Network adapters section. If you disable the virtual adapter for troubleshooting, note that it will most likely disable Wi-Fi Direct support as well.

```
C:\LabFiles>netsh wlan show drivers

Interface name: Wi-Fi

    Driver                        : Intel(R) Wireless-AC 9560 160MHz
    Vendor                        : Intel Corporation
    Provider                      : Intel
    Date                          : 2020-02-25
    Version                       : 21.80.2.1
    INF file                      : oem131.inf
    Type                          : Native Wi-Fi Driver
    Radio types supported         : 802.11b 802.11g 802.11n 802.11a 802.11ac
    FIPS 140-2 mode supported     : Yes
    802.11w Management Frame Protection supported : Yes
    Hosted network supported      : No
    Authentication and cipher supported in infrastructure mode:
                                    Open            None
                                    Open            WEP-40bit
                                    Open            WEP-104bit
                                    Open            WEP
                                    WPA-Enterprise  TKIP
                                    WPA-Enterprise  CCMP
                                    WPA-Personal    TKIP
                                    WPA-Personal    CCMP
                                    WPA2-Enterprise TKIP
                                    WPA2-Enterprise CCMP
                                    WPA2-Personal   TKIP
                                    WPA2-Personal   CCMP
                                    Open            Vendor defined
                                    WPA3-Personal   CCMP
                                    Vendor defined  Vendor defined
    IHV service present           : Yes
    IHV adapter OUI               : [00 00 00], type: [00]
    IHV extensibility DLL path: C:\WINDOWS\system32\IntelIHVRouter08.dll
    IHV UI extensibility ClSID    : {00000000-0000-0000-0000-000000000000}
    IHV diagnostics CLSID         : {00000000-0000-0000-0000-000000000000}
    Wireless Display Supported: Yes (Graphics Driver: Yes, Wi-Fi Driver: Yes)
```

Figure 4-13   Netsh output to determine wireless adapter driver's capabilities

Wi-Fi Direct is similar to Bluetooth technology and its capability to connect dynamically; however, the technology is faster than Bluetooth (up to 250 MBps) and has a greater range (currently up to 200 meters). Some common devices that can be certified for Wi-Fi Direct include wireless display adapters, Miracast display adapters, digital audio players, printers, televisions, projectors, cameras, phones, routers, computers, and tablets to name a few categories.

A computer that has a traditional Wi-Fi connection to a Wi-Fi network or hotspot can use that connection for traditional Internet access, what the Wi-Fi Direct program would call an infrastructure connection. Wi-Fi Direct allows that infrastructure connection to be shared with the Wi-Fi Direct connections, because the security of the Wi-Fi Direct peer-to-peer group is managed separately from the infrastructure network. Currently, most Wi-Fi Direct solutions use a custom vendor app or a third-party app you can purchase from the Windows Store to configure and use Wi-Fi Direct devices with Windows.

WIRELESS NETWORKING

Network connections allow data to flow from the local computer to other computers that share that network. Many networking technologies rely on a wire-based physical data connection to the local computer. Different types of cables, connectors, and expansion equipment make up the wired network. Instead of relying on wires to connect computers, a wireless network transfers data without a physical connection. The most common type of wireless technology uses radios to transmit and receive data. Many different types of radios have been developed for wireless technology.

The **Wireless Fidelity (Wi-Fi) Alliance** was created in 1999 as a nonprofit body to help manufacturers test and certify wireless products that would work together. These wireless standards are summarized in Table 4-10. IEEE 802.11n performance is fast and currently preferred because it is more tolerant of interference and supports a wide range of devices. Many portable devices, such as smartphones and newer laptops, include support for IEEE 802.11ac, which is becoming a popular alternative to 802.11n.

Table 4-10   IEEE 802.11 Wireless Standard Comparison

Wireless Standard	Primary Radio Frequency	Maximum Data Throughput (MBps)
IEEE 802.11a	5 GHz	54
IEEE 802.11b	2.4 GHz	11
IEEE 802.11g	2.4 GHz	54
IEEE 802.11n	2.4 and 5 GHz	600
IEEE 802.11ac	5 GHz	3466
IEEE 802.11ad	60 GHz	6757
IEEE 802.11ax	2.4, 5, 6 GHz	9608

Windows 10 provides a strong foundation for wireless technology, leaving the manufacturer with less responsibility for code development and a smaller chance of creating unstable software. Wireless adapters now appear as their own media type, not as an Ethernet 802.3 connection.

Even though Windows 10 supports a range of IEEE 802.11 standards, several are becoming obsolete. For example, it is rare to find 802.11a and 802.11b hardware in use. Each standard defines limits on how many devices can interact at once, resistance to radio interference, how fast they transfer data, and over what range they can operate. Exceeding any of those limits can cause performance issues that Windows 10 cannot compensate for with software alone. For example, the 802.11ad standard can operate at a very high data rate but only for a short distance, typically within the same room (11 feet). Some newer standards, such as 802.11ax are not supported in older versions of Windows 10, being first introduced as supported in Windows 10 version 2004.

A computer running Windows 10 may have a wireless adapter installed in the computer. It may be installed as an add-on card, plugged into a USB port, or built into the system itself. If the wireless adapter is built in, such as in a laptop, there is often a power switch that toggles the adapter on or off to save power or ensure privacy.

The wireless adapter can communicate with a base station or other wireless adapters. A base station is commonly called a **wireless access point (WAP)**. The WAP itself connects to the wired network and allows wireless clients to ultimately use that wired connection. The WAP may be part of a firewall device sharing access to the Internet, or it may be a stand-alone unit. The WAP and wireless adapter in the Windows 10 computer must use the same 802.11 standard to communicate with each other. If they are not compatible, one or the other hardware component may need to be replaced. When a WAP is purchased, consider that many will support a combination of IEEE 802.11 standards, which can give them a price or feature set competitive advantage over other WAPs.

Most WAP devices have a web server built into them that allows the device to be configured initially using a wired network connection. The manufacturer's instructions provide connection details and initial sign-in credentials. The manufacturer identifies a default management IP address, an initial connection URL (for example, http://192.168.0.1/admin), and a default administrator ID and password.

The most common configuration details for a WAP include:

- *Security Set Identifier (SSID)*—The Security Set Identifier (SSID) is the name assigned to the WAP to identify itself to clients. The SSID may or may not be configured to broadcast its identity to all wireless clients. If the SSID is not broadcast, the wireless client can still connect if it knows the name ahead of time and has the right connection settings preconfigured.
- *802.11 mode*—This includes the versions of 802.11 in which the radio operates, such as 802.11n. Choices will be limited to the modes supported by the WAP hardware.
- *Security method*—This includes the methods used to encrypt and restrict wireless client connections to the WAP.

Wireless encryption methods and client connection restrictions are required because the range of a wireless signal does not have a specific boundary. A private system may be detected by clients in unauthorized and unexpected areas. Newer technology has a greater range than ever before. Simply upgrading existing wireless hardware may expose companies to risks they did not think about before. A wireless client must be configured with correct security settings to enable it to communicate with a secured WAP. If the WAP is unsecured, it is referred to as an open or unsecured system.

Connecting to an open system may be dangerous because your computer may be connecting to an untrusted WAP that has been configured purposely to help unauthorized users gain access to your system or monitor the traffic you move through the WAP. If no choice is available, ensure that the connection is identified as a Public network connection to maximize the protection of Windows Defender Firewall and to disable your computer's advertising of its identity.

Creating a Wireless Connection

Wireless network connections can be created using several methods:

- *Manually connect to a wireless network*—This wizard is available by clicking Set up a new connection or network in Network and Sharing Center from Control Panel and selecting the Manually Connect to a Wireless Network option. All settings are manually configured.
- *Connect to a network*—By clicking the network icon in the notification area of the taskbar, a list of wireless networks is displayed, as shown in Figure 4-14. The list of visible networks shows the signal strength of each connection, if it is secure or open (no security), and if Windows 10 is connected to one of them. Selecting a network from the list and clicking the Connect button triggers the client to attempt a connection. If a security passphrase is requested, the user must enter a correct value before the connection is fully established.
- *Use a command-line utility*—The netsh command-line utility supports a command section for wireless LAN configuration, wlan. This advanced utility is not typically used in day-to-day network administration, but it is available for advanced management. More options can be seen by issuing the netsh wlan /? command.
- *Configure in Group Policy*—Wireless network settings can be applied to domain computers using Group Policy settings defined in Active Directory. A list of allowed or denied wireless networks can be specified.
- *Provision via a website*—Windows 10 version 2004 introduced the capability to configure a website so that a user can browse the website and provision a Wi-Fi profile for a Passpoint or normal network. Passpoint is a Hotspot 2.0 technology term, covered later in this module.
- *Use Wi-Fi Sense*—Wireless network settings could be shared among contacts using Outlook.com, Skype, and Facebook contacts who decide to share certain Wi-Fi connections with their contacts; however, this feature has been disabled by Microsoft due to its complexity and low demand for this feature.

Windows 10 keeps a list of SSIDs sorted by preference based on what you connected to in the past. The last used SSID is the preferred connection to connect to by default. If you are connected to one SSID in the list but you want to select a different one, simply select the other one from the list and connect to it. Windows 10 will remember that choice for next time.

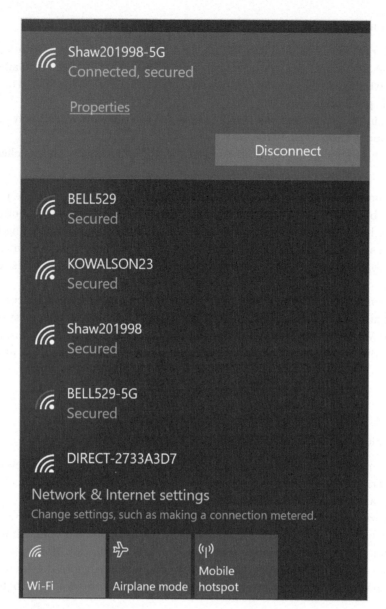

Figure 4-14 Wireless networks displayed from taskbar notification area

Wireless Connection Properties

When a new wireless connection is created, the key settings stored to describe it in Windows 10 are:

- *Network name*—The name of the wireless connection and its profile in the operating system
- *Security type*—The type of security methods the WAP expects the wireless client to use
- *Encryption type*—The method used to encrypt data, if a choice exists, as a customization of the selected security type
- *Security key*—A passphrase that acts as a password, allowing the wireless client to authenticate and connect
- *Connect automatically when this connection is in range*—The setting that identifies this SSID as preferred; tries to connect automatically once the client detects the WAP is operating in range
- *Look for other wireless networks while connected to this network*—A setting that allows the client to attempt to connect to a preferred wireless connection if it becomes available while connected to this SSID
- *Connect even if the network is not broadcasting its name (SSID)*—A setting that allows the client to attempt to connect even if it does not notice the WAP broadcasting its SSID wirelessly

Note that the last three connection settings enable a preference to be set for connecting to WAPs. A preferred connection can be set to automatically connect. A secondary connection can be used, but the client can change to a preferred WAP if it becomes available. If none of those is available, Windows can search for a specifically named WAP that is not broadcasting its name to clients. A WAP that is not configured to broadcast its name is sometimes seen as a security measure; however, applications are available that can spot the SSID from other types of packets the WAP generates, making the name known to others if they really want to look for it.

Wireless Network Security

A wireless network connection has settings for both security type and encryption type. The security type defines how authentication is performed. The encryption type defines the algorithm that is used to encrypt data while in transit over the wireless network. In general, these settings are automatically detected when you connect to a wireless network for the first time.

The following security types are available:

- *No authentication (open)*—This service type is used by public Wi-Fi networks where you are not required to provide credentials.
- *WPA3-Personal*—**WPA3-Personal** support was added with Windows 10 version 1903. Like WPA2, it also uses a pre-shared key exchange with improved 128-bit encryption and a new handshake protocol to make it harder to attack.

 **CAUTION** WPA3 security issues collectively called Dragonblood were discovered and allowed attackers to crack Wi-Fi network passwords and access encrypted network traffic exchanged among connected devices. Windows 10 version 2004 includes fixes to address those issues. As always, consider keeping device firmware and drivers up to date to ensure that the latest security patches are applied to all components of the wireless network.

- *WPA2-Personal*—**WPA2-Personal** uses a pre-shared key (password) for authentication and is suitable only for small environments.
- *WPA2-Enterprise*—**WPA2-Enterprise** uses 802.1x for authentication and is suitable for larger environments.
- *802.1x*—This option defines port-based network access control that uses the physical characteristics of the LAN infrastructure to authenticate devices attached to a LAN port.

The **802.1x** protocol is a standard for network devices, such as a Windows 10 computer, to be authenticated by switches or WAPs. Windows 10 provides authentication credentials to the WAP and then the WAP queries a **RADIUS server** to verify the credentials. In a Windows-based environment, the RADIUS server can verify authentication for Active Directory user accounts or computer accounts.

The three encryption types available are as follows:

- *None*—Data is transmitted as cleartext. This option is available only for open networks.
- *Wired Equivalent Privacy (WEP)*—This older encryption protocol has known flaws and should be avoided whenever possible. This option is available only for open networks and 802.1x.
- *Advanced Encryption Standard (AES)*—This is the preferred encryption type and is used by WPA2-Personal and WPA2-Enterprise.

Managing Wireless Connections

Managing a wireless network connection is similar to managing a wired network connection. Typically, very few tasks are required to manage a wireless network after it is configured, except for troubleshooting when connectivity issues occur.

If connectivity issues occur, you can view the status of the wireless network, as shown in Figure 4-15. This shows which wireless network you are connected to and the signal strength. In the unlikely event you need to change the settings for the wireless network, you can do it manually in the wireless properties; however, it is typically faster and easier to forget the existing network and reconnect to autodetect the settings again.

Figure 4-15   Network and Sharing Center, wireless connection status

Forget Wireless Networks

Windows 10 keeps a record of all wireless networks that it has connected to, including the settings that were used. To delete older wireless networks that are no longer in use or you want to reset, you can choose to forget them from Network and Internet settings, Wi-Fi, Manage known networks, as shown in Figure 4-16.

Airplane Mode

From a user perspective, temporarily disabling Wi-Fi can be useful for air travel. If you activate Airplane mode, it disables Wi-Fi and Bluetooth connectivity. You can enable Airplane mode in the Network and Internet Settings, as shown in Figure 4-17, or from the network icon on the taskbar, as shown previously in Figure 4-14.

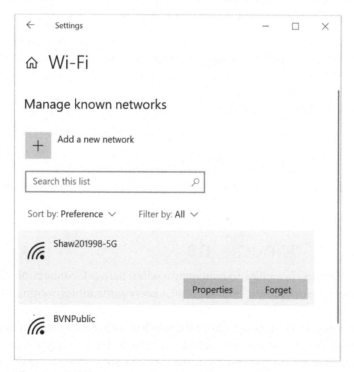

Figure 4-16   Manage known Wi-Fi networks

Figure 4-17 Airplane mode settings

Hotspot 2.0 Networks

Cellular networks have the convenience of working wherever a cell phone has reception from a compatible carrier's tower and antennas. As you physically move away from one cell tower and approach another, your connection is handed off from one tower to the next, and you would likely not notice the temporary change in your voice call or browsing the network for data. Unlike typical Wi-Fi, you did not need to browse a list of local cell towers, pick one to login, and then enter credentials. Hotspot 2.0 is a technology that tries to provide a similar experience using public Wi-Fi provided by major carriers (i.e., the same companies most likely supplying your cell phone connection).

Hotspot 2.0 is a standard managed by the Wi-Fi Alliance and is based in large part on the IEEE 802.11u standard. Security on conversations between Windows 10 and the access point providing access to the hotspot network is based on end-to-end WPA2-Enterprise and WPA3 enhanced encryption. After the user signs up for a provider's Hotspot 2.0 service and makes the first connection to a Hotspot 2.0 access point, the credentials and login process is remembered and automated for that service provider. For the user to connect to a hotspot network, **Online Sign-Up** must be enabled in the Network and Internet settings, Wi-Fi settings, as shown in Figure 4-18.

After the user activates the feature, this can potentially provide that cell-like experience but with Wi-Fi instead. For example, as the user moves from a hotel, to a café, and to an airport, his or her computer might find a compatible hotspot network at each location and seamlessly connect at each site to provide Internet connectivity. The user would not have to check which access point to use and configure a login at each location. Note that this would work only

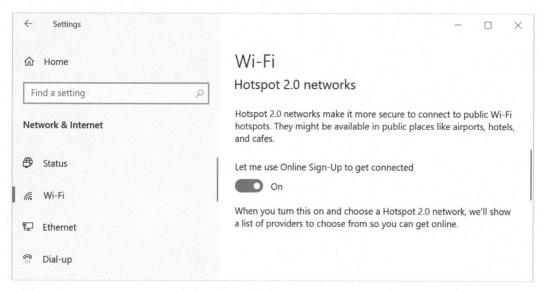

Figure 4-18   Hotspot 2.0 settings

with access points that are set up to support that user's carrier or service provider. The technology is designed to be secure and trusted so not just any access point could advertise and fake the secure connection.

Hotspot networks are supported by other computers and devices as well. If a device supports Hotspot 2.0, it will have a Passpoint certification to identify it as a compatible device.

Troubleshooting Wireless Connections

Wireless technology is flexible, but several issues commonly arise. The first thing to check is whether the wireless radio on the device running Window 10 is turned on. This can be controlled by a switch, key, or just plugging in an antenna.

A common problem for travelers is that they forgot that they turned on airplane mode, which disables the Wi-Fi and Bluetooth radios on the computer. It's also possible that the computer has a keyboard key combination that turns airplane mode on or off and somebody just pressed it by accident.

Before advanced wireless settings or configurations are changed, you should consider that the ISP hardware or any hardware between that and the WAP could be malfunctioning to block access to Internet data. It is common to start with power cycling these devices (i.e., turning off a device, wait at least 30 seconds, then turn it back on again), working your way from the ISP modem, ISP router, firewall, network switch, to the wireless access point. If you are not sure about the impact to the network environment, for example in a client's office, this needs to be planned out carefully. Some ISP support technicians may ask you to reset their equipment to factory default settings as part of troubleshooting Wi-Fi built into their equipment. If the configuration has been customized for an installation, be prepared to back up and reapply custom settings after a factory reset. A simple ping test between your computer and the default gateway could show if network traffic is getting at least that far.

Wireless technologies are typically radios restricted to specific radio frequencies as referenced in Table 4-10. Each of the 802.11 standards is designed to operate on one or perhaps more frequencies. Other devices, such as microwaves and cordless telephones, power lines, and nearby signal towers can interfere with the radio signal. If the interference cannot be eliminated, the signal between the computer and WAP might need to be improved with better antennas or better antenna placement. If that does not help enough, the WAP and wireless network adapter might have to be reconfigured to use a different frequency or IEEE 802.11 standard.

Some 802.11 standards are limited to what channels, in addition to specific frequencies, they can use to communicate. For example, the 802.11b standard works with 2.4 GHz radio frequencies. Each channel represents a small change of frequency from the original 2.4 GHz. Each channel is numbered, starting at 1, up to a maximum number of channels for that standard. Each country has rules about how many channels a standard can use on radios sold in that country. For example, IEEE 802.11b based radios can have up to 11 channels in North America and 14 in Japan.

Channels are designed to overlap in frequency ranges, so you may experience interference when someone else is also on your channel or close to it. For example, your computer may be on channel 1 and someone next door is on channel 2. The channel frequency ranges are very close together and the radio signal can experience overlap. Perhaps the person next door has a more powerful antenna and it is causing your radio to retry communications with your WAP. You have a working Wi-Fi connection, but it appears slow and maybe it even drops the connection occasionally. If the previous suggestions of upgrading antennas, or moving antennas did not help, you could change the Wi-Fi adapter to another channel in the advanced wireless adapter settings, picking a channel further away and eliminating the conflict. Channel selection may be limited by the number of active clients and sources of interference nearby. In a crowded environment like an office or apartment building, finding a free channel without heavy interference may be difficult. Making changes to the channel used might also require updates to the WAP configuration, as well.

Note that channel interference is a dynamic problem. The nature of the interference can change over time. For example, someone moves into the office next door and installs a new Wi-Fi system that interferes with yours. How can you determine if channel competition and interference is a problem? There is no native utility in Windows 10 to analyze overall Wi-Fi channel use. Another option is trial and error, testing the use of a different channel and seeing if the situation improves, but that is not efficient. Best-practice advice to explore channel use is to use the Microsoft Store app to search for third-party Wi-Fi analyzers. Several are free and support basic features, but paid editions can be more elaborate and functional.

Purchasing new hardware might be a requirement in some situations where the existing hardware and its supported 802.11 settings fail to operate effectively. Options are limited by the manufacturer's support for both the WAP and wireless network adapter, so you may have to replace both. If the device has built-in Wi-Fi, like a notebook, you may have to buy an updated notebook or add a new USB wireless network adapter.

A Wi-Fi problem can also be caused by a misconfiguration of the WAP. For example, the SSID assigned to a WAP identifies that device, but there is no automatic method to force two WAP devices in the same area to have different SSID values assigned. If they have the same SSID, the wireless client may become confused about which one to connect to and unreliable connectivity will result. This is common when WAP devices are installed with factory settings in areas where multiple offices or homes are clustered together. A WAP's SSID and administrator credentials (i.e., user ID and password) should always be changed when it is installed for the first time.

A Windows 10 client can be configured to connect to a WAP automatically when it is in range. This can be configured in Network and Internet Settings, Status, Change connection properties link, as shown in Figure 4-19. It can also be updated in the Network and Internet Control Panel app, wireless adapter's wireless properties as shown in Figure 4-20.

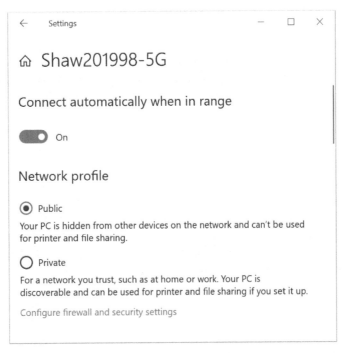

Figure 4-19   Network and Internet settings, Wi-Fi connection details

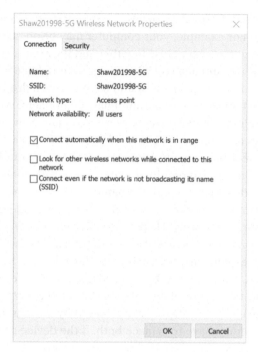

Figure 4-20 Network and Sharing Center, wireless adapter network properties

Note the advanced option in Figure 4-20 to look for other wireless networks while connected to this network. If the computer is configured for multiple WAPs and they are all active and in range, it may disconnect from one WAP and reconnect to another as the signal strength varies. This can cause the client to appear slow and unresponsive as the connection toggles. The wireless client can be moved closer to one of the WAPs to change the signal strength—the closer it is, the stronger the signal will appear. Another strategy is to set one wireless SSID as preferred and all others enabled with the option to connect to a more preferred network if it is available.

WAP devices in public places may be untrusted, even if they have a passphrase configured. If a computer is being connected to an untrusted network, always consider setting the network location type as Public and confirming that Windows Defender Firewall is up to date and configured without unsafe exceptions. Not all open WAPs are considered dangerous; some are designed to be open to allow devices to connect and access a paid secure wireless connection.

If the problem doesn't seem to be the external wireless environment, the user can trigger the network trouble-shooter by right-clicking the network icon in the taskbar and selecting Troubleshoot problems on the shortcut menu. This wizard is designed to work with users who are not as technically inclined; however, it should not be dismissed as a superficial troubleshooting tool. Microsoft has compiled a great deal of intelligence into the network troubleshooter, and it can correct many conditions with little effort from the user.

Windows 10 includes advanced troubleshooting tools for wireless connections that are used by network administrators and normally not by the average user. A history of wireless activity is collected by Windows 10 and can be used to generate a report called the Wireless LAN Report, or WlanReport for short. This is an .html and .xml file created by opening an elevated administrative command prompt and issuing the netsh wlan show wlanreport command. The report will be generated and include the date that the report was run in the file name. The location of the report will be reported by the command, but it is typically stored in the hidden folder C:\ProgramData\Microsoft\Windows\WlanReport.

The WlanReport.html file can be viewed in a browser and contains an interactive summary graph, general system information, user information, network adapter inventory details, output of an ipconfig /all command, ; and details of the wireless devices, drivers, and wireless profiles.

Some Windows 10 computers that have been updated from an earlier operating system might have an old device driver installed for the wireless network adapter that is not fully compatible with Windows 10. In that case, consider updating the device drivers for the wireless network driver using Device Manager.

If you are struggling to find a stable version of the device driver, look for a new device driver and advice from the wireless card manufacturer's website. Ensure you are downloading the correct driver based on the manufacturer, make, and model number of the wireless adapter and its compatibility with the installed Windows version. Some embedded wireless adapters might even require a firmware update for the computer as well.

Even if a wireless network card driver is correct, the problem with connectivity can be caused by malicious software (malware), poorly written software, or people making low-level changes to network settings in the registry and making a mistake. This is not that common, but the attempted fix is fairly straightforward. Several command-line commands can reset the basic TCP/IP configuration of the computer. These commands should be run in the sequence listed below in an elevated administrative command prompt window:

- *Netsh winsock reset*—Reset the Winsock catalog tracking what applications are associated with ports linked to TCP/IP interfaces.
- *Netsh int ip reset*—Reset the TCP/IP protocol (i.e., re-install it).
- *Ipconfig /release*—Discard any previously obtained DHCP IP address information.
- *Ipconfig /renew*—Attempt to obtain new DHCP IP address information.
- *Ipconfig /flushdns*—Purge any previous DNS cached responses, which map names to IP addresses or "name not found" responses.
- *Shutdown /r /f /t 60*—Restart the computer (i.e., /r), forcing open applications to close (i.e., /f), waiting for 60 seconds to elapse before triggering the actual restart (i.e., /t 60).

If the network settings on the network adapter and the TCP/IP protocol are not the problem, it is possible that antivirus, Windows Defender Firewall settings, or anti-malware settings may have contributed to the problem. Antivirus and anti-malware performance and configuration issues should be escalated to their vendor for support. Windows Defender Firewall settings are reviewed in the next section.

As a last resort, consider the option of triggering a full network reset. This can be triggered by running the netcfg–d command from an elevated command prompt, or you can use the network reset feature introduced with Windows 10 version 1607. Network reset can be found in the Network and Internet settings, Status, Network reset link. This cleans up and removes all network devices plus customizations from the Windows 10 computer, and then triggers a restart. The Windows 10 computer detects the installed network devices it can see and attempts to reinstall drivers to default settings. This can help if the computer has been upgraded from an older operating system and old VPN software components or devices no longer used litter the system settings, causing a general network failure. Remember that after the network reset you will need to reconfigure network connections, reinstall custom VPN software, and update network discovery settings and network location profiles. Best practice is to document old settings if they are important before you trigger a network reset.

WINDOWS DEFENDER FIREWALL

Many businesses have a firewall appliance at the network perimeter, managed by corporate administrators and beyond the control of a user within that site. Legacy network design assumed that the computers within the corporate site were static and did not move out of the building. The problem with this way of thinking is that attention is focused on the idea that network threats and their malicious traffic are outside the company site, not inside, and you should spend most of your focus protecting the site's main data connection to the outside. The reality is that computers today are mobile, and the corporate boundary is extended to all the places you can take that computer—a café, a hotel, the airport, your car with shared Wi-Fi, Hotspot 2.0 networks, or even your home.

As ransomware and malware proliferate, attackers can sneak into corporate networks by infecting machines and using those infected machines to steal corporate intellectual property, as well as look for unprotected paths to elevate their access to other computers and systems within the corporate network. Having an active firewall on each computer is more important than ever.

A host-based firewall, like Windows Defender Firewall in Windows 10, protects your computer by restricting what network traffic (i.e., packets) comes in or goes out. It evaluates each packet as it arrives or leaves and determines whether that packet is allowed or denied. By default, all packets are denied when they arrive from external sources, and only a few are allowed for specific purposes. For example, when you join a domain, Windows 10 automatically configures Windows Defender Firewall to allow the correct packets through for domain-based communication, but other packets are denied.

The Windows Defender Firewall can be augmented with third-party firewall software that is certified to work with Windows Defender Firewall. Some parts of, or all of, the Windows Defender Firewall functionality could be turned off because the third-party firewall will provide the equivalent or enhanced function. This is by design; however, consider that turning off Windows Defender Firewall functions without an alternate firewall provider is a risky decision.

>  **CAUTION** Stopping the Windows Defender Firewall service (i.e,. service name MpsSvc) associated with Windows Defender Firewall is not supported by Microsoft. Disabling Windows Defender Firewall profiles is not the same as turning off that service in the services snap-in. Turning off the actual service can result in newer applications failing to install or update, Start menu malfunctions, and trusted connection failures to back-end services among other unexpected issues. The proper way to disable the firewall is to disable the Windows Defender Firewall profiles and leave the service running.

Basic Firewall Configuration

Microsoft has designed Windows Defender Firewall to be active on every Windows 10 computer right from the start and to support common programs. The user does not have to manage cryptic network traffic rules to be protected. When applications are installed, most installers are designed to update Windows Defender Firewall settings as required.

Basic controls for Windows Defender Firewall are found in the Settings app (Figure 4-21). The Settings app is preferred to access these basic controls, navigated to by clicking Settings, Update and Security, Windows Security, then Firewall & network protection. The Windows Defender Firewall Control Panel app is becoming deprecated but is still used for some advanced operations.

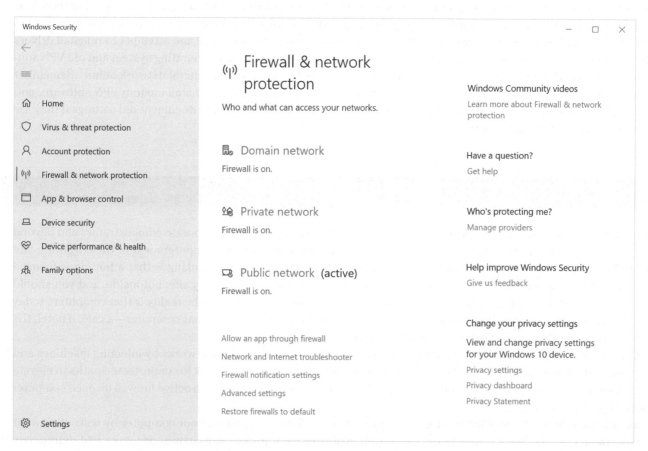

Figure 4-21 Windows Security settings, Firewall & network protection

Windows 10 allows custom firewall settings for each type of network location (i.e., domain, private, or public), as was shown in Figure 4-21. When a network interface becomes active, it has a specified network location assigned to it. The matching firewall settings for that type of network location applies to traffic through that interface. If a Windows 10 computer has multiple network interfaces active, each can be assigned a different network location, each with different firewall settings based on that type of assigned network location.

If you select a network location profile from the Firewall & protection settings you will be shown which active network interfaces are using that type of network location, and you will have the option to turn Microsoft Defender Firewall on or off for that type of network location, as shown in Figure 4-22. Disabling Windows Defender Firewall should be done only for troubleshooting and not left as a permanent configuration. Many administrators regret the day they got lazy and left the firewall disabled on all local computers after a ransomware attack ran amok within a site.

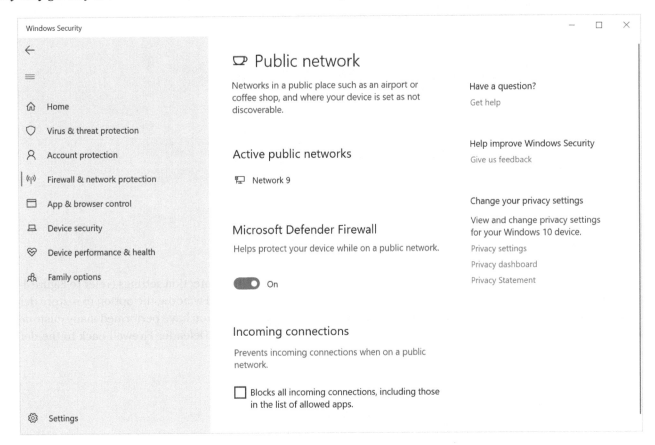

Figure 4-22   Windows Security settings, Firewall & network protection, network profile settings

An option also is provided to block all incoming connections for that type of network location. When this option is selected, no exceptions are allowed. You are still able to initiate communication with other computers, but other computers cannot initiate communication with your computer. This is recommended only when you are connected directly to public networks, such as the wireless network in a café.

When you select Allow an app through Firewall in the Firewall & network protection settings, the Allowed apps window opens, as shown in Figure 4-23. This allows you to configure which programs are able to accept network communication requests. A program can be allowed access through the firewall depending on the network location type, private or public. The firewall exception can be enabled for one, both, or none of the network location categories.

This allows some applications, such as Remote Assistance, to be available when the user is connected in supported situations. Many corporate offices do not want Remote Assistance enabled when the user is connected in unsupported locations or in locations where other support methods are available. The choice of what application to make an exception for and the type of network location to enable it for are defined by situational requirements. When you create an exception for a program, the exception applies to that program no matter what port number it uses. The exception is also valid only when the program is running. If the program is stopped, the exception poses no risk.

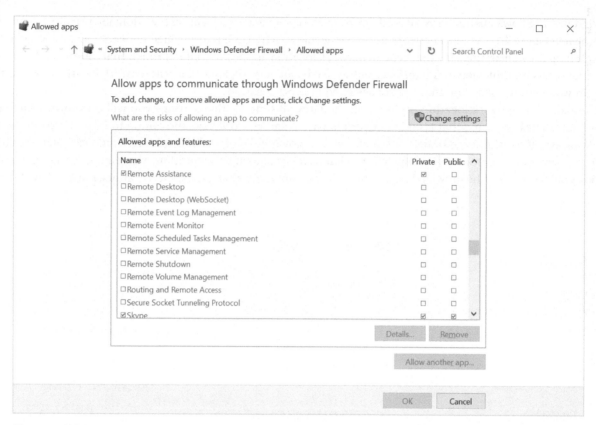

Figure 4-23   Windows Defender Firewall, allowed apps

When Restore firewalls to default is selected from the Firewall & network protection settings (refer to Figure 4-21), or Restore defaults is selected from the Windows Defender Firewall Control Panel window, the option to restore default settings for Windows Defender Firewall is presented, as shown in Figure 4-24. If you have performed many customized configurations and did not document them, you might want to reset Windows Defender Firewall back to the default configuration as part of the troubleshooting process.

Figure 4-24   Windows Defender Firewall, restore defaults

Advanced Firewall Configuration

Advanced firewall configuration allows you to configure more complex rules, outgoing filtering, and IPSec rules. Advanced firewall configuration is useful in corporate and enterprise computing situations. The basic firewall settings are usually sufficient in home and small business situations. The tools available to perform advanced firewall configuration are:

- *Windows Defender Firewall with Advanced Security utility*—This utility is a graphical tool to configure all of the Windows Defender Firewall features on a single computer.

- *Netsh*—This is a command-line utility for managing network configuration. It is also capable of configuring all of the Windows Defender Firewall features on the local computer. This tool can be used in a script that is run on multiple computers.
- *Group Policy*—To quickly and easily manage the Windows Defender Firewall settings in a corporate environment, you should use Group Policy. It allows firewall settings to be applied to hundreds or thousands of computers very quickly. Some Windows 10 Group Policy configuration options were not available for previous versions of Windows, and these settings are ignored by previous versions of Windows.
- *Windows PowerShell*—Windows PowerShell cmdlets can be used to configure advanced firewall settings. To view the list of cmdlets, use Get-Command *firewall* and Get-Command *ipsec*.
- *Intune/Endpoint Configuration Manager*—Settings that alter the Windows Defender Firewall are managed in the cloud by a tenant administrator and applied to a cloud-managed Windows 10 workstation. This topic is beyond the scope of this book and is not covered here.

 TIP If you find that Windows Defender Firewall is not enabled for all network location types, you can enable it using a script from an elevated command prompt with the netsh advfirewall set allprofiles state on command or from an elevated PowerShell prompt by running the Set-NetFirewallProfile -Name Domain,Public,Private -Enabled True command.

When Advanced settings is selected in the Firewall & network protection settings (refer to Figure 4-21), or from the Windows Defender Firewall Control Panel window, the Windows Defender Firewall with Advanced Security utility window opens, as shown in Figure 4-25.

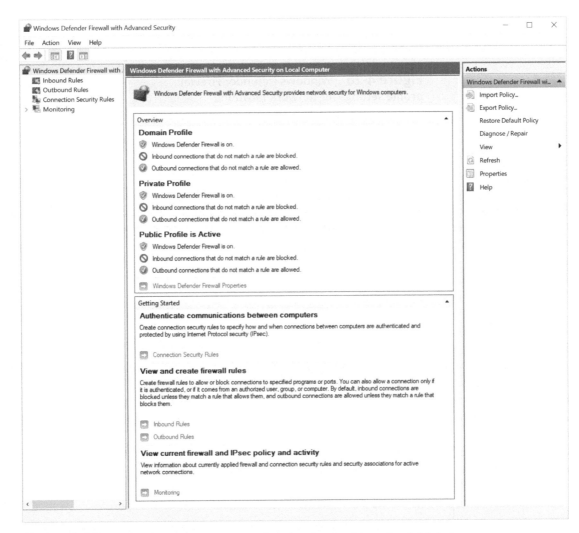

Figure 4-25 Windows Defender Firewall with Advanced Security, initial view

Configuring Firewall Properties

When the Windows Defender Firewall with Advanced Security on Local Computer node is selected at the top of the left pane, a summary is displayed in the center pane showing the configuration of each network location profile. You can click Properties below Actions in the right pane or Windows Defender Firewall Properties in the center-pane to edit location profile settings and IPSec settings, as shown in Figure 4-26. The tabs for editing each profile have exactly the same options.

Figure 4-26   Windows Defender Firewall, profile settings for network locations

In each network location profile tab, you can:

- Enable or disable Windows Defender Firewall.
- Configure inbound connections.
  - *Block (default)*—All inbound connections are blocked unless specifically allowed by a rule.
  - *Block all connections*—All inbound connections are blocked regardless of the rules.
  - *Allow*—All inbound connections are allowed unless specifically blocked by a rule.
- Configure outbound connections.
  - *Allow (default)*—All outbound connections are allowed unless specifically blocked by a rule.
  - *Block*—All outbound connections are blocked unless specifically allowed by a rule.
- Customize protected network connections.
  - *Select which network interfaces this firewall state applies to*—All interface types (e.g., Ethernet) found on the computer are selected by default.
- Customize settings.
  - *Display notifications to the user when a program is blocked from receiving inbound connections*—This is useful for users to be notified when something unusual is happening on the network.
  - *Allow unicast response to multicast or broadcast network traffic*—Some network attackers use multicast and broadcast requests to map out the network and determine client IP addresses. Disabling this reduces that possibility.
  - *Apply local firewall rules*—This option allows firewall rules from Group Policy and the local computer to both be applied. If there is a conflict between Group Policy-based rules and local rules, the Group Policy-based rules are effective. You can configure this option only in Group Policy.

○ *Apply local connection security rules*—This option allows connection security rules from Group Policy and the local computer to both be applied. If there is a conflict between Group Policy-based rules and the local rules, the Group Policy-based rules are effective. You can configure this option only in Group Policy.

- Customize logging.
  ○ *Name*—This identifies the name and location of the Windows Defender Firewall log. By default, this is C:\Windows\system32\LogFiles\Firewall\pfirewall.log.
  ○ *Size limit*—This limits the size of the Windows Defender Firewall log to ensure you do not run out of disk space.
  ○ *Log dropped packets*—This specifies whether blocked packets are logged. By default, this option is turned off and blocked packets are not logged.
  ○ *Log successful connections*—This specifies whether successful connections are logged. By default, this option is turned off and successful connections are not logged.

Configuring IPSec Settings

By using the Windows Defender Firewall with Advanced Security utility, you can configure IPSec settings, as shown in Figure 4-27. IPSec allows you to create connection security rules as a logical barrier between devices even if they are on the same local area network. Think of non-IPSec firewall rules as controlling traffic based on properties of the network traffic itself, for example, port numbers, which side started the conversation (e.g., inbound/outbound), and what network interface is involved, maybe even the application involved in the conversation. IPSec-based security connection rules are separate from the general traffic firewall rules, as they limit communication based on the identity of each computer involved in a conversation, each computer's capability to prove that identity, as well as encrypt and authenticate the actual conversation among them. For a complete organization security solution, you would plan and deploy both types of rules. Due to the complexity of security connection rules and the ability to impact the ability of computers to talk to one another within an organization, it requires a lab environment and rigorous testing to ensure you get the results the situation demands.

The IPSec default settings you can configure are:

- *Key exchange*—This setting controls which method is used to securely transmit the keys used for data encryption between both computers.
- *Data protection*—This setting controls which methods are used to encrypt and protect the integrity of data.
- *Authentication method*—This setting controls which method is used to authenticate the two computers creating an IPSec connection. The simplest method is a pre-shared key (password), but it is also the least secure and is not recommended. By default, Kerberos authentication is used.

The IPSec exemption settings you can configure are:

- *Exempt ICMP from IPsec*—This is a Yes or No setting. ICMP packets are commonly used by troubleshooting tools (such as ping), and if they are exempted from IPSec by the network administrator, it could assist in diagnosing issues during troubleshooting. Note that exempting ICMP packets from IPSec doesn't automatically allow them through the firewall. The Windows Defender Firewall rules must be enabled separately to allow ICMP traffic as well.

The IPSec tunnel authorization settings you can configure are:

- *None*—No user or computer authorization is required to use a tunnel mode connection from a remote computer to the local computer.
- *Advanced, Custom*—List specific users or computers that are either allowed (i.e., authorized) or denied (i.e., exceptions) the use of the tunnel mode connection from a remote computer to the local computer.

NOTE 15

Creating and applying a secure isolation design with Windows Defender Firewall and Advanced Security is beyond the scope of this book. To learn more about advanced design and application for Windows Defender Firewall with Advanced Security, see: https://docs.microsoft.com/en-us/windows/security/threat-protection/windows-firewall/windows-firewall-with-advanced-security-design-guide.

NOTE 16

If the settings are configured as the value Default, they can be overridden by Group Policy-based settings. This is the preferred approach in a domain environment, while custom settings are preferred when the computer is not domain joined.

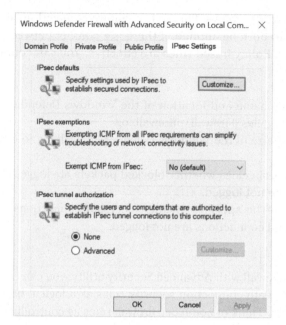

Figure 4-27   Windows Defender Firewall, global IPSec settings

Viewing and Editing Firewall Rules

A large number of inbound and outbound network traffic rules are created by default in Windows 10. Figure 4-28 shows a sample list of inbound rules. In the list of rules, you can see the name of the rule, a group of rules it belongs to, profiles the rule can belong to, if the rule is enabled, and whether the rule allows or denies packets. Additional columns can be added to the view by selecting more columns in the view options if desired.

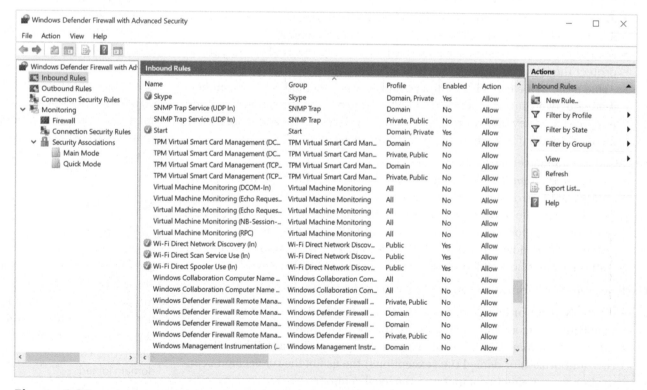

Figure 4-28   Windows Defender Firewall, sample inbound rule listing

The icons for each rule also give you information about that rule. Rules that are enabled and allow packets have a green arrow icon. Rules that are enabled and deny packets have a red circle with a slash. If the icon is blank, the rule is disabled.

You modify an existing rule by changing its properties. Figure 4-29 shows the properties of the Echo Request ICMPv4-In rule.

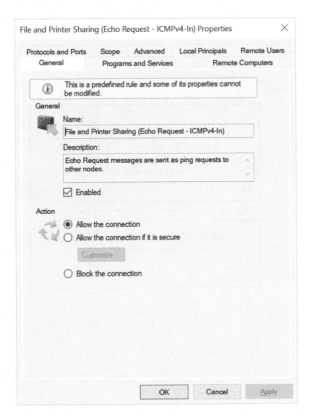

Figure 4-29   Windows Defender Firewall, sample inbound default rule properties

The tabs in the properties of an inbound rule are:

- *General*—This tab allows you to configure the rule name, configure the rule description, enable or disable the rule, and choose the rule action (e.g., allow, block, or allow if secured by user or computer identity).
- *Programs and Services*—This tab allows you to select programs, application packages, and services that this rule applies to.
- *Remote Computers*—This tab allows you to restrict connections to include or exclude specific computers or groups of computers. IPSec authentication is required.
- *Remote Users*—This tab allows you to restrict connections to include or exclude specific users or groups of users. IPSec authentication is required.
- *Local Principals*—This tab allows you to restrict connections to include or exclude specific users or application package properties.
- *Protocols and Ports*—This tab allows you to specify the protocol type this rule applies to, the local port this rule applies to, the remote port this rule applies to, and which ICMP packet types this rule applies to.
- *Scope*—This tab allows you to specify the source and destination IP addresses this rule applies to.
- *Advanced*—This tab allows you to specify which profiles (e.g., domain, private, public) and interface types (e.g., local area network, wireless, remote access) this rule applies to. Edge traversal settings enable you to allow or block traffic that came from the other side of a NAT router (i.e., most likely from the Internet) or let the user or an application decide if that's acceptable.

Creating New Firewall Rules

You can create firewall rules using all the methods mentioned at the start of this section. If you use the Windows Defender Firewall with Advanced Security interface to create a new firewall rule, a wizard guides you through the process. The wizard for creating an outbound rule is shown in Figure 4-30. Using a wizard simplifies the process of rule creation because it limits the options during the creation process to only those options you need for the particular type of rule you are creating.

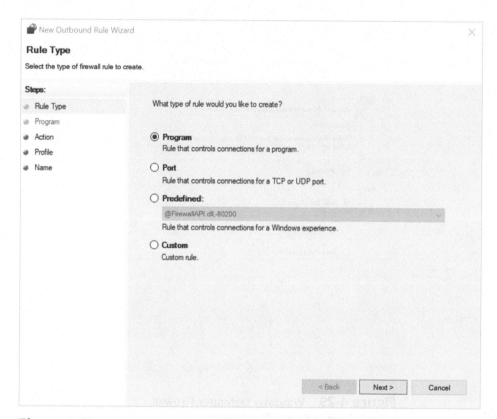

Figure 4-30   Windows Defender Firewall, new outbound rule wizard

The rule types you can create with the Outbound Rule wizard are:

- *Program*—A program rule allows or denies traffic for a specific program that is specified by selecting an executable file. You can specify which profiles this rule applies to.
- *Port*—A port rule allows or denies traffic for a specific TCP or UDP port. You can specify which profiles this rule applies to.

 TIP   You should know common TCP/IP application port numbers, with several common values listed in Table 4-11, or refer to a recent listing from IANA to understand which port numbers are used with common TCP/IP applications at https://www.iana.org/assignments/service-names-port-numbers/service-names-port-numbers.xhtml.

- *Predefined*—A predefined rule creates a group of rules to allow or deny Windows functions, such as file and printer sharing or Remote Assistance. In most cases, these rules are already created and do not need to be re-created. These rules allow you to define source and destination computers (endpoints) that the rule applies to. You can also specify to which profiles this rule applies.
- *Custom*—A custom rule lets you configure programs, ports, protocols, endpoints, and profiles. You can use this type of rule when the other rule types do not meet your needs.

Table 4-11   Common TCP/UDP Application Port Numbers

Program or Application	Server-Side Port Value
echo	7
ftp-data	20
ftp	21
ssh	22
telnet	23
smtp	25
DNS	53
HTTP	80
POP3	110
IMAP	143
HTTPS	443

When you define the actions for a rule, as shown in Figure 4-31, you can specify the following:

- *Allow the connection*—This option allows connections based on this rule.
- *Allow the connection if it is secure*—This option allows connections based on this rule only when an IPSec connection is configured. By default, this option requires that IPSec authenticates the connection and ensures integrity; however, you also have the option to require data encryption. Additionally, because a secure connection is based on an IPSec rule, you can select to have this rule override other block firewall rules.
- *Block the connection*—This option denies all connections based on this rule; however, a rule with this option selected can be overridden by another rule that allows only secure connections.

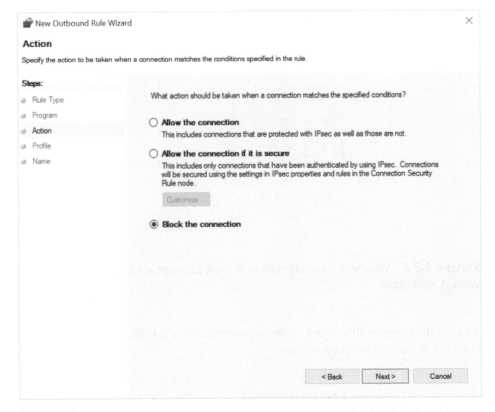

Figure 4-31   Windows Defender Firewall, new outbound rule wizard, rule actions

Creating New Computer-Connection Security Rules

Computer-connection security rules use IPSec to authenticate and secure communication between two computers. Remember that these rules combine with the general inbound and outbound traffic rules to create a customized security experience at the firewall level. The computer-connection security rule types, shown in Figure 4-32, are:

- *Isolation*—An isolation rule restricts communication with other computers to only those that can be authenticated. You can specify the method of authentication. The rule can apply to inbound connections, outbound connections, or both.
- *Authentication exemption*—An authentication exemption rule specifies IP addresses or IP address ranges that do not need to be authenticated when communicating with this computer. Effectively, this creates exceptions to an isolation rule.
- *Server-to-server*—A server-to-server rule is used to enforce IPSec settings between two computers. Typically, this type of rule is used to require encryption between two computers, such as a client and server; however, it can also be configured to apply only for certain connection types, such as wireless connections.
- *Tunnel*—A tunnel rule is used to configure Windows 10 as the endpoint of a secure communication tunnel. Other computers use the Windows 10 computer as their default gateway to secure communication through the IPSec tunnel. This type of rule is seldom used.
- *Custom*—A custom rule allows you to configure a customized rule if the standard rule types do not meet your needs.

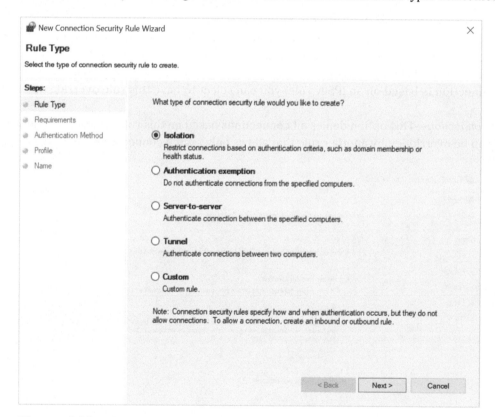

Figure 4-32   Windows Defender Firewall, New Connection Security Rule Wizard, rule types

PowerShell Cmdlets for Network Security

Table 4-12 shows some of the common IP network security PowerShell cmdlets that can be used to update the Windows Defender Firewall and the Advanced Security settings.

Monitoring Windows Defender Firewall Rules and Connections

When you view the inbound or outbound rules for Windows Defender Firewall, there is a large list of rules that includes enabled or disabled rules. The Firewall node below Monitoring in Windows Defender Firewall with Advanced Security, shown in Figure 4-33, allows you to see all of the rules that are enabled in one screen. This quickly shows you how your system is configured. This is also useful to see the rules that are being applied by Group Policy.

Table 4-12   PowerShell Windows Defender Firewall and Related Network Security Cmdlets

PowerShell Cmdlet	Description
Copy-NetFirewallRule	Copies an entire firewall rule, and associated filters, to the same or to a different policy store.
Disable-NetFirewallRule	Disables a firewall rule.
Enable-NetFirewallRule	Enables a previously disabled firewall rule.
Get-NetFirewallProfile	Displays settings that apply to the per-profile configurations of the Windows Defender Firewall with Advanced Security.
Get-NetFirewallRule	Retrieves firewall rules from the target computer.
Get-NetFirewallSetting	Retrieves the global firewall settings of the target computer.
New-NetFirewallRule	Creates a new inbound or outbound firewall rule and adds the rule to the target computer.
Remove-NetFirewallRule	Deletes one or more firewall rules that match the specified criteria.
Rename-NetFirewallRule	Renames a single firewall rule.
Set-NetFirewallProfile	Configures settings that apply to the per-profile configurations of the Windows Defender Firewall with Advanced Security.
Set-NetFirewallRule	Modifies existing firewall rules.
Set-NetFirewallSetting	Modifies the global firewall settings of the target computer.

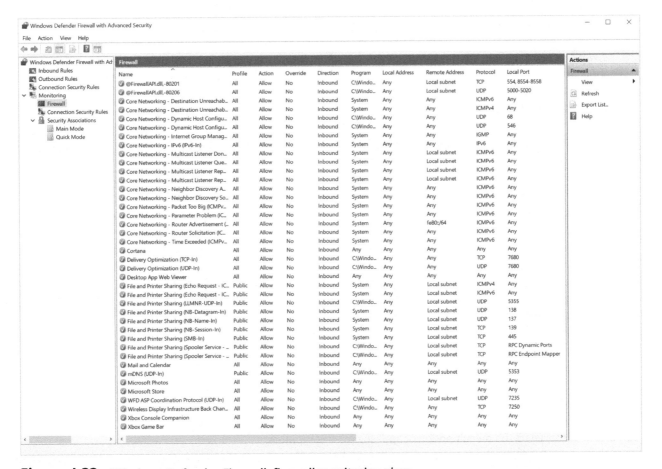

Figure 4-33   Windows Defender Firewall, firewall monitoring view

The Connection Security Rules node below Monitoring allows you to see the computer connection security rules that are enabled and any security associations that are active. A security association is the set of rules for communication negotiated between two computers. If two computers have a security association, they are using IPSec to communicate.

Security associations are listed in the following two categories:

- *Main Mode*—Used for the initial configuration of an IPSec connection, including authentication
- *Quick Mode*—Signifies a secure IPSec communication channel has been negotiated

Activity 4-5: Configuring Windows Defender Firewall

Time Required: 15 minutes

Objective: Configure Windows Defender Firewall by using the Windows Defender Firewall with Advanced Security utility

Description: Windows Defender Firewall in Windows 10 is capable of performing outbound filtering as well as inbound filtering. In this activity, you create a rule to block access to Internet websites and then disable the rule.

1. If necessary, start your computer and sign in.
2. On the taskbar, click **Microsoft Edge**.
3. In the Search or enter web address box, type **http://www.microsoft.com** and then press **Enter**. When the Microsoft website displays, it confirms that your computer is able to connect to the Internet properly right now.
4. Exit Microsoft Edge.
5. Click the **Start** button, in the search box type **firewall**, and then press **Enter**. This displays the Firewall and network protection system settings.
6. Click the **Advanced settings** link in the left pane. This opens the Windows Defender Firewall with Advanced Security utility.
7. If you are prompted with a User Account Control window, click **Yes**.
8. Read the overview of Windows Defender Firewall configuration. Windows Defender Firewall is on for all network location profiles, inbound connections that do not match a rule are blocked by default, and outbound connections that do not match a rule are allowed by default. In the Overview pane, click the **Windows Defender Firewall Properties** link.
9. Click the **Private Profile** tab. These settings apply for all Private networks.
10. In the Settings area, click the **Customize** button. Here, you can configure whether notifications are displayed when inbound connections are blocked and how local firewall rules are combined with firewall rules defined in Group Policy.
11. Click **Cancel** to close the Customize Settings for the Private Profile dialog box.
12. In the Logging area, click the **Customize** button. Here, you can configure logging for Windows Defender Firewall.
13. In the Log dropped packets box, select **Yes** and then click OK. Now all blocked connections will be logged to C:\Windows\system32\LogFiles\Firewall\pfirewall.log.
14. Click OK to close the Windows Defender Firewall with Advanced Security on Local Computer Properties dialog box.
15. In the left pane, click **Outbound Rules**. These are the rules that control outbound communication. However, none of the default rules block outbound communication.
16. In the left navigation pane, right-click **Outbound Rules** and then click **New Rule**.
17. In the Rule Type window, click **Custom** and then click **Next**.
18. In the Program window, if necessary click **All programs** and then click **Next**.
19. In the Protocol type box, click TCP.
20. In the Remote port box, click to select **Specific Ports** and then type **80,443**. This rule will apply to outbound packets addressed to port 80 and port 443. Ports 80 and 443 are used by web servers.
21. Click **Next**.
22. Click **Next** to select the default option of applying to all computers.
23. If necessary, click **Block the connection** and then click **Next**. This rule will block connections to port 80 and port 443.

24. Click **Next** to accept the default configuration of this rule applying to all profiles. You can also limit it to specific profiles.
25. In the Name box, type **Block Web** and then click **Finish**. The Block Web rule is now at the top of the list of outbound rules. Notice that it is enabled and the action is block.
26. On the taskbar, click **Microsoft Edge**. Note that some cached content may still be displayed; however, this is content that was downloaded before you created the rule blocking outbound connections to web servers.
27. In the Search or enter web address box, type **http://www.microsoft.com** and then press **Enter**. You are unable to load the Microsoft website because the Block Web rule is blocking access to all websites.
28. Exit Microsoft Edge.
29. Click the **Start** button, in the search box type **cmd**, right-click **Command Prompt**, and then click **Run as administrator** on the shortcut menu.
30. If you are prompted with a User Account Control window, click **Yes**.
31. At the command prompt, type **netsh advfirewall firewall set rule name="Block Web" new enable=no** and then press **Enter**. This will disable the rule called "Block Web" that we created earlier using netsh instead of using the GUI interface to show the power of using netsh with advanced configurations.
32. In Windows Defender Firewall with Advanced Security, below Actions click **Refresh** to refresh the view. Note that the "Block Web" rule is not enabled.
33. On the taskbar, click **Microsoft Edge**.
34. In the Search or enter web address box, type **http://www.microsoft.com** and then press **Enter**. This verifies that web connectivity is working again.
35. Close the Microsoft Edge window.
36. Click the **Start** button, in the search box type **powershell**, right-click the result **Windows PowerShell**, and then click **Run as administrator** on the shortcut menu.
37. If you are prompted with a User Account Control window, click **Yes**.
38. At the PowerShell prompt, type **Remove-NetFirewallRule -DisplayName "Block Web"** and then press **Enter**. In the future, Microsoft will deprecate the netsh utility and use PowerShell cmdlets as a preference for script-based configurations. The netsh syntax and operation is specific to netsh, whereas PowerShell cmdlets have common programming behavior. For example, netsh has to refer to firewall rules by name; however, PowerShell logic can interact with rules based on their settings, using firewall properties to trigger updates.
39. In the Windows Defender Firewall with Advanced Security window, below Actions in the right-most actions pane click **Refresh** to refresh the view. Note that the "Block Web" rule is no longer listed.
40. Close the Administrator Windows PowerShell window.
41. Switch to the Administrator command prompt window. At the command prompt type **netsh advfirewall reset ?** and then press **Enter**. This will show the help screen for the netsh command to reset Windows Defender Firewall with Advanced Security policy to default values.

> **⚠ CAUTION** The netsh advfirewall reset command will reset default firewall rules and remove firewall customizations for previously installed applications and updated operating system components, which could result in broken functionality. Resetting firewall settings is a nontrivial decision but could be useful in a lab setting while you are testing custom settings for an organization.

42. Close the Administrator Command Prompt window.
43. Close the Windows Defender Firewall with Advanced Security window.
44. Switch to the Windows Security window that is open to the Firewall & network protection settings. Click the **Restore firewalls to default** link at the bottom.
45. This will open the Restore Defaults window for Windows Defender Firewall. This will have the same effect as the netsh advfirewall reset command but with less options than netsh. Click **Cancel** to abort the operation and close the window.
46. Close all open windows.

SUMMARY

- Network and Internet from the Settings app as well as Network and Sharing Center from Control Panel allow you to view and access networking information, such as viewing active networks, network status, and connection status, and to access configuration and troubleshooting wizards.

- Windows 10 is network-aware and can sense which type of network location it is connected to and change settings accordingly. Network location types are Private, Public, or Domain. These network location profiles can be applied to newly discovered and past remembered network locations.

- Network connections are composed of clients, services, protocols, and network drivers. Windows 10 includes both IPv4 and IPv6 protocols, neither of which can be removed.

- The important configuration concepts in IPv4 are IP addresses, subnet masks, default gateways, DNS, and WINS. If any of these components are configured incorrectly, network communication may be affected.

- Windows 10 can obtain IP configuration information from static configuration data, DHCP, APIPA, or an alternate IP configuration. DHCP is the most common.

- Windows 10 uses IPv6 to support peer-to-peer and general networking applications. IPv6 is becoming more common, and the address types can be recognized based on their prefix values. The most common method used for configuring IPv6 is based on stateful or stateless automatic configuration.

- The primary technologies for connecting a single computer or device to the Internet are cable, DSL, cellular, and dial-up. Cable and DSL are high-speed connection methods, while dial-up is slow. DSL commonly requires the configuration of PPPoE. Cellular requires a broadband device to supply Internet connectivity, potentially a cable to tether (connect) the computer to the mobile device, and a paid contract from the broadband supplier to use the feature.

- When an Internet connection is shared by multiple computers, there must be a mechanism to share the single IP address assigned by your ISP. You can use a router or Internet Connection Sharing (ICS). For sharing over Wi-Fi, the preferred standard is to configure your computer as a mobile hotspot or use Wi-Fi Direct technology. The older Wireless Ad Hoc feature has limited security and is difficult to configure in comparison. Windows also supports wireless hosted network as a similar but more advanced solution compared to wireless ad hoc, but it is still harder to configure and has weaker security than the preferred solutions.

- Wireless networking in Windows 10 supports different versions of the IEEE 802.11 standard that defines how a wireless adapter in a computer connects to a wireless access point (WAP). The WAP's SSID and security settings must be correctly configured to enable the wireless client to connect. Wireless clients can automatically reconnect when they are in range of a WAP. Network location settings and Windows Defender Firewall can help secure the data connection. Cell-like convenience for public roaming WiFi is enabled by the newer Hotspot 2.0 technology.

- Windows Defender Firewall is a host-based firewall included with Windows 10 and can perform inbound and outbound filtering. Also, IPSec security connection rules are combined with firewall rules in Windows 10. Windows Defender Firewall can be configured by local settings and utilities, Group Policy, or cloud-based Intune.

Key Terms

802.11
802.1x
address prefix
alternate IP configuration
Automatic Private IP Addressing (APIPA)
autonegotiation
broadcast address
classless interdomain routing (CIDR)
client

Client for Microsoft Networks
default gateway
Domain Name System (DNS)
domain network
Dynamic Host Configuration Protocol (DHCP)
eSIM
File and Printer Sharing for Microsoft Networks
fully qualified domain name (FQDN)

hostname
Hotspot 2.0
Institute of Electrical and Electronics Engineers (IEEE)
Internet Connection Sharing (ICS)
Internet Protocol Version 4 (TCP/IPv4)
Internet Protocol Version 6 (TCP/IPv6)
IP address
ipconfig

IPSec
ISP
Link-Local Multicast Name
   Resolution (LLMNR)
location type
loopback address
multicast
nbtstat
NetBIOS
netsh
netstat
Network Address Translation (NAT)
Network and Internet Settings
Network and Sharing Center
network discovery
network driver
network location awareness
nslookup
octet

Online Sign-Up
Passpoint
pathping
Personal Area Network (PAN)
ping
Point-to-Point Protocol over
   Ethernet (PPPoE)
private network
protocol
public network
Quality of Service (QoS)
RADIUS server
route
routing table
Security Set Identifier (SSID)
Server Message Block (SMB)
SIM
stateful automatic address
   configuration

stateless automatic address
   configuration
subnet mask
Time To Live (TTL)
tracert
unicast
Wi-Fi Direct
Windows Defender Firewall
Windows Defender Firewall and
   Advanced Security utility
Windows Internet Naming Service
   (WINS)
wireless access point (WAP)
Wireless Ad Hoc
Wireless Fidelity (Wi-Fi) Alliance
Wireless Hosted network
WPA2-Enterprise
WPA2-Personal
WPA3-Personal

Review Questions

1. Your computer is configured to obtain an IPv4
   address and DNS server address automatically.
   What utility will help you to find the IPv4 address of
   your computer? (Choose all that apply.)
   a. Get-NetIPAddress
   b. ipconfig
   c. Get-NetIPConfiguration
   d. netsh
   e. arp

2. _____ provides you with a way to
   control how your computer views other computers
   on the network and advertises its presence on the
   network.
   a. Windows Defender Firewall
   b. SMB
   c. Network discovery
   d. IPv6
   e. Network location

3. Your computer is configured to obtain an IPv4
   address and DNS server address automatically.
   Network traffic is not flowing as expected. You
   are asked by your manager to output the current
   IPv4 routing table. What commands can you use
   to display the IPv4 routing table? (Choose all that
   apply.)
   a. route
   b. netstat
   c. nslookup

   d. Get-NetRoute
   e. Get-RouteIPv4Table

4. Which protocol is used by the Client for Microsoft
   Networks and File and Printer Sharing for Microsoft
   Networks to communicate with one another and
   share files?
   a. FTP
   b. IPv4
   c. IPv6
   d. HTTP
   e. SMB

5. For a Class C IPv4 address, what is the correct
   default subnet mask value, specified as either a
   dotted decimal address or a CIDR value? (Choose
   all that apply.)
   a. 255.0.0.0
   b. /24
   c. 255.255.255.0
   d. C::/24
   e. 255.255.256.0

6. Which of these addresses represents a valid IPv6
   link-local address?
   a. 169.254.12.1
   b. ::1
   c. FE80::2cab:2a76:3f57:8499
   d. 2001:0:4137:9e74:2cab:2a76:3f57:8499
   e. FF::1:2

7. Which IPv4 configuration options must be configured properly to communicate with websites on the Internet? (Choose all that apply.)
   a. IP address
   b. subnet mask
   c. default gateway
   d. DNS
   e. WINS

8. Which of the following IP addresses is a valid IPv4 address and can be used by a host on the global Internet? (Choose all that apply.)
   a. 192.168.0.55
   b. 172.32.0.1
   c. 169.254.99.208
   d. 38.15.222.299
   e. 99.99.99.99

9. Which method can be used to assign IPv4 configuration settings when a DHCP server is not available? (Choose all that apply.)
   a. static configuration
   b. DNS
   c. WINS
   d. APIPA
   e. alternate IP configuration

10. To convert host names to IP addresses on the Internet, _____ is used.

11. Which of the following IPv4 addresses is a valid IPv4 address and has the same network ID as 192.168.112.45 given the subnet mask 255.255.255.0?
    a. 10.0.0.45
    b. 192.168.113.46
    c. 192.168.112.257
    d. 172.16.112.45
    e. 192.168.112.5

12. Your company is looking at securing connectivity between an internal server and workstations on the local area network. The network infrastructure does not support VLAN technology to compartmentalize network traffic, so they ask you for an overall design plan using Windows Defender Firewall with Advanced Security. Computers are required to confirm their identity when they communicate with one another using IPSec. For which of the following should your plan reference specific rules? (Select all that apply.)
    a. connection security rules
    b. IPSec token rules

c. inbound rules
d. outbound rules
e. routing table rules

13. Which of the following IPv4 addresses have the same network ID as 10.16.112.45 given the subnet mask 255.255.0.0? (Choose all that apply.)
    a. 10.16.160.45
    b. 192.168.172.46
    c. 10.16.122.2
    d. 10.16.185.45
    e. 10.18.114.3

14. Your company requires computers to authenticate to one another and enforces this requirement with Windows Defender Firewall with advanced security rules. You are asked to customize exceptions based on specific IP ranges. This can be done with a(n) _____ connection security rule.
    a. isolation
    b. outbound
    c. authentication exemption
    d. server-to-server
    e. inbound

15. A Wi-Fi access point with a non-broadcasting SSID is not discoverable through any means unless a Wi-Fi client is configured to connect to it in advance. (True or False)?
    a. True
    b. False

16. Which Internet connection type is most likely to require the use of PPPoE?
    a. cable
    b. DSL
    c. dial-up
    d. wireless hotspot

17. Which of these addresses represents a valid IPv6 global unicast address?
    a. 169.254.12.1/64
    b. 2001::1::FEA
    c. FE80::2cab:2a76:3f57:8499
    d. 2001:0:4137:9e74:2cab:2a76:3f57:8499
    e. FF::1:2

18. Which of these addresses represents a valid loopback address? (Choose all that apply.)
    a. ::1
    b. ::/0
    c. FF::1

d. 127.0.0.1

e. 127::1/32

19. Which utilities can be used to perform advanced firewall configuration? (Choose all that apply.)

   a. Device security

   b. netsh

   c. Group Policy

   d. Windows Defender Firewall and Advanced Security

   e. Windows PowerShell

20. A computer has the IPv4 address 192.168.0.23 and a subnet mask of 255.255.255.0. Which of these addresses represents a possible default gateway address? (Choose all that apply.)

   a. 192.168.0.254

   b. 193.168.0.1

   c. 0.0.0.1

   d. 127.0.0.1

   e. 192.168.0.1

Case Projects

Case Project 4-1: Networking Concepts

Superduper Lightspeed Computers helps many customers configure small home networks. A new staff person has started with very limited networking experience. How would you explain the basics of Windows 10 networking to the new person?

Case Project 4-2: Configuring Windows Defender Firewall

Gigantic Life Insurance has thousands of desktop computers and has just completed a major security audit. One of the recommendations in the security audit was to implement a host-based firewall on all workstations. Explain how Windows Defender Firewall could be used by Gigantic Life Insurance and the method you would use to configure Windows Defender Firewall on all the workstations.

MANAGING DISKS AND FILE SYSTEMS

After reading this module and completing the exercises, you will be able to:

1. Describe disk technologies and partition styles
2. Distinguish between basic, dynamic, and Storage Spaces disk types
3. Use disk management tools
4. Describe and manage physical disks
5. Create and manage virtual hard disks (VHDs)
6. Describe Storage Spaces components such as storage pools, storage space volumes, and resilience
7. Describe Windows 10 supported file systems and their features, limits, and tasks
8. List file and folder attributes used in Windows 10 file systems
9. Understand Windows 10 file and folder permissions
10. Describe Windows 10 file sharing methods and monitoring

This module looks at how storage is managed by Windows. Windows 10 combines old and new disk management technology, such as basic MBR disks, that have been around for decades and new software-controlled Storage Spaces technology with resiliency options. The module looks at how space on local disks is divided into units of storage called partitions or volumes. These volumes must be formatted with a file system to store and organize data, and Windows 10 has several file systems from which to choose. Different file systems include different management features. The management features can be basic, such as including management attributes to mark data as read-only, or hidden. Other management features can offer advanced security settings that control what specific identities can do with the data. In this module, you learn the factors involved in choosing various storage solutions.

DISK TECHNOLOGY

Disk technology can be categorized by how it is connected to the computer and how it is presented to Windows 10. When you are reviewing disk technology available on a computer for use with Windows 10, consider these disk technologies:

- Internal disk
- External disk
- Virtual hard disk (VHD)
- Multiple disks as one logical disk

Internal Disk

Devices that run Windows 10 are usually designed with consumer-grade technology and not server-grade components. Internal disks are commonly realized with electromechanical drives, solid-state drives, or custom embedded chip memory. Electromechanical drives are an older technology that rotate physical disks to read and write data, so they are slower, bulkier, and consume more power but provide storage at a lower cost. Solid-state drives (SSDs) with no moving parts are smaller and faster than electromechanical drives, but they are also more expensive and have a limited operational lifetime. Device manufacturers often embed chip memory into tablet devices running Windows 10 at the factory, some of which is used to emulate an internal disk drive. These common, nonremovable disk types are attached to the device's internal interface(s) and provide a suitable location to store operating system files required to start the computer.

External Disk

External interfaces are used to connect removable, portable disk storage. External storage is useful for expanding a computer's bulk file storage to contain application and user data files, but it is not typically suitable for operating system files that are essential and must always be present. Windows 10 is not normally installed on removable disk media.

Virtual Hard Disk (VHD)

A **virtual hard disk (VHD)** is a file format that can be used by the operating system to emulate the function of a hard drive, with all the data and structural elements of a drive. Files can be stored in a VHD storage location just like any other disk technology once the VHD is attached and made available through the Windows 10 operating system. A VHD may contain thousands of individual files from the user's perspective, but it still appears as only one physical file on the disk hosting that VHD file.

 TIP   All versions of Windows 10 support VHD operations. For example, double-clicking a VHD file automatically opens the VHD file as a mounted drive on the local operating system.

Multiple Disks as One Logical Disk

A logical disk appears to the Windows 10 operating system as one disk drive. Internal, external, and VHD disks are all examples of individual logical disks. Multiple drives can also be grouped together to appear as one logical disk to Windows 10. Two reasons for grouping multiple drives in this way include creating a logical disk that has more combined space than one disk alone could have and adding fault tolerance. The fault tolerance allows for a disk in a combined set to fail without losing access to the group's logical disk and its data. Windows 10 includes Storage Spaces, which can also combine multiple disks as one logical disk using technology that is similar to RAID (Redundant Array of Independent Disks) but is enhanced beyond that legacy technology.

NOTE 1

For simplicity, the remainder of this module uses the term disk to refer to a logical disk.

DISK PARTITION STYLES

When you configure a disk for use by Windows 10, you need to select a partition style. A partition style specifies how data can be organized on the disk. The **GUID Partition Table (GPT)** is used with new computers that use UEFI firmware to start the computer. For backward compatibility with older computers using BIOS firmware, you can use disks with the **Master Boot Record (MBR)** partition style. Table 5-1 summarizes the differences between GPT and MBR partition styles.

Table 5-1   Disk Partition Styles

GPT	MBR
Bootable only from UEFI firmware	Bootable from BIOS or UEFI firmware
Maximum 18 million TB (theoretical)	Maximum 2 TB usable space
Maximum 128 partitions	Maximum 4 partitions

Like the older BIOS standard, UEFI firmware controls the startup process of the computer and eventually loads the operating system. New computers designed to run Windows 10 are sold with UEFI firmware. Computers with UEFI typically support the option of emulating legacy MBR-based boot firmware to run older operating systems; however, this reintroduces the legacy limitations of the MBR standard for device support. UEFI firmware that is up to date and running in full UEFI mode provides the best support for Windows 10 operation and management, including features that require UEFI firmware operating in full UEFI mode, such as Secure Boot, Device Guard, and Credential Guard.

Prior to Windows 10 Version 1703, the only way to upgrade an MBR partition to GPT was to back up the data, reinitialize the disk using MBR as GPT, then restore data from the backup. Windows 10 Version 1703 introduced the command-line tool **MBR2GPT**, which is designed to work offline in the recovery environment as part of the Windows boot upgrade process from BIOS/MBR to UEFI/GPT. It is important to note that even though MBR2GPT can be run from the regular Windows 10 environment, it is not recommended because misconfiguration issues can arise.

> **! CAUTION**   Before you use MBR2GPT on a boot disk, verify that the computer is using UEFI firmware.

DISK TYPES

Empty space on disk drives can be identified by the type of storage using three different types in Windows 10: basic disks, dynamic disks, and Storage Spaces.

Basic Disks

When a new hard disk is added to a computer, it is initially configured as a **basic disk**. A basic disk can be partitioned using either MBR or GPT. Because basic disks have been in use for so long, many people and most computer utilities understand how to work with basic disks.

A basic disk is organized into one or more defined areas of storage called partitions. Each partition is identified by its size and the type of data it is supposed to hold. Most of these partition attributes are stored in a data table on the disk that is part of the MBR or GPT specifications. This table is commonly called the **partition table**.

Dynamic Disks

Dynamic disks are an older technology that were introduced as an alternative to basic disks using an MBR partition style. A primary advantage of dynamic disks at the time was the ability to create many **volumes** on a disk and avoid the MBR limitation

NOTE 2

To simplify disk management terminology, many disk management utilities refer to partitions on basic disks as volumes.

of four partitions. On Dynamic disks, volumes provide similar functionality to partitions on basic disks. Dynamic disks also have support for distributing a volume over multiple hard drives, with or without fault tolerance.

The use of dynamic disks never really caught on and their use is not recommended for Windows 10. Microsoft recommends that the only reason to use dynamic disks with Windows 10 is for mirrored boot volumes. The advanced features and resilience enabled when using dynamic disks for data are now available in Storage Spaces.

 TIP If you need the advanced features and resilience available when using dynamic disks, use Storage Spaces instead.

Storage Spaces

In Windows 10, the **Storage Spaces** feature is an inexpensive way to combine, or pool, the storage of multiple physical disk drives. Storage Spaces can also provide fault tolerance with data redundancy across multiple disks. Implementing Storage Spaces is easier and less expensive than most consumer-level, hardware-based solutions for disk redundancy.

For disk pooling and fault tolerance, older operating systems typically relied on custom software or hardware-based RAID technology installed on the local computer, which could require expensive or proprietary mechanisms. Storage Spaces is a software-based storage technology that doesn't need specialized storage hardware.

You can't use Storage Spaces for the Windows 10 boot drive. So, to obtain any benefit from Storage Spaces, at least two extra drives are required, in addition to the drive where Windows was installed. Multiple disk technologies (e.g., SATA, SAS, USB) can be used at the same time. Storage Spaces can be configured to store multiple copies of data on more than one drive to mitigate the risk of a hard drive failure. Another benefit of using Storage Spaces as a software-based solution is that you can move Storage Spaces disks to another Windows 10 computer and still get access to the data.

① CAUTION Storage Spaces on Windows 10 is designed to work with common consumer-grade disk components. If a disk is attached to the computer using a RAID-based technology, it should not be used with Storage Spaces.

NOTE 3

The terms Storage Spaces volume and storage space are commonly used interchangeably to describe a volume hosted by Storage Spaces technology.

Storage Spaces technology combines selected individual disks into a managed logical group called a **storage pool**. The storage pool acts as a container for data storage and can grow or shrink as physical disks are added or removed from the pool. The storage pool, in turn, presents the user a portion of that space as a **Storage Spaces volume**—a virtualized representation of a disk capable of storing the user's files.

Storage Pool

The first step in configuring Storage Spaces is creating a storage pool. You do this by identifying one or more disks that should be assigned to the pool. Once disks are assigned to a storage pool, Storage Spaces has access to the disks. More than one storage pool can reside on the same computer; however, a disk can be assigned to only one storage pool. Disks can be added and removed from a storage pool, making the storage technology flexible to the capacity needs of the user.

If a storage pool is running low on free drive space, you can add another disk to the computer while it is up and running and then assign it to the storage pool to increase its capacity. To accommodate this flexible technology, Microsoft designed Storage Spaces to work with a wide variety of disks at the same time. Some disk technologies are limited by the number of physical devices that can be added or by speed limitations built into those technologies (such as USB). Storage Spaces does not remove those limitations, but it allows multiple disks to be combined using different interface technologies simultaneously.

Disks can be removed from a storage pool if the remaining disks in the pool can store the information that was on the disk being removed. During the removal process, that disk has its data moved to the remaining disks in the pool. If the pool does not have enough space to hold that data, the disk removal fails.

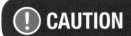 **CAUTION**   When a disk is assigned to a storage pool, all its previous contents are erased. If desired, back up the contents before adding it to a storage pool.

The storage pool hides the details of the physical disks it combines into what appears as one large reservoir of storage. Users don't interact directly with the storage pool and have no way of knowing which disks in the pool their data is stored on.

Storage Space

After disks have been added to a storage pool, you need to allocate space from the pool for data storage. The space you allocate from the storage pool is called a storage space, otherwise known as a Storage Spaces volume. To users, a storage space is a single logical disk, but it can contain space from one or more disks that are members of the storage pool.

Storage Spaces technology allows for the overallocation, or overbooking, of storage spaces created from storage pools. The size of the storage pool does not restrict the specified maximum size of the storage space created from it. The maximum size of a storage space volume is a logical limit and can be larger than the storage pool disk capacity. For example, if a storage pool has 500 GB of capacity, a 900 GB storage space volume can be created from it without generating an error. This maximum volume size is a theoretical limit, not a measured quantity in this case.

The size of the physical storage pool does set a practical limit of how much actual data can be saved to a storage space volume. If the storage pool used to create a 900 GB volume has only 500 GB of physical disk space available, Windows 10 completes write operations to the volume without an issue as long as free space exists in the pool hosting that volume. As the available free space in the physical storage pool gets low, Windows warns users that they need to add more disks to the storage pool, delete some other data in the pool, or save less data to the pool.

The data written to a Storage Space volume is organized and spread by Windows 10 among the disk drives in the storage pool to maximize efficiency and redundancy in an automated fashion. All the disks that belong to a storage pool are known to one another as members of the same group. If one physical disk member fails, the storage space volumes created from the pool may fail or survive depending on how the volume was configured for resiliency.

DISK MANAGEMENT TOOLS

Windows 10 includes multiple tools that you can use to manage disks. End users are typically most comfortable using the graphical Disk Management console. Administrators might use the command-line DiskPart utility or Windows PowerShell cmdlets for scripting.

Disk Management Console

The **Disk Management console** is an MMC snap-in (diskmgmt.msc) that is also part of the Computer Management utility. To use Disk Management and make changes to the disk configuration, you need to be a member of the Administrators group. Disks that are part of a storage pool are not visible in the Disk Management console, but Storage Spaces volumes are.

The Disk Management console allows changes to be made interactively and usually takes effect immediately without requiring the computer to be restarted.

As shown in Figure 5-1, the Disk Management console is divided into two views, a top view and a bottom view. The top view defaults to a summary of the volumes and partitions on the computer. The bottom view defaults to a graphical view of the disks and the volumes/partitions they contain.

DiskPart

DiskPart, shown in Figure 5-2, is a command-line tool that allows disk, partition, volume, and virtual hard disk management operations to be performed from a text-based screen interactively or from within a scripted file using command-line parameters.

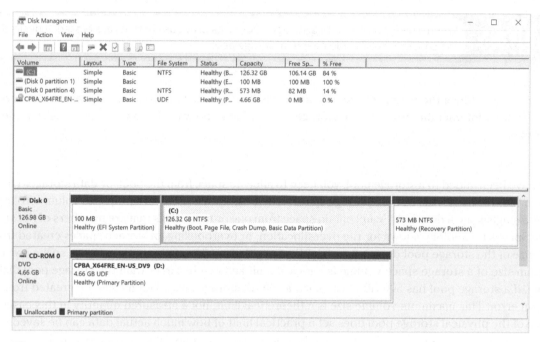

Figure 5-1   Disk Management console

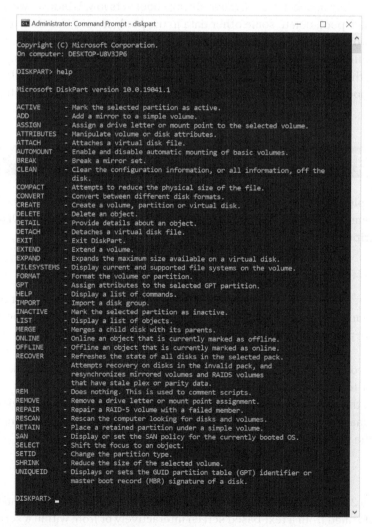

Figure 5-2   DiskPart running in interactive mode

Operations in the DiskPart utility are driven by a sequence of commands. Each command must have a specific object on which to focus its action. For example, before a partition can be created, the DiskPart utility must be told which disk the partition will be created on. Items such as disks and partitions are usually numbered, with the first disk or partition object starting at 0. If you set the focus incorrectly, destructive operations can remove or delete data unexpectedly.

 TIP   To see a list of DiskPart commands, type help at the DiskPart command prompt. To see more details about a specific DiskPart command, type help command_name, where command_name is the command of interest.

The DiskPart utility is powerful; it can contain a series of maintenance or repair commands that can be executed as part of a scheduled task or automated response on the local computer or remotely from another computer. It is considered an advanced tool that is not normally used for day-to-day administration. The tool can be run only in the security context of a user with local Administrator rights.

Activity 5-1: Using DiskPart

Time Required: 10 minutes
Objective: Start the DiskPart utility, browse its help menu, and use DiskPart to explore fundamental disk properties
Description: In this activity, you start the DiskPart utility, browse its help utility, and try out basic DiskPart commands.

1. If necessary, start your computer and sign in.
2. Click the **Start** button, in the search box type **cmd**, and then click **Run as administrator** in the details pane.
3. In the User Account Control dialog box, click **Yes**.
4. Type **diskpart** and then press **Enter** to start the DiskPart utility in its interactive mode. Note that the prompt changes to DISKPART>.
5. Type **help** and then press **Enter** to see a list of DiskPart commands.
6. Type **help select** and then press **Enter** to see information about the select command.
7. Type **help select disk** and then press **Enter** to see information and examples for the select disk command.
8. To see what disks can be selected, type **list disk** and then press **Enter**.
9. The DiskPart utility has not been focused on a particular disk yet, so some commands will not be able to run. For example, type **list partition**, press **Enter**, and note the error message.
10. To focus attention on the first disk, type **select disk = 0** and then press **Enter**.
11. Type **list partition**, press **Enter**, and note that the error message is gone.
12. To see what volumes are visible to the DiskPart utility, type **list volume** and then press **Enter**.
13. To leave the DiskPart utility, type **exit** and then press **Enter**.
14. Close the Administrator: Command Prompt window.

Storage Cmdlets in Windows PowerShell

Windows PowerShell cmdlets can be used to manage the Windows 10 storage subsystem, including Storage Spaces. Using Windows PowerShell cmdlets to manage storage avoids the quirks and older syntax of the DiskPart utility.

One advantage of using storage cmdlets in PowerShell is that configuration steps can be deployed without clicking around in the graphical consoles. This is very useful in more complicated server environments, such as virtual servers or cloud computing, but it can also be used in the Windows 10 environment for advanced management, automation, and troubleshooting.

Activity 5-2: Use Windows PowerShell to Manage Storage

Time Required: 10 minutes

Objective: Use Windows PowerShell to view basic storage properties for disks, volumes, and partitions.

Description: In this activity, you view the storage cmdlets available in Windows PowerShell and then use them to view storage information.

1. If necessary, start your computer and sign in.
2. Right-click the **Start** button and then click **Windows PowerShell (Admin)**.
3. In the User Account Control dialog box, click **Yes**.
4. Type **Get-Command -Module Storage** and then press **Enter**. This lists all the cmdlets available in the currently installed Windows Storage module.
5. At the Windows PowerShell prompt, type **Get-Disk** and then press **Enter**. This lists all physical disk objects, like basic disks, organized in a table.
6. Type **Get-Disk | FL Number, FriendlyName, PartitionStyle, BusType** and then press **Enter**. This lists specific attributes for each drive, including some additional information that was not shown in the default table format. Note that not all data returned by a straightforward PowerShell command like Get-Disk is displayed on the screen by default.
7. Type **Get-Partition** and then press **Enter**. This shows all the partitions, organized by disk, even if they are not formatted as a volume to store files.
8. Type **Get-Volume** and then press **Enter**. This returns a table of all volumes on all partitions for all disks.
9. Type **Get-Volume | Where-Object {$_.DriveLetter -ne $null}** and then press **Enter**. This shows the power of PowerShell to generate a filtered view, in this case only the volumes that have a drive letter assigned.
10. Close the Windows PowerShell prompt window.

MANAGING PHYSICAL DISKS

When you have a computer with a single hard drive, that hard drive is prepared for use during the installation of Windows 10. On a computer that already has Windows 10 installed, you might add one or more hard drives for additional storage. When you add a hard drive that's connected internally, it's typically connected via SATA. When you connect a hard drive externally, it's typically connected via USB.

Adding a New Drive

When you add a new SATA drive, it is connected to cabling inside your computer when the computer is turned off. When you restart the computer, it needs to be identified by the firmware in your computer and then Windows 10 has access to the drive. If a newly connected SATA drive is not visible in Disk Management, then you should verify that the SATA port is enabled in firmware. Even though it is common for computers to have multiple SATA ports, manufacturers often only enable the SATA ports with devices connected.

When you add a new USB drive, it is connected to an external USB port when the computer is turned on. Plug and Play functionality in Windows 10 detects the new USB drive, loads the appropriate drivers, and then Windows 10 has access to the drive. In rare cases, a USB drive requires unique drivers not included in Windows 10 and you need to install the appropriate drivers. You might need to go into Device Manager and scan for new hardware changes for the embedded storage controller to be detected properly.

Sometimes Plug and Play doesn't identify new drives properly even when the storage driver is loaded. In many cases, it is easiest to restart the computer and then the drive is usually detected properly. Alternatively, you can use Disk Manager and scan for new disks to trigger the discovery process. If a new disk appears in Disk Manager but is offline, you can bring it online in Disk Manager. You can also bring a disk online by using the Set-Disk cmdlet.

Most new hard disks can't be used to store files until you **initialize** them with the MBR or GPT partition style. When you initialize a disk, it applies the selected partition style and marks the disk with a digital signature that Windows 10 can use for identification. Some new hard disks are initialized by the manufacturer.

 TIP   If you are adding a new disk to a storage pool, then you don't need to initialize it.

In Disk Management, a new disk that is not initialized has a status of Unknown. If necessary, you can trigger the disk initialization process manually in Disk Management or by using the Initialize-Disk cmdlet. Disk Management prompts you for the partition style. You can specify a partition style when using Initialize-Disk, but if you don't specify a partition style then GPT is used by default.

 CAUTION   If you initialize a disk that already has data on it, that data is erased.

Moving Drives

There are no special considerations for moving basic disks. When you move a basic disk to another computer, all the data on the disk is available in the new computer, but the drive letters assigned to each volume might be changed.

If you move a dynamic disk to another computer, you need to import it. Before the disk is imported, the Disk Management console reports the status of the disk as a **Foreign Disk** and you don't have access to data on the disk. You must right-click the disk name in Disk Management and then select Import Foreign Disk to initiate the import process.

If a dynamic disk contains a volume that is spread across multiple dynamic disks, all member disks must be moved at the same time. Failure to do so leaves the volume broken, even if the dynamic disk is correctly imported.

Storage Spaces technology is similar to dynamic disk technology in that it keeps track of each disk that is a member of a storage pool. When a storage pool is moved from one computer to another, all disk members of the pool should be moved at the same time. Once the disks are connected to the target Windows 10 computer, the pool and its Storage Spaces volumes mount automatically as read-write storage.

 CAUTION   Moving multiple disks between computers is always risky. If the data is important, back up the data at the source before the move as a precaution.

 **VIRTUAL DISK MANAGEMENT TASKS**

Windows 10 provides native support for working with VHDs. Disk Management and DiskPart are automatically available for creating and managing VHDs. The Windows PowerShell cmdlets for managing VHDs are installed as part of the Hyper-V Module for Windows PowerShell feature. If you have installed Hyper-V on the computer, this module is included by default. Otherwise, you can install the module by itself as an additional feature.

 TIP   Windows 10 Home edition does not include the Hyper-V Module for Windows PowerShell.

Creating VHDs

A VHD in Windows 10 is created as a single file on a physical disk drive. All versions of Windows 10 support the capability to create a VHD. VHDs can be created using the Disk Management snap-in, the New-VHD cmdlet, or the DiskPart command-line utility.

To create a VHD, you must specify the following information:

- *Location*—This includes the name and physical location of the file that will hold the VHD data. The location needs to be large enough to hold the VHD file and all its data.
- *Virtual Hard Disk Format*—This specifies VHD or VHDX. VHD is an older format that supports virtual disks up to 2 TB. VHDX is a newer format that supports virtual disks up to 64 TB and has better performance.
- *Virtual Hard Disk Size*—This states a maximum storage limit specified in MB, GB, or TB.
- *Virtual Hard Disk Type*—This specifies whether the type is dynamically expanding or fixed size. A dynamically expanding VHD takes up only the disk space required to hold the data inside it and has a maximum size allocated. A dynamically expanding VHD behaves much like a compressed folder (.zip) that expands as you add content to it. A fixed-size VHD immediately takes up the full size allocated to the VHD.

VHD disks created by using Disk Management automatically attach to the operating system and appear as a new disk drive that is uninitialized. The drive must be initialized, just like a new hard drive, before it can be configured with partitions to store files. VHDs are restricted to basic disk technology due to their transient existence in the operating system.

 **CAUTION** Because VHDs are not automatically reattached after signing out, shutting down, or restarting, you should not sign out, shut down, or restart during an activity that involves a VHD unless instructed otherwise.

Activity 5-3: Creating VHD Disks

Time Required: 10 minutes

Objective: Create a new VHD disk

Description: In this activity, you perform the typical steps required to create a new VHD disk hosted on drive C:.

1. If necessary, start your computer and sign in.
2. Right-click the **Start** button and then select **File Explorer**.
3. Click to select **Local Disk (C:)** in the left-pane and create a new folder in the root of C: called **VHD Storage**.
4. Right-click the **Start** button and then select **Disk Management**.
5. In the Disk Management window, click **Disk 0**, click **Action** on the menu bar, and then select **Create VHD**. This displays the Create and Attach Virtual Hard Disk dialog box.
6. Click the **Browse** button and navigate to **C:\VHD Storage**. In the File name field, enter the text **VHDExample** and then click the **Save** button.
7. In the Create and Attach Virtual Hard Disk dialog box, in the Virtual hard disk size, type **5**, and then change the unit size to **GB**.
8. In the Virtual hard disk format area, click **VHDX**.
9. In the Virtual hard disk type area, verify that **Dynamically expanding** is selected.
10. Click **OK** to create the VHD and automatically attach it.
11. Note that a new disk appears in the graphical disk view with an Unknown disk type and a status of Not Initialized. The free space on the drive appears as 5 GB of unallocated space and the graphical drive icon next to the disk identifier is light blue.

12. Right-click anywhere within the 5 GB block of unallocated space shown as part of the newly created VHD disk, and note the available volume creation options are all dimmed and unavailable.

13. Right-click the VHD's disk name next to the blue drive icon and then select **Initialize Disk** on the shortcut menu.

14. In the Initialize Disk dialog box, select **MBR** and then click **OK**.

15. Right-click the unallocated space from the VHD disk and then select **New Simple Volume**.

16. When the first wizard screen is displayed, click **Next**.

17. On the Specify Volume Size screen, click **Next** to accept the suggested volume size.

18. On the Assign Drive Letter or Path screen, note the drive letter assigned to the new simple volume and then click **Next**.

19. On the Format Partition screen, in the Volume label box, type **VHDVOL**, click **Next**, and then click **Finish**.

NOTE 4

During the creation and formatting of the drive, Windows might mistakenly prompt you to format the new volume even though the wizard is performing that task for you. If that happens, just click **Cancel** at the prompt asking Do you want to format it?

20. Note the size of the newly created partition in Disk Management. It is reported as the full size of 5 GB you specified in the New Volume Creation Wizard.

21. Switch to the File Explorer window and browse to **C:\VHD Storage**. Note the size of the VHD file in that folder and the fact that it is much smaller than the reported volume size.

22. In the File Explorer window, right-click the drive letter assigned to the VHD disk and select **Properties**. Note the Used Space and Free Space values shown on the General tab. Compare this with the actual size of the VHD file noted in the previous step.

23. Click **OK** to close the drive Properties dialog box.

24. Close all open windows, but do not sign out or restart.

 **CAUTION** Activity 5-4 relies on the VHD created and mounted in Activity 5-3. Do not sign out, restart, or shutdown between Activity 5-3 and Activity 5-4.

Attaching and Detaching VHDs

A VHD must be attached, or mounted, to be available to the operating system and the user. When a VHD is attached, it can be managed with typical disk and partition operations. All versions of Windows 10 can attach an existing VHD file. VHDs can easily be attached by double-clicking the VHD file name in File Explorer.

VHDs can also be attached using methods that offer more control, such as the Mount-VHD cmdlet, Disk Management, or the DiskPart command-line utility. When a VHD file is attached via these methods, it can optionally be opened in read-only mode where its file contents cannot be accidentally modified.

When a Windows 10 computer is restarted, the VHD files currently attached do not automatically reattach. They must be manually attached again after the computer restarts. The only time a VHD automatically mounts as the computer starts is the special case in which Windows 10 is configured to boot from a VHD file.

A VHD must be detached, or dismounted, to make it unavailable to the operating system and the user. All versions of Windows 10 support the capability to detach an existing VHD file. VHDs can be detached using the Disk Management snap-in, the Dismount-VHD PowerShell command, or the DiskPart command-line utility.

Activity 5-4: Managing VHD Disks

Time Required: 5 minutes

Objective: View VHD attributes using DiskPart and detach a VHD

Description: In this activity, you use DiskPart to view a VHD's details, detach it, and confirm that it is no longer visible as an active disk.

1. Right-click the **Start** button and then click **File Explorer**.
2. Confirm that you can see the drive letter associated with the VHD created and mounted in Activity 5-3.
3. Click the **Start** button, in the search box type **cmd**, right-click the result **Command Prompt**, and then click **Run as administrator** on the shortcut menu.
4. In the User Account Control dialog box, click **Yes**.
5. At the command prompt, type **diskpart** and then press **Enter**.
6. To focus attention on the VHD created in the previous activity, type **select vdisk file= "C:\VHD Storage\ VHDExample.vhdx"** and then press **Enter**.
7. Type **detail vdisk** and then press **Enter** to display detailed information about the VHD. Note the Virtual size and Physical size attributes listed in the output of the command.
8. Type **detach vdisk** and then press **Enter** to dismount the VHD.
9. Type **exit** and then press **Enter** to exit DiskPart.
10. Switch to the File Explorer window. Confirm that you can no longer see the drive letter associated with the VHD created and mounted in Activity 5-3.
11. Close all open windows.

MANAGING STORAGE SPACES

Management of Storage Spaces is not integrated into Disk Management or DiskPart. A new graphical control interface called Manage Storage Spaces is found in the System and Security section of Control Panel. This tool allows administrative users to create and manage storage pools and storage spaces.

Manage Storage Spaces allows changes to be made interactively and take effect immediately without requiring the computer to be restarted. Physical disks that are added to storage pools can be managed with the Disk Management console before they are added to a storage pool, but once they are added to a storage pool, they must be managed within the Manage Storage Spaces view.

Creating an Initial Storage Pool and Storage Space

Initially, Manage Storage Spaces shows only a link to create a new storage pool and storage space.

If no disks exist except for the system disk (i.e., drive C:), the Storage Spaces wizard notifies the user that no drives are available for use with the technology. Before a storage pool can be created, at least one additional drive must be added to the computer and must be recognized by the system. Once a storage pool exists, the Manage Storage Spaces view changes to provide management options for existing storage pools and storage spaces, as shown in Figure 5-3.

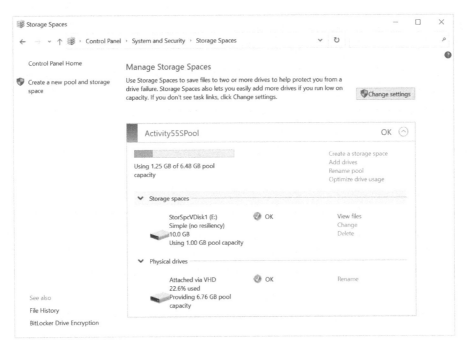

Figure 5-3   Storage Space settings after the initial setup

> **⚠ CAUTION**   Activity 5-6 relies on a VHD that is mounted in Activity 5-5. Do not shut down, restart, or sign out between Activity 5-5 and 5-6.

Activity 5-5: Creating the Initial Storage Pool and Storage Space Volume

> **⚠ CAUTION**   VHDs are not officially supported for Microsoft Storage Spaces because they do not automatically remount in Windows 10. They are used in this lab only to illustrate Storage Spaces concepts and should never be used in a production environment with Storage Spaces. Because of their unsupported nature, we will use the precision of PowerShell commands to build our Storage Spaces environment.

Time Required: 15 minutes

Objective: Create a storage pool and storage space volume using the initial Storage Spaces Wizard

Description: In this activity, you create a new virtual disk that is attached and empty. Using PowerShell, you create a new storage space pool and volume from that virtual disk. Finally, you confirm the storage space volume's settings in the Disk Management console to note key information.

1. If necessary, start your computer and sign in.
2. Right-click the **Start** button and then click **Disk Management**.
3. In the Disk Management window, click **Action** on the menu bar and then click **Create VHD**.
4. In the Create and Attach Virtual Hard Disk dialog box, click the **Browse** button and navigate to the location **C:\VHD Storage**, which was created in Activity 5-3.
5. In the File name box, type **VHDPoolDisk1** and then click **Save**.
6. In the Virtual hard disk size box, type **7** and then change the unit size to **GB**.
7. Confirm that **VHD** is the virtual hard disk format selected.
8. In the Virtual hard disk type area, select **Dynamically expanding** and then click **OK**. Note that the disk appears in Disk Management as an uninitialized disk with 7 GB of unallocated space.
9. Click the **Start** button, in the search box type **control panel**, and then click **Control Panel**.

10. Click **System and Security** and then click **Storage Spaces**.
11. Click the **Create a new pool and storage space** link. When you are prompted by User Account Control for permission to run the application, click **Yes**.
12. Note that the Storage Spaces agent has discovered the newly created and attached VHD as an available disk and has already selected it by default. Click **Create pool**.
13. In the Create a storage space window, enter the following information and then click **Create storage space**.
    - Name: **Simple space**
    - Drive letter: **D:**
    - File system: **NTFS**
    - Resiliency type: **Simple (no resiliency)**
    - Size (maximum): **10 GB**
14. In the Storage Spaces window, expand **Physical drives**. Read the information displayed to see information about the storage space and the physical drives it is located on.
15. Switch to the Disk Management window and note that the VHD is no longer displayed as a disk visible to Disk Management. Instead, you can see a new basic disk with a volume named Simple space. Simple space is the storage space that you created.
16. Right-click the newly created disk name and then select **Properties**.
17. Click to select the **General** tab if it is not selected. Note that the Location is specified as on Microsoft Storage Spaces Controller.
18. Click to select the **Volumes** tab. Note that the default partition style was defaulted to GUID PartitionTable (GPT).
19. Click **OK** to close the Microsoft Storage Spaces Device Properties window.
20. Right-click the **Start** button and then select **File Explorer**.
21. Navigate to the folder **C:\Program Files**, right-click the **Common Files** folder and then click **Copy**.
22. Navigate to the drive letter for the Simple space volume and paste the Common Files folder. This content is used to provide some data within the storage space volume for later activities.
23. Close all windows but do not sign out or restart your computer.

Maintaining Storage Pools and Storage Spaces

Each storage pool is identified by the physical disk members that are grouped within that pool. Metadata about the pool and its members is stored on each physical disk that is a member of the pool. The end user has the option to customize a storage pool by:

- *Renaming a storage pool*—The default name for the first storage pool is just the name Storage pool. If you intend to have multiple storage pools, it might be desirable to rename this pool based on some attribute of the data or disks that are contained within the pool.
- *Adding disk drives to the pool*—You can add more disks to the storage pool after the disk is connected to the computer and visible to Windows 10. The physical disk must be at least 4 GB in size; if it is smaller, Storage Spaces does not allow that disk to be selected. If the disk contains any previous data, it is destroyed once the disk is joined to a storage pool.
- *Creating or deleting a storage space volume assigned to the pool*—The maximum size of a volume created from the storage pool is not limited by the storage pool, and similarly, the number of volumes created from one storage pool is not limited by just having one storage pool. The biggest limitation to the number of storage space volumes is the availability of free drive letters to assign to those volumes.
- *Optimizing drive usage within the pool*—When data is written to a storage pool, Windows 10 manages the placement of the data on the physical disks. As physical disks are assigned to the pool, Windows by default tries to rebalance the data across all the disks that belong to the pool. If a storage pool was created with an earlier version of Windows and upgraded for use with Windows 10, or automatic rebalancing was not enabled when a disk was added to a storage pool, you can manually trigger the optimization and rebalancing of data across all drives in the pool as a background activity.

Activity 5-6: Managing Storage Pools and Storage Space Volumes

Time Required: 20 minutes

Objective: Investigate options to manage a storage pool and storage space volumes using the Storage Spaces section in Control Panel

Description: In this activity, you rename the storage pool to aid the end user's recognition of the storage pool, plus look at the option to add a second virtual disk to the existing storage pool. The activity looks at the options to create a new simple storage volume.

1. You should already be signed in from the previous activity.
2. Right-click the **Start** button and then select **Disk Management**.
3. In the Disk Management window, click **Action** on the menu bar and then click **Create VHD**.
4. In the Create and Attach Virtual Hard Disk window, click the **Browse** button and navigate to the location **C:\VHD Storage**. In the File name box type **VHDPoolDisk2** and then click **Save**.
5. In the Virtual hard disk size box, type **6** and then change the unit size to **GB**.
6. Confirm that VHD is the virtual hard disk format selected.
7. In the Virtual hard disk type area, select **Dynamically expanding** and then click **OK**.
8. Click the Start button, type **storage**, and then click **Manage Storage Spaces**.
9. Click the **Change settings** button.
10. When you are prompted by a User Account Control dialog box for permission to run the application, click **Yes**. Note that the links to manage the existing storage pool and its storage spaces are now active.
11. Click the **Rename pool** link.
12. In the Name box, type **Archive Storage** and then click **Rename pool**.
13. Click the **Add drives** link.
14. Note that a list of available unformatted drives is presented in the Add drives wizard. Confirm that the **Optimize drive usage to spread existing data across all drives** option is selected.
15. Confirm that the virtual disk added earlier in the activity is selected and then click **Add drives**.
16. In the Storage Spaces window, in the Archive Storage area, expand Physical Disks. Note that two disks are shown.
17. Click the **Optimize drive usage** link and then click the **Optimize drive usage** link button to trigger the process manually. Optimization is a background task that will proceed until it completes.
18. Click the link **Create storage space**.
19. In the Name and drive letter settings area, in the Name box, type **STORVOL2**.
20. In the Resiliency area, in the Resiliency type box, select **Simple (no resiliency)**.
21. In the Size area, in the Size (maximum) box, type **20 GB** and then click **Create storage space**.
22. Close all windows and sign out.

NOTE 5

After this activity, you can shut down, restart, or sign out.

Configuring Storage Spaces Fault Tolerance

Individual physical disks configured as basic disks are not fault tolerant themselves. If the data is not backed up, the loss of a basic disk results in permanent data loss.

A storage space volume can be configured for fault tolerance when it is initially created if the proper starting conditions are met. Individual drives within the storage pool are used by Windows 10 transparently to provide the level of fault tolerance requested. Different levels of fault tolerance are available that are similar to traditional RAID levels but are customized to operate with additional functionality not normally found in traditional RAID. These fault-tolerant options are listed in Table 5-2.

NOTE 6

This module provides disk fault-tolerance information specific to Windows 10 and Storage Spaces. If you would like to review generic RAID fault tolerance, please see Standard RAID levels on Wikipedia at https://en.wikipedia.org/wiki/Standard_RAID_levels.

Table 5-2   Storage Spaces Resiliency Types

Resiliency Types	Description
Simple (no resilience)	- Needs one drive minimum in the pool - Good for temporary data and where performance is more important than resilience - If a drive in the pool fails and contains part of this volume, the volume is not available to the end user
Two-way mirror	- Needs two drives minimum - A volume's data is copied to at least two separate disks in the pool; each disk holds a synchronized copy of the volume's data - Good performance with disk read and write operations - Can handle a single drive failure and still be operational - Supported volume size is limited to the size of the smallest drive member
Three-way mirror	- Needs five drives minimum - Three copies of a volume's data are spread across all five drives - Good performance with disk read and write operations - Can handle multiple drive failures and still be operational
Parity	- Similar to RAID 5 in that parity information is calculated and can determine data that is lost from a drive failure - Needs three drives minimum to handle a single drive failure - Needs seven drives minimum to handle a double drive failure - Slow performance during a disk failure while the system calculates missing data; best used for low data that needs fault tolerance but not high performance, such as archive data

FILE SYSTEMS

Once a volume is available to store data, its free space must be organized into files and folders using a file system. A user typically has different file storage requirements for different devices. For example, some files must be portable and interchangeable with other operating systems, while other files must be secure and efficiently stored. Some devices, such as hard disks, support multiple file systems on one device. This section discusses the common file systems used in Windows 10, the properties of files stored on them, and securing those files.

A file system allows the operating system to store and organize files. The choice of file system can limit the total amount of data stored in a partition or volume, the number of files, the size of the files, their names, attributes, and other properties. Windows 10 supports several common file systems:

- File Allocation Table (FAT)
- NT File System (NTFS)
- Resilient File System (ReFS)
- Universal Disk Format (UDF)

NOTE 7

The choice of basic or dynamic disk technology has no impact on the system features described in this section.

File Allocation Table (FAT)

The earliest file system used for hard disks by the MS-DOS operating system is the **File Allocation Table (FAT)**. All Microsoft operating systems since MS-DOS support a version of this file system. Different versions of FAT can be used with Windows 10: FAT, FAT32, and exFAT.

FAT is a simple and basic method to organize files on partitions that are no larger than 4 GB in size. FAT32 was introduced with Windows 95 OSR2 to support hard disks that were becoming much larger than 2 GB in size. Windows 10 does not use FAT32 as a file system for new partitions or volumes larger than 32 GB.

Microsoft introduced exFAT with Windows Vista Service Pack 1 and continues to license the technology to memory device manufacturers, such as USB memory sticks. ExFAT has the simplicity of the FAT file system but with capacity limits that are so large that it can be used with almost any portable bulk storage device. As memory device sizes exceed 32 GB, exFAT could be the file system of devices preformatted at the factory.

In Windows 10, FAT should be used for file systems only when portability to non-Microsoft operating systems is a concern. Generally, this means that FAT is used only for portable media such as USB memory sticks and memory cards for phones and digital cameras. FAT does not provide file system security. To provide enhanced features for security, usability, and larger partitions, NTFS is a better alternative.

New Technology File System (NTFS)

The **New Technology File System (NTFS)** was first introduced with Windows NT, and a newer version of it is supported by Windows 10. NTFS stores files and folders in a way that looks very similar to the FAT file system. The difference is in how that data is secured, reliably managed, and allowed to grow. The major advantages of NTFS are listed in Table 5-3.

NOTE 8

A volume can't be formatted with exFAT using graphical tools; however, the format K: /FS:exFAT command formats the specified volume, K:, with the exFAT file system from the command line. The format utility supports the FS (i.e., file system) parameters FAT, FAT32, exFAT, NTFS, UDF, ReFS.

Table 5-3   Advantages of the NTFS File System over FAT

Advantage	Description
File and Folder permissions	Each file and folder has its own discretionary access control list (DACL) of who (i.e., user or group) can do what to the file system object. Permissions include configurable inheritance through the folder structure. Permissions can be basic or advanced using allow or deny assignments. Ownership of a file system object is tracked and always allows access to file system objects owned by that user or group.
Audit controls	Each file and folder can have its own custom system access control list (SACL) to define who is audited in the Security event log when they succeed or fail at accessing a file system object.
Compression	Files can optionally have their contents compressed.
Encrypting File System (EFS)	Files can optionally have their contents encrypted.
Disk quotas	Optionally track how much data is used on the file system by a user and potentially apply storage limits.
Automatic bad cluster management	Bad clusters that fail to store data reliably are tracked and not reused.
File names in Unicode format	File and folder names can contain international languages and symbols, not just ASCII characters.
Alternate data streams	Support for multiple data streams that link to the same file but have different purposes (e.g., file data for one stream, a bitmap in another stream for the app that is registered to open that type of file).
Transactional NTFS	This is used to protect data files with log files and checkpoint consistency checks.
Log file and checkpoint consistency checks	Changes made to key files can be rolled back in the event of a problem to a known good state.
Extendable/shrinkable partitions and volumes	As long as free space allows on the disk or volume, the partition or volumes can be extended or shrunk.
Volume mount points	You can link an empty folder in one volume to another volume.
Symbolic links	A symbolic link points to another file or folder, similar to a shortcut. To the user or application, it appears as if the file is in that folder.

Disk Quotas

Disk quotas are primarily used on file servers to limit or monitor the amount of storage consumed by specific users. The ability to configure disk quotas is included as part of the NTFS files system, but it is seldom implemented on a computer running Windows 10. If you decide to implement quotas, you can do so on the Quotas tab in the Properties of a volume via File Explorer or Disk Management. You can also use the **fsutil** command-line utility.

NOTE 9

Compressed files count against the user's quota based on their uncompressed size, not the compressed size.

The Quota tab displays quota settings for that partition or volume, as shown in Figure 5-4.

Once disk quotas are enabled for a partition, the operating system calculates the amount of disk space used by each unique owner listed for all files on the volume. The first time quota management is turned on, the system takes some time to identify all the owners and tally all the file sizes attributed to each owner. If the owner of a file changes, then the size of that file is applied to the quota of the new owner.

Figure 5-4 NTFS-formatted disk properties, disk Quota tab

Even if disk quotas are enabled, the initial configuration reports only the amount of data in use by different owners; no limits or warnings are enforced. The options on the Quota tab allow for limits to be configured as a default setting for all users.

As users approach those limits, warnings can be issued; when they finally reach the maximum limit, they are denied additional disk space within the partition. Warnings to users can be ignored, misinterpreted, and not noticed, so the warnings can be optionally recorded to the application event log as a permanent reference of the event for administrators.

Some users may require special consideration and should have a different warning or deny limit in place. The Quota Entries button on the Quota tab opens a Quota Entries window where user-specific limits can be defined that override the default settings. The Quota Entries window is shown in Figure 5-5.

> **! CAUTION** Activity 5-7 relies on a VHD that is mounted. Do not shut down, restart, or sign out during this activity.

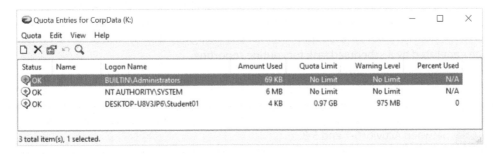

Figure 5-5   Quota entries for an NTFS-formatted disk

Activity 5-7: Enabling Disk Quotas for an NTFS Partition

Time Required: 15 minutes

Objective: Enable disk quotas

Description: Disk quotas can be used to limit disk utilization, but they can also be used just to identify the amount of disk space that each user is using. For example, if you enable quotas on the C: drive of a computer running Windows 10, you can see how much application data and profile space is used. In this activity, you enable disk quotas on the C: drive of your computer and log events when limits are reached.

1. If necessary, start your computer and sign in.

NOTE 10

This activity uses a VHD created earlier in Activity 5-3.

2. On the taskbar, click **File Explorer** and browse to **C:\VHD Storage.**
3. To attach the VHD, right-click the **VHDExample.vhdx** file and then click **Mount.** Note the drive letter it was mounted as in relation to This PC.
4. Right-click **VHDVOL (*driveletter*)** and then click **Properties.**
5. In the VHDVOL (*driveletter*) Properties dialog box, click the **Quota** tab and then click the **Show Quota Settings** button. Note that the traffic light indicator on the Quota tab is red and that the status is reported as Disk quotas are disabled.
6. Select the **Enable quota management** check box and then click **Limit disk space to.**
7. In the Limit disk space to box, type **2** in the numeric field and then select **GB** in the units list.
8. In the Set warning level to box, check that **1** is entered in the numeric field and select GB from the units list.
9. Select the **Log event when a user exceeds their quota limit** and **Log event when a user exceeds their warning level** check boxes and then click **Apply.**
10. A warning appears that enabling the disk quota system will take some time to complete. Click **OK** in the warning window to continue.
11. When the traffic light indicator on the Quota tab turns green and the status is reported as Disk quota system is active, click the **Quota Entries** button.
12. The Quota Entries for VHDVOL (*driveletter*) window dialog box displays and lists the current owners who have files on the volume. On slower systems, the Logon Name column is initially populated with the security identifiers (SIDs) of the owners found on the volume which is later updated to the friendly names.
13. Click the **Start** button, in the search box type **cmd**, right-click the result **Command Prompt**, and then click **Run as administrator** on the shortcut menu.
14. In the User Account Control dialog box, click **Yes.**

15. Using the drive letter you noted in Step 2, at the command prompt, type **fsutil quota query** *drive-letter* (for example, fsutil quota query e:) and then press **Enter**. Note the detail reported in the text output by the command in comparison to the detail visible in the Quota Entries for (C:) dialog box displayed in Step 12. Consider which report could be generated by a scheduled task for routine reporting.

16. Close all open windows and dialog boxes.

 **CAUTION**   Activity 5-8 relies on a VHD that is mounted in Activity 5-7. Do not shut down, restart, or sign out between Activity 5-7 and 5-8.

Volume Mount Points

A partition or volume has a finite amount of space available. The partition or volume can be extended or spanned, but in some cases, this is not an option. Volume mount points allow an empty folder in an NTFS-formatted file system to point to another partition or volume in the local computer. You can configure volume mount points by using the Disk Management console. The user performing the task must have administrator privileges on the local computer.

To the users, it appears they are accessing a folder in the original NTFS partition, but in fact they are accessing the file system on the other partition. The partition connected via the volume mount point can be formatted with a different file system. The disk space reported for the NTFS volume hosting the mount point does not increase; the volume mount point is just a pointer. The free space and control of the target pointed at by the volume mount point is separately reported and managed.

A folder must be empty before it can be converted into a volume mount point. A single volume mount point can only point to one partition or volume; however, multiple mount points can point to the same target partition or volume. Volume mount points can be added or removed for a partition, but they cannot be modified. If a partition or volume is deleted and it is pointed to by one or more mount points, those mount points will appear as broken links and will not revert to empty folders.

 **CAUTION**   Activity 5-8 relies on a VHD that is mounted. Do not shut down, restart, or sign out during this activity.

Activity 5-8: Managing Mount Points

Time Required: 15 minutes

Objective: Link additional space to an existing volume using a volume mount point and observe the changes to the view in File Explorer

Description: You can use a mount point to expand the capacity of an existing partition or volume. This can be useful when you need to add a large amount of storage space and no space is available on the physical disk. For example, you can create a mount point for application data. In this activity, you create a mount point on the C: drive to hold data for an application.

1. You should already be signed in from the previous activity.
2. On the taskbar, click **File Explorer** and browse to C:\.
3. In File Explorer, on the **Home** tab, click **New folder**, type **MyAppData**, and then press **Enter**.
4. Browse to VHDVOL, click the **Home** tab, click **New item**, and click **Text Document**.
5. Type **DataFile** and then press **Enter** to name the file.
6. Close the File Explorer window.
7. Right-click the **Start** button and then click **Disk Management**.

8. Right-click **VHDVOL** (*driveletter:*) and then click **Change Drive Letter and Paths**.
9. In the Change Drive Letter and Paths for *driveletter:* (VHDVOL) dialog box, select the drive letter and then click **Remove**.
10. In the Disk Management window, click **Yes** to acknowledge the warning.
11. Right-click **VHDVOL** and click **Change Drive Letter and Paths**.
12. In the Change Drive Letter and Paths for VHDVOL dialog box, click **Add**.
13. In the Add Drive Letter or Path dialog box, click **Mount in the following empty NTFS folder**, type **C:\MyAppData** in the text box, and then click **OK**.
14. On the taskbar, click **File Explorer** and browse to C:\. Notice that MyAppData is displayed with a different icon and shows a size.
15. Close File Explorer.
16. Click the **Start** button, in the search box type **cmd**, right-click the result **Command Prompt**, and then click **Run as administrator** on the shortcut menu.
17. In the User Account Control dialog box, click **Yes**.
18. At the command prompt, type **dir C:\my*** and then press **Enter**. Notice that MyAppData is identified as a junction point.
19. Type **cd \MyAppData** and then press **Enter**.
20. Type **dir** and then press **Enter**. Verify that DataFile.txt is there.
21. Close the command prompt window.
22. In Disk Management, scroll down in the list of disks, right-click the disk containing VHDVOL, and then click **Detach VHD** on the shortcut menu.
23. In the Detach Virtual Hard Disk dialog box, click **OK**.
24. Close the Disk Management window.

Symbolic Links

A symbolic link can point to a file or folder on the local computer or to a remote location identified with a UNC path. If the target is remote, the other computer hosting the target must also support symbolic links. The two special types of symbolic links are known as hard links and junction points. Only administrators can create symbolic links using the command-line utility mklink.

Symbolic links are different from a shortcut because a shortcut is a file that defines how Windows can locate content somewhere else. To other applications, the shortcut appears as just another file with a .lnk extension. Symbolic links appear as a file or folder with a given name that may be different or the same as the target. The majority of applications would be oblivious to the fact that the file or folder they are accessing is really located somewhere else.

A hard link can point only to a file on the same partition or volume as the hard link object. A hard link is a duplicate directory entry that points to the *contents* of a target file. When users or applications access a hard link, they believe the file content exists in the folder holding the hard link. Multiple hard links can point to the same target file. If the hard link's target file is deleted from the target's original location, the content can still be accessed through any hard link that still points to the content. The file's content is preserved until the original file and all hard links that point to it are deleted.

A junction point is a special type of symbolic link that points to folders only. The path to the target folder must be specified using an absolute path. The absolute path points to a target that can be located without needing to know the location of the original junction point object. Windows 10 makes frequent use of junction points to organize and optimize system data such as user profile folders, for example. Most end users are not aware of, or recognize the use of, junction points.

Resilient File System (ReFS)

Resilient File System (ReFS) is a newer file system introduced with Windows Server 2012 that is included in Windows 10 but in a restricted capacity. It was originally envisioned as a candidate to replace NTFS as the default file system for persistent local storage. After many revisions, the capability to create ReFS volumes was removed from Window 10 v1709 (2017 Fall Creator's Update) except for Enterprise and Pro for Workstation editions. All versions of Windows 10 retain the capability to read and write to existing ReFS disks. ReFS is not a general-purpose file system that is ready to replace NTFS.

The ReFS file system on a Windows 10 system is complementary to the resilient nature of storage spaces. ReFS is designed to verify and autocorrect data faults on the volume without having to bring the volume down for maintenance. Data integrity and correction testing is performed routinely as a background task to ensure that the file system has the highest level of uptime possible. This is considered practical for advanced Windows 10 configurations in an enterprise but not for the typical small/medium business or consumer configuration.

ReFS cannot be used to format the system boot volume, or on removable media. Some NTFS features are not included in the current ReFS file system in Windows 10, including some major features such as 8.3 file name support, file and folder compression, disk quotas, extended attributes, and Encrypting File System (EFS).

Universal Disk Format (UDF)

The Universal Disk Format (UDF) is a file system developed as a standard to allow file interchange between different operating systems. This makes it ideal for storing files on portable CD-ROM and DVD media. Windows 10 supports both reading and writing of files to the UDF file system.

FILE SYSTEM TASKS

After a partition or volume is formatted with a file system, few changes to the filesystem's base configuration are possible. The most common file system changes are changing the assigned drive letter and converting the installed file system.

Changing Drive Letters

Drive letters are used by applications and users as a quick reference to locate files. A drive letter points to a partition or volume formatted with a file system.

Once a drive letter has been used to reference a particular group of files, users and their applications expect the same drive letter to be used when the files are accessed again. This is especially true for a drive where Windows and apps are installed. Changing the drive letter for those drives can result in a broken system or apps that fail to run.

In some instances, the drive letter assigned to a partition or volume must change. For example, a new application might be installed that requires a specific drive letter to access data files, perhaps to mirror old settings hard-coded into an application. You can change the drive letter, or assign a new one, to a partition or volume by using the Disk Management console.

 **CAUTION** Some partitions, such as recovery and system partitions, should not be assigned a drive letter, as they are not meant to be accessed by users.

When a new partition or volume is created, one of the New Simple Volume wizard's tasks asks if a drive letter should be assigned. Any unused drive letter can be selected. A single drive letter can be assigned to only one partition or volume.

Drive letters can also be removed from a partition or volume. If a drive letter is removed, the files might become inaccessible to the user.

Converting File Systems

The only file system conversion that you can perform in Windows 10 that retains data is converting a volume from FAT/FAT32 to NTFS. You can use the convert command-line utility for this purpose. You can also change the file system for a volume when you reformat the volume, but all data on the volume is deleted during this process.

To convert a FAT file system to NTFS, perform these general steps:

1. Back up the data on the partition.
2. Ensure free space remains on the partition.
3. Convert the partition using the convert command-line utility.

 **CAUTION** Any file system conversion has a risk of failure, and, as a best practice, before you start you should have a backup available to recover the data or roll back the change.

The convert command-line utility has the syntax of convert drive_id /FS:NTFS.

The drive_id is the drive letter, mount point, or volume name used to identify which partition to convert. The command-line option /FS:NTFS tells the utility to convert the existing file system to NTFS.

For example, the command to convert drive N: to NTFS is:

convert N: /FS:NTFS

Converting a partition requires that the convert utility runs with full administrative access to the local computer. If the file system is currently in use, the computer might have to reboot several times to complete the conversion process.

To retain data when you convert a ReFS or NTFS file system to FAT, perform the following general steps:

1. Back up the data on the partition.
2. Reformat the partition with FAT32.
3. Restore the data originally backed up from the NTFS partition.

FILE AND FOLDER ATTRIBUTES

When you view the properties of a file or folder you can see a variety of useful information, as shown in Figure 5-6. The details reported for the properties of a file or folder change slightly depending on the type of item, file, or folder, and the file system (FAT, NTFS, or ReFS). For the most part, however, they have the same general information.

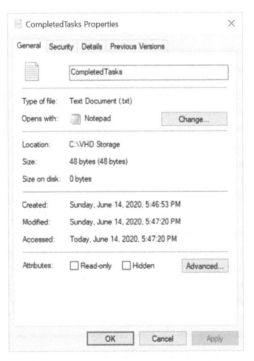

Figure 5-6 Properties of a file on an NTFS file system, General tab

A few items worth noting in the properties of a file:

- The Size and Size on disk are not exactly the same. This is because disk space is allocated based on the cluster size you chose when you formatted the drive.
- Created, Modified, and Accessed time can all be useful when trying to identify the current version of file that users are working on.
- If you modify the application that a file type opens with, it is changed for all files with that file extension, not just the file you are modifying.

Each file or folder also has attributes. Attributes control how the operating system interacts with the file or folder. For example, when the read-only attribute for a file is turned on, the contents of the file can't be modified. The General tab in the Properties of a file allows you to control the following attributes:

- Read-only—When a file is marked as read-only, the contents of the file can't be modified. When you turn on the read-only attribute for a folder, it configures existing files in that folder and subfolders as read-only. New files created in the folder will not have the read-only attribute enabled.
- Hidden—The hidden attribute controls visibility of the file when using File Explorer or other utilities. Files with the hidden attribute enabled are not visible by default, but you can configure File Explorer to show hidden files, as shown in Figure 5-7.

Figure 5-7   File Explorer, View tab, option to show hidden items

File Explorer also gives you access to advanced attributes. Figure 5-8 shows the advanced attributes available for a file on the NTFS file system. The advanced attributes are as follows:

- *File is ready for archiving*—The archive attribute is automatically enabled by Windows 10 when a file is modified. This attribute is used by backup software to identify files that should be backed up. You can manually enable or disable the archive attribute, but this is rarely required.
- *Allow this file to have contents indexed in addition to file properties*—You can disable this option to prevent the contents of a file from being indexed by Windows search. This affects search results returned by File Explorer.
- *Compress contents to save disk space*—When you enable the compress attribute on a file, a compression algorithm is applied by Windows 10 and storage space required by the file is reduced. When you enable the compress attribute on a folder, you get the option to compress existing files in that folder and all new files created in the folder have the compress attribute enabled by default.
- *Encrypt contents to secure data*—The encrypt attribute is used to secure file contents with Encrypting File System (EFS). By default, an EFS encrypted file is accessible only to the user that encrypts it, but access can be granted to additional users. When you enable the encrypt attribute on a folder, you get the option to encrypt existing files in that folder and all new files created in the folder have the encrypt attribute enabled by default.

TIP   You can't combine the compress and encrypt attributes.

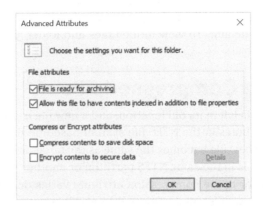

Figure 5-8   Properties of a file on an NTFS file system, General tab, Advanced Attributes

To make it easier to identify compressed and encrypted files and folders, they are displayed with a unique icon in File Explorer, as shown in Figure 5-9. Compressed files and folder have two arrows pointing at each other. Encrypted files and folders have a lock symbol.

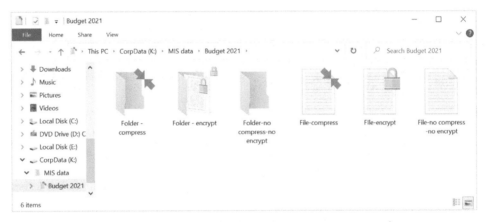

Figure 5-9   Modified icons to indicate compressed files and folders in File Explorer

The system attribute is used by Windows 10 to identify files that should not be accessed or modify by users. When a file has the system and hidden attributes set, it is not displayed by File Explorer unless you disable the Hide protected operating system files (Recommended) folder option. You cannot modify the system attribute by using File Explorer.

NOTE 11

For more information about EFS, see Module 6 Windows 10 Security Features.

Managing Attributes

Most attribute flags can be viewed in File Explorer as part of the object's properties. The **attrib** command-line utility is used to manage the System and other advanced attributes, such as no scrub and integrity attribute flags, which cannot be accessed using File Explorer (advanced attributes, such as no scrub and integrity are relevant only with the ReFS file system when it is used with Storage Spaces; therefore, it's not necessary to make those attributes generally available through File Explorer). The compression and encryption attribute flags cannot be managed by using the attrib command. Instead, the **compact** command-line utility is used to manage the compress attribute flag, and the **cipher** command-line utility is used to manage the encrypt attribute flag.

When you are at a command prompt and using the dir command, files or folders with the hidden attribute are not displayed by default. You can use dir to display files and folders with specific attributes set. For example, dir /as shows files and folders with the system attribute set.

In Windows PowerShell, the dir command is an alias for the Get-ChildItem cmdlet. The Get-ChildItem cmdlet does not show hidden files and folders by default. To view hidden files and folder, you need to use the -Force parameter, for example, Get-ChildItem -Force.

Copying and Moving Compressed Files

When a file is copied, the original file is left in its old location, and a new file is created in the target folder. The newly created file always receives new attributes in the NTFS file system based on the attributes of the target folder. This means the compress attribute on the new file becomes the same as the target folder's compress attribute setting. This is true whether the destination folder is in the same NTFS partition or another NTFS partition.

When a file is moved, the behavior of the compression attribute varies depending on whether the file is moved within the same partition or moved to a different partition. When a file is moved to a new location in the same NTFS partition, its attributes don't change. This means the compress attribute on the file remains the same regardless of the target folder default setting.

When a file is moved from its current location to a new location in a different NTFS partition, new attributes are created in the destination's NTFS system files. This means the compress attribute on the file becomes the same as the target folder's compress attribute setting.

 TIP When a file is copied or moved to a destination folder that does not support compression (formatted with the FAT or ReFS file system, for example), the new copy of the file is uncompressed.

FILE AND FOLDER PERMISSIONS

Every file and folder stored on an NTFS or ReFS partition has its own **access control list (ACL)**. Each **access control entry (ACE)** in the ACL identifies a specific user or group and what action they can perform to a file or folder. Each ACE uses a security identifier (SID) to identify the user or group, but the user interface for managing permissions displays the name of the user or group instead. Files and folders stored with other file systems such as FAT or FAT32 do not have an ACL. In the following section, note that NTFS permission settings apply equally to ReFS security.

NOTE 12

Refer to command-line parameters for the icacls utility by visiting https://docs.microsoft.com/windows-server/administration/windows-commands/icacls.

NTFS permissions apply security to files and folders that impact any user trying to access the object. This applies equally to local users and network users. For example, if the ACL in a file system specifies deny access to a file, then access is denied regardless of how the file is being accessed.

NTFS permissions are typically modified with File Explorer, but advanced changes can also be made from PowerShell using the cmdlets Get-ACL and Set-ACL, or the command-line utility **icacls**. The icacls utility is very powerful but can be cryptic in its usage.

 TIP The icacls utility parameter /reset can replace permissions with default inherited ACLs, which can be very useful if custom permissions are badly broken and need to be reset.

Windows 10 applies specific default permissions to folders when a partition is first formatted with the NTFS file system.

Default Folder Permissions

The first level of folder in an NTFS partition is the root folder. The default permissions assigned to this folder on the C: drive are as follows:

- Members of the computer's Administrators group have full control.
- The operating system has full control.

- Members of the computer's Users group have the ability to read and execute programs.
- Authenticated users have the ability to create folders in this folder.
- Authenticated users have the ability to create files and write data in subfolders only.

 TIP By default, users do not have the ability to create files in the root folder of the C: drive.

You can view the permission for a file or folder by using File Explorer. The Security tab in the Properties of the file or folder, shown in Figure 5-10, displays a summary of the permissions. Select a specific user or group to view the permissions assigned to that user or group.

Figure 5-10 Security tab for an NTFS drive's properties

The default permissions assigned to subfolders on the C: drive, and the root folder on all other NTFS partitions are as follows:

- Members of the computer's Administrators group have full control.
- The operating system has full control.
- Members of the computer's Users group have the ability to read and execute programs.
- Authenticated users have the ability to create, modify, and delete files and folders in this folder and its subfolders.

As additional folders and files are created, they inherit permissions from the parent object that contains them. Inheritance allows a permission setting to be configured at a higher level in the file system and have it propagate to lower subfolders and files.

NTFS permissions are assigned using the following two formats:

- Basic NTFS permissions
- Advanced NTFS permissions

NOTE 13

Basic NTFS permissions were called standard NTFS permissions in previous versions of Windows. Likewise, advanced NTFS permissions were called individual NTFS permissions in previous versions of Windows.

Basic NTFS Permissions

Basic NTFS permissions represent a collection of predetermined advanced NTFS permissions. The combination of advanced permissions provides a general level of access specific to the type of basic permission assigned. For example, the basic NTFS permission of Modify is a collection of advanced NTFS permissions that allows a file to be read, written to, renamed, or deleted. The names of basic NTFS permissions are meant to be intuitive and easy to understand. The basic NTFS permissions are listed in Table 5-4.

Table 5-4   Basic NTFS Permissions

Permission	Description
Write	This permission used for folders allows new files and folders to be created in the current folder. The folder attributes can be changed and the folder's ownership and security can be viewed.
	This permission used for files allows file data to be rewritten. The file's attributes can be changed and the file's ownership and security can be viewed.
Read	This permission used for folders allows files and folder data, attributes, ownership, and security to be viewed. This permission used for files allows the file's data, attributes, ownership, and security to be viewed.
List folder contents	This permission applies only to folders. Without this permission, the files and folders contained in a folder cannot be listed. The user or application can still access the files if they have permission and know the exact file or folder name.
Read & execute	This permission used for folders allows read access to files and folders below this point. This is the equivalent of enabling Read and List folder contents.
	This permission used for files allows read access to the file's information and, if it is an executable file, the user is allowed to run it. This permission automatically includes the Read permission.
Modify	This permission used for folders allows the same actions as Write and Read & execute permissions combined. The folder can also be deleted.
	This permission used for files allows the same actions as Write and Read & Execute permissions combined. Files can also be deleted.
Full Control	This permission used for folders allows the same actions as Modify plus the ability to change permissions and allow a user to take ownership of the folder.
	This permission used for files allows the same actions as Modify plus the ability to change permissions and allow a user to take ownership of the file.
Special permissions	Special permissions are the advanced permissions that can be assigned when the predefined basic permissions are not adequate to achieve desired results.

Advanced NTFS Permissions

Many advanced NTFS permissions exist to fine-tune access and control for files and folders. The list of advanced permissions is visible only when editing a permission entry in the Advanced security view, shown in Figure 5-11.

It is much more complex to configure advanced NTFS permissions because the name and purpose of the individual advanced permissions are often not intuitive. It is a best practice to use basic NTFS permissions wherever possible. This avoids complex special security settings that are unnecessarily difficult to manage.

Permission Scope

When an NTFS permission setting is applied to a file or folder, it also has a scope assigned. The scope determines what other objects are impacted by the assigned permission. For files, the scope is limited to this object only, which is just the file itself. For folders, you can configure the scope in the Applies to box of the advanced security view, as shown in Figure 5-12. When you configure basic NTFS permissions on a folder the scope is automatically configured as This folder, subfolders and files.

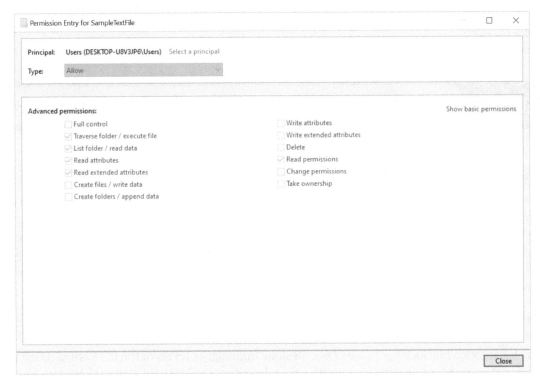

Figure 5-11   Viewing advanced NTFS permissions on a file for one ACL entry

Figure 5-12   Viewing advanced NTFS permissions on a folder for one ACL entry

For folders, the scope can be set to:

- This folder only
- This folder, subfolders, and files
- This folder and subfolders
- This folder and files

- Subfolders and files only
- Subfolders only
- Files only

 **CAUTION** Consider the permission scope carefully to ensure that you obtain the desired inheritance effect.

Permission Inheritance

NTFS permissions are inherited to files and subfolders based on the permission scope defined on the parent folder. Typically, permissions propagate from a parent folder to all files and folders below that point. When viewing the Permissions tab in advanced security settings for a folder, the Inherited from column shows where a permission setting was first applied, as shown in Figure 5-13. Further changes to those permission assignments automatically propagate through folders and files below that point. Any files created in those folders inherit permissions from the folder in which they are located.

Inheritance of permissions is convenient, but it might not be desired for all situations. Each file or folder has a Disable inheritance option in the Advanced Security Settings dialog box to disable inheritance of that object.

Disabling inheritance blocks inheritance of permissions from higher levels of the file system. Once inheritance is disabled, a prompt appears asking if the old inherited permissions should be copied to the object or removed entirely so that you can start with new permissions. If the previous permissions are copied, they provide a starting point and can be customized to meet any requirements. If the permissions are removed, new permissions must be configured from scratch.

Any file or folder can have additional permissions assigned directly to the object that combine with the inherited permissions. This combination of inheritance and explicit permissions at any level allows for flexibility, but you must be very careful that the combination of permissions gives you the desired security result.

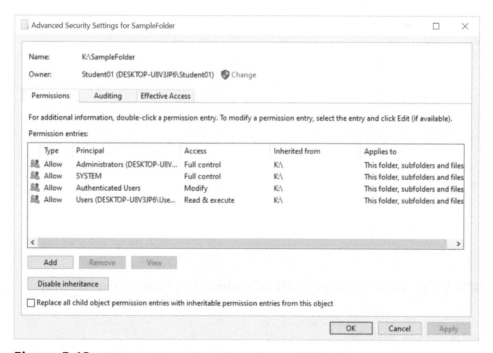

Figure 5-13 Advanced security settings for an NTFS folder

Effective Permissions

Effective permissions are the combination of permissions assigned to the user and permissions assigned to groups that the user is a member of. You need to add the user and group permissions to determine the effective permissions. If a user is assigned read permission and a group the user is a member of is assigned write permission, then the effective permissions for the user are read and write.

 TIP   Permissions assigned to groups are easier to manage and audit than assigning permissions directly to users. The user's group membership is much easier to manage than remembering all the places that need to be updated in the file system's permissions.

Effective permissions include permissions directly assigned to the file and folder, as well as inherited permissions. If permissions are assigned directly to a file for a specific user, then those permissions override any inherited permissions that were assigned for that user. For example, if a user is assigned full control permissions to a folder and the user is also assigned read permission directly to a file inside that folder, then the effective permission is Read, because it is changing the user specific permission. If some of the permissions are assigned to a group and some permissions are assigned to the user, then they're not overridden. For example, if the Users group is assigned full control permissions to a folder and the user is assigned read permission directly to a file inside that folder, then the effective permission is full control.

You also need to consider that permissions can allow permissions or deny permissions. When some permissions are allow and other permissions are deny, you need to understand the order of precedence:

1. Explicit deny
2. Explicit allow
3. Inherited deny
4. Inherited allow

Some other considerations for permissions are as follows:

- Each permission has a scope that determines what range of objects to which it applies.
- Users that do not have explicit permission assigned to an object and are not part of any inherited permission have no permission to the object.
- Users can be members in multiple groups that have different permissions to the same object.
- Owners of a file or folder have full control of the object.

To simplify the analysis of effective permissions, the Advanced Security Settings window for any file or folder includes an Effective Access tab, as shown in Figure 5-14. When you select a user or group on the Effective Access tab, the advanced NTFS permissions which are effective for that group or user are displayed. This tool doesn't show how those effective permissions were obtained; it shows only what they are. You still need to review permissions on folders above to identify how the permissions were obtained.

 **CAUTION**   The Effective Access tab in a file or folder's Advanced Security Settings does not include ownership as part of its effective permission calculations.

Ownership

Each NTFS file or folder has an owner assigned to it. The owner of a file or folder always has the ability to assign permissions to that file or folder, regardless of which existing permissions are assigned. This ensures that the owner can always assign himself Full control permission and modify a file.

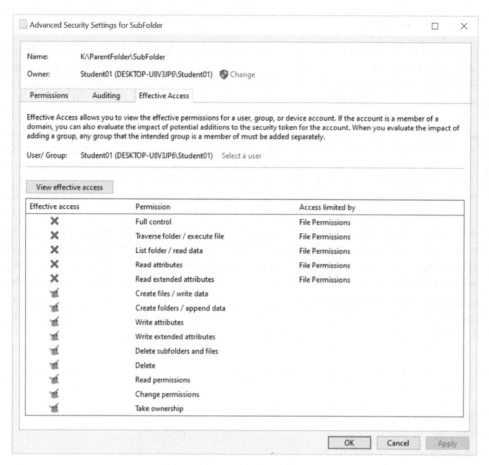

Figure 5-14   Effective Access tab in advanced file or folder security settings

Members of the Administrators group have the right, by default, to assign or take ownership of a file or folder. Users with the Full control basic permission or the advanced NTFS permission Take ownership can also assume ownership of a file.

You can view or modify the owner of a file or folder in the Advanced Security Settings window when using File Explorer. At a command prompt, you can use the icacls or **takeown** utilities to configure ownership. In Windows PowerShell, you can use the Get-Acl and Set-Acl cmdlets to view and modify ownership.

Permission Changes when Content Is Copied or Moved

When files and folders are first created in a volume that is formatted with NTFS, they take on the permission settings of the folder in which they are created. Copy operations always create new versions of the content that is being copied. Those new versions take on the permission settings of the target location, which might be different than the permission settings of the source content. Move operations affect permissions differently depending on the destination location relative to the source location.

Each single volume or partition formatted with the NTFS file system has its own database to track permissions and attributes for each file and folder it stores. When files and folders are moved from one location on the volume to another location on the same volume, new content is not created; only pointers to the content are moved in the database. In that case, the destination content keeps whatever permissions it originally had, regardless of the destination folder's permissions.

When files and folders are moved from one volume to a different volume formatted with NTFS, new content is created in the destination location. Just like a copy operation, the new content takes on the permission settings of the target location. Any permission settings assigned to the source content are lost.

Permission Strategy Considerations

Assigning and managing file permissions is seldom required for computers running Windows 10. Administrators have full access to the entire file system as required for any maintenance. Users have full access to their own profiles to store documents and application data. Users do not have access to the profiles of other users or the ability to modify system files. In the vast majority of scenarios, this is what you want.

In rare cases, an application might require you to modify the file system permissions to run properly. For example, some applications that use a nonstandard update process require you to give users modify permission to the application folder. Then, the user is able to run the script that copies files and updates the application.

Most of the detailed considerations about applying file and folder permissions are more relevant for configuring permissions on a shared folder on a server. On a server, you might have a shared folder with multiple folders inside it. Each of the folders in the shared folder might have different permissions for different departments.

Activity 5-9: Managing File and Folder Permissions

Time Required: 30 minutes

Objective: Configure a new folder with unique NTFS security settings

Description: In this activity, you create a new folder called Marketing Documents on the C: drive. The default permissions are removed and replaced with permissions that allow only your user account to access the folder. You then create a file in the folder and investigate its resulting inherited permissions.

1. You should already be signed in from the previous activity.
2. Right-click the **Start** button and then click **File Explorer**.
3. In the left pane, click **Local Disk (C:)**.
4. Create a new folder called **Marketing Documents** in C:\.
5. Right-click the **Marketing Documents** folder and then click **Properties**.
6. In the Marketing Documents Properties dialog box, click the **Security** tab and review the users and groups assigned permissions.
7. Click the **Advanced** button and review the specific permissions that have been applied to the users and groups.
8. In the Advanced Security Settings for Marketing Documents dialog box, click the **Effective Access** tab.
9. Click the **Select a user link** to display the Select User or Group dialog box.
10. Type your user name and then click **OK** to continue.
11. Click the **View effective access** button. On the Effective Access tab, notice which advanced NTFS permissions have a check mark next to them. You have all available permissions because your account is a local administrator.
12. Note the current owner of the folder. Your account is the owner of the folder because you created it. Click the **Change** link to the right of the name in the Owner field.
13. In the Select User or Group dialog box, type **Administrators** and then click **OK** to change the owner of the folder to the local Administrators group and any user that belongs to that group.
14. Select the **Replace owner on subcontainers and objects** check box.
15. If necessary, click the **Change Permissions** button to enable the controls for changing permissions.
16. Click the **Disable inheritance** button.
17. In the Block Inheritance warning dialog box, click **Remove all inherited permissions from this object** to start with blank security settings for the Marketing Documents folder.
18. Click the **Add** button in the Advanced Security dialog box to display the **Permission Entry** dialog box.
19. Click **Select a principal** link.
20. Enter your user name and then click **OK** to continue.
21. In the list of basic permissions, place a check next to the **Full control** permission.
22. Note that all other basic permissions are automatically assigned and that the permission scope is set to **This folder, subfolder and files**.
23. Click **OK** to continue.
24. Note the new permission entry on the Permissions tab in the Advanced Security Settings dialog box.
25. Notice that the Inherited from column shows as None for the directly assigned permission.
26. Click **OK** to close the Advanced Security Settings dialog box.

27. Click **OK** to close the Marketing Documents Properties dialog box. This is required to refresh the contents of that window.
28. Right-click the **Marketing Documents** folder and then click **Properties**.
29. Click to select the **Security** tab. Notice the new permission setting and the simpler view.
30. Click **OK** to close the Marketing Documents Properties dialog box.
31. Create a new text document called **First Quarter Report.txt** in the **C:\Marketing Documents** folder.
32. Right-click **First Quarter Report.txt**, click **Properties**, and then click the **Security** tab. Notice that the permissions from the Marketing Documents folder are inherited by this file, as indicated by the grey check marks.
33. Click **Cancel** and close all windows and dialog boxes.
34. To release all open and attached VHDs, plus the active storage pool created with virtual disks, restart your computer. These virtual disks will not reattach automatically the next time you sign in.

FILE SHARING

Windows 10 provides multiple ways to share files from one computer to another. The best method for sharing files will depend on the scenario. For example, the Share tab in File Explorer is a simple interface for sharing individual files, but shared folders are a better mechanism for keeping many files in a central location.

> **⊘ CAUTION** Early versions of Windows 10 included the HomeGroup feature to simplify file sharing in a home or workgroup environment. This feature was removed in Windows 10 version 1803, but you might still find documentation that references it.

Sharing Individual Files

The Share tab in File Explorer, shown in Figure 5-15, is designed for users with basic needs, users who are not trying to fine-tune or tweak shared item security. It simply enables the users to get what they want—the selected file(s) sent to somewhere or someone else. This method of file sharing sends a copy of the file to the recipient. If you update the source file, the recipient won't get the updated version unless you send it again.

Figure 5-15   Share tab in File Explorer

After selecting the files you want to share, click the Share button to select a sharing method. It will open a window, as shown in Figure 5-16, where:

- The recipient can be selected from the signed in user's contact list and a copy is sent via email.
- The content is shared through Bluetooth or Wi-Fi. For this feature to work, nearby sharing must be enabled in Setting's Shared experiences, as shown in Figure 5-17.
- Files can be shared via an app, such as OneNote, Mail, or Skype. Additional apps like Dropbox can be added to the list of Apps by visiting the Microsoft Store.

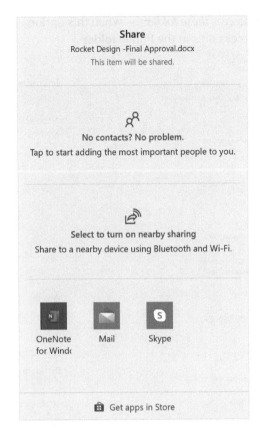

Figure 5-16   File Explorer, Share tab, Send group, Share option, possible recipients

Figure 5-17   Settings app, System, Shared experiences

You can also access these file sharing options by right-clicking a local file in File Explorer and then clicking Share on the shortcut menu. This is a convenience for quickly sharing files—if you right-click a local folder you will not see that option.

> **⊙ CAUTION**   If you right-click a file in a folder that is synchronized with OneDrive, you may see a cloud symbol next to the word Share on the shortcut menu. Selecting this opens a window to craft a custom link that you can send to someone, which they will use to access the shared content in that user's OneDrive. This is not the same Share experience mentioned earlier for local files, and the link can be used with folders and files.

Sharing the Public Folder

The Public folder is typically located at C:\Users\Public. Sharing the Public folder is a simplified way to perform file sharing on home and small office networks. By default, all files in the Public folder are shared among users who sign in sitting at the same local computer, giving those users a way to share data locally. The Public folder, however, can also be shared with network users. Sharing for the Public folder is configured by using the Public folder sharing option in Advanced sharing settings in the Network and Sharing Center, as shown in Figure 5-18.

The options for sharing the Public folder are as follows:

- *Turn on sharing so that anyone with network access can read and write files in the Public folders*—When this option is selected, all network users are able to read, change, delete, and create files in the Public folder. A Public folder configured this way could be used as a central storage location for business documents in a small business to ensure that files can be easily found and are able to be backed up each night.

- *Turn off Public folder sharing (people signed in on this computer can still access these folders)*—When this option is selected, only local users (i.e., those sitting at the computer) can access files in the Public folder.

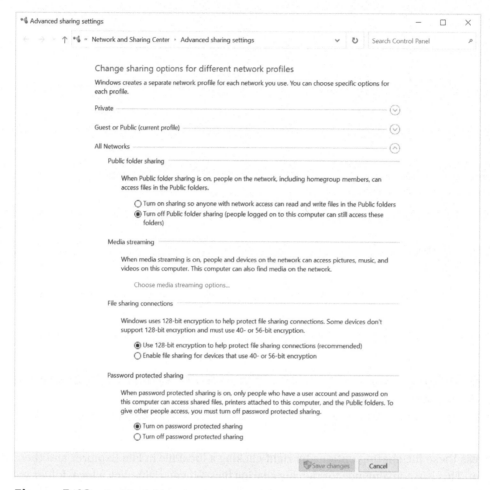

Figure 5-18   Public folder sharing controls

You also have options for Password protected sharing that also apply to the Public folder, also shown in Figure 5-18. Password protection offers two options. These options also apply to other shared folders and printers.

- *Turn on password protected sharing*—When this option is selected, network users must sign in to the sharing computer by using a user account that has been granted access to the sharing computer. The account can be either a local user account or a domain user account. This allows you to restrict access to the shared Public folder to valid user accounts, but you cannot select which user accounts have access. All valid user accounts are able to access the shared Public folder.
- *Turn off password protected sharing*—When this option is selected, anyone can access the information in the Public folder, even if they do not have a valid user account on the sharing computer. Effectively, this allows anonymous users access to the Public folder.

Creating and Managing Shared Folders

Sharing files from specific folders on your computer gives you more options to manage which users have access to those files and what those users can do to those files. You can set the permissions for users when you share individual folders. For example, in a small business, the users in your project team may be given permission to view and change your shared project files, but your other coworkers are able only to view the files.

The ability to configure shared folder permissions may be confusing for inexperienced users, but for experienced users the level of control allows you to configure file sharing just the way you want it. In a domain-based network, you can select users from the domain to share files with. In a workgroup-based network, you must create local accounts for the users you want to share files with. For example, if you want to share files with Bob, who signs in to another computer, you must create a user account for Bob on your Windows 10 computer, and then give the local user Bob permission to access files.

Simplified Folder Sharing

Simplified folder sharing provides a limited set of security options to configure shared folders. The folder sharing wizard, shown in Figure 5-19, manages the shared folder settings and NTFS permissions based on the options that you select. This hides the details behind a user-friendly interface that is suitable for end users without complex needs.

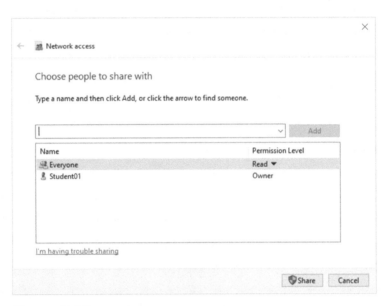

Figure 5-19   Folder sharing wizard

The folder sharing wizard contains an arrow that you can use to select the users or groups to which you want to assign permissions. By default, only the Everyone group and local user accounts are displayed in the list. If you want to add other users or groups, you need to type the user or group name instead of selecting from the list. The following permission levels are shown in the folder sharing wizard:

- Owner—This identifies the user that is the owner of the folder. You can't assign which user is the owner; this permission is just displayed.
- Read/Write—This permission grants users the Full Control NTFS permission.
- Read—This permission grants users the Read & Execute NTFS permission.

 **CAUTION**   The NTFS permissions configured by the folder sharing wizard remove any existing NTFS permissions in the folder being shared and any subfolders.

After the folder sharing wizard creates the share, it displays the Universal Naming Convention (UNC) path for the shared folder. The UNC path includes the name of the Windows 10 computer and the name of the share. For example, \\Desktop48\Data. You need to give this UNC path to other users so that they know where to access the shared folder over the network.

The folder sharing wizard can be triggered in multiple ways:

- Use the Share button on the Share tab in the Properties of a folder.
- Right-click a folder, point to Give access to, and select Specific people.
- Select Specific people in the Share with area on the Share tab in File Explorer.

Advanced Folder Sharing

Advanced folder sharing allows you precise control over the permissions assigned to the shared folder and the NTFS permissions in the file system. The interface for advanced folder sharing allows you to configure only the share permissions. You need to configure the NTFS permissions as a separate task. You access advanced folder sharing by clicking the Advanced Sharing button on the Sharing tab in the Properties dialog box of a folder, as shown in Figure 5-20.

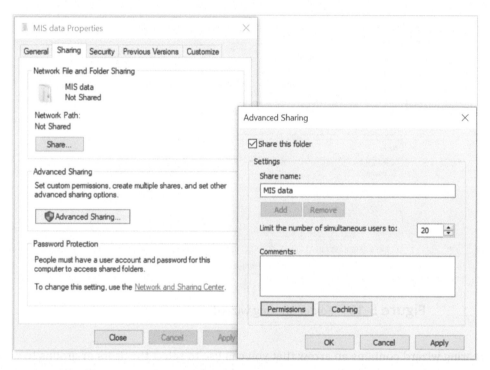

Figure 5-20 Folder properties, Advanced Sharing

Following are the settings you can configure in Advanced Sharing:

- *Share this folder*—This option enables the folder as shared.
- *Share name*—This option allows you to specify one or more names that the folder is shared as. By default, the share name matches the folder name. Users access the shared folder by using the UNC path \\computername\ sharename. Each additional share name is associated with its own set of shared folder permissions and limits on concurrent users. For example, if the folder has two share names, it is accessible using two different UNC paths. The UNC path a user uses to access the shared folder will determine which shared folder permission and limits apply to that shared folder connection over the network.

 TIP Share names ending in a dollar sign ($) are hidden shares that cannot be seen by browsing the network. You can use the dollar sign at the end of your own shared folder names so that the folder will be accessible only if the user knows the appropriate UNC path to use. This is not considered a strong security mechanism alone, as there are numerous ways to discover these so-called hidden shares.

- *Limit the number of simultaneous users to*—Windows 10 supports up to 20 concurrent connections from network users. With this setting, you can reduce this to a lower number to ensure that the computer is not overwhelmed by network users; however, this is typically not done because sharing files has very little effect on performance.
- *Comments*—This box contains text that is displayed for users when they view the share on the network. Typically, the text describes the content in the shared folder.
- *Permissions*—This button lets you configure the share permissions for the shared folder.
- *Caching*—This button lets you control how network clients cache files from this share as offline files. You can prevent file caching, allow users to select files for caching, or force file caching. Caching files for offline use is typically done only for mobile computers.

When you configure share permissions, the permissions can be allow or deny permissions, as shown in Figure 5-21. When a permission is denied, it overrides any permissions that are allowed. For example, if the Everyone group is given Read permission and the user Bob is denied Read permission, Bob will not have access to the share.

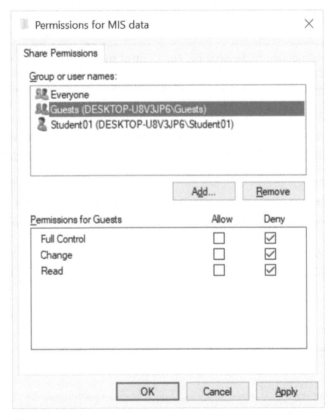

Figure 5-21   Folder properties, Advanced Sharing, Permissions

The share permissions available in Windows 10 are the following:

- *Full Control*—Allows users complete control over files and folders in the share and sets permissions on files and folders in the share. In addition, Full Control allows users to configure the share permissions on the shared folder.
- *Change*—Allows users complete control to create, modify, and delete files in the shared folder, but not to set permissions.
- *Read*—Allows users to read the contents of files in the shared folder, but not to modify the files in any way.

If the local file system does not support additional security, for example the FAT file system, the shared folder permissions are the only security settings that apply when that folder is accessed from the network. The Security tab won't even show up on the folder's properties, only the Sharing tab. That's why most administrators prefer the custom security provided by combining shared folder permissions with local NTFS file and folder permissions.

Some special considerations should be taken when shared folder permissions combine with NTFS permissions—the most restrictive permissions are effective when the file is accessed over the network. If the user is sitting at the keyboard and signing in locally (i.e., interactively), only the NTFS file and folder permissions apply.

For example, if a user is assigned Read share permissions and Full control NTFS permissions, the user will have only read access when accessing the folder over the network. If a user is assigned Full Control share permissions and Read NTFS permissions, the user will also have only read access when accessing the folder over the network. Both of these permission combinations result in the same effective permission for accessing files in the folder over the network—read; however, consider that when the user signs in directly to that computer, the user's permission to the folder and its contents are different in each case.

To simplify the management of permissions, you can assign the Full Control share permission to the Everyone group and then use NTFS permissions to apply more restrictive access to the folders and files in the shared folder. This has the added benefit of ensuring that user permissions are the same for accessing folders and files whether a user accesses the content over the network or by signing in to the local computer.

 TIP When you use simplified folder sharing, Full Control share permissions are assigned and NTFS permissions are used to control access.

Create A Shared Folder Wizard

Computer Management includes the capability to create, manage, and monitor shared folders. When you create a shared folder from within Computer Management, it triggers the Create A Shared Folder Wizard.

 TIP The Create A Shared Folder Wizard can also be running the shrpubw.exe utility.

You can select an existing local folder or create a new folder on the computer with this wizard. Once a folder is selected, the options to configure for the share, shown in Figure 5-22, are similar to the advanced sharing wizard's configuration options.

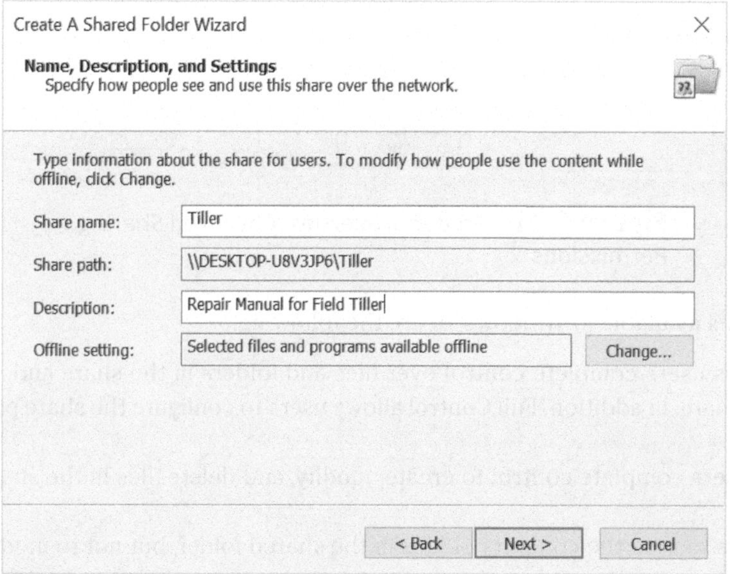

Figure 5-22 Create A Shared Folder Wizard, Specify folder settings

The Create A Shared Folder Wizard will ask if you want to configure one of the more common shared folder permission combinations or enable you to configure custom permissions that conveniently include shared folder permissions and NTFS file permissions, as shown in Figure 5-23.

 **CAUTION** This wizard can be used to create multiple shares for the same local folder, but you do not manage existing shared folder settings from here—you must use the advanced sharing button from the shared folder's properties.

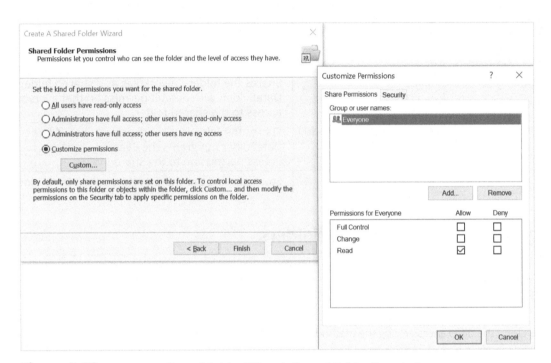

Figure 5-23 Create A Shared Folder Wizard, Shared Folder Permissions

PowerShell for Sharing Folders

You can use Windows PowerShell cmdlets to create and manage shared folders. It is more common to use graphical tools, but if you need to automate the creation of shared folder on multiple computers, then using the cmdlets can be useful. The cmdlets include Smb because Windows 10 file sharing is based on the **Server Message Block (SMB)** protocol. The primary cmdlets for managing shared folders are listed in Table 5-5.

Table 5-5 PowerShell Cmdlets for Managing Shared Folders

PowerShell Cmdlet	Description
Get-SmbShare	Retrieves the properties of the SMB shares on the computer.
Get-SmbShareAccess	Retrieves the share permissions of the SMB share.
Grant-SmbShareAccess	Adds or modifies share permissions for a user or group.
New-SmbShare	Creates an SMB share.
Remove-SmbShare	Deletes the specified SMB share.
Revoke-SmbShareAccess	Removes the share permissions for a user or group.
Set-SmbShare	Modifies the properties of the SMB share.

Net Commands to Share Folders

The **net command-line utility** is a legacy tool that can be used to perform a wide variety of tasks, such as creating users and creating shared folders. You might see this utility used in older scripts that were created many years ago but are still in use. Examples of net commands to manage shared folders are listed in Table 5-6.

 **CAUTION**   The net command-line tool still works with Windows 10; however, it has been deprecated since Windows 8.

Table 5-6   Net Command Examples for Managing Shared Folders

Example Net Commands	Description
Net Share DataFolder=C:\workfiles	Shares the folder C:\workfiles as a shared folder called DataFolder, with default permission that everyone has read access to the shared folder.
Net Share DataFolder=C:\workfiles /grant:everyone,full	Shares the folder C:\workfiles as a shared folder called DataFolder but grants the Everyone built-in group full access permission to the shared folder.
Net Share DataFolder /delete	Stops sharing the shared folder called DataFolder.

Activity 5-10: Creating Shared Folders

Time Required: 15 minutes

Objective: Create shared folders for network users

Description: Multiple methods are available to create shared folders. To ensure that shared folders meet your needs, you need to understand the differences among the methods for creating shared folders. In this activity, you create shared folders using multiple methods.

1. If necessary, start your computer and sign in.
2. Right-click the **Start** button and then click **File Explorer**. In the left pane, click to select the **Documents** location.
3. Right-click the empty area in the right pane, point to **New**, and then click **Folder**.
4. Type **SimpleShare1** and then press **Enter**.
5. Click **SimpleShare1** and then click the **Share** menu on the toolbar.
6. Select **Specific people** in the Share with area on the toolbar. Click the arrow in the box next to the Add button, click **Everyone**, and then click the **Add** button. Notice that the default permission given to Everyone is Read.
7. To the right of Everyone, click **Read** and then click to select **Read/Write**. This allows Everyone to modify files.
8. Click the **Share** button.
9. If you are prompted to turn on network discovery and file sharing for all public networks, click **Yes, turn on network discovery and file sharing for all public networks**. This is a suitable choice for a lab environment, but this would likely not be a good idea if the computer were going to be used in an untrusted environment, such as an Internet café.
10. Read the results in the File Sharing window. Notice that the UNC path for this share is long and goes through the C:\Users folder. All folders shared by using simple file sharing in your Documents folder use this long UNC path.
11. Click **Done**.
12. In the File Explorer window currently displaying the Documents library, double-click **Local Disk (C:)** below Computer in the left pane.
13. Right-click an open area in the right-hand pane, point to **New**, and then click **Folder**.
14. Type **SimpleShare2** and then press **Enter**.

15. Right-click an open area, point to **New**, and then click **Folder**.
16. Type **AdvancedShare** and then press **Enter**.
17. Right-click **SimpleShare2**, point to **Give access to**, and then click **Specific people**.
18. On the Choose people to share with screen, click the arrow, click **Everyone** in the list, and then click the **Add** button.
19. To the right of Everyone, click **Read** and then click **Read/Write**.
20. Click the **Share** button.
21. On the Your folder is shared screen, read the results and notice that the UNC path is directly to the shared folder when the folder is not inside your Documents folder.
22. Click **Done**.
23. Right-click the **AdvancedShare** folder and then click **Properties**.
24. Click the **Sharing** tab and then click **Advanced Sharing**.
25. Select the **Share this folder** check box. Notice that the Share name setting is the same name as the folder by default, but it can be changed.
26. Click the **Permissions** button to view the share permissions.
27. Select the **Allow** check box next to the **Change** permission and then click **OK**. This allows all users to modify files through the share, but not to change the share permissions.
28. Click **OK** to close the Advanced Sharing dialog box.
29. Click the **Security** tab and then click the **Edit** button.
30. Click **Add**, type **Everyone**, click **Check Names**, and then click **OK**.
31. In the Group or user names box, click **Everyone** to select the built-in group.
32. In the Permissions for Everyone box, select the **Allow** option next to the **Modify** permission and then click **OK**. NTFS permissions work with the share permissions to control what tasks a user is able to perform on a network share. These steps have configured the Everyone group and its members to have the same permission to the folder when accessed over the network, and locally at the keyboard, granting read/write access to its contents.
33. Click **Close** to close the AdvancedShare Properties dialog box.
34. Close all open windows and/or dialog boxes.

Monitoring Shared Folders

Over time, you might lose track of all the folders that are shared on your computer. You can use PowerShell cmdlets, net commands, and the Computer Management console to review what is shared and who is connecting to it.

PowerShell to Monitor Shared Folders

The primary PowerShell cmdlets for managing SMB-based shares are listed in Table 5-7. Using PowerShell cmdlets for folder monitoring requires administrative rights to the computer.

Table 5-7   PowerShell Cmdlets for Monitoring Shared Folders

PowerShell Cmdlet	Description
Get-SmbConnection	Retrieves the connections established from the SMB client to an SMB server.
Get-SmbOpenFile	Retrieves basic information about the files that are open on behalf of the clients of the SMB server.
Get-SmbSession	Retrieves information about the sessions that are currently established between the SMB server and the associated clients.
Get-SmbShare	Retrieves the SMB shares on the computer.
Get-SmbShareAccess	Retrieves the Access Control List of the SMB share.

Net Commands to Monitor Shared Folders

Viewing shared folder details from the command prompt can be accomplished with the legacy net command, even without administrative rights to the computer. Examples of net commands to monitor shared folders are listed in Table 5-8.

Computer Management to Monitor Shared Folders

The most comprehensive way to monitor shares is by using Computer Management, shown in Figure 5-24. The Shared Folders system tool has the following three nodes for monitoring and managing shared folders:

Table 5-8   Net Command Examples for Monitoring Shared Folders

Example Net Commands	Description
Net Session	Displays information about all sessions with the local computer, including computer names, user names, number of files open, and session idle time.
Net Share	Displays information about all the resources that are shared on the local computer.
Net view \\localhost	Displays a list of resources that are being shared by the specified computer.
Net view \\localhost /ALL	Displays a list of resources that are being shared by the specified computer, including the hidden shares with $ at the end of their name.

- *Shares*—This node allows you to create new shares, configure existing shared folders, and optionally stop sharing them. It shows all of the shared folders on this computer, including hidden shares. The summary view here even allows you to see how many clients are connected to each share.
- *Sessions*—This node allows you to see which users are connected to this computer. The summary view shows which computer each user is connecting from, how many files each user has open, and how long each user has been connected. If your system has the maximum of 20 sessions already connected and you need to allow another user access, you can disconnect an existing session from here.
- *Open Files*—This node allows you to see which files and folders are opened through file shares on this computer. You can see which users have the files open and whether the file is open for writing. Occasionally, due to system problems, users will be disconnected from files, but Windows 10 keeps the file locked. You can force a file to close here so that it can be reopened and modified.

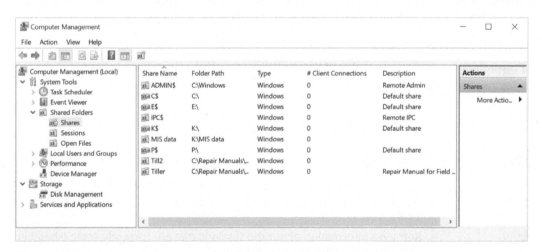

Figure 5-24   Shares view in Computer Management

Activity 5-11: Monitoring Shared Folders

Time Required: 5 minutes

Objective: Monitor shared folders by using Computer Management

Description: When you share folders on your computer, it is useful to see who is using those files. For example, if you want to reboot your computer, you must be sure that no files are open. Rebooting a computer with shared files open can corrupt the files. In this activity, you monitor shared folders on your computer.

1. If necessary, start your computer and sign in.
2. Right-click the **Start** button and then click **Computer Management**.
3. In the left pane, expand **Shared Folders** and then click **Shares**. This displays all the shares on your computer, including the hidden shares. You can see the Users, SimpleShare2, and AdvancedShare shares from previous activities. You can also see the number of clients connected to each share and the folder each is sharing.
4. Right-click **SimpleShare2** and then click **Properties**. The General tab allows you to configure the name of the share, description, user limit, and offline settings.
5. Click the **Share Permissions** tab and then, if necessary, click **Everyone**. This tab allows you to configure the share permissions for the share. Notice that the Everyone group has Full Control.
6. Click the **Security** tab, and in the Group or user names box, if necessary, click **Everyone**. This tab displays the NTFS permissions for the folder. Notice that Everyone has Full Control NTFS permissions. These NTFS permissions were automatically configured by the Grant access to simple sharing wizard in the previous activity.
7. Click **Cancel** to close the SimpleShare2 Properties dialog box.
8. In the left pane of the Computer Management window, click **Sessions**. The Sessions folder shows you which users are connected to your computer and from which computer they are connected.
9. In the left pane of Computer Management, click **Open Files**. The Open Files folder shows you which files and folders are open on your computer and by which user.
10. Close all open windows.

SUMMARY

- Windows 10 supports internal, external, virtual, and pooled disks (dynamic and Storage Spaces).
- Windows 10 supports MBR and GPT partition styles to organize data into partitions and volumes on physical and virtual disks.
- Disk management tools include the Disk Management Tools, Diskpart, and storage cmdlets in Windows PowerShell.
- When you add a new physical disk to a computer, you might need to adjust firmware settings or scan for new drives. You also need to initialize the new disk to define the partition style for the disk. When you move a physical disk to a new computer, initialization is not required.
- VHDs are natively supported by Windows 10 and can be managed as a basic disk once the VHD is attached in the operating system. VHD files can either be a fixed size or allowed to grow dynamically to a maximum size. You need to attach a VHD in Windows to view and modify the contents.
- Storage Spaces technology is software based and is used to combine physical disk drives into a managed storage pool, which is then used to create virtual volumes from that combined space. Depending on the number of physical disks in the pool, Storage Spaces volumes can be created with a selected resiliency level.

- The NTFS file system is preferred in Windows 10 because it supports advanced features, such as security, ownership, disk quotas, compression, and encryption that FAT does not. Small partitions can still benefit from the legacy support and simplicity of FAT. ReFS has a subset of NTFS features but does not support disk quotas, compression, or encryption.
- When you format a partition or volume, you select a drive letter and a file system. It is possible to change the drive letter afterwards if required. You can also convert use the convert utility to change the file system from FAT to NFTS without data loss.
- Files stored in FAT, ReFS, and NTFS partitions use attributes to control and limit file access. Some attributes are: read-only, hidden, archive, compress, and encrypt.
- Given an NTFS-formatted source location, a copy operation will create content in a destination location. A move operation will only create content in a destination location when the destination is in a different NTFS volume. Newly created content will take on the permissions of the destination folder in which they were created.
- NTFS and ReFS share a security model that is configured by assigning permissions to users or groups. Basic permissions are suitable for most scenarios, but advanced permissions can be used for more specific control if required. To properly calculate effective permissions, make sure that you understand permission scope and inheritance.
- File sharing allows you to share files and folders on one computer with another user on a different computer. The Share button in File Explorer allows you to send individual files. Simplified and advanced folder sharing make a folder and its contents available over the network. Advanced folder sharing allows you to configure share permissions and NTFS permissions separately.

Key Terms

access control entry (ACE)	fsutil	Server Message Block (SMB)
access control list (ACL)	GUID Partition Table (GPT)	storage pool
attrib	hard link	Storage Spaces
basic disk	icacls	Storage Spaces volume
cipher	initialize	symbolic link
compact	junction point	takeown
Disk Management console	Master Boot Record (MBR)	Universal Naming Convention
disk quotas	MBR2GPT	(UNC) path
DiskPart	mklink	virtual hard disk (VHD)
dynamic disks	net command-line utility	volume mount points
Encrypting File System (EFS)	New Technology File System (NTFS)	volumes
File Allocation Table (FAT)	partition table	
Foreign Disk	Resilient File System (ReFS)	

Review Questions

1. A user has been given Full Control permission to a shared folder. The user has been given Modify permission at the NTFS level to that folder and its contents. What is that user's effective permissions to that folder when they access it through the shared folder from another computer?
   a. Full Control
   b. Modify
   c. Read
   d. No access

2. Which sharing method should you recommend if a user wants to configure share and NTFS permissions for another user that wants to access a folder on their computer in a single simple process?
   a. Public folder sharing
   b. Grant access to
   c. Advanced sharing
   d. Create A Shared Folder Wizard

3. Which sharing method does not allow you to pick the folder that is being shared?

    a. Public folder sharing

    b. Simple sharing

    c. Advanced sharing

    d. Create A Shared Folder Wizard

4. What is the most accurate way to view all the shares on your system?

    a. Browse your computer on the network.

    b. View the shares in Computer Management.

    c. Use the Show me all the shared network folders on this computer link.

    d. Use the Show me all the files and folders I am sharing link.

    e. View the shares in the Network and Sharing Center.

5. Which type of startup firmware best supports Windows 10 with regard to device operation and management?

    a. BIOS

    b. GPT

    c. UEFI

    d. MBR

6. A VHD has been created using the Disk Management utility. Before the newly created VHD can be used to store files, it must be _____.

    a. detached

    b. configured as a dynamic disk

    c. set to GPT partition style

    d. initialized

    e. set to MBR partition style

7. A storage _____ acts as a logical container grouping multiple physical disks.

8. You have just plugged a USB portable hard drive into an older laptop and the disk has not appeared as available. You are concerned that the hard disk controller hardware has not been recognized by the computer. Which utility would you use to verify that the controller is functioning correctly?

    a. DiskPart

    b. Disk Management console

    c. USB Management console

    d. Device Manager

    e. none of the above

9. The number of physical disks required to implement three-way resilience for a Storage Spaces volume is _____.

    a. 1

    b. 2

    c. 3

    d. 5

    e. 7

10. The preferred technology to set up disk storage with mirrored fault tolerance for a user's backup data is _____

    a. basic disks

    b. dynamic disks

    c. hardware-based RAID 5

    d. Storage Spaces

    e. hardware-based RAID 1

11. An NTFS partition has disk quotas enabled. You would like to run a weekly report that summarizes how much space each user is consuming. The _____ utility allows you to review quota details from the command line.

    a. convert

    b. fsutil

    c. get-diskquota

    d. diskpart

    e. dsquota

12. Windows 10 supports locally encrypted files stored on these types of partitions (Select all that apply).

    a. NTFS

    b. ReFS

    c. FAT

    d. FAT32

13. The _____ file system is the only one that supports file compression in Windows 10.

    a. FAT32

    b. ReFS

    c. NTFS

    d. FAT

14. A file is currently compressed in its local file system. For security reasons, the file is required to be encrypted. The file can be both compressed and encrypted. True or False?

    a. True

    b. False

15. A user is given Read permission to a file stored on an NTFS-formatted volume. The file is then moved to a different folder on a different NTFS-formatted

volume where the user has been given Modify permission for that folder. The file is then moved to a folder on a FAT32-formatted volume. When the user signs in to the computer holding the file and accesses it via a drive letter, what is the user's effective permission to the file?

a. Read
b. Change
c. Full control
d. Modify
e. It will lose its permissions

16. A user is assigned Read permission to the NTFS folder C:\ACCOUNTING as required by company policy. The user requires full access to the subfolder C:\ACCOUNTING\FORMS and its contents. This can be best accomplished by _____.

a. not possible
b. blocking permission inheritance at C:\ACCOUNTING\FORMS and assigning the user ownership of C:\ACCOUNTING\FORMS
c. assigning the user Full control to C:\ACCOUNTING
d. blocking permission inheritance at C:\ACCOUNTING and assigning the user Full control to C:\ACCOUNTING\FORMS
e. assigning the user Full control to C:\ACCOUNTING\FORMS

17. A user checks the free space in a folder on their local computer, Y:\BusReports, and notices that 3 GB of disk space is reported as available. When the user checks free space in Y:\BusReports\Archive, he notices that 50 GB of disk space is reported as available. The difference in available disk space is probably because the folder Y:\BusReports\Archive is _____.

a. archived
b. compressed

c. encrypted
d. dynamic
e. a mount point

18. Upon opening the Disk Management console, you notice a disk whose status is reported as Foreign Disk. This is most likely because _____.

a. the disk must be initialized
b. the disk has been corrupted
c. the disk is shared on the network
d. the disk was moved from another computer

19. A user is given Read permission to a file stored on an NTFS-formatted volume. The file is then moved to a different folder on a different NTFS-formatted volume where the user has been given Full control permission to that folder. When the user signs in to the computer holding the file and accesses its new location via a drive letter, what is the user's effective permission to the file?

a. Read
b. Full control
c. No access
d. Modify
e. none of the above

20. A user is given Read permission to a file stored on an NTFS-formatted volume. The file is then moved to a folder on the same NTFS-formatted volume, where the user has been given Modify permission to that folder. When the user signs in to the computer holding the file and accesses its new location via a drive letter, what is the user's effective permission to the file?

a. Read
b. Full control
c. No access
d. Modify
e. none of the above

Case Projects

Case Project 5-1: Selecting a File System and Security Settings

You decide to share the annual report for your company from your computer. You decide that the data will be stored in its own partition, so you create a 20 MB partition for the report. If a user signs in to your computer locally, they must have read-only access to the files. What file system would you select for the partition? What security settings would you use to achieve the desired results?

Case Project 5-2: Designing a Shared File System with Security

You are responsible for creating a shared file system to support a new branch office. The manager has requested shared locations for branch staff to access files. An area is required for all staff to access common forms and notices. Staff members are required to have read-only access to this location, but the manager will require full access to all content. A different area is required for all staff to share files without restrictions. The last area required is for the manager's private files, and only the manager has access to this location. A second manager will be hired in the next month to share the current manager's duties for job training. Both managers will require the same access throughout the file system. Only the IT administrator should have the ability to change file and folder permission settings for any area. Network permissions are not a concern because they will be configured appropriately based on the NTFS permissions you select. What groups would you create to simplify permission assignment? What folder structure and corresponding file-level permission settings would you use to achieve the desired results?

Case Project 5-3: Designing Storage Spaces

You have created a new storage space using a single 500 GB external USB 3.0 drive. The drive is becoming full, so you add another external 1 TB USB 2.0 drive to the storage pool. Now that you have two drives, you would like to create a volume with storage space resiliency set to two-way mirror. You create the new volume with two-way resiliency and a size limit of 1 TB. As you are copying files from C: to this new volume, you receive a warning that you are running out of space. Only a few hundred megabytes have been copied; why might you be receiving the warning so quickly? What can you do about it?

WINDOWS 10 SECURITY FEATURES

After reading this module and completing the exercises, you will be able to:

1. Use the Local Security Policy to secure Windows 10
2. Enable auditing to record security events
3. Configure User Account Control
4. Describe the malware security features in Windows 10
5. Implement the data security features in Windows 10
6. Secure Windows 10 by using Windows Update

Security is a crucial consideration for how you configure Windows 10. Computers that are not secure are susceptible to malware that can destroy data and steal passwords. Windows 10 includes many security features, most of which are enabled by default; you also have options to optimize them for your environment.

In this module, you learn how to configure security by using the Local Security Policy, including AppLocker, and how to enable auditing. You also learn about User Account Control, which requires approval to perform administrative actions. Windows Defender Antivirus, for malware protection, is covered, along with using Encrypting File System and BitLocker Drive Encryption for data encryption. Finally, using Windows Update and the new Windows 10 update processes are discussed.

WINDOWS 10 SECURITY POLICIES

Windows 10 includes a **Local Security Policy**, shown in Figure 6-1, which can be used to control many facets of Windows. You can access the Local Security Policy in Administrative Tools.

The Local Security Policy contains the following categories of settings:

- Account Policies
- Local Policies
- Windows Defender Firewall with Advanced Security
- Network List Manager Policies
- Public Key Policies
- Software Restriction Policies
- Application Control Policies
- IP Security Policies on Local Computer
- Advanced Audit Policy Configuration

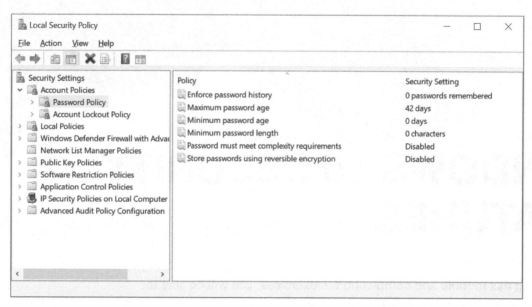

Figure 6-1   Local Security Policy

The Local Security Policy is part of a larger Windows management system called Group Policy, which can be implemented on a local computer but is more commonly part of a domain-based network. A variety of tools and security templates can be used to configure and analyze security policies.

Account Policies

The Account Policies category contains the Password Policy and the Account Lockout Policy. The Account Policies in the Local Security Policy affect only local user accounts. The account policies do not affect domain accounts. To control domain accounts, the account policies must be configured at the domain level.

Password Policy

The **Password Policy** controls password characteristics for local user accounts. The available settings are:

- *Enforce password history*—This setting specifies the number of password changes that must occur before a password can be reused. For example, if the setting is 3, a password can be reused only every fourth time. The default value is 0 passwords remembered, and the maximum is 24 passwords remembered.
- *Maximum password age*—This setting is the maximum amount of time that a user can keep the same password without changing it. Forcing password changes reduces the risk of a shared or hacked password being used over an extended period of time. The default value is 42 days.
- *Minimum password age*—This setting is the shortest amount of time that a user can use a password before changing it. A minimum password age is often used to ensure that users do not change their password several times in quick succession to continue using a single password. The default value is 0 days, which allows passwords to be changed again immediately.
- *Minimum password length*—This setting is the minimum number of characters that must be in a password. In general, longer passwords are more secure. A minimum password length of 8 or 10 characters is typical for most organizations. The default value is 0 characters, which allows any password length.
- *Password must meet complexity requirements*—This setting applies a number of tests to a new password to ensure that it is not too easy to guess or hack. This setting is enforced when a password change is made but is not applied to existing passwords. The default value is Disabled. The complexity requirements include the following:
  - Cannot contain part of the user's account name
  - Must be at least six characters long
  - Must contain characters meeting three of the following characteristics: uppercase characters, lowercase characters, numerals (0–9), nonalphanumeric characters (e.g., !, @, #, $)

- *Store passwords using reversible encryption*—This setting controls how passwords are encrypted in the Security Accounts Manager (SAM) database that stores user credentials. By default, this setting is disabled, and passwords are encrypted in a nonreversible format. Storing passwords by using reversible encryption is required for compatibility only with specific applications that require it. Enabling this option stores passwords in a less secure way and should not be enabled unless absolutely required to support a specific application.

Account Lockout Policy

The **Account Lockout Policy** is used to prevent unauthorized access to Windows 10. Using the Account Lockout Policy, you can configure an account to be temporarily disabled after a number of incorrect sign-in attempts. This prevents automated password-guessing attacks from being successful.

The settings available to control account lockouts are:

- *Account lockout duration*—This setting determines how many minutes an account remains locked. The default value is 30 minutes; however, this value is not configured until the Account lockout threshold has been configured.
- *Account lockout threshold*—This setting determines the number of incorrect sign-in attempts that must be performed before an account is locked. The default value is 0 invalid sign-in attempts, which means that account lockouts are disabled.
- *Reset account lockout counter after*—This setting determines within what time frame the incorrect sign-in attempts must occur to trigger a lockout. The default value is 30 minutes; however, this value is not configured until the Account lockout threshold has been configured.

Activity 6-1: Implementing a Password Policy

Time Required: 10 minutes

Objective: Implement a password policy that applies to local users

Description: A password policy is used to control the passwords that can be selected by users. One of the most effective password policy settings for increasing security is requiring complex passwords that are difficult to hack. In this activity, you configure a password policy to require complex passwords.

1. If necessary, start your computer and sign in.
2. Click the **Start** button, type **local**, and then click **Local Security Policy**.
3. In the Local Security Policy window, in the left pane, expand **Account Policies** and then click **Password Policy**. This shows all the password policy settings that are available to you.
4. Double-click **Password must meet complexity requirements**, click **Enabled**, and then click **OK**. Now all passwords must meet complexity requirements when they are changed.
5. Close all open windows.
6. Press **Ctrl+Alt+Delete** and then click **Change a password**. Note that you can't use this method to change your password if you are signed in by using a Microsoft account.
7. In the Old password box, type **password**.
8. In the New password and Confirm password text boxes, type **simple** and then press **Enter**. You will receive an error indicating that the new password is not acceptable due to length, complexity, or history requirements.
9. Click **OK**.
10. In the Old password text box, type **password**.
11. In the New password and Confirm password text boxes, type **S1mpl3** and then press **Enter**. This time, the password will be changed successfully.
12. Click **OK**.

> **⚠ CAUTION** Passwords with simple letter number substitution like S1mpl3 are still not very secure because hacking tools include that functionality. When you add numbers and symbols to make a password more complex, do your best to make it an unpredictable pattern.

Local Policies

Local Policies are for auditing system access, assigning user rights, and configuring specific security options. Auditing lets you track when users sign in and which resources are used. Details about auditing are covered later in this module. User rights control which system tasks a particular user or group of users can perform. The specific security options are a variety of settings that can be used to make Windows 10 more secure. Figure 6-2 shows some of the settings available in User Rights Assignment.

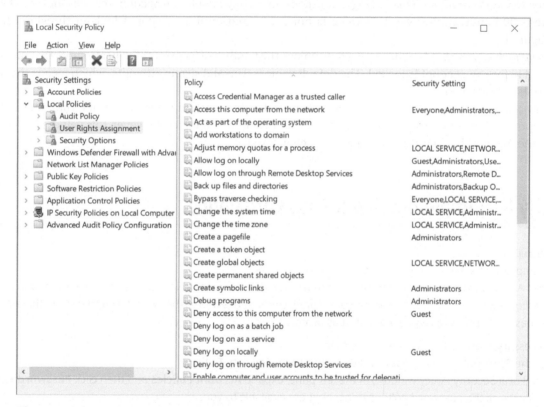

Figure 6-2   User Rights Assignment settings

Some of the settings available in User Rights Assignment are:

- *Allow log on locally*—This setting controls which users are allowed to sign in to the computer at the console but does not affect who can access the computer over the network. Administrators, Backup Operators, Guest, and Users are assigned this right by default.
- *Back up files and directories*—This setting controls which users are allowed to back up files, regardless of whether they have the necessary file permissions to read those files. Administrators and Backup Operators are assigned this right by default.
- *Change the system time*—This setting controls which users are allowed to change the system time. Administrators and Local Service are assigned this right by default.
- *Load and unload device drivers*—This setting controls which users are able to install and remove device drivers. Only Administrators are assigned this right by default.
- *Shut down the system*—This setting controls which users are able to shut down Windows 10. For a public access computer, you might restrict this right. Administrators, Backup Operators, and Users are assigned this right by default.

Some of the settings available in Security Options are:

- *Devices: Prevent users from installing printer drivers*—This setting controls whether standard users are allowed to install printer drivers from a shared printer. It does not affect the installation of local printer drivers. The default value is disabled, which allows all users to install network printer drivers.
- *Interactive logon: Don't display last signed-in*—This setting allows you to remove the last user name from the sign-in screen. This makes sign-in more secure by not revealing user names to potential hackers. The default value is Disabled.
- *Interactive logon: Message text for users attempting to log on*—This setting allows you to display a message for users before they sign in. The message can be instructions about how to sign in or a warning against unauthorized use. By default, no message is displayed.
- *Shutdown: Allow system to be shut down without having to log on*—This setting allows you to require sign-in before allowing the system to be shut down. This is important for public access computers when you want to restrict which users can shut down the system. The default value is Enabled.

Activity 6-2: Configuring a Sign-In Message

Time Required: 10 minutes
Objective: Configure a warning message that appears for users before signing in
Description: The security policy of some organizations dictates that users are presented with a warning message about appropriate use before signing in. This warning is used to ensure that users are properly informed about organizational policies. In this activity, you configure Windows 10 with a warning message that appears before users sign in.

1. If necessary, start your computer and sign in. Recall that the password has been changed to S1mpl3.
2. Click the **Start** button, type **Local**, and then click **Local Security Policy**.
3. In the Local Security Policy window, in the left pane, expand **Local Policies**, and then click **Security Options**.
4. Scroll down and then double-click **Interactive logon: Message title for users attempting to log on**.
5. In the text box, type **Acceptable Use** and then click **OK**.
6. Double-click **Interactive logon: Message text for users attempting to log on**.
7. In the text box, type **This computer should be used only for approved company business**. **Please see the acceptable use policy for more details.** and then click **OK**.
8. Close Local Security Policy.
9. Sign out and then press **Ctrl+Alt+Delete**. Notice that the warning message appears.
10. Click **OK** to display the sign-in screen.

AppLocker

AppLocker is used to define which programs are allowed or disallowed in the system. Its most common use is for malware prevention. Much malware installs itself by running from within a user profile. You can use AppLocker to restrict the locations that allow executables to run, thereby potentially avoiding the problem.

 TIP   A particularly nasty type of malware is known as ransomware. Ransomware encrypts files and requires payment for a key to decrypt the files. AppLocker is an effective tool to prevent ransomware.

You can audit or enforce AppLocker rules. When you audit an AppLocker rule, an event is logged when an action matching the rule is performed, but the software is allowed to run. When you enforce an AppLocker rule, software is blocked from running. If you do not define whether rules are enforced or audited, the default is enforced. When you first implement AppLocker rules, it is a good idea to use audit rather than enforce the rules. This allows you to review the logs and verify that your rules allow all the necessary software to run. Figure 6-3 shows the configuration of AppLocker auditing and enforcement.

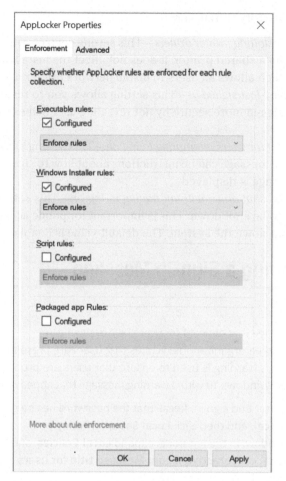

Figure 6-3   Configuring AppLocker enforcement

The enforcement or auditing of AppLocker rules relies on the configuration of appropriate rules and the Application Identity service. The Application Identity service must be running for AppLocker rules to be evaluated. This service is configured for Manual startup and is stopped by default. If you are implementing AppLocker rules, you should configure the Application Identity service for Automatic startup.

 TIP   In a domain-based environment, you can use Group Policy to easily configure the Startup Type for the Application Identity service on multiple computers.

Rule Collections

AppLocker rules are divided into categories called rule collections, as shown in Figure 6-4. Each rule collection applies to different types of files.

The rule collections are:

- *Executable*—These rules apply to .exe and .com files. Use these rules to control which applications users can run.
- *Windows Installer*—These rules apply to .msi and .msp files. Use these rules to control which users can install applications and from what locations.
- *Script*—These rules, which apply to .ps1, .bat, .cmd, .vbs, and .js files, are used to control which users can run scripts.
- *Packaged app*—These rules apply to .appx files. Use these rules to control which users can run Windows Store apps.
- *DLL*—These rules apply to .dll and .ocx files. Use these rules to verify that the dynamic link library (DLL) and ActiveX (OCX) files used by applications are not modified or unknown. These rules are not enabled by default due to negative performance impact.

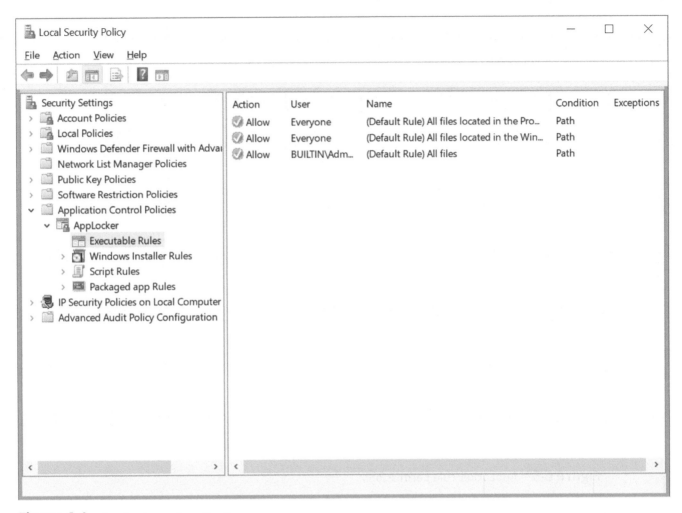

Figure 6-4   AppLocker rule collections

Many Windows applications use DLL files when they are executing programs. DLL files contain code that is shared across many applications, and many DLLs are included as part of the operating system. DLL files are considered a lower risk than executable files and are not evaluated by default. Evaluating DLL files creates a significant performance impact because DLLs are accessed many times during program execution, and the DLL must be evaluated each time it is accessed. If performance is not a concern, however, you can choose to evaluate DLL files in addition to executable files to enhance security.

For each rule collection, you can:

- *Create a New Rule*—This allows you to manually specify the characteristics of a rule. To create rules in this way, you must understand the exact end results that you are trying to achieve.
- *Automatically Generate Rules*—This option scans your computer and creates rules that match its current configuration. In a larger corporate environment, you can create the rules on a standardized reference computer and then apply them to all computers in the organization. You should review the rules before applying them.
- *Create Default Rules*—This creates standardized rules for a rule collection that meets the needs of many users and organizations. Because these rules are very general, they provide less security than automatically generated rules but are usually easier to manage. The default rules created vary for each rule collection.

Rule Permissions

Each rule contains permissions that define whether the rule allows or denies software the capability to run, as shown in Figure 6-5. It is important to remember that until a rule is created in a rule collection, the default permission is Allow. For example, if no executable rules are specified, all executables are allowed. As soon as a single executable rule is

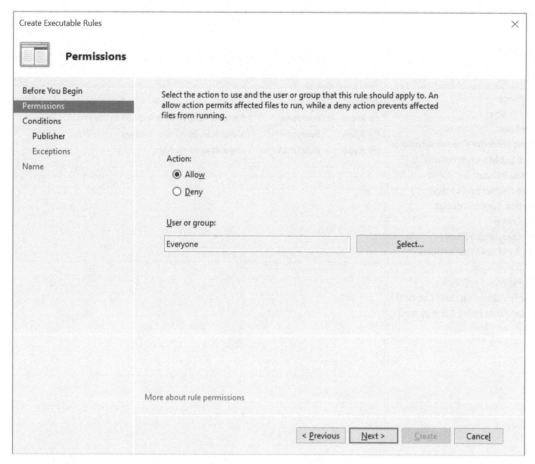

Figure 6-5   AppLocker rule permissions

created, the default permission is Deny, and only specifically allowed executables can run. For example, if you create a rule that prevents users from running cmd.exe, access to all other applications without an Allow rule is prevented.

Permissions also define to which users the rule applies. A rule can be applied to an individual user or group but not multiple users or groups. This means it is crucially important to plan which groups to use for allowing access.

In general, the best strategy for applying rules is to begin by creating rules that allow access for larger groups of users. Then, you can restrict smaller groups or individuals with a rule that denies access, or you create an exception within the original rule. The Deny permission overrides the Allow permission when multiple rules apply for a user.

Rule Conditions

A rule condition defines the software that is affected by the rule. The three conditions that can be used are as follows:

- Publisher
- Path
- File Hash

The Publisher rule condition, shown in Figure 6-6, identifies software by using a digital signature in the software. If the software is not digitally signed, you cannot use a Publisher rule condition to identify it. In that case, consider using a File Hash rule condition instead.

To begin configuration of a Publisher rule condition, you specify a reference file. The wizard reads the digital signature from this reference file as the basis for the condition. After a reference file has been defined, you can use the slider to select the specific information that must be matched. You can make it as specific as a particular file and file version or make it more generic and restrict it only to a specific product name or publisher. You can also define custom values that do not match the information read from the reference file.

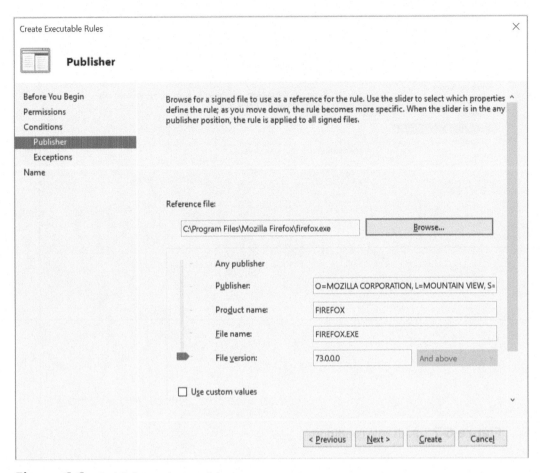

Figure 6-6   Publisher rule condition

 TIP   If you include the file version in a publisher rule, you might need to update the rule each time you update the application. For easier maintenance, create rules that trust common publishers like Microsoft, and don't specify further details.

The Path rule condition, shown in Figure 6-7, identifies software by file location. You can specify a single file or a folder path from which software can be run. This type of rule condition tends to be much less secure than a Publisher rule condition. For example, if you use a Path rule condition that allows software to be run from C:\Program Files\, any malware accidentally installed by a user and located in C:\Program Files\ can be run. At a minimum, you should avoid using Path rule conditions that allow executables to be run from file locations where standard users can copy files. Variables can be used as part of the path to simplify rule creation.

The File Hash rule condition generates a unique identifier for the specified files called a hash value. If the file is modified in any way, the hash value of the file no longer matches the hash value in the rule, and the software is blocked from running. If you use a File Hash rule condition, application updates will require the rule to be updated.

Rule Exceptions

An AppLocker rule exception defines software to which the rule does not apply. In general, you use rule conditions to define a large set of software and then use exceptions to define a smaller set of software to which the rule does not apply. Similar to rule conditions, when you add an exception, it can be based on publisher, path, or file hash. You can add multiple exceptions to a single rule.

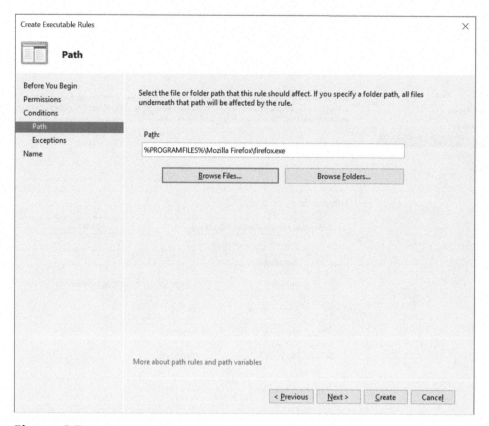

Figure 6-7   Path rule condition

Activity 6-3: Configuring AppLocker

Time Required: 10 minutes

Objective: Implement AppLocker rules

Description: AppLocker rules can be used to limit which software is allowed to run on a workstation. An administrator can use this to prevent a particular piece of software from running or allow only specific software to run. In this activity, you create and review default AppLocker rules and audit the use of cmd.exe.

1. If necessary, start your computer and sign in. Remember that the password is changed to S1mpl3.
2. Click the **Start** button, type **local**, and then click **Local Security Policy**.
3. In the left pane, expand **Application Control Policies** and then click **AppLocker**.
4. Scroll down and notice that no rules are created by default, but they are enforced.
5. Click **Executable Rules**.
6. Right-click an open area in the right pane and then click **Create Default Rules**.
7. Review the default rules. These rules allow administrators to run all applications and allow Everyone to run applications in C:\Program Files\ and C:\Windows\.
8. Right-click an open area in the right pane and then click **Automatically Generate Rules**.
9. On the Folder and Permissions screen, click **Next** to accept the default of scanning C:\Program Files\.
10. On the Rule Preferences screen, read the default options that are selected and then click **Next**. Notice that the rules are being created based on digital signatures and file hashes rather than the file path.
11. On the Review Rules page, click **View Rules that will be automatically created**.
12. Read the rules and then click **OK**. These rules are based on the software installed on your computer.
13. On the Review Rules page, click **Cancel**.
14. In the left pane, right-click **Executable Rules** and then click **Create New Rule**.
15. On the Before You Begin screen, click **Next**.

16. On the Permissions screen, click **Deny** and then click **Next**.
17. On the Conditions screen, click **Path** and then click **Next**.
18. On the Path screen, in the Path box, type **C:\Windows\System32\cmd.exe** and then click **Next**.
19. On the Exceptions screen, click **Next** to accept the default of no exceptions.
20. In the Name box, delete the existing name, type **Deny Command Prompt**, and then click **Create**.
21. In the left pane, click **Windows Installer Rules**, right-click **Windows Installer Rules**, and then click **Create Default Rules**.
22. Review the default rules that are created. These rules allow Everyone to install digitally signed software and allow administrators to install any software.
23. In the left pane, click **AppLocker** and then click **Configure rule enforcement**.
24. Under Executable rules, select the **Configured** check box, select **Audit only** in the list, and then click **OK**.
25. Close the Local Security Policy window.
26. Right-click the **Start** button and then click **Computer Management**.
27. Expand **Services and Applications** and then click **Services**.
28. Click the **Application Identity** service, read the description, and then click the **Start** button.
29. Wait a few seconds for the service to be completely initialized then click the **Start** button. Type **cmd** and then click **Command Prompt**.
30. In the left pane of Computer Management, expand **Event Viewer**, expand **Applications and Services Logs**, expand **Microsoft**, expand **Windows**, expand **AppLocker**, and then click **EXE and DLL**.
31. Click the **Warning** event and read the description. Notice that cmd.exe was allowed to run because it is only being audited rather than enforced. If you don't see any events, it's possible that the Application Identity service was not completely initialized. Close the command prompt and then repeat Step 29.
32. In the left pane of Computer Management, scroll down and then click **Services**.
33. Click the **Application Identity** service and then click **Stop**.
34. Close all open windows.

Software Restriction Policies

Software Restriction Policies are an older technology that you can use to control application usage in a fashion similar to AppLocker. Software Restriction Policies are still functional in Windows 10. If both AppLocker rules and Software Restriction Policies are defined on a Windows 10 computer, only the AppLocker rules are enforced.

AppLocker is preferred over Software Restriction Policies because it provides the following enhancements:

- Rules can be applied to specific users and groups rather than all users.
- The default rule action is Deny to increase security.
- A wizard is available to help create rules.
- You can use audit-only mode for testing that writes only events to the event log.

To use AppLocker, you must implement Windows 10 Enterprise or Windows 10 Education; however, many smaller organizations use Windows 10 Pro instead, because they receive it with new computers. For these smaller organizations that cannot use AppLocker, Software Restriction Policies offer an effective way to restrict malware from running.

 TIP Software Restriction Policies have been deprecated starting with Windows 10 version 1803 (March 2018). Questions about this functionality are not likely to appear on the exam.

Other Security Policies

Windows Defender Firewall with Advanced Security is used to configure the firewall in Windows 10. This policy lets you configure both inbound and outbound rules for packets. In addition, you can configure specific computer-to-computer rules. In Windows 10, this area can also be used to configure IP Security (IPsec) rules.

The Network List Manager Policies are used to control how Windows 10 categorizes networks to which it is connected and how users can interact with the process. For example, unidentified networks can be automatically defined as either public or private, and the user can restrict the ability of other users to change it. These policies also control whether users can rename networks to which they connect.

Public Key Policies have settings for the Encrypting File System (EFS), BitLocker Drive Encryption, and certificate services. You can add recovery agents for EFS files or BitLocker-encrypted drives. A recovery agent is allowed to decrypt files protected by EFS or BitLocker. More detailed information about EFS and BitLocker Drive Encryption is provided later in this module.

IP Security Policies on Local Computer are used to control encrypted network communication. By default, network communication is not encrypted. You can, however, configure encrypted network communication for certain hosts or communication on certain port numbers. This policy is deprecated in Windows 10 and is included only for backward compatibility with previous versions of Windows. When configuring IPsec rules, you should use Windows Defender Firewall with Advanced Security.

Advanced Audit Policy Configuration is a simplified way to configure advanced audit policies in Windows 10. These policies first appeared in Windows Vista but needed to be edited at a command-line level.

AUDITING

Auditing is the security process that records the occurrence of specific operating system events in the Security log. Every object in Windows 10 has audit events related to it. Log entries can be recorded for successful events or failed attempted events. For example, logging all failed sign-in attempts may warn you when an attack that might breach your security is occurring. In addition, monitoring sensitive documents for read access lets you know who is accessing the documents and when.

It is more common to use auditing to monitor access to server-based resources than resources on desktop computers. In some cases, however, you might want to know which users are signing in to a specific workstation. For example, if security logs indicate that someone was attempting unauthorized access to resources from a particular workstation, it is useful to see which user was signed in at the time.

Windows 10 has basic audit policy settings and advanced audit policy settings. Both sets of audit policy settings allow you to capture similar information, but the advanced audit policy settings have more detailed configuration options than the basic audit policy settings. Using the advanced audit policy settings allows you to limit the amount of audit data that you capture. In this way, you capture only relevant data and simplify the task of reviewing the audit logs. Table 6-1 describes the categories for Advanced Audit Policy settings.

Table 6-1   Event Categories for Advanced Audit Policy Settings

Event Category	Description
Account Logon	Tracks when users are authenticated by a computer. If a local user account is used, the event is logged locally. If a domain user account is used, the event is logged at the domain controller. Account Logon events are not audited by default.
Account Management	Tracks when users and groups are created, modified, or deleted. Password changes are also tracked. Success events for user management and group management are audited by default.
Detailed Tracking	Tracks how a computer is being used by tracking application activity. This includes identifying the creation and termination of processes, encryption events, and remote procedure call (RPC) events. No events are audited by default.
DS Access	This category is not relevant for Windows 10 and is not audited by default. It is used only for domain controllers.
Logon/Logoff	Tracks user activity events, including local and domain log-ons (sign-in) attempts, at the local computer. This category is similar to, but different from, auditing account log-on events. Signing in with a local account generates both an account log-on event and a log-on event on the local computer. Signing in with a domain account generates an account log-on event at the domain controller and a log-on event at the workstation where the sign in occurred. Success events for log off and account lockout are audited by default. Success and failure events for logon and network policy server are audited by default.

Object Access	Tracks access to files, folders, printers, and registry keys. Each individual object being accessed also must be configured for auditing. Files and folders can be monitored only if they are on NTFS-formatted volumes. Object access is not audited by default.
Policy Change	Tracks changes to user rights assignments, audit policies, and trust policies. Success events for audit policy changes and authentication policy changes are audited by default.
Privilege Use	Tracks when tasks are performed that require a user-rights assignment, such as changing the system time. You can define which categories of privilege use are audited; none is audited by default.
System	Tracks when system events occur, such as restarting the system. By default, success and failure events are audited for system integrity and other system events. Only success events are audited for security state change.
Global Object Access Auditing	Provides an easy way to specify that all access to files or registry keys should be audited. This avoids the need to configure auditing at the file, folder, or registry-key level after enabling auditing for object access to files or registry keys; however, this must still be used in combination with auditing enabled for object access. This category does not appear when using auditpol.exe.

> **⚠ CAUTION** You should not combine basic audit policy settings and advanced audit policy settings because the results are unpredictable. To prevent conflicts, you can enable the Security Options policy setting Audit: Force audit policy subcategory settings (Windows Vista or later) to override audit policy category settings.

Basic auditing is enabled through the Local Security Policy or by using Group Policy. The **audit policy** for basic auditing is located in the Local Policies node of the Local Security Policy.

Advanced auditing is enabled through the Local Security Policy, by using Group Policy, or by using auditpol.exe. The tool auditpol.exe provides the most accurate view of which Advanced Audit Policy settings are applied. Figure 6-8 shows the Advanced Audit Policy settings in the Local Security Policy.

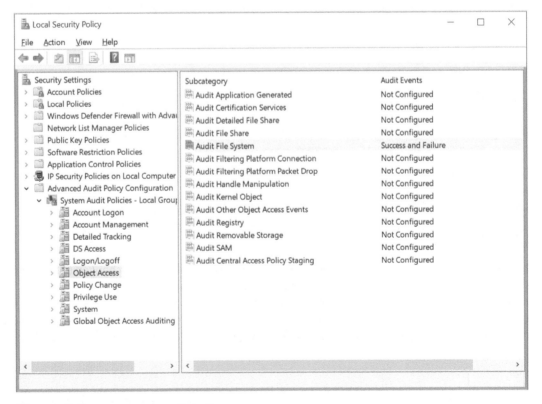

Figure 6-8 Advanced Audit Policy

The default configuration for the Advanced Audit Policy settings can be viewed only by using the auditpol.exe utility. If you review the configuration in the Local Security Policy, it appears that no settings are enabled. Be aware that after you enable settings in the Local Security Policy, the default configuration is lost and does not return if the Advanced Audit Policy settings are removed from the Local Security Policy. Refer to Table 6-1 for the default configuration for the Advanced Audit Policy settings.

After the audit policy is configured, the audited events are recorded in the Security log that is viewed by using Event Viewer. Event Viewer is available as part of the Computer Management MMC console or as a stand-alone MMC console in Administrative Tools. Security events are listed by selecting the Windows Security log, as shown in Figure 6-9.

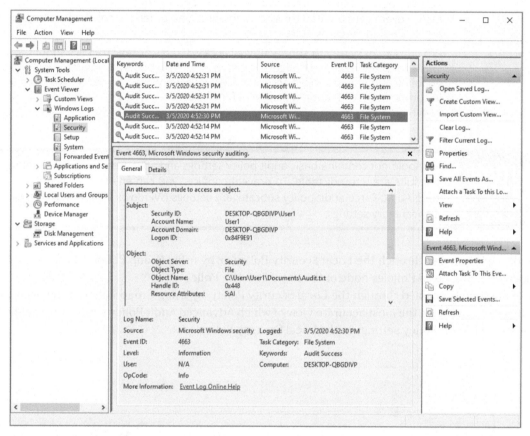

Figure 6-9   Windows Security log

Activity 6-4: Auditing File Access

Time Required: 15 minutes

Objective: Audit file modification for users

Description: In a corporate environment, it is useful to track all the users who have modified sensitive files. You can use auditing to track file modification. In this activity, you enable auditing of file modification creation, configure a file to be audited, and view user modification of that file.

1. If necessary, start your computer and sign in. Remember that the password is changed to S1mpl3.
2. Right-click the **Start** button and then click **Windows PowerShell (Admin)**.
3. In the User Account Control dialog box, click **Yes**.
4. At the Windows PowerShell prompt, type **auditpol /get /category:*** and then press **Enter**. This displays a list of all the advanced audit policy settings and their configurations.

5. Read the list of policy settings that are enabled. This is the default configuration for Windows 10. Notice that below Object Access, File System auditing is not enabled. After you enable policy settings in the local security policy, these settings are removed, and only the settings explicitly applied in the policy are effective.

6. Close the Windows PowerShell prompt window.

7. Click the **Start** button, type **local**, and then click **Local Security Policy**.

8. In the left pane, expand **Local Policies** and then click **Audit Policy**. Review the list of categories for basic auditing and notice that none is enabled in the local security policy.

9. In the left pane, expand **Advanced Audit Policy Configuration**, expand **System Audit Policies - Local Group Policy Object**, and then click **Object Access**.

10. Double-click **Audit File System**. This option enables auditing for file access.

11. In the Audit File System Properties dialog box, select the **Configure the following audit events** check box and then select the **Success** and **Failure** check boxes.

12. Click the **Explain** tab, read the explanation, and then click **OK**. The system is now able to track successful file access when users have permission to access a file and unsuccessful file access when users do not have permission to access a file; however, auditing must still be enabled for the individual files.

13. Close Local Security Policy, and close all open windows.

14. On the taskbar, click **File Explorer** and then click **Documents**.

15. Right-click an open area in the **Name** column, point to **New**, and then click **Text Document**.

16. Type **Audit** and then press **Enter**.

17. Right-click **Audit**, click **Properties**, and then click the **Security** tab.

18. In the Audit Properties dialog box, click **Advanced** and then click the **Auditing** tab. Notice that auditing information is protected by UAC.

19. Click **Continue** to open the auditing information. Notice that no auditing is configured by default.

20. Click **Add**, click **Select a principal**, type **Everyone**, click **Check Names**, and then click **OK**. This configures auditing to track access by all users. You can limit auditing to certain users or groups.

21. In the Type box, select **All**. This configures auditing of successful and failed access.

22. Below Basic permissions, select the **Full control** check box. This configures auditing to track all changes to the file.

23. Click **OK** three times to close all open dialog boxes.

24. Double-click **Audit** to open the file and then add some content to the file.

25. Click **File** on the menu bar, click **Exit**, and then click **Save**.

26. Close the File Explorer window.

27. Right-click the **Start** button and then click **Computer Management**.

28. In the left pane, expand **Event Viewer**, expand **Windows Logs**, and then click **Security**. This displays all the events in the security log.

29. Right-click **Security** and then click **Filter Current Log**.

30. In the Event sources box, select **Microsoft Windows security auditing**.

31. In the <All Event IDs> box, type **4663** and then click **OK**. Notice that multiple events are listed. These events were generated by editing the file.

32. Starting with the first event, read the Account Name identified in the event. Continue down until the Account Name referenced is User$x$. Read the description of the event. The description indicates that a file was written by User$x$, where x is the number assigned to you; the file opened was Audit.txt; and the program used to write the file was notepad.exe.

33. Close the Computer Management window.

USER ACCOUNT CONTROL

User Account Control (UAC) is a feature that makes running applications more secure. Security is enhanced by reducing the need to sign in and run applications using administrator privileges. Reducing the use of administrative privileges makes it less likely that malicious software can adversely affect Windows 10.

In some organizations, all user accounts are configured as administrators on the local workstations. This is done to ensure that users are able to perform any local maintenance tasks that may be required, such as installing printers or software. In Windows 10, major efforts have been put forth to ensure that most common tasks do not require administrative privileges; however, even if users are still given administrative privileges, UAC increases security.

When UAC is enabled and an administrative user signs in, the administrative user is assigned two access tokens. One access token includes standard user privileges and the other access token includes administrative privileges. The standard user access token is used to launch the Windows 10 user interface; therefore, all applications started by using the user interface also start with standard user privileges. This approach keeps any malicious software from having access to restricted areas, like system files.

Admin Approval Mode ensures that the access token with administrative privileges is used only when required. When you use an application that requires administrative privileges, you are prompted to continue or cancel running the program with administrative privileges. If you select to continue, the program is run using the access token with administrative privileges. The Application Information Service is responsible for launching programs by using the access token with administrative privileges.

When UAC is enabled and a standard user signs in, the user is assigned only one access token with standard user privileges. If the user attempts to run an application that requires administrative privileges, the user is prompted to supply credentials for a user with administrative privileges.

Application Manifest

Newer Windows applications use an application manifest to describe the structure of an application. The application manifest file identifies required DLL files and whether they are shared. The file can also include information about UAC. To trigger the privilege elevation prompt for an application that requires administrative privileges, an entry must be included in the application manifest.

Applications that are not designed for Windows 10 and that require administrative privileges do not properly request elevated privileges, which generates an error. You can eliminate this error by using the Application Compatibility Toolkit.

UAC Configuration

Windows 10 limits the number of UAC prompts presented to administrative users with a default configuration that does not prompt if the user initiated the action. If a program initiates the action, a UAC prompt is still presented; however, you can modify the default configuration as shown in Figure 6-10. Four options are available, as listed below:

- *Always notify me*—This setting is equivalent to the configuration in Windows Vista in which even administrative users are prompted every time an administrative task is attempted.
- *Notify me only when apps try to make changes to my computer*—Administrative users are prompted only when a program attempts to perform an administrative task. When the administrative task is initiated by the user, a prompt is not displayed. This is the default setting.
- *Notify me only when apps try to make changes to my computer (do not dim my desktop)*—This setting is the same as the default setting except that when the UAC prompt is displayed, the screen is not dimmed.
- *Never notify me*—This setting disables UAC and is not recommended because UAC is an important security feature.

For advanced configuration, UAC is configured by using either the Local Security Policy or Group Policy. The policy settings for configuring UAC are listed in Table 6-2. The default settings for UAC work well for most scenarios. Carefully consider the ramifications before you modify the advanced configuration settings for UAC.

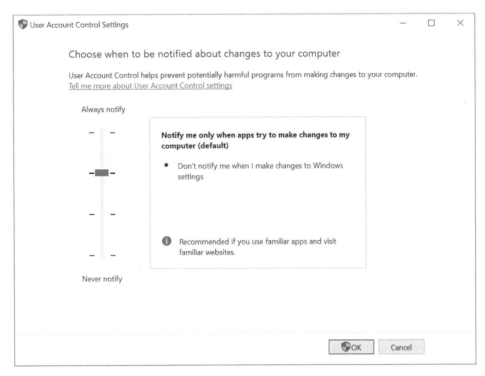

Figure 6-10   UAC settings

Table 6-2   UAC Configuration Options

Option (User Account Control)	Description
Admin Approval Mode for the built-in Administrator account	Used to enable or disable Admin Approval Mode for the built-in administrator account. The default configuration is disabled.
Allow UIAccess application to prompt for elevation without using secure desktop	Used to allow UIAccess programs, such as Remote Assistance, to automatically disable the screen dimming that normally occurs when a UAC prompt is displayed. This is a less secure configuration but can speed up screen drawing over slow connections. This is disabled by default.
Behavior of the elevation prompt for administrators in Admin Approval Mode	Used to configure the elevation prompt for Administrators only. The default configuration is to prompt for consent for non-Windows binaries; however, you can also configure a prompt for administrative credentials instead of a simple approval or you can disable the prompt. Entirely disabling the prompt effectively disables UAC for administrators because applications can then request elevation to administrative privileges and are automatically approved. Applications still run with standard user privileges until they request elevation.
Behavior of the elevation prompt for standard users	Used to configure the elevation prompt for standard users only. The default configuration is to prompt for credentials. You can also select Automatically deny elevation requests, in which case the user must manually use the Run as administrator option to elevate the privileges of the application.
Detect application installations and prompt for elevation	Used to automatically detect whether an application is being installed and generate a prompt to elevate privileges. The default configuration is enabled. If this option is disabled, many legacy application installations will fail.
Only elevate executables that are signed and validated	Used to limit privilege elevation to only applications that are digitally signed. The default configuration is disabled, which allows older unsigned applications that require administrative privileges to be elevated.
Only elevate UIAccess applications that are installed in secure locations	Used to force applications using the UIAccess integrity level in their application manifest to be located from a secure location. Secure locations are C:\ProgramFiles\ and C:\Windows\System32\ and their subfolders. The default configuration is enabled.

(continues)

Table 6-2   UAC Configuration Options (*Continued*)

Option (User Account Control)	Description
Run all administrators in Admin Approval Mode	Used to limit all user processes to standard user privileges unless they are elevated to administrator privileges. The default configuration is enabled. When this option is disabled, UAC is disabled for administrators and standard users.
Switch to the secure desktop when prompting for elevation	Used to secure communication between the elevation prompt and other processes. When enabled, the UAC elevation prompt is limited to communication with processes that are part of Windows 10. This prevents malware from approving elevation. The default configuration is enabled.
Virtualize file and registry write failures to per-user locations	Used to enable non-UAC compliant applications to run properly. Applications that write to restricted areas are silently redirected to space in the user profile. The default configuration is enabled.

Activity 6-5: Configuring UAC

Time Required: 5 minutes

Objective: Identify the differences in simplified UAC settings

Description: In most cases, UAC with the default configuration makes using a computer more secure for administrative users because many tasks performed by administrative users do not need administrative privileges, such as reading email or researching on the Internet. The default configuration does not prompt administrative users for approval when they initiate the action. In some cases, however, you might want administrators to be prompted so that they realize they are performing an administrative task. In this activity, you review how the simplified UAC settings modify the user experience.

1. If necessary, start your computer and sign in.
2. Click the **Start** button, type **local**, and then click **Local Security Policy**.
3. Expand **Local Policies** and then click **Security Options**.
4. Scroll down to the bottom of the list of security options and read the options available for User Account Control.
5. Close Local Security Policy.
6. Click the **Start** button and then click **Settings**.
7. In the Settings window, in the Find a setting box, type **uac** and then click **Change User Account Control settings**.
8. In the User Account Control Settings dialog box, move the slider up to **Always notify** and then click **OK**.
9. Click **Yes** to allow the changes. Notice that you are prompted by UAC because a program is changing the setting. Also notice that the screen is dimmed (hidden) when you are prompted by UAC which indicates that the secure desktop is being used.
10. In the Find a setting box, type **uac** and then click **Change User Account Control settings**. Notice that this time you are prompted to elevate.
11. In the User Account Control dialog box, click **Yes**.
12. In the User Account Control Settings dialog box, move the slider down to **Notify me only when apps make changes to my computer (do not dim my desktop)** and then click **OK**.
13. Click **Yes** to allow the changes.
14. Click the **Start** button, type **diskpart**, and then press **Enter**. Notice that a UAC dialog box appears, but the desktop is not dimmed. Secure desktop is not being used.
15. In the User Account Control dialog box, click **No**.
16. In the Find a setting box, type **uac** and then click **Change User Account Control settings**.
17. Move the slider back to the default setting and then click **OK**.
18. Click **Yes** to approve the change.
19. Close all open windows.

MALWARE PROTECTION

Malware (malicious software) is unwanted software on a computer that you did not choose to install. As the name indicates, this software performs actions you don't approve.

Some of the things malware can do include:

- Sending spam from your computer to the Internet
- Capturing user names and passwords for websites, including online banking
- Stealing personal information for identity theft
- Allowing others to remotely control your computer and use it as a launching point for illegal activities
- Using your processor to mine digital currency

Windows Security, shown in Figure 6-11, is a console that brings together most security settings, including those related to malware. The Home screen displays the status of security services. A green check mark indicates that everything is working properly. A yellow warning exclamation sign indicates that you should review the status of the service and might need to perform an action. A red x indicates that an error with the services needs to be fixed.

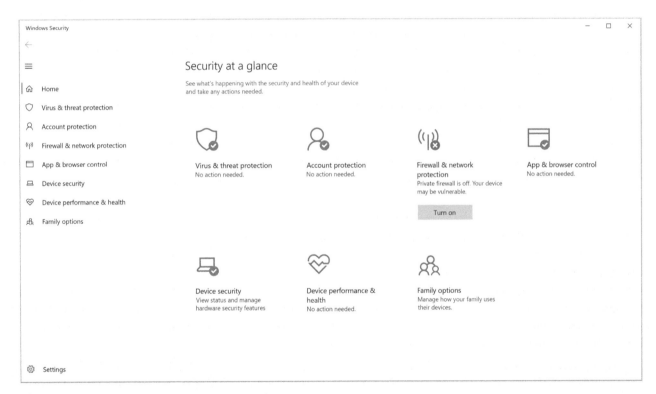

Figure 6-11   Windows Security

Windows Defender Advanced Threat Protection (ATP) is the collection of features that protects Windows 10 from malware, and you can configure anti-malware features from within Windows Security.

Other functionality in Windows Security includes:

- *Account protection*—This screen provides links to configure sign-in options and dynamic lock.
- *Firewall & network protection*—This screen provides status information about Windows Defender Firewall and links to configure Windows Defender Firewall.
- *Family options*—For home users, this screen provides links to configure family settings for Microsoft accounts. Once enabled, you can set limits on specific accounts that restrict access to websites and limit screen time. You can also obtain weekly activity reports to monitor activity.

Virus and Threat Protection

The Virus & threat protection screen, shown in Figure 6-12, provides the settings for managing traditional anti-malware scanning in **Windows Defender Antivirus**. The anti-malware scanning provided by Windows Defender Antivirus is as good as that found in third-party anti-malware software. Home users typically don't need to buy additional anti-malware software.

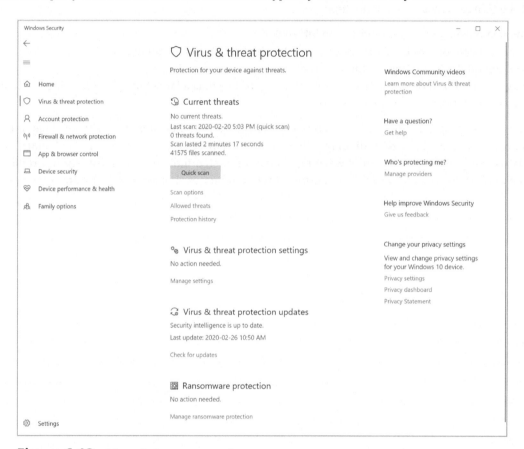

Figure 6-12   Virus & threat protection screen

In an enterprise environment, you might choose to use third-party anti-malware software, not because that software detects and removes malware better than Windows Defender Antivirus, but because it offers better management capabilities. Most corporate anti-malware software has a centralized console for distributing signature updates and monitoring computers. Windows Defender Antivirus provides no centralized monitoring or control. Consequently, it is best suited to small environments.

 TIP   Microsoft does provide centralized monitoring for Windows Defender Antivirus as part of Microsoft Configuration Manager Endpoint Protection enterprise management software and Microsoft Intune cloud service.

Scanning

Real-time scanning constantly monitors activity on your computer. It monitors actions, files that are being downloaded, and disk activity. The goal of real-time scanning is to detect malware before it executes on your computer. For example, if you run a program that contains malware, real-time scanning identifies the malware when the file is read from disk and prevents it from executing. It will also quarantine the file.

 TIP   If you are performing a disk-intensive activity, temporarily disabling real-time scanning can increase overall storage performance.

On-demand scanning is used to identify malware that is already present on your computer. A quick scan looks for malware in the most common locations. When a quick scan is running, user performance is not affected. A full scan looks at the entire disk system and running processes to find malware. This type of scan is more complete, but it might affect system performance. A full scan is typically performed when you think that malware is on your computer. You can run a custom scan if you want to check a specific folder or file for malware.

Some malware is capable of hiding itself when resident in memory and avoiding detection. In some cases, the malware is capable of restarting itself after infection and remaining undetectable by anti-malware software, such as Windows Defender Firewall. For this type of malware, you need to do an offline scan where Windows is not running so that the malware is not in memory. For this scenario, use Windows Defender Offline. Windows Defender Offline restarts your computer and performs a scan while your installation of Windows 10 is not running. You can run a Windows Defender Offline scan manually or it might be suggested when Windows Defender Antivirus detects malware.

Windows 10 automatically runs scheduled scans in the background. This is important to detect malware that has been saved to disk before malware definitions were updated. A default schedule is in place for running quick scans and remediation scans (full scan), but you can configure your own schedule by using the Set-MpPreference cmdlet or by using Group Policy. No graphical interface is available for configuring scheduled scans.

Definitions

Windows Defender Antivirus uses definitions to identify known and potential malware. The definitions should be updated regularly to ensure you can detect the most recent malware. By default, definitions are updated automatically by Windows Update; however, you also have the option to manually update the definitions on the Virus & threat protection screen.

Protection History

In Windows Defender, you can view the history of items that were detected. In the list of detections, you can expand the event, as shown in Figure 6-13. Expanding the event allows you to read more information about what was detected and the action subsequently performed by Windows Defender Antivirus.

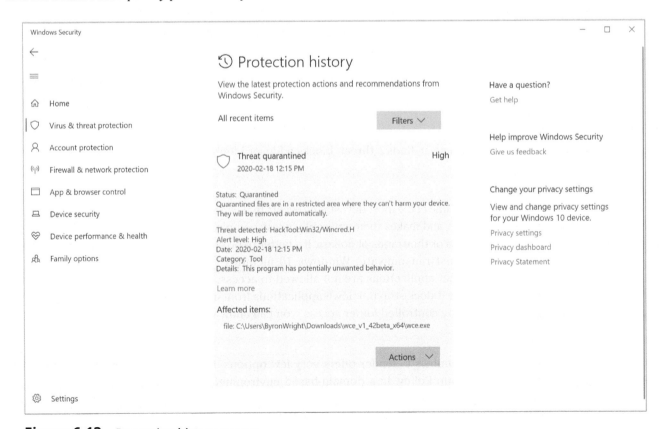

Figure 6-13   Protection history screen

Sometimes antivirus software can be overly aggressive and quarantine files that you legitimately want to use and access. This is common with tools that analyze Windows security or scan the network. On the Actions button, you can restore a quarantined file that appears as a false positive. Alternatively, after you've verified that the file was a threat, you can remove it using the Actions button.

 TIP   If you identify a false positive detection and allow a program to run, it is listed in Allowed threats.

In most cases, only a few items should be listed in the protection history; however, if you have an unfortunate event (or a few of them) and many items are listed in the protection history, you can use filtering to identify the items you want to view. The Filters button lets you view items based on recommendations, quarantined items, cleaned items, blocked actions, and severity.

Virus and Threat Protection Settings

Windows Defender Antivirus has a very limited set of configuration options available in the Update & security settings. In most cases, you want to leave these options at the default setting. The settings you can configure are:

- *Real-time protection*—Unless you have a specific need to disable real-time protection, you should leave this on. If you are copying a large number of files, disabling real-time protection might speed up the copying process. Also, if you are trying to download a file that you know is safe, and Windows Defender is seeing the file as a false positive, you can temporarily disable real-time scanning.
- *Cloud-based protection*—This option allows Windows Defender Antivirus to communicate with Microsoft to report malware and scanning activity on your computer. This information is used by Microsoft to improve Windows Defender Antivirus. Cloud-based protection is enabled by default.
- *Automatic sample submission*—When this option is enabled, samples of detected malware are sent back to Microsoft for further analysis. This is particularly important for malware identified by heuristics. Heuristics identifies malware based on pattern of behavior instead of signature. After submission to Microsoft, the malware signature can be included in definitions. Automatic sample submission is enabled by default.
- *Tamper protection*—When this option is enabled, applications can't modify Windows Defender Antivirus settings. This helps to prevent malware from evading Windows Defender Antivirus by adding an exclusion or disabling real-time protection.
- *Exclusions*—Some applications, such as databases, might not run properly when real-time scanning is performed on them. In such a case, you can create an exclusion for specific files or folders. No exclusions are configured by default.
- *Notifications*—You control which events generate notifications. By default, you get notified when Windows Defender Antivirus completes a scan, finds a threat, blocks a file, or blocks an action.

Ransomware Protection

Losing all the data files on a computer is one of the most devastating events that can occur for a computer user. Ransomware is a type of malware that encrypts files and makes them unusable unless you pay a fee to the hacker(s). The charge to decrypt might be a few hundred dollars or thousands of dollars. It's better to protect yourself than to pay the ransom.

To protect your computer against ransomware, Windows 10 includes **controlled folder access**, shown in Figure 6-14. You can specify folders that applications are not allowed to access. This doesn't prevent you from opening a data file using Word or Excel, but it does stop unknown applications from modifying or deleting files. If you have a trusted application that is blocked by controlled folder access, you can allow it.

Group Policy Configuration

The user interface for configuring Windows Defender offers very few options. If you need fine-grained control over Windows Defender, you can use Group Policy. In a domain-based environment, the Group Policy settings can be easily deployed to multiple computers. The Group Policy settings for Windows Defender are located in Computer Configuration\Administrative Templates\Windows Components\Windows Defender Antivirus. Each of the settings is documented in the Group Policy editor.

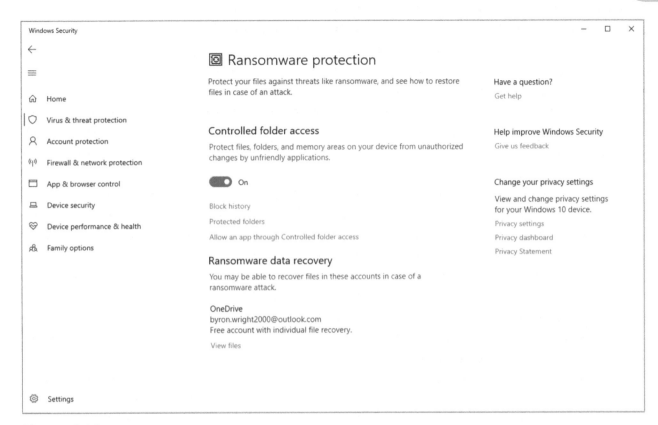

Figure 6-14   Ransomware protection screen

Windows PowerShell Configuration

The graphical interface for managing Windows Defender Antivirus does not give you all the available management options. To view and modify the detailed configuration settings for a local instance of Windows Defender Antivirus, you can use Windows PowerShell cmdlets. You can use Windows PowerShell scripts to configure multiple computers, but Group Policy is better suited for that task. Table 6-3 lists some of the cmdlets for managing Windows Defender Antivirus.

Table 6-3   Windows PowerShell cmdlets for Managing Windows Defender Antivirus

Cmdlet	Description
Get-MpPreference	Views the current configuration settings for Windows Defender Antivirus
Set-MpPreference	Modifies the settings for Windows Defender Antivirus
Get-MpComputerStatus	Views the current status of Windows Defender Antivirus
Get-MpThreat	Views threats that have been detected by Windows Defender Antivirus; this identifies the threat but not the specific incident information
Get-MpThreatDetection	Views incident information, such as time of the incident, where threats have been detected by Windows Defender Antivirus
Remove-MpThreat	Removes active threats; in most cases Windows Defender Antivirus removes threats by default and the cmdlet is not required
Start-MpScan	Starts a Windows Defender Antivirus scan
Start-MpWDOScan	Starts a Windows Defender offline scan
Update-MpSignature	Updates definitions for Windows Defender Antivirus

Activity 6-6: Using Windows Defender Antivirus

Time Required: 10 minutes

Objective: Use Windows Defender Antivirus to prevent spyware on a computer

Description: Windows Defender Antivirus is used to prevent malware installation and remove malware. You can test the functionality of anti-malware software by using the EICAR anti-malware test file. The test file has a specific text string that all anti-malware software detects but poses no risk of a malware infection. In this activity, you test real-time scanning and on-demand scanning.

1. If necessary, start your computer and sign in.
2. On the taskbar, click **Microsoft Edge**.
3. In the Search or enter web address box, type **www.eicar.org** and then press **Enter**.
4. On the Eicar website, click the **DOWNLOAD ANTI MALWARE TESTFILE** icon in the upper-right corner and then click **DOWNLOAD** in the left navigation menu.
5. On the Download page, scroll down and below the Download area using the secure, SSL enabled protocol https heading, click **eicar_com.zip** and then click **Save**. You should be notified that Windows Defender detected malware and deleted it.
6. Leave the Microsoft Edge window open for later in this activity.
7. Click the **Start** button and then click **Settings**.
8. In the Settings window, click **Update & Security** and then click **Windows Security**.
9. On the Windows Security screen, click **Virus & threat protection**.
10. In the Windows Security window, below Virus & threat protection settings, click **Manage settings**.
11. Click the **Real-time protection** switch to turn it **Off**. If necessary, click **Yes** in the User Account Control prompt to confirm the action.
12. In Microsoft Edge, click **eicar_com.zip** and then click **Save**.
13. Click **Open folder** and verify that the file is downloaded.
14. In the Windows Security window, click the **Real-time protection** switch to turn it **On**. Notice that the eicar_com.zip file is not detected immediately because the file hasn't been accessed yet.
15. In the left navigation pane, click **Virus & threat protection** and then click **Scan options**.
16. On the Scan options screen, click **Custom scan** and then click **Scan now**.
17. In the Select Folder dialog box, browse to **Local Disk (C:)**, select the **Users** folder, and then click **Select Folder**.
18. When the scan is complete, the EICAR test file is shown as a detected threat. Click **Virus:DOS/EICAR_Test_File** to view the details.
19. Click **See details** and then click **Yes** in the User Account Control prompt.
20. Read the detailed information about the EICAR test file and then click **OK**.
21. Click **Start actions** to apply the default action.
22. Close all open windows.
23. Click the **Start** button, type **PowerShell**, right-click **Windows PowerShell**, and then click **Run as administrator**.
24. In the User Account Control dialog box, click **Yes**.
25. At the Windows PowerShell prompt, type **Get-MpThreat** and then press **Enter**. Read the threat information.
26. At the Windows PowerShell prompt, type **Get-MpThreatDetection** and then press **Enter**. Read the threat detection information.
27. At the Windows PowerShell prompt, type **Get-MpPreference** and then press **Enter**. Read the configuration information.
28. At the Windows PowerShell prompt, type **Get-MpComputerStatus** and then press **Enter**. Read the status information.
29. Close the Windows PowerShell window.

App & Browser Control

Because the Internet is one of the primary sources of malware, it's important that access to the Internet is monitored for malware. **Windows Defender Smartscreen** is included in Windows 10 to monitor unrecognized apps and files, malicious websites, and web content downloaded by Microsoft Store apps. For these options, you can configure content to be blocked, a warning displayed, or no action (off), as shown in Figure 6-15.

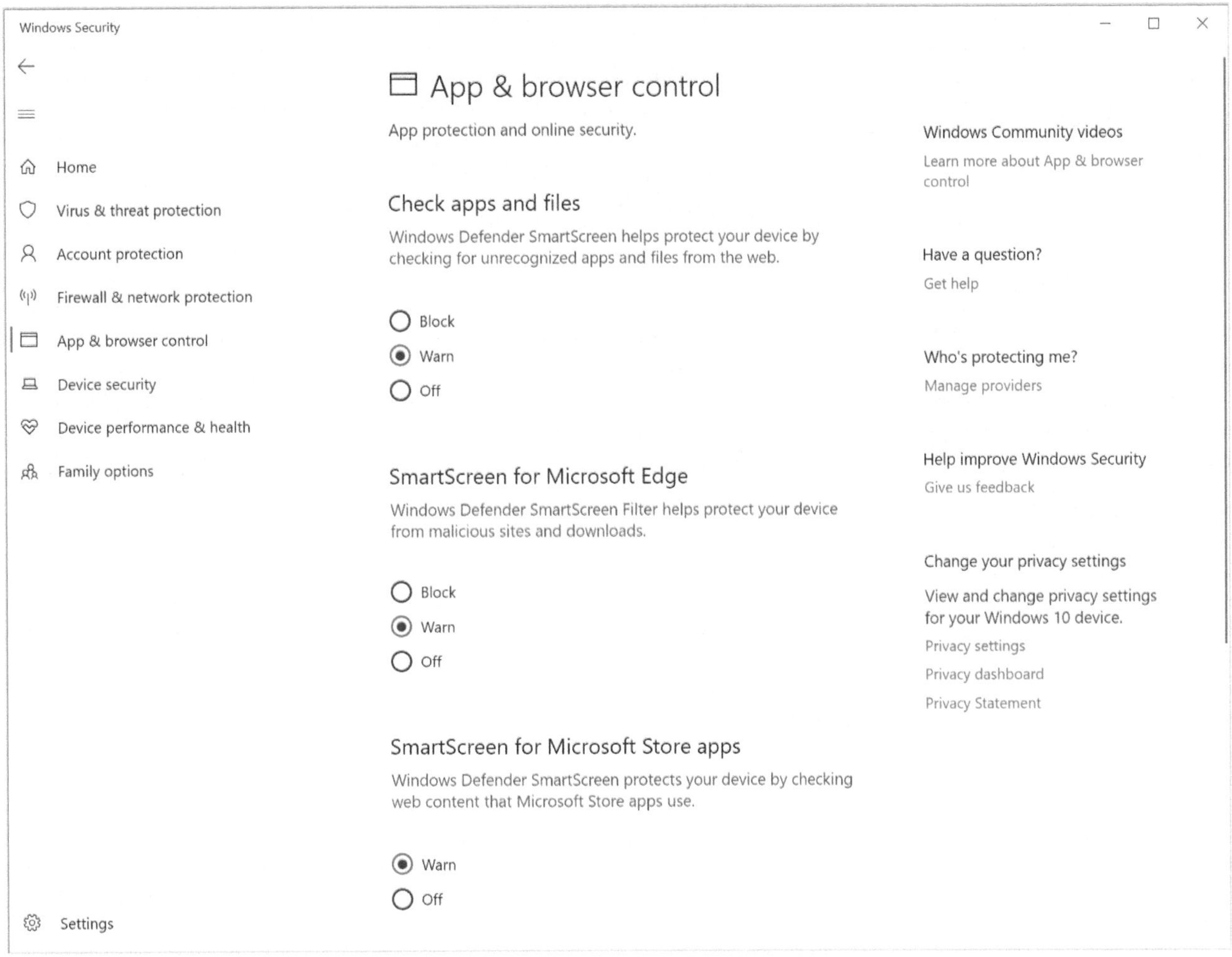

Figure 6-15   App & browser control screen

Not all malware will be detected by Windows Defender Smartscreen because it identifies known malicious files. Malware developers are constantly developing new methods to exploit Windows 10. **Windows Defender Application Guard** can mitigate some malware risk by running Microsoft Edge in an isolated browsing environment. The isolated browsing environment is a Hyper-V enabled container that is in a separate environment from the operating system. This prevents an unknown exploit from affecting the operating system and infecting Windows 10. It also prevents the exploit from accessing credentials currently in use.

Windows 10 Pro includes Windows Defender Application Guard, but you need to configure it for each device. To centrally manage Windows Defender Application Guard by using management software, such as Microsoft Intune, you need to use Windows 10 Enterprise or Windows 10 Education. You also need to have a computer that supports Hyper-V virtualization.

Known exploit mitigation techniques can be enabled or disabled in Windows 10. Many of them are enabled by default because they generally do not cause application compatibility issues. For example, Data Execution Prevention (DEP), which ensures that code is not run from data-only memory, is on by default. Other mitigations are not enabled by default because they can cause compatibility issues; because of this, you should evaluate your applications before enabling the mitigation.

In addition to system-level exploit protection mitigations, you can configure application-specific settings. If you have one application that is not compatible with a mitigation, you can disable the mitigation for that specific application and enable the mitigation and the system level.

You can deploy customized mitigation settings to multiple computers by using an XML file with the customized mitigation settings. First, you configure a reference computer with the customized settings and then export those settings as an XML file. You can export the XML file from exploit-protection settings or by using the Get-ProcessMitigation cmdlet with the -PolicyFilePath parameter. You can import the XML file on a destination computer by using the Set-ProcessMitigation cmdlet or by using the Use a common set of exploit protection settings setting in Group Policy. After you import the XML file, you can view the settings in Windows Security.

Device Security

The content on the Device security screen, shown in Figure 6-16, in Windows Security varies depending on the capabilities of your computer. The options supported by your computer automatically appear if applicable.

Core isolation includes memory protection techniques that are available only if your computer supports Hyper-V virtualization. Memory integrity enforces the requirement for code running kernel mode to be trusted. Memory access protection prevents drive-by direct memory access (DMA) attaches that can occur when hot-plug PCI devices are connected via Thunderbolt 3 ports. Memory access protection is enabled automatically if your computer has a Thunderbolt 3 port.

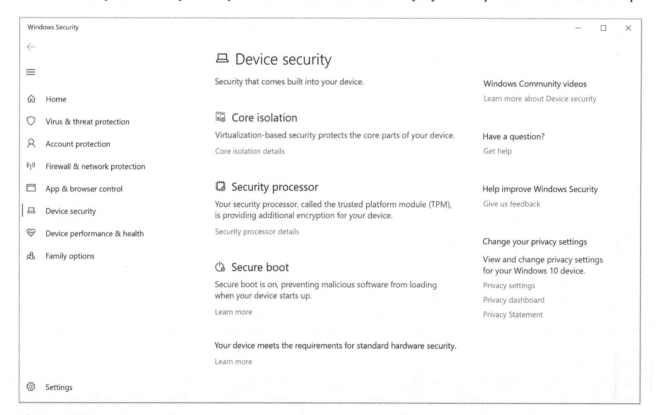

Figure 6-16   Device security screen

Security processor contains the settings for the trusted platform module (TPM) in your computer. You can use this area to view information about the TPM, including the manufacturer and TPM specification version. If you want to view error messages or clear the TPM to default settings, select the Security processor troubleshooting link.

 Data encryption keys are often stored in the TPM. Make sure you back up TPM data before you clear it back to default settings.

Secure boot is a system that ensures the integrity of files used early in the Windows 10 startup process. If startup files are modified, Windows 10 will not start in order to ensure that malware is not being loaded. Newer computers using UEFI firmware support using secure boot.

At the bottom of the Device security screen is a status message about the support your computer has for standard hardware security, including the following:

- *Your device meets the requirements for standard hardware security*—When you see this message, your device supports memory integrity and core isolation. Your device also has a TPM-meeting specification version 2.0, secure boot enabled, DEP enabled, and UEFI memory attributes table (MAT).
- *Your device meets the requirements for enhanced hardware security*—When you see this message, your device meets the requirements for standard hardware security and has memory integrity enabled.
- *Your device exceeds the requirements for enhanced hardware security*—When you see this message, your device meets the requirements for enhanced hardware security and has System Management Mode (SMM) protection turned on. SMM protection monitors operating system memory and ensures that it is not modified.
- *Standard hardware security not supported*—When you see this message, at least one of the requirements for standard hardware security is not met.

Often, when a computer does not meet the requirements for standard hardware security, it is due to the TPM configuration. It is common for lower-end computers to not include a TPM. Older computers also might not have a TPM that is specified as version 2.0.

UEFI firmware configuration can also prevent a computer from meeting standard hardware security requirements. Most newer computers have UEFI firmware that supports secure boot and UEFI MAT. Sometimes, however, the UEFI firmware is configured to run in BIOS-compatibility mode, which doesn't support secure boot or UEFI MAT. Also, you might need to enable secure boot in the UEFI firmware. Secure boot might not be enabled by default.

DATA SECURITY

The most basic level of data security in Windows 10 is NTFS permissions. NTFS permissions stop signed-in users from accessing files and folders for which they do not have read or write permission; however, NTFS permissions are effective in protecting data only when the original operating system is running.

You can work around NTFS permissions and gain access to data in several ways. The following are two examples:

- You can start a computer from a USB drive or DVD and run Linux with an NTFS driver. Linux with an NTFS driver can read NTFS-formatted partitions and ignore the security information. This allows you to copy or modify data on the NTFS-formatted volume even without a valid user name.
- You can attach a hard drive from one Windows 10 computer to another. Local administrators always can take ownership of files and then read or modify them. When you move a hard drive, the local administrators of the new system can take ownership of files and then read or modify them.

As you can see, it is relatively easy to work around NTFS permissions when you have physical access to the computer. NTFS permissions are a reliable method of securing data when files are accessible only over a network, but not when there is physical access to the computer storing the files. This makes NTFS permissions excellent for servers, which are typically physically secured, but not as effective for desktop computers and laptops. Laptops are particularly at risk because they are more often lost or stolen.

To secure data on desktop computers and laptops, encryption is required. Windows 10 includes Encrypting File System (EFS) and BitLocker Drive Encryption to encrypt files.

Encryption Algorithms

Encryption is the process of taking data and rendering it unreadable. In most cases, encryption is a two-way process; first, data is encrypted to make it unreadable, then it is decrypted to make it readable again. The process for encrypting data uses an algorithm. For computerized encryption of data, algorithms are math formulas that scramble the data into an unreadable format.

Different types of encryption algorithms are suited to different purposes. Some algorithms are faster than others and best suited to encrypting large volumes of data. Other algorithms require two separate keys for encryption and decryption and are well suited to operations performed by two separate users or processes.

Symmetric Encryption

A **symmetric encryption algorithm** uses the same key to encrypt data and decrypt data. This is very similar to how a deadbolt lock works. When you leave your house, you lock the door with your key; when you return, you unlock the door with the same key. Figure 6-17 shows Bob and Susan accessing encrypted data by using the same key.

In computerized encryption, the key is a long number that is extremely difficult to guess. The longer the key, the harder it is to guess. One of the most common key lengths for symmetric encryption is 128 bits. Data that is symmetrically encrypted with a 128-bit key will take years to decrypt by guessing the key. Other solutions offer stronger encryption, with longer keys of 4096 bits or more.

Symmetric encryption is strong and fast, which makes it well suited to encrypting large volumes of data, such as that contained in files. Most file encryption is done with a symmetric encryption algorithm. Both EFS and BitLocker Drive Encryption use symmetric encryption to secure data.

The biggest problem with symmetric encryption is securing the key. Anyone who has a copy of the encryption key can decrypt the data. In Figure 6-17, both Bob and Susan need to have a copy of the same symmetric key. EFS and BitLocker Drive Encryption both use different methods to secure the key.

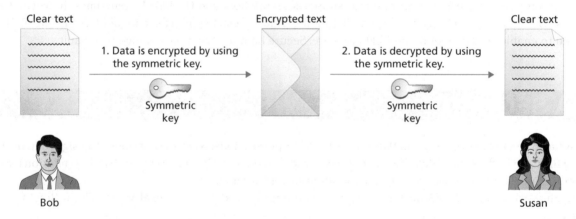

Figure 6-17   Symmetric encryption

Asymmetric Encryption

An **asymmetric encryption algorithm** uses two related, but unique, keys to encrypt and decrypt data. Data encrypted by one key is decrypted by the other key. This is similar to an electronic safe, where one person has a code that allows him or her to deposit money, but the other person has a code that allows him or her to remove money from the safe.

The keys used in asymmetric encryption are part of a digital certificate. Digital certificates are obtained from certificate authorities (sometimes also called certification authorities). Some of the better-known certificate authorities are Comodo, Digicert, and Let's Encrypt. Companies can also generate their own digital certificates internally. Most server operating systems, including Windows Server 2019, have certificate authority functionality as an option.

The digital certificate from a certification authority contains a public key and a private key. The public key is meant to be known to other people. The private key is protected and known only to you. By using both keys, encrypted data can be sent securely without the risk of transferring a symmetrical key. For example, in Figure 6-18, Bob is encrypting data for Susan. When Bob performs the encryption, he uses Susan's public key. Then, Susan—and only Susan—can decrypt the data by using her private key because only Susan has the private key.

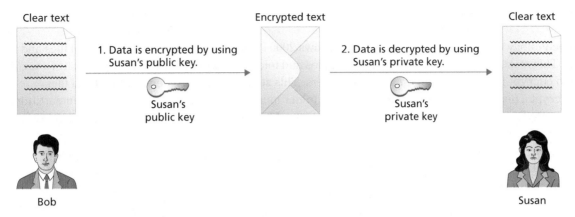

Figure 6-18 Asymmetric encryption

Asymmetric encryption requires more processing power and is less secure than symmetric encryption. This makes asymmetric encryption unsuitable for large volumes of data. Asymmetric encryption is typically used to encrypt small amounts of data. Many systems for encrypting data use symmetric encryption to encrypt the data and then use asymmetric encryption to protect just the symmetric key because a symmetric key is relatively small compared to the data it has encrypted.

Hashing

Hashing algorithms are used for a very different purpose than symmetric and asymmetric encryption algorithms. A hashing algorithm is one-way encryption, which means that it encrypts data, but the data cannot be decrypted.

Hashing is used to uniquely identify data rather than prevent access to data. Sometimes, hash values for data are referred to as fingerprints. When you download software, some websites give you an MD5 value for the file. MD5 is a hashing algorithm. The MD5 value is the unique value that is created when the MD5 hashing algorithm is run on the downloadable software. You can verify that the software has not been modified or corrupted by verifying the MD5 value after you download the software. If the software has been changed in any way, the MD5 value is also changed. Figure 6-19 shows how a hash value is used to verify that software has not been modified.

Hashing algorithms are also used for storing passwords. The passwords entered by users are not actually checked. The operating system verifies that the hash value of the password entered by the user matches the hash value that is stored for the user's password. When passwords are stored only as a hash value, it is impossible to decrypt the password. The password can be guessed only by brute force (trying all possible combinations).

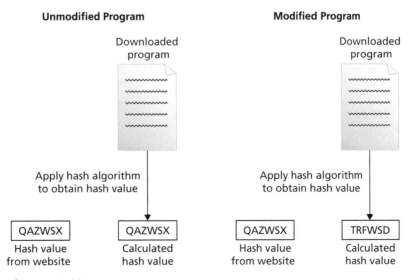

Figure 6-19 Hash encryption

Encrypting File System

EFS is a technology that was first included with Windows 2000 Professional. It encrypts individual files and folders on a volume. This makes it suitable for protecting data files and folders on workstations and laptops; however, it can also be used to encrypt files and folders on network servers. This section focuses on encrypting local files.

To encrypt a file or folder by using EFS, the file or folder must be located on an NTFS-formatted partition. FAT- and FAT32-formatted partitions cannot hold EFS-encrypted files. FAT and FAT32 file systems are not capable of holding the information required to decrypt the files.

When a file is encrypted, the data in the file is encrypted using a symmetrical key that is randomly generated for that specific file. The symmetrical key is then encrypted by asymmetric encryption, based on user-specific keys. This protects the symmetrical key from unauthorized users.

To use EFS, users must have a digital certificate with a public key and a private key. Unless specifically configured otherwise, users do not have a digital certificate by default. If a user encrypts a file and does not have a digital certificate, Windows 10 generates a certificate automatically. The public key from the digital certificate is used to encrypt the symmetrical key that encrypted the file. Only the user who encrypted the file is able to decrypt the symmetrical key because only that user has access to the private key required to decrypt the symmetrical key. The EFS encryption and decryption process is shown in Figure 6-20.

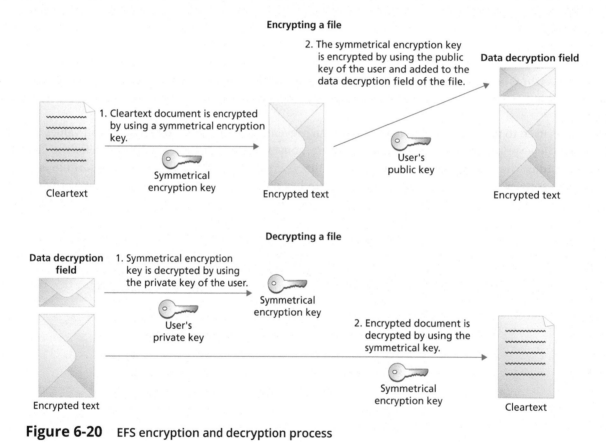

Figure 6-20   EFS encryption and decryption process

> 💡 **TIP**   User certificates are stored in the user profile.

From the user perspective, encryption is a file attribute, like compression, hidden, or read-only. To encrypt a file, a user needs to access the Advanced Attributes of the file, as shown in Figure 6-21.

> 💡 **TIP**   Files that are encrypted cannot also be compressed.

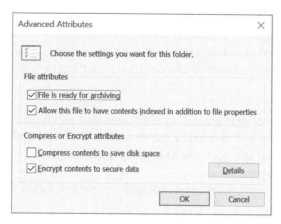

Figure 6-21 Advanced attributes of a file

Files can also be encrypted using the cipher command-line utility. Cipher is useful for scripting or making changes to many files at once. For more information about cipher options, run cipher with the /? switch from a command prompt.

Lost Encryption Keys

If a user loses the certificate that secures an EFS key, the encrypted file is unrecoverable with the default configuration. The encrypted file can be recovered only if the user has backed up the EFS certificate or if a recovery certificate has been created and installed.

The following are some ways EFS certificates may be lost:

- The user profile is corrupted.
- The user profile is deleted accidentally.
- The user is deleted from the system.
- The user password is reset.

User Accounts in Control Panel provides an option for you to manage your file encryption certificates that allows you to view, create, and back up certificates used for EFS. You can also configure EFS to use a certificate on a smart card and update previously encrypted files to use a new EFS certificate. After a certificate is backed up, it can be used whenever required. This certificate can be imported back into a new user profile or even to a different user.

 TIP You can back up and import EFS certificates by using the Certificates snap-in in a Microsoft Management Console.

Creating a recovery certificate allows the files encrypted by all users to be recovered if required. When a recovery certificate is in place, the symmetric key for all files is stored twice. The first copy of the symmetric key is encrypted by using the public key of the user encrypting the file. The second copy of the symmetric key is encrypted by using the public key of the recovery certificate.

The steps for creating and using a recovery certificate are as follows:

1. *Create the recovery certificate*—This is done by running cipher with the /r:filename option, where filename is the name of the recovery certificate.
2. *Install the recovery certificate*—This is done by importing the recovery certificate into the local security policy as a data recovery agent. After this point, all newly encrypted files will include a symmetric key that is accessible to a user using the recovery certificate.
3. *Update existing encrypted files*—This is done by running cipher with the /u option. Encrypted files can be updated only by a user who is able to decrypt the files. This means that multiple users might need to update files. Updating encrypted files adds an extra encrypted copy of the symmetric key that is accessible to a user using the recovery certificate.

To recover files, you import the recovery certificate into a user profile using the Certificates MMC snap-in. After the recovery certificate is imported, that user can decrypt any files necessary.

In a domain-based environment, the recovery certificate is deployed by using Group Policy rather than individually on each computer. To do this, navigate to Computer Configuration\Windows Settings\Security Settings\Public Key Policies\Encrypting File System, right-click Encrypting File System, and then click Add Data Recovery Agent. A wizard then guides you through the process of importing the certificate that will be used as a data recovery agent.

Sharing Encrypted Files

In a domain-based environment, it is easy to store encrypted files on a server and access them from multiple workstations or share them with other users. The necessary certificates are automatically created and stored on the remote server, and the files are encrypted and shared. On workstations that are part of a workgroup or local users in a domain, the process takes more work.

For a single user to work with encrypted files on multiple computers, follow these steps:

1. Encrypt the file on the first computer.
2. Export the EFS certificate, including the private key from the first computer.
3. Import the EFS certificate, including the private key on the second computer.
4. Open the encrypted file on the second computer.

To share encrypted files with other users, follow these steps:

1. Export the EFS certificate of the first user but do not include the private key.
2. Import the EFS certificate of the first user into the profile of the second user as a trusted person.
3. The second user encrypts the file and shares it with the first user. A copy of the symmetric key is encrypted with the public key of each user.

 TIP   In an environment without an internal certificate authority, the EFS certificate for a user is created automatically the first time he or she encrypts a file.

Encrypted files are typically not shared within a workgroup because of the complex process required. Sharing encrypted files is more common among domain users where no additional configuration is required.

Moving and Copying Encrypted Files

The encryption of files and folders behaves differently than NTFS permissions and compression when files and folders are moved and copied. When files and folders are copied, they always take on the NTFS permissions or compression attribute of the folder they are copied into; however, this is not the case for encrypted files.

The following rules apply for moving and copying encrypted files:

- An unencrypted file copied or moved to an encrypted folder becomes encrypted.
- An encrypted file copied or moved to an unencrypted folder remains encrypted.
- An encrypted file copied or moved to a FAT or FAT32-formatted volume becomes unencrypted if you have access to decrypt the file. If you do not have access to decrypt the file, you receive an access-denied error.

Activity 6-7: Using EFS

Time Required: 10 minutes
Objective: Use EFS to encrypt and protect files
Description: EFS is used to encrypt individual files and folders. After a file is encrypted, only authorized users are able to read the data in the file. In this activity, you encrypt a file and test it to ensure that only authorized users can decrypt the file.

1. If necessary, start your computer and sign in.
2. On the taskbar, click **File Explorer**.
3. In the File Explorer window, navigate to **C:\Users\Public\Public Documents**.
4. Right-click an open area in the **Name** column, point to **New**, and then click **Text Document**.

5. Type **encrypt** as the file name and then press **Enter**.
6. Double-click **encrypt** to open it and then type a line of text.
7. Click **File** on the menu bar, click **Exit**, and then click **Save**.
8. Right-click an open area in the **Name** column, point to **New**, and then click **Text Document**.
9. Type **other** as the file name and then press **Enter**.
10. Double-click **other** to open it and then type a line of text.
11. Click **File** on the menu bar, click **Exit**, and then click **Save**.
12. Right-click **encrypt** and then click **Properties**.
13. Click the **Advanced** button, select the **Encrypt contents to secure data** check box, and then click **OK**.
14. Click **OK**, click **Encrypt the file only**, and then click **OK**. Notice that the file encrypt now has a lock icon to indicate that it is encrypted.
15. Close the File Explorer window.
16. Switch the user to **Bob**.
17. On the taskbar, click **File Explorer**.
18. In File Explorer, navigate to **C:\Users\Public\Public Documents**.
19. Double-click **other**. Notice that you are able to open and read this file.
20. Exit Notepad.
21. Double-click **encrypt**. You receive an error indicating that access is denied because the file is encrypted.
22. Click **OK** to close the error dialog box and then exit Notepad.
23. Sign out as **Bob**.

Activity 6-8: Recovering Lost Encryption Keys

Time Required: 10 minutes
Objective: Back up and restore an EFS encryption key
Description: A lost EFS encryption key means that an encrypted file cannot be accessed. To avoid this problem, you can back up the encryption key of a user. If a user's encryption key is backed up, you can restore it and then the user regains access to his or her files. In this activity, you back up and restore the encryption key for a user.

1. If necessary, start your computer and sign in.
2. Click the **Start** button, type **control** and then click **Control Panel**.
3. Click **User Accounts** and then click **User Accounts**.
4. In the left pane, click **Manage your file encryption certificates**.
5. Click **Next** to start the Manage your file encryption certificates wizard.
6. Click **Next** to accept the default certificate.
7. If necessary, click **Back up the certificate and key now**.
8. To set the Backup location, click the **Browse** button, type **CertBak**, and then click **Save**. The default location is your Documents directory. Typically, you would save the backed-up certificate on removable storage and keep it in a secure location.
9. In the Password and Confirm password boxes, type **password** and then click **Next**. It is important to secure the backup with a password because it contains your private key.
10. Click **Next** to skip updating encrypted files with a new key.
11. Click **Close**.
12. Click the **Start** button, type **mmc**, and then press **Enter**.
13. Click **Yes** to start the Microsoft Management Console.
14. Click **File** on the menu bar and then click **Add/Remove Snap-in**.
15. In the Available snap-ins area, click **Certificates** and then click **Add**.
16. Click **Finish** to accept managing certificates for your user account and then click **OK**.
17. In the left pane, expand **Certificates—Current User**, expand **Personal**, and then click **Certificates**.

18. In the middle pane, right-click the **Userx** certificate, and then click **Delete**. If multiple certificates appear, delete all of them.
19. Read the warning message about losing the ability to decrypt files and then click **Yes**.
20. Sign out and sign in again. This clears the certificate from memory.
21. On the taskbar, click **File Explorer**.
22. In File Explorer, below Recent files, double-click **encrypt**. You should receive an error indicating that access is denied because the file is encrypted.
23. Click **OK** to close the error dialog box and then exit Notepad.
24. Click the **Start** button, type **mmc**, and then press **Enter**.
25. Click **Yes** to start the Microsoft Management Console.
26. Click **File** on the menu bar and then click **Add/Remove Snap-in**.
27. In the Available snap-ins area, click **Certificates** and then click **Add**.
28. Click **Finish** to accept managing certificates for your user account and then click **OK**.
29. In the left pane, expand **Certificates - Current User** and then click **Personal**.
30. Right-click **Personal**, point to **All Tasks**, and then click **Import**.
31. Click **Next** to start the Certificate Import Wizard.
32. Click the **Browse** button, change the file type to **Personal Information Exchange (*.pfx,*.p12)**, click **CertBak**, and then click **Open**.
33. Click **Next**.
34. In the Password box, type **password**.
35. Select the **Mark this key as exportable. This will allow you to back up or transport your keys at a later time.** check box and then click **Next**.
36. Click **Next** to accept the default certificate location, click **Finish**, and then click **OK**. Now you have a personal certificate again.
37. Close the MMC and then click **No** to saving the console settings.
38. In the File Explorer window, double-click **encrypt**. Now you are able to open the file because you have restored the certificate that contains your private key. Your public key was used to encrypt the symmetrical key that was used to encrypt the file.
39. Close all open windows.

BitLocker Drive Encryption

BitLocker Drive Encryption is a data encryption feature included with Windows 10 that addresses some of the short-comings of EFS. EFS is designed to encrypt only specified files. Some files, such as the operating system files, cannot be encrypted by using EFS. In addition, in some cases it might be possible to introduce low-level software that is able to steal EFS certificates.

When you use BitLocker Drive Encryption, an entire volume is encrypted. This protects not only your data, but also the operating system. Protecting the operating system ensures that additional software is not placed on the drive when the operating system is shut down. Figure 6-22 shows the screen used to enable BitLocker Drive Encryption.

BitLocker Drive Encryption is designed to be used with a TPM. A TPM is part of the motherboard in a computer and is used to store encryption keys and certificates. Not all computers have a TPM module, and you should verify whether a TPM is present when buying a newer computer. BitLocker Drive Encryption can be used on computers without a TPM, in which case the encryption keys are stored on a USB drive or you need to enter a PIN at startup.

When a TPM is used, BitLocker Drive Encryption has two modes:

- *TPM only*—In this mode, the user is not aware that BitLocker is activated because the keys stored in the TPM are automatically used to start Windows 10. This option protects data from offline modification but does not add any extra protection to the boot process to prevent password guessing.
- *Startup key*—In this mode, the user must supply a startup key to boot Windows 10. The startup key can be configured on a USB drive or as a PIN entered by the user. This adds extra protection because password guessing to sign in to the operating system cannot be performed without first obtaining the startup key.

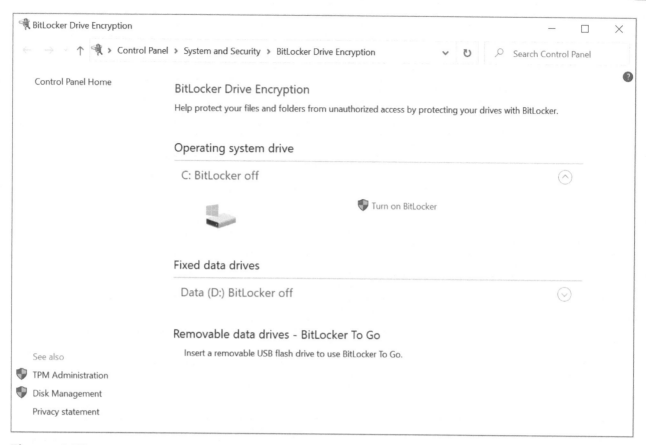

Figure 6-22   BitLocker Drive Encryption

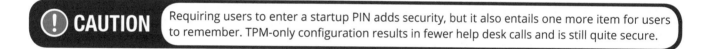

CAUTION   Requiring users to enter a startup PIN adds security, but it also entails one more item for users to remember. TPM-only configuration results in fewer help desk calls and is still quite secure.

BitLocker Hard Drive Configuration

To use BitLocker Drive Encryption, a hard drive must be divided into two partitions. One partition is used as the operating system volume. The operating system volume is the volume that is encrypted. This volume is the C: drive that contains both the operating system and user data.

The second required volume is the system volume. The system volume is not encrypted and contains the necessary files to boot the operating system. This volume must be at least 300 MB and formatted as an NTFS volume. Windows 10 automatically creates this volume as part of the installation process unless you specifically prevent it.

BitLocker Encryption Keys

BitLocker uses two keys to protect data. The **Volume Master Key (VMK)** is used to encrypt the data on the operating system volume. The VMK is then encrypted using a **Full Volume Encryption Key (FVEK)**. This multiple-key method for data encryption makes it faster to change the encryption key. Changing the VMK would require re-encrypting all the data, which is time consuming. Changing the FVEK requires re-encrypting only the VMK, which is very fast. Figure 6-23 illustrates how the encryption keys are used to protect data.

Accessing BitLocker-encrypted data is seamless for the user. A filter driver is used by Windows 10 to encrypt and decrypt data transparently as it is accessed from the hard drive. All data saved on the operating system volume is encrypted, including the paging files and hibernation file. Although a slight decrease in disk performance occurs, it should not be noticeable to users in most circumstances. Microsoft claims that BitLocker has a performance impact of less than 10%.

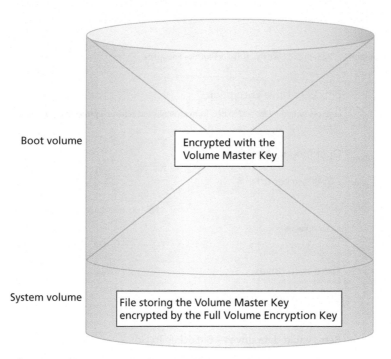

Boot volume

Encrypted with the
Volume Master Key

System volume

File storing the Volume Master Key
encrypted by the Full Volume Encryption Key

Figure 6-23   BitLocker encryption keys

Activity 6-9: Enabling BitLocker Drive Encryption

Time Required: 15 minutes

Objective: Enable BitLocker Drive Encryption

Description: BitLocker Drive Encryption encrypts the contents of a hard drive so that unauthorized users cannot gain access to it. This is typically implemented in mobile computers. For the best experience, you should use a computer with a TPM; however, you can enable BitLocker on computers without a TPM. In this activity, you encrypt the C: drive of a computer without a TPM.

1. If necessary, start your computer and sign in.
2. Click the **Start** button, type **mmc**, and then press **Enter**.
3. Click **Yes** to start the Microsoft Management Console.
4. Click **File** on the menu bar and then click **Add/Remove Snap-in**.
5. In the Available snap-ins area, click **Group Policy Object Editor**, and then click **Add**.
6. Click **Finish** to edit the Local Computer Group Policy object and then click **OK**.
7. Expand **Local Computer Policy**, expand **Computer Configuration**, expand **Administrative Templates**, expand **Windows Components**, expand **BitLocker Drive Encryption**, and then click **Operating System Drives**.
8. Double-click **Require additional authentication at startup**.
9. In the Require additional authentication at startup window, click **Enabled**.
10. Select the **Allow BitLocker without a compatible TPM (requires a password or startup key on a USB flash drive)** check box and then click **OK**.
11. Close the MMC and then click **No** to saving the settings.
12. Click the **Start** button and then click **Settings**.
13. In the Find a setting box, type **BitLocker** and then click **Manage BitLocker**.
14. In the BitLocker Drive Encryption window, for the C: drive, click **Turn on BitLocker**.
15. On the Choose how to unlock your drive at startup screen, click **Enter a password**.
16. On the Create a password to unlock this drive screen, in the Enter your password and Reenter your password boxes, type **password** and then click **Next**.

17. On the How do you want to back up your recovery key screen, click **Print the recovery key**.
18. In the Print window, click **Microsoft Print to PDF** and then click **Print**.
19. In the Save Print Output As window, in the File name box, type **BitLocker** and then click **Save**.
20. On the How do you want to back up your recovery key screen, click **Next**.
21. On the Choose how much of your drive to encrypt screen, click **Encrypt used disk space only (faster and best for new PC's and drives)** and then click **Next**.
22. On the Choose which encryption mode to use screen, click **New encryption mode (best for fixed drives on this device)** and then click **Next**.
23. On the Are you ready to encrypt this drive screen, click **Continue**.
24. Restart your computer.
25. On the BitLocker screen, in the Enter the password to unlock this drive box, type **password** and then press **Enter**.
26. Sign in to your computer.
27. Right-click the **Start** button and then click **Windows PowerShell (Admin)**.
28. In the User Account Control dialog box, click **Yes**.
29. At the Windows PowerShell prompt, type **manage-bde -status** and then press **Enter**. This shows the percentage of encryption completed.
30. At the Windows PowerShell prompt, type **Get-Command | *BitLocker*** and then press **Enter**. This displays the Windows PowerShell cmdlets available for managing BitLocker.
31. At the Windows PowerShell prompt, type **Get-BitLockerVolume** and then press **Enter**. This provides status information about the BitLocker encrypted volume.
32. Close the Windows PowerShell prompt window.

BitLocker Network Unlock

One potential issue with BitLocker-encrypted systems is maintenance. If TPM and a PIN are required for startup, it prevents remote maintenance. For example, if a wake-on-LAN is used to start a computer remotely, it remains at the BitLocker screen waiting for the PIN to be entered, which means an administrator cannot remotely control it and updates cannot be installed. To resolve this issue, BitLocker Network Unlock allows computers to start automatically when connected to the corporate network.

When Network Unlock is enabled, the computer requests a certificate from the network during startup. A Windows Deployment Services (WDS) server provides a certificate capable of unlocking BitLocker. This functionality is possible only if the computer has UEFI firmware. BIOS firmware is not supported for Network Unlock.

NOTE 2

For detailed information about enabling Network Unlock, see BitLocker: How to enable Network Unlock at https://docs.microsoft.com/en-us/windows/security/information-protection/bitlocker/bitlocker-how-to-enable-network-unlock.

Recovering BitLocker-Encrypted Data

When BitLocker Drive Encryption is enabled, a recovery password is generated automatically. The recovery password is a random number that you can save to a USB drive or folder, display on the screen, or print. It is important to keep the key in a secure location because it can be used to access data on the BitLocker-encrypted volume.

Windows 10 also provides an option to configure a data recovery agent for BitLocker. Like a data recovery agent for EFS, a data recovery agent for BitLocker can access BitLocker-encrypted data even if a user forgets the PIN or password. In domain-based environments, this is configured by importing a certificate for a data recovery agent into Group Policy at Computer Configuration\Windows Settings\Security Settings\Public Key Policies.

In domain-based environments, you have the option to store the recovery password for BitLocker-encrypted drives in Active Directory. When this option is enabled, the recovery password is stored as an attribute of the computer object in Active Directory. You can also configure BitLocker to not allow encryption unless the recovery password is successfully stored in Active Directory. In a Group Policy object, enable Store BitLocker recovery information in Active Directory Domain Services (Windows Server 2008 and Windows Vista) in Computer Configuration\Administrative Templates\Windows Components\BitLocker Drive Encryption.

The recovery password is required when the normal decryption process for BitLocker Drive Encryption is unable to function. The most common reasons that the recovery password is required are:

- *Modified boot files*—If one of the boot files on the system volume is modified, BitLocker Drive Encryption stops the system from starting because the operating system has experienced tampering.
- *Lost encryption keys*—If the TPM has a problem, and the encryption keys stored in it are lost or corrupted, the encrypted volume cannot be decrypted normally. The recovery password is also required if the encryption keys are stored on a USB drive that is lost or erased.
- *Lost or forgotten startup PIN*—If the requirement for a startup PIN is selected and the user forgets the startup PIN, the recovery password is required to access the encrypted data.

The recovery process is as follows:

1. Turn on the computer.
2. Enter the BitLocker Drive Encryption Recovery Console.
3. Provide the recovery password by inserting a USB key or typing it in.
4. The computer restarts and boots normally.

Disabling BitLocker Drive Encryption

If you no longer need BitLocker Drive Encryption, you can turn it off or disable it. Turning off BitLocker Drive Encryption decrypts all the data on the hard drive and makes it readable again. After BitLocker Drive Encryption is turned off, the drive can be moved to another computer and read by other operating systems.

Disabling BitLocker Drive Encryption does not decrypt the files on the volume. Instead, BitLocker Drive Encryption stores the FVEK as a clear key, which effectively removes the data protection associated with using BitLocker Drive Encryption. A clear key is one that is not encrypted or protected in any way. Disabling BitLocker Drive Encryption is not sufficient for other operating systems to read the BitLocker-encrypted data.

Activity 6-10: Recovering a BitLocker-Encrypted Drive

Time Required: 20 minutes
Objective: Recover a BitLocker-encrypted drive
Description: BitLocker Drive Encryption protects your data from anyone who might steal your computer; however, it can also render your data unavailable if the keys in the TPM are corrupted or you forget a startup password. In this activity, you recover the C: drive of a computer after forgetting the password.

1. If necessary, start your computer and sign in.
2. On the taskbar, click **File Explorer**, and below Recent files, double-click **BitLocker**.
3. Read the contents of BitLocker.pdf. This content should be stored in a safe location that is not on the encrypted drive.
4. Print a copy of BitLocker.pdf so that you can use it later in this activity to recover the drive. If you do not have access to a printer, copy the recovery key on a piece of paper. If you are working with a virtual machine, you can take a screenshot.
5. Restart your computer.
6. On the BitLocker screen, press **Esc** to enter BitLocker Recovery.
7. On the BitLocker recovery screen, in the Enter the recovery key for this drive box, type the recovery key from BitLocker.pdf and then press **Enter**.
8. Sign in to your computer.
9. Click the **Start** button and then click **Settings**.
10. In the Find a setting box, type **BitLocker** and then click **Manage BitLocker**.
11. For the C: drive, click **Suspend protection**.
12. In the BitLocker Drive Encryption dialog box, click **Yes**.
13. Restart your computer and then sign in. Notice that you did not need to enter the password even though the drive is still encrypted.

14. Click the **Start** button and then click **Settings**.
15. In the Find a setting box, type **BitLocker** and then click **Manage BitLocker**.
16. For the C: drive, click **Turn off BitLocker**.
17. In the BitLocker Drive Encryption dialog box, click **Turn off BitLocker**.
18. Close all open windows.

BitLocker To Go

Windows 10 includes **BitLocker To Go** as a method for protecting data on removable storage, such as USB drives. When you choose to enable removable storage for BitLocker To Go, you are prompted for how the storage will be unlocked. This process for unlocking the encryption keys is different for BitLocker To Go because you must be able to unlock the removable drive on multiple computers.

The options for unlocking removable storage are:

- *Use a password to unlock the drive*—When this option is selected, you enter a password that protects the encryption key for the data. When you take the removable storage to another computer, you are prompted for the password before getting access to the data on the removable drive.
- *Use my smart card to unlock the drive*—When this option is selected, you identify a smart card that will protect the encryption key for the data. When you take the removable storage to another computer, you must provide the smart card and the PIN for the smart card before getting access to the data on the removable drive. This method is the most secure, but the second computer must have a smart card reader, which is not common.

When you enable BitLocker To Go for a removable drive, you are prompted to save or print the recovery key, just as you are when you enable BitLocker for a fixed hard drive.

BitLocker To Go can be enabled for a device only when using Windows 10 Pro, Enterprise, or Education editions, although any edition of Windows 10 can view or modify data encrypted by BitLocker To Go. This means you can configure Windows To Go on a USB drive at work with Windows 10 Pro and use the encrypted data on your home computer running Windows 10 Home.

BitLocker To Go can be configured to automatically unlock a protected drive when it is connected to a specific computer when a particular user is signed in. This simplifies access to the drive when used in a trusted environment, but still prompts for a password when the protected drive is used in another location.

Many BitLocker and BitLocker To Go settings can be managed through Group Policy. For example, you can force all removable storage to be encrypted with BitLocker To Go.

WINDOWS UPDATE

Scheduling automatic updates with Windows Update is the most important security precaution you can take with Windows 10. The vast majority of exploits used by viruses, worms, and other malware are addressed by updates available from Microsoft. Often, computers are vulnerable to many of these threats only because the necessary updates have not been applied.

When a Windows security flaw is found by a security company or an ethical hacker, the flaw is reported to Microsoft. The person or company that found the flaw does not release their findings until Microsoft has created and released an update to fix the problem, which typically takes a few weeks or months.

After the update has been released, the person or company that found the flaw releases detailed information about the flaw. Microsoft releases the information on their website, as well. Malware creators then begin to create software that takes advantage of the flaw. Computers that do not apply patches in a timely way are still vulnerable to malware using the flaw. In contrast, computers that are updated regularly are not vulnerable.

Servicing Branches

Microsoft has fundamentally changed the update process in Windows 10. In previous versions of Windows, Microsoft released security updates for varying service pack levels, which made it difficult for Microsoft to test and verify compatibility. Microsoft now releases updates for specific builds of Windows 10 only for a specified period of time. Before the end of the support period, a new build is released and computers upgrade to the new build, which then gets new updates until the next build is released.

The three distinct servicing branches are:

- *Windows Insider Preview Branch*—This branch is updated at irregular intervals depending on when Microsoft has a new preview ready for release. Consider this branch beta software. Windows Insider Preview should be used only on test computers if you want an early look at new features. You need to join the Windows Insider Program to use this service branch.
- *Semi-Annual Channel*—Approximately every six months, Microsoft releases feature updates that include new functionality in Windows 10. These releases have a version number that identifies when it was released. For example, version 1909 was released in September of 2019.
- *Long Term Servicing Branch*—This branch is a specific edition of Windows 10 that does not receive feature updates. Windows Updates are provided for Long Term Servicing Branch for 10 years. This is meant for controlled environments, such as equipment controllers, where changes cannot be tolerated.

Microsoft provides monthly updates that include fixes and security updates for the Semi-Annual Channel releases for 18 months. This allows organizations to keep Windows 10 in a supported state if they choose to skip a feature update to avoid a change in their environment. For Enterprise and Education editions of Windows 10, updates are provided for 30 months, which provides additional time for testing and controlled deployment.

 TIP Feature updates for early versions of Windows 10 took 30–45 minutes to install on many devices. Starting with version 1909, feature updates can be incremental and take only a few minutes to install.

Controlling Windows Updates

The default configuration of Windows Update uses the Semi-Annual Channel and installs updates automatically when they are available. When updates are available, they are listed in Windows Update, as shown in Figure 6-24. You have the option to check for updates immediately, but typically this is not required. You also have the option to view your update history there. Viewing the update history can be useful when trying to identify if a recent update introduced instability.

In the settings for Windows Update, you can view the active hours defined for your computer. When you define active hours, your computer will not be automatically restarted during those active hours. You can change these active hours to match when you use the device so that it doesn't restart when you want to use it. You can also turn on the Automatically adjust active hours for this device based on activity option that automatically sets the active hours based on when the device is typically used. Other advanced options are shown in Figure 6-25.

In the Advanced options, you can configure additional settings, such as:

- *Receive updates for other Microsoft products when you update Windows*—In most cases, you will want to leave this option on to get updates for a wide variety of Microsoft products. Malware is capable of taking advantage of flaws in multiple products, not just the operating system.
- *Download updates over metered connections*—This option is off by default and should generally remain off. On metered connections you usually have a limited amount of data and usage, and additional costs might be incurred. For example, you probably don't want to download large windows updates when your laptop is tethered to your mobile phone for data.
- *Restart this device as soon as possible when a restart is required to install an update*—This option is off by default and should generally remain off. When you enable this option, your computer will restart after an update is installed, even if it is during active hours. Windows displays a notice that the restart will happen. If your device is on battery power, a restart is not performed.

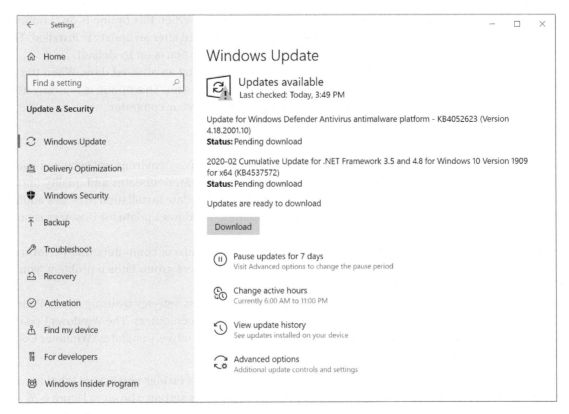

Figure 6-24   Windows Update screen

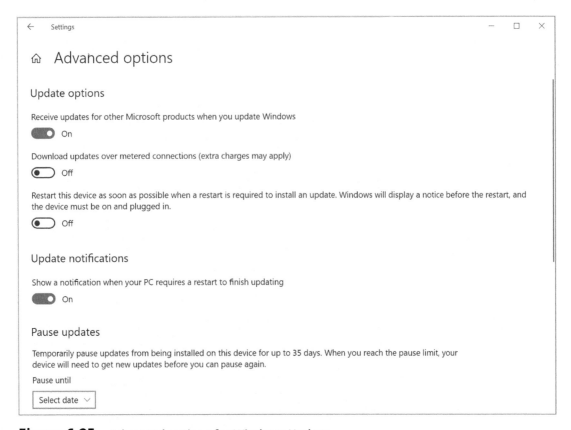

Figure 6-25   Advanced options for Windows Update

- *Show a notification when your PC requires a restart to finish updating*—When this option is on, a notification is displayed in the system tray to indicate that a system restart is required after an update is installed. This gives users an option to restart during active hours if they want to. This option is on by default.
- *Pause updates*—You can pause updates for up to 35 days by selecting an allowed date. When the pause is completed, pending updates must be installed before you can pause again. This option is typically used when you have identified an update that you think will cause problems on your computer.

Windows Update for Business

To allow more detailed control of update delivery to computers in a business environment, you can use **Windows Update for Business**. Windows Update for Business allows you to defer feature updates and quality updates by up to 365 days. By default, each update type is deferred for 7 days. Delaying update installation provides additional time to determine if new updates cause any problems with your computers. Windows Update for Business is not available for Windows 10 Home.

The purpose of Windows Update for Business is to create separate groups of computers that perform updates at different times. The first group is the testers in the organization. If the testers group finds a problem, you can pause updates to everyone else until the issue is resolved.

In a domain-based network, you can apply Windows Update for Business settings by using Group Policy. You can create multiple configurations to apply different settings to different sets of computers. The Windows Update for Business Group Policy settings are located in Computer Configuration\Administrative Templates\Windows Components\ Windows Update\Windows Update for Business. The available settings are:

- *Manage preview builds*—Use this setting to allow or disallow Windows Insider versions of Windows 10.
- *Select when Preview Builds and Feature Updates are received*—Use this setting, shown in Figure 6-26, to define how long Feature Updates are delayed. You can also pause Feature Updates until a specified date.
- *Select when Quality Updates are received*—Use this setting to define how long Quality Updates are delayed. You can also pause Quality Updates until a specified date.

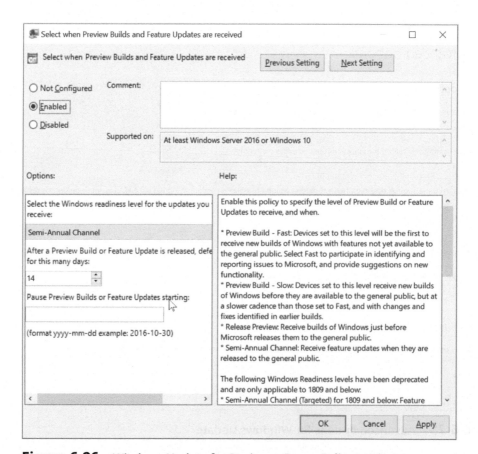

Figure 6-26 Windows Update for Business Group Policy setting

The standard Windows Update process can also be modified to use Windows Server Update Services (WSUS). WSUS provides greater control over the update process by allowing individual updates and upgrades to be approved for delivery to groups of computers. When WSUS is used, the Defer Upgrades and Updates setting is not used.

Delivery Optimization

Delivery optimization allows Windows Updates to be delivered among Windows 10 devices rather than all devices downloading the updates from Microsoft. This can reduce network data consumption when Internet speed is limited or data caps are in place.

By default, this setting is on, but it is limited to computers on the local network. You have the option to allow sharing with computers on the Internet also, but most organizations won't allow this due to security concerns.

An activity monitor for delivery optimization allows you to see download and upload statistics. You can verify how much data has been sent and received from Microsoft, computers on the local network, and computers on the Internet.

If you think that delivery optimization for Windows updates is causing network problems, rather than disabling it, you can implement bandwidth limits for uploading and downloading updates. These are configured in the advanced options within delivery optimization.

Removing Windows Updates

If you believe that a Windows update is causing a problem on your computer, you can remove it. The simplest way to remove an update is through the graphical interface, shown in Figure 6-27, which you can access through Control Panel or the update history in Settings. The Uninstall an update screen categorizes updates by product, such as Microsoft Windows or Adobe Acrobat Reader. To remove an update, you select the update and then click Uninstall.

In a larger environment, you might want to script a solution for removing an update from computers. This is faster than manually visiting many computers. To do this, you can use the Windows Update Standalone Installer (wusa.exe). This tool can install or remove Windows Updates from the command prompt or a Windows PowerShell prompt; however, you need to specify the KB number of the update.

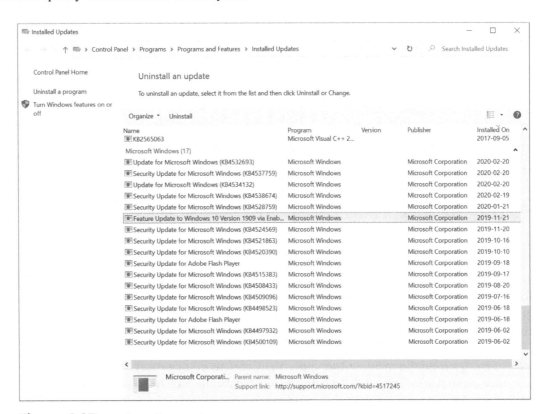

Figure 6-27   Uninstall an update screen

You can identify the KB number of an update from the title of the update in update history or on the Uninstall an update screen. At a Windows PowerShell prompt, you can use the Get-HotFix cmdlet. You can also use the command wmic qfe list at a command prompt or in the Windows PowerShell window.

Activity 6-11: Protecting Your Computer by Using Windows Update

Time Required: 5 minutes

Objective: Protect your computer by configuring Windows Update

Description: One of the simplest methods for protecting your computer from malware that uses known exploits is regular installation of patches and security updates. For better stability in a business environment, you can configure Windows Update for Business to delay Windows Updates for a few days. In this activity, you view available options and configure Windows Update.

1. If necessary, start your computer and sign in.
2. Click the **Start** button and then click **Settings**.
3. In the Settings window, click **Update & Security**. This screen indicates whether Windows 10 is up to date or not.
4. Click **Change active hours** and read the available options.
5. On the Change active hours screen, click the **Back** button in the upper-left corner.
6. Click **Advanced options** and read all the available options.
7. Scroll down to the Choose when updates are installed area, specify **30** days for feature updates, and then specify **5** days for quality updates.
8. Click **Delivery Optimization** and read the available options.
9. Click **Advanced options**, read the available options, and then click the **Back** button.
10. Click **Activity monitor** and review the statistics.
11. Click the **Back** button three times or until you are on the Windows Update screen and then click **View update history**.
12. Scroll down and read the list of updates. Notice that categories for Feature Updates, Quality Updates, Driver Updates, Definition Updates, and Other Updates are listed. If your installation of Windows 10 is new, no updates might be installed.
13. At the top of the View update history screen, click **Uninstall updates**. You can remove updates from this window.
14. Close all open windows.
15. Click the **Start** button, type **PowerShell**, and then click **Windows PowerShell**.
16. At the Windows PowerShell prompt, type **Get-HotFix** and then press **Enter**. Read the results of this command.
17. At the Windows PowerShell prompt, type **wmic qfe list** and then press **Enter**. Read the results of this command.
18. At the Windows PowerShell prompt, type **wusa.exe /?** and then press **Enter**.
19. In the Windows Update Standalone Installer dialog box, read the help information and then click **OK**.
20. Close the Windows PowerShell window.

Updating Microsoft Store Apps

Microsoft Store apps are not updated by using Windows Update. Windows Store apps are updated through the Microsoft Store. To access settings related to Microsoft Store app updates, click the Start button, start the Microsoft Store app, and then click the Downloads and updates icon in the upper-right corner. From the Downloads and updates screen, shown in Figure 6-28, you can check for updates, download all updates, or download specific updates.

If you select Settings from the menu in the upper-right corner, you can turn on or off automatic updates for Microsoft Store apps, as shown in Figure 6-29. Update apps automatically is on by default which is the preferred option in most scenarios.

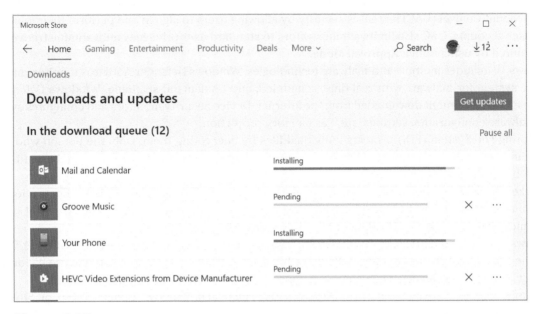

Figure 6-28   Windows Store Downloads and updates

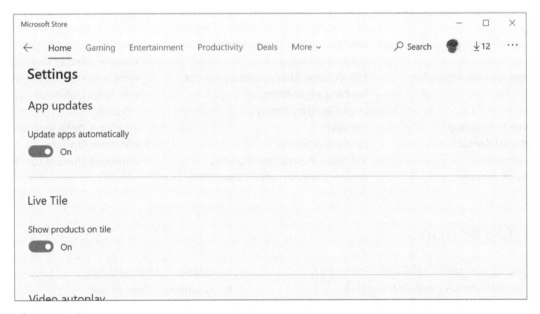

Figure 6-29   Microsoft Store Settings

SUMMARY

- The Local Security Policy in Windows 10 is used to configure a wide variety of security settings. Account policies control password settings and account lockout settings. Local policies configure auditing, user rights, and other security options. Software restriction policies and AppLocker control what software is allowed to run on a computer. Other security policies configure Windows Defender Firewall and EFS certificates and encrypt network communication.
- Auditing is used to record specific operating system events to the security log. Event categories that can be configured are Account Logon, Account Management, Detailed Tracking, DS Access, Logon/Logoff, Object Access, Policy Change, Privilege Use, System, and Global Object Access.

- User Account Control (UAC) increases security by allowing users to sign in and perform their jobs with standard user accounts. UAC also limits administrators to standard user privileges until administrative privileges are required by using Admin Approval Mode.
- Windows 10 includes multiple anti-malware technologies. Windows Defender Antivirus monitors memory and the file system for malware with real-time, scheduled, and on-demand scanning. Windows Defender Smartscreen monitors content downloaded from the Internet. Device Security monitors and configures system-level anti-malware configuration settings, such as memory protection.
- Encrypting File System (EFS) protects individual files by encrypting them. Only the person who encrypted a file can decrypt it, unless that file has been properly shared. A recovery certificate can be used to decrypt files if the certificate is configured.
- BitLocker Drive Encryption is used to encrypt an entire volume. To use BitLocker Drive Encryption, the hard drive must contain at least two partitions. BitLocker Drive Encryption also protects the operating system from being modified. BitLocker To Go allows removable storage to be encrypted.
- Windows Update is used to ensure that updates are applied to Windows 10 as they are made available. Windows 10 uses the semiannual channel update of Windows 10 by default, but it can be configured to use Windows Insider Preview Branch. You can delay installation of updates by using Windows Update for Business.
- Microsoft Store apps are updated by the Microsoft Store instead of Windows Update. Microsoft Store apps are automatically updated by default.

Key Terms

Account Lockout Policy	Encrypting File System (EFS)	User Account Control (UAC)
AppLocker	feature updates	Volume Master Key (VMK)
asymmetric encryption algorithm	Full Volume Encryption Key (FVEK)	Windows Defender Antivirus
audit policy	hashing algorithms	Windows Defender Application
auditing	Local Security Policy	Guard
BitLocker Drive Encryption	malware	Windows Defender Smartscreen
BitLocker Network Unlock	password policy	Windows Update
BitLocker To Go	Software Restriction Policies	Windows Update for Business
controlled folder access	symmetric encryption algorithm	

Review Questions

1. Which security feature in Windows 10 prevents malware by limiting user privilege levels?
   a. Windows Defender Antivirus
   b. User Account Control (UAC)
   c. Microsoft Security Essentials
   d. Service SIDs

2. Which of the following passwords meet complexity requirements? (Choose all that apply.)
   a. passw0rd$
   b. ##$$@@
   c. ake1vyue
   d. a1batr0$$
   e. A%5j

3. Which password policy setting should you use to prevent users from reusing their passwords too quickly?

   a. Maximum password age
   b. Minimum password age
   c. Minimum password length
   d. Password must meet complexity requirements
   e. Store passwords using reversible encryption

4. Which Account Lockout Policy setting is used to configure the time frame in which incorrect logon attempts must be conducted before an account is locked out?
   a. Account lockout duration
   b. Account lockout threshold
   c. Reset account lockout counter after
   d. Account lockout release period

5. The _____ local policy controls the tasks users are allowed to perform.

6. Which type of AppLocker rule condition can uniquely identify any file regardless of its location?
   a. Publisher
   b. Hash
   c. Network zone
   d. Path

7. You must configure a certificate authority on your network to use EFS. True or False?

8. How would you create AppLocker rules if you wanted to avoid updating the rules when most software is already installed?
   a. Manually create rules for each application.
   b. Automatically generate rules.
   c. Create default rules.
   d. Download rule templates.

9. Evaluating DLL files for software restrictions has a minimal impact on performance because of caching. True or False?

10. To which event log are audit events written?
    a. Application
    b. Security
    c. System
    d. Audit
    e. Advanced Audit

11. A(n) _____ is used to describe the structure of an application and trigger UAC when required.

12. What are you disabling when you configure UAC to not dim the desktop?
    a. Admin Approval Mode
    b. file and registry virtualization
    c. user-initiated prompts
    d. secure desktop

13. Which type of encryption is the fastest, strongest, and best suited to encrypting large amounts of information?
    a. symmetric
    b. 128-bit
    c. asymmetric
    d. hash
    e. public key

14. To encrypt a file by using EFS, the file must be stored on an NTFS-formatted partition. True or False?

15. How can you recover EFS-encrypted files if the user profile holding the digital certificate is accidentally deleted? (Choose all that apply.)

    a. Restore the file from backup.
    b. Restore the user certificate from a backup copy.
    c. Another user that has access to open the file can decrypt it.
    d. Decrypt the file by using the recovery certificate.
    e. Decrypt the file by using the EFS recovery snap-in.

16. Which of the following is not true about BitLocker Drive Encryption?
    a. BitLocker Drive Encryption requires at least two disk partitions.
    b. BitLocker Drive Encryption is designed to be used with a TPM.
    c. Two encryption keys are used to protect data.
    d. Data is still encrypted when BitLocker Drive Encryption is disabled.
    e. You must use a USB drive to store the startup PIN.

17. BitLocker Drive Encryption is user aware and can be used to protect individual files on a shared computer. True or False?

18. How long are quality updates provided for a specific version of Windows 10 Pro?
    a. 6 months
    b. 12 months
    c. 18 months
    d. 24 months
    e. 30 months

19. Which command-line tool can be used to remove Windows Updates?
    a. Remove-HotFix
    b. wusa.exe
    c. wmic qfe
    d. wuauclt.exe
    e. Updates can be removed only from the graphical interface.

20. Which setting should you configure to minimize data usage from downloading Windows Updates each time you travel and tether your laptop to your mobile phone for data connectivity?
    a. Pause updates for 7 days.
    b. Delay installation of feature updates for 14 days in Windows Update for Business.
    c. Limit bandwidth utilization in delivery optimization.
    d. Turn off Download updates over metered connections.
    e. Disable the Windows Update service.

Case Projects

Case Project 6-1: Virus Prevention

Buddy's Machine Shop's computers have been infected with a virus for the second time in six months. Several computers cannot run antivirus software with real-time scanning (even Windows Defender Antivirus) because it interferes with specialized software used to fabricate machine parts from blocks of metal. What can you do to mitigate the risk of viruses infecting the computers?

Case Project 6-2: Controlling Windows Updates

Angela's Printing Services has 50 Windows computers that are used for various purposes, such as graphical design and general office productivity. All computers are running Windows 10 Pro with the default settings for Windows Update. Last month an update caused an unexpected problem with critical printing software. How should Windows Update be configured to minimize the risk of problems from future updates?

Case Project 6-3: Data Encryption

The salespeople at Hyperactive Media sales all use laptop computers so that they can have easy access to important data on the road. The salespeople regularly take customer lists and other sensitive company information with them; unfortunately, a laptop occasionally is lost or stolen. Which data encryption features in Windows 10 can prevent hard drive data from being used after a laptop is stolen? Which features would you implement and why?

Case Project 6-4: Enterprise Virus Protection

You are the new system administrator for Precision Accounting Services, which has 45 computers on its network running Windows Defender Antivirus. All the computers have access to the Internet and update antivirus definitions as required.

Last week, several users received an email with a link to an executable file stored on a cloud-based file sharing service. One user was tricked into downloading and running the malware. This malware was detected by Windows Defender Antivirus, but it couldn't be removed from memory while running. The user didn't understand the malware detection messages and didn't inform you. This created a security risk because the malware ran for an extended period and began accessing network file shares. How can you prevent this in the future?

USER PRODUCTIVITY TOOLS

After reading this module and completing the exercises, you will be able to:

1. Describe features for file management in File Explorer

2. Use OneDrive to store documents

3. Explain and configure Windows 10 printing

4. Describe the features in Microsoft Edge and Internet Explorer

5. Identify useful Windows 10 applications and keyboard shortcuts

Windows 10 includes a variety of tools that are required in a modern operating system in order to be productive. You certainly need specialized apps like Microsoft Office to create and consume content, but the operating system also needs to provide some core tools for tasks such as managing files and accessing the Internet.

In this module, you learn how to use File Explorer for file management, including how to configure libraries. You also learn about how cloud-based storage provided by OneDrive can be used to make your files portable. OneDrive also serves as a backup solution if your computer's hard drive fails. Despite the promise of a paperless office, printing is still important functionality in Windows 10, so you will learn how to configure printing. To help support using web-based applications, you will identify the features available in the Microsoft Edge browser, including Enterprise Mode, which supports backward compatibility with Internet Explorer. Finally, you will identify useful application and shortcut keys in Windows 10.

FILE EXPLORER

File Explorer, shown in Figure 7-1, is the interface used to view the file system in Windows 10. The left navigation pane provides a way to move quickly to various locations where files might be stored. The right pane displays the files and folders in the location that is selected in the navigation pane.

In the navigation pane, several file storage locations are available by default:

- *Quick access*—When you select this node, a list of recently accessed files and folders are displayed. You also have the option to pin folders in Quick access. For example, if you are working on several projects, you can pin the folder that stores files for each project in Quick access.
- *OneDrive*—This node provides access to OneDrive cloud storage that is associated with a Microsoft account.

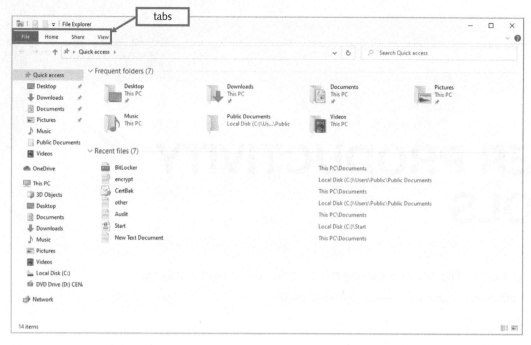

Figure 7-1   File Explorer

- *This PC*—This node displays the files and folder for locally attached storage. This includes hard drives, USB drives, and DVDs.
- *Network*—Use this node to display computers on the local area network (LAN). If the computers have shared resources, you can browse file shares and shared printers.

 TIP   Some third-party products, such as Dropbox, also integrate into the navigation pane. Dropbox is cloud storage similar to OneDrive.

If you are double-clicking folders in the right pane to drill down into the folder structure, the navigation pane is not updated. You can configure the navigation pane to keep in sync with the folders to which you browse. Some people prefer this because it simplifies moving between folders in the navigation pane.

Ribbon Tabs

Above the navigation pane and the right pane are tabs on the ribbon for various functions. The tabs available on the ribbon vary depending on the content that you have selected.

When you are viewing the file system, the following tabs are available:

- *File*—This tab provides options to open a new File Explorer window or to display a Windows PowerShell prompt that is focused on the current folder. The Windows PowerShell prompt option can be significantly faster than opening a prompt and then changing to the directory that you want. This tab also allows access to folder and search options.
- *Home*—This tab has buttons for manipulating files and folders. For example, it contains buttons to copy, paste, and delete, along with options to view file and folder properties and select items. Many of the options here are similar to the shortcut menu that is displayed when you right-click a file or folder.
- *Share*—This tab provides options to configure folder sharing and file permissions. It also has options to share files via email or with an app that you specify. Options to send files to a zipped folder, burn to disc, print, or fax also are offered.
- *View*—This tab has options that control how files and folders are displayed. For example, you can select whether file details are displayed, you can display only file names, or you can specify various sizes of icons.

You can enable display of a Details pane or a Preview pane with additional information when files are selected. You can also choose to view hidden items and hide items.

One common user complaint is the inability to distinguish between files of different types that have the same name. For example, you may have a Word document and an Excel spreadsheet that are both named Project1. Both documents have different icons, but it can be difficult to interpret the icons when files are displayed in List view. To make it easier for users to distinguish between files of different types, you can configure Windows 10 to display the file name extensions. This is done on the View tab by selecting the File name extensions check box. This is not selected by default.

Activity 7-1: Configuring File Explorer

Time Required: 5 minutes
Objective: Customize the display in File Explorer
Description: For many users, the default display in File Explorer is acceptable. You have the option, however, to customize it in many ways to better suit your preferences. In this activity, you perform some of the commonly implemented modifications to the default view in File Explorer.

1. If necessary, start your computer and sign in.
2. On the taskbar, click **File Explorer**.
3. In the File Explorer window, click the **View** tab, click the **Navigation pane** button, and then, if necessary, click **Expand to open folder** to enable it.
4. In the navigation pane, click **This PC**.
5. In the right pane, double-click **Local Disk (C:)** and then double-click **Windows**. Notice that the navigation pane reflects the content of the location you are browsing.
6. Scroll down in the right pane, and notice that most of the file extensions are hidden.
7. Click the **View** tab and, if necessary, select the **File name extensions** check box.
8. Scroll down in the right pane, and notice that most of the file extensions are now visible, which makes it easier to identify the type of file.
9. Click the **View** tab and then click **List** in the Layout group. Notice that you can now see more files and folders at one time.
10. Click the **View** tab and then click the **Options** button.
11. In the Folder Options dialog box, click the **View** tab, click **Restore Defaults**, and then click **OK**. This disables viewing of file extensions.
12. Close the File Explorer window.

Libraries

Libraries were introduced in Windows 7 to simplify access to files in multiple locations. Each library contains multiple file system locations and the content from all locations is placed together into a single view. A library can contain local folders or file shares.

You can modify the locations included in a library, but the location must be indexed by Windows Search. This means that if you add a file share, it must be indexed by Windows Search on the computer that is hosting the file share. This requirement ensures that content can be categorized and displayed quickly.

Some file management issues to consider for libraries are:

- When you browse down into a folder from the root of a library, you are viewing a specific location, and any files created are in that specific location.
- When you are viewing the root of a library and create a new file or folder, the new item is created in the location specified as the default save location in the properties of the library.

Activity 7-2: Using Libraries

Time Required: 5 minutes

Objective: Use libraries to organize files in File Explorer

Description: In Windows 10, libraries are not visible by default. Some users who upgrade from Windows 7 or Windows 8.1 may prefer to continue using this feature. In this activity, you enable libraries in File Explorer and verify their functionality.

1. If necessary, start your computer and sign in.
2. On the taskbar, click **File Explorer**.
3. In the File Explorer window, click the **View** tab, click the **Navigation pane** button, and then click **Show libraries** to place a check mark before that item.
4. In the navigation pane, expand **Libraries** and then click **Documents**.
5. Right-click **Documents** and then click **Properties**.
6. In the Documents Properties window, click **Add**.
7. In the Include Folder in Documents window, in the address bar, type **C:\Users\Public** and then press **Enter**.
8. Click **Public Documents** and then click **Include folder**.
9. In the Document Properties dialog box, the single green check mark identifies the Documents folder as your default save location. The green check mark with the users identifies the Public Documents folder as the public save location.
10. Right-click **Public Documents**, click **Set as default save location**, and then click **OK**. Notice that the view now includes both locations.
11. Click the **Home** tab, click **New item**, click **Text Document**, type **NewPublicFile** as the file name, and then press **Enter**. Notice that the file was created in the Public Documents folder because that is the default save location for the Documents library.
12. Click the **View** tab, click **Navigation pane**, and then click **Show libraries** to remove the check mark from that item.
13. Close the File Explorer window.

Search

Windows 10 includes search functionality that can be used to find files and folders. Search is made faster by an indexing function included in Windows 10. It is context sensitive, so you do not need to choose whether the search occurs inside or outside the index. If you are searching content that is indexed, the index is used. If you are searching content that is not indexed, the index is not used.

Indexing is automatically enabled so that all users can immediately get the benefit of index-based searches. Each time a file is updated, the index is also updated. When a user performs a search, the search results include only files to which the user has access.

By default, only the most common file system locations are indexed. This is the Classic search option selected in Figure 7-2. Classic search prevents the index from incorporating less relevant files, such as operating system files, for which users are unlikely to search. Search speed is improved, and indexing time is decreased by indexing only specified files.

The Enhanced search option indexes all files on your computer unless they are in excluded folders. If you store files outside of your user profile that you want to be indexed, this can be a fast way to ensure that they are indexed. When you enable the Enhanced search option, some user profile folders for application data are excluded. Content in C:\Program Files, C:\ProgramData, and C:\Windows also is excluded.

The file locations indexed by Classic search are the Start menu and C:\Users (except the AppData subfolder in each profile). Other locations are indexed for specific applications if the application is in use. For example, if you are using Microsoft Outlook in cached mode, the cached mailbox is indexed. You can specify additional search locations depending on your needs, as shown in Figure 7-3.

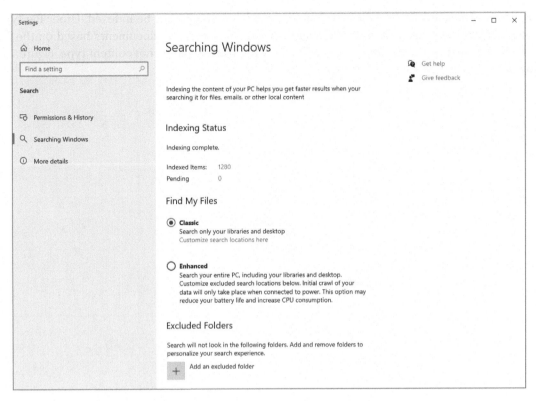

Figure 7-2 Search settings

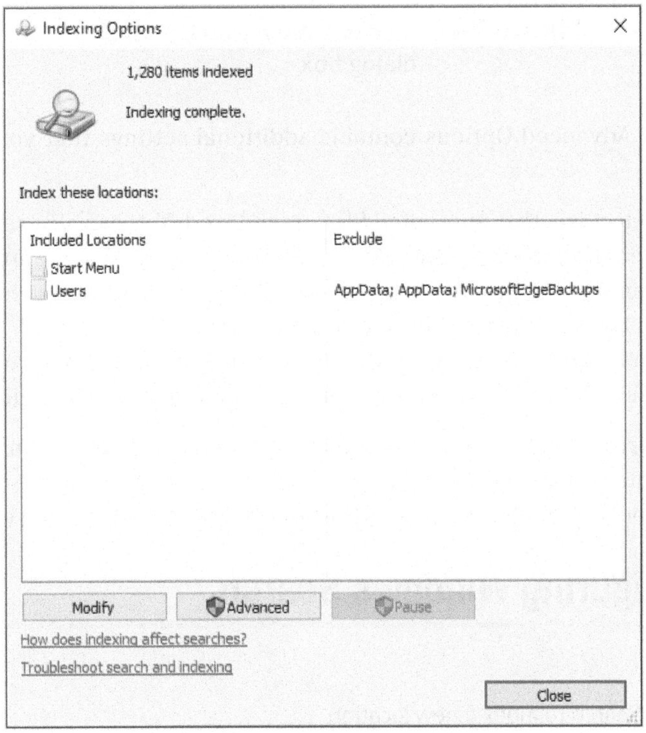

Figure 7-3 Indexing Options dialog box

The Advanced Options in Indexing Options apply to both Classic search and Enhanced search. You can define which file types are indexed and how those files are indexed. For each file type (defined by file extension), you specify whether the contents of the files or only the files' metadata is indexed. For some file types, such as pictures, the content of the files is meaningless from a search perspective and should not be indexed. Other file types, such as Word documents, can have their content indexed so that you can search for documents based on the content. The filter for each file type is responsible for understanding how to properly index that content type. Figure 7-4 shows the configuration of file types in Advanced Options.

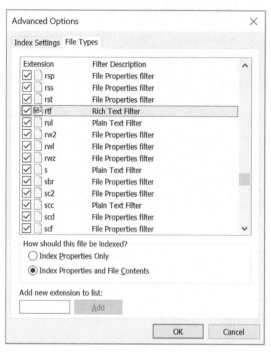

Figure 7-4   Indexing Advanced Options
dialog box

The Index Settings tab in Advanced Options contains additional settings that you can configure, including the following:

- *File Settings*—You can select whether encrypted files are indexed. You can also select whether words with different accents are treated the same, for example, whether *resume* and *resumé* are indexed as the same word.
- *Troubleshooting*—You can rebuild the index if you believe it has become corrupted. You can also run a trouble-shooter that guides you through the troubleshooting process.
- *Index location*—You can move the index from the default location of C:\ProgramData\Microsoft to another location. This can be useful if the C: drive is becoming full and free space is available on a different partition.

The most basic file metadata are characteristics such as file name, creation date, and modified date. Depending on the type of file, additional metadata may be included. For example, pictures taken with a digital camera have additional metadata that is appropriate only for pictures, such as the shutter speed and lighting conditions.

Activity 7-3: Configuring Windows Search

Time Required: 10 minutes
Objective: Configure Windows Search to index a new location
Description: Indexing files makes it much faster to find specific files you are seeking. If you store files outside of your User file, they are not indexed by default. In this activity, you specify an additional indexing location for Windows Search and then verify that it is searchable.

1. If necessary, start your computer and sign in.
2. On the taskbar, click **File Explorer**.
3. If necessary, expand **This PC** and then click **Local Disk (C:)**.

4. Click the **Home** tab, click **New folder**, type **NewData** as the folder name, and then press **Enter**.

5. Double-click the **NewData** folder, click the **Home** tab, click **New item**, click **Text Document**, type **SearchFile** as the file name, and then press **Enter**.

6. Double-click **SearchFile** to open the file in Notepad.

7. In the Notepad window, type **Kangaroo**, click **File** on the menu bar, and then click **Save**.

8. Exit Notepad.

9. On the taskbar, click the **Type here to search** button and then type **Kangaroo**. This displays web searches for Kangaroo.

10. At the top of the search box, click **Documents** and then click **Kangaroo**. The search should not find any matches.

11. Close all open windows.

12. Click the **Start** button and then click **Settings**.

13. In the Settings window, in the Find a setting box, type **index** and then click **Windows Search settings**.

14. On the Searching Windows screen, below the Classic option, click **Customize Search locations here**.

15. In the Indexing Options window, click **Modify**.

16. In the Indexed Locations window, expand **Local Disk (C:)**, select the **NewData** check box, and then click **OK**.

17. In the Indexing Options dialog box, click **Close**.

18. On the taskbar, click the **Type here to search button**, type **Kangaroo**, and then click **Documents**. This time, the search found the file because it has been indexed.

19. Close all open windows.

ONEDRIVE

OneDrive is cloud-based storage that is automatically included free of charge when you create a Microsoft account. Each Microsoft account is allocated 5 GB of storage space that can be used for file storage in OneDrive. Additional storage can be purchased if required.

Files stored in OneDrive can be accessed directly from the OneDrive website or by using the OneDrive client. The OneDrive client is included with Windows 10 and integrates into File Explorer as a separate node for accessing files.

Using OneDrive has several benefits, including the following:

- Access files from anywhere
- Back up automatically to the cloud
- Recover deleted or modified files
- Edit files from a browser
- Edit files on mobile devices
- Share files with others

OneDrive Client

If you sign in to Windows 10 using a Microsoft account, the OneDrive client automatically uses that account to sign in to OneDrive also. Then, any files you save on the OneDrive node in File Explorer are automatically synchronized to OneDrive where they can be accessed from another computer, a mobile phone, or tablet. Because OneDrive files are accessible by browser, they can be accessed from almost any device.

 TIP   If you don't sign in to Windows 10 using your Microsoft account, you need to configure the OneDrive client with the credentials for your OneDrive account.

The OneDrive node in File Explorer contains Documents and Pictures folders by default, but you can create additional folders to organize your files. Local files and folders that are synchronized with OneDrive have a green check mark to indicate that they are successfully synchronized. When you make changes to a file, the icon changes to two arrows in a circle to indicate that the file is synchronizing. While you have a file open for editing, it is typical for the synchronizing icon to appear for the file. If the icon is a cloud, then the file is available in OneDrive but not synchronized locally. If a small icon with the outline of a person appears as part of the status, then the file or folder is shared. Figure 7-5 shows the status icons.

The default location for files synchronized by the OneDrive client is C:\Users\%username%\OneDrive in the user's profile. If you have a folder with preexisting data, you can change synchronization to use that folder instead. When you select a folder with preexisting data, that data is merged with the data already stored in OneDrive.

☁	**In cloud**
⟳	**Syncing**
⊘ᴿ	**Synced locally and shared**
◉	**Always keep on this device**

Figure 7-5 Sync status icons

In the properties for the OneDrive client, you can also configure the following settings:

- *Start OneDrive automatically when I sign in to Windows*—This option is on by default and should be left on. If you turn off this option, files stop synchronizing with OneDrive because the client is not enabled the next time you sign in.
- *Let me use OneDrive to fetch any of my files on this PC*—This option is disabled by default. Enable this option if you want to be able to browse the file system on the computer and access files through the OneDrive website.
- *Use Office to work on files with other people at the same time*—This option is on by default and should be left on. When this option is on, you can collaborate with other users on a shared Microsoft Office document at the same time. Two or more users can perform simultaneous editing.

The OneDrive client also has a backup option. For your local computer, you can back up the Desktop, Documents, and Pictures folder to OneDrive. When you configure backup, those folders become part of OneDrive, and you don't need to manage your OneDrive documents separately. You also have the option to automatically store pictures and videos from cameras and phones in OneDrive when you retrieve them using your computer. Finally, you can configure screenshots to be saved in OneDrive automatically.

 TIP During profile creation for a Microsoft account, you are asked whether you want to back up your files with OneDrive. The backup feature is enabled if you click Next. If you select the Only save files to this PC option, then backup is not enabled.

OneDrive Web Interface

The web interface for OneDrive, shown in Figure 7-6, provides access to all the features of OneDrive. In the web interface, you have access to all the files that have been synchronized to OneDrive, but in addition you can do the following:

- Recover deleted files from the Recycle Bin
- Access previous versions of files
- View a list of all files that you have shared
- View the amount of storage space you have remaining in OneDrive
- Access files on computers with the OneDrive client installed and configured

 TIP You can access OneDrive at https://onedrive.live.com.

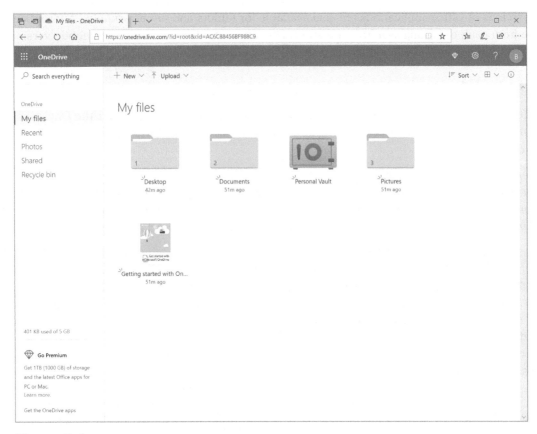

Figure 7-6   OneDrive web interface

The web interface for OneDrive is not merely a way to download your files on different computers. You can also use the web versions of Microsoft Office applications, such as Word and Excel, to view and edit the files online. When you open a file on the OneDrive website, it automatically opens in the appropriate online Office application in read-only mode. If you choose to edit the file, you are prompted as to whether to edit in the online Office application or use a locally installed Office application.

If you choose to use the online Office application to edit a file, you get a functional, but not full-featured, version of the application. The online Office applications work with a variety of browsers across platforms, such as Microsoft Edge, Internet Explorer, Firefox, Chrome, and Safari.

 TIP   Files in online Office applications are automatically saved as you edit them. It is initially disconcerting that you don't have the option to save files manually, but you can verify that the file has been saved by checking the title bar.

If you choose to use a locally installed Office application to edit a file, the file is opened directly from OneDrive. Office applications are capable of opening files over the Internet by using the HTTP protocol. When you save the file, it is saved directly back in OneDrive.

 TIP   When you store files on OneDrive, you can use the AutoSave feature in Microsoft Office desktop apps that saves file changes in near real-time.

Mobile versions of Office applications are also available for tablets and phones running Android and iOS. These apps are free from each operating system's app store. This means that you can install a mobile version of Word on your iPad or Android device and edit a document stored in OneDrive.

Managing Files

You can perform basic file management tasks by using both the OneDrive website and the OneDrive client in File Explorer. Both these tools can delete, copy, move, and rename files; however, the following two functions can be performed only on the OneDrive website:

- *Recover deleted files*—Files deleted from OneDrive are placed in the Recycle Bin and then deleted after approximately 90 days. If a file has not been deleted from the Recycle Bin, you can restore it and regain access to it.
- *Previous file versions*—As you modify files, OneDrive keeps multiple versions of the file, not just the most recently saved version. You can access and recover previous versions if an incorrect modification has been made.

NOTE 1

You can find more information about various OneDrive plans on Compare OneDrive Plans at https://products.office.com/en-us/onedrive/compare-onedrive-plans.

If you upgrade to a paid version of OneDrive in Office 365, you also have the option to restore your entire OneDrive to a point in time up to 30 days ago. Microsoft will also notify you if it appears that ransomware is affecting your OneDrive files. After you eliminate the ransomware, you can restore your files in OneDrive back to the point before the ransomware infected your computer.

Sharing Files and Folders

When you store files in OneDrive, you also have the option to share files and folders with other users. You can share files anonymously with users so that they can access files in your OneDrive without authenticating. You send other users a URL for the specific file or folder that you shared. When they follow the URL, they can either view or edit the files, depending on the level of permissions that you specified.

 **CAUTION** If you share files anonymously, you control to whom you send the URL, but you can't control to whom they send it. Because of this, you shouldn't use anonymous sharing for important files.

Instead of sharing with anonymous users, most of the time you should share with specific users. When you share with specific users, you specify an email address. The email address you specify must be associated with a Microsoft account or an Azure AD account. That user then is required to authenticate before accessing the file.

Managing Synchronization

The Files On-Demand feature in OneDrive controls which files are synchronized to the local computer. By default, the Save space and download files as you use them option is enabled. With this configuration, files are synchronized to the local device only when you open them. Until that point, they remain only in the cloud.

You can force files or folders to synchronize locally if you right-click and select Always keep on this device. Forcing local synchronization is useful when you want to ensure that you always have the latest version of a file for offline use. For example, you can edit the latest version when you are on an airplane as long as you allowed it to sync before you take off.

If you need to free up disk space on a device, you can right-click and then select Free up space. This removes the local copy of the file. You can do this for files that were synced dynamically by Files On-Demand or files that you forced to sync locally.

Controlling Network Utilization

On a mobile device with a metered network, you might be concerned about using too much data for OneDrive synchronization. For example, if you tether your laptop through the mobile phone you probably wouldn't want to download 1 GB of file changes that exist in OneDrive. To prevent network utilization on a metered network you can enable the Automatically pause sync when this device is on a metered network option.

TIP   Remember that Windows 10 does not designate Wi-Fi networks as metered by default. When tethering to a mobile device, you need to manually identify the network as a metered network.

On some networks, the total volume of data is not a concern, but the speed of data synchronization is. For example, an office with a slow Internet connection with multiple computers attempting to synchronize as quickly as possible might slow down other important services, such as email. By default, upload and download rates are not limited, but you can specify a limited rate, such as 125 KB/s for either.

 **CAUTION**   If you have a slow Internet connection, consider an appropriate value for limiting upload and download rates. The rate of 125 KB/s is equivalent to 1 Mbps.

Personal Vault

To help store highly secure personal information, Microsoft has created Personal Vault for personal and home plans of OneDrive. To access the files you store in the Personal Vault, you need to provide additional authentication information beyond your user name and password. You need to be further authenticated by a strong authentication method, such as fingerprint, face recognition, PIN, or a code sent by text message.

When you unlock your personal vault, it relocks after a period of inactivity to ensure that your data remains safe. On a mobile device, the personal vault locks again after 3 minutes. On a computer running Windows 10, the personal vault locks again after 20 minutes by default, but you can set longer values up to 4 hours.

 **CAUTION**   If you disable Personal Vault, all files inside Personal Vault are removed and can't be recovered. Copy files out of Personal Vault before you disable it.

OneDrive for Business

Business plans of Office 365 or Microsoft 365 include OneDrive for Business, which is similar to the consumer version of OneDrive but with different features. Some differences with OneDrive for Business include:

- OneDrive for Business does not allow remote access to files on computers with the OneDrive client.
- OneDrive for Business does not include Personal Vault.
- OneDrive for Business requires an Azure AD account rather than a Microsoft account.
- OneDrive for Business has a starting size of 1 TB that can be unlimited in size, depending on the specific plan.
- OneDrive for Business can be centrally managed by the administrator of your Office 365 or Microsoft 365 tenant.

Activity 7-4: Using OneDrive

Time Required: 10 minutes

Objective: Use OneDrive to manage files

Description: OneDrive is a cloud-based service that you can use to back up and share files. In this activity, you save files in OneDrive and explore the recovery options.

1. If necessary, start your computer and sign in by using your Microsoft account.
2. On the taskbar, click **File Explorer**.
3. In File Explorer, in the navigation pane, click **OneDrive** and read the list of files. Notice that the status for Getting started with OneDrive is a cloud icon. This .pdf file should be in the root of OneDrive unless you previously deleted it.

4. Double-click **Getting started with OneDrive** to open it, quickly scan through the document, and then exit Microsoft Edge.
5. In the File Explorer window, read the status of Getting started with OneDrive. The status icon is now a green check mark to indicate that the file is stored locally because you opened it.
6. In the navigation pane, expand **OneDrive** and then click **Documents**.
7. In the right pane, right-click an open area, point to **New**, click **Text Document**, type **OnlineFile**, and then press **Enter**.
8. Double-click **OnlineFile**.
9. In the Notepad window, type **First edit**, exit Notepad, and then save the changes. When the file icon has a green check mark, it has finished synchronizing to OneDrive.
10. In the File Explorer window, right-click **OnlineFile** and then click **Delete**.
11. On the taskbar, click **Microsoft Edge**.
12. In the Microsoft Edge window, in the address bar, type **https://onedrive.live.com** and then press **Enter**. Notice that you do not need to provide authentication credentials if you signed in to Windows 10 by using a Microsoft account.
13. If necessary, on the Welcome to OneDrive screen, click **FINISH LATER**.
14. If necessary, on the Get the premium experience screen, close the screen.
15. On the My files screen, read the list of files and folders. Notice that these match those in OneDrive on your computer except for the Personal Vault.
16. In OneDrive, click **Recycle bin**. Notice that OnlineFile.txt is listed here.
17. Click **OnlineFile.txt** and then click **Restore**.
18. Click **My files** and then click **Documents**. Notice that the file is restored to the Documents folder.
19. Click **OnlineFile.txt** and wait for the file contents to be displayed. A simple online text editor is used because this is a text file rather than a Word document.
20. Click **Open** on the menu bar and then click **Open in Text Editor**.
21. Add the text **Second edit** as a new line in the file and then click **Save**.
22. In File Explorer, right-click **OnlineFile** and then click **Always keep on this device**.
23. Verify that a green check mark appears next to OnlineFile and then double-click **OnlineFile**.
24. In Notepad, verify that the text Second edit appears and then exit Notepad.
25. In OneDrive, in the top ribbon menu, click **OneDrive** and then click **Documents**.
26. In OneDrive, click **New** and then click **Word document**. This creates a new Word document named Document1.
27. In Word Online, if a Welcome to Word on the web dialog box appears, close it.
28. In Document1, type **Version 1**, wait for the document to finish saving, and then close the Document1.docx tab in Microsoft Edge.
29. In OneDrive, click **Document1.docx**.
30. In Word Online, click **Edit Document** and then click **Edit in Word Online**.
31. Add a new line with the text **Version 2**, wait for the document to finish saving, and then close the Document1.docx tab in Microsoft Edge.
32. In OneDrive, right-click **Document1.docx** and then click **Version history**. The current version is automatically selected, and you will see a preview.
33. Select the most recent previous version. Notice that this document has only the Version 1 text. You have the option to restore this version or download it.
34. Exit Microsoft Edge.
35. In the File Explorer window, if necessary, expand **This PC**, right-click **Desktop**, and then click **Properties**.
36. In the Desktop Properties dialog box, click the **Location** tab. Notice that the location of the Desktop folder has been redirected inside the OneDrive folder because backup has been configured.
37. Click **Cancel** and then close the File Explorer window.

PRINTING

Despite the promise of the paperless office, most organizations still do quite a bit of printing. Maintaining printers and troubleshooting their functionality can be a significant portion of your job when doing desktop support. To support printers and troubleshoot them, you need to understand the following:

- Printing scenarios
- Printer drivers
- Printer management tools

Printing Scenarios

As a network administrator, you need to be able to troubleshoot the printing process. One of the keys to troubleshooting is understanding how printers can be connected to Windows 10. Figure 7-7 shows the physical layout of local printing, network printing directly to a printer, and network printing to a shared printer.

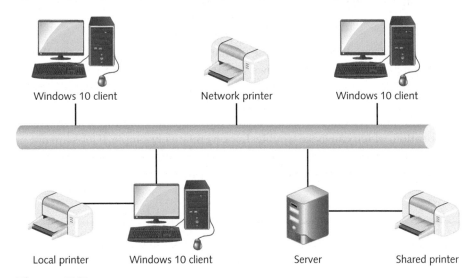

Figure 7-7   Printing scenarios

Local Printing

Local printing requires that a printer be connected directly to a Windows 10 computer by using a cable. The type of cable you select depends on which connection type is physically available on the printer. Most newer printers connect to a computer by using a USB cable. Some older printers and specialty printers are connected by using parallel or serial cables.

USB printers are automatically installed in Windows 10 when they are connected because they are Plug and Play. Before you connect a USB printer for the first time, however, read the documentation included with the printer. Some USB printers (particularly multifunction printers) require you to install the driver before attaching the printer for the first time. If you connect the printer before the proper driver is installed, Windows 10 attempts to load a compatible driver, which might not have full functionality for the printer. The installation process for serial and parallel printers must be triggered manually.

The most common reasons to use local printing are simplicity and security. The entire printing process occurs within the local computer, so troubleshooting is easier. Having a local printer makes printing secure because users are able to print sensitive documents in their office from the local printer rather than in an open area on a shared network printer where other users might see the documents' contents.

To install a local printer, you need administrator permissions if the driver is not already installed. After a local printer is installed, it is available to all users on that computer.

Printing Directly to a Network Printer

A high percentage of printers can be configured to communicate directly on a wired or wireless network. This functionality is available even in many lower-end printers for home users. When a printer is connected directly to the network, computers can send it print jobs over the network. Many computers can be connected to the network printer at the same time, but only one computer can be printing at a time.

Sharing a printer on the network saves money in the long run. Typically, it costs less to purchase a single high-capacity printer rather than many low-capacity printers for many computers. The per-page consumables cost for the high-capacity printer is typically much lower than for low-capacity printers.

In this scenario, print jobs are queued at the local computer and sent to the printer when the printer is not busy. This is a contention-based system, and jobs are not serviced in any specific order. No central queue controls the order or priority of print jobs; however, a key benefit is the lack of any single computer as a single point of failure.

When you print directly to a network printer, it behaves similarly to a local printer except that connectivity is through a network port or wireless network adapter instead of a USB port. To install this type of printer in Windows 10, you need administrator permissions if the driver is not already installed on the computer. After this type of printer is installed, it is available to all users on the computer.

Printing to a Shared Printer

Both Windows servers and Windows clients are capable of sharing printers on the network. When a printer is shared, multiple computers on the network can use it. Windows 10 attempts to find printers shared on the local network and install them automatically; however, if the shared printers are not on the local subnet, you need to install the printer manually.

In this scenario, all print jobs are queued on the computer that is sharing the printer. This allows all jobs to be controlled in a central location, which can make troubleshooting relatively simple. If jobs are not printing, you start by looking at the computer that is sharing the printer; however, the computer sharing the printer also becomes a central point of failure. If the computer sharing the printer is disabled or turned off, it is not possible to print documents on the shared printer.

 TIP   Shared printers can be connected directly to the sharing computer or be network printers.

NOTE 2

For detailed information about print driver versions, see Printer Sharing Technical Details at https://docs.microsoft.com/en-us/previous-versions/windows/it-pro/windows-server-2012-R2-and-2012/jj590748(v=ws.11).

Standard users can install a shared printer, even if the printer driver is not already installed. For older version 3 printer drivers (Windows 7), the printer driver is copied from the computer sharing the printer. For newer version 4 printer drivers (Windows 8, 8.1, or 10), the print job can be rendered completely on the server side, and no driver installation is required. If the client can identify the correct version 4 printer driver through Plug and Play, however, the driver can be installed from local files or Windows Update to allow client-side rendering with full functionality.

After installation, a shared printer is installed only for the user who installed it. Other users on the same computer also need to install the printer to be able to use it.

Printer Drivers

A basic **printer driver** is software that Windows 10 uses to understand and use the features of a printer. A key part of driver functionality is formatting print jobs so that they print properly. When an incorrect printer driver is used, print jobs might have small formatting errors, like misalignment, or you might get what appear to be random characters printing.

Windows 10 supports **printer driver packages** that include the basic printer driver but can also include additional software. For example, a printer driver package could include additional software that shows printer status, such as remaining toner, in the notification area. Generally, printer packages are still referred to as printer drivers.

Page Description Languages

Many printers have support for multiple page description languages, and different printer drivers are available for each of the languages. A **page description language** defines the layout of content for a print job. It is not uncommon to find that some applications work properly with a printer driver using one page description language but have small formatting errors when using the printer driver for another page description language. You might need to experiment with different versions of printer drivers to find one that works best with your applications.

Some commonly available page description languages are:

- *PostScript*—**PostScript** is the oldest and best supported page description language. If you are having issues with printer driver versions, try using the PostScript driver, because printer manufacturers often put the most effort in ensuring that the PostScript drivers work properly.
- *Printer Command Language*—**Printer Command Language (PCL)** is the most common page description language besides PostScript. In general, PCL offers faster printing than PostScript but is also more prone to odd formatting errors because many printer manufacturers put less time into developing PCL drivers. Because PCL 5 and PCL 6 drivers can provide varying results, you should try both when troubleshooting if your printer supports both.
- *Portable Document Format*—**Portable Document Format (PDF)** is most often thought of as a document format, but it is also supported by some printers as a page description language. This allows .pdf documents to be sent directly to a printer without any processing.
- *XML Paper Specification*—Microsoft designed **XML Paper Specification (XPS)** as both a document format and page description language. Microsoft uses XPS internally as part of the printing process, but most printers do not include native support for XPS.

To support using XPS as a document format, Windows 10 includes a virtual printer named Microsoft XPS Document Writer. New in Windows 10 is a virtual printer for PDF documents named Microsoft Print to PDF. Both these printers let you print from any application and save the output as a file in either XPS or PDF format. XPS and PDF documents can both be viewed by using Microsoft Edge.

> 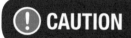 **CAUTION** Beginning with Windows 10 version 1803, the XPS Viewer is no longer installed by default. You can still install XPS Viewer as a feature.

Printer Driver Store

Windows 10 has a **printer driver store** where installed printer drivers are added. Printer drivers can be added to the store before the printer is attached. This can be useful in corporate environments by preconfiguring computers with all printer drivers that may be required.

Adding a driver to the store is known as staging a driver. If a printer driver is added during the printer installation process, the driver is automatically staged as part of the process. Drivers can also be staged manually by a user with administrative rights using the pnputil.exe utility. Drivers can also be added to the store by users who have been granted device installation rights by a group policy. Table 7-1 has examples of using the pnputil.exe utility.

Table 7-1   Pnputil.exe Examples

Example	Description
pnputil.exe /add-driver *driverINFfile*	Add a printer driver to the store
pnputil.exe /enum-drivers	Enumerate (list) all third-party drivers in the store
pnputil.exe /delete-driver *driverINFfile*	Delete a printer driver from the store
pnputil.exe /?	Display the help information for pnputil.exe

When drivers are added to the store, they are stored side by side. This means that multiple versions of the same driver can be contained in the store, which is useful when testing new printer drivers. Occasionally, new printer drivers result in print quality problems for specific reports or documents. When this occurs, you can change the printer driver back to a previous version.

After a printer driver is in the printer driver store, standard users can install local and network printers that use that driver. By default, standard users cannot install new printer drivers unless it is a shared printer and the driver is downloaded from the computer sharing the printer.

 **CAUTION**   You should remove old printer driver versions from the driver store to ensure that users don't accidentally install obsolete versions.

Activity 7-5: Staging a Driver

Time Required: 10 minutes

Objective: Stage a printer driver in the driver store

Description: Standard users are not able to download and install their own printer drivers from a manufacturer's website. If a driver is staged in the driver store before the printer is installed, however, Windows 10 uses the driver automatically when the printer is installed. In this activity, you download and stage a printer driver.

1. If necessary, start your computer and sign in.
2. On the taskbar, click **Microsoft Edge**.
3. In the Search or enter web address box, type **support.hp.com** and then press **Enter**.
4. Click **Software and Drivers** and then click **Printer**.
5. On the Identify your printer screen, in the Enter your product name box, type **hp universal print driver** and then click **HP Universal Print Driver Series for Windows**.
6. In the search area, click **Search all support** and then select **Software, Drivers, and Updates**.
7. Expand **Driver – Universal Print Driver (3)**, and for HP Universal Print Driver for Windows PCL6 (64-bit), click **Download** and then click **Save**.
8. When the download is complete, close the Microsoft Edge window.
9. On the taskbar, click **File Explorer** and then click **Downloads**.
10. Double-click the file you just downloaded.
11. In the WinZip Self-Extractor window, in the Unzip to file box, type **C:\HPDriver**, deselect the When done unzipping open: .\install.exe check box, and then click **Unzip**.
12. Click **OK** and then close all open windows.
13. Right-click the **Start** button, click **Windows PowerShell (Admin)**, and then click **Yes**.
14. Type **pnputil /?** and then press **Enter**. This command displays the list of available options for pnputil.exe.
15. Type **pnputil /enum-drivers** and then press **Enter**. This command displays the list of third-party driver packages that have been installed. The HP Universal Print Driver package is not listed.
16. Type **dir C:\HPDriver*.inf** and then press **Enter**. This command displays all INF files in the HPDriver directory.
17. Type **pnputil /add-driver C:\HPDriver\hpcu240u.inf** and then press **Enter**. This command installs the printer driver package into the printer driver store. If the command prompt is not running as an administrator, this command fails. This file might not be available in your downloaded version of the driver. If this file is not available, select an alternative .inf file.
18. After the package is added, type **pnputil /enum-drivers** and then press **Enter**. Notice that the driver is now listed and named oem*x*.inf, where *x* is a number. The .inf file for each driver is renamed when it is added to the driver store. This guarantees that all .inf files have a unique name.
19. Close all open windows.

Printer Management Tools

Windows 10 has several tools for managing printers. You can choose the method based on your scenario and tool preference. The **Print Management snap-in** and Devices and Printers were introduced in Windows 7. The option to manage printers in Settings is new for Windows 10.

Printers and Scanners

The Printers & scanners screen, accessed from Devices in the Settings window and shown in Figure 7-8, is a new interface for managing printers in Windows 10. You can add or remove printers here. You can also set the default printer. When the Let Windows manage my default printer check box is selected, the default printer is always the last printer you used at a location, rather than a printer specifically defined as the default printer.

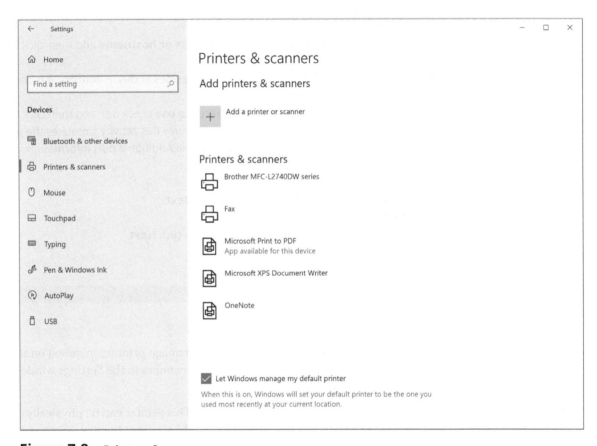

Figure 7-8 Printers & scanners screen

When you click Add a printer or scanner, Windows 10 scans the network looking for printers and displays a list of available printers. If the printer you want to install is found, you select the printer name from the list and click Add device to install it. If Windows 10 does not find the printer on the network, you can click The printer that I want wasn't listed, which starts the Add Printer Wizard that provides more advanced option for installing a printer.

After adding a printer, if you click the printer name, an Open queue option allows you to manage print jobs. A Manage option also is provided where you can perform the following tasks:

- Print a test page
- Run the troubleshooter
- View printer properties
- View printing preferences
- View hardware properties

Activity 7-6: Adding a Printer

Time Required: 10 minutes

Objective: Add a new printer from Settings

Description: In Windows 10, a USB printer will be detected automatically, but you need to manually install network printers. In this activity, you install a new network printer from Settings.

1. If necessary, start your computer and sign in.
2. Click the **Start** button and then click **Settings**.
3. In the Settings window, click **Devices** and then click **Printers & scanners**.
4. Click **Add a printer or scanner**. Windows takes a few minutes to scan the network to attempt to find printers and display any printers that are found.
5. Click **The printer that I want isn't listed**.
6. In the Add Printer dialog box, click **Add a printer using a TCP/IP address or hostname** and then click **Next**.
7. In the Device type list, select **TCP/IP Device**.
8. In the Hostname or IP address text box, type **172.16.99.99**. No printer resides at this IP address; it is chosen for the purposes of this activity only to see the interface.
9. Deselect the **Query the printer and automatically select the driver to use** check box and then click **Next**. In most cases, you want to leave this option on. You are deselecting it because this activity simulates the process.
10. After the TCP/IP port is detected (which might take a few minutes), on the Additional port information required screen, click **Standard** and then click **Next**.
11. In the Manufacturer area, click **HP**.
12. In the Printers box, select **HP Universal Printing PCL 6** and then click **Next**.
13. In the Printer name box, type **HP Printer PCL6** and then click **Next**.
14. On the Printer Sharing screen, click **Do not share this printer** and then click **Next**.
15. Click **Finish**.

Devices and Printers

Devices and Printers in Control Panel, shown in Figure 7-9, allows you to manage printers installed on the local computer. The functionality of Devices and Printers is the same as Printers & scanners in the Settings window. The major tasks that you can perform in Devices and Printers include:

- *Add a printer*—This option adds a new printer to the local computer. This printer can be physically attached or a network printer. This option scans the network just as when you add a printer through Printers & scanners.
- *See what's printing*—This option allows you to see jobs in the print queue for the selected printer. Within the queue, you can pause or delete individual print jobs.
- *Set as default printer*—This option allows you to configure a printer as the default printer for apps. In an app, such as Microsoft Word, when you click the Print button on the toolbar, the default printer is used.
- *Select printing preferences*—This option allows you to configure basic printer settings and paper configuration.
- *Configure printer properties*—This option allows you to edit all printer properties, including those for printing preferences, sharing, and security.
- *Configure print server properties*—This option allows you to edit print server properties for the local computer. This includes setting available forms (page sizes), configuring ports, and managing drivers.
- *Remove device*—This option removes the printer from your computer.

 TIP   When you right-click a printer name, most of the commonly used configuration options are accessed by selecting the Printer Properties option. The Properties option allows you to view some summary information.

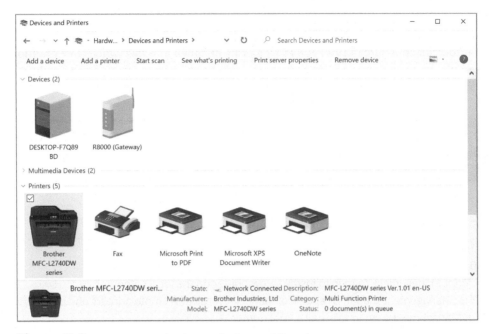

Figure 7-9   Devices and Printers in Control Panel

Print Management Snap-In

The Print Management snap-in, shown in Figure 7-10, allows you to manage printers for your entire network from a single computer. This is a big benefit for any organization with multiple print servers. Typically, you use the Print Management snap-in to manage print servers rather than individual computers.

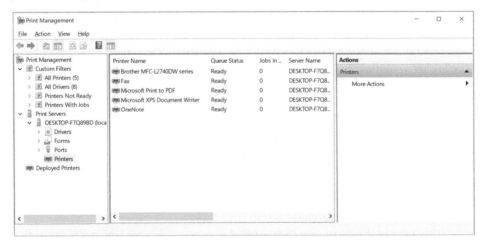

Figure 7-10   Print Management snap-in

Some features of the Print Management snap-in are:

- *Manage multiple print servers*—You can manage and configure not only printers, but also print server configuration, such as adding standard TCP/IP ports or printer drivers.
- *Filter views*—You can filter views to display only the printers in which you are interested. This can include showing only printers in an error state or in one physical location. Four filters exist by default: All Printers, All Drivers, Printers Not Ready, and Printers With Jobs.
- *Automatic installation of printers on a print server*—You can trigger an automatic printer installation process that scans the local subnet for network printers. If the appropriate drivers are located on the print server, all printers will be installed automatically. This can make configuring a new print server much faster.
- *Bulk printer management*—You can perform management operations on multiple printers at one time. For example, you can pause all the printers on a print server before you take it down for maintenance.

- *Use Group Policy to deploy printers*—You can add printer deployment information to Group Policy objects to automatically install printers on workstations.
- *Notification*—You can configure notifications to generate an email message when the conditions of a filter are met. For example, you can create a filter that shows only those printers in an error condition and set a notification on that filter. Then, when any printer experiences an error condition, you will be notified by email.

 **CAUTION**   The Use Group Policy to deploy printers option in the Print Management snap-in is outdated and should not be used. The updated method for deploying printers by using Group Policy is by configuring Group Policy Preferences.

Activity 7-7: Using the Print Management Snap-In

Time Required: 10 minutes

Objective: Use the Print Management snap-in to install a new printer on the local computer

Description: The Print Management snap-in is capable of managing local and remote printers and print servers. In this activity, you use the Print Management snap-in to install a local printer.

1. If necessary, start your computer and sign in.
2. Click the **Start** button, type **print**, and then click **Print Management**.
3. If necessary, in the left pane, expand **Custom Filters** and then click **All Printers**. This filter displays all the printers installed on every print server that is being monitored. In this case, only the local printers are displayed because only the local computer is being monitored.
4. In the left pane, click **All Drivers**. This filter displays all the printer drivers that are installed on every print server that is being monitored. This allows you to see if different printer driver versions are installed on various print servers.
5. In the left pane, if necessary, expand **Print Servers**, expand your computer, and then click **Drivers**. This node displays only the printer drivers that are installed on your computer.
6. In the left pane, click **Forms**. This node displays the forms that are configured on your computer. Forms are the paper sizes the printer is configured to use. You can add, edit, or delete forms by right-clicking the Forms node and then clicking Manage Forms.
7. In the left pane, click **Ports**. This node displays all the ports configured on your computer that can be used for printing. You can add additional ports or manage existing ports from here.
8. In the left pane, click **Printers**. This node displays all of the printers that are installed on your computer. You can manage the printers from here and install new printers.
9. In the left pane, right-click **Printers** and then click **Add Printer**.
10. Click **Add a new printer using an existing port**, if necessary, select **LPT1: (Printer Port)**, and then click **Next**. After printer installation, this printer will generate an error message when you attempt to print because no printer is physically attached to your computer on LPT1.
11. Click **Use an existing printer driver on the computer**, if necessary, click **HP Universal Printing PCL6**, and then click **Next**.
12. In the Printer Name box, type **Local**.
13. Leave the option **Share this printer** checked, type **Local** in the Share Name box, and then click **Next**.
14. On the Printer Found screen, click **Next**.
15. When the printer installation is finished, click **Finish**.
16. In the left pane, click **Printers**. The new printer named Local is installed here now.
17. Right-click **Local** and then click **Pause Printing**.
18. Right-click **Local** and then click **Print Test Page**.
19. In the Local dialog box, click **Close**.
20. In the left pane, click **Printers With Jobs**. Notice that this screen now displays the printer Local because a job is in the queue.
21. Close all open windows.

Printer Configuration

In many cases, after installing a printer, no further configuration is required. If you install a local USB printer, all the available options might already be configured for you. When you install more complex printers with multiple paper trays and finishing options like duplexing, however, you often need to configure the printer. You might also need to manage print jobs, configure location-aware printing, or configure branch office printing.

Configuration Options

Each printer you install in Windows 10 can be configured independently. Most of the options available for configuration are standardized by Windows 10; however, the Device Settings tab, shown in Figure 7-11, has device-specific settings. These settings typically indicate whether specific hardware options, such as duplexers and paper trays, have been installed. The Device Settings tab might not be included for all printers.

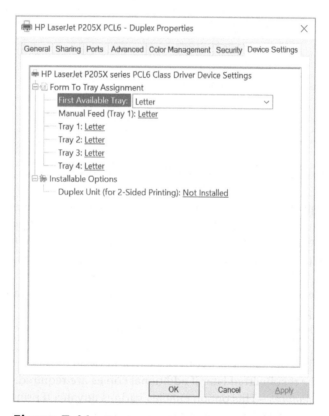

Figure 7-11   Device Settings tab of a printer

The Advanced tab, shown in Figure 7-12, has a number of options that are typically only implemented for server-based printing; however, these settings are also available for Windows 10. The options on this tab are the same regardless of the printer driver that is installed.

Options on the Advanced tab are:

- *Availability*—You can schedule the time of day that the printer is available. This is typically used for large print jobs that are deferred until after regular work hours to prevent the printer from being busy for an extended period of time during the workday.
- *Priority*—This option is used when multiple printers are configured to use the same port. The printer with the highest priority will print first. Printers with lower priority are able to print through the port only when printers with higher priority have completed all of their jobs. This is used on busy print servers to give a few users faster access to the printer.
- *Driver*—You can update or change the printer driver here.

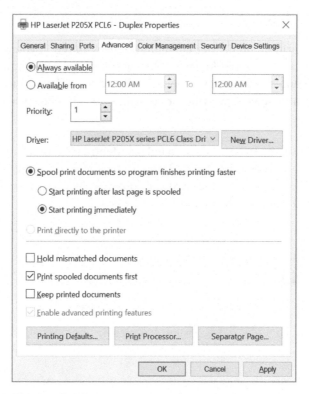

Figure 7-12   Advanced tab of a printer

- *Spooling configuration*—Spooling allows you to begin using an application faster after printing by storing the print job as a file and sending the print job to the printer as a background process. If you print directly to the printer, you cannot begin using your application again until the print job is complete. When spooling is enabled, you can prevent printing from starting until the last page is spooled as a troubleshooting mechanism when print jobs are being corrupted.
- *Hold mismatched documents*—This option holds print jobs in the queue if the paper type of the print job is not correctly matched to the paper in the printer.
- *Print spooled documents first*—This option gives priority to print jobs that have completed spooling over those that are still spooling.
- *Keep printed documents*—This option keeps a copy of each print job in the queue even after the job is complete. This allows print jobs to be resubmitted later if additional copies are required.
- *Enable advanced printing features*—This option enables various advanced printing options depending on the application that you are using and the printer driver that is installed.
- *Printing Defaults*—This option includes the default configuration options for print jobs, such as duplexing, paper orientation, and print quality. These options vary based on the printer driver that is installed.
- *Print Processor*—This option allows you to choose the format of the print jobs. This is typically used when troubleshooting print job corruption issues.
- *Separator Page*—This option allows you to specify a separator page that is included at the beginning of each document. Large organizations sometimes include these on busy printers where the separator page includes the user name of the person who printed the job.

Other standard tabs in a printer's Properties window are:

- *General*—Used to view information about the printer, configure printing preferences, and print a test page.
- *Sharing*—Used to configure printer sharing.
- *Ports*—Used to select and configure ports that are used by this printer.
- *Color Management*—Used to configure color profiles that are used to control how screen colors are translated to colors for printers. In some cases, color profiles for specific printers are available for download.
- *Security*—Used to configure user and group permissions for printing.

Printer Sharing and Security

Just as you can create file shares to share files with other users and computers over the network, you can also create shared printers. This is useful in a small office when you want to share the printer attached to a workstation. Sharing is enabled and controlled on the Sharing tab, shown in Figure 7-13.

Figure 7-13   Sharing tab of a printer

The Sharing tab allows you to:

- Enable sharing for the printer.
- Define the share name for the printer.
- Specify whether print jobs are rendered on the client computer or print server.
- Add drivers for other operating systems to download.

Whether a printer is shared or local, you can also configure security on that printer to control who is allowed to use and manage the printer. The Security tab is shown in Figure 7-14. You can allow or deny user and group permissions to print, manage printers, and manage documents.

The default permissions for printing are:

- *Everyone*—Allowed to print.
- *All Application Packages*—Allowed to print and manage documents. This allows Windows Store apps to print and manage print jobs.
- *Creator Owner*—Allowed to manage documents. This allows all users to manage their own print jobs.
- *User who installed printer (Userx)*—Allowed to print, manage printers, and manage documents.
- *Administrators*—Allowed to print, manage printers, and manage documents.

Branch Office Direct Printing

In Windows Server 2012 and Windows 8, Microsoft introduced **Branch Office Direct Printing** as a way to improve print performance for users in remote offices. Branch Office Direct Printing is designed for use when the client doing the printing and the printer are in the same physical location, but the print server that shares the printer is in a different location. Print configuration information from the print server is cached on the client computer, and the client prints directly to the printer instead of sending print jobs to the print server.

Figure 7-14   Security tab of a printer's Properties dialog box

Consider the following for Branch Office Direct Printing:

- You can centralize the administration of printers for remote offices but still keep WAN link utilization low because the print jobs stay local within the branch office.
- Intermittent WAN outages are not a problem because the printer configuration is cached on the client.
- The client computer is responsible for rendering the print job and must have the correct printer driver installed locally.
- Branch Office Direct Printing is enabled on a shared printer by using the Print Management snap-in.

Managing Print Jobs

In addition to controlling printers, you can also manage the individual jobs in a print queue. For each print job, you can perform the following tasks:

- *Pause*—Prevents the job from printing. If a job is partially finished printing, it stops at the end of a page.
- *Resume*—Allows a paused print job to continue printing.
- *Restart*—Restarts printing a job from the first page.
- *Cancel*—Stops a print job and removes it from the queue. The print job might not stop immediately, as it might take a few moments for the printer to remove the job from memory and complete printing the final page.
- *Edit job properties*—Allows you to change the priority of a print job or schedule the job.

Some of the situations where you might want to manage print jobs include:

- Restarting a print job when a paper jam has occurred and some pages have been destroyed
- Pausing a large print job to let several other smaller print jobs be completed
- Raising the priority of a print job to ensure that it prints next
- Changing the schedule of a large print job to prevent it from printing during main office hours
- Canceling a corrupted print job that is blocking other jobs in the queue

Print jobs are managed in Windows 10 by the spooler service. When printing has inexplicably stopped for a printer on a Windows computer, a reboot usually fixes the problem, unless a corrupted print job is blocking the queue. Instead of rebooting the computer, stop and start the print spooler service to accomplish the same result faster. This can be done by using the Services snap-in or opening a command prompt as Administrator and using the net stop spooler and net start spooler commands. You can also use the Windows PowerShell commands Stop-Service Spooler and Start-Service Spooler or Restart-Service Spooler.

If a corrupted print job occurs, it is possible that you will not be able to cancel the job. In such a case, stop the spooler service and delete the job manually in the file system. Print jobs are stored in C:\Windows\System32\spool\PRINTERS. Each print job is composed of two numbered files (.spl and .shd). Delete both files for the corrupted print job and then start the spooler service.

 TIP Sometimes corrupted print jobs cause the Spooler Service to hang and stop processing print jobs. If you can't stop the spooler service, you can kill the spoolsv.exe process by using Task Manager.

Activity 7-8: Managing Print Jobs

Time Required: 5 minutes

Objective: Manage print jobs

Description: Managing individual print jobs is seldom required; however, it can be useful for troubleshooting. In this activity, you manage a print job in the queue.

1. If necessary, start your computer and sign in.
2. Click the **Start** button and then click **Settings**.
3. Click **Devices**, click **Printers & scanners**, and then click **Local**. Note that the Printer local is paused.
4. Click **Open queue**. Notice that a Test Page job exists from Activity 7-7.
5. Right-click **Test Page** and then click **Pause**. Notice that the status of the job changes to Paused.
6. Right-click **Test Page** and then click **Resume**.
7. Right-click **Test Page** and then click **Properties**.
8. Click the **General** tab. You can modify the priority and schedule of the job here.
9. Click **OK** to close the Test Page Document Properties dialog box.
10. Right-click **Test Page** and then click **Cancel**.
11. When prompted, click **Yes** to confirm canceling the job.
12. Close all open windows.

BROWSERS

Microsoft includes the Edge browser in Windows 10. This is the default browser and is designed to be used for everyday browsing. Some organizations, however, have older intranet applications or access websites with ActiveX controls that are not supported in Microsoft Edge. To support those older applications, Internet Explorer 11 is also included in Windows 10.

Microsoft Edge

Over the years, Internet Explorer gained a reputation as an unsecure browser. Despite huge security improvements in Internet Explorer during later years, the reputation was hard to shake, and Microsoft determined that it would be best to create a completely new browser that is not limited by the requirement to support legacy technologies. Microsoft Edge in Windows 10 is that browser.

Microsoft Edge works well for browsing on the Internet and is focused on supporting Internet standards, such as HTML5. This browser is not designed to support older web applications designed for specific versions of Internet Explorer. Any web-based application that requires an older version of Internet Explorer to be rendered properly on the screen will not work properly in Microsoft Edge.

The other major feature not in Microsoft Edge is ActiveX controls. ActiveX controls were a method to allow code to be downloaded from a website and executed in the browser. Due to their design, however, ActiveX controls were a large security risk. Many older web-based applications used ActiveX controls.

Finally, Java applets are not supported in Microsoft Edge. No compatible plug-in or extension allows you to run Java applets. Because Java applets were an ongoing security concern, this is a positive development. Other major browsers, such as Chrome and Firefox, have also ended support for Java applets.

Chromium-Based Microsoft Edge

In January of 2020, Microsoft released a new version of Microsoft Edge based on the open source Chromium browser. The Google Chrome browser is also based on Chromium. This should result in better website compatibility with Microsoft Edge, because the functionality in Chromium is more widely supported than the previous page-rendering technology in the older version of Microsoft Edge.

Microsoft documentation refers to the Chromium-based version of Microsoft Edge as version 77 or later. The older version of Microsoft Edge is referred to as version 45 or earlier. To identify which version of Microsoft Edge is installed, you can look at the icon. Figure 7-15 shows the icon for the versions of Microsoft Edge.

The Chromium-based version of Microsoft Edge is not included in Windows 10 version 1909, but an automatic update upgrades Microsoft Edge to the Chromium-based version. Windows 10 version 2004 and later include the Chromium-based version of Microsoft Edge.

Version 45 or earlier   **Version 77 or later**

Figure 7-15
Microsoft Edge
versions

Configuration Settings

Most of the settings available in Microsoft Edge are common across almost all browsers. You can view the history of websites you have visited or save commonly visited websites to your list of favorites.

Collections is a new feature in the Chromium-based version of Microsoft Edge. You can create collections to store a list of websites that share a theme. This is similar to using folders in Favorites to organize webpages. Within a collection, you can also add notes, which is not possible within Favorites. This might be useful when researching, because you can create notes to identify what you still need to research or indicate what useful content a website contained.

Microsoft Edge can also save user names and passwords for websites. This password manager functionality makes it easier for you to maintain a unique user name and password combination for each website that you visit because you don't need to remember it.

If you use multiple devices, you should consider configuring profile synchronization in Microsoft Edge. If you sign in to Microsoft Edge with a Microsoft account or an Azure AD account, you can enable synchronization among devices that includes information such as favorites, settings, and saved passwords. This makes it easier to work seamlessly across multiple devices.

Activity 7-9: Configure Microsoft Edge

Time Required: 10 minutes
Objective: Configure settings and features in Microsoft Edge
Description: The Chromium-based version of Microsoft Edge is an updated browser for Windows 10. You should be aware of a number of configuration settings to support users. In this activity, you review and configure settings in Microsoft Edge. If necessary, you update your browser to the Chromium-based version of Microsoft Edge.

1. If necessary, start your computer and sign in.
2. Look at the Microsoft Edge icon on the taskbar and compare it to the icons in Figure 7-15. If you are using version 77 or later, skip to Step 13.
3. On the taskbar, click **Microsoft Edge**.
4. In the Search or enter web address box, type **https://www.microsoft.com/en-us/edge** and then press **Enter**.

5. Click **DOWNLOAD for Windows 10**.
6. In the Download the new Microsoft Edge dialog box, click **Accept and download** and then click **Close**.
7. In the What do you want to do with MicrosoftEdgeSetup.exe dialog box, click **Run**.
8. In the User Account Control dialog box, click **Yes** and then wait for the download to complete.
9. In the Close Microsoft Edge to install the new version dialog box, click **Close and continue**.
10. If necessary, on the Someone else is signed in to this PC screen, click **Install anyway**.
11. On the Welcome to the new Microsoft Edge screen, click **Get started** and then click **Done**.
12. Close the Microsoft Edge window.
13. On the taskbar, click **Microsoft Edge**. Notice that the default page that opens is content from Microsoft.
14. In the upper-right corner, click **Settings and more** and then click **Settings**.
15. Read the information on the Your profile screen. You can sign in by using a Microsoft account or an Azure AD account to synchronize Microsoft Edge settings such as favorites and saved credentials between devices.
16. In the navigation pane, click **Privacy and services** and read through the available options. Notice, at the bottom of the screen, that Microsoft Defender SmartScreen is enabled by default.
17. In the navigation pane, click **Appearance** and read the available options.
18. In the navigation pane, click **On startup** and read the available options. Notice that the Open a new tab option is selected by default.
19. In the navigation pane, click **New tab page** and then click **Customize**.
20. In the Page layout dialog box, click **Inspirational** and identify how the layout has changed.
21. Click **Focused** and close the Page layout dialog box.
22. In the Search or enter web address box, type **edge://settings** and then press **Enter**.
23. In the navigation pane, click **Site permissions** and read the list of permissions.
24. In the Search or enter web address box, type **edge://edge-urls** and then press **Enter**. This is a list of URLs that you can use to get additional information about Microsoft Edge configuration.
25. Scroll down and click **edge://system** and read the system information.
26. Close the Microsoft Edge window.

Security Zones

Windows 10 uses security zones to apply different levels of security to websites. The interface for managing the websites assigned to zones was originally designed for Internet Explorer but are also effective for Microsoft Edge; however, not all options, such as Protected Mode, apply to Microsoft Edge. The settings for zones and the sites in each zone are configured by using the Security tab in the Internet Options dialog box, shown in Figure 7-16.

The security zones are:

- *Internet*—The Internet zone includes all Internet websites that are not specifically assigned to another zone. The default security level is Medium-high.
- *Local intranet*—The Local intranet zone is meant to be all computers on the internal corporate network. The internal corporate network is defined by default as all sites in the local domain; however, this is relevant only if the workstation is joined to a domain. For workstations that are not part of a domain, the Intranet zone is treated the same as the Internet zone. The default security level is Medium-low.
- *Trusted sites*—The Trusted sites zone contains no sites by default; you must add sites that you consider trusted. This is useful when the Internet zone settings block functionality, such as pop-up windows, that are required for a site you know and trust. Adding the site to the Trusted sites zone allows that site to function properly. The default security level is Medium.
- *Restricted sites*—The Restricted sites zone is a specific list of sites that you do not trust. No sites are in this list by default. The default security level is High and cannot be changed except through custom settings.

The Local intranet zone is used primarily to support older web-based applications that require lowered security to function properly. By default, any website accessed by using a server name without dots (periods) is part of the Local

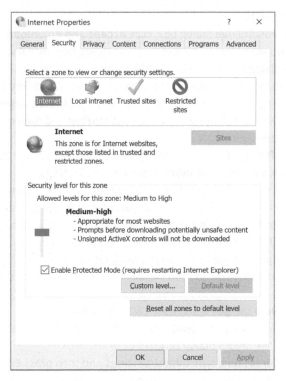

Figure 7-16   Security zones

intranet zone. For example, http://webserver/app is part of the Local intranet zone, but http://webserver.mydomain .com/app is not part of the Local intranet zone. You can also manually add websites to the Local intranet zone.

    When a website is part of the Local intranet zone, Microsoft Edge can pass sign-in credentials from the local workstation to the web server for authentication. Some companies use this as a method for automatically authenticating users to web-based applications. Users are prompted for sign-in credentials if the website is not part of the Local intranet zone.

 TIP   The Seamless Single Sign-On feature in Azure AD that allows automatic sign-in to Office 365 services requires a website to be placed in the Intranet zone.

Group Policy Settings for Microsoft Edge

In larger organizations, it's not reasonable to visit each computer to configure Microsoft Edge to meet organizational standards. Instead, on domain-joined computers Group Policy is used to apply settings. The necessary policy files, however, are not included with Windows 10. Instead, you need to download the policy files that define the Group Policy settings. After you download the policy files, you can configure Microsoft Edge settings by using Group Policy.

    The three groups of Microsoft Edge settings that you can configure after installing the policy files include:

- *Microsoft Edge*—Settings for Microsoft Edge where the setting from Group Policy is authoritative and can't be changed by users. Some of these are security related and should not be adjusted by users.
- *Microsoft Edge-Default Settings (users can override)*—This is a smaller group of settings that users are more likely to want to customize. For example, the settings for the Startup page and new tabs are included here.
- *Microsoft Edge Update*—These settings control how automatic updates for Microsoft Edge are performed, including configuration of a proxy server.

IE Mode

To support legacy web-based applications that still require the use of Internet Explorer, you can use **IE Mode** in Microsoft Edge. IE Mode allows you to create a list of websites that require Internet Explorer and have those websites automatically open in IE Mode for your users. This avoids the user frustration of needing to remember which browser to use for which websites.

> **⚠ CAUTION**   IE Mode uses the components of Internet Explorer 11, which is included as part of Windows 10. If you uninstall the Internet Explorer 11 optional feature, then IE will not work.

You can specify which websites to open in IE Mode by using an XML file to list specific websites or enable the Send all intranet sites to Internet Explorer setting for Microsoft Edge in Group Policy. It is recommended to create the XML instead, because not all intranet sites are likely to require IE Mode.

Although you can manually create the XML file for Enterprise Mode, it is faster and easier to use Enterprise Mode Site List Manager, shown in Figure 7-17, to create the XML file. When you specify the websites, you can also select the mode of Internet Explorer. For example, to support an older web-based application, you can specify that the site be opened in IE 7 Enterprise Mode, which emulates Internet Explorer 7.

NOTE 4

Enterprise Mode Site List Manager for Windows 10 can be downloaded from http://go .microsoft.com/fwlink/p/? LinkId=716853.

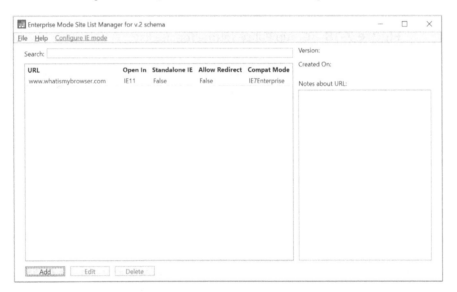

Figure 7-17   Enterprise Mode Site List Manager for v.2 schema

The final step in configuring Enterprise Mode is configuring the clients to use the XML file. This is done by enabling the Configure the Enterprise Mode Site List Group Policy setting in \Administrative Templates\Windows Components\ Microsoft Edge, shown in Figure 7-18. This setting is available for users and computers. When you enable this setting, you provide the location of the XML files. The location can be a website, network share, or local file.

You also need to configure how Internet Explorer is integrated with Microsoft Edge. You configure this in Group Policy with the Configure Internet Explorer integration setting. The three options for this setting include the following:

NOTE 5

For detailed information about configuring IE mode in Microsoft Edge, see Use Microsoft Edge with IE mode at https://go.microsoft .com/fwlink/?linkid=2094210.

- *Internet Explorer 11*—A new Internet Explorer 11 window is opened.
- *Internet Explorer mode*—The Internet Explorer components run from inside the Microsoft Edge window.
- *None*—Websites are opened only in normal Microsoft Edge rendering.

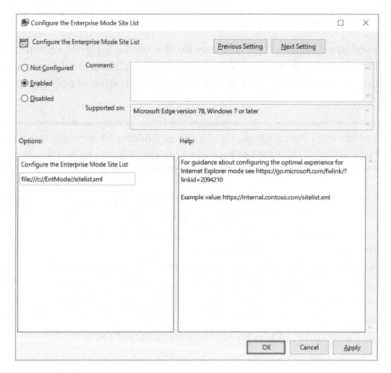

Figure 7-18   Group Policy setting for site list

Activity 7-10: Using IE Mode for Compatibility

Time Required: 20 minutes
Objective: Implement Enterprise Mode to provide backward compatibility for web-based applications
Description: Many organizations have web-based applications that are not compatible with Microsoft Edge. You can use IE Mode to configure a list of websites that will open by using Internet Explorer components. In this activity, you implement IE Mode to support legacy web-based applications.

1. If necessary, start your computer and sign in.
2. On the taskbar, click **Microsoft Edge**.
3. In the Search or enter web address box, type **http://go.microsoft.com/fwlink/p/?LinkId=716853** and then press **Enter**.
4. On the Enterprise Mode Site List Manager (schema v.2) page, click **Download**.
5. When the download is complete, click **Open file**.
6. In Enterprise Mode Site List Manager Setup dialog box, click **Next**.
7. Select the **I accept the terms in the License Agreement** check box and then click **Next**.
8. On the Destination Folder screen, click **Next**.
9. Click **Install** and then click **Yes** in the User Account Control dialog box.
10. Click **Finish**.
11. Click the **Start** button, type **enterprise**, and then click **Enterprise Mode Site List Manager**.
12. In Enterprise Mode Site List Manager for v.2 schema window, click **Add**.
13. In the Add new website window, in the URL box, type **www.whatismybrowser.com**.
14. In the Open In box, select **IE11**.
15. In the Compat Mode box, select **IE7 Enterprise Mode** and then click **Save**.
16. In Enterprise Mode Site List Manager for v.2 schema window, click **File** on the menu bar and then click **Save to XML**.
17. In the Save as dialog box, click **Local Disk (C:)**, click **New Folder**, type **EntMode**, and then press **Enter**.
18. Double-click **EntMode**.
19. In the File name box, type **sitelist.xml** and then click **Save**.

20. Close the Enterprise Mode Site List Manager for v.2 schema window.
21. In Microsoft Edge, in the Search or enter web address box, type **https://www.microsoft.com/en-us/edge/business/download** and then press **Enter**.
22. On the Download and deploy the new Microsoft Edge for business page, in the Select channel/build box, select the newest Stable option.
23. Click **GET POLICY FILES** and then click **Accept and download**.
24. When the file download is complete, click **Open file**.
25. In the File Explorer window, right-click **MicrosoftEdgePolicyTemplates** and then click **Extract**.
26. In the Select A Destination dialog box, in the navigation pane, below This PC access, click **Local Disk (C:)**, click **New folder**, type **PolicyFiles**, and then press **Enter**.
27. Double-click **PolicyFiles** and then click **Extract**.
28. In the File Explorer window, navigate to **C:\PolicyFiles\MicrosoftEdgePolicyTemplates\windows\admx**.
29. Use Ctrl+click to select **msedge.admx**, **msedgeupdate.admx**, and the **en-US** folder.
30. Click the **Home** tab and then click **Copy**.
31. Navigate to **C:\Windows\PolicyDefinitions**, click the **Home** tab, and then click **Paste**.
32. In the Destination Folder Access Denied dialog box, select the **Do this for all current items** check box and then click **Continue**.
33. Close the File Explorer window.
34. In Microsoft Edge, in the Search or enter web address box, type **www.whatismybrowser.com** and then press **Enter**. Notice that your browser is identified as Microsoft Edge.
35. Close the Microsoft Edge window.
36. Click the **Start** button, type **group**, and then click **Edit group policy**.
37. In the Local Group Policy Editor window, navigate to **\Local Computer Policy\Computer Configuration\Administrative Templates\Microsoft Edge** and then double-click **Configure Internet Explorer integration**.
38. In the Configure Internet Explorer integration dialog box, click **Enabled**.
39. In the Configure Internet Explorer integration box, select **Internet Explorer mode** and then click **OK**.
40. Double-click **Configure the Enterprise Mode Site List**.
41. In the Configure the Enterprise Mode Site List window, click **Enabled**.
42. In the Type the location (URL) of your Enterprise Mode IE website list box, type **file:///c://EntMode//sitelist.xml** and then click **OK**.
43. On the taskbar, click **Microsoft Edge**.
44. In the Search or enter web address box, type **edge://compat** and then press **Enter**. Notice that the site list is being used.
45. In the Search or enter web address box, type **www.whatismybrowser.com** and then press **Enter**. Notice that the browser version is reported as an old version.
46. Close all open windows.

ACCESSORIES AND SHORTCUTS

Windows client operating systems have always included some programs for performing simple editing of graphics and text. Some of these programs can be found in a Windows Accessories folder on the Start menu. These programs have limited utility but ensure that you don't need to install expensive software, such as Microsoft Office, to perform simple tasks. To aid productivity, Windows 10 also includes a wide variety of shortcuts that you can use to quickly perform tasks instead of clicking in several places. Table 7-2 lists some shortcuts for Windows.

NOTE 6

A comprehensive list of shortcuts in Windows 10 can be found on the Keyboard shortcuts on the Windows page at https://support.microsoft.com/en-us/help/12445/windows-keyboard-shortcuts.

Table 7-2 Windows Shortcuts

Shortcut	Description
Win+D	Minimize all windows
Win+L	Lock the screen
Win+I	Open Settings
Win+Ctrl+Shift+B	Attempt to fix display issues, such as a blank screen
Win++	Turn on Magnifier for a quick closeup during presentations

Text Editing

Notepad is a basic text editor included in Windows 10. This program can edit text files but does not include any text formatting, which means you cannot have multiple fonts, bold type, or italics. It also means that while Notepad is a poor choice for writing a report, it can be an excellent choice for editing text-based configuration files.

 TIP Many support professionals use Notepad++ as an alternative to Notepad. Notepad++ includes many advanced features for searching and editing text. It can be downloaded for free from https://notepad-plus-plus.org.

WordPad is a more advanced text editor that can be used to create simple documents that include text formatting. In addition to text formatting, you can also insert graphics. It does not have many of the advanced features found in a word processor like Microsoft Word, but you can create simple reports. You should avoid using WordPad when editing text-based configuration files because it might add unnecessary formatting information and corrupt the data file.

Windows 10 allows you to use many text-editing shortcuts, which are listed in Table 7-3.

Most of these shortcuts have not changed from previous versions of Windows, but one new option is Win+V for clipboard history. The default clipboard in Windows 10 retains only a single item. When you enable **clipboard history**, you can copy multiple items and then paste them later. Clipboard history can be enabled in Settings, as shown in Figure 7-19. You can also enable syncing of clipboard data across multiple devices.

Table 7-3 Text Editing Shortcuts

Shortcut	Description
Ctrl+C	Copy selected text or item to clipboard
Ctrl+X	Cut selected text or item and place on clipboard
Ctrl+V	Paste clipboard contents
Win+V	Open clipboard history and select item to paste
Ctrl+Z	Undo previous action (for many applications)
Ctrl+Y	Redo previous action (for many applications)
Ctrl+Home	Move to top of document (for many applications)
Ctrl+End	Move to end of document (for many applications)
Double-click text	Select whole word (for many applications)
Triple-click text	Select whole paragraph or line (for many applications)
Shift+arrow key	Move cursor one character at a time and select text
Win+.	Displays emoji keyboard

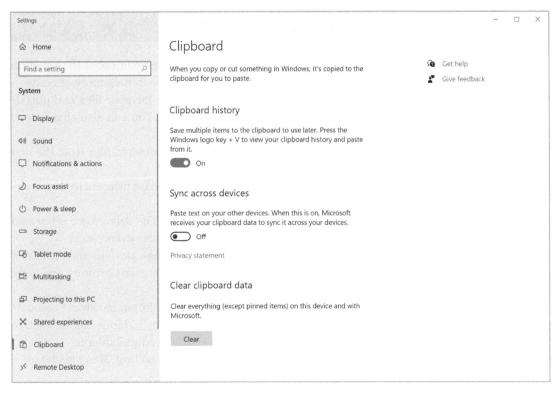

Figure 7-19   Clipboard settings

Graphics Editing

The Paint application in Windows 10 is a quick and easy want to do some very basic picture editing. If you capture a screenshot and want to crop or annotate it before you paste it into a document, the Paint application works well. Paint, however, does not have more advanced tools for editing pictures, such as adjusting brightness or coloring.

Paint 3D is a newer application that can accomplish the same simple editing as Paint but also apply color filtering and add stickers. You also can add a variety of 3D shapes. When you add a 3D shape, you can rotate it to the position you prefer.

When you double-click a picture, such as a JPG file, it opens in the Photos application. Photos is suitable for simple picture editing. In addition to cropping and rotating, you can also apply filters and light and color adjustments, as well as fix red eye. You can also combine multiple photos with music to create a video.

As a technical support professional, it's a common requirement to create documentation. The best documentation provides sufficient screenshots to make a process easier to understand. Table 7-4 describes the options included in Windows 10 for taking screenshots.

Table 7-4   Screenshot Shortcuts

Shortcut	Description
Print Screen	Take a screenshot of the entire screen
Win+Print Screen	Take a screenshot of the entire screen and automatically save it to Pictures\Screenshots
Shift+Print Screen	Take a screenshot of the in-focus window
Win+Shift+S	Open the snipping tool to capture a region of the screen, a window, or the entire screen
Win+G	Open the Xbox Game Bar to capture video

SUMMARY

- File Explorer is used to manage and access files in Windows 10. You can enable libraries to provide additional functionality. You can also index additional file system locations to make searching more effective.
- OneDrive is cloud-based storage for files that provides a backup location for your files and portability. You can access files in OneDrive through File Explorer or by using a browser. You can also share files stored in OneDrive with other people.
- In the web interface for OneDrive, you can view file versions and recover deleted files from the Recycle Bin. You can also edit files by using online Microsoft Office applications.
- Printing can be implemented with local or network printers. You can also share printers from a computer running Windows 10 or Windows Server.
- Printer drivers allow Windows 10 to use the full capabilities of a printer. The drivers are often available for PostScript and PCL. After installation, printer drivers are stored in the printer driver store.
- Printers can be installed and managed by using Printers & scanners in Settings, Devices and Printers in Control Panel, and the Print Management snap-in. Some of the configuration settings for printers are standardized, while others are specific to the capabilities of each printer.
- The Microsoft Edge browser is the primary browser in Windows 10. To maintain backward compatibility for older web-based applications, you can configure IE Mode in Microsoft Edge. IE Mode can be used to identify websites that should automatically be opened using compatibility with Internet Explorer.
- Windows 10 includes many useful programs for text editing and graphics editing. Many keyboard shortcuts also can be used to accomplish tasks quickly.

Key Terms

Branch Office Direct Printing
Clipboard history
IE Mode
libraries
metadata
Microsoft Edge

OneDrive
OneDrive for Business
page description language
Personal Vault
Portable Document Format (PDF)
PostScript

Print Management snap-in
Printer Command Language (PCL)
printer driver
printer driver packages
printer driver store
XML Paper Specification (XPS)

Review Questions

1. Which document format is similar to XPS?
   a. PDF
   b. TXT
   c. DOC
   d. RTF

2. Which of the following are languages used by printers? (Choose all that apply.)
   a. WPF
   b. XPS
   c. PCL
   d. PostScript

3. Which utility is used to add printer drivers to the printer driver store?

   a. pdriver.exe
   b. pnputil.exe
   c. PushPrinterConnections.exe
   d. Print Management snap-in

4. Which utilities can be used to manage printers? (Choose all that apply.)
   a. Devices and Printers in Control Panel
   b. Computer Management
   c. Device Manager
   d. Print Management snap-in
   e. Printers & scanners in Settings

5. Which of the following are features available only in the Print Management snap-in? (Choose all that apply.)

    a. Manage remote printers

    b. Manage local printers

    c. Configure notifications

    d. Bulk printer management

    e. Update printer drivers

6. When a printer is configured with a lower priority value, the print jobs for that printer are printed first. True or False?

7. By default, all users are able to manage their own print jobs because the _____ group has the manage documents permission.

8. When you create a new document in the root of a library, where is the document created?

    a. in the highest priority location with free space

    b. in the first location listed in the library properties

    c. in a location you specify when prompted

    d. in the default save location of the library

9. Which file locations are indexed by default? (Choose all that apply.)

    a. the Temp folder

    b. the Windows folder

    c. the Start menu

    d. the Users folder

10. For each type of file, you can specify whether the contents of the file are indexed. True or False?

11. Which security zone is relevant only if the computer is joined to a domain?

    a. Internet

    b. Local intranet

    c. Trusted sites

    d. Restricted sites

12. What is the default folder synchronized with OneDrive?

    a. C:\OneDrive

    b. C:\Users\%username%\SkyDrive

    c. C:\Users\%username%\OneDrive

    d. C:\Users\%username%\Cloud

13. Which actions for OneDrive can be performed only when accessing files through the web interface? (Choose all that apply.)

    a. Recover deleted files from the Recycle Bin.

    b. Share files with other people.

    c. Edit files by using web-based applications.

    d. Simultaneously edit files at the same time as other people.

    e. Access previous versions of files.

14. Access to shared files in OneDrive can be restricted to specific people. True or False?

15. Which of the following are characteristics of Branch Office Direct Printing? (Choose all that apply.)

    a. WAN utilization is reduced.

    b. The print server is responsible for rendering the print job.

    c. WAN outages prevent jobs from starting because the print server cannot be contacted.

    d. You can centrally manage printers for multiple locations from a single print server.

    e. The Print Management snap-in is used to enable Branch Office Direct Printing on a printer.

16. Which steps are required to configure IE Mode with Microsoft Edge? (Choose all that apply.)

    a. Create a text file with a list of websites requiring Internet Explorer 11.

    b. Create an XML file with a list of websites requiring Internet Explorer 11.

    c. Enable IE Mode in Group Policy.

    d. Enable IE Mode in Microsoft Edge settings.

17. The _____ service is responsible for processing print jobs.

18. Which application included in Windows 10 is the best to use for editing text-based configuration files?

    a. Notepad

    b. Word

    c. Edit.exe

    d. WordPad.exe

    e. Notepad++

19. Which keyboard shortcut takes a screenshot of the in-focus window?

    a. Print Screen

    b. Ctrl+P

    c. Shift+Print Screen

    d. Win+P

    e. Win+Print Screen

20. What is the version number for the new version of Microsoft Edge that is Chromium-based?

    a. 25 and higher

    b. 42 and higher

    c. 55 and higher

    d. 77 and higher

    e. 86 and higher

Case Projects

Case Project 7-1: Printing to PDF

The accountant for Buddy's Machine Shop has just received a new Windows 10 computer. His accounting software has been installed and is working well; however, he asks you to install a PDF printer that he uses to generate invoice PDFs to send out via email. This PDF printer is quite expensive. Explain why this PDF printer is not necessary for Windows 10.

Case Project 7-2: Website Compatibility

Gigantic Life Insurance is planning the implementation of Windows 10 for its internal staff. As part of the migration process, you want to standardize using the Microsoft Edge browser for the enhanced security over Internet Explorer. Several important web-based applications, however, run properly only in Internet Explorer. How can you implement IE Mode to make this process easy for users?

Case Project 7-3: Data Backup with OneDrive

The salespeople at Hyperactive Media Sales all use laptop computers so that they can have easy access to important data on the road. A concern has arisen, however, that the salespeople keep data on their laptop computers and the data is never backed up. Because of this, if the hard drive in the laptop fails, important information would be lost. Explain how OneDrive can help in this situation.

WINDOWS 10 APPLICATION SUPPORT

After reading this module and completing the exercises, you will be able to:

1. Describe the application environments supported by Windows 10
2. Modify and back up the registry
3. Install various types of apps
4. Describe and implement options for app compatibility
5. Configure clients for virtual desktops and RemoteApp

As a technology support worker, it is easy to lose track of the real purpose of computers. The purpose of computers is to run applications that allow workers to be more productive. Installing and troubleshooting those applications is core to the role of desktop support.

In this module, you review the different application environments available in Windows 10, which in turn identify the types of apps supported by Windows 10. You also learn about the structure of the registry and how to edit it. Then, you learn about different installation processes for apps, including automated deployment for larger organizations. You also identify the different options for mitigating app compatibility problems when migrating to Windows 10. Finally, you learn about how to access virtual desktops and RemoteApp programs when Remote Desktop Services has been configured.

APPLICATION ENVIRONMENTS

Apps are written by developers to interact with a specific **application environment subsystem**. The application environment subsystem provides access to operating system services through an **application programming interface (API)**. The application environment subsystem is then responsible for communicating with the operating system to accomplish tasks, such as communicating on the network or saving files to disk.

To install and use an app, the application environment it is written for must be present. If the application environment is not present, the APIs necessary for the app to request operating system functions are not available. Some application environments have multiple versions, and you need to ensure that the correct version is present for apps. You might need to install Windows Updates to ensure you have the most recent version of the desired application environment.

NOTE 1

For an overview of applications environments oriented at programmers, see Choose your app platform at https://docs.microsoft.com/en-us/windows/apps/desktop/choose-your-platform.

All the application environments in Windows 10 restrict apps to running in user mode where they are isolated from the core functionality of the operating system. Running apps in user mode ensures that a poorly written app does not affect system stability. This compares with hardware drivers that operate in kernel mode where a poorly written driver can impact system stability.

Windows API

The Windows API provides a way for apps to request services and functionality from Windows 10. Apps written in various programming languages can use this API. The modern variation of the Windows API is Win64. Win64 is implemented on 64-bit versions of Windows 10. In 32-bit versions of Windows, the Win32 version of the Windows API is implemented.

 TIP   Sometimes the Windows API is generically referred to as Win32 even on 64-bit versions of Windows.

Most organizations use the 64-bit version of Windows 10 rather than the 32-bit version of Windows 10. Both versions support Win32, but the 64-bit version of Windows 10 supports 32-bit applications by using a Windows on Windows 64 (WOW64) virtualized environment to host Win32 apps. The calls to Win32 APIs are translated to an equivalent Win64 API call in the 64-bit version of Windows 10 to provide compatibility.

It is common for organizations to have a mix of 32-bit and 64-bit applications. On a 64-bit version of Windows 10, the apps installed to C:\Program Files (x86)\ are 32-bit applications.

Activity 8-1: Identifying Win32 and Win64 Apps

Time Required: 10 minutes

Objective: Run Win32 and Win64 apps and review how they appear in Task Manager

Description: The core apps included in the 64-bit version of Windows 10 are all 64-bit applications; however, 32-bit versions of some system apps are included for backward compatibility for some programs. In this activity, you run a Win32 app and a Win64 app to confirm how they are individually presented on the Processes tab in Task Manager.

1. If necessary, start your computer and sign in.
2. Click the **Start** button, type **notepad**, and then click **Notepad**.
3. On the taskbar, click **File Explorer**.
4. In the File Explorer window, browse to **C:\Windows\SysWOW64** and then double-click **notepad**.
5. Compare the two Notepad windows. Notice that no visual difference is apparent between the two Notepad windows.
6. Right-click the taskbar and then click **Task Manager**.
7. If Task Manager is in the simplified view, click **More details**.
8. On the Processes tab, if necessary, click the Name column to sort by name, and notice that two Notepad apps are listed. One of the Notepad apps has (32 bit) appended to the name. The text (32 bit) identifies Win32 processes.
9. Right-click **Notepad (32 bit)** and then click **Properties**.
10. In the notepad Properties window, notice that the location for this app is C:\Windows\SysWOW64 and then click **Cancel**.
11. Close all open windows.

.NET Framework

The **.NET Framework** is a commonly used application environment for apps on Windows 10. You can identify whether the .NET Framework is required for an app from the documentation for the app. Most applications that require the .NET Framework verify that the correct version of .NET Framework is available during installation. Some apps even distribute the .NET Framework during installation if required.

Multiple versions of the .NET Framework exist. At the time of this writing, the current version is .NET Framework 4.8. In theory, the latest version of .NET Framework is compatible with previous versions, but the reality is that some apps require specific versions. In general, .NET Framework 3.5 supports apps written for .NET versions 2.0, 3.0, and 3.5. Apps requiring .NET 4.0 or later are generally compatible with the latest version of the .NET Framework. Windows 10 provides .NET Framework 3.5 and .NET Framework 4.8 as features.

Updates for the .NET Framework are delivered through Windows Update. If your organization has .NET applications, you should test any new .NET Framework updates before deploying them to user computers. Updates for the .NET Framework are issued regularly.

 TIP   For instructions on how to identify which version of the .NET Framework is installed, see How to: Determine which .NET Framework versions are installed at https://docs.microsoft.com/en-us/dotnet/framework/migration-guide/how-to-determine-which-versions-are-installed.

Activity 8-2: Installing .NET Framework 3.5

Time Required: 10 minutes
Objective: Install .NET Framework 3.5 on Windows 10
Description: Some applications require an older version of .NET Framework to be installed. In Windows 10, .NET Framework 3.5 is available for backward compatibility. In this activity, you install the .NET Framework 3.5 feature on Windows 10.

1. If necessary, start your computer and sign in.
2. Click the **Start** button, type **control**, and then click **Control Panel**.
3. In the Control Panel window, click **Programs** and then click **Turn Windows features on or off**.
4. In the Windows Features dialog box, notice that .NET Framework 4.8 Advanced Services is already installed by default.
5. Select the **.NET Framework 3.5 (includes .NET 2.0 and 3.0)** check box and then click **OK**.
6. In the Windows Features window, click **Let Windows Update download the files for you**. The installation files are not included with Windows 10. In most cases, the file download takes only a few minutes.
7. When Windows has completed the requested changes, click **Close** and then close the Control Panel window.

Universal Windows Platform

To make application development easier across multiple types of devices, Microsoft created **Universal Windows Platform (UWP)**. UWP apps are designed with a more modern interface that is flexible enough to accommodate multiple form factors, like a desktop computer and tablets. These apps have been known as Metro apps, Modern apps, Windows Store apps, Microsoft Store apps, and UWP apps.

Many of the apps included in Windows 10 are UWP apps. For example, the Calculator app is a UWP app. A defining characteristic of UWP apps is that they are distributed and updated from the Microsoft Store. This enhances app security because Microsoft verifies that the app does not contain malware and meets development standards.

Legacy Applications

If you are running a 64-bit version of Windows 10, you cannot run DOS or Win16 applications. DOS was the command-line precursor to Windows, and Win16 was used for apps in Windows 3.1. Because both these platforms were popular in the 1980s and early 1990s, very few apps in production were designed for DOS or Win16.

If you do have a legacy DOS or Win16 application that you need to run, you can use a 32-bit version of Windows 10. To support Win16 applications, a 32-bit version of Windows 10 translates Win16 API calls to Win32 API calls in the same way that 64-bit versions of Windows 10 support 32-bit applications. DOS applications are supported by a virtual instance of DOS (Ntvdm.exe).

THE REGISTRY

Windows 10 has the **registry** as a central store for application and operating system configuration information. Applications and Windows 10 read their configuration information from the registry during startup and when running. When you make configuration changes to applications or Windows 10, those changes are stored in the registry so that they can be retrieved later.

In most cases, you don't need to manually edit or view the registry. Applications and Windows 10 properly understand the structure of the registry and how their own information is stored in it. Sometimes, however, you will find support documents that identify registry keys that need to be verified or modified. In those cases, you need to understand the structure of the registry and how to modify it.

Registry Structure

The registry is divided into sections and levels of data. Multiple sections exist to organize data by purpose. The individual sections are called hives. Each **hive** has a specific role to play and is stored in memory while it is in use. When the computer is shut down, the memory versions of the hives are written to files and folders typically found in the C:\Windows\System32\config folder. Each hive is composed of one or more files.

Within a single hive, the data is stored in keys and values identified by their name and position relative to one another. Figure 8-1 shows an example of the registry structure when viewed with a registry editing tool.

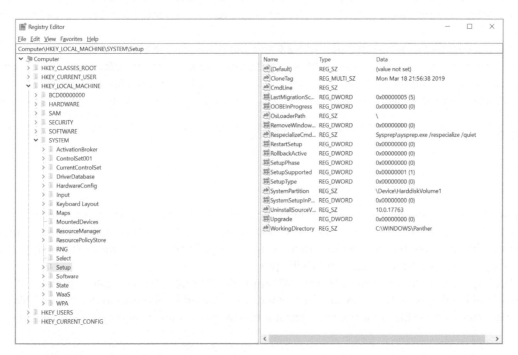

Figure 8-1   View of the registry structure

The left navigation pane displays a hierarchical folder structure. Each hive appears as a top-level folder in the left pane. In the hives, each folder in the left pane is referred to as a **registry key**. Each registry key is identified by the hive it belongs to, its position relative to other keys in the hive, and its name.

The right pane shows the data values that are stored at a specific level in the registry hierarchy (i.e., within a registry key). Each registry key can store multiple data values. The data values are defined by a name that is case sensitive, a type indicating how the data is formatted (e.g., binary, string, word), and the actual data stored by the value.

 TIP   In documentation, it is common for the registry hive names to be abbreviated. For example, HKEY_LOCAL_MACHINE is often referred to as HKLM. Also, HKEY_CURRENT_USER is often referred to as HKCU.

To aid in troubleshooting and understanding why changes might be requested by a support document, it is useful to understand the contents of each registry hive. Table 8-1 describes the contents of each registry hive.

Table 8-1   Registry Hives

Hive Name	Description
HKEY_CLASSES_ROOT	This hive defines file types (classes) and properties associated with those types. For example, file type associations are stored here. This hive is a combination of HKCU\Software\Classes and HKLM\Software\Classes. If settings for a file type are defined in both locations, the user-specific settings take precedence.
HKEY_CURRENT_USER	This hive contains the user-specific registry information from ntuser.dat stored in the user profile. Any application or operating system settings that are user specific are stored in this hive. If you are attempting to fix a user-specific application issue, the support document will have you review and modify keys here.
HKEY_LOCAL_MACHINE	This hive contains global settings for the entire computer and the applications installed on it. If you are attempting to fix any operating system or application issue that is not user specific, the support document will have you review and modify keys here. More details about HKLM are provided later in this module.
HKEY_USERS	This hive contains the user-specific settings for the current user and several system services. The name of the registry key for the currently signed-in user is the security identifier (SID) of the user. The content of the key for the currently signed-in user is also available in HKCU.
HKEY_CURRENT_CONFIG	This hive contains details about the current hardware profile in use. The details report the differences between the standard configuration defined in HKLM\System and HKLM\Software and those in the active hardware profile. This hive is also a mapped view to information stored in HKLM\System\CurrentControlSet\Hardware Profiles\Current.

HKEY_USERS

The HKEY_USERS hive contains several registry keys, as shown in Figure 8-2. The .DEFAULT key contains the default registry settings that are copied for new user profiles. The shorter registry keys, such as S-1-5-18, are for system services. The registry keys with a full SID are for the currently signed-in user.

HKEY_LOCAL_MACHINE

This hive contains important settings for Windows 10 and applications, as well as all of the general settings. Some of the important keys in this hive are as follows:

Figure 8-2   HKEY_USERS hive

- *BCD00000000*—This key contains information from the boot configuration database that defined the Windows 10 boot process. Instead of editing these keys, you should use the bcdedit.exe utility.
- *HARDWARE*—This key contains hardware information that is detected at startup. You should not edit this information.

- *SOFTWARE*—This key contains information for applications. Application data is typically located in a key with the following naming structure: HKLM\SOFTWARE*vendor**application*\\.
- SYSTEM—This key contains information about Windows 10 and hardware drivers. Device driver and service information is in HKLM\SYSTEM\CurrentControlSet. A backup copy of this key named ControlSet001 is updated each time a user signs in. This backup can be used by Windows 10 during a recovery.

Registry Editing Tools

The preferred method for configuring applications and Windows 10 is to use the interfaces provided for that purpose. Applications typically have settings or options that you can use to configure the application. Windows 10 has Settings, Control Panel, and various Microsoft Management Console (MMC) snap-ins.

If you do need to view and modify the registry entries, take the following precautions:

- Back up the portion of the registry you will be changing before you make any changes.
- Restrict the number of changes made at one time to limit the impact, and identify which change actually fixed the problem.
- When possible, use a test system rather than a user's computer to verify that changes resolve the issue.
- If you are adjusting registry entries for services or drivers, ensure that the computer can boot properly after the changes have been made.

Registry Editor

The most commonly used tool for viewing and modifying the registry is the graphical **Registry Editor** (regedit). In addition to basic editing functionality, you can use this tool to search the registry and modify permissions. You can also export and import sections of the registry. The Registry Editor is shown in Figure 8-1.

When you export registry keys for a backup, it is done to a .reg file. If you want to restore the contents of the .reg file, you can import it by using the Registry Editor; however, you can also double-click the file in File Explorer to restore the registry keys.

Activity 8-3: Using Regedit to Back Up and Modify the Registry

Time Required: 10 minutes
Objective: Use regedit to view and change registry information
Description: Startup information for services is stored in the registry. Although you should normally edit service startup information by using the Services administrative tool, you can also edit directly in the registry. In this activity, you modify the startup setting for a server by using regedit.

1. If necessary, start your computer and sign in.
2. Click the **Start** button, type **services**, and then click **Services**.
3. Scroll down and then double-click the **Print Spooler** service.
4. In the Print Spooler Properties (Local Computer) dialog box, read the information for the service and then click **Cancel**. Notice that the Startup type is Automatic.
5. Click the **Start** button, type **regedit**, and then click **Registry Editor**.
6. In the User Account Control dialog box, click **Yes**.
7. In the Registry Editor, navigate to HKEY_LOCAL_MACHINE\SYSTEM\CurrentControlSet\Services\Spooler.
8. Right-click **Spooler** and then click **Export**.
9. In the Export Registry File window, click **This PC** and then double-click **Local Disk (C:)**.
10. In the File name box, type **SpoolerBak** and then click **Save**.
11. In the Registry Editor, double-click **Start**.
12. In the Edit DWORD (32-bit) Value dialog box, in the Value data box, type **4** and then click **OK**.
13. In the Services window, press F5 to refresh the view, verify that the value in the Startup Type column for the Print Spooler service is now Disabled, and then close the Services window.
14. In the Registry Editor, collapse all the hives so that no keys are visible and then close the Registry Editor window.

Activity 8-4: Restoring a Registry Backup

Time Required: 10 minutes

Objective: Restore registry settings from a .reg file

Description: Before modifying the registry, you should export any keys that you will be changing to a .reg file. If the registry change does not go as planned, you can import the .reg file to restore the previous level of functionality. In this activity, you restore a .reg file and verify that the contents imported properly.

1. If necessary, start your computer and sign in.
2. On the taskbar, click **File Explorer**, navigate to **C:**, and then double-click **SpoolerBak**.
3. In the User Account Control dialog box, click **Yes**. Notice that the Registry Editor is being started.
4. In the Registry Editor window, click **Yes** to continue.
5. Click **OK** to acknowledge the successful import and then close the File Explorer window.
6. Click the **Start** button, type **regedit**, and then click **Registry Editor**.
7. In the User Account Control dialog box, click **Yes**.
8. In the Registry Editor, expand **HKEY_LOCAL_MACHINE** and then click **SYSTEM**.
9. Click **Edit** on the menu bar and then click **Find**.
10. In the Find dialog box, in the Find what box, type **spooler**.
11. In the Look at area, deselect all check boxes except **Keys** and then click **Find Next**.
12. Keep pressing **F3** to Find Next until the Print Spooler service identified in Activity 8-3 is located. This will take about 5–10 presses, but review the information that is found along the way.
13. Read the Start value and verify that it has been set back to 2.
14. Click the **Start** button, type **services**, and then click **Services**.
15. Scroll down to the Print Spooler service and verify that the Startup Type is Automatic.
16. Close all open windows.

Reg.exe

If you need to read or write registry entries from batch files, you can use reg.exe, as shown in Figure 8-3. Reg.exe is a command-line utility with similar functionality to regedit. You may see some support documents that advise you to use reg.exe when modifying the registry. This is because it is easier to type out a single command in support documentation

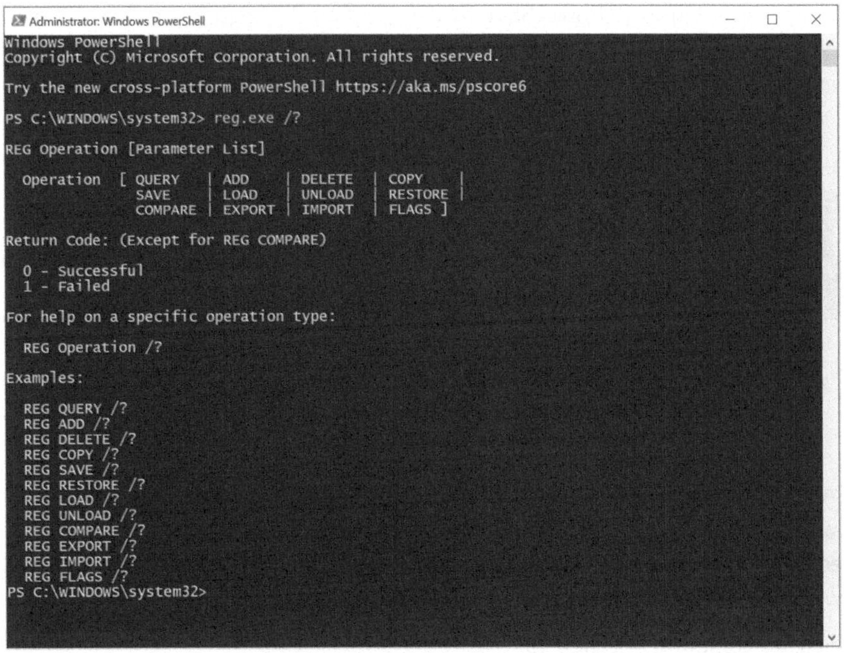

Figure 8-3   Reg.exe command-line utility

than to provide multiple steps to perform the task using a graphical interface. Regardless of the registry editing tool used, the end result is the same.

Activity 8-5: Using Reg.exe

Time Required: 10 minutes

Objective: Use reg.exe to view and modify registry entries

Description: If you need to query or modify the registry from a command-line or batch file, you can use reg.exe. In this activity, you view and modify registry entries by using reg.exe.

1. If necessary, start your computer and sign in.
2. Right-click the **Start** button, click **Windows PowerShell (Admin)**, and then click **Yes** in the User Account Control dialog box.
3. At the Windows PowerShell prompt, type **reg /?** and then press **Enter** to view the general help information.
4. Type **reg query /?** and then press **Enter** to view the query help information. Scroll up and down to read all of it.
5. Type **reg query HKLM\SYSTEM\CurrentControlSet\Services\Spooler** and then press **Enter**. Verify that the Start value is 0×2.
6. Type **reg add /?** and then press **Enter** to view the add help information. Scroll up and down to read all of it.
7. Type **reg add HKLM\SYSTEM\CurrentControlSet\Services\Spooler /v Start /d 0×4** and then press **Enter**. This sets the Start value to 0×4.
8. Press **Y** and then press **Enter** to confirm overwriting the value.
9. Type **reg query HKLM\SYSTEM\CurrentControlSet\Services\Spooler** and then press **Enter**. Verify that the Start value is 0×4.
10. Type **reg import /?** and then press **Enter** to view the import help information.
11. Type **reg import C:\SpoolerBak.reg** and then press **Enter**.
12. Type **reg query HKLM\SYSTEM\CurrentControlSet\Services\Spooler** and then press **Enter**. Verify that the Start value is 0x2 as it was restored from the backup.
13. Close the Windows PowerShell prompt window.

Windows PowerShell

In Windows 10, you can also use Windows PowerShell to view and modify registry values. This is important, as administrators are more likely to create new scripts in Windows PowerShell than to create batch files and use reg.exe.

In Windows PowerShell, the registry is accessible in a similar fashion to the file system. Both HKCU and HKLM are configured as drives. You can navigate through these drives by using the cd and dir commands. These, however, are actually aliases to the PowerShell cmdlets Set-Location and Get-ChildItem.

 **CAUTION**   Windows PowerShell doesn't include any built-in functionality to export or import a section of the registry to a .reg file. It can be done by using a script, but it's much easier to use reg.exe or the Registry Editor.

Activity 8-6: Viewing the Registry by Using Windows PowerShell

Time Required: 10 minutes

Objective: Use Windows PowerShell to view and modify registry entries

Description: If you need to query or modify the registry from a command-line or batch file, you can use Windows PowerShell. In this activity, you view and modify registry entries by using Windows PowerShell.

1. If necessary, start your computer and sign in.
2. Right-click the **Start** button and then click **Windows PowerShell (Admin)**.

3. In the User Account Control dialog box, click **Yes**.
4. At the Windows PowerShell prompt, type **Get-PSDrive** and then press **Enter**. You can see that HKCU and HKLM are available.
5. Type **Set-Location HKLM:** and then press **Enter**. Notice that the prompt has changed to indicate you are in HKLM.
6. Type **Get-ChildItem** and then press **Enter**. You can see the same registry keys as in regedit.
7. Type **Set-Location SYSTEM\CurrentControlSet\Services\Spooler** and then press **Enter**.
8. Type **Get-ItemProperty.** and then press **Enter**. The period in this command represents the current folder of Spooler. Notice that Start has a value of 2.
9. Type **Set-ItemProperty. -Name Start -Value 4** and then press **Enter**.
10. Type **Get-ItemProperty.** and then press **Enter**. Verify that Start has a value of 4.
11. Type **reg import C:\SpoolerBak.reg** and then press **Enter**.
12. Close the Windows PowerShell prompt window.

INSTALLING APPS

Apps can be packaged for deployment in multiple ways. The most common way traditional Win32 or .NET Framework apps are packaged is in an MSI file. This type of file is read by the Windows Installer service to perform the installation. The MSI file has all the files for the app and instructions for file locations and registry keys.

For app developers, the Windows Installer service takes care of the details of app installation, repair, and removal. All the developers need to do is package the application properly.

 TIP Even though many apps have a setup.exe file, typically that setup.exe just starts the installation by using an MSI file.

Some app developers do not use MSI files for their apps. Typically, you see this for small developers that want to execute very simple deployment of their apps. These apps often lack repair functionality once they are installed. The installation and uninstallation are handled completely by the setup.exe file.

Automating MSI Installation

In a small organization, you can go to each computer and install apps manually. This process is typically faster than figuring out how to automate the process. In a larger organization, however, it is worth the time to identify how apps can be automatically deployed to computers. Even if it takes only 5 minutes to install an app, 5 minutes for each of 1000 computers is a long time.

The simplest automated deployment method is to create a batch file that does a silent install of the application. Many applications have a /q or /quiet option for the setup.exe file. You can configure the command to run setup.exe / quiet in a sign-in script. This is not very sophisticated, but it can work for some simple scenarios.

The msiexec.exe command-line utility, shown in Figure 8-4, also can be used with MSI files in a script. When you run msiexec.exe, you can specify a /quiet option to suppress prompting users for input. If the app requires some input during installation, you can provide a transform file (.mst) that provides the additional information necessary for the app to install.

A more manageable way to deploy MSI-based applications in smaller environments is by using Group Policy. In Group Policy, you can deploy MSI-based apps to users or computers. If you deploy apps to users, the apps get installed on each computer that they use. If you deploy apps to computers, they are available to all users on that computer. Figure 8-5 shows the Group Policy settings for application deployment to a computer.

Apps installed by Group Policy do not prompt the user for input. So, if the app typically requires user input, you need to create a transform file to provide the necessary information or repackage the app with the information already provided.

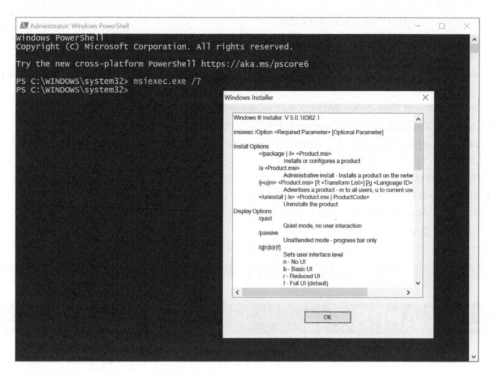

Figure 8-4   Msiexec.exe command-line utility

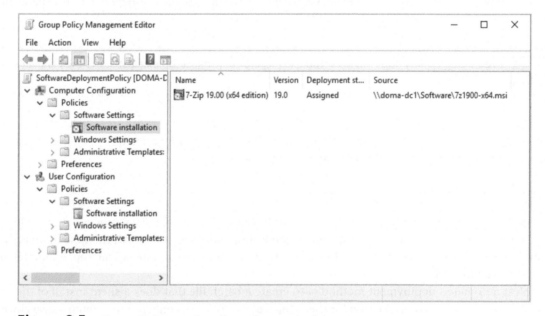

Figure 8-5   Group Policy settings for software deployment

Apps can install even if the signed-in user does not have administrative permissions. This is because the Windows Installer service does the work, and it has Local System privileges.

When you deploy software by using Group Policy, you can update it afterwards by applying an MSP file to the application. Or, you can create a new version of the app and replace the existing version for upgrades.

In large environments, a better option for software deployment is Microsoft Endpoint Configuration Manager. Microsoft Endpoint Configuration Manager has many other functions, but it also performs software deployment. It can deploy both MSI-based apps and newer UWP and MSIX apps. Like Group Policy, it can include transform files and perform updates based on version; however, Microsoft Endpoint Configuration Manager is much more flexible in selecting the users and computers for which the apps are deployed. It also has centralized reporting about app deployment and can even monitor licensing. You can also use Microsoft Intune to manage Azure AD-joined devices.

Activity 8-7: Installing and Removing an MSI-Based App

Time Required: 10 minutes

Objective: Install and remove an MSI-based app by using msiexec.exe

Description: You can use msiexec.exe to silently install MSI-based applications. In this activity, you download an MSI-based app, install the app, and also remove it.

1. If necessary, start your computer and sign in.
2. On the taskbar, click **Microsoft Edge**.
3. In Microsoft Edge, in the address bar, type **https://www.7-zip.org/download.html** and then press **Enter**.
4. On the Download page, in the first table, in the row with Type of .msi and Windows 64-bit x64, click **Download** and then click **Save**.
5. When the download is complete, click **Open folder**.
6. In the File Explorer window, double-click the file you downloaded. This starts an installation with the standard user interface.
7. Click **Cancel** to stop the installation, click **Yes** to confirm, and then click **Finish**.
8. Close the File Explorer window.
9. Click the **Start** button, type **cmd**, and then click **Run as administrator** below Command Prompt. It is preferable to use a command prompt for this task because the syntax is not interpreted properly by a Windows PowerShell prompt.
10. In the User Account Control dialog box, click **Yes**.
11. At the command prompt, to change to the downloads folder, type **cd \users\user1\downloads** and then press Enter. If necessary, substitute user1 with the name of your user account.
12. To view the MSI files in the current directory, type **dir *.msi** and then press **Enter**. Verify that the file you just downloaded is listed.
13. To view the options for misexec.exe, type **msiexec.exe /?** and then press **Enter**.
14. In the Windows Installer dialog box, scroll down, read the available options, and then click **OK**.
15. At the command prompt, to install 7-Zip silently, type **msiexec.exe /i 7z1900-x64.msi INSTALLDIR="C:\Program Files\7-Zip" /quiet** and then press **Enter**. The INSTALLDIR variable could also be set by using a transform file. If necessary, substitute 7z1900-x64.msi with the name of the file you downloaded.
16. Click the **Start** button and then click **Settings**.
17. In the Settings window, click **Apps** and then verify that 7-Zip is in the list of installed apps.
18. Close the Settings window.
19. At the command prompt, to remove 7-zip silently, type **msiexec.exe /x 7z1900-x64.msi /quiet** and then press **Enter.** If necessary, substitute 7z1900-x64.msi with the name of the file you downloaded.
20. Click the **Start** button and then click **Settings**.
21. In the Settings window, click **Apps** and then verify that 7-Zip is not in the list of installed apps.
22. Close all open windows.

UWP Apps

UWP apps are designed for distribution through the Microsoft Store. These apps are not designed to be installed manually in the same way traditional apps are. No option to run setup.exe or distribute a UWP app by using Group Policy exists.

If the app you want is in the Microsoft Store, users can install it from the Microsoft Store. It is not very manageable, however, to instruct users to obtain apps directly from the Microsoft Store. If you have obtained the **APPX file** for a UWP app, you can sideload the app; that is, you can install an app from a source other than the Windows Store, such as your workplace.

You can manually sideload Windows Store apps much more easily in Windows 10 than you could in Windows 8.1. You can allow sideloading of apps on the Settings > Update & Security > For developers screen, as shown in Figure 8-6.

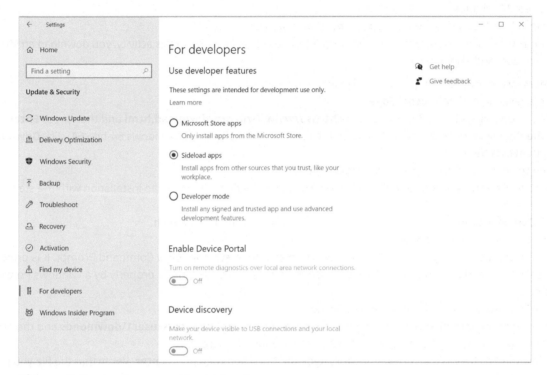

Figure 8-6   Setting to enable sideloading

After sideloading is enabled, the certificate used to sign the UWP app must be trusted by the Windows 10 computer. If the app was signed by using a certificate from a public certification authority, no configuration is required. If the app was signed by using a self-signed certificate, that certificate needs to be imported on the computer running Windows 10 as a trusted root certification authority. Finally, you can install the app by using the Add-AppPackage cmdlet. To automate the deployment of UWP apps to computers running Windows, you can use Microsoft Endpoint Manager or Microsoft Intune.

 TIP   Older documentation for installing APPX apps refers to using the Add-AppxPackage cmdlet. This is equivalent to the Add-AppPackage cmdlet.

Microsoft has also created a **Microsoft Store for Business**. Each business has its own private portal with approved apps. This makes it much easier for users to find the correct apps than if users had to find the same apps in the Microsoft Store. The other benefit is that custom apps can be placed in the Microsoft Store for Business and installed without sideloading. The custom apps you place in the Microsoft Store for Business do not have to go through an approval process the way that apps for the Windows Store do.

Activity 8-8: Installing and Removing a Microsoft Store App

Time Required: 10 minutes

Objective: Install and remove an app from the Microsoft Store

Description: Many of the apps you obtain from the Microsoft Store are APPX-based apps. In this activity, you install an app from the Microsoft Store and then remove it by using Windows PowerShell.

1. If necessary, start your computer and sign in.
2. On the taskbar, click **Microsoft Store**.
3. In the Microsoft Store window, in the Search box, type **Whiteboard** and then press **Enter**.
4. In the list of search results, click **Microsoft Whiteboard**.
5. Read the information about Microsoft Whiteboard and then click **Get**.
6. In the Use across your devices dialog box, click **No, thanks**.
7. Wait while Microsoft Whiteboard downloads and installs.
8. Close the Microsoft Store window.
9. Right-click the **Start** button and then click **Windows PowerShell (Admin)**.
10. In the User Account Control dialog box, click **Yes**.
11. At the Windows PowerShell prompt, to view a list of installed packages, type **Get-AppPackage** and then press **Enter**. Microsoft Whiteboard appears at the end of the list.
12. To display a simplified list, type **Get-AppPackage | Format-List Name** and then press **Enter**.
13. To view only information about Microsoft Whiteboard, type **Get-AppPackage -Name Microsoft.Whiteboard** and then press **Enter**.
14. To remove Microsoft Whiteboard, type **Get-AppPackage -Name Microsoft.Whiteboard | Remove-AppPackage** and then press **Enter**.
15. Close the Windows PowerShell window.

MSIX Deployment

MSIX, a new app packaging option created by Microsoft to improve application deployment, supports Win32 apps, .NET Framework apps, and UWP apps. It is intended to be a universal packaging option that is less restrictive than APPX but still provides some of the APPX advantages.

MSIX apps are containerized. This means that the apps run in an isolated environment that redirects file system and registry access. This ensures that files and registry keys used by MSIX apps do not conflict with one another or with different apps.

App developers can distribute MSIX apps for consumers and businesses through the Microsoft Store. The apps then can be updated automatically through the Microsoft Store.

Larger organizations might have apps that are not distributed from the Microsoft Store or Microsoft Store for Business. To install these apps, you need to enable sideloading, just like what is required for APPX apps. The same setting applies for both types of apps. In addition, you can install and manage MSIX apps by using the same *-AppPackage cmdlets. You can automate distribution MSIX apps by using Microsoft Endpoint Configuration Manager or Microsoft Intune.

 TIP You can also double-click APPX and MSIX apps to install them.

NOTE 2

For detailed information about MSIX app packaging, see What is MSIX at https://docs.microsoft .com/en-us/windows/msix/ overview.

MSIX can also be distributed from a web server by using App Installer. This method for delivery can be useful for internally developed apps. As part of the MSIX package, you can specify a location to check for updates to keep the app automatically updated.

Windows 10 in S Mode

Windows 10 in S mode is a configuration of Windows 10 that allows only apps from the Microsoft Store to be installed and run. This version of Windows 10 is designed to make a computer more like using a tablet or phone where all apps are installed from a trusted source. Existing MSI apps can be repackaged as MSIX apps for use with Windows 10 in S mode.

The choice to deploy Windows 10 in S mode must be made at initial deployment. In most cases, computers are received from the manufacturer using Windows 10 in S mode. As an administrator, however, you can configure a starting system image that deploys Windows 10 in S mode. Windows 10 in S mode is available for all editions of Windows 10. A computer with Windows 10 in S mode can be converted to the full operating system that can run all apps, but it cannot be switched to Windows 10 in S mode. To switch out of S mode, go to the Microsoft Store and install the Switch out of S mode app.

In addition to limiting which apps can run, Windows 10 in S mode has the following limitations:

- *Can't be domain joined*—A computer running Windows 10 in S mode can't be joined to a domain-based network for management or authentication. It can be joined to Azure AD. You can use a local user account, a Microsoft account, or an Azure AD account to sign in.
- *Limited support for peripherals*—Due to the limitations on software, much of the advanced peripheral management software does not work with Windows 10 in S mode. Basic functionality provided by the drivers in Windows 10 is supported for most peripherals.

NOTE 3

For detailed information about deploying Windows 10 in S mode, see Windows 10 in S mode manufacturing overview at https://docs.microsoft.com/ en-us/windows-hardware/ manufacture/desktop/ windows-10-s-overview.

Microsoft 365 Apps Click-to-Run Deployment

For some Microsoft 365 and Office 365 licensing plans, Microsoft 365 Apps is included for users. At the time of this writing, Microsoft 365 Apps has equivalent functionality to Microsoft Office Professional Plus 2019. This is the full Microsoft Office suite that includes Word, PowerPoint, Excel, Outlook, Publisher, and Access. Both versions of the Microsoft Office Suite are distributed by using Click-to-Run.

Click-to-Run streams the installation of Microsoft 365 Apps. This means that it delivers the critical components first and allows the users to begin using apps before installation is complete. This is important because Microsoft 365 Apps is designed to be deployed by users from the Microsoft 365 or Office 365 website.

The Click-to-Run deployment method is also responsible for deploying updates. When updates are available, those updates are streamed to clients when they start the apps. Updates for these apps are not installed by Windows Update. By default, the apps are updated via the Internet from Microsoft servers. If you want to control network utilization or clients don't have direct access to the Internet, however, you can configure clients to obtain updates from a shared folder.

 **CAUTION**   Applying Microsoft 365 Apps updates from a shared folder requires significantly more administrative effort than allowing updates to be downloaded from Microsoft.

When users install Microsoft 365 Apps, no customization is possible. All the components are installed by default. If you need to limit components that are installed, you can use the Office Deployment Tool for Click-to-Run. This tool creates an XML file that can be used to limit the components that are installed. You can modify an existing installation of Microsoft 365 Apps or download a local installation source so that users can access the initial installation files locally.

Licensing for Microsoft 365 Apps is on a per-user basis. Users have an account in Office 365 or Microsoft 365, and they need to authenticate using their account every 30 days to keep their installation of Microsoft 365 Apps active. This is an alternative to the traditional license key and activation process used by volume-licensed copies of Microsoft Office. At the time of writing, one user can install Microsoft 365 Apps on up to five devices. This allows users to install Microsoft 365 Apps on their work desktop computer, a mobile computer, and their home computer with a single license.

APP COMPATIBILITY

One of the primary concerns when planning a deployment of Windows 10 is application compatibility. The good news is that the vast majority of apps designed for Windows 7 and newer run properly on Windows 10. Most compatibility issues are for very old legacy apps created for Windows XP.

If you have older apps that do not run properly on Windows 10, the preferred option is to upgrade the app to a newer version that works properly. Unfortunately, some apps might not have an upgraded version available. For example, a line-of-business app may have been custom developed many years ago and no easy alternative exists. If no path for upgrading is possible, you need to explore alternate options for compatibility.

Compatibility Settings for Executables

Windows 10 includes some basic features for application compatibility that you can set when viewing the properties of an executable file, shown in Figure 8-7. Some of the common issues that can be addressed are:

- *Reliance on older Windows versions*—Some Windows apps specifically verify which version of Windows they are running on and do not run if the reported version is not recognized. For example, an app might look for Windows 7 as an acceptable version and not recognize Windows 10. To resolve this issue, you can set the compatibility mode as Windows Vista (RTM, Service Pack 1, or Service Pack 2), Windows 7, or Windows 8. When you set the compatibility mode, and an app queries the operating system version, the configured compatibility level is reported back to the app.

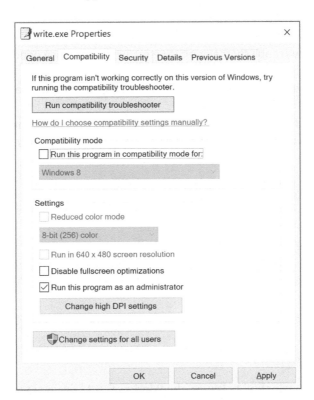

Figure 8-7   Compatibility settings for an executable

- *Display issues*—Many older apps were designed for smaller and lower-resolution displays. These apps don't display properly on newer displays with higher resolution and operating systems that expect higher color depth. Windows 10 can force the app to run in a 640 × 480 resolution window, eliminate scaling on high-resolution displays, and reduce color depth.
- *Reliance on administrator permissions*—Some apps require administrative permissions to run properly. This is due to poor programming practices by developers that require the user to write to privileged areas of the file system or the registry. In Windows 10, with User Access Control (UAC), even if you are an administrator of the local computer, apps are run with standard user permissions unless a manifest file for the application indicates that the app requires elevated privileges. Older apps do not have this manifest file; however, you can force apps to run with elevated privileges by selecting the Run this program as an administrator option. This avoids the need to manually select Run as administrator each time you start the app. The user still needs to be a local administrator on the computer.

If you are unsure of how to resolve compatibility issues for an application, you can run the compatibility trouble-shooter. This wizard attempts to automatically detect the compatibility problem. If automatic detection fails, you can utilize a wizard that asks you a series of questions to identify a likely resolution. After the wizard is complete, the applied settings are visible on the Compatibility tab and can be disabled there.

Activity 8-9: Configuring App Compatibility

Time Required: 10 minutes

Objective: Configure compatibility settings for an app

Description: Some older apps do not run properly in newer versions of Windows, including Windows 10. In this activity, you configure compatibility settings for an app.

1. If necessary, start your computer and sign in.
2. On the taskbar, click **File Explorer** and then navigate to **C:\Windows**.
3. In the File Explorer window, right-click **write**, click **Copy**, and then exit File Explorer.
4. Right-click the desktop and then click **Paste**.
5. On the desktop, right-click **write** and then click **Troubleshoot compatibility**.
6. In the Program Compatibility Troubleshooter, on the Select Troubleshooting option screen, click **Troubleshoot program**.
7. On the What problems do you notice? screen, select the **The program requires additional permissions** check box and then click **Next**.
8. On the Test compatibility settings for the program screen, click **Test the program**.
9. In the User Account Control dialog box, click **Yes**. The UAC dialog box may be minimized on the taskbar. If so, click it to make it active.
10. Exit WordPad.
11. In the Program Compatibility Troubleshooter, click **Next**.
12. On the Troubleshooting has completed screen, click **Yes, save these settings for this program**.
13. On the Troubleshooting has completed screen, click **Close**.
14. On the desktop, right-click **write** and then click **Properties**.
15. In the write Properties window, click the **Compatibility** tab, and read the options.
16. Verify that the **Run this program as an administrator** check box is selected and then click **Cancel**.

Windows ADK Tools

To help identify and resolve app compatibility issues, the Windows 10 Assessment and Deployment Kit (ADK), shown in Figure 8-8, includes Compatibility Administrator and the Standard User Analyzer Tool (SUA). If you have an older application that you can't get to run by using the basic compatibility settings, these tools provide more detailed fixes.

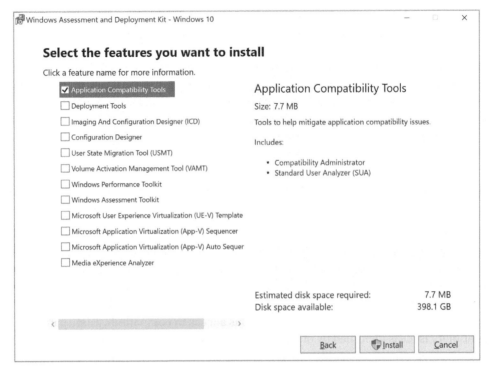

Figure 8-8   Windows 10 ADK Application Compatibility Tools

⊗ CAUTION   You might see some references to Windows 10 ADK containing the Application Compatibility Tool kit. This has been removed from newer versions of the Windows 10 ADK. Only Compatibility Administrator and SUA are still included.

Compatibility Administrator, shown in Figure 8-9, contains a list of older commercial applications and known fixes for them. Most of these applications were produced prior to 2010. If you don't have the budget to replace these applications with newer versions, you can use Compatibility Administrator to create a compatibility database for the apps.

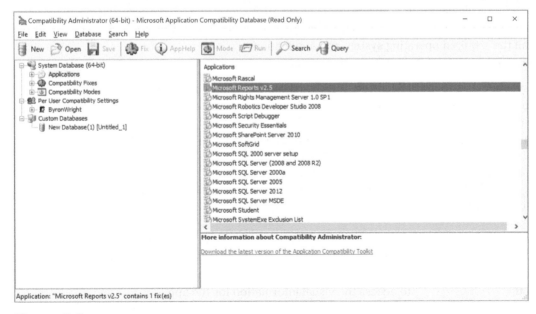

Figure 8-9   Compatibility Administrator

The bitness of Compatibility Administrator needs to match the bitness of the application you are mitigating. For example, you need to use the 32-bit version of Compatibility Administrator to create a compatibility database for 32-bit applications.

For noncommercial apps that are not part of Compatibility Administrator, you might be able to identify what is required for compatibility by using SUA. SUA monitors application activity and identifies potential fixes. Those potential fixes are saved as a compatibility database in the same format generated by Compatibility Administrator.

In some cases, compatibility issues with custom apps can be resolved by using the Standard User Analyzer (SUA). This tool, which is included with Compatibility Monitor, is used to closely monitor the activity of a single app and provide a resolution for problems if possible. SUA also generates a compatibility-fix database.

To apply a compatibility database (.sdb) to multiple computers, you can use sdbinst.exe. This tool can be scripted and run at sign-in or by a software management tool, such as Microsoft Endpoint Configuration Manager.

Desktop Analytics

Desktop Analytics is a cloud-based solution to identify compatibility problems with applications and suggest mitigations. This service integrates with Microsoft Endpoint Configuration Manager to leverage existing application inventory data and provide an infrastructure for deploying mitigations. Because the deployment of Windows Desktop operating systems is based on new feature updates, this solution is optimized for that purpose.

Because Desktop Analytics is cloud-based, the service has access to compatibility data gathered by many customers. When a compatibility issue is identified by other customers, you can be warned about this same issue even before you do any testing. Desktop Analytics can identify this based on the hardware and software inventory collected by Configuration Manager.

Another key benefit of Desktop Analytics is identifying a pilot group for testing. Desktop Analytics uses the hardware and software inventory to identify the smallest possible group of computers that include the largest possible range of configurations. This makes it more likely that you identify issues with software updates before you perform organization-wide deployment.

Client Hyper-V

If an app is not compatible with Windows 10 and there is no way to mitigate the issue, you need to run an older operating system to keep using that application. For example, if all users are being upgraded to a 64-bit version of Windows 10, another operating system is required to support a legacy 16-bit Windows app. Although it is possible to maintain an older physical computer for the purpose of running the older app, that older computer will be prone to failure over time.

Client Hyper-V is virtualization software for Windows 10. It allows you to create virtual machines with a completely independent operating system that shares the hardware on the computer running Windows 10. In the virtual machine, you can install the required operating system and application.

The potential downsides to using Client Hyper-V are as follows:

- No easy way exists to move data from the virtual machine to the host computer.
- The operating system in the virtual machine still needs to be managed with software updates and any other management considerations.
- Some users find it confusing to use a separate virtual machine for some tasks.

NOTE 4

For more information, see Introduction to Hyper-V on Windows 10 at https:// docs.microsoft.com/en-us/ virtualization/hyper-v-on-windows/about/.

Virtual Desktop Infrastructure and RemoteApp

Windows Server can host and provide access to virtual desktops. This functionality is provided by Remote Desktop Services. Several variations exist, but for all of them, the application runs on a computer and the Remote Desktop Protocol (RDP) is used to access the visual information for the app.

By running the app on a remote computer, any application conflicts on the local computer are avoided. For example, when Microsoft 365 Apps is installed on a computer, you can't have older MSI-based versions of apps, such as Visio, installed locally. By using Remote Desktop Services, you can remote control the application running elsewhere while it appears to run locally.

App-V

Application Virtualization (App-V) is a technology that both deploys and manages apps. Instead of a standard installation, apps are streamed to computers and can begin executing before all the app files are on the destination computer. Updates are never installed directly on the client computers. Instead, the source app is updated and the updates stream to the clients. This is similar to how Microsoft 365 Apps is distributed because the Click-to-Run functionality for Microsoft 365 Apps is based on App-V.

Apps distributed by using App-V run in a virtualized environment within the operating system. From a user perspective, the app appears to be installed like a normal application, but conflicts with other applications running on the computer are avoided. You can use App-V to resolve compatibility conflicts when two apps cannot both be installed on the same computer. The apps, however, must still be compatible with the operating system.

> **① CAUTION** App-V is no longer being developed as a technology. Microsoft hopes that the virtualization within MSIX packaging will meet this need instead.

REMOTE DESKTOP SERVICES

The Remote Desktop Services role in Windows Server provides a way to run apps on a remote server or virtual machine and have the display appear on the local computer. This way, users can run apps without ever installing them on their local computer. This system can be used when app compatibility might cause concerns, but more often, it is used to provide remote access to apps.

The remote desktop protocol (RDP) used by Remote Desktop Services is very efficient. This makes it feasible to provide access to remote desktops and apps over the Internet and even over public Wi-Fi. It also provides the flexibility to use apps from anywhere and on any device that has an RDP client. Microsoft provides Remote Desktop clients not only for Windows, but also for iOS and Android devices.

Remote Desktop Services can provide these two types of virtual desktops:

- *Session-based virtual desktops*—This type of virtual desktop is hosted on a Remote Desktop Session Host (RD Session Host). An RD Session Host is running a Windows Server operating system, such as Windows Server 2019. A single RD Session Host is shared by multiple users at one time. When the users connect, each gets their own independent desktop and runs their own applications; however, the core operating system services are shared, which allows many users to share the same server.
- *Virtual machine-based virtual desktops*—This type of virtual desktop is hosted on a Windows server running Hyper-V. Each user has an independent virtual machine with a completely independent operating system, which is typically Windows 10. The hardware of the server is shared among the virtual machines, but each virtual machine is independent. This type of virtual desktop has lower density than session-based virtual desktops. Figure 8-10 illustrates the difference between session-based virtual desktops and virtual machine-based virtual desktops.

RemoteApp

Providing users with full remote desktops can sometimes be confusing for the users if they don't understand conceptually how they can have two desktops at the same time. To simplify access to apps, there is also RemoteApp. RemoteApp still uses either session-based virtual desktops or virtual machine-based virtual desktops to execute

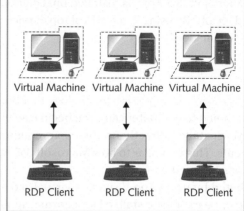

Figure 8-10   Types of virtual desktops

apps, but the user interface is different. When users start a RemoteApp running on a virtual desktop, it behaves like a regular application. A window opens only for that application. For most users, this is a simpler interface and easier to understand than a full desktop.

Accessing Virtual Desktops and RemoteApp

The most popular configuration to access virtual desktops and RemoteApp programs requires you to sign in to a website. This website is hosted on a Remote Desktop Web Access (RD Web Access) server. Unlike older virtual desktop solutions, like Terminal Services, you do not directly access an RD Session Host.

After the users authenticate to RD Web Access, they see a webpage with the RemoteApp programs and virtual desktops to which they have been given access. Users click the RemoteApp program or virtual desktop that they want to access, and Remote Desktop Connection is run to access it. Remote Desktop Connection is the RDP client included in Windows 10.

RemoteApp and Desktop Connections is an alternative to RD Web Access for accessing RemoteApp programs and virtual desktops hosted by Remote Desktop Services. This client reads the list of RemoteApp programs and virtual desktops by accessing a web feed URL on the RD Web Access server. The web feed URL is https://<servername>/RDWeb/Feed/webfeed.aspx, where <servername> is the host name of the RD Web Access server.

The three ways to configure RemoteApp and Desktop Connections with the URL for the web feed are as follows:

- *Manually enter the URL*—You can provide users with instructions on how to configure the URL the first time they start it. This solution is not very scalable and runs the risk of users making typing errors, but it is simple to implement.
- *Use Group Policy*—You can configure the URL in a Group Policy Object at \User Configuration\Policies\Administrative Templates\Windows Components\Remote Desktop Services\RemoteApp and Desktop Connections. If all your computers are domain joined, this is a fast way to configure all of them in a single step.
- *Based on email address*—The initial configuration for RemoteApp and Desktop Connections can use a DNS record based on an email address provided by the user. For the domain of the email address, RemoteApp and Desktop Connections looks for an _rdac TXT record. The value of that record is the URL for the web feed. This solution requires users to initiate it, but it works for internal domain-joined computers and devices that are not domain joined.

The wizard for configuring RemoteApp and Desktop Connections prompts for either a URL or email address, as shown in Figure 8-11. Based on this information, the wizard connects with the web feed and downloads the list of RemoteApp programs and virtual desktops to which the user has access.

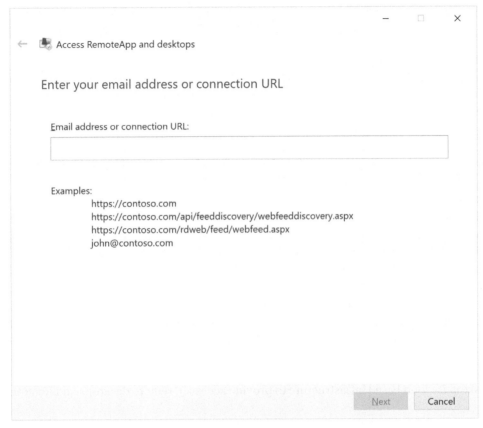

Figure 8-11 Configuring RemoteApp and desktops

 TIP RemoteApp and Desktop Connections refreshes data from the web feed only once per day. It can be refreshed manually if required.

Windows Virtual Desktop

For organizations that are moving to cloud-based services, Microsoft provides Windows Virtual Desktop in Microsoft Azure. This is a similar configuration for Remote Desktop Services, but the virtual machines that build the infrastructure are hosted in Microsoft Azure. Like Remote Desktop Services, Windows Virtual Desktop can provide access to full desktops or RemoteApp programs.

Because Windows Virtual Desktop is hosted as a cloud service, it is much faster to deploy and easier to license. You can deploy RD Session hosts based on Windows Server 2012 R2 or later. You can configure VDI by using Windows 7 with extended support until 2023 or Windows 10. A new multisession version of Windows 10 also is available as an RD Session Host. This provides some of the scalability and cost effectiveness of using Windows Server as an RD Session Host with application compatibility of using Windows 10. Windows 10 multisession is not available for use on premises.

 TIP To deploy Microsoft Office Suite on a server-based RD Session Host, you need to use a perpetual license version. Using Microsoft 365 Apps is supported on Windows 10 virtual desktops (including Windows 10 multisession).

SUMMARY

- Windows 10 supports running apps by providing various application environments. You can run Win32, Win64, .NET Framework, and UWP apps.
- The registry is a central store of configuration information for apps and the operating system. It is composed of hives that contain registry keys and values. Two commonly accessed hives are HKCU and HKLM.
- To edit the registry, you can use the graphical Registry Editor, reg.exe, or Windows PowerShell cmdlets. Before editing the registry, you should export the keys so that you can restore them if required.
- MSI-based apps are installed by the Windows Installer service. You can automate installation of MSI-based apps by using Group Policy or Configuration Manager.
- Installation of AWP apps on desktop computers can be automated by using Microsoft Endpoint Configuration Manager. For phones, tablets, and non-domain-joined computers, you can automate deployment by using mobile device management software, such as Microsoft Intune. The Microsoft Store for Business is a customizable website that you can use to provide your users with access only to specific apps.
- MSIX is a newer app packaging option that can be used to deploy Win32 apps, .NET Framework apps, and UWP apps. This packaging format can also be distributed through the Microsoft Store.
- Microsoft 365 Apps installs by using a new technology called Click-to-Run.
- Windows 10 provides some basic functionality for resolving app compatibility issues; however, you can also use Compatibility Administrator, Client Hyper-V, Remote Desktop Services, and App-V.
- Remote Desktop Services provides access to virtual desktops and RemoteApp programs. A virtual desktop is a complete desktop with applications. RemoteApp provides access to only an app in a single window. Windows Virtual Desktop is cloud-based infrastructure to provide access to remote desktops and RemoteApp programs.

Key Terms

.NET Framework	Compatibility Administrator	RemoteApp
application environment	Desktop Analytics	Remote Desktop Services
subsystem	hive	Standard User Analyzer (SUA)
application programming interface (API)	Microsoft Store for Business	Universal Windows Platform (UWP)
	MSI file	
Application Virtualization (App-V)	MSIX	Windows 10 in S mode
APPX file	registry	Windows API
Click-to-Run	Registry Editor	Windows on Windows 64 (WOW64)
Client Hyper-V	registry key	Windows Virtual Desktop

Review Questions

1. Which types of apps are not supported by a 64-bit edition of Windows 10? (Choose all that apply.)
   a. DOS
   b. Win16
   c. Win32
   d. Win64
   e. .NET Framework

2. Which registry hive is used to store global information about apps regardless of the user who is signed in?
   a. HKEY_CLASSES_ROOT
   b. HKEY_CURRENT_USER
   c. HKEY_LOCAL_MACHINE

   d. HKEY_DYN_DATA
   e. HKEY_GLOBAL_CONFIG

3. On a 64-bit version of Windows 10, where are 32-bit apps typically installed?
   a. C:\Program Files
   b. C:\Windows\SysWOW64
   c. C:\Program Files (WOW64)
   d. C:\Program Files (x86)
   e. C:\Windows\WOW64

4. Which versions of .NET Framework are included with Windows 10? (Choose all that apply.)
   a. .NET Framework 1.1
   b. .NET Framework 2.0

    c. .NET Framework 3.5

    d. .NET Framework 4.0

    e. .NET Framework 4.8

5. All Microsoft Store apps are UWP apps. True or False?

6. You can use a 32-bit version of Windows 10 to run legacy Win16 apps. True or False?

7. Which registry hive contains settings that are imported from ntuser.dat?

    a. HKEY_CLASSES_ROOT

    b. HKEY_CURRENT_USER

    c. HKEY_LOCAL_MACHINE

    d. HKEY_DYN_DATA

    e. HKEY_GLOBAL_CONFIG

8. Which tools or methods can you use to import a .reg file? (Choose all that apply.)

    a. Registry Editor (regedit)

    b. regimp.exe

    c. reg.exe

    d. double-click the .reg file in File Explorer

    e. Import-Registry

9. You can automate installation of Microsoft Store apps by using Group Policy. True or False?

10. Which cmdlet do you use to sideload UWP apps?

    a. Add-AppxPackage

    b. Install-WinApp

    c. Install-WinStoreApp

    d. Add-WinApp

    e. New-Sideload

11. Microsoft 365 Apps never receives updates through Windows Update. True or False?

12. Which compatibility issues can be fixed for an app by using the capabilities included in Windows 10? (Choose all that apply.)

    a. wrong version of .NET Framework

    b. a version check to verify that the app is running on Windows 7

    c. poor display quality on full screen when the screen resolution is 1920 × 1024

    d. required to select Run as administrator

    e. odd colors when the color depth is greater than 16-bit

13. Which tool is used to deploy compatibility fixes to multiple computers?

    a. Compatibility Administrator

    b. fixinst.exe

    c. Runtime-analysis package

    d. Standard User Analyzer

    e. sdbinst.exe

14. If you have a computer running a 64-bit version of Windows 10 with Client Hyper-V, it is possible to run a 16-bit Windows app in a virtual machine. True or False?

15. Which of the following are true about App-V? (Choose all that apply.)

    a. Apps are streamed for installation.

    b. RDP is used to access the app.

    c. Virtual environments prevent conflicts between apps.

    d. Virtual environments allow a 16-bit app to be run on a 64-bit operating system.

    e. Apps are updated when the source on the server is updated.

16. Microsoft Store for Business contains Azure RemoteApp programs. True or False?

17. Which three methods can you use to configure RemoteApp and Desktop Connections with the URL of the web feed? (Choose all that apply.)

    a. Manually enter the URL during configuration.

    b. Create a CNAME record in DNS that includes the URL and have users enter their email address during configuration.

    c. Configure a Group Policy Object with the correct URL.

    d. Create a TXT record in DNS that includes the URL and have users enter their email address during configuration.

    e. Package an MSI file with the correct configuration information.

18. Which PowerShell cmdlet is used to modify a registry key value?

    a. Set-ItemProperty

    b. Set-RegKeyValue

    c. Set-ChildItem

    d. Set-LocationValue

    e. Set-ChildItemValue

19. Which of the following are true about Windows 10 multi-session? (Choose all that apply.)

    a. It is available only as part of Windows Virtual Desktop.

    b. It is available for on-premises installation.

    c. It supports up to 5 simultaneous RDP sessions.

    d. It supports up to 10 simultaneous RDP sessions.

    e. It can be used to provide RemoteApp programs.

20. Developers can use MSIX packaging to distribute .NET Framework and UWP apps, but not Win32 apps. True or False?

Case Projects

Case Project 8-1: Application Compatibility

Gigantic Life Insurance has thousands of desktop computers running a wide variety of apps. Many desktops are still running Windows 7 due to concerns about application compatibility with Windows 10. Many legacy apps simply don't run on Windows 10. What are your options to address this problem and allow an upgrade to Windows 10?

Case Project 8-2: Remote Access to Apps

Hyperactive Media now has more than 40 salespeople on the road meeting with customers. The salespeople currently have laptops with locally installed apps; however, this means that salespeople need to come back to the office and transfer sales orders from their laptops to the central order system. Describe how salespeople could be given remote access to this system by using RemoteApp. What concerns might you have about using RemoteApp?

Case Project 8-3: .NET Framework Updates

Gigantic Life Insurance has thousands of desktop computers running many .NET Framework apps. As a best practice, you realize that you need to apply security updates as quickly as possible. A colleague is rightly concerned that apps might start to fail if .NET Framework updates are applied. What can you do to ensure that .NET Framework updates can be deployed as quickly as possible?

PERFORMANCE TUNING AND SYSTEM RECOVERY

After reading this module and completing the exercises, you will be able to:

1. Describe performance-tuning concepts
2. Use Task Manager
3. Use Resource Monitor
4. Use Performance Monitor
5. Configure Performance Options
6. Control application startup
7. Describe tools that you can use for troubleshooting errors in Windows 10
8. Understand recovery and backup of user data
9. Describe recovery options for an unstable Windows 10 computer

On most Windows 10 computers, the default configuration provides acceptable performance. When users run applications, the applications respond quickly. When users access files, the files open quickly. On some systems, however, performance can start to deteriorate over time. Performance tuning lets you optimize the performance of Windows 10 to function at acceptable standards. Keep in mind that poor performance and improper operations might not simply be a matter of tweaking the system; problems might have appeared that require corrective actions to remedy.

In this module, you begin by learning about the performance-tuning process and how Performance Monitor allows you to find system bottlenecks. Additionally, you learn how to use Task Manager and Event Viewer to troubleshoot system performance. If you recognize that the problems are significant enough to require a repair of the Windows operating system, this module investigates your options—including recovering old versions of data and application components, or ultimately repairing or reinstalling a Windows operating system.

PERFORMANCE TUNING OVERVIEW

Performance tuning is a process that you can use to improve the speed of a computer system. In an ideal world, an effective performance-tuning process is initiated well before problems occur; in most cases, however, performance tuning is not even considered until a performance problem exists.

The performance tuning process consists of:

- Establishing a baseline
- Recognizing bottlenecks
- Tuning performance

Establishing a Baseline

To recognize the system bottlenecks that are limiting performance, you must first establish a baseline that defines normal performance. A **baseline** is a set of performance indicators captured when system performance is acceptable. Effectively, the baseline defines normal performance. The baseline values are compared with future values of performance indicators to isolate performance problems.

Windows 10 reports on a wide variety of performance indicators. Performance indicators are often called **counters** because they display values for system characteristics. Some examples of counters are:

- % Processor Time
- Disk Read Byte/sec
- Memory: Available Mbytes
- IPv4: Datagrams/sec

When you establish a baseline, it's important to ensure that you're measuring the normal state of the performance indicators. If unusual activity is occurring, the baseline performance measurement is not valid, and it will be difficult to use the baseline to identify abnormal activity in the future.

To ensure that you are measuring the normal state when establishing a baseline, you should:

- Verify that no unusual activity is happening on the computer. For example, ensure that no applications are performing large queries to databases or processing batch jobs, unless that is the normal state of the computer.
- Measure performance indicators over time. By measuring performance indicators over time, you can see an average value for the indicators. Average values are less volatile and more accurate than measuring with snapshots of short duration.

Recognizing Bottlenecks

A **bottleneck** occurs when a limitation in a single computer system component slows down the entire system. For any application, one component in the computer system always is the limiting factor for performance. This component is the bottleneck. Performance tuning attempts to eliminate bottlenecks.

For each activity you perform and each application that you run, the bottleneck might be different. For example, a database application may require fast access to the hard drive, and older spinning disk drives are a common bottleneck. A 3-D rendering program may experience limited processing power as the most common bottleneck. The most common bottlenecks to system performance are in the areas of disk, memory, processor, or the network.

Disk Bottlenecks

Disk bottlenecks occur when Windows 10 and running applications want to read and write information to the physical disk in the system faster than the disk can manage. For desktop computers running Windows 10, disk bottlenecks are not that common.

You can identify disk bottlenecks by monitoring active time for the disk or the disk queue length. If the active time is at 100% for a sustained period of time, then the disk is too slow. Disk queue length identifies the number of disk requests queued to be serviced. If the disk queue length is consistently greater than one, then the disk is too slow.

If required, disk performance can be increased in a few different ways, such as:

- *Upgrade the disks*—Disks are capable of certain speeds of data transfer. In less-expensive computers, it is common for manufacturers to include spinning hard drives that perform much slower than solid-state drives (SSDs). In lower-end laptops, slow 5400 RPM hard drives with low power consumption are often used, which are slow even when compared to the 7200 RPM hard drives used in most desktop computers. Upgrading a spinning hard drive to an SSD is a huge performance improvement at minimal cost; it also uses less power.

- *Implement mirrored Storage Spaces*—Mirrored Storage Spaces volumes increase read and write performance by spreading data manipulation tasks across multiple hard drives. Because it's not typical for a Windows 10 computer to have multiple hard drives, this option is rarely used.
- *Move the paging file to a nonsystem disk*—By default, the paging file, which is accessed often by the system, resides on the same disk as the operating system files, which are also accessed often by the system. Putting the paging file on a different physical disk (not just a different partition) can increase performance by reducing the data manipulation that any one disk needs to perform. This is most commonly an issue when a computer has limited memory and forces the paging file to be used more often.

Memory Bottlenecks

Most memory bottlenecks occur when the applications you are running require more memory than is physically available in the computer. This forces Windows 10 to use virtual memory to accommodate the memory requirements of all the running applications. Virtual memory is a system wherein memory is simulated on disk with a paging file. The least used memory areas are stored in the paging file. When information in the paging file is required, it is taken out of the paging file and placed in physical memory.

Accessing information from disk is much slower than accessing information from physical memory. Reducing the need for virtual memory can significantly improve system performance. You can recognize when virtual memory is being heavily used by a high volume of disk activity.

To reduce the use of virtual memory, you can do the following:

- *Increase the amount of physical memory*—Adding physical memory to a computer allows more information to be kept in physical memory, which reduces the need for virtual memory.
- *Run fewer applications at once*—If you are running multiple applications, more information is kept in memory. Reducing the number of applications running at the same time reduces the amount of memory used and, consequently, the need for virtual memory.

If heavy utilization of the paging file is occurring, moving the paging file to a faster disk, such as an SSD, can improve performance. Windows 10 also allows some USB drives to be used for ReadyBoost. ReadyBoost uses a USB drive as a memory cache similar to a paging file. The USB drive is faster than a mechanical disk but offers no performance improvement when an SSD is being used.

Processor Bottlenecks

A processor bottleneck occurs when a processor has too much work to do. In a newer computer, processors typically have four or more cores. Each core in a processor can work on only one task at a time. The combination of applications and operating system services running in Windows 10 are typically greater than the number of processor cores. To run multiple applications and perform system tasks, the processor switches between the required tasks very quickly to give the illusion of all activities happening at the same time. When too many tasks must be performed, or an individual task requires too much processor time, the processor becomes a bottleneck.

To identify a processor bottleneck, you monitor the percentage of CPU utilization. If CPU utilization is consistently at 100% then the CPU is a bottleneck.

To resolve a processor bottleneck, do the following:

- *Change to a processor with higher clock speed*—Processor performance is traditionally measured by clock speed. When comparing processors with the same architecture and number of cores, a processor with a higher clock speed can perform more work in a given time frame. For example, a 3 GHz processor is faster than a 2 GHz processor.
- *Change to a processor with more cores*—Because so many processes are running in Windows 10 at the same time, it might be beneficial to have additional processor cores. With more processor cores, more tasks can be performed at the same time.
- *Add additional processors*—Some computers can contain multiple physical processors. Windows 10 Professional and Windows 10 Enterprise can support more than one physical processor. Windows 10 Home can support only one. Having multiple processors means that tasks can be completed more quickly because the second processor provides additional cores for processing.

 **CAUTION** The motherboard in a computer supports a limited range of processors. In most cases, it is not cost-effective or practical to upgrade only the processor. Purchasing a new computer with more processing capacity is typically required.

Network Bottlenecks

Network bottlenecks are more common for servers than computers running Windows 10. In the rare circumstance where the network is simply too slow, you can replace the existing network with a faster one. For example, if an old 100 Mbps network is slowing down file sharing between computers, you could replace it with a 1 Gbps network. This might involve replacing network cards, cabling, and switches. The slowest networking component between two systems determines the fastest speed that the two computers can communicate with each other. It is common that the maximum speed of a network connection (for example, 1 Gbps) is not fully realized because overhead and random delays occur that use up some of the network's capacity to carry data. A 1 Gbps network connection might end up limited to around 800 Mbps of effective data transfer, which is not a bottleneck; it is expected because of administrative and operational overhead on the data stream. As wireless networks become more common at home, problems with wireless performance may have less to do with the local computer and more to do with the networking equipment's age, component position, and local interference.

Tuning Performance

The process for performance tuning is consistent regardless of the problems being experienced. In each case, you perform the following steps:

1. Create a baseline for the computer.
2. Compare the baseline with current performance indicators.
3. Identify possible causes for variations from the baseline.
4. Identify possible fixes for variations from the baseline.
5. Select a fix to implement.
6. Implement the fix and monitor for changes.
7. If the problem is not resolved, undo the fix and repeat Step 5.
8. If the problem is resolved, document the solution for future reference.

When selecting a fix to implement, you should take into account the time involved and the likelihood that the fix will resolve the problem. Sometimes, it is better to attempt several simple fixes, even if they are less likely to fix the problem, before attempting a complex fix that is likely to solve the problem.

Documentation during the performance-tuning process is essential. As you attempt each fix, you should document the changes you are making. This allows you to undo each fix before you try the next one.

PERFORMANCE MONITORING TOOLS

To identify performance bottleneck in Windows 10, you can use performance monitoring tools included in Windows 10. The tool you select for troubleshooting will depend on the situation. For a quick overview of current performance, Task Manager is a good choice. For a more detailed look at current performance, you can use Resource Monitor. For the most detailed understanding of system performance, you can use Performance Monitor to view current performance statistics and log performance data to file for later analysis.

Task Manager

Task Manager provides an overview of the current state of a computer. You often use Task Manager when a computer starts performing poorly and you want to get a quick idea of where the bottleneck might be. The default view in Task Manager shows the applications you are running, but no performance information. You need to switch to the Details view, shown in Figure 9-1, to see the performance information.

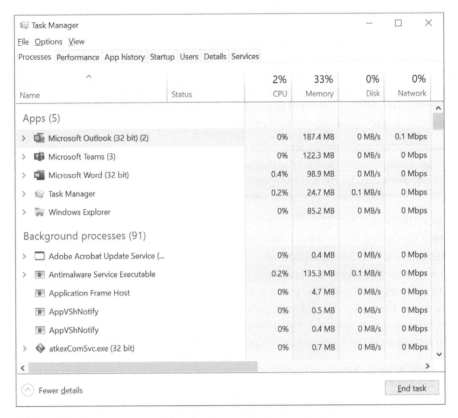

Figure 9-1   Task Manager Processes tab in Details view

You can access Task Manager in any of the following ways:

- Press Ctrl+Alt+Delete and then click Task Manager.
- Press Ctrl+Shift+Esc.
- Right-click an empty area of the taskbar and then click Task Manager.
- Run taskmgr.exe from a command prompt.

Processes

The Processes tab in Task Manager shows all user applications running on the computer and background processes. For example, the process Microsoft Word (32-Bit) appears in the list of Apps in Figure 9-1 because it is actively running on that computer. This view provides an easy way to see how much CPU, Memory, Disk, and Network resources are being used overall and by each process. For example, if you see that CPU utilization is at 100%, you can sort the processes by CPU utilization to identify the offending process and then stop it.

The Details tab provides even more detailed information about each process. The process name listed on the Details tab is the name of the executable file instead of the friendly name used on the Processes tab.

 TIP   To easily find the detailed information about a process, right-click the process on the Processes tab and then select Go to details. This displays the Details tab and highlights the detailed information for the selected process.

For each process on the Details tab, you can see:

- *Name*—The process executable file.
- *PID*—The process identifier (PID) is a unique number that is assigned to each process. When multiple instances of an application are running, each has the same name but a unique PID.
- *Status*—Identifies whether a process is running or suspended. Windows 10 suspends unused processes to save power.

- *User name*—The user who started the process. You can use this to identify whether a process was started by a user or the system.
- *CPU*—The percentage CPU utilization of the process.
- *Memory*—The memory used exclusively by the process.
- *UAC virtualization*—Identifies whether a process uses UAC virtualization redirect write requests to restricted areas in the file system or registry. For most processes, this is set to Not allowed or Disabled. You can try enabling UAC virtualization for legacy applications that are not able to run properly in Windows 10 with default settings.

 TIP   You can customize the view on the Processes tab or Details tab by adding more columns of information. Columns are added by right-clicking on any column header and then clicking Select columns.

For each process on the Details tab, you can set the priority of the process. You might be able to boost the performance of an application by raising its priority; however, this is not recommended because raising the priority of one application can be detrimental to other applications.

You can also end a specific process or process tree. Ending a process tree stops the process and all other processes that were started by the process. Ending just the process allows other processes started by the process to continue running.

You can configure a process to run on a specific processor core by setting processor affinity. In the vast majority of situations, system performance will be better if you do not set processor affinity for a process. When processor affinity is not set, Windows 10 optimizes system performance automatically by moving processes among processors as required.

 TIP   You can view process information similar to Task Manager details in Windows PowerShell by using the Get-Process cmdlet.

Performance

The Performance tab, shown in Figure 9-2, provides a quick overview of system performance for CPU, memory, disk, Ethernet, Wi-Fi, and GPU (graphics processor). When you select each item on the left side, more detailed information appears on the right side. For example, if you select Disk 0, you see detailed information, such as the brand and model of disk, active time, read and write speed, and response time. As a convenience, a link is also available to start Resource Monitor from this tab.

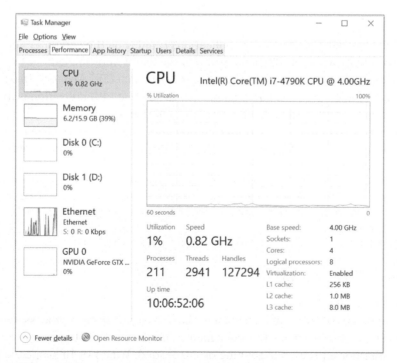

Figure 9-2   Task Manager Performance tab

Other Task Manager Information

The App history tab shows a summary of what applications have been using resources since the last startup and the total usage of those resources in comparison with one another.

The Startup tab shows a list of applications that start automatically when Windows starts and lets you mark them as enabled or disabled for startup.

The Users tab has a list of users who are currently signed in to the system. If multiple users share a computer and use fast user switching to stay signed in, the users appear in this list. If you expand a user, you can see the processes started by that user. If your account is an administrator, you can sign out users that are disconnected. Signing out users can free up additional memory for better performance or gain access to files that are locked because a user has them open.

The Services tab provides a list of the services running on Windows 10. The information here is approximately the same as the information found in the Services node in Computer Management. From this tab, you can also locate the process associated with a particular service and can start and stop services.

Activity 9-1: Using Task Manager

Time Required: 10 minutes

Objective: Use Task Manager to view system information

Description: The primary purpose of Task Manager is to provide a quick overview of system and process performance information. In this activity, you view system information and manage processes by using Task Manager.

1. If necessary, start your computer and sign in.
2. Click the **Start** button, in the search box type **cmd**, and then press **Enter**.
3. In the command prompt window, type **mspaint** and then press **Enter**.
4. Right-click the taskbar and then click **Task Manager**.
5. Note that the initial view for Task Manager lists the running applications but no details. Click the down arrow next to **More details** to expose all of Task Manager's details if they are not already visible.
6. If necessary, click the **Processes** tab. You can see that both the command prompt and Paint are listed in the Apps section.
7. Expand **Windows Command Processor (2)**. Notice that two processes are listed for this App.
8. Right-click **Windows Command Processor** and then click **Go to details**. This switches to the Details tab, with cmd.exe selected.
9. Right-click **cmd.exe** and then click **End process tree**.
10. Read the warning and then click **End process tree**. This closes both the command prompt and Paint because Paint was started by the command prompt.
11. Click the **CPU** column header once. This sorts the processes by CPU utilization. A down arrow above the column title indicates that the processes are sorted in descending order with the highest CPU utilization at the top of the list.
12. Click the **Services** tab. This tab displays the status of services running on the computer.
13. Click the **Performance** tab. This tab provides some basic CPU and memory utilization information.
14. Click **Ethernet** on the left side of the window. This displays an overview of network utilization and status.
15. Click the **Users** tab. This tab displays a list of all users who are signed in. Multiple users can be signed in at the same time when fast user switching is used.
16. Close the Task Manager window.

Resource Monitor

Resource Monitor, shown in Figure 9-3, provides real-time monitoring of the most common system performance indicators that is more detailed than what is provided by Task Manager. On the Overview tab, you can view performance indicators for CPU, disk, network, and memory. Key performance indicators are also summarized in graphs at the side of the screen.

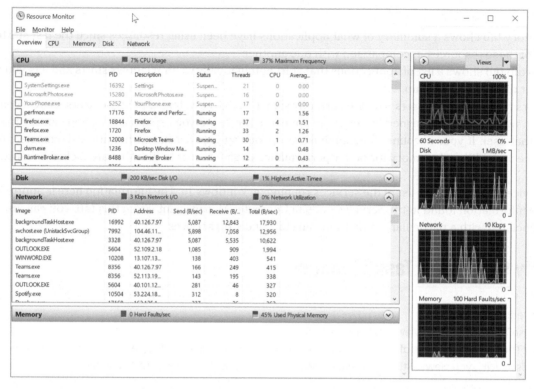

Figure 9-3   Resource Monitor

The data displayed in Resource Monitor are updated in real time while monitoring is active. The constant updating sometimes makes it hard to read the data. Monitoring can be stopped to freeze the displayed values. If you want to view information for only a few processes, you can select those processes to filter the information.

CPU

The CPU tab is used to monitor processor performance and determine whether the processor is a bottleneck. When you select the CPU tab, a list of running processes is displayed. From this tab, you can sort the list of active processes by their CPU activity, threads spawned, status, or PID.

Selecting a specific process populates the Associated Handles and Associated Modules summary sections with information from that process. The Associated Handles section displays files, registry keys, and other system resources that are being used by the process. The Associated Modules section displays DLL files that are being used by the process.

You can suspend, resume, or end a process. By suspending the operation of a process, you can quickly test its effect on the computer's performance. Note that suspending a process can cause instability, so this advanced feature should be used with caution.

Memory

The Memory tab is used to monitor memory performance and determine whether the memory subsystem is a bottleneck. The Memory tab displays memory information for each process. The Physical Memory area displays overall memory usage information in a graphical form detailing how portions of memory have been allocated. The graphical view can help you get a general awareness of the current memory demands.

Disk

The Disk tab is used to monitor disk performance and determine whether the disk subsystem is a bottleneck. When you select the Disk tab, a list of processes performing disk activity is displayed. When a process has not accessed the disk for 60 seconds, it is removed from the list. The disk activity shown for each process includes which files are being accessed. Sometimes this helps to identify which activity is causing high disk utilization.

The Storage section reports overall activity of each storage location, organized by logical disk. Each logical disk reports the physical disk it is on, the percentage of time that disk is active, space usage, and the number of disk operations waiting to be completed in the disk queue. A high disk queue length is usually indicative of a disk subsystem that is overwhelmed or experiencing technical issues.

Network

The Network tab is used to monitor network performance and determine whether the network subsystem is a bottleneck. On the Network tab you can see information about network activity and the endpoints that are generating traffic or are capable of receiving network data. TCP connection details are provided and include statistics about packet loss and latency in milliseconds between a listed local and remote address. Heavy packet losses or high latency is a sign that the network connection is oversaturated or experiencing faults somewhere between the two addresses.

Activity 9-2: Using Resource Monitor

Time Required: 5 minutes

Objective: Use the Resource Monitor tool to view performance data

Description: The Resource Monitor gives you a quick overview of what is happening on your system with regard to the CPU, disk, network, and memory. In this activity, you use Resource Monitor.

1. If necessary, start your computer and sign in.
2. Click the **Start** button, type **resource**, and then click **Resource Monitor**.
3. Click the **Overview** tab if it is not already selected. Review the graphs at the right side of the screen for CPU, Disk, Network, and Memory.
4. Expand the **CPU** summary bar if it is not already expanded and review the listed processes in the Image column. Scroll down to view processes that are running. Review the column information available for each process.
5. Click the **CPU** column header so that a down arrow appears in the header just to the left of the column title. This sorts the processes from highest to lowest based on their current CPU utilization. If you click again, the sort order is reversed.
6. Collapse the **CPU** summary bar and expand the **Disk** summary bar. Read the information about each process. This area provides disk usage information for each process running on the system.
7. Collapse the **Disk** summary bar and expand the **Network** summary bar. Read the information about each process. This area provides network usage information for each process running on the system.
8. Collapse the **Network** summary bar and expand the **Memory** summary bar. Read the information about each process. This area provides memory usage information for each process running on the system.
9. Click the **CPU** tab, and in the Processes area, click the **Image** column header twice to sort alphabetically from A to Z.
10. Select the **explorer.exe** process and expand the **Associated Handles** summary bar. Scroll down and review the resources being used by explorer.exe.
11. Collapse the **Associated Handles** summary bar and expand the **Associated Modules** summary bar. Scroll down and review the DLL files being used by explorer.exe.
12. In the Processes area, uncheck **Image** in the column header to show information for all processes again.
13. Click the **Memory** tab and review the available information.
14. Click the **Disk** tab and review the available information.
15. Click the **Network** tab and review the available information.
16. Close all open windows.

Performance Monitor

Performance Monitor, shown in Figure 9-4, is a tool that provides access to highly detailed performance information in Windows 10. When you open Performance Monitor, a summary screen with the more commonly monitored counters is displayed, but more advanced functions are typically used. You can create reports or capture and log information over time and display it in a variety of graph types. You can also configure alerts that are triggered by performance counter values.

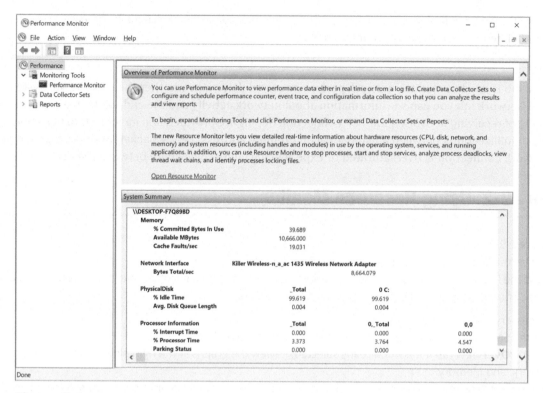

Figure 9-4   Performance Monitor

Counters

Unlike Resource Monitor, Performance Monitor allows you to select the individual counters you want to view. This helps you to focus monitoring on a specific operating system element. In some cases, after finding a general problem by using Resource Monitor, you might want to find more detailed information by using the Performance Monitor. Performance Monitor can also monitor many counters that are not shown in Resource Monitor.

When you add a counter, it can be from the local computer or another computer available over the network. In most cases, you will monitor the local computer. Some counters, however, should be monitored over the network to prevent monitoring from affecting the validity of the data. For example, if you are logging disk activity, you should monitor it over the network to ensure that the logging process is not creating disk activity that affects your results.

Counters are divided into categories, as shown in Figure 9-5. Common counter categories include processor, memory, physical disk, TCPv4, system, and logical disk. Many other categories are also available that offer specialized counters of interest. Some applications, such as Microsoft SQL Server, add new counters when you install the application.

For each counter, there might be multiple instances of that counter to choose from. For example, in a computer with multiple processors, each processor is an instance. This allows you to monitor the information about each processor separately, or you can choose to view a combined total for all processor instances. Selecting a counter displays information about that counter's collected data as a chart type.

Five different chart types are available for viewing performance data, including:

- *Line*—Displays a line for each selected counter. Each line is displayed in a different color to help distinguish them. This chart type allows you to visualize performance over time. This is the default chart type.
- *Histogram bar*—Displays a vertical bar for the current value of each performance counter. This chart type is useful for comparing similar types of counters with one another at the same time.
- *Report*—Displays the current value of each performance counter in decimal format. This is useful when you want to see the exact value of a performance counter rather than compare it with other performance counters.
- *Area*—Shows data in a similar format to a line chart, but the area below the line is a solid color. This can be useful to identify variances between two values, but a high value for one counter can hide the data for another counter.
- *Stacked area*—Displays a combined total of the selected counters and each counter's portion of the total. This can be useful when monitoring parts of a whole resource, such as the cores in a CPU. The total of all cores stacked is equal to the overall CPU utilization.

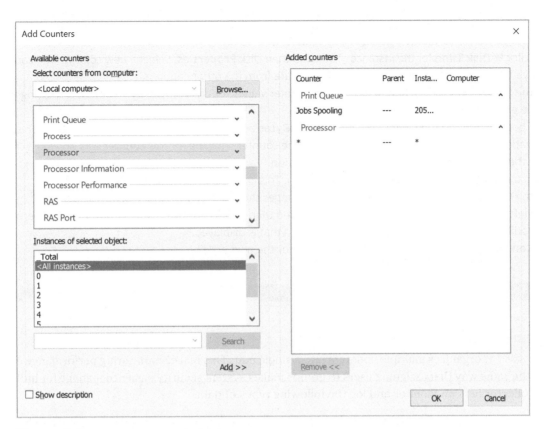

Figure 9-5   Add Counters dialog box

Activity 9-3: Using Performance Monitor

Time Required: 10 minutes

Objective: Use Performance Monitor to view counter values

Description: Performance Monitor allows you to view the value of performance counters. You can choose to display the values in several different formats. The counters allow you to monitor system performance. In this activity, you use Performance Monitor to view system activity.

1. If necessary, start your computer and sign in.
2. Click the **Start** button, type **Performance**, and then click **Performance Monitor**.
3. In the Performance Monitor window, read the information on the summary screen.
4. If necessary, expand **Monitoring Tools**, and select **Performance Monitor**. You can see that by default % Processor Time is displayed. The default report type shown is a line chart.
5. In the toolbar, click the **Add** button (the plus symbol).
6. In the list of Available counters, expand **PhysicalDisk** and click **% Disk Time**. This counter monitors how often the disk is busy.
7. In the Instances of selected object box, click **<All instances>**. This selects disk 0 for monitoring. If multiple disks were present in this computer, multiple instances would be listed.
8. Select the **Show description** check box to enable it. This displays a description of each counter as you select it.
9. Click **Add**.
10. In the list of Available counters, expand **Memory** and then click **Available MBytes**. This counter monitors how much physical memory is free for use by processes.
11. Click **Add** and then click **OK**. Notice that new lines are added to the graph. The graph is scaled from 0 to 100, but the new counters might provide values outside that range.
12. At the bottom of the screen, click **% Disk Time** for the instance _Total. The Last, Average, Minimum, and Maximum values now reflect what has been measured for % Disk Time. Note the average value. A small value

here might not register on the scrolling line graph. A scale value adjusts the counter values to better fit in the graph range from 0 to 100. The default scale value is 1.

13. Right-click **% Disk Time** for the instance _Total and then click **Properties**. Select a new color for the counter's displayed line that will be easy to see and differentiate from the other counters.

14. Click the **Scale** arrow, select **10.0** to multiply all counter values for this counter by 10 before displaying them on the line graph, and then click **OK**.

15. At the bottom of the screen, right-click **Available MBytes** and then click **Scale Selected Counters**. This automatically changes the scale used to measure the counter. The line for this counter was previously at the very top of the chart and did not provide useful information.

16. On the toolbar, click the **Change graph type** button. This changes the graph to a bar chart.

17. Click the **Change graph type** button again. This changes the graph to a report.

18. In the left pane, right-click **Performance Monitor** and then click **Properties**. Notice that on the General tab, you can modify the graph sample rate and the time span that is displayed.

19. Click **Cancel** and leave Performance Monitor open for the next activity.

Data Collector Sets

A **Data Collector Set** organizes multiple counters into a single unit. This makes monitoring performance easier to manage in much the same way that assigning users to groups makes system security easier to manage for individual users.

A Data Collector Set can monitor and log the following types of data:

- *Performance counters*—This records data on a timed basis. The value of selected performance counters is recorded at defined intervals, such as 1 second.
- *Event trace*—This tracks when system events occur. In this way, real-time information is collected about the system rather than samples. The information collected is based on the selection of an event trace provider. For each provider, you can select which specific events are tracked.
- *Configuration*—This tracks changes to the registry and when they occurred. You can use this to monitor changes made by application installations.

When you configure a Data Collector Set, it is often to log performance information to disk. For event trace data and configuration data, the changes must be logged to disk.

Data Collector Sets are not always running. If they were, very large log files would be generated and system performance would suffer. You can manually start Data Collector Sets when you are performing troubleshooting, or you can start them with an alert. If you are collecting a baseline, you should schedule the Data Collector Set to run at a consistent time.

Data Collector Set scheduling is very flexible, allowing you to create multiple schedules based on a start date, end date, day of week, and time of day. Stopping a Data Collector Set is configured most often based on overall collection duration or a maximum collected data limit. When a Data Collector Set stops, you can run a task. This can be used to process the log files after data collection is complete. For example, you might have a script that looks for specific event values within the logs, or you might simply copy logs to a network location for further analysis.

Activity 9-4: Logging Performance Data

Time Required: 15 minutes

Objective: Log performance data by using a Data Collector Set

Description: Data Collector Sets allow you to group counters for easier manageability. If you want to log performance data, it must be done with a Data Collector Set. In this activity, you create a Data Collector Set and log performance data to disk.

1. In the left pane of Performance Monitor, expand **Data Collector Sets** and then click **System**. You can see that two predefined Data Collector Sets are created by the system to perform common maintenance tasks.

2. In the left pane, click **Event Trace Sessions**. These are trace providers used by the system to collect system performance data.

3. In the left pane, click **User Defined**. When you create new Data Collector Sets, they are placed in this folder.

4. Right-click **User Defined**, point to **New**, and then click **Data Collector Set**.

5. In the Name box, type **CPU and Disk logging** and then click **Next**. This Data Collector Set will be created from a template.

6. In the Template Data Collector Set box, select each option and read the description.

7. Click **Basic** and then click **Next**.

8. Accept the default Root directory and then click **Next**.

9. Click **Open properties for this data collector set** and then click **Finish**.

10. In the CPU and Disk logging Properties dialog box, on the General tab, read which user the Data Collector Set will run as.

11. Click the **Directory** tab. This tab shows you where the log files will be stored.

12. Click the **Stop Condition** tab. Notice that, by default, the Data Collector Set will stop after 1 minute.

13. Click **OK**.

14. In the left pane, expand **User Defined** and then click **CPU and Disk logging**.

15. Right-click **Performance Counter** in the right pane and then click **Properties**. Notice that all processor-related counters are selected by default.

16. Click **Add**, in the Available counters box, expand **PhysicalDisk**, select **PhysicalDisk** to select all counters, click **Add**, and then click **OK**. This adds all of the counters for the physical disk.

17. Notice that the log format is binary in the Performance Counter Properties dialog box and then click **OK**.

18. In the left pane, click **User Defined**. Notice that CPU and Disk logging has a status of stopped in the right pane.

19. Right-click **CPU and Disk logging** in the right pane and then click **Start**.

20. Wait 1 minute for the data collection to complete.

21. In the left pane, click **Performance Monitor** and, on the toolbar, click the **View Log Data** button. Note that if you hover the cursor over each toolbar button, the name of the button is displayed as a ScreenTip.

22. Under Data source, click **Log files**, click **Add**, double-click the **Admin** folder, double-click the **CPU and Disk logging** folder, double-click the folder with today's date, click the file **Performance Counter.blg**, and then click **Open**.

23. Click **Time Range**. This displays the time range in the log file. You can select just a subset of the time range to view if you desire. The default setting is to display the entire time range.

24. Click the **Data** tab to select the counters to display from the log file, click **Remove** as required to remove any existing counters, and then click **Add**.

25. Expand **PhysicalDisk**, click **% Idle Time**, and then click **Add**. This adds the total % Idle Time for all physical disks that were logged.

26. Expand **Processor**, click **% Idle Time**, and click **Add**. This adds the total % Idle Time for all processors that were logged.

27. Click **OK**. Notice that the counters are now listed under Counters.

28. Click **OK** to save the settings and display the data on the Performance Monitor graph. If necessary, change the chart view's graph type to **Line**.

29. Click the **Add** button on the toolbar. Notice that only the PhysicalDisk and Processor counters are available because only those counters were logged.

30. Expand **PhysicalDisk**. Notice that you can select any counter in the category because they were all logged.

31. Click **Cancel** to close the Add Counters window.

32. Leave Performance Monitor open for the next activity.

Alerts

For performance counters, you can configure an alert instead of logging to disk. After selecting the performance counter you desire for an alert, you also state a threshold value and configure whether the alert is triggered by going above or below the threshold value. For example, you can trigger an alert when the \Memory\AvailableBytes counter drops below 50 MB.

When an alert triggers, the following can be performed:

- *Log an entry in the application event log*—Placing an event in the application log allows you to search for the event later and incorporate it into your normal system monitoring process.
- *Start a Data Collector Set*—If you have an ongoing problem that you are trying to monitor, you can start a Data Collector Set when the alert is triggered. For example, if disk utilization is high, you can start a collector set with various counters that help you find the source of the problem.
- *Run a scheduled task*—Running a task can start any program. In most cases, you will want to run a script. For example, you could run a script that sends the administrator an email notification.

Data Manager

Data Manager allows you to automatically control the log files and reports that can be generated by Data Collector Sets, as shown in Figure 9-6. You can apply a policy and specify actions. Using Data Manager, you can specify parameters such as minimum free disk space, maximum number of folders, report generation, and deletion preferences to make room for new data.

Figure 9-6 Data Manager settings

Reports

Reports are used to process log file data and display it in a meaningful way. You add rules for report processing in Data Manager for the Data Collector Set. In theory, you could create your own rules for processing log files, but most administrators will never need to do so. Windows 10 includes the rules you are likely to need and runs them automatically.

Activity 9-5: Viewing Reports

Time Required: 10 minutes

Objective: View a report generated by Performance Monitor

Description: Performance Monitor can generate reports from log files. To do this, XML-based rules files are applied to the log data. Several system reports are available. In this activity, you view an existing system report.

1. In the left pane of Performance Monitor, below Data Collector Sets, click **User Defined**.
2. Right-click **CPU and Disk logging** in the right pane and then click **Start**.

3. Wait approximately 1 minute for data collection to complete.
4. Right-click **CPU and Disk logging** and then click **Latest Report** on the shortcut menu. The left navigation pane changes focus to highlight the most recent report, and the report's details are opened in the right pane.
5. Review the information available in the report. Locate the Summary section and read the information available there.
6. Expand **Application Counters** and read the information.
7. Expand each remaining section of the report and read the information.
8. Close Performance Monitor and close all other open windows.

PERFORMANCE OPTIONS

Windows 10 includes the Performance Options dialog box, shown in Figure 9-7, to optimize visual effects, processor scheduling, and virtual memory. To access the Performance Options dialog box, search for the word *performance* in Settings, and then select Adjust the appearance and performance of Windows.

The Visual Effects tab allows you to configure a wide variety of settings that improve how the Windows 10 interface performs. On systems with poor graphics processing performance, disabling some of these features can improve performance. By default, the Let Windows choose what's best for my computer option is selected.

The Advanced tab lets you select whether processor time is allocated to optimize performance for programs or background services. If Programs is selected, the program running in the active window is given a slightly higher priority than other applications. This ensures that the program you are using is the most responsive on the system. If you select Background services, all programs are given the same priority.

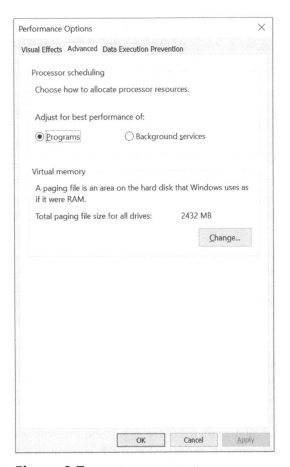

Figure 9-7   Performance Options

The Advanced tab also gives you access to the settings for virtual memory. Virtual memory settings control how the paging file that is used to simulate memory on disk is configured. By default, the paging file is managed automatically by Windows. As more of the paging file is required, it is expanded from the minimum size to the maximum size.

You can manually configure the paging file if you prefer. This allows you to optimize the placement of the paging file. Moving the paging file to its own hard disk optimizes system performance because less contention for disk resources when accessing the paging file will occur. Alternatively, you can spread the paging file over multiple disks to speed access to the file.

Most Windows 10 computers have only a single hard disk, and increasing performance is not possible by adjusting the virtual memory settings. You might, however, want to move the paging file to a different partition to free space on the C: drive if it is almost full.

It is also possible to specify that no paging file is to be used; however, this is not recommended as performance will suffer. Even when systems have sufficient physical memory to hold all active processes and their data, system performance suffers when the paging file is disabled.

 CAUTION Moving the paging file to another volume on the same physical disk provides no performance improvement.

Data Execution Prevention (DEP) is a processor feature that Windows 10 is capable of using. DEP monitors processes to ensure that they do not access unauthorized memory spaces, which is done by various types of malware, to take control of systems. Despite the value of DEP in preventing malware, there is a performance cost. By default, DEP is enabled for only essential Windows programs and services. This protects the core components of the operating system that are likely to be targeted by malware and still preserves system performance. You can enable DEP for all programs and services (and specify exceptions), but this has a significant performance impact and is not recommended.

CONTROLLING APPLICATION STARTUP

When you sign in to Windows 10, some applications are started automatically. Most of these applications are small utilities that provide status information or run in the background waiting for communications. For example, messaging clients like Microsoft Teams typically start automatically so that they can provide notifications and accept incoming communication.

On computer systems with limited resources, you might find that having too many applications running at startup causes performance issues. During startup, many applications attempting to start simultaneously can cause a high level of disk activity that overwhelms traditional hard drives and causes the sign-in process to be very slow. After signing in, too many applications running simultaneously might use a large amount of memory and not leave enough for applications you are actively using. To resolve these issues, you might want to stop some applications from starting automatically.

 **TIP** Some malware configures Windows 10 to start the malware executable automatically at startup. Understanding all of the methods for controlling automatic startup can be useful when removing malware.

Tools for Managing Application Startup

Most applications that start automatically when you sign in have an option in the application settings to enable or disable automatic startup. If an application has this setting, then modifying this setting is the preferred method for controlling automatic startup. Applications can use multiple methods to configure automatic startup, and using the setting in the application avoids the need to determine which method is being used.

Task Manager is another tool that allows you to control application startup without knowing the exact mechanism that the application is using. On the Startup tab, shown in Figure 9-8, you can enable or disable startup for applications. You can also see the startup impact caused by applications.

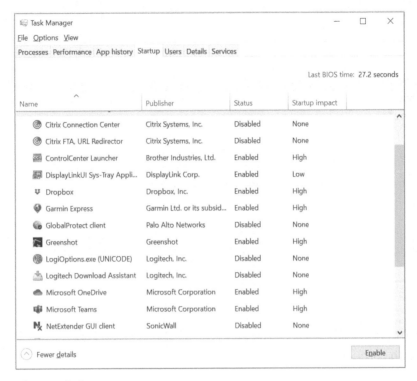

Figure 9-8   Task Manager Startup tab

For more advanced management of applications and add-ons that start in Windows 10, you can use Autoruns, shown in Figure 9-9. The main advantage of using this tool is that it goes beyond identifying and managing simple application startup. Autoruns also analyzes add-ons that are hooked into networking, File Explorer, and other Windows functions.

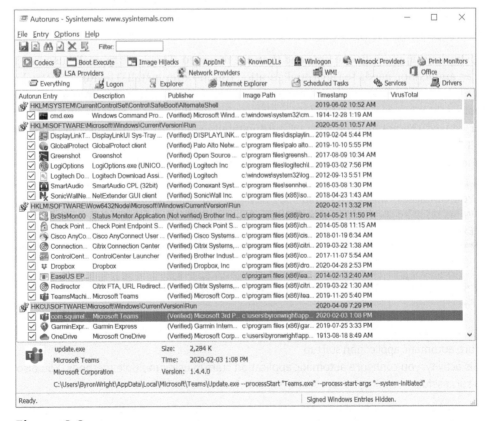

Figure 9-9   Autoruns

NOTE 1

Autoruns is not included as part of Windows 10, but you can download it from the Microsoft website at https://docs.microsoft.com/en-us/sysinternals/downloads/autoruns.

Autoruns is particularly useful when looking for malware that has embedded itself in Windows. It shows how the add-on or application is starting, the file location, and whether the application publisher is verified. Files in nonstandard locations and with unverified publishers should be investigated. You have the option to delete an item listed in Autoruns if you determine it shouldn't be there.

Startup Methods Used by Applications

Applications can be started by a scheduled task that is triggered at sign in. Figure 9-10 shows a scheduled task that is configured to start when any user signs in. You can disable or delete the scheduled task to stop this behavior, but carefully consider the impact on the application before you make this change.

Name	Status	Triggers	Next Run Time	Last Run Time
Office Feature Updates	Ready	Multiple triggers defined	2020-05-04 12:10:43 PM	2020-05-04 8:42:03 AM
Office Feature Updates Logon	Ready	Multiple triggers defined		2020-05-04 8:54:30 AM
Office Subscription Maintenance	Ready	At 12:26 PM every day	2020-05-04 12:26:12 PM	2020-05-03 12:26:13 PM
OfficeBackgroundTaskHandlerLogon	Ready	At log on of any user		1999-11-30 12:00:00 AM
OfficeBackgroundTaskHandlerRegistration	Ready	When the task is created or modified - After triggered, rep...		2020-05-04 9:27:01 AM
OfficeTelemetryAgentFallBack	Ready	At log on of any user - After triggered, repeat every 12:00:...		2020-05-04 9:28:41 AM
OfficeTelemetryAgentFallBack2016	Ready	At log on of any user - After triggered, repeat every 12:00:...		1999-11-30 12:00:00 AM
OfficeTelemetryAgentLogOn	Ready	At log on of any user - After triggered, repeat every 08:00:...		2020-05-04 8:58:41 AM

Figure 9-10   Scheduled tasks

Several registry keys can be used to automatically start applications. They exist in both HKEY_LOCAL_MACHINE and HKEY_CURRENT_USER. If they are configured in HKEY_LOCAL_MACHINE, the applications start automatically for all users. If they are configured in HKEY_CURRENT_USER, the applications start automatically for only the current user.

The registry keys for starting applications automatically are:

- HKEY_LOCAL_MACHINE\Software\Microsoft\Windows\CurrentVersion\Run
- HKEY_CURRENT_USER\Software\Microsoft\Windows\CurrentVersion\Run
- HKEY_LOCAL_MACHINE\Software\Microsoft\Windows\CurrentVersion\RunOnce
- HKEY_CURRENT_USER\Software\Microsoft\Windows\CurrentVersion\RunOnce

The RunOnce registry keys apply only one time and then are removed. These are typically used as part of application installation when an application needs to run a configuration routine after install. The Run registry keys are permanent and are triggered each time a user signs in. These keys are ignored if you start in Safe Mode.

In earlier versions of Windows, a Startup folder was visible on the Start menu. Placing a shortcut to an application in this folder caused the application to start automatically when the user signed in. This folder still exists in Windows 10, but it is not visible on the Start menu; however, shortcuts in this folder are still automatically started at sign in. Items in the notification area are commonly started from here.

 TIP   You can access the Startup folder by navigating to C:\Users*username*\AppData\Roaming\Microsoft\Windows\Start Menu\Programs\Startup. You can also type shell:startup in the address bar in the File Explorer window and then press Enter.

Activity 9-6: Configuring Automatic Application Startup

Time Required: 15 minutes

Objective: Configure automatic application startup

Description: In this activity, you configure automatic application startup using multiple methods. You also verify that your configuration was successful.

1. If necessary, start your computer and sign in.
2. Click the **Start** button, type **registry**, and then click **Registry Editor**.

3. In the User Account Control dialog box, click **Yes**.
4. In the Registry Editor window, navigate to HKEY_CURRENT_USER\Software\Microsoft\Windows\CurrentVersion\RunOnce.
5. Click **Edit** on the menu bar, point to **New**, and then click **String Value**.
6. Type **Paint** and then press **Enter** to name the value.
7. Double-click **Paint**, in the Value data box, type **C:\Windows\System32\mspaint.exe**, and then click **OK**.
8. Close the Registry Editor window.
9. On the taskbar, click **File Explorer**.
10. In the File Explorer window, in the address bar, type **shell:startup** and then press **Enter**.
11. Right-click an open area, point to **New**, and then click **Shortcut**.
12. In the Create Shortcut wizard screen, in the Type the location of the item text box, type **C:\Windows\System32\notepad.exe** and then click **Next**.
13. In the Type a name for this shortcut text box, type **AutoNotepad** and then click **Finish**.
14. Close the File Explorer window.
15. Right-click the taskbar and then click **Task Manager**.
16. In the Task Manager window, click the **Startup** tab and read the items listed. Notice that the Notepad shortcut you created is present but not the Paint application in the RunOnce registry key.
17. Close the Task Manager window.
18. Sign out and then sign in again. Both Notepad and Paint start automatically.
19. Exit Notepad and Paint.
20. Click the **Start** button, type **registry**, and then click **Registry Editor**.
21. In the User Account Control dialog box, click **Yes**.
22. In the Registry Editor window, if necessary, navigate to HKEY_CURRENT_USER\Software\Microsoft\Windows\CurrentVersion\RunOnce. Notice that the value you created has been deleted.
23. Close the Registry Editor window.
24. Right-click the taskbar and then click **Task Manager**.
25. In the Task Manager window, click the **Startup** tab and read the items listed. Notice that the Notepad shortcut you created is still present.
26. Click **Notepad** and then click **Disable**.
27. Close the Task Manager window.
28. Sign out and then sign in again. Neither Notepad nor Paint start automatically.
29. On the taskbar, click **File Explorer**.
30. In the File Explorer window, in the address bar, type **shell:startup** and then press **Enter**.
31. Right-click **AutoNotepad** and then click **Delete**.
32. Close the File Explorer window.

TROUBLESHOOTING WINDOWS 10 ERRORS

Sometimes Windows 10 or apps installed on Windows 10 become unstable and start to generate errors. Sometimes an error message is displayed on the screen that provides an obvious solution, but more often you need to use additional tools to troubleshoot further. The more information you have about a problem, the more likely it is that you can find a solution. Using precise search terms in a search engine generates results that are most likely to be applicable to your specific problem.

Steps Recorder

When a user reports an error, the information provided by the user is not always accurate. Rather than accepting a description of the error at face value, you are better off to have the user demonstrate the steps to reproduce the error. If you cannot visit or view the user desktop, you can ask the user to record the steps with Steps Recorder.

When Steps Recorder is activated, it captures a screenshot each time the user clicks on a screen item. The screenshots and user actions are saved in a report that can be sent via email or saved to a shared storage location. The report is an .mht file that contains both text and the screenshots. To keep the report size small, it is compressed in a .zip file.

Text typed by the user is not captured by Steps Recorder. If information being typed is important, the user needs to add a comment that includes the information being typed.

Reliability Monitor

Sometimes a computer has become unstable over time and you would like to identify when the stability problem began. **Reliability Monitor**, shown in Figure 9-11, rates the system stability of Windows 10 and lets you monitor the events that contribute to system stability.

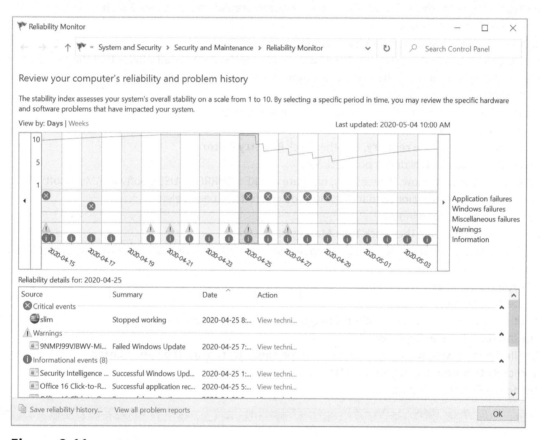

Figure 9-11 Reliability Monitor

Reliability Monitor collects the following data:

- *Software installs and uninstalls*—Software tracked here includes driver and operating system updates.
- *Application failures*—Any application that stops responding is logged here.
- *Windows failures*—Any system failure that results in blue screen errors and boot failures is logged here.
- *Miscellaneous failures*—Any event not included in other categories is logged here. One type of failure recorded here is improper shutdowns.

The Reliability Monitor graph lets you see the point in time at which significant reliability events occurred. You can use the graph to drill down and find out what event occurred in that time frame and correct the problem. For example, if frequent failures occur after adding a new driver, the driver is the likely cause of the stability problem and it should be removed.

Event Viewer

Event Viewer is used to browse and manage events stored in system event logs, as shown in Figure 9-12. You can start Event Viewer as a stand-alone administrative tool or use it in Computer Management. When you are troubleshooting, events in these logs can be a valuable source of information. Sometimes, Error events provide a description of how to fix the problem. In other cases, you can use Error event information in an Internet search engine to find a solution.

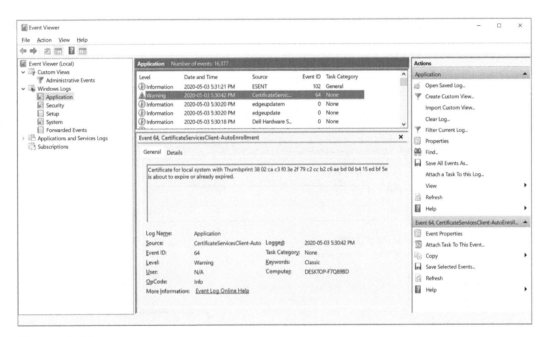

Figure 9-12   Event Viewer

The logs in the Windows Logs node of Event Viewer are the most commonly used for troubleshooting. Most non-Microsoft apps and many Microsoft apps write their events to the Application log. The Security log contains Audit Success and Audit Failure events. The System log contains general operating system events, such as services starting and stopping or IP address conflicts.

The Applications and Services Logs node contains event logs for many operating system services. It also contains logs for some management software, such as User Experience Virtualization and App-V. In general, each service or app has its own log.

The Custom Views node is used to create filtered views that can contain specific event types from specific sources. You can create a view that gathers events you require for working with a specific application that writes information to various logs. The Administrative Events view shows Critical, Error, and Warning events from all logs.

You can use the Subscriptions node to copy events from a remote computer to yours. This can be useful when you are monitoring several computers. By default, the events from a subscription are copied into the Forwarded Events log.

Finding Events

By default, when you view an event log, you see all of the events listed in it. Sometimes, you can scroll up and down in the list of events to find helpful information, but it can be useful to limit the visible events to only those in which you're interested.

If you have a general idea of what you're looking for during troubleshooting, but you don't know the event ID or event source, then you can search for a specific word by using the Find option. When you use Find, the search applies to all text in the events for a single log.

You can also filter individual logs to find the events you want to see, as shown in Figure 9-13. You can use this dialog box to filter by time, event level, event source, event ID, keyword, user, and computer. It is most common to filter by:

- Event level to see only errors or warnings when searching for general information
- Event ID to see instances of only specifically identified events that you know are relevant
- Event source to see all events from a subsystem you are troubleshooting

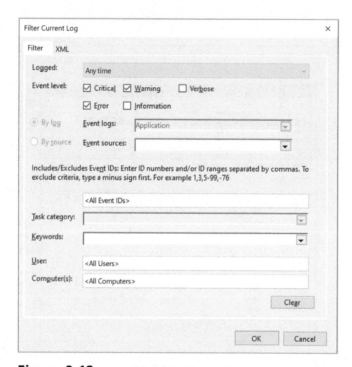

Figure 9-13   Event log filtering options

If you are using a filter often, you can create a custom view that applies that filter. Then you can select the view instead of recreating the filter each time. When you create a custom view, you can include events from multiple logs. This is useful when you are troubleshooting an application or subsystem that writes events in multiple logs.

Managing Event Logs

Most of the time you don't need to do anything to manage event logs. The default configuration is sufficient in most cases; however, you can configure the following:

- *Maximum log size*—Sometimes on a busy system you increase the maximum log size to allow more events to be retained.
- *Log behavior when maximum log size is reached*—By default, the oldest events in the log are removed when new events are added. If you want to ensure that older events are not lost before you can review them, you can archive the log when full or choose not to overwrite events. If you archive the log when full, you'll need to periodically remove the archives to ensure that the C: drive does not run low on space. If you choose Do not overwrite events, then new events are not recorded when the log is full, and you need to manually clear the log before new events are recorded.

Triggering Scheduled Tasks

You can also attach a scheduled task to a specific event. When the event appears in the event log, the scheduled task is triggered. This can be useful if you want to be notified when a specific event occurs. This can also be used to resolve problems that can be resolved simply with a script. For example, the script could restart a service when the service generates an error.

Event Log Forwarding

Most of the time, you use Event Viewer to view events generated on the local computer, but sometimes it's useful to see events generated on multiple computers in a single place. For example, you might want to monitor performance for a specific application that is installed on multiple computers. Event subscriptions allow events to be copied from the computer that generates the event to another computer that collects the events.

When you configure a collector-initiated subscription, the collector computer queries Windows Remote Management (WinRM) on the event source to retrieve the events. Windows 10 does not configure WinRM by default; you need to configure it by issuing the winrm quickconfig command at a command prompt or a Windows PowerShell prompt.

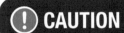 **CAUTION** The quick configuration for WinRM allows any computer to connect. You can use advanced configuration options to limit connections to only allowed IP addresses.

On the collector computer, you also need to enable and configure Windows Event Collector Service. If you do not configure it before attempting to create a subscription, you will be prompted to configure it automatically. If you issue the wecutil qc command at a command prompt or Windows PowerShell prompt, it will be configured before starting the subscription.

On a domain-based network, to give the collector computer permission to access event logs, you need to make the computer account of the collector computer a member of the Event Log Readers Group on the source computer. In a workgroup environment, you need to configure a user account as a member of the Event Log Readers Group instead.

NOTE 2

For more detailed information about event log subscriptions see the Windows Event Collector page at https://docs.microsoft.com/en-us/windows/win32/wec/windows-event-collector.

 TIP Security events are not accessible to members of the Event Log Readers Group. If you want to collect security events, the user account needs to be a member of the Administrators group.

Activity 9-7: Using Event Viewer

Time Required: 10 minutes
Objective: Use Event Viewer to view logged events
Description: In this activity, you configure automatic application startup using multiple methods. You also verify that your configuration was successful.

1. If necessary, startup your computer and sign in.
2. Click the **Start** button, type **event**, and then click **Event Viewer**.
3. In the Event Viewer window, in the Summary of Administrative Events area, expand **Error**, and scroll down to review the events. You can use this to get an overview of Error events in all logs.
4. In the navigation pane, expand **Windows Logs** and then click **System**.
5. Double-click the top event to view the details and then click **Close**.
6. Right-click **System** and then click **Filter Current Log**.
7. In the Filter Current Log dialog box, click the Event sources arrow, scroll down, select **Kernel-General,** and then click **OK**. Only events from the Kernel-General source are displayed.
8. Right-click **System** and then click **Clear Filter**.
9. Right-click **System** and then click **Find**.
10. In the Find dialog box, in the Find what text box, type **Time** and then click **Find Next**.
11. Click **Cancel** and then double-click the selected event to view it.
12. Read the event information and identify where the word time is located. It might be part of a larger word.

13. Click the Details tab, read through the detailed information, and then click **Close**.
14. In the left navigation pane, expand Applications and Services Logs, expand Microsoft, click **Windows**, and then read the list of event logs for Windows services.
15. In the left navigation pane, expand Custom Views and then click **Administrative Events**. This view shows Error and Warning events from multiple event logs.
16. Close the Event Viewer window.

NOTE 3

For detailed information about how to use Get-WinEvent, see the Get-WinEvent page at https://docs.microsoft.com/en-us/powershell/module/microsoft.powershell.diagnostics/get-winevent?view=powershell-5.1

Viewing Events by Using Windows PowerShell

You can use Windows PowerShell to view event log contents on the local computer or remote computers. Most people find it much easier to work with Event Viewer than the Get-WinEvent cmdlet in Windows PowerShell. So, Get-WinEvent is typically used only when you have a specific need to create a script that analyzes event log contents.

Activity 9-8: Use Windows PowerShell to View Events

Time Required: 10 minutes

Objective: Use Windows PowerShell to view logged events

Description: In this activity, you configure automatic application startup using multiple methods. You also verify that your configuration was successful.

1. If necessary, start your computer and sign in.
2. Right-click the **Start** button and then click **Windows PowerShell (Admin)**.
3. In the User Account Control window, click **Yes**.
4. At the Windows PowerShell prompt, type **Get-WinEvent -Listlog *** and then press **Enter**. This lists all event logs.
5. Type **Get-WinEvent -Listlog S*** and then press **Enter**. This lists all event logs that start with the letter S.
6. Type **Get-WinEvent -LogName System -MaxEvents 10** and then press **Enter**. This lists the most recent 10 events from the System log.
7. Type **Get-WinEvent -LogName System -MaxEvents 1 | Format-List *** and then press **Enter**. This shows the details of the most recent event in the System log.
8. Close the Windows PowerShell prompt window.

LOCAL FILE RECOVERY AND BACKUP

If user data is stored on a Windows 10 computer, it should be backed up to ensure that it can be recovered in case of a hardware failure. In most large organizations, files are stored on central servers where they can easily be backed up and restored by administrators. When users need to keep files locally on their computer, such as when they are in a workgroup or while using a mobile computer while traveling, the best solution is to store data in a cloud service, such as OneDrive. When you synchronize files with OneDrive, they are stored locally and automatically backed up offsite. Your data is protected if you lose you device or if there is a major disaster, such as your house burning down.

File History is the current tool that you should use to make local backups of data to an external hard drive or network location. Backup and Recovery (Windows 7) is still present in Windows 10, but it is primarily there to support restoring data from older Windows 7 backups.

Configuring File History

File History backs up data to an external hard drive or a network location. The configuration of File History is user specific and is meant to backup only user data. File History does not perform a complete system backup. You configure File History from the Backup settings shown in Figure 9-14. File History is disabled by default, because you need to pick a location to store backup data that will be available if the primary drive fails.

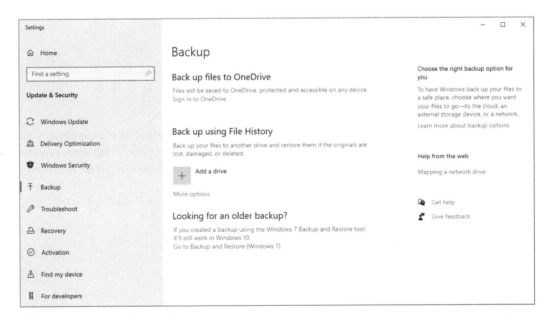

Figure 9-14   Backup settings

 TIP   To specify a network location for File History, you need to use the File History settings in Control Panel.

When you attach an external hard drive and configure it for use by File History, the drive does not get erased. Backup data is added to the drive using the drive's free space. Note that if the source files include any EFS-protected files, the external drive should be formatted with NTFS to back up the source data properly.

File History creates a series of folders at the root of the drive selected to hold File History data. The path is F:\FileHistory*username**workstationName* where F: is replaced with the drive letter assigned to the external drive selected for use by File History on that system.

You can customize File History to include or exclude specific folders, but the default configuration includes Libraries, Desktop, Contacts, and Favorites. Libraries includes common folders, such as Documents and Pictures.

The first backup takes a copy of all files monitored by File History. The backup process happens in the background and doesn't require monitoring. The initial backup generates disk activity that might be noticed on systems with poor disk performance but is not noticeable on most systems. Future backups are much smaller and copy only files that have changed. New instances of a file are saved in the same backup folder, but with a different date and time stamp within parentheses added to the title.

 **CAUTION**   File History content is not compressed or encrypted on the external drive. Anyone who steals the drive will have ready access to the drive's contents unless it is encrypted with a technology, such as BitLocker.

Files are backed up every hour by default. The backup frequency can be changed to as little as every 10 minutes or as much as every 24 hours. The retention period for backup data can be changed so the oldest backup data will be deleted when space is needed for newer backup files, kept for a range from one month to two years, or to be kept forever (the default).

 **CAUTION**   If the external drive selected for File History runs out of space, backups stop. To avoid this, select to keep backups Until space is needed.

Only one backup drive can be configured for use by File History at a time. If you want to switch from using one drive to another, you must first stop using the current drive and add the new one. When you stop using a drive with File History, the backed-up data on that drive is not deleted.

Activity 9-9: Configuring File History

Time Required: 10 minutes
Objective: Configure File History settings
Description: In this activity, you simulate a separate internal disk drive by adding a virtual disk to the system and then configuring it for use with File History. Note that using a virtual disk drive is for lab purposes only and is not recommended for backing up production machines, because the virtual disk does not remain attached after the system is restarted.

1. If necessary, start your computer and sign in.
2. Right-click the **Start** button and then click **Disk Management**.
3. Click **Action** on the menu bar and then click **Create VHD**.
4. In the Location box, type **C:\VHD Storage\VHDFileHistory.vhdx**.
5. Change the Virtual hard disk size unit from MB to GB.
6. In the Virtual hard disk size text box, type **4**.
7. In the Virtual hard disk format area, click **VHDX**.
8. Confirm that **Dynamically expanding (recommended)** in the Virtual hard disk type area is selected and then click **OK**.
9. In the bottom pane, scroll to the new 4 GB disk, right-click the disk name, and then click **Initialize disk**. Accept the default settings in the Initialize Disk dialog box and then click **OK**.
10. Right-click the 3.98 GB of unallocated space on that disk and then select **New Simple Volume**.
11. In the new Simple Volume Wizard, click **Next** twice to accept the default volume size, and note the assigned drive letter here: _____.
12. Click **Next** to accept the assigned drive letter.
13. In the Volume label box, type **File History Data** and then click **Next**.
14. Click **Finish** to create the new virtual disk. If you are prompted to format the disk before using it, you can safely cancel the prompt.
15. Close the Disk Management window.
16. Click the **Start** button and then click the **Settings**.
17. Click **Update & security** and then click **Backup**.
18. Under the heading Back up using File History, click **Add a drive**.
19. When the drive search completes, click the drive labeled **File History Data**. Note that the Add a drive section is replaced with a toggle switch to enable or disable automatic back up of files.
20. Click the **More options** link.
21. In the Back up my files box, select **Every 10 minutes**.
22. In the Keep my backups box, select **Until space is needed**.
23. Below Overview, click **Back up now**. Note that the status changes in the Overview section, but no progress window opens.
24. Close the Settings window.

Configuring Backup and Restore (Windows 7)

Backup and Restore (Windows 7) is included in Windows 10 primarily to allow access to older backups created in Windows 7. A common scenario for using this would be migrating data from an older computer running Windows 7 to a new computer running Windows 10. It is possible to configure Backup and Restore (Windows 7) to perform daily backups to an external disk, just like you could in Windows 7, but you should use File History instead.

One feature available in Backup and Restore (Windows 7) that's not found in File History is a complete system backup. This is referred to as a system image in Backup and Restore (Windows 7). A system image is a complete copy of the computer, including the operating system, applications, and data.

 **CAUTION** The System Image Backup option is deprecated beginning in Windows 10 version 1709. Microsoft recommends using a third-party backup solution if you want to back up system images.

Restoring Previous Versions of Files and Folders

If File History or Backup and Restore (Windows 7), or both, have been configured to protect data, that data can be recovered using a feature called **Previous Versions**. You can browse to a location in File Explorer and open the properties of a file or folder to view the Previous Versions tab, as shown in Figure 9-15. A list of known previous versions is displayed. You can recover an old version of the content and restore it in the same place or to an alternate location for inspection.

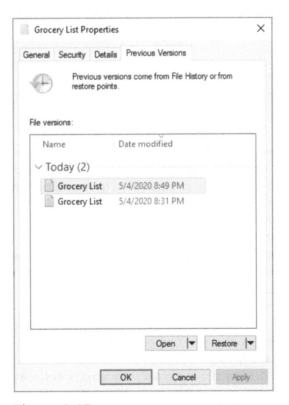

Figure 9-15   Previous Versions of a file

If a file has been deleted, you can't view the previous versions by selecting the file in File Explorer. You can, however, view the previous versions for a folder to display files that have been deleted, as shown in Figure 9-16. In this window, you use arrows to move back and forth between available versions and click the green arrow to restore.

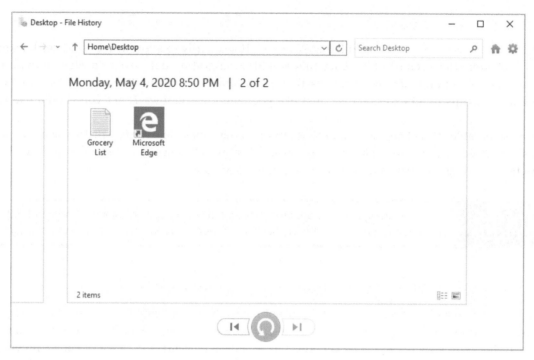

Figure 9-16   File History for a folder

Activity 9-10: Restoring Previous Versions of Files

Time Required: 20 minutes

Objective: Restore files from File History

Description: In this activity, you create a sample Grocery List file that will be backed up with multiple versions and restored to identify supporting backup data elements.

1. If necessary, start your computer and sign in.
2. Right-click anywhere on the Desktop, point to **New**, and then click **Text Document**.
3. Edit the name of the new document to be **Grocery List** and then press **Enter** to save the change.
4. Double-click the **Grocery List** text document on the desktop to open it. In the Notepad editor window, enter the text **Version one – eggs**.
5. Exit Notepad and when prompted to save your changes, click **Save**.
6. Click the **Start** button, type **backup**, and then click **Backup settings**.
7. Below Back up using File History, click **More options** and then click **Back up now**. You are triggering a manual backup to avoid waiting 10 minutes for the file to be backed up.
8. Leave the Settings window open for later in the Activity.
9. On the Desktop, double-click the **Grocery List** text document.
10. In the Notepad editor window, edit the text to read **Version two – eggs, apples**.
11. Exit Notepad and when prompted to save your changes, click **Save**.
12. In the Settings window, click **Back up now**.
13. On the Desktop, right-click the **Grocery List** document and then click **Restore previous versions**. Note that the Properties window for the file opens and the Previous Versions tab is selected by default.
14. Select the oldest version of the file in the list and then click **Restore**.
15. In the Replace or Skip Files dialog box, click **Replace the file in the destination**. Note that a progress indicator is temporarily displayed and then File Explorer opens to show the restored content.
16. In File Explorer, double-click the **Grocery List** file and note that the original version of the document has replaced version two.
17. Exit Notepad and close the Grocery List Properties dialog box.
18. In File Explorer, click the **Home** tab on the ribbon and then click **History** in the Open group on the ribbon.

19. If necessary, in the address bar, remove **Grocery List.txt** from the path and then press **Enter**. The previous versions for the Desktop folder are shown.

20. Click the **left arrow** at the bottom of the File History window until you reach the first File History backup. Note that the Grocery List file is not listed because the first File History backup was made before the file existed.

21. Click the **right arrow** at the bottom of the File History window until you reach the latest File History backup.

22. Double-click the **Grocery List** file within the last File History backup, which previews the contents of the file in the File History window. In this preview mode, the arrows at the bottom of the screen allow you to examine different versions of the content.

23. Confirm that version two of the Grocery List content is displayed and then click the **Restore to original location** (green circular arrow) button.

24. In the Replace or Skip Files dialog box, click **Replace the file in the destination**.

25. Close the File History window.

26. In the Settings window, scroll to the bottom and click **Stop using drive**. If you receive an error here, a window is open that is viewing File History information.

27. On the taskbar, click File Explorer and then browse to the drive letter you noted in Step 11 of Activity 9-9.

28. Navigate to the folder H:\FileHistory*UserX**PcX*\Data\C\Users*UserX*\Desktop, where H: is the drive letter noted in Step 11, *UserX* is the user you are signed in as, and *PcX* is the name of your computer.

29. Review the versions of the Grocery List file in that folder and note the difference in the file names based on time.

30. Close all open windows.

31. Do not restart your computer or sign out before proceeding to the next activity to ensure that the File History Data virtual hard drive remains attached and available.

SYSTEM RECOVERY

If a computer running Windows 10 has minor problems, you might be able to resolve those errors by researching the issue and finding help online. Sometimes, however, it is not an effective use of time to spend hours troubleshooting and tinkering when you can perform a system recovery instead. If a computer running Windows 10 does not boot, you must perform a system recovery.

Windows 10 has two primary recovery options, shown in Figure 9-17. Reset this PC sets your computer back to the state of a newly installed instance of Windows 10. This is much like performing a factory reset on a tablet or phone. Advanced startup provides a number of options for troubleshooting startup or recovering from backup.

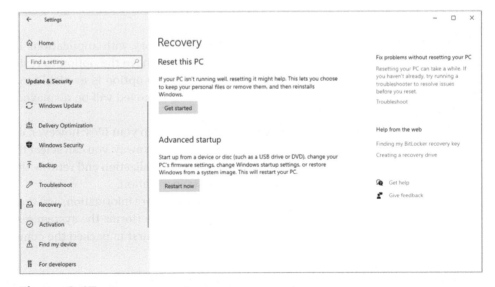

Figure 9-17   Recovery options

Reset this PC

When you choose Reset this PC as a recovery method, it removes all apps and puts settings back at their default values; however, you have the option to keep your data files and settings, as shown in Figure 9-18. When you keep files and settings, all user accounts and profiles are retained, but not application files in AppData.

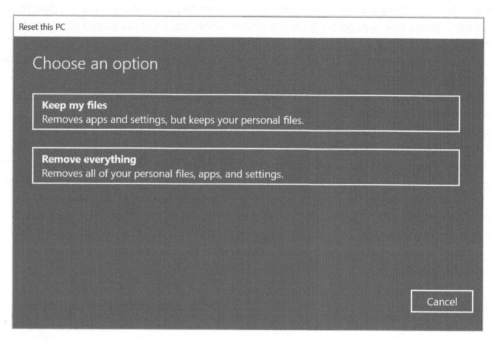

Figure 9-18   Reset this PC options

You also get the option to choose whether to perform a local reinstall or a cloud download. A local reinstall uses Windows 10 installation files that are already cached on your computer. A local reinstall avoids downloading installation files, but if you're concerned that malware might have infected those files, you should choose to perform a cloud download. A cloud download obtains the Windows 10 installation files over the Internet from Microsoft to avoid any risk of malware infecting the installation files.

 **CAUTION**   A cloud download will take significantly longer to perform than a local reinstall on a slow network connection because a large amount of data must be downloaded.

NOTE 4

For a detailed description of the steps performed during a reset, see Optimize Windows 10 PC reset using the cloud at https://insider.windows.com/en-us/articles/optimize-windows-10-pc-reset-using-the-cloud/.

If your computer came from the factory with applications installed and you selected to keep your files, you will likely have the option to restore the apps and settings that came with the computer. No option is available to retain apps that you have installed. A list of apps being removed will be displayed before the reset is performed.

Most of the time, you will choose to keep your files; however, if you are resetting the computer so that you can sell it or give it away, you can select the option to erase everything. This option removes all personalization and returns the computer to its initial configuration after a Windows installation.

Some vendors include customized restore information, and the option to restore factory settings might be displayed. This performs the system reset and takes you back to an experience similar to when you first unpacked the computer.

Activity 9-11: Performing a System Reset

Time Required: 60 minutes

Objective: Perform a system reset

Description: In this activity, you identify the reset options available in Settings and then perform a system reset. After performing a system reset, user data will be retained, but all custom settings will be removed.

1. If necessary, start your computer and sign in.
2. Click the **Start** button and then click **Settings**.
3. In the Settings window, click **Update & Security** and then click **Recovery**.
4. Below Reset this PC, click **Get started**.
5. In the Reset this PC window, click **Remove everything**.
6. Select **Local reinstall**.
7. On the Additional settings screen, click **Change settings**.
8. On the Choose settings screen, read the available options and then click **Cancel**.
9. In the Settings window, below Reset this PC, click **Get started**.
10. In the Reset this PC window, click **Keep my files**.
11. Select **Local reinstall**.
12. On the Additional settings screen, click **Change settings**.
13. On the Choose settings screen, read the available options and then click **Confirm**.
14. On the Additional settings screen, click **Next**.
15. On the Ready to reset this PC screen, click **View apps that will be removed**.
16. Read the list of apps and then click **Back**.
17. Click **Reset**.
18. Wait for the reset to be performed. This may take from 30 to 60 minutes depending on processing capacity and disk speed. The system will reboot several times as the Windows installation files are extracted and then Windows is reinstalled.
19. Sign in to your computer and verify that the **Grocery List** file is still on the desktop. Notice that a Removed Apps webpage has been added to the desktop.

Windows Recovery Environment

The Advanced startup option in recovery settings allows you to restart your computer in the Windows Recovery Environment (WinRE). WinRE is a small instance of Windows 10 that includes several options for troubleshooting and repairing Windows 10. During installation, Windows 10 creates a recovery partition to store WinRE (winre.wim). If Windows 10 is in a state where it does not start properly, the system might start in WinRE automatically. Figure 9-19 shows some of the options available in WinRE.

Some of the available options in WinRE are:

- *Use a device*—This option allows you to select an alternate boot device. You can use this to boot from a USB drive, network connection, or a recovery DVD. To use a recovery DVD, you must have manually created one before you need to perform a recovery.
- *Reset this PC*—This provides the same options as Reset this PC within Windows 10, but is accessible when Windows 10 doesn't start properly.
- *Startup Repair*—This is an automated tool that attempts to fix common issues that prevent Windows 10 from starting.
- *Startup Settings*—This allows you to select from a variety of startup modes with limited functionality, such as low-resolution video or Safe Mode. Sometimes you can use these limited modes to start Windows 10 and perform further troubleshooting when Windows 10 won't start.

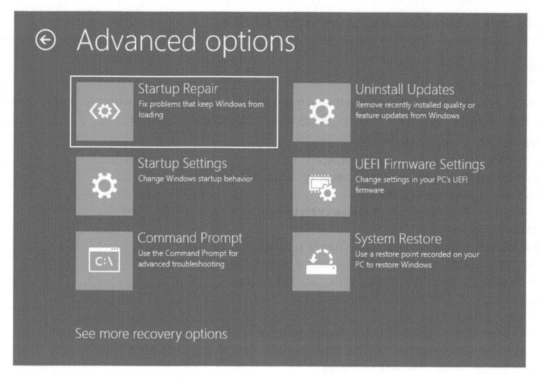

Figure 9-19   WinRE, Advanced options

- *Uninstall Updates*—Use this option to remove the most recent quality or feature update. This is useful when a recent update has created a problem and Windows won't start.
- *UEFI Firmware Settings*—Restarts your computer to edit UEFI settings. This is an alternative to pressing a function before Windows starts to access these settings.
- *System Restore*—Allows you to restore system files to a point in time. To use this option, you need to have previously enabled restore points. Restore points are not enabled by default.
- *Command Prompt*—This starts a limited version of Windows 10 that includes command-line utilities, such as bcdedit.exe and bootrec.exe, that can be used to repair Windows 10. Attempt a fix by using Startup Repair before using this option.
- *System Image Recovery*—This option allows you to restore Windows 10 from a system image created by using Backup and Recovery (Windows 7).

Activity 9-12: Using WinRE

Time Required: 20 minutes

Objective: Use WinRE to repair Windows 10

Description: In this activity, you start WinRE and explore recovery options. You will perform a startup repair, use startup settings, and access a command prompt.

1. If necessary, start your computer and sign in.
2. Click the **Start** button and then click **Settings**.
3. In the Settings window, click **Update & Security** and then click **Recovery**.
4. Below Advanced startup, click **Restart now**.
5. On the Choose an option screen, click **Use a device**. This displays possible boot devices that you can use to boot recovery media.
6. Click the back arrow and then click **Troubleshoot**.
7. On the Troubleshoot screen, click **Advanced options**.
8. On the Advanced options screen, click **Startup Repair**.

9. On the Startup Repair screen, click **User1**, type your password, and then click **Continue**. To perform this task, you need to sign in as a user that is an administrator.

10. Wait a few moments for the repair to complete and then read the results onscreen. It reports that no repairs are necessary.

11. Click **Advanced options**, click **Troubleshoot**, and then click **Advanced options**.

12. On the Advanced options screen, click **Startup Settings**.

13. Read the information about Startup Settings and then click **Restart**.

14. Read the list of available options, consider when each of these might be useful, and then press **F4** to enter Safe Mode. Safe Mode has a limited set of drivers to avoid most startup problems related to Windows 10 configuration.

15. Sign in to your computer. Safe Mode text is displayed on the Desktop.

16. On the taskbar, click **Microsoft Edge**. An error is displayed indicating that no network connectivity is found. This is expected in Safe Mode.

17. Click the **Start** button and then click **Settings**.

18. In the Settings window, click **Update & Security** and then click **Recovery**.

19. Under Advanced startup, click **Restart now**.

20. Click **Troubleshoot** and then click **Advanced options**.

21. On the Advanced options screen, click **Command Prompt**.

22. On the Command Prompt screen, click **User1**, type your password, and then click **Continue**. To perform this task, you need to sign in as a user that is an administrator.

23. At the command prompt, type **bcdedit** and then press **Enter**.

24. Read the boot information provided by bcdedit. Windows 10 is configured to boot from the C: drive. The X: drive currently used at the command prompt is a limited version of Windows 10 used for recovery.

25. Type **bcdedit /?** and then press **Enter**. Review the help information for bcdedit.

26. Type **dir *.exe** and then press **Enter**. Review the list of executables available in the recovery environment.

27. Type **bootrec /?** and then press Enter. Review the help information for bootrec.

28. Type **dism /image:C:\ /cleanup-image /scanhealth** and then press **Enter**. If this command reports errors, you can use the /restorehealth option to attempt to repair it.

29. Type **exit** and then press **Enter**.

30. On the Choose an option screen, click **Continue**.

Restore Points

Restore points can offer a quick way to recover from an application or operating system update that is causing stability problems in Windows 10. A **restore point** is a snapshot of system files and settings created at a specific point in time. User data files are not included in a restore point.

You can create restore points manually, but they are typically done automatically when an application or operating system update is performed. More than one restore point can be saved, creating a series of point-in-time snapshots of the system. When the storage space dedicated to restore points becomes too large, the oldest restore point is automatically removed.

System protection, shown in Figure 9-20, is disabled by default. You need to enable system protection before you can create restore points. The most important drive to be protected by System Restore is C: because it contains the operating system and applications.

An administrator can also use PowerShell commands in an elevated PowerShell session to update and automate the configuration of System Restore. The five cmdlets available include:

- *Enable-ComputerRestore*—Turn System Restore on for specified drives.
- *Disable-ComputerRestore*—Turn System Restore off for a specified drive.
- *Checkpoint-Computer*—Create a new restore point.
- *Get-ComputerRestorePoint*—Show all available restore points.
- *Restore-Computer*—Roll back to a specified restore point.

You can also start the Restore system files and settings utility from an elevated command prompt using the rstrui.exe command. This can be useful when you can only start the computer in Safe Mode with Command Prompt.

Figure 9-20   System Properties, System Protection tab

Activity 9-13: Configuring System Restore Points

Time Required: 15 minutes

Objective: Configure system restore points

Description: In this activity, you configure system restore points and create an initial restore point manually. After the restore point is created, you use it to roll back the computer configuration to that earlier configuration.

1. If necessary, start your computer and sign in.
2. Click the **Start** button, type **restore**, and then click **Create a restore point**.
3. In the System Properties dialog box, click **Local Disk (C:) (System)** and then click the **Configure**.
4. Move the slider in the Disk Space Usage section to change the maximum usage to **10%**.
5. Click **Turn on system protection** and then click **OK**.
6. Click **Create** to manually create a restore point.
7. In the System Protection dialog box, type **First manual restore point** and then click **Create**.
8. Wait for the status message that the restore point was created successfully and then click **Close**.
9. Click **System Restore**.
10. On the Restore system files and settings screen, click **Next**.
11. Select **First manual restore point** and then click **Scan for affected programs**. This checks to see if any programs or drivers will change as a result of rolling back the computer configuration to this restore point.
12. Verify that no changes to programs or drivers are detected and then click **Close**.
13. Click **Next** to proceed to the review screen.
14. On the Confirm your restore point screen, click **Finish**, and when prompted to confirm the action, click **Yes**.
15. Wait for the restore to complete and then sign in.
16. Note the message that the restore has completed successfully and then click **Close**.

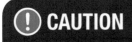 **CAUTION** It is common for computer accounts to lose their trust relationship with the domain when you roll back to a restore point. This is because the password for the computer account has changed since the restore point was configured. You can rejoin the domain to fix this error.

Recovery Drive

A **recovery drive** is bootable media that you can use to repair or reinstall Windows 10. Using a recovery drive is an alternative when you can't access the recovery partition for your Windows 10 installation. When you boot from a recovery drive, you see the same WinRE interface as when you choose the Advanced startup option in recovery settings.

 **CAUTION** A recovery drive does not contain applications or user data.

To create a recovery drive, you use an external drive. All data on the external drive is erased when you create the recovery drive. So, verify the external drive contents before you create the recovery drive.

When you create a recovery drive, the WinRE files take about 500 MB of disk space. If you select to backup system files, a full copy of Windows 10 is also stored on the recovery drive and about 16 GB of disk space is used.

A recovery drive is bit-specific. If you create a recovery drive from a 64-bit version of Windows 10, then that recovery drive can be used to repair only a 64-bit version of Windows 10 and not a 32-bit version of Windows 10.

If a local drive in the computer already was identified as a recovery drive, you might be asked if you want it deleted now that you have an external recovery drive. Unless you need to reclaim disk space, leave the existing recovery drive. It is more convenient to use the local recovery drive when possible.

 TIP The option create a recovery drive is available in Control Panel.

SUMMARY

- Establishing a baseline for performance tuning allows you to recognize variations from normal system behavior and identify system bottlenecks. The four main areas that cause bottlenecks are disk, memory, processor, and network.
- Task Manager allows you to quickly view system process information. Process information includes memory utilization and processor utilization. In addition, you can monitor network utilization.
- Resource Monitor provides more detailed information than Task Manager, such as the network utilization of each process. You can also filter by process to monitor all the resources a specific process is using.
- Performance Monitor can be used to monitor system performance and reliability, create alerts, log performance activity, and generate reports.
- Performance Options allow you to configure visual effects, processor scheduling, virtual memory, and Data Execution Prevention (DEP). In most cases, the default configuration for these settings is acceptable.
- Applications that start automatically can affect system performance. To configure application startup, you can use application settings, Task Manager, or Autoruns. Applications can be configured to start automatically in registry keys, the Startup folder of the Start menu, and scheduled tasks.
- To gather information to help troubleshoot errors in Windows 10 or apps, you can use Steps Recorder, Reliability Monitor, and Event Viewer.
- To protect user data, you can use Windows 10 features such as File History and Backup and Restore (Windows 7). After these options are configured, you can access previous versions of files.
- The Windows 10 operating system has many tools available for improved operating system recovery, including recovery disk, system image backup, system restore points, and the WinRE environment.

Key Terms

Alert	File History	restore point
Backup and Restore (Windows 7)	Performance Monitor	Steps Recorder
baseline	performance tuning	Task Manager
bottleneck	Previous Versions	virtual memory
counters	recovery drive	Windows Recovery Environment
Data Collector Set	Reliability Monitor	(WinRE)
Data Execution Prevention (DEP)	Reset this PC	
Data Manager	Resource Monitor	

Review Questions

1. Performance monitoring is the act of changing a system's configuration systematically and carefully observing performance before and after such changes. True or False?

2. Which of the following can Task Manager monitor? (Choose all that apply.)
   a. memory utilization for each process
   b. network utilization for each process
   c. CPU utilization for each process
   d. disk utilization for each process

3. Which of the following can be used to start Task Manager? (Choose all that apply.)
   a. Ctrl+Alt+Delete
   b. running taskman.exe
   c. Ctrl+Shift+Esc
   d. right-clicking the taskbar
   e. restart in Safe Mode

4. In Performance Monitor, all performance objects have the same counters. True or False?

5. Which Performance Monitor component records log files?
   a. Performance Monitor
   b. Reliability Monitor
   c. Data Collection Sets
   d. Alerts
   e. Reports

6. Each Data Collector Set can contain only a single counter. True or False?

7. What is the most common physical symptom of insufficient memory?
   a. excessive heat coming from the computer
   b. graphics displayed incorrectly on the monitor
   c. a memory error code displayed on the screen
   d. high levels of disk activity
   e. three short beeps from the computer

8. File History is designed to roll back device drivers. True or False?

9. When a component is the slowest part of a process, it is referred to as a(n) _____.

10. You know that you will be making some major changes to your computer and you want to back up all your user data and the local operating system. This can be accomplished by selecting all drive data to create a:
    a. recovery drive
    b. WinRE environment
    c. System Image disk
    d. File History
    e. previous version

11. The event logs most commonly used for troubleshooting are located in the Applications and Services Logs node. True or False?

12. Which backup and restore function can you use to set a computer back to its factory default settings without any additional media?
    a. System Restore
    b. File History
    c. Windows Recovery Environment (WinRE)
    d. Recovery Drive
    e. Reset this PC

13. Which backup and restore function can you use to create a system image that includes the apps you have installed?
    a. System Restore
    b. File History
    c. Windows Recovery Environment (WinRE)
    d. third-party backup software
    e. System Reset

14. Which tool can you use to gather screenshots of a user demonstrating a problem?
    a. Remote Desktop
    b. Steps Recorder
    c. Reliability Monitor
    d. Event Viewer
    e. Remote Assistance

15. Which tool can you use to identify the point in time at which a computer running Windows 10 started to become unstable?
    a. Remote Desktop
    b. Steps Recorder
    c. Reliability Monitor
    d. Event Viewer
    e. Remote Assistance

16. Resource Monitor can be used to monitor the amount of data sent over various network connections. True or False?

17. Which is the best solution for backing up user data?
    a. OneDrive
    b. File History
    c. Backup and Restore (Windows 7)
    d. Previous Versions
    e. Cloud History

18. What is the first option you should investigate when you want a program to stop running when users sign in?

    a. a registry value in HKLM:\Software\Microsoft\Windows\CurrentVersion\Run
    b. a shortcut in the Startup menu of the Start menu
    c. a registry value in HKCU:\Software\Microsoft\Windows\CurrentVersion\Run
    d. the application settings
    e. schedule tasks

19. Which Event Viewer feature should you use to view events in multiple logs?
    a. Filter
    b. Find
    c. Custom view
    d. Subscription
    e. Custom log

20. Which command do you need to run on the source computer to allow remote access to event logs for a subscription?
    a. wecutil qc
    b. winrm quickconfig
    c. eventvwr subsetup
    d. net set event
    e. enable-WinRM

Case Projects

Case 9-1: Collecting Performance Data

Gigantic Life Insurance has several batch jobs that run on Windows 10 computers overnight. The batch jobs are scheduled overnight because they require all the performance capability of the computers and must be completed by morning for staff to perform their regular work. The batch jobs always use approximately the same amount of data, but occasionally they are not finished in the morning, resulting in lost productivity. Describe how you would determine the cause of the slow processing.

Case 9-2: Identifying Data Recovery Methods

You are interviewing for a job as a system administrator at Deep Woods Campers and Trailers, a manufacturer of recreation trailers for camping. All 150 office staff and 600 manufacturing staff use computers. The office staff have a mix of desktop computers and mobile computers. The mobile computers are regularly used outside of the office at home and on sales calls. The manufacturing staff share computers located on the production floor to track the production process. The interviewer has asked for your opinion on the best way to protect user data and recover it when a computer running Windows 10 fails.

ENTERPRISE COMPUTING

After reading this module and completing the exercises, you will be able to:

1. Understand Active Directory
2. Use Group Policy to control Windows 10
3. Describe enterprise management tools for Windows 10
4. Configure enterprise file services for Windows 10
5. Describe Microsoft cloud services

In the computer industry, the term enterprise is used to describe large companies with needs that are different from smaller companies. Enterprise products typically have much better features for manageability than those used by smaller companies. Enterprise deployments of Windows 10 have unique challenges that need to be addressed.

In this module, you learn how Active Directory and Group Policy can be used to manage hundreds or thousands of Windows 10 computers. Enterprise management tools for Windows 10 can also be used to deploy software and configure Windows 10 computers in large environments. You'll also learn how enterprise file services differ from simple file sharing. Finally, Microsoft cloud services and how they are used by enterprises is described.

ACTIVE DIRECTORY

Microsoft includes Active Directory as a centralized directory service that can be used to control a network of Windows computers. When you implement a domain-based network by using Active Directory, you enable centralized management that is much more scalable than a workgroup-based network. To allow for centralized management, computers running Windows 10 are joined to the domain, and a computer account is created in the domain. User accounts are also managed centrally in the domain, rather than on each computer.

A **domain controller** is a server that holds a copy of Active Directory information. Domain controllers are responsible for authenticating users when they sign in to a workstation. After users are authenticated, they can access network resources. Domain controllers also respond to requests for other domain information, such as printer information or application configuration.

NOTE 1

Microsoft rebranded several services under the Active Directory name and uses the term Active Directory Domain Services (AD DS) to refer to what was previously known as Active Directory. The term Active Directory is still commonly used by IT professionals and is used throughout this book.

Active Directory Structure

The key feature of Active Directory is a **domain**. A domain has a central security database that is used by all computers that are members of the domain. This central database means that user accounts can be created once in the domain and then used to sign in at any workstation in the domain. No matter which workstation the user signs in at, the user gains access to all the appropriate network resources. There are no concerns about synchronizing passwords because only one central account is used.

In addition to user account information, domains also store information about computers. Each computer that is a member of the domain has an account in Active Directory. Information about applications and printers is also found in Active Directory. DNS information is often stored in Active Directory, too.

Active Directory uses the same naming convention for domains and objects contained in these domains as DNS. For example, an Active Directory domain can be named GiganticLife.com. Active Directory domains and DNS domains, however, contain very different content. Many organizations use the same DNS domain name for Active Directory and the Internet email, but it is not required.

Organizational Units

Each domain can be subdivided into **organizational units (OUs)**. Using OUs allows you to organize the objects in a domain. For example, you can organize the users in a domain by department by creating an OU for each department. This makes it easier to find the user accounts that you are looking for. Figure 10-1 shows how OUs are displayed when using the Active Directory Users and Computers administrative tool on the server.

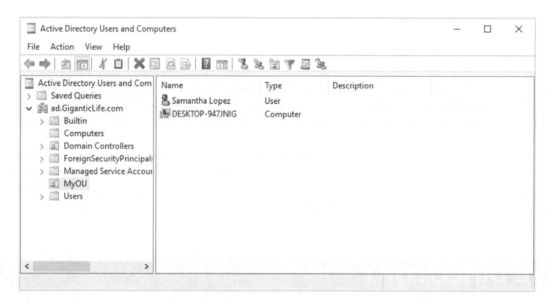

Figure 10-1   Active Directory Users and Computers

OUs can also be used for delegating management permissions. For example, you can delegate the capability of creating and managing objects in the Marketing OU to an administrator assigned to the Marketing department. That administrator will not be able to create and manage objects in the OUs of other departments.

Finally, OUs are used to apply group policies. Group policies can be applied to a specific OU, which applies Group Policy settings to the user accounts or computer accounts in the OU. For example, you could create a group policy with marketing-specific settings and apply it to the Marketing OU.

Trees and Forests

In most cases, a single domain subdivided into OUs is sufficient to manage a network; however, you can create more complex Active Directory structures by combining multiple domains into a tree and multiple trees into a **forest**. Figure 10-2 shows a single Active Directory forest with two trees. The domains using ad.GiganticLife.com are one tree and the domains in EnormousLife.com are another tree. Europe.ad.GiganticLife and Asia.ad.GiganticLife are subdomains of ad.GiganticLife.com.

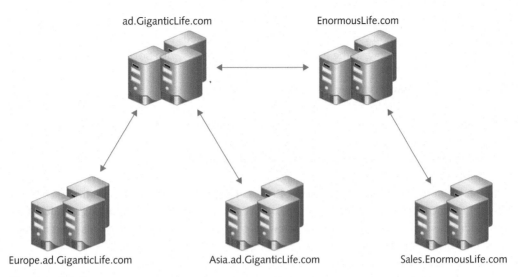

ad.GiganticLife.com   EnormousLife.com

Europe.ad.GiganticLife.com   Asia.ad.GiganticLife.com   Sales.EnormousLife.com

Figure 10-2   Domains, trees, and trusts

When multiple domains exist in a forest, trust relationships are automatically generated among the domains. This allows administrators to give users in one domain access to resources in another domain.

Server Roles

Within Active Directory, Windows servers can be either member servers or domain controllers. Member servers are integrated into Active Directory and can participate in the domain by sharing files and printers with domain users. Windows 10 computers integrate into Active Directory in the same way as member servers. Windows 10, however, is a desktop operating system and is not able to function as either a member server or a domain controller.

Activity 10-1: Installing a Domain Controller

Time Required: 1.5 hours
Objective: Install a Windows Server 2019 domain controller
Description: To create a single centralized security database, you must have a computer running Windows Server configured as a domain controller. In this activity, you install Windows Server 2019 and configure the server as a domain controller.

NOTE 2

The preferred method for implementing this activity is for students to have their own virtual machines in an isolated environment. Client Hyper-V can be used for the server installed in this activity; however, you can use a single server shared by multiple students. In such a case, you need to modify the activities slightly to ensure that each student is not affecting other students. Some parts, such as this activity, must be demonstrated.

1. Place the Windows Server 2019 DVD in the computer and start it.
2. Press a key to boot from the DVD when prompted.
3. In the Windows Setup window, click **Next** to accept the default language, time, and keyboard settings.
4. Click **Install now**.
5. If necessary, on the Activate Windows screen, click **I don't have a product key**. This screen does not appear when you install the evaluation version of Windows Server 2019.
6. On the Select the operating system you want to install screen, click **Windows Server 2019 Standard Evaluation (Desktop Experience)** and click **Next**. This name will not include the word Evaluation if you are using volume license media.
7. On the Applicable notices and license terms screen, select the **I accept the license terms** check box and then click **Next**.
8. On the Which type of installation do you want screen, click **Custom: Install Windows only (advanced)**.

9. On the Where do you want to install Windows screen, if any preexisting partitions exist, delete them all, click **Drive 0 Unallocated Space**, and then click **Next**. The install proceeds and will reboot.

10. In the Customize settings window, in the Password and Reenter password boxes, type **Passw0rd** (0 is zero) and then click **Finish**.

11. Sign in to your server as **Administrator** with a password of **Passw0rd**.

12. In the Networks area, click **Yes** to make the server discoverable and then wait for Server Manager to start.

13. In the Server Manager dialog box, select the **Don't show this message again** check box and then close the dialog box.

14. In Server Manager, in the navigation pane, click **Local Server**.

15. Next to Ethernet, click **IPv4 address assigned by DHCP, IPv6 enabled**.

16. Right-click **Ethernet** and then click **Properties**.

17. In the Ethernet Properties window, click **Internet Protocol Version 4 (TCP/IPv4)** and then click **Properties**.

18. In the Internet Protocol Version 4 (TCP/IPv4) Properties window, click **Use the following IP address** and then enter an IP address, subnet mask, and default gateway assigned by your instructor. This server needs to be on the same IP network as the client you will be connecting to it.

19. In the Preferred DNS server box, type **127.0.0.1** and then click **OK**. This server will be configured as a DNS server.

20. In the Ethernet Properties window, click **Close**.

21. Close the Network Connections window.

22. Next to Computer name, click the computer name.

23. In the System Properties window, on the Computer Name tab, click **Change**.

24. In the Computer Name/Domain Changes window, in the Computer name box, type **DC** and then click **OK**. If your environment is coexisting with other students, obtain a unique name from your instructor.

25. In the Computer Name/Domain Changes dialog box, click **OK**.

26. In the System Properties window, click **Close**.

27. In the Microsoft Windows dialog box, click **Restart Now**.

28. Sign in to your server as **Administrator** with the password of **Passw0rd**.

29. In Server Manager, click **Manage** and then click **Add Roles and Features**.

30. In the Add Roles and Features Wizard, click **Next**.

31. On the Select installation type screen, click **Role-based or feature-based installation** and then click **Next**.

32. On the Select destination server screen, click **DC** and then click **Next**.

33. On the Select server roles screen, select the **Active Directory Domain Services** check box.

34. In the Add Roles and Features Wizard dialog box, click **Add Features**.

35. On the Select server roles screen, click **Next**.

36. On the Select features screen, click **Next**.

37. On the Active Directory Domain Services screen, read the information and then click **Next**.

38. On the Confirm installation selections screen, click **Install**.

39. Wait a few minutes for installation to complete and then click **Close**.

40. In Server Manager, click **Notifications** and then click **Promote this server to a domain controller**.

41. In the Active Directory Domain Services Configuration Wizard, on the Deployment Configuration screen, click **Add a new forest**.

42. In the Root domain name, type **ad.GiganticLife.com** and click **Next**. If your environment is coexisting with other students, obtain a unique name from your instructor.

43. On the Domain Controller Options screen, in the Password and Confirm password boxes, type **Passw0rd** and then click **Next**.

44. On the DNS Options screen, click **Next**.

45. On the Additional Options screen, click **Next**. If your environment is coexisting with other students, obtain a unique name from your instructor.

46. On the Paths screen, click **Next**.

47. On the Review Options screen, read the information and then click **Next**.

48. Wait for the prerequisite check to complete and then click **Install**.

49. In the You're about to be signed out dialog box, click **OK**.

50. After the reboot, sign in as **AD\Administrator** with a password of **Passw0rd**. The first startup might take a few minutes.

 This domain controller is suitable for use by a single student. If the domain controller is being shared by multiple students, you can enable the server as an RD Session Host to allow multiple students to connect simultaneously. Alternatively, you can have students install the Remote Server Admin Tools (RSAT) to perform Active Directory management tasks from Windows 10.

Active Directory Partitions

Active Directory is not a single monolithic database with all the information about the network. To make Active Directory more manageable, it is divided into the domain partition, configuration partition, and schema partition:

- The **domain partition** holds the user accounts, computer accounts, and other domain-specific information. This partition is replicated only to domain controllers in the same domain.
- The **configuration partition** holds general information about the Active Directory forest. Also, applications, such as Exchange Server, use the configuration partition to store application-specific information. This partition is replicated to all domain controllers in the Active Directory forest.
- The **schema partition** holds the definitions of all objects and object attributes for the forest. This partition is replicated to all domain controllers in the Active Directory forest.

NOTE 3

Active Directory also contains application partitions, but they are outside the scope of this course.

One special case for replication of information in the domain partition is global catalog servers. A **global catalog server** is a domain controller that holds a subset of the information in all domain partitions. For example, a global catalog has information about all users in the entire Active Directory forest, but only some of the information that is available about the users in each domain. Global catalog servers are used to hold the membership of universal groups and by applications, such as Microsoft Exchange Server. Exchange Server uses global catalog servers to perform address book lookups and locate user mailboxes.

Active Directory Sites and Replication

Active Directory uses multimaster replication. This means that Active Directory information can be changed on any domain controller and those changes will be replicated to other domain controllers. This process ensures that all domain controllers have the same information. Replication, however, is not immediate, and the amount of time required to replicate data depends on whether domain controllers are in the same site or different sites.

An **Active Directory site** represents a physical location in your network; however, Active Directory is not aware of physical locations, and sites are defined by IP subnets. As administrator, you create sites and define the IP subnets in each site. In most cases, you should create an Active Directory site for each physical location in your network. If you have fast (10 Mbps) and reliable WAN links, however, you can consider making separate physical locations part of the same site.

Within a site, Active Directory replication is uncontrolled. The replication process is completely automatic. When a change is made to an Active Directory object, the change replicates to all domain controllers in the site after five seconds.

Between sites, Active Directory replication is controlled by site links. By default, all replication is controlled by a single site link that allows replication to occur every 180 minutes, but this can be shortened to 15 minutes.

Active Directory and DNS

One of the more common configuration problems in Active Directory networks is incorrect DNS configuration on servers and workstations. Proper configuration of DNS is essential for using Active Directory. Active Directory stores information about domain controllers and other services in DNS. Workstations use the information in DNS to find domain controllers in their local site and sign in.

Incorrect DNS configuration can result in:

- Slow user sign-ins
- Inability to apply group policies
- Failed replication among domain controllers

All domain-joined workstations and servers should be configured to use an internal DNS server. This ensures that all domain controllers register their information in the correct location and that all workstations have access to domain controller information. The internal DNS server can resolve Internet DNS records on behalf of clients, as well. An external DNS server that is provided by an Internet service provider is typically unable to accept dynamic registration of DNS records, which is required for Active Directory.

Activity 10-2: Viewing Active Directory DNS Records

Time Required: 10 minutes
Objective: View the DNS records for Active Directory
Description: Active Directory DNS records are used by Windows 10 to locate domain controllers and other domain services. In this activity, you use the DNS management tool console to view the DNS records registered by a domain controller.

> **(!) CAUTION** If you are using a shared server, use Remote Desktop Connection to sign in to the domain controller from your Windows 10 computer or the DNS RSAT tool.

1. Sign in to the DC as **AD\Administrator** with a password of **Passw0rd**.
2. If necessary, click the **Start** button and then click **Server Manager**.
3. In Server Manager, click **Tools** and then click **DNS**.
4. In the left pane, expand **DC**, expand **Forward Lookup Zones**, and then click **_msdcs.ad.GiganticLife.com**. This is the DNS domain that holds DNS records for Active Directory.
5. Expand **_msdcs.ad.GiganticLife.com**, expand **dc**, and then click **_tcp**. Notice that DC.ad.GiganticLife.com is listed for the _kerberos and _ldap services. These records are used by clients to find a domain controller for sign-in.
6. Expand **Sites**, expand **Default-First-Site-Name**, and then click **_tcp**. Notice that DC.ad.GiganticLife.com is listed for the _kerberos and _ldap services in this Active Directory site.
7. Close all open windows.

Joining a Domain

When a workstation joins a domain, it is integrated into the security structure for the domain. Administration of the workstation can be performed centrally by using Group Policy. Also, domain administrators are automatically given the ability to manage the workstation.

The following security changes occur when a workstation joins a domain:

- The Domain Admins group becomes a member of the local Administrators group.
- The Domain Users group becomes a member of the local Users group.
- The Domain Guests group becomes a member of the local Guests group.

The process of joining a workstation to a domain creates a computer account. It is this computer account that allows the workstation to integrate with Active Directory. If the computer account is removed, the workstation can no longer be used to access domain resources by users with domain-based accounts.

By default, all domain users can create 10 computer accounts in Active Directory. To increase security, many organizations change this limit to zero and prevent standard users from joining computers to the domain. If your organization makes this change, then only users that are assigned the appropriate permissions can create computer accounts. A standard user can still join a computer to the domain if an administrator creates the computer account in Active Directory before the computer is joined to the domain. The pre-staged computer account needs to have the same name as the computer running Windows 10.

By default, a computer account changes its password in the domain every 30 days. This happens in the background automatically. If the computer operating system is restored, the password that is restored might be an old password, which prevents the computer from authenticating. At this point, Windows 10 might present a message indicating that the trust relationship with the domain has been lost. One way to fix this is to put the computer back in a workgroup and rejoin the domain.

You can also use the Test-ComputerSecureChannel PowerShell cmdlet. The Test-ComputerSecureChannel cmdlet reports the status of the trust relationship with the domain. If the trust relationship is broken, you can use the -Repair parameter to fix it.

Activity 10-3: Joining a Domain

Time Required: 15 minutes

Objective: Join Windows 10 to an Active Directory domain

Description: Joining a domain integrates Windows 10 into the security system for Active Directory. In this activity, you join a Windows 10 workstation to an Active Directory domain and view the security changes.

 **CAUTION**   This activity can be performed with a physical computer or a virtual machine with Windows 10 installed. The computer must be on the same IPv4 network as the domain controller and must be using the domain controller for the DNS server. Make these changes before beginning the activity.

1. If necessary, start your computer and sign in.
2. Click the **Start** button and then click **Settings**.
3. In the Settings window, click **Accounts** and then click **Access work or school**.
4. On the Access work or school screen, click **Connect**.
5. In the Microsoft account window, click **Join this device to a local Active Directory domain**.
6. In the Join a domain window, in the Domain name box, type **ad.GiganticLife.com** and then click **Next**.
7. Sign in as **Administrator** with a password of **Passw0rd**.
8. On the Add an account screen, click **Skip**. This screen provides you the opportunity to give a domain user account administrator permissions if required.
9. Click **Restart now**.
10. Sign in to your computer as **AD\Administrator** with a password of **Passw0rd**. Be sure to include the domain name to ensure you don't attempt to sign in as the local Administrator account.
11. Right-click the **Start** button and then click **Computer Management**.
12. In the Computer Management window, expand **Local Users and Groups**, click **Groups**, and then double-click **Administrators**.
13. In the Administrator Properties window, verify that AD\Domain Admins has been added to the Administrators group and click **OK**.
14. Double-click **Users**, verify that AD\Domain Users has been added to the Users group, and then click **OK**.
15. Close the Computer Management window.
16. Right-click the **Start** button and click **Windows PowerShell (Admin)**. You are not prompted by UAC because you are signed in as the domain administrator account.
17. At the Windows PowerShell prompt, type **Test-ComputerSecureChannel** and then press **Enter**. The status True indicates that the trust relationship with the domain is working properly.
18. Close the Windows PowerShell prompt window.

Time Synchronization

Time synchronization is a critical part of Active Directory authentication. If the clock on a computer running Windows 10 is more than five minutes different from the domain controller, authentication to Active Directory fails. To ensure that time settings don't prevent authentication, domain-joined computers synchronize their time with domain controllers. Time is synchronized at startup and periodically afterwards. The time synchronization is based on network time protocol (NTP).

Before a Windows 10 computer is domain-joined, it synchronizes time with time.windows.com. This is a time server provided by Microsoft and available on the Internet. If the domain time and the time provided by time.windows.com are not within 5 minutes, you might need to manually set the time on the computer to match the domain to successfully join the domain. As a best practice, your domain should synchronize time with a time server on the Internet. This avoids potential time mismatches when joining a domain.

Time synchronization in Windows 10 is performed by the Windows Time service. This service is configured by setting registry key values, but you can view and modify the configuration by using w32tm.exe. If you need to force Windows 10 to resync time, the simplest method is restarting the Windows Time service.

 TIP   To complete reset time synchronizations settings, run w32tm /unregister and then w32tm /register.

Activity 10-4: View Time Synchronization Settings

Time Required: 5 minutes
Objective: View time synchronization settings for Windows 10
Description: Accurate time synchronization is a critical part of Active Directory authentication. In this activity, you verify the configuration of time synchronization on a domain-joined Windows 10 computer.

1. If necessary, start your computer and sign in as **AD\Administrator**.
2. Right-click the **Start** button and then click **Windows PowerShell (Admin)**.
3. At the Windows PowerShell prompt, type **Get-Service W32Time** and then press **Enter**. Verify that the Windows Time service is running.
4. To view help information for w32tm.exe, type **w32tm** and then press **Enter**. Scroll up and down to read the help information for w32tm.exe.
5. To view the configuration of time synchronization, type **w32tm /query /configuration** and then press **Enter**. Verify that below [TimeProviders] the Type is set to NT5DS. The type NT5DS means that time is being obtained from a domain controller.
6. To force Windows Time service to read new configuration settings, type **w32tm /resync /rediscover** and then press **Enter**.
7. Close the Windows PowerShell prompt window.

Offline Domain Join

In enterprise environments, sometimes a need arises to automate the domain join process and have it occur very quickly. The offline domain join process allows a Windows 10 computer to be joined to an Active Directory without ever directly communicating with the domain controller. This can also be required in high security environments where only domain-joined computers can connect to the local network.

NOTE 4

To see examples of using djoin .exe, see the Djoin page at https: //docs.microsoft.com/en-us/ previous-versions/windows /it-pro/windows-server-2012- r2-and-2012/ff793312(v=ws.11).

The high level steps to perform an offline domain join are as follows:

1. Run djoin.exe on Windows Server with the /provision option to create a computer account and a blob file. The blob file contains authentication information for the Windows 10 computer.
2. Copy the blob file to the Windows computer.

3. Run djoin.exe on the Windows 10 computer with the /requestodj option to import the blob file.

4. Reboot to apply the changes.

 **CAUTION**   You can use only local users for authentication until a domain controller is reachable.

GROUP POLICY

Group Policy is a feature integrated with Active Directory that can be used to centrally manage the configuration of a Windows 10 computer. You can use thousands of Group Policy settings to control almost any aspect of Windows 10, so many, in fact, that you shouldn't browse through them to find something useful. Instead, you configure specific settings based on documentation that instructs you how to accomplish a task. Or, you might browse a specific category of Group Policy settings to see if anything can help you to accomplish a specific task.

NOTE 5

If you want to browse a list of Windows 10 Group Policy settings, download the Group Policy Reference Spreadsheet at https://www.microsoft.com/en-us/download/101451.

The Group Policy settings used by Windows 10 are contained in a **Group Policy object (GPO)**. A GPO is a collection of registry settings applied to the Windows 10 computer. To apply GPO settings, the GPO is linked to an OU, Active Directory site, or domain. A GPO can also be applied locally to a single computer. Configuration of Group Policy Objects is performed with the Group Policy Management Console, as shown in Figure 10-3.

The settings in a GPO are divided into user settings and computer settings. The user settings are applied to any user accounts in the OU to which the GPO is linked. Computer settings in the GPO are applied to any computer accounts in the OU to which the GPO is linked. In Figure 10-4, if Bob signs in to WS1, the user settings from the GPO linked to the Marketing OU and the computer settings from the GPO linked to the Head Office OU are applied.

Windows workstations and member servers download Group Policy settings during startup and approximately every 90 minutes thereafter. If you are testing GPO settings, you can use the gpupdate utility to trigger faster Group Policy Object downloads and application. Domain controllers download Group Policy settings every 5 minutes.

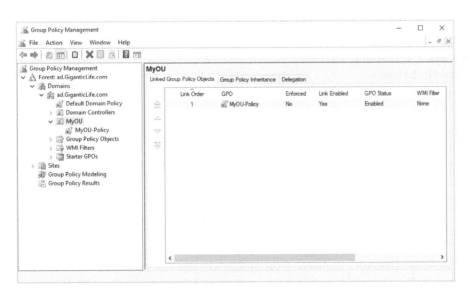

Figure 10-3   Group Policy Management

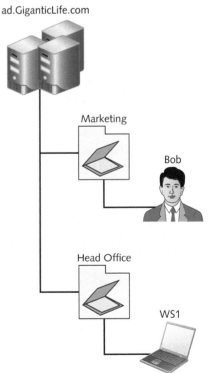

Figure 10-4   Group Policy application

Activity 10-5: Creating a GPO

Time Required: 15 minutes

Objective: Create and apply a Group Policy Object (GPO)

Description: You can create GPOs to control users and their workstations. In this activity, you create an OU, link a GPO to the OU, and verify that it is applied to your Windows 10 computer.

1. If necessary, start DC and sign in as **AD\Administrator** with a password of **Passw0rd**.
2. If necessary, start **Server Manager**.
3. In Server Manager, click **Tools** and then click **Active Directory Users and Computers**.
4. In the Active Directory Users and Computers window, expand **ad.GiganticLife.com** and then click **ad.GiganticLife.com**.
5. Right-click **ad.GiganticLife.com**, point to **New**, and then click **Organizational Unit**.
6. In the New Object - Organizational Unit dialog box, in the Name box, type **MyOU** and then click **OK**. If you are sharing the domain with other students, get a unique name for your OU from your instructor.
7. Right-click **MyOU**, point to **New**, and then click **User**.
8. In the New Object - User dialog box, in the First name box, type **Samantha**.
9. In the Last name box, type **Lopez**.
10. In the User logon name box, type **SLopez** and then click **Next**. If you are sharing the domain with other students, get a unique sign-in name from your instructor.
11. In the Password and Confirm password boxes, type **Passw0rd**.
12. Deselect the **User must change password at next logon** check box and then click **Next**.
13. Click **Finish** and then close the Active Directory Users and Computers window.
14. In Server Manager, click **Tools** and then click **Group Policy Management**.
15. In the Group Policy Management window, expand **Forest: ad.GiganticLife.com**, expand **Domains**, expand **ad.GiganticLife.com**, and then click **MyOU**.
16. Right-click **MyOU** and then click **Create GPO in this domain, and Link it here**.
17. In the New GPO dialog box, in the Name box, type **MyOU-Policy** and then click **OK**. If you are sharing the domain with other students, get a unique GPO name from your instructor.
18. In the Group Policy Management window, expand **MyOU**, right-click **MyOU-Policy** and then click **Edit**.
19. In the Group Policy Management Editor window, browse to **\User Configuration\Policies\Administrative Templates\System\Ctrl+Alt+Del Options.**
20. Double-click **Remove Task Manager**, click **Enabled**, and then click **OK**.
21. Close all open windows.
22. On your Windows 10 computer, sign in as **AD\Administrator** with a password of **Passw0rd**.
23. Right-click the **Start** button and then click **Windows PowerShell (Admin)**.
24. At the Windows PowerShell prompt, type **gpupdate** and then press **Enter**.
25. Sign out and sign in as **AD\SLopez** with a password of **Passw0rd**.
26. After the profile is ready, press **Ctrl+Alt+Delete**.
27. Verify that Task Manager is not available and then sign out.
28. Sign in as **AD\Administrator** with a password of **Passw0rd**.
29. Press **Ctrl+Alt+Delete**, verify that Task Manager is an option, and then click **Cancel**.

Group Policy Inheritance

Group Policy Objects can be linked to the Active Directory domains, OUs, and Active Directory sites. In addition, each Windows 10 computer can have local Group Policy Objects. It is essential to understand the precedence given to each of these policies. For example, when a local policy configures the home page for Microsoft Edge as http://www.microsoft.com

and a domain policy configures the home page for Microsoft Edge as http://intranet, which one is effective? The precedence determines what settings apply when there are conflicting settings between policies.

When a Windows computer starts, GPOs are applied in the following order:

1. Local computer
2. Site
3. Domain
4. Parent OU
5. Child OU

All the individual GPO settings are inherited by default. For example, a Group Policy setting on a parent OU is also applied to child OUs and to all users and computers in the child OUs. One computer or user can process many policies during startup and sign-in.

At each level, more than one GPO can be applied to a user or computer. If more than one GPO per container exists, the policies are applied in the order specified by the administrator. The following steps are used to determine which policy settings to apply:

1. If no conflict exists, the settings for all policies are applied.
2. If a conflict does exist, later settings overwrite earlier settings. For example, the setting from a domain policy overrides the setting from a local policy. This means that a child OU would be applied last and have the greatest priority by default.
3. If the settings in a computer policy and user policy conflict, the settings from the computer policy are applied.

When you are troubleshooting Group Policy application, it can be difficult to track down which policies are being applied. You can generate an HTML report to identify which Group Policy Objects are being applied. Use gpresult /h report.html to generate the report.

Activity 10-6: Generating a Report for GPO Troubleshooting

Time Required: 5 minutes

Objective: Generate and view a report for GPO troubleshooting

Description: When Group Policy settings are not being applied as you think they should be, it can be difficult to identify why. The gpresult.exe command can be used to generate a report that shows which GPOs and specific settings are being applied. In this activity, you use gpresult.exe to generate a report and then view the contents of the report.

1. Sign in to your Windows 10 computer as **AD\SLopez** with a password of **Passw0rd**.
2. Right-click the **Start** button and then click **Windows Powershell**.
3. At the Windows PowerShell prompt, type **gpresult /h report.html** and then press **Enter**.
4. Type **.\report.html** and then press **Enter**. In Windows PowerShell you need to use .\ to refer to the current directory when attempting to run an app.
5. Review the contents of the report. Notice that MyOU-Policy is an applied GPO. Also notice that no computer settings are reported because SLopez is not a local administrator and does not have the necessary permissions to view information about the computer.
6. Close all open windows.

Group Policy Preferences

A typical Group Policy setting is applied to a computer and cannot be changed by the user, even if the user has full administrative privileges to the computer. **Group Policy Preferences** are pushed down to the computer as part of the same process as Group Policy settings; however, a Group Policy Preference can be changed by the user. For example, you can use Group Policy Preferences to configure power options, such as configuring the computer to sleep after 10 minutes of inactivity. The user can manually change this; however, the next time the computer is restarted, the Group Policy Preference is reapplied.

Group Policy Preferences provide a way to configure many Windows 10 features that might have been done with scripting in the past. Many organizations have replaced logon scripts with Group Policy Preferences. Some of the things you can configure with Group Policy Preferences include:

- ODBC data sources
- Enable and disable devices
- Printers
- Drive mappings
- Scheduled tasks
- Service configuration
- VPN and dial-up connections
- Registry keys

One of the unique features of Group Policy Preferences is the ability to target them. By using targeting, you can have a single Group Policy Object that provides different settings for different users. For example, you can configure a drive mapping that is applied only if you are a member of the Sales group.

Activity 10-7: Configuring Group Policy Preferences

Time Required: 15 minutes

Objective: Configure and test Group Policy Preferences

Description: One of the common tasks performed by sign-in scripts is creating drive mappings. Management of drive mappings can be simplified by using Group Policy Preferences to apply the drive mappings. In this activity, you create a file share and then create a drive mapping to that file share that is distributed by using Group Policy Preferences.

1. If necessary, sign in to DC as **AD\Administrator** with a password of **Passw0rd**.
2. If necessary, open **Server Manager**.
3. In Server Manager, click **Tools** and then click **Computer Management**.
4. In Computer Management, expand **Shared Folders** and then click **Shares**.
5. Right-click **Shares** and then click **New Share**.
6. In the Create A Shared Folder Wizard, click **Next**.
7. In the Folder path box, type **C:\MyFolder** and then click **Next**. If you are sharing the domain with other students, obtain a unique folder name from your instructor.
8. Click **Yes** in the dialog box to create the folder.
9. On the Name, Description, and Settings screen, click **Next** to accept the default settings. Notice the Share path.
10. On the Shared Folder Permissions screen, click **Customize permissions** and then click **Custom**.
11. In the Customize Permissions window, with **Everyone** selected, select the **Allow Change** check box and then click **OK**.
12. Click **Finish** and then click **Finish** again.
13. On the taskbar, click **File Explorer** and browse to **C:**.
14. Right-click **MyFolder** and then click **Properties**.
15. In the MyFolder Properties dialog box, click the **Security** tab and then click **Edit**.
16. In the Permissions for MyFolder dialog box, click **Users (AD\Users)**, select the **Allow Modify** check box, and then click **OK** twice.
17. Close the File Explorer window.
18. In Server Manager, click **Tools** and then click **Group Policy Management**.
19. In the Group Policy Management window, click **Group Policy Objects**, right-click **MyOU-Policy**, and then click **Edit**.
20. In the Group Policy Management Editor window, below **User Configuration**, expand **Preferences**, expand **Windows Settings**, and then click **Drive Maps**.

21. Right-click **Drive Maps**, point to **New**, and then click **Mapped Drive**.
22. In the New Drive Properties dialog box, in the Location box, type **\\DC\MyFolder**.
23. In the Drive Letter area, click **Use** and then select **S** in the drop-down list.
24. Click the **Common** tab and review the options. Item-level targeting is the option used to apply preferences to specific groups of users.
25. Click **OK**.
26. Close all open windows.
27. On your Windows 10 computer, sign in as **AD\SLopez** with a password of **Passw0rd**.
28. Right-click the **Start** button and then click **Windows PowerShell**.
29. At the Windows PowerShell prompt, type **gpupdate** and then press **Enter**.
30. After the Group Policy update is complete, close the Windows PowerShell prompt window.
31. On the taskbar, click **File Explorer** and then click **This PC**. Notice that the S: drive is listed. If the S: drive is not listed, sign out and sign in again.
32. Close the File Explorer window.

Multiple Local Policies

In a nondomain environment, it can be useful to have different Group Policy settings applied to administrative and nonadministrative users. Typically, this functionality is useful when you are trying to set up a public computer that is locked down when signed in with a public account, but unlocked when signed in with an administrative user.

You can create a local GPO for any local group or local user. You cannot create a local GPO directly for domain users; however, a domain user can be a member of a local group, which has a local GPO. You select who a local GPO applies to in the Microsoft Management Console (MMC) when you are adding the Group Policy Object Editor snap-in, as shown in Figure 10-5. Creating a local GPO is typically done for special-purpose computers that are not connected to a domain.

Figure 10-5   Selecting a local Group Policy object

NOTE 6

By default, restrictions on device installation do not apply to users with local administrator permissions.

Controlling Device Installation

In a security-conscious organization, there are often concerns about users having the ability to remove organizational data by using a USB drive. One of the ways you can mitigate that risk is by controlling device installation. You can use Group Policy to define specific device types that are allowed or not allowed on the computer.

Identifying Devices

When a new device is installed in a Windows 10 computer, the operating system uses a device identification string and device setup class to properly install the new device. The **device identification string** is used to find an appropriate driver for the device. The **device setup class** controls how the device driver software is installed. Both the device identification string and the device setup class can be used when controlling the installation of devices.

A device often reports multiple device identification strings when queried by the operating system. A hardware ID is the most specific device identification string. When multiple hardware IDs are reported, there is typically one very specific hardware ID that includes make, model, and revision, then other less-specific hardware IDs, such as make and model. Figure 10-6 shows the hardware IDs for a disk drive.

Figure 10-6   Hardware IDs for a disk drive

Including multiple hardware IDs in a device allows the best available driver to be installed from those that are available. From a device installation control perspective, you can use the more generic hardware IDs to control installation rather than the very specific ones.

Device setup classes are used during the installation process for a new device to describe how the installation should be performed. The device setup class identifies a generic type of device rather than a specific make or model. Each device setup class is identified by a globally unique identifier (GUID).

Some devices have multiple GUIDs defined if they are multifunction devices, such as scanner/fax/printer devices. The parent device (overall device) has one GUID, and other functions (scanner, fax, printer) each have their own GUID.

Device Installation Group Policy Settings

Windows 10 includes Group Policy settings specifically to control device installation, as shown in Figure 10-7. They control which devices can and cannot be installed. Also, you can define a default option for whether users are allowed to install new devices. All of these settings are located in Computer Configuration\Policy\Administrative Templates\System\Device Installation\Device Installation Restrictions.

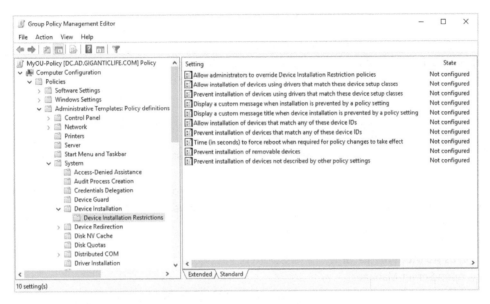

Figure 10-7   Device installation Group Policy Settings

Removable Storage Group Policy Settings

Because access to removable storage is a concern for many organizations, there are additional Group Policy settings, as shown in Figure 10-8, which can be used to control access to different types of removable storage, rather than preventing installation. With these policy settings, you can deny read or write access to specific removable storage types. All of these settings are located in Computer Configuration\Policies\Administrative Templates\System\Removable Storage Access and User Configuration\Policy\Administrative Templates\System\Removable Storage Access.

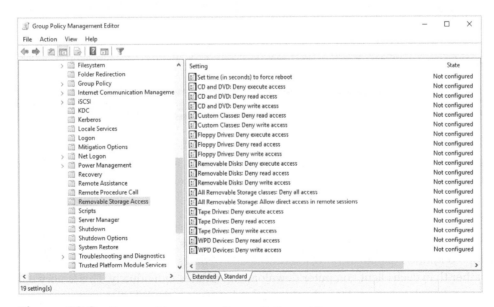

Figure 10-8   Removable storage Group Policy settings

In some cases, a reboot is required to enforce removable storage Group Policy settings. This is normally a problem only when a device is in use. In such a case, you can define how long the system waits to apply the changes before rebooting the system. Rebooting the system allows the policy changes to be applied.

Activity 10-8: Controlling Device Installation

Time Required: 15 minutes

Objective: Use Group Policy settings to control device installation

Description: Windows 10 includes a number of Group Policy settings to control the installation of devices and access to removable storage. In this activity, you use Group Policy settings to prevent the installation of any new disks, including portable storage devices, such as USB drives.

1. On your Windows 10 computer, sign in as **AD\Administrator** with a password of **Passw0rd**.
2. Right-click the **Start** button and then click **Device Manager**.
3. In the Device Manager window, expand **Disk drives**, right-click a disk installed in your system, and then click **Properties**.
4. In the disk Properties dialog box, click the **Details** tab, and in the Property box, select **Hardware Ids**. This displays the hardware IDs reported by your disk. Notice that the lowest value in the list is GenDisk. This is the least specific reference to your disk.
5. Close all open windows.
6. On DC, sign in as **AD\Administrator** with a password of **Passw0rd**.
7. If necessary, open Server Manager.
8. In Server Manager, click **Tools** and then click **Group Policy Management**.
9. In Group Policy Management, right-click **MyOU-Policy** and then click **Edit**.
10. In the Group Policy Management Editor, browse to Computer Configuration\Policies\Administrative Templates\System\Device Installation\Device Installation Restrictions.
11. Select each Group Policy setting and read the description.
12. Double-click **Prevent installation of devices using drivers that match these device setup classes**.
13. In the Prevent installation of devices using drivers that match these device setup classes window, click **Enabled** and then click **Show**.
14. In the Value box, type **GenDisk** and then click **OK**.
15. In the Prevent installation of devices using drivers that match these device setup classes dialog box, click **OK**.
16. Close all open windows.

ENTERPRISE MANAGEMENT TOOLS

Larger organizations need automated tools to simplify management of their desktop computers. Group Policy is a useful tool for many tasks, but it doesn't meet all the needs of large organizations. Three areas that often require additional tools are applying updates, deploying software, and managing BitLocker.

Windows Server Update Services

Windows Server Update Services (WSUS) is a role included in Windows Server to manage the deployment of Windows updates to desktop computers and servers. WSUS downloads updates from Microsoft Update and stores them in a local datastore, rather than each client computer downloading updates individually. This is very efficient for network utilization because each update is downloaded only once and stored on the WSUS server.

Client computers are configured to contact a WSUS server for updates rather than contacting the Microsoft update service directly. This can be configured by editing the registry or by using a Group Policy object.

WSUS is significantly more flexible than automatic updates downloaded directly from Microsoft. You can organize computers into groups to control the update process and generate reports to view which computers have been updated and which have not. The ability to test updates before they are generally applied to workstations significantly reduces the risk of an update causing system downtime. You can also use WSUS to remove updates that have already been installed. The WSUS update process is shown in Figure 10-9.

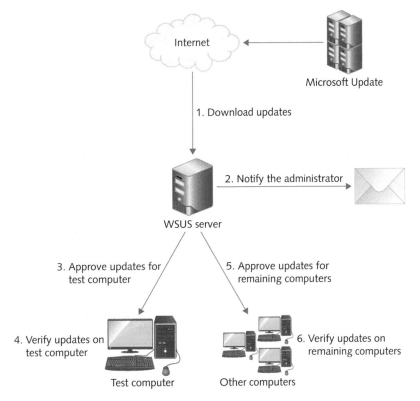

Figure 10-9   WSUS update process

The WSUS update process still relies on the client computers to trigger the installation of updates. After updates are approved for a specific computer, the update is downloaded by that computer from the WSUS server the next time Automatic Updates is triggered.

You can configure rules on the WSUS server to automatically approve some updates for specific computers. For example, you might want to automatically approve all updates for your test computers to reduce administrative work.

The updates downloaded automatically from Microsoft can be controlled by product, product family, update classification, and language. For example, you can choose to download only English updates or only critical updates. You can manually specify to download an update that is not configured to download automatically.

Activity 10-9: Configuring Clients for WSUS

Time Required: 10 minutes
Objective: Use Group Policy settings to configure clients to use WSUS
Description: After installing and configuring a WSUS server, you need to configure clients to use the WSUS server. In this activity, you use Group Policy settings to configure clients to use a WSUS server.

NOTE 7

This Activity performs only the steps required to configure the WSUS client, because configuring a WSUS server is outside the scope of the course.

1. On DC, sign in as **AD\Administrator** with a password of **Passw0rd**.
2. If necessary, open Server Manager.

3. In Server Manager, click **Tools** and then click **Group Policy Management**.
4. In the Group Policy Management window, right-click **MyOU-Policy** and then click **Edit**.
5. In the Group Policy Management Editor, browse to **Computer Configuration\Policies\Administrative Templates\Windows Components\Windows Update**.
6. Select each of the Group Policy settings and read the description.
7. Double-click **Specify intranet Microsoft update service location**.
8. In the Specify intranet Microsoft update service location dialog box, click **Enabled**.
9. In the Set the intranet update service for detecting updates and Set the intranet statistics server text boxes, type **http://wsus.ad.GiganticLife.com** and then click **OK**. This step assumes that you have a Windows server with WSUS installed with the name wsus.ad.GiganticLife.com.
10. Close all open windows.

Microsoft Endpoint Configuration Manager

Many large organizations use **Microsoft Endpoint Configuration Manager** to help manage on-premises desktop computers that are domain-joined. In small organizations, it's possible to configure computers manually or have a single standardized configuration. In large organizations, many different variations are required to support the needs of different user groups. Configuration Manager provides management flexibility for groups of users and computers.

 TIP Microsoft Endpoint Configuration Manager is part of Microsoft Endpoint Manager. This product was formerly known as System Center Configuration Manager.

NOTE 8

For more information on Microsoft Endpoint Configuration Manager, see the product documentation at https://docs.microsoft.com/en-us/mem/configmgr/.

You can use Configuration Manager to help with the following tasks:

- Desktop analytics, which includes hardware and software inventory
- Deploy updates for Windows operating systems and non-Microsoft apps
- App deployment with greater flexibility than Group Policy, including APPX and MSIX apps
- Operating system deployment with task sequences to perform complex configuration, including app deployment
- Manage BitLocker deployment

Microsoft BitLocker Administration and Monitoring

Microsoft BitLocker Administration and Monitoring (MBAM) is used to simplify the deployment and management of BitLocker. By default, BitLocker is enabled individually on each computer. There is no centralized management of BitLocker except for storage of recovery passwords in Active Directory. When you implement MBAM, you enable centralized deployment and monitoring of BitLocker.

To enable centralized management of BitLocker, you need to install the MBAM agent on each computer. After this is done, Group Policy settings are read and applied by the MBAM agent. The Group Policy settings are part of an .admx template that is part of MBAM. The .admx template allows you to configure the new Group Policy settings in a GPO.

To simplify recovery of encrypted drives, MBAM includes a self-service web portal to look up recovery keys. In some cases, this means that users will be able to perform their own recovery without needing to call support.

MBAM is part of the Microsoft Desktop Optimization Pack that is included with subscriptions to Windows 10 Education and Windows 10 Enterprise. This product has ceased development and is slated for retirement in 2026. For new deployments, you should use the BitLocker functionality in Configuration Manager.

ENTERPRISE FILE SERVICES

The file-sharing functionality in Windows provides a high level of control for security but can be difficult to use in a large organization with multiple locations. In particular, if locations are connected by slow WAN links, opening files over those links is very slow. Distributed File System (DFS) and BranchCache help to mitigate this issue.

Distributed File System

Distributed File System (DFS) is composed of DFS replication and DFS namespaces. DFS replication is used to synchronize data among file shares. DFS namespaces are used to virtualize access to shared folders and hide the true location of the shared folder. When you implement DFS, you can have multiple replicated copies of data and provide highly available access to that data. Figure 10-10 shows how DFS replication and DFS namespaces work together. The namespace \\ad.GiganticLife.com\Shares\Marketing points to two file shares with data replicated between them.

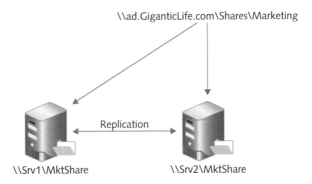

Figure 10-10 DFS folder with multiple targets

Some scenarios for using DFS are:

- *High availability in a single location*—In this scenario, file shares are replicated between two servers in the same site. The namespaces point at both servers. If one server goes down, clients continue using the other server.
- *Close data access among locations*—In this scenario, file shares are replicated between two servers in different locations. The namespaces point at both servers. When users roam between the two sites, they automatically use the file share in the local location.
- *Data backup off-site*—In this scenario, file shares are replicated between two locations. The namespaces point at both servers. The file shares for remote users are backed up in the central location.

DFS replication is very efficient between locations. When a file is changed, only the changes to that file are replicated between the two servers.

Windows 10 includes DFS client software for accessing DFS namespaces. A DFS namespace appears to be a single, large file structure, but it can really be composed of shared folders on multiple servers. This allows administrators to change the location of file shares without impacting client computers. When the DFS namespace is updated, clients automatically begin using the new location.

You can customize the connection process, but by default, when a DFS namespace refers to multiple file shares (targets), the client is directed to a file share in the local Active Directory site. If multiple file shares are in the local Active Directory site, one file share is randomly selected. If connectivity to the first file share fails, the client connects to another available file share identified by the namespace.

The list of targets provided by a DFS namespace is known as a referral list. The order of targets in the referral list determines the order in which the client attempts to access the targets. If the target being used by a client becomes unavailable, the client switches over to another target almost immediately.

When changes are made to the list of targets, clients are not updated immediately. By default, clients cache the folder referral list for 30 minutes before refreshing it. If you remove a target from a folder, clients continue to use it until the cache for that folder is updated. Similarly, if you add a new target for a folder, the clients might not be informed for up to 30 minutes. You can change the cache time in the properties of a folder, but it is seldom required because changes to DFS namespaces are typically well planned and can be implemented over the span of a few hours or days. Figure 10-11 shows the properties of a folder in DFS Management.

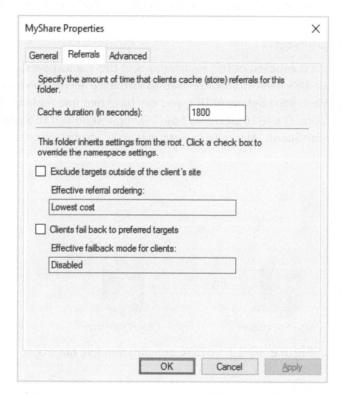

Figure 10-11   DFS folder properties, Referrals tab

If Windows 10 connects to a nonoptimal target in a remote site due to a short-term error, Windows 10 remains connected to the nonoptimal target unless the Clients fail back to preferred targets option has been enabled on the folder. If this option is enabled, Windows 10 fails back to the preferred target at the next refresh. If the option is not enabled, you can cause clients to fail back by restarting, sleeping, or hibernating. As part of the Windows 10 startup process, the cache is cleared.

 TIP   No interface for managing the DFS client in Windows 10 exists. The folder settings are retrieved from Active Directory.

BranchCache

BranchCache is a file-caching technology for domain-joined computers in remote locations with slow WAN links. Files are stored in a file share in a central location but are cached at the remote site to make it faster to open the files. In addition to files in file shares, BranchCache can also cache data from web servers and application servers using Background Intelligent Transfer Service (BITS).

BranchCache has these two modes:

- *Distributed cache mode*—In this mode, each computer running Windows 10 maintains a cache and the computers in a single site share cache data. If a computer with cached data is turned off, other clients obtain the data from the file share over the slow WAN link.
- *Hosted cache mode*—In this mode, a Windows server is used as a central cache by all computers in the remote site. This maximizes the availability of cached data because the server will always be on.

When you open a file that has been cached, BranchCache verifies with the server hosting the file share that the file has not been modified since it has been cached. If the file has not been modified, it is opened from the cache. If the file has been modified, it is opened from the file share over the WAN link. This process ensures that an out-of-date file is never used, but it also means that if the WAN link is down, cached data cannot be accessed. Saving a file is always done back to the file share and the cache.

In most cases, you enable BranchCache on clients by using a GPO. It is possible, however, to manually enable BranchCache and view BranchCache configuration by using the netsh command and Windows PowerShell cmdlets. To view the Windows PowerShell cmdlets available for managing BranchCache, run Get-Command *-BC*.

> **! CAUTION** BranchCache is available only in the Enterprise and Education editions of Windows 10.

Activity 10-10: Configuring Clients for BranchCache

Time Required: 10 minutes
Objective: Use Group Policy settings to configure clients to use BranchCache
Description: To use BranchCache, it needs to be enabled on the client and the server hosting the data. To enable clients to use BranchCache, you use Group Policy settings. In this activity, you enable clients to use BranchCache in distributed cache mode.

NOTE 9

This activity does not configure the server hosting data for BranchCache because it is outside the scope of this course.

1. On DC, sign in as **AD\Administrator** with a password of **Passw0rd**.
2. If necessary, open Server Manager.
3. In Server Manager, click **Tools** and then click **Group Policy Management**.
4. In Group Policy Management, right-click **MyOU-Policy** and then click **Edit**.
5. In the Group Policy Management Editor, browse to **Computer Configuration\Policies\Administrative Templates\Network\BranchCache**.
6. Click each setting and read the description.
7. Double-click **Turn on BranchCache**, click **Enabled**, and then click **OK**.
8. Double-click **Set BranchCache Distributed Cache mode**, click **Enabled**, and then click **OK**.
9. Close all open windows.

MICROSOFT CLOUD SERVICES

Many organizations are starting to use cloud-based applications and services, including device management. **Cloud services** are available over the Internet using infrastructure provided by the vendor. In general, using cloud services is simpler to manage than deploying the same service on-premises. To deploy a new service on-premises, you need to purchase and maintain hardware, install operating systems, install apps, and maintain apps. When you use cloud-based services, all those tasks are the responsibility of the vendor.

Another key benefit of cloud services is availability over the Internet. To allow access to on-premises apps from the Internet requires complex security configurations in an on-premises data center. A cloud service is available over the Internet automatically with no additional configuration.

Microsoft is a large vendor in the cloud services space. Some of the cloud services available from Microsoft are listed in Table 10-1 below.

Table 10-1 Microsoft Cloud Services

Service	Description
Microsoft Azure	Provides online hosting of virtual machines and services for applications, such as storage and databases. Services and virtual machines hosted in Azure can be securely integrated with on-premises networks.
Office 365 Enterprise	This is a suite of cloud-hosted services that includes email (Exchange Online), file storage (SharePoint Online and OneDrive for Business), collaboration (Microsoft Teams), and online versions of Office apps. Some licensing plans also include the desktop version of Microsoft Office Suite (Microsoft 365 Apps).
Microsoft 365 Business	This suite of cloud-hosted services includes similar functionality to Office 365 Enterprise, but it is focused on small organizations of up to 300 users. Some plans include the desktop version of Microsoft Office Suite. These plans do not include Windows 10 Enterprise.
Microsoft 365 Enterprise	This suite of cloud-hosted services includes all the features in Office 365, along with additional security features and Windows 10 Enterprise.

For smaller organizations, using cloud services is an easy way to get complex services for a minimal cost. For example, a small business can buy five licenses for Microsoft 365 Business and start using all the features right away without ever hiring IT staff or purchasing servers. Then, if the organization grows, they can easily purchase additional licenses as required.

Even larger organizations benefit from cloud services. They can increase capacity without expanding their data center. They also have the option to cut costs by reducing the number of licenses that they purchase for the month. This means that a seasonal business can expand capacity in the busy season and then reduce capacity in the slower season.

Azure AD

Azure AD is the online directory service used for Microsoft cloud services. To give a user access to Office 365 or Microsoft 365, you create a user account in Azure AD and then assign the appropriate license. Similar to Active Directory on-premises, you can also create groups to organize users.

Small organizations often have cloud-only user accounts in Azure AD. These are user accounts that exist only in Azure AD and are not synchronized with on-premises Active Directory. This is suitable for very small organizations that don't have on-premises Active Directory or don't want the complexity of synchronizing user accounts from Active Directory to Azure AD.

Larger organizations synchronize user accounts from Active Directory into Azure AD. This simplifies the logon process for users because they have the same user name and password for the cloud services as they use on-premises with Active Directory. Administrators install Azure AD Connect on a Windows server to perform directory synchronization.

Azure AD Join

In the same way that you can join a computer to Active Directory, you can join a computer to Azure AD. After a device is Azure AD-joined, it can be managed by using services integrated with Azure AD. The most common tool for management is Microsoft Intune.

In small organizations, users might join their device to Azure AD manually based on instructions provided by the IT department or Microsoft. Larger organizations can automate the process during initial system setup or by using a provisioning package.

Azure AD join is designed for devices that are not joined to Active Directory. This can be used by small organizations for centralized management. Azure AD join is also useful for larger organizations that have devices that seldom connect to the corporate network, for example, sales staff that are outside the office. Users sign into an Azure AD-joined device by using an Azure AD account.

If your organization has services that rely on Active Directory, but you also want to introduce cloud-based management, you can configure Windows 10 as hybrid Azure AD-joined. In this configuration, the computer running Windows 10 is joined to Active Directory and Azure AD.

NOTE 10

For more information about Azure AD join, see Azure AD-joined devices at https://docs.microsoft.com/en-us/azure/active-directory/devices/concept-azure-ad-join.

 TIP If your Azure AD-joined computer has BitLocker enabled, the BitLocker recovery key is automatically backed up to Azure AD.

Microsoft Intune

Microsoft Intune is a cloud-based management solution that is integrated with Azure AD. This service is included as part of Microsoft Endpoint Manager to manage mobile devices while Configuration Manager is used to manage on-premises devices. Microsoft Intune is also available as a stand-alone service. In many ways, Microsoft Intune is a cloud-based version of Configuration Manager but can manage Android and iOS devices in addition to Windows 10 devices.

The tasks that you perform with Windows 10 devices by using Microsoft Intune include:

- Deploy and update apps
- Manage Windows updates
- Deploy profiles for VPN, certificates, email, and Wi-Fi
- Enforce policies, like those provided by Group Policy
- Enable and disabled device features
- Reset or wipe devices
- Monitor and manage anti-malware status (including Windows Defender)

To support communication between Windows 10 and Microsoft Intune, you need to install the client software for Microsoft Intune. Administrators can download the client from the administration portal and provide it to users, but it's typically more convenient for users to install it from the Microsoft Store. In the Microsoft Store, the app is called Company Portal.

NOTE 11

To see what the management portal for Windows Intune looks like, see Tutorial: Walkthrough of Microsoft Intune in the Azure portal at https://docs.microsoft.com/en-CA/mem/intune/fundamentals/tutorial-walkthrough-intune-portal.

NOTE 12

For a video that shows the Company Portal installation process, see Enroll your Windows 10 Device in Microsoft Intune at https://youtu.be/TKQxEckBHiE.

SUMMARY

- Active Directory is a database of network information about users, computers, and applications. A network based on Active Directory is far more scalable than workgroup-based networks. The components of Active Directory are domains, OUs, trees, and forests.
- Servers in an Active Directory domain can be either domain members or domain controllers. A domain member is integrated into the security structure of the domain. A domain controller holds a copy of the Active Directory information for the domain.

- Active Directory is composed of a domain partition, configuration partition, and schema partition. The replication of the information in each partition is controlled by Active Directory sites.
- Clients use DNS to locate domain controllers. If DNS is not configured properly, client performance suffers and group policies may not be applied.
- Group Policy is used to configure and control workstations. Group Policy settings are stored in Group Policy Objects. The order of application for Group Policy Objects is: local, site, domain, parent OU, and child OU. If a conflict occurs, the last applied policy has the highest priority. Multiple local policies can be created.
- You can use Group Policy settings to control device installation and the use of removable storage devices. Both of these enhance the ability of organizations to control data leaving the organization.
- Enterprise environments need additional tools to help manage Windows 10 computers. Commonly used management tools include WSUS, Configuration Manager, and MBAM.
- Enterprise environments often use advanced file services functionality. DFS is used to replicate file shares and virtualize access to the file shares with namespaces. BranchCache is used to speed up file access in remote locations.
- Microsoft provides cloud services that are used by small organizations and large enterprises. Azure AD stores user and computer identities. Microsoft Intune is used to manage devices.

Key Terms

Active Directory site
BranchCache
cloud services
configuration partition
device identification string
device setup class
Distributed File System (DFS)
domain
domain controller

domain partition
forest
global catalog server
Group Policy
Group Policy object (GPO)
Group Policy Preferences
Microsoft BitLocker Administration
  and Monitoring (MBAM)

Microsoft Endpoint Configuration
  Manager
Microsoft Intune
organizational units (OUs)
schema partition
Windows Server Update Services
  (WSUS)

Review Questions

1. Which type of server is used to sign in clients that are joined to an Active Directory domain?
   a. domain controller
   b. member server
   c. global catalog server
   d. Azure AD server

2. Which type of server holds some of the domain information for all domains in the forest?
   a. domain controller
   b. member server
   c. global catalog server
   d. Azure AD server

3. Which Active Directory partitions are replicated to all domain controllers in the Active Directory forest? (Choose all that apply.)
   a. domain partition
   b. configuration partition
   c. schema partition
   d. global catalog partition

4. The _____ partition contains the definition of the objects and their attributes that can exist in Active Directory.

5. Which network service is used by workstations to find domain controllers?
   a. Active Directory
   b. DHCP
   c. DNS
   d. NetBIOS

6. Group Policy can be used to distribute software to a Windows 10 computer. True or False?

7. Approximately how often does a Windows 10 computer download Group Policy Objects?
   a. every 5 minutes
   b. every 90 minutes
   c. only at shutdown
   d. only at startup

8. Which Group Policy setting location has the lowest priority and will always be overridden by other GPOs when there is a conflict?
   a. Local
   b. Site
   c. Domain
   d. Parent OU
   e. Child OU

9. Which Windows technology requires an agent to be installed?
   a. DFS
   b. BitLocker
   c. MBAM
   d. BranchCache

10. A DFS folder can have a maximum of two targets. True or False?

11. Group Policy Preferences can be overridden by users. True or False?

12. By default, how long do DFS clients cache the referral list for a folder?
   a. 30 seconds
   b. 5 minutes
   c. 15 minutes
   d. 30 minutes
   e. 90 minutes

13. Which methods can you use to fix a Windows 10 computer that has a broken trust relationship with the domain? (Choose all that apply.)
   a. Move the workstation to a workgroup and then rejoin the domain.
   b. Run Repair-ComputerTrust.
   c. Run dism /rejoin.
   d. Synchronize the time with the domain controller.
   e. Run Test-ComputerSecureChannel -Repair.

14. After a computer has been joined to a domain, all domain users can sign in to that computer. True or False?

15. Which tool or command can you use to view time synchronization settings in Windows 10?
   a. Computer Management
   b. WinTime.exe
   c. w32tm.exe
   d. Get-TimeConfig
   e. Event Viewer

16. Which management tools can you use to approve the deployment of Windows Updates to computers? (Choose two.)
   a. WSUS
   b. BranchCache
   c. Configuration Manager
   d. Group Policy
   e. DFS

17. Which enterprise file system allows you to create duplicate copies of files for high availability?
   a. WSUS
   b. BranchCache
   c. Configuration Manager
   d. Group Policy
   e. DFS

18. Which cloud service can you use to deploy software to Windows 10 computers?
   a. Microsoft Intune
   b. Configuration Manager
   c. Azure AD
   d. Microsoft 365
   e. Group Policy

19. Companies can synchronize users from Active Directory into Azure AD. True or False?

20. Which tool or utility can you use to perform an offline domain join?
   a. dism.exe
   b. djoin.exe
   c. Group Policy
   d. w32tm.exe
   e. Azure AD

Case Projects

Case 10-1: Enterprise Group Policy Application

Gigantic Life Insurance is planning to implement Group Policy to control user desktops. Some of the desired settings are to be implemented for the entire organization, while other settings apply only to specific regions or departments.

Active Directory for Gigantic Life Insurance is organized as a single domain. The network manager is concerned that dividing into multiple domains to apply individual group policies will entail a lot of work and disrupt users. Explain why this is not a concern.

Case 10-2: Small-Office Group Policy Application

Buddy's Machine Shop has a kiosk computer located in the lobby for customers to use. The kiosk computer is not part of a domain. The local computer policy severely restricts the use of the computer, so that customers can use only the browser.

Occasionally, an administrator needs to sign in to the kiosk computer to perform maintenance and update software. This is awkward, though, because the administrator needs to disable settings in the local policy before performing any task. Then, when the tasks are complete, the administrator needs to re-enable the settings in the local policy. Explain how this system can be improved.

Case 10-3: Controlling Software Updates

Currently, all computers at Enormous Financial Corporation download updates directly from Microsoft. You have heard that many other companies use WSUS to download and apply updates. You would like to use WSUS in your organization. To justify implementing WSUS, describe the benefits of using WSUS and your plan for implementing it.

Case 10-4: Enterprise Management of Windows 10

Enormous Financial Corporation has thousands of computers running Windows 10. Many of these are at the head office, but thousands of mobile computers also are used by salespeople outside the office. Many of the salespeople are independent and never come into the office; therefore, they can't be joined to the domain and managed by the standard tools. To install software on these computers, you send the individual users instructions on how to download and install the apps. This is a time-consuming and error-prone process. Explain how cloud services could be used to improve management of the mobile computers.

MANAGING ENTERPRISE CLIENTS

After reading this module and completing the exercises, you will be able to:

1. Troubleshoot and manage enterprise clients
2. Manage profiles for roaming users
3. Configure clients for virtual private networks
4. Describe and configure data synchronization for mobile clients

When you manage clients in an enterprise environment, you need to consider the best ways to scale up your ability to provide support. Small challenges for a few people in a 100-user environment become big issues in an enterprise. In an enterprise, users are more likely to roam among computers, require remote access, and have mobile computers. You need to understand how these services are implemented for Windows 10.

In this module, you learn about methods for remotely managing Windows 10 computers so that you can quickly provide help to users without physically visiting them. You also learn how to centralize profile data to support users that don't sign in to the same computer each day. For users outside the office, you learn about remote access by using a virtual private network (VPN), including the various protocols that can be used. Finally, you learn about data synchronization options that can be used by mobile computers to provide data access when they are not connected to a network.

TROUBLESHOOTING AND MANAGING ENTERPRISE CLIENTS

In smaller companies, you can manually go to each computer to perform troubleshooting when a problem arises. It takes you only a few minutes to go from your desk to where the problem is. In larger companies, desktop support staff need to work remotely from the computer where the problem is occurring.

The physical size of large companies makes it impractical to visit each computer to perform troubleshooting. Whether it's just a physically large building or an organization with multiple physical locations, it takes a lot of time to visit each desktop computer. Desktop support staff are much more efficient when they can work from their own desk. The tools available for remote management are shown in Table 11-1.

Table 11-1   Remote Management Tools

Tool	Description
Remote Desktop	Enables you to remotely sign in to a computer and work with it just as if you were at the console. The main benefit of using Remote Desktop is that it gives you full access to the remote computer and its software; however, you are signed in as your user account and not as the user that needs help. So, if any of the problems are related to configuration information in the user profile, then Remote Desktop won't help. Also, when you sign in by using Remote Desktop, the user at the console is disconnected.
Remote Assistance	Allows you to connect to the console of the remote computer where a user is signed in. The main benefit of remote assistance is that you can see what users are doing when they are experiencing issues. You can ask to remote control the session to perform troubleshooting. Because the remote computer is signed in as the user, you can repair problems caused by settings stored in the user profile.
Quick Assist	Allows you to connect to the console of the remote computer where a user is signed in. This is a replacement for Remote Assistance that is included only in Windows 10 and not previous versions of Windows. This tool is easy to use over an Internet connection without any firewall configuration.
Microsoft Management Console (MMC) snap-ins	Enables you to connect to a remote computer with an MMC snap-in to manage specific settings on the remote computer. Because MMC snap-ins, such as Event Viewer and Services, are the most common way to manage a local instance of Windows 10, using the same tool to manage remote systems is convenient. More commonly used MMC snap-ins can connect to remote systems. You need to allow remote management of systems to use an MMC snap-in remotely.

Connecting remotely with MMC snap-ins can be done while users are signed in and working. Users are not prompted to accept connections and do not see you performing any actions. |
| Registry Editor (regedit.exe) | Option that lets you connect to the registry of a remote computer and modify registry keys. This performs similarly to MMC snap-ins. When in Registry Editor, select a remote computer to connect to. Be aware that many registry changes don't take effect until the computer, apps, or services are restarted.

Connecting remotely with Registry Editor can be done while users are signed in and working. Users are not prompted to accept connections and do not see you performing any actions. |
| Windows PowerShell remoting | Enables you to connect to a remote computer with a Windows PowerShell prompt. Then, when connected through PowerShell remoting, you can run Windows PowerShell cmdlets as if you were at a Windows PowerShell prompt on the console of the remote system. This is similar to a system such as Telnet where you remotely control a computer system through a text-based interface.

Connecting remotely with Windows PowerShell can be done while users are signed in and working. Users are not prompted to accept connections and do not see you performing any actions. |
| Group Policy | Option that allows you to configure multiple computers quickly and easily in a domain-based network. Group Policy is useful for standardizing computer configuration quickly. Group Policy is applied to computer objects in Active Directory. When a setting is configured by using Group Policy, users cannot change that setting. |

Remote Desktop

NOTE 1

When you use Remote Desktop to connect to a computer where a user is already signed in, the user is prompted whether to allow you access or not.

Remote Desktop provides functionality that is similar to an RD Session host, but it does not require additional licensing or servers. It is often used by desktop support staff to connect to a computer running Windows 10 and run troubleshooting tools or perform configuration tasks. When you connect by using Remote Desktop, you sign in as yourself and see your own desktop, as well as the application you are running. You are not able to view what a user is seeing on the desktop. In fact, when you connect to a Windows 10 computer by using Remote Desktop, it disconnects a locally signed in user.

You can enable Remote Desktop on a computer running any edition of Windows 10 except Home edition. When Remote Desktop is enabled, as shown in Figure 11-1, local administrators and members of the local Remote Desktop Users group have permission to connect. By default, Remote Desktop Users contain no members. To give standard users access to connect, they must be members of this group.

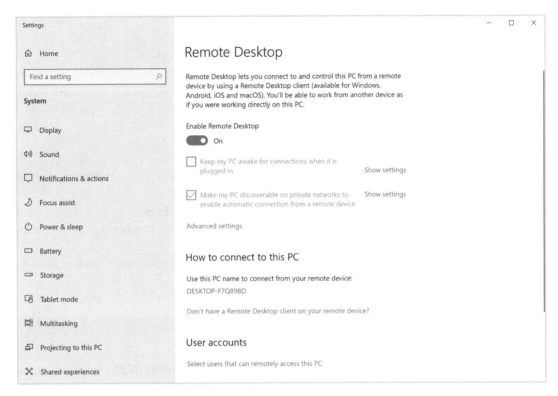

Figure 11-1 Remote Desktop settings

Remote Desktop listens on TCP port 3389. When you enable Remote Desktop, Windows Firewall is automatically configured to allow connectivity on port 3389. It is possible to change the port used by Remote Desktop by editing the registry, but this is seldom required. If you change the port for Remote Desktop, you need to manually create a Windows Defender Firewall rule to allow it.

By default, Remote Desktop uses Network Level Authentication. When Network Level Authentication is enabled, Remote Desktop Connection obtains sign-in information from users before connecting to the remote computer. This prevents users from connecting until the connection is authenticated. If Network Level Authentication is not used, you can connect to a computer and see the sign-in screen before you authenticate. This is a security risk because that screen might display the last signed-in user. Also, if the RDP protocol or Remote Desktop contains a flaw, it could be exploited by an unauthenticated user.

Activity 11-1: Enabling Remote Desktop

Time Required: 5 minutes
Objective: Enable Remote Desktop for a computer
Description: You want to be able to connect to a Windows 10 computer remotely by using Remote Desktop to perform remote administration. In this activity, you enable Remote Desktop.

NOTE 2

This activity assumes you have access to the desktop of the domain controller that your Windows client is joined to.

1. If necessary, start your Windows 10 computer and sign in as AD\Administrator.
2. Click the **Start** button and then click **Settings**.

3. In the Settings window, click **System**, in the System pane, scroll down if necessary, and select **Remote Desktop**.
4. Click the Enable remote desktop toggle and then click **Confirm** in the Remote Desktop Settings dialog box.
5. In the Settings window, read the information in the How to connect to this PC heading. Take note of the computer name.
6. Click **Advanced settings** and read the information. Notice that Network Level Authentication is required and the Remote Desktop port is 3389.
7. Close the Settings window.
8. On your domain controller, sign in as AD\Administrator.
9. Click the **Start** button, type **remote**, and then click **Remote Desktop Connection**.
10. In the Remote Desktop Connection dialog box, in the Computer box, type the computer name you recorded in Step 5, and then click **Show Options**.
11. Click the **Display** tab and read the options.
12. Click the **Local Resource** tab and read the options.
13. Click the **Experience** tab and read the options.
14. Click the **Advanced** tab, read the options, and then click **Connect**.
15. In the Windows Security window, type the password for AD\Administrator and then click **OK**. You are now connected to the Windows 10 desktop in Remote Desktop Connection.
16. In the Remote Desktop Connection window, on the taskbar, click **Microsoft Edge**.
17. Close the Remote Desktop Connection window and then click **OK** in the dialog box warning about disconnecting from the session.
18. On your Windows 10 computer, sign in as AD\Administrator. Notice that Microsoft Edge remains open from your remote session.
19. Exit Microsoft Edge.

Remote Desktop Connection, shown in Figure 11-2, is the Remote Desktop Protocol (RDP) client that you use to connect to a remote desktop. You can configure many different settings in Remote Desktop Connection, and you might want these settings to be different when connecting to different computers. To simplify using different settings, you can save settings, including the remote computer name, in .rdp files. Then, you can double-click the .rdp file name to initiate the connection.

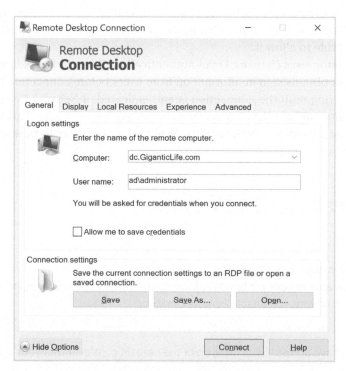

Figure 11-2   Remote Desktop Connection

The Display tab in Remote Desktop Connection lets you select the screen resolution and color depth for the remote session. The larger the values are, the more data will be sent back and forth between the two computers. On slow connections, consider reducing the screen resolution and color depth. If you select Use all my monitors for the remote session, you can have a multimonitor connection to the remote computer.

 TIP   On slow network connections, consider reducing the screen resolution and color depth. A solid color desktop can also reduce data requirements.

The Local Resources tab in Remote Desktop Connection, shown in Figure 11-3, controls which resources in the local computer are available for the session. These settings provide better integration between the local and remote computers to provide a better experience. Some of the things you can configure are:

- Enable playback of sound from the remote computer on the local computer.
- Allow printers from the local computer to be used in the remote session.
- Allow copying of Clipboard data between the local and remote computers.
- Allow hard drives from the local computer to be accessed in the remote session.
- Allow smart cards on the local computer to be used in the remote session.

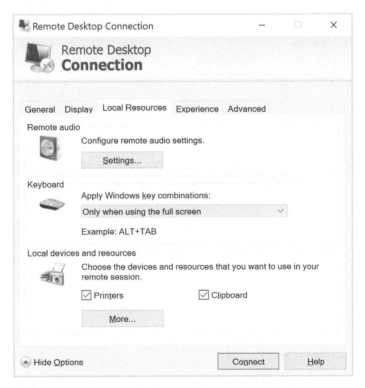

Figure 11-3   Remote Desktop Connection, Local Resources tab

The Experience tab in Remote Desktop Connection allows you to enable and disable various display-related settings that can impact the amount of data sent between the local and remote computers. On slower network connections, you can disable some of these settings to reduce delays in seeing results after you click items or move them around. By default, Remote Desktop Connection detects the connection quality automatically and adjusts the features as necessary. Automatic configuration works well in most cases, but for very slow connections, you might find the experience better if you manually disable most of the features.

On the Advanced tab in Remote Desktop Connection, you can configure server authentication settings and Remote Desktop Gateway (RD Gateway) settings. The server authentication settings control how Remote Desktop Connection behaves when the certificate used by the server does not match the name you use when connecting. By default, a warning is displayed. To increase security, you can prevent mismatched names from being allowed, but this means that you will not be able to connect directly by IP address.

An RD Gateway server is used to secure access to Remote Desktop from public networks, such as the Internet. When Remote Desktop Connection is configured to use an RD Gateway, RDP traffic is tunneled in HTTPS packets to the RD Gateway server. The RD Gateway server sends the RDP packets on to the internal network. Effectively, this is like an SSL VPN that is specifically designed for Remote Desktop and RDS. Figure 11-4 shows the settings for RD Gateway in Remote Desktop Connection.

Figure 11-4   Remote Desktop Connection, RD Gateway server settings

Most of the time, you will start Remote Desktop Connection from the Start button; however, you can start Remote Desktop Connection from a command prompt by running mstsc.exe. You can view all of the options available by running mstsc.exe /?. Table 11-2 lists some configuration options that are available at the command prompt but not in the graphical interface.

Table 11-2   Mstsc.exe Options

Option	Description
/admin	Connects to the console of a remote computer rather than an RDP session. This can be useful in some cases when you are troubleshooting and a typical RDP is not working properly.
/public	Prevents Remote Desktop Connection from saving information to the local computer. For example, credentials and the name of the remote computer are not cached for later use.
/restrictedAdmin	Prevents the remote computer from accessing your credentials. The session uses the local computer account for permissions instead, which might not allow you to access network resources. This is useful when a remote system may have been compromised.
/remoteGuard	Prevents the remote computer from accessing your credentials similarly to /restrictedAdmin. This mode, however, allows connectivity to network resources by routing requests back through Remote Desktop Connection.
/shadow	Allows you to connect to an existing session and view what another user is doing.
/control	Allows someone else to control your session if that person is viewing it with you.
/noConsentPrompt	Allows someone to shadow your session without prompting you for consent.

Activity 11-2: Customizing Settings for Remote Desktop Connection

Time Required: 10 minutes

Objective: Customize settings for Remote Desktop Connection

Description: You want to create a set of customized settings for connecting to a specific remote desktop. In this activity, you configure settings in Remote Desktop Connection and save them as an .rdp file for later use.

1. If necessary, start your computer and sign in.
2. Click the **Start** button, type **mstsc**, and then click **Remote Desktop Connection**.
3. In the Remote Desktop Connection window, in the Computer box, type **w10-45.giganticlife.com** and then click **Show Options**.
4. Click the **Display** tab and in the Display configuration area, select **1024 by 768 pixels**.
5. Click the **Local Resources** tab and then clear the **Printers** check box.
6. Click the **Experience** tab and then in the Choose your connection speed to optimize performance box, select **Low-speed broadband (256 kbps - 2 Mbps)**.
7. Click the **Advanced** tab and then in the Connect from anywhere area, click **Settings**.
8. In the RD Gateway Server Settings dialog box, click **Use these RD Gateway server settings**.
9. In the Server name box, type **RD-Gateway.giganticlife.com** and then click OK.
10. In Remote Desktop Connection, click the **General** tab and then click **Save As**.
11. In the Save As dialog box, in the File name box, type **w10-45** and then click **Save**.
12. Close the Remote Desktop Connection window.

Remote Assistance

Remote Desktop allows you to connect to a remote computer for troubleshooting. For the best results when troubleshooting, however, it is often useful to have users show you the problem they are experiencing, which is not possible with Remote Desktop. You can use **Remote Assistance**, shown in Figure 11-5, to view what a user is doing and even take control to resolve the issue.

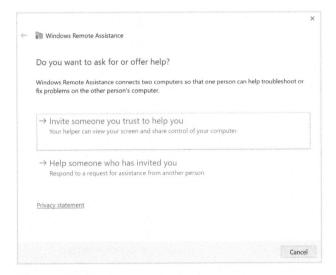

Figure 11-5   Windows Remote Assistance

Remote Assistance can be initiated in the following ways:

- *Invitation file*—Users can create an invitation file that they send to a helper. When the helper opens the file, remote assistance starts. This method does not work over routers that perform Network Address Translation (NAT) because the IP address information in the invitation file is the internal IP address of the computer that is not accessible over the Internet.

- *Easy Connect*—When users select Easy Connect instead of an invitation, the user is provided with a password that needs to be sent to the helper. The helper enters that password to be connected. This type of connection works over the Internet and through NAT. Easy Connect tunnels IPv6 packets over IPv4 networks and relies on the Teredo Adapter Interface, which is not installed by default.
- *Administrator initiated*—As a helper, you can offer remote assistance to users if you know the IP address or computer name. After the connection to the computer is established, the user is prompted to allow the connection. This method is used on internal networks and not over the Internet.

After an invitation has been created or Easy Connect has been initiated, the user needs to leave Windows Remote Assistance open. If the Windows Remote Assistance window is closed, the helper cannot connect. On the remote system, you also need to have allowed Remote Assistance, as shown in Figure 11-6.

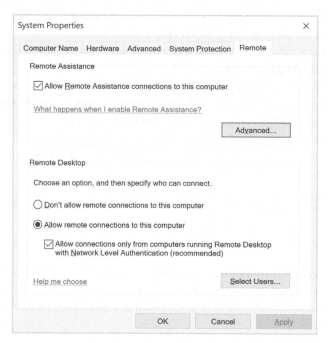

Figure 11-6   Allow Remote Assistance

 TIP   To open Windows Remote Assistance, run msra.exe.

Activity 11-3: Creating a Remote Assistance Request

Time Required: 5 minutes
Objective: Create a Remote Assistance request
Description: You want to create a Remote Assistance request so that you can send it to a colleague to work through a problem together on your computer. In this activity, you create a Remote Assistance request.

 TIP   If there is time, consider working with a partner to test Remote Assistance. The two computers must be able to communicate over the network.

1. If necessary, start your computer and sign in.
2. Click the **Start** button, type **msra**, and then click **msra**.
3. In the Windows Remote Assistance dialog box, click **Invite someone you trust to help you**.

4. On the How do you want to invite your trusted helper screen, click **Save this invitation as a file**.
5. In the Save As dialog box, note the location and file name and then click **Save**.
6. Note the password that is displayed that must also be given to your helper.
7. Close the Windows Remote Assistance window and then click **Yes** when prompted for confirmation.

Quick Assist

Quick Assist is a simplified and improved tool in Windows 10 to remote control another computer. Like Remote Assistance, Quick Assist lets you view what the user is doing, but the connectivity process is simplified and works well over the Internet without the requirement to install or configure any additional software.

Authentication for Quick Assist is based on a security code that is generated by the helper. If you want to assist someone else, you need to sign in by using a Microsoft Account or an Azure AD account. After you are signed in, a security code is displayed, and you need to send the security code to the person you are helping. The person you are helping enters the security code into Quick Assist on their computer to complete the connection, as shown in Figure 11-7. Once connected, you can see their screen. If the user allows it, you can control the mouse and keyboard.

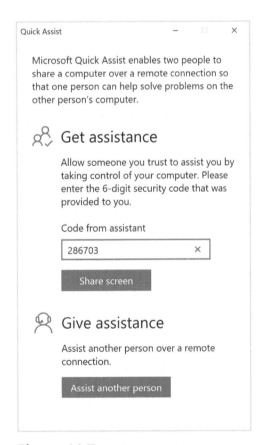

Figure 11-7   Quick Assist

Computers using Quick Assist do not communicate directly with each other. They each connect to a Microsoft server that mediates the communication. No special firewall configuration is required because Quick Assist connects to port 443 on the Microsoft server just like a browser connecting to a secure website.

 TIP   Quick Assist is an excellent tool for any environment, but it is very well suited for novice users because of the minimal configuration requirements.

Activity 11-4: Using Quick Assist

Time Required: 5 minutes

Objective: Use Quick Assist for remote control

Description: You are working at the help desk and want to provide assistance to a staff member in your company. This person is working at home using a computer running Windows 10. In this activity, you provide remote assistance by using Quick Assist.

 TIP   If there is time, consider working with a partner to test Quick Assist. The two computers must have access to the Internet.

1. If necessary, start your computer and sign in.
2. Click the **Start** button, type **quick**, and then click **Quick Assist**.
3. In the Quick Assist window, read the information and then click **Assist another person**.
4. Sign in by using your Microsoft Account.
5. When prompted to stay signed in, click **No**.
6. On the Share security code screen, read the information. The security code must be given to the person you are helping.
7. Close the Quick Assist window.

MMC Snap-Ins

Older MMC snap-ins use **remote procedure calls (RPC)** to connect to computers running Windows 10 over the network. RPC communication is no longer preferred for new snap-ins and apps because it uses randomly selected port numbers that are difficult to regulate using network firewalls. The following general process is used to create an RPC connection:

1. The client connects to the RPC Endpoint Mapper service (TCP port 135) on the remote computer.
2. The RPC Endpoint Mapper service identifies the TCP port for the requested app or service.
3. The RPC Endpoint Mapper service sends the client the TCP port for the requested app or service.
4. The client connects to the app or service on the remote computer using the supplied TCP port.

For RPC communication in Windows 10, the RPC Endpoint Mapper service and the Remote Procedure Call (RPC) service must be running. Both services are set to start automatically in Windows 10.

To allow connectivity for MMC snap-ins, you might need to enable Windows Defender Firewall rules, such as the following:

- Remote Event Log Management (RPC)
- Remote Scheduled Tasks Management (RPC)
- Remote Service Management (RPC)
- Windows Defender Firewall Remote Management (RPC)

Activity 11-5: Viewing Event Logs Remotely by Using RPC

Time Required: 10 minutes

Objective: View event logs remotely by using RPC

Description: The Event Viewer MMC snap-in can connect to remote computer systems by using RPC. This allows you to see the contents of event logs on other computers without visiting the desktop. In this activity, you verify RPC connectivity for Event Viewer.

NOTE 3

This activity assumes you have access to the desktop of the domain controller to which your Windows client is joined.

1. Sign in to your domain controller as AD\Administrator.
2. Click the **Start** button, type **event**, and then click **Event Viewer**.

3. In the Event Viewer window, right-click **Event Viewer (Local)** in the left pane and then click **Connect to Another Computer**.

4. In the Select Computer dialog box, click **Browse** and then click **Advanced**.

5. Click **Find Now**, select your Windows 10 computer, and then click **OK** three times.

6. Wait until the connection fails, read the information, and then click **OK**.

7. On your Windows 10 computer, sign in as AD\Administrator.

8. Right-click the **Start** button and then click **Windows PowerShell (Admin)**.

9. At the Windows PowerShell prompt, type **Get-Service rpc*** and then press **Enter**. Notice that the status for RPC Endpoint Mapper service and the Remote Procedure Call (RPC) service show they are Running.

10. Close the Windows PowerShell prompt window.

11. Click the **Start** button, type **defender**, and then click **Windows Defender Firewall with Advanced Security**.

12. In the Windows Defender Firewall with Advanced Security window, select **Inbound Rules**.

13. In the list of inbound rules, scroll down and click **Remote Event Log Management (RPC)** for the **Domain** profile.

14. In the Actions pane, click **Enable rule**. Notice that a green check mark now appears beside the rule to indicate that it's enabled.

15. Close the Windows Defender Firewall with Advanced Security window.

16. On the domain controller, in Event Viewer, right-click **Event Viewer (Local)** and then click **Connect to Another Computer**.

17. In the Select Computer dialog box, click **Browse** and then click **Advanced**.

18. Click **Find Now**, select you Windows 10 computer, and then click **OK** three times. Notice that the Windows 10 computer name now appears in the navigation pane.

19. In the navigation pane, expand **Windows Logs**, click **System**, and then double-click an event to open it.

20. In the Event Properties dialog box, read the computer attribute, and verify that the name listed is your Windows 10 computer.

21. Close all open windows.

Newer MMC snap-ins and some other management tools use a web-based protocol for remote management. **Windows Remote Management (WinRM)** is the Microsoft implementation of the WS-Management protocol for remote management. WS-Management defines how messages are passed between the client and the remote computer.

WinRM is implemented as the Windows Remote Management (WS-Management) service. By default, this service is set for manual startup. Before you can access WinRM on a remote computer, you need to configure it. This process can be done manually, but the simplest method for configuring WinRM is to run one of the following commands:

- winrm quickconfig
- Set-WSManQuickConfig

The quickconfig commands perform the following steps for you:

1. Starts the WinRM service.

2. Configures the WinRM service to start automatically.

3. Creates a listener that accepts requests from any IP address.

4. Enables the firewall rule to allow access to WinRM.

The WinRM service listens on port 5985. You may see some out-of-date documentation that refers to WinRM listening on port 80, but that documentation was relevant only for Windows XP.

WinRM is not configured to use secure sockets layer (SSL) or transport layer security (TLS) to secure communication. Authentication to WinRM is protected by Kerberos, but data sent over the network is unencrypted. If you do decide to enable SSL/TLS for WinRM, the port used is 5986 and you need to create the firewall rule to allow it. You also need to deploy certificates to the computers that will be running WinRM.

Activity 11-6: Enabling WinRM

Time Required: 5 minutes

Objective: Enable WinRM

Description: You have purchased a new management tool for Windows 10. This tool uses WinRM to remotely connect to Windows 10. To enable this tool to work, you need to enable WinRM and verify it is listening on the network. In this activity, you enable WinRM and verify which port it is listening on.

1. If necessary, turn on your computer and sign in as AD\Administrator.
2. Right-click the **Start** button and then click **Windows PowerShell (Admin)**.
3. At the Windows PowerShell prompt, type **Set-WSManQuickConfig** and then press **Enter**.
4. Read the information that is displayed, type **Y**, and then press **Enter**.
5. Type **winrm /?** and then press **Enter**. Read the options available with the tool.
6. Type **winrm get winrm/config** and then press Enter.
7. Scroll through the output and read the settings.
8. Close the Windows PowerShell prompt window.
9. Click the **Start** button, type **resource**, and then click **Resource Monitor**.
10. In the Resource Monitor window, click the **Network** tab and then expand **Listening Ports**.
11. Scroll down in the list of ports and verify that the System image for Windows 10 is listening on port 5985.
12. Close the Resource Monitor window.

You can also use Group Policy to enable WinRM. To enable WinRM by using Group Policy, you need to create a Group Policy object that performs the same tasks as the quickconfig option, as follows:

- Set the WinRM service to start automatically
- Configure a WinRM listener
- Enable the Windows Remote Management (HTTP-in) firewall rule

The Group Policy setting for configuring a WinRM listener is Allow remote server management through WinRM located in Computer Configuration\Policies\Administrative Templates\Windows Components\Windows Remote Management\ WinRM Service\. You need to enable this setting and define a filter for client connections. Using a filter of * allows connections from any IP address.

Registry Editor

To use the Registry Editor to edit the registry of a remote computer running Windows 10, you need to enable the Remote Registry service on the remote computer. The Remote Registry service is disabled by default so that you cannot start it accidentally. This also prevents malware from starting the Remote Registry service. The Remote Registry service does not need to be started manually; when you connect to the computer, a trigger starts it automatically.

Connections to the Remote Registry service are on TCP port 445. You typically do not need to configure the firewall to allow access to this port because it is already allowed for file sharing. The rule is File and Printer Sharing (SMB-In).

Activity 11-7: Enabling Remote Registry Editing

Time Required: 10 minutes

Objective: Enable remote registry editing

Description: To simplify troubleshooting with users in your organization, you want to view and modify registry settings remotely. You want to use the Registry Editor because it is easier than running scripts while you are investigating. In this activity, you enable the Remote Registry service and test the capability to view the registry remotely.

NOTE 4

This activity assumes you have access to the desktop of the domain controller to which your Windows client is joined.

1. If necessary, turn on your computer and sign in as AD\Administrator.
2. Right-click the **Start** button and then click **Computer Management**.
3. In the Computer Management window, expand **Services and Applications** and then click **Services**.
4. Scroll down in the list of services and then click **Remote Registry**. Notice that this service is disabled.
5. Right-click **Remote Registry** and then click **Properties**.
6. In the Remote Registry Properties dialog box, in the Startup type box, select **Automatic** and then click **OK**.
7. Close the Computer Management window.
8. Click the **Start** button, type **defender**, and then click **Windows Defender Firewall with Advanced Security**.
9. In the Windows Defender Firewall with Advanced Security window, select **Inbound Rules**.
10. In the list of inbound rules, scroll down and then click **File and Printer Sharing (SMB-In)** for the **Domain** profile.
11. If the rule is disabled, in the Actions pane, click **Enable rule**. Notice that a green check mark now appears beside the rule to indicate that it's enabled.
12. Close the Windows Defender Firewall with Advanced Security window.
13. On your domain controller, sign in as AD\Administrator.
14. Click the **Start** button, type **regedit**, and then click **Registry Editor**.
15. In the Registry Editor window, click **File** and then click **Connect Network Registry**.
16. In the Select Computer dialog box, click **Advanced** and then click **Find Now**.
17. Select your Windows 10 computer and then click **OK** twice. Your Windows 10 computer name appears.
18. Under your Windows 10 computer name, expand **HKEY_LOCAL_MACHINE.**
19. Close the Registry Editor window.

Windows PowerShell Remoting

You can use **Windows PowerShell remoting** to run Windows PowerShell cmdlets and scripts on remote computer systems. For any tasks that you can use Windows PowerShell at the desktop, you can perform that same task remotely over the network by using Windows PowerShell remoting. By default, Windows PowerShell remoting is disabled in Windows 10.

To enable Windows PowerShell remoting, you need to run the Enable-PSRemoting cmdlet. This command performs all the following tasks:

1. Enables WinRM if not already configured (same as quickconfig).
2. Registers Windows PowerShell with WinRM.
3. Restarts the WinRM service to force settings to take effect.

To remotely access a computer by using PowerShell Remoting, run the Enter-PSSession -ComputerName RemoteComputer command. In a domain-based network, no further configuration is required because Kerberos authentication is successful. Your current credentials are used to authenticate to the remote computer. In a workgroup-based network you need to perform these two extra steps:

- Configure TrustedHosts on the client.
- Provide credentials when connecting.

By default, WinRM only allows Kerberos authentication using HTTP. In a workgroup-based network this is not possible. To allow authentication, you can either enable HTTPS for WinRM or configure TrustedHosts. The client will transmit unencrypted credentials to the remote computer only if the remote computer has been added to TrustedHosts. To add a trusted host, use the following PowerShell command:

- Set-Item WSMAN:\localhost\Client\TrustedHosts -Value "IPAddress"

Or add a trusted host at a command prompt, as follows:

- wsman set winrm/config/client @{TrustedHosts="IPAddress"}

To be prompted for credentials when connecting, use this modified command to connect to the remote host:

- Enter-PSSession -ComputerName RemoteComputer -Credential (Get-Credential)

Activity 11-8: Enabling Windows PowerShell Remoting

Time Required: 10 minutes

Objective: Enable Windows PowerShell remoting

Description: Your organization has hundreds of desktop computers, and you want to use Windows PowerShell remoting to help perform troubleshooting on those computers. Before you use Group Policy to enable Windows PowerShell remoting on all the computers, you want to enable Windows PowerShell remoting manually and try it out. In this activity, you enable Windows PowerShell remoting on Windows 10 and test the functionality.

NOTE 5

This activity assumes you have access to the desktop of the domain controller to which your Windows client is joined.

1. If necessary, turn on your computer and sign in as AD\Administrator.
2. Right-click the **Start** button and then click **Windows PowerShell (Admin)**.
3. At the Windows PowerShell prompt, type **Enable-PSRemoting** and then press **Enter**. Notice that WinRM is already configured from a previous Activity.
4. Close the Windows PowerShell prompt window.
5. On your domain controller, sign in as AD\Administrator.
6. Right-click the **Start** button and then click **Windows PowerShell (Admin)**.
7. At the Windows PowerShell prompt, type **Enter-PSSession -ComputerName *<Win10Computer>***, where <Win10Computer> is the name of your Windows 10 computer, and then press **Enter**.
8. Read the text at the prompt. Notice that the computer name is now displayed to indicate that you are connected to a remote session.
9. Type **Get-ComputerInfo** and then press **Enter**.
10. Scroll through the displayed computer information and verify that the operating system is Windows 10 and the computer name matches the name of your Windows 10 computer.
11. Type **Exit-PSSession** and then press **Enter**.
12. Close the Windows PowerShell prompt window.

MANAGING PROFILES FOR ROAMING USERS

A roaming user is a person who does not use the same computer each day. This has long been common in businesses such as call centers, but you can now see this in open office environments also. An important concern for roaming users is consistent computer configuration. Users strongly prefer a consistent work environment, including files and settings.

Windows has long supported roaming user profiles that are stored on a file server, but roaming users profiles have never worked well. They are prone to corruption, which requires intervention by an administrator. If a large amount of data is stored in a roaming profile, the sign-in and sign-out process can be very slow.

Mapped Drive Letters

Even though roaming user profiles don't work well, the concept of centrally storing data so that it's accessible from multiple locations is a sound one. One of the first measures that any organization should implement is centralized file shares for data storage. Computers can be configured with mapped drive letters that connect to the file shares so that files are accessible from any computer. All users in a department will have access to the same files for collaboration.

 TIP Cloud storage services are quite popular, but large organizations still keep many files on premises in shares.

For personal data, users can be given a private home drive on a file server. Again, this would be available from any computer when the user signs in.

Folder Redirection

You can use **folder redirection** to store some profile information on a file server so that it's accessible from any computer. This is better than a roaming profile because the data is used directly from the network location and isn't synchronized locally. You typically configure folder redirection by using Group Policy.

Some of the folders you can synchronize include:

- AppData\Roaming
- Documents
- Desktop
- Downloads
- Favorites

 TIP Redirecting the Documents folder to a network share makes it easy for users to store documents in a central location.

Credential Roaming

Some organizations issue certificates to users for authentication to resources. In Windows 10, user certificates are stored in the user profile but are not part of any folder that can be redirected. You can implement credential roaming to allow certificates to synchronize to the profile on multiple computers when roaming users profiles are not implemented.

When you implement Credential Roaming, the user certificates are stored in Active Directory. Then, during sign in, certificates are synchronized with the local user profile. You enable Credential Roaming by using Group Policy.

User Experience Virtualization

User Experience Virtualization (UE-V) provides user state virtualization similar to roaming profiles. When users sign in to different domain-joined computers, their settings follow them from computer to computer; however, UE-V provides more advanced functionality that is not provided by roaming profiles, such as:

- Synchronization is based on templates for fine-grained control of specific application settings.
- Synchronization can be performed between multiple operating systems where user profiles would not be compatible.
- Settings are synchronized while the user is signed in rather than at sign-in or sign-out.

The UE-V agent is included with Windows 10 Enterprise and Education. To enable UE-V, you configure Group Policy settings to configure the client. Two important settings are as follows:

- *Setting storage location*—This location is a file share where the settings for users are stored by the agent.
- *Settings template catalog location*—This location is a file share where settings location templates that describe how to synchronize settings for specific applications are stored. The agent reads the settings location templates.

You do not need to create settings location templates for all apps for which you want to synchronize settings. UE-V includes the ability to synchronize settings for Microsoft Office and many Windows settings. Settings location templates typically need to be created for custom apps and non-Microsoft apps.

NOTE 6

For detailed information about UE-V, see User Experience Virtualization (UE-V) for Windows 10 overview at https://docs.microsoft.com/en-us/windows/configuration/ue-v/uev-for-windows.

Profile Synchronization with Microsoft Account or Azure AD

You can use a Microsoft Account or an Azure AD account to synchronize profile settings to multiple computers. The profile settings are stored online as part of the Microsoft Account or Azure AD account. When you use the cloud-based account to sign in to another computer, the settings are downloaded and used in the local copy of the profile, as shown in Figure 11-8.

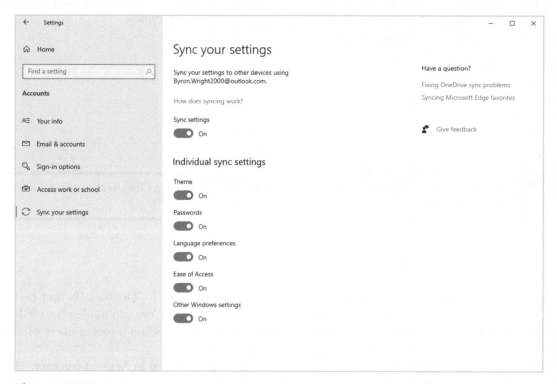

Figure 11-8   Sync settings with Microsoft account

If a computer is Azure AD joined, you can't manually enable the Sync your settings option. On an Azure AD-joined device, an administrator needs to enable Enterprise State Roaming in Azure AD.

USING A VPN FOR REMOTE ACCESS

Remote access consists of a dedicated computer acting as a remote access server and clients connecting to that server. After clients are connected to the remote access server, the clients have access to resources on the network where the remote access server is located. For example, remote access clients can open and save files on a file server back in the main office, as shown in Figure 11-9. In fact, the client gets an IP address for the organizational network.

NOTE 7

For a detailed list of Windows 10 settings that can be synced, see Windows 10 roaming settings reference at https://docs.microsoft.com/en-us/azure/active-directory/devices/enterprise-state-roaming-windows-settings-reference.

The oldest technology for remote access is dial-up networking. Dial-up networking clients have a modem and connect to the remote access server over telephone lines. This technology is seldom used now because it is very slow when compared with Internet connectivity. Dial-up connectivity is limited to approximately 56 KBps (kilobits per second). A 4G data plan on most mobile phones is over 1000 times faster.

It is much more common for remote access to be done over a **virtual private network (VPN)**. A VPN creates an encrypted connection between the VPN clients and the remote access server over a public network, such as the Internet. Because the connection is encrypted, anyone between the VPN client and the remote access server is prevented from viewing the data in transit.

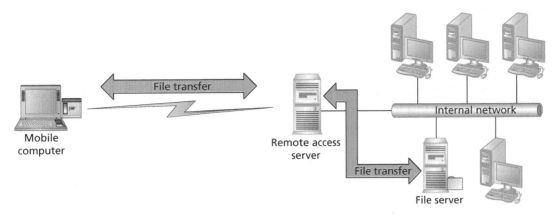

Figure 11-9 Remote access

A VPN is much faster than dial-up because it operates at almost the same speed as the Internet connection; however, latency is still much higher over a VPN than on a local area network (LAN). Therefore, even with a fast connection, accessing data is slower over a VPN than it is locally. Opening and saving files, such as Word documents, is a noticeably slower process over a VPN, but users might find it tolerable. For many apps that use a central database for data storage, a VPN is not practical because the app running on the client generates many small requests, and each request has high latency, which delays processing in the app.

Configuring VPN Clients

One of the main concerns when you allow remote access to resources is security. A VPN encrypts communication between the VPN clients and the remote access server, as shown in Figure 11-10. On the internal network, the remote access server sends the data as unencrypted cleartext just as if the client were located on the internal network. When you evaluate VPN security, you need to be aware of the different protocols and authentication methods that can be used.

Figure 11-10 Windows Remote Assistance

Windows Server 2019 can be configured as a remote access server by installing the Remote Access server role. When you use Windows Server as a remote access server, the required protocols for connectivity with Windows 10 are included in Windows 10. It's not necessary to deploy additional software on the clients.

Many organizations use a non-Microsoft solution for their VPN. Often, these solutions are provided by network equipment vendors, such as Cisco, Juniper, Palo Alto, SonicWALL, Fortinet, and WatchGuard. Most of the non-Microsoft solutions require you to install a VPN client that is specific to their solution.

VPN Protocols

The VPN protocols that are supported by Windows 10 are the protocols supported when you use Windows Server as a remote access server. When you are planning a VPN deployment, you decide which protocols will be offered based on your analysis of how secure they are and how easy they are to use. When you configure the VPN clients, you need to select a protocol that is already configured on the server.

PPTP

Point-to-Point Tunneling Protocol (PPTP) is one of the easiest protocols to use for a VPN. Authentication for PPTP is typically based on a user name and password, which is easy for users to work with. It is possible to configure certificate-based authentication, which is more secure, but this is seldom done.

Most remote locations, such as hotels, allow PPTP packets to pass through their firewalls. PPTP is widely supported because it is an older protocol that has been available since the 1990s; however, it is also one of the most insecure protocols. A determined hacker who has captured authentication traffic for PPTP can easily determine the user name and password. Despite the security concerns, PPTP is still used for some networks with low security requirements.

The PPTP protocol is initiated by the VPN client communicating with the remote access server on TCP port 1723. At this point, a Generic Routing Encapsulation (GRE) tunnel is created. The GRE packets are IP protocol type 47 and need to be allowed through any firewalls. The GRE packets have a source and destination IP address, but they are not TCP (6) or UDP (17) packets. This is why they require special consideration.

L2TP

Layer 2 Tunneling Protocol (L2TP) is only an authentication protocol. When you create an L2TP VPN connection, IPSec is used with L2TP to provide data encryption. The authentication provided by L2TP is based on user credentials. IPSec includes authentication for the VPN client and remote access server. The combination of the two authentication levels increases security, but it also makes it more difficult to manage L2TP VPN connections. As a consequence, the Microsoft implementation of L2TP has never become very popular.

The authentication for IPSec can be based on:

- *Pre-shared key*—This is a password that needs to be configured on both the VPN client and the remote access server. A pre-shared key is relatively easy to implement, but, because a single password is shared by all clients and the remote access server, this is not very secure.
- *Certificates*—If the VPN client and the remote access server have both been configured with certificates that are trusted, certificate authentication can be used. This is more secure than a pre-shared key, but it can be awkward to deploy certificates to all the VPN clients.
- *Kerberos*—Windows-based networks use Kerberos to authenticate users and computers. This same protocol can be used by IPSec. Using IPSec is possible only if the VPN client computer and the remote access server are members of the same Active Directory forest.

To allow L2TP connectivity through a firewall, you need to allow UDP port 500, UDP port 4500, and IP protocol type 50. IP protocol type 50 is Encapsulating Security Payload (ESP) that is used by IPSec.

SSTP

To simplify firewall configuration and ensure the best compatibility with remote locations, many VPNs are now based on Secure Sockets Layer (SSL). An SSL VPN uses TCP port 443, which is also used by secure websites. All public networks allow connectivity using TCP port 443. Microsoft has implemented **Secure Socket Tunneling Protocol (SSTP)** as an SSL VPN.

 TIP   SSL is an obsolete protocol for network encryption. SSL VPNs have been updated to use the new Transport Layer Security (TLS) protocol for network encryption, but retain SSL in the name.

An SSTP connection is authenticated by a user name and password to make it easier for users. In addition, the remote access server is authenticated because the certificate installed on the remote access server for encryption must be trusted.

IKEv2 Tunneling Protocol

Internet Key Exchange v2 Tunneling Protocol (IKEv2) is a newer VPN protocol that allows IPSec to be used for data encryption. Unlike L2TP, authentication for an IKEv2 VPN connection does not require that IPSec authentication be configured separately. You can use authentication based only on a user name and password.

The main benefit of IKEv2 is better support for unreliable network connections. Microsoft refers to this feature as **VPN Reconnect**. Unlike a typical VPN connection, which may lose connectivity when a network interruption occurs, IKEv2 can reconnect automatically when network connectivity is restored. In some cases, users might not notice that the VPN was ever disconnected.

Firewall configuration for IKEv2 is the same as for L2TP. You need to allow UDP port 500, UDP port 4500, and IP protocol type 50.

Creating a VPN Connection

In most cases, a typical user will have only one VPN connection back to the main office to access data; however, a support technician with multiple clients may have a VPN connection for each client. Your specific scenario determines which method for creating VPN connections will work best for you.

Individual Windows 10 users can create a VPN connection from Settings, as shown in Figure 11-11. You can also create a new connection from Network and Sharing Center by selecting Set up a new connection or network. When users configure a VPN connection manually, you will need to provide instructions on how to create the VPN connection, including any settings that are necessary. Even with instructions, the process tends to be error-prone because users make mistakes in the configuration.

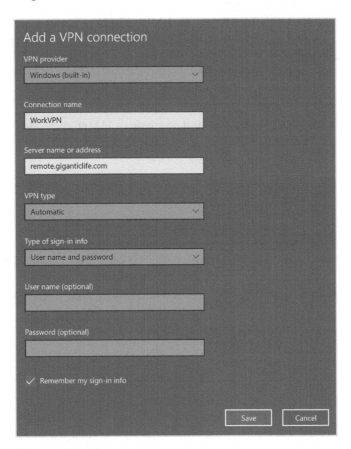

Figure 11-11 Creating a VPN connection in Settings

When you configure a VPN from Settings, you need to provide the following information:

- *VPN provider*—The VPN provider is the software that creates and controls the VPN connection. Windows 10 includes the Windows VPN provider, but other vendors can make providers available to support their specific type of VPN. Other VPN providers need to be installed as additional software because they are not included in Windows 10.
- *Connection name*—Each VPN connection needs a name to identify it. This should be given a name that relates to its purpose.
- *Server name or address*—This is the FQDN or IP address of the remote access server that the VPN client connects to.
- *VPN type*—The default value for VPN type is Automatic, which attempts to detect the type of VPN automatically. This avoids the need for the user to know the specific VPN type. If the type of VPN is not detected properly, you can select a specific VPN type, such as PPTP or SSTP, as defined on the remote access server.
- *Type of sign-in info*—Many organizations allow users to sign in by using a user name and password; however, you can enhance sign-in security by using smart cards, one-time passwords, or certificates.

An option to enter and save credentials (user name and password) is provided when you create the VPN connection. If you save the credentials, any user who gains access to your computer could remotely access over the VPN. This is less of a risk if BitLocker is being used to protect the hard drive.

Activity 11-9: Creating a VPN Connection

Time Required: 5 minutes

Objective: Create a VPN connection that connects to a remote access server

Description: You want to connect to the remote access server at your office to access files securely over the Internet. In this activity, you configure a VPN connection.

1. If necessary, start your computer and sign in.
2. Click the **Start** button and then click **Settings**.
3. In the Settings window, click **Network & Internet** and then click **VPN**.
4. Below the VPN heading, click **Add a VPN connection**.
5. In the Add a VPN connection window, in the VPN provider box, select **Windows (built-in)**.
6. In the Connection name box, type **WorkVPN**.
7. In the Server name or IP address box, type **vpnserver.giganticlife.com**.
8. In the VPN type box, select **Automatic**.
9. In the Type of sign-in info box, select **User name and password** and then click **Save**.
10. In the Settings window, click **WorkVPN** and then click **Advanced options**.
11. Review the list of options and close all open windows.

Automated VPN Deployment

Many organizations provide users with a list of instructions to create VPN connections manually on their computers. If you want to simplify VPN deployment for your users and reduce the chance of configuration errors, you can automate VPN deployment.

Several methods are available for deploying VPN connections automatically. These methods are listed in Table 11-3.

Table 11-3 Methods to Deploy VPN Connections

Deployment Method	Description
Group Policy Preferences	You can distribute VPN connections by using Group Policy Preferences. For domain-joined computers, this is the simplest way to configure VPN connections automatically. This method cannot be used for computers that are not domain joined.
Connection Manager Administration Kit (CMAK)	Connection Manager Administration Kit (CMAK) is a feature that can be installed on Windows 10 or Windows Server. You use CMAK to create VPN connections that are packaged as an executable file. Users can run the executable file to create VPN connections on their computer. Computers do not need to be domain joined.
Windows PowerShell	Although it is possible to create and manage VPN connections by using Windows PowerShell cmdlets, it is beyond the scope of this book to identify the cmdlet details for occasional use. You could, however, create a script that creates VPN connections as an alternative to distributing an executable created with CMAK. Computers do not need to be domain joined, but users need to be knowledgeable enough to run the Windows PowerShell script.
Windows Configuration Designer	You can use Windows Configuration Designer to create VPN connectivity profiles that are deployed to client computers as provisioning packages. Provisioning packages can be distributed to clients as a file that needs to be installed, via Microsoft Intune or via Microsoft Endpoint Configuration Manager.

Activity 11-10: Using CMAK

Time Required: 15 minutes

Objective: Use CMAK to create a deployment package for a VPN connection

Description: You would like to create a deployment package for a VPN connection that can be used by Windows 10 computers that are domain joined or not domain joined. In this activity, you install CMAK and create a deployment package for a VPN connection.

1. If necessary, start your computer and sign in as AD\Administrator.
2. Click the **Start** button and then click **Settings**.
3. In the Settings window, click **Apps**, click **Apps & features**, and then click **Optional features**.
4. On the Optional features screen, click **Add a feature**.
5. In the Add an optional feature window, select the **RAS Connection Manager Administration Kit (CMAK)** check box and then click **Install (1)**.
6. When installation is complete, close the Settings window.
7. Click the **Start** button, type **cmak**, and then click **Connection Manager Administration Kit**.
8. In the Connection Manager Administration Kit Wizard window, click **Next**.
9. On the Select the Target Operating System screen, click **Windows Vista or above** and then click **Next**.
10. On the Create or Modify a Connection Manager profile screen, click **New profile** and then click **Next**.
11. On the Specify the Service Name and the File Name screen, in the Service name text box, type **GiganticLifeVPN**.
12. In the File name text box, type **GLvpn** and then click **Next**.
13. On the Specify a Realm Name screen, click **Do not add a realm name to the user name** and then click **Next**.
14. On the Merge Information from Other Profiles screen, click **Next**.
15. On the Add Support for VPN Connections screen, select the **Phone book from this profile** check box.
16. In the VPN server name or IP address area, click **Always use the same VPN server**, type **remote.giganticlife.com** in the text box, and then click **Next**.
17. On the Create or Modify a VPN Entry screen, click **GiganticLifeVPN Tunnel <Default>** and then click **Edit**.
18. In the Edit VPN Entry window, click the **Security** tab.
19. In the VPN Strategy box, select **Try Secure Socket Tunneling Protocol First**.
20. In the Logon security area, click **Use Extensible Authentication Protocol (EAP)**, select **Microsoft: Protected EAP (PEAP) (encryption enabled)**, and then click **OK**.
21. On the Create or Modify a VPN Entry screen, click **Next**.
22. On the Add a Custom Phone Book screen, clear the **Automatically download phone book updates** check box and then click **Next**.
23. On the Configure Dial-up Networking Entries screen, click **Next**.
24. On the Specify Routing Table Updates screen, click **Next**.
25. On the Configure Proxy Settings for Internet Explorer screen, click **Next**.
26. On the Add Custom Actions screen, click **Next**.
27. On the Display a Custom Logon Bitmap screen, click **Next**.
28. On the Display a Custom Phone Book Bitmap screen, click **Next**.
29. On the Display Custom Icons screen, click **Next**.
30. On the Include a Custom Help File screen, click **Next**.
31. On the Display Custom Support Information screen, click **Next**.
32. On the Display a Custom License Agreement screen, click **Next**.
33. On the Install Additional Files with the Connection Manager profile screen, click **Next**.
34. On the Build the Connection Manager Profile and Its Installation Program screen, click **Next**.
35. On the Your Connection Manager Profile is Complete and Ready to Distribute screen, verify the location of the .exe file and then click **Finish**.

Activity 11-11: Using Windows PowerShell to View VPN Connections

Time Required: 5 minutes

Objective: Use Windows PowerShell to view the VPN connections on a computer

Description: As an administrator, you want a quick way to see the VPN connections that have been created on a computer. In this activity, you use Windows PowerShell to view the VPN connections on a computer.

1. If necessary, start your computer and sign in as AD\Administrator.
2. Right-click the **Start** button and then click **Windows PowerShell (Admin)**.
3. At the Windows PowerShell prompt, type **Get-Command *vpn*** and then press Enter.
4. Type **Get-VpnConnection -AllUserConnection** and then press **Enter**.
5. Close all open windows.

Authentication Protocols

When you create a VPN connection in Settings, you are required to specify the type of sign-in information. This setting defines the options that are used for authentication, which are shown in Figure 11-12. These advanced security settings can be edited from the properties of the VPN adapter. In most cases, you should configure the type of sign-in info through Settings rather than modifying the authentication settings directly.

Figure 11-12   VPN security settings

For the purpose of understanding documentation and using other tools, such as Windows PowerShell, for VPN management, it is useful to understand the authentication protocols.

Extensible Authentication Protocol (EAP) is a framework that allows multiple authentication methods to be integrated with the sign-in process. Multiple authentication methods are included with Windows 10, and more can be added by vendors. EAP can be used by the newer VPN protocols. IKEv2 requires the use of EAP.

Windows 10 includes Password Authentication Protocol (PAP) and Challenge Handshake Authentication Protocol (CHAP). Both of these protocols should be used only if there is no other choice. PAP transmits unencrypted credentials during authentication and CHAP has serious security flaws that make it easy to obtain the credentials. Microsoft CHAP version 2 (MS-CHAP v2) provides significantly better security than PAP and CHAP, but it is also known to be vulnerable to hacking with minimal effort and should be avoided whenever possible.

PAP, CHAP, and MS-CHAP v2 are used with PPTP VPNs. A preferred alternative is to use another VPN type for better security. If that is not possible, evaluate the possibility of using PEAP-MS-CHAP v2 with PPTP. This authentication method uses MS-CHAP v2 within **Protected EAP**. Protected EAP uses TLS to protect the authentication process and make it secure.

Network Settings

A VPN connection has network settings just like an Ethernet or Wi-Fi connection, as shown in Figure 11-13. The Client for Microsoft Networks and File and Printer Sharing for Microsoft Networks can be disabled, but there are no configuration settings. IPv4 and IPv6 have configuration options similar to a standard network adapter.

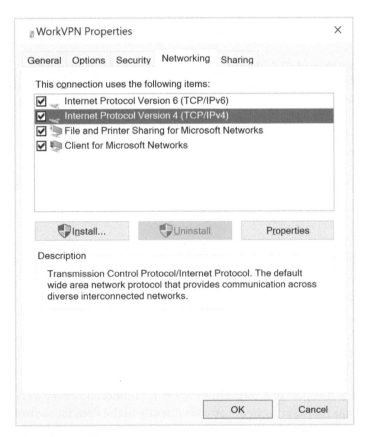

Figure 11-13 VPN network settings

By default, IPv4 is configured to obtain an IP address from DHCP automatically. In most cases, this is the preferred configuration; however, if you need to, you can configure a static address for the VPN connection. One setting that can be useful to change in the Advanced TCP/IP Settings is for the default gateway, as shown in the next activity.

NOTE 8

Configuring a VPN client to route some traffic through the VPN and some through the local default gateways is known as split tunneling.

The setting Use default gateway on remote network is selected by default. When this setting is enabled, all network access is done through the VPN. This is on by default to ensure that VPN clients can access resources on remote networks where the remote access server is located; however, this also means that all Internet access goes through the VPN, which might make Internet access slow. The remote access server can be configured to provide static routes to the VPN clients for internal resources and then allow VPN clients to continue using their normal default gateway.

Activity 11-12: Disabling the VPN as Default Gateway

Time Required: 5 minutes

Objective: Disable a VPN from being used as a default gateway

Description: You want to optimize Internet connectivity for a VPN client. The VPN server provides static routes for all of the internal networks, and the VPN clients use the local Internet connection as a default gateway. In this activity, you disable the use of the VPN as a default gateway.

1. If necessary, start your computer and sign in as AD\Administrator.
2. Click the **Start** button and then click **Settings**.
3. In the Settings window, click **Network & Internet**, click **VPN**, and then click **Change Adapter options**.
4. In the Network Connections window, right-click **WorkVPN** and then click **Properties**.
5. In the WorkVPN Properties dialog box, click the **Networking** tab, click **Internet Protocol Version 4 (TCP/IPv4)**, and then click **Properties**.
6. In the Internet Protocol Version 4 (TCP/IPv4) Properties dialog box, click **Advanced**.
7. In the Advanced TCP/IP Settings dialog box, on the IP Settings tab, clear the **Use default gateway on remote network** check box and then click **OK**.
8. In the Internet Protocol Version 4 (TCP/IPv4) Properties dialog box, click **OK**.
9. In the WorkVPN Properties dialog box, click **OK**.
10. Close all open windows.

Always On VPN

Always On VPN is a VPN configuration that is available only for Windows 10 clients. When you configure Always On VPN, client computers can automatically connect to the VPN whenever connectivity is available. Benefits of this configuration are:

- *Easier for users*—Users do not need to do anything for Always On VPN to work. Access to all resources can be maintained with the only difference being slower access.
- *Clients are manageable*—Because the VPN is always on, the clients are manageable even when they are on the road. Group Policy Objects (GPOs) can still be applied and software deployment technologies still work. Generally, with a VPN, clients are not considered to be manageable.

You can implement device tunnel as part of Always On VPN. Device tunnel allows the VPN to connect and authenticate before users sign in. This means that user authentication is directly to the domain controller rather than using cached credentials. In this state, the help desk can reset user passwords and have them take effect immediately.

 **CAUTION**   To implement device tunnel, you need to be using Windows 10 Enterprise or Education and the computers must be domain joined.

If you are using Windows 10 Pro, then only user tunnel is available for Always On VPN. User tunnel authenticates automatically after the user signs in to Windows 10. This still provides an excellent user experience but does not provide some of the management options available with device tunnel.

Always On VPN uses the IKEv2 protocol whenever possible, but will fallback and use SSTP when IKEv2 cannot be used. IKEv2 is preferred due to the VPN Reconnect functionality. Authentication is based on certificates issued to users and computers by an internal certification authority configured on a Windows Server.

 **CAUTION** The server configuration for Always On VPN is complex and should be carefully planned before you attempt to deploy.

To configure Always On VPN for Windows 10 computers, you need to create an XML configuration file with the settings for your deployment. Then, you run a Windows PowerShell script (typically VPN_Profile.ps1) that uses the settings in the XML file to create the Always On VPN profile. To automate this process, you can use a logon script or Microsoft Endpoint Configuration Manager. There is no support to deploy Always On VPN by using Group Policy.

DirectAccess

DirectAccess is a technology similar to Always On VPN that is based on using a device tunnel. Authentication is performed automatically in the background whenever there is connectivity between the roaming client and the DirectAccess server. The initial release of DirectAccess for Windows 7 required certificates to be issued for authentication, but Windows 10 does not require certificates. Instead, a Kerberos proxy can be used for Windows 10 if some advanced features, such as high availability, are not required.

The client connectivity for DirectAccess is based on IPv6. Because most DirectAccess clients do not have IPv6 connectivity directly to the DirectAccess server, the IPv6 packets are tunneled in IPv4 packets over the Internet. On the internal network, there is no requirement for servers accessed by clients to have IPv6 configured.

Windows 10 is configured for DirectAccess by using GPOs. The GPOs are created on the server side during the DirectAccess configuration process. So, no manual configuration is required on the Windows 10 clients. In most cases, after DirectAccess is properly configured on the server, there is nothing to do on the client side.

The GPOs for DirectAccess are applied to a specific Active Directory group that is selected during configuration. For DirectAccess GPOs to apply to computers, the computer accounts need to be added to that group.

 **CAUTION** It is strongly recommended to implement Always On VPN instead of DirectAccess because it does not require the Enterprise or Education edition of Windows 10. If you need to support Windows 8.1, then DirectAccess is required.

SYNCHRONIZING DATA FOR MOBILE CLIENTS

When you are in a location without network connectivity or with poor network quality, you cannot use a VPN or other forms of remote access. Sometimes locations do not provide guest Wi-Fi access, and hotels are notorious for having poor quality Wi-Fi.

When there is either no connectivity or poor connectivity, **data synchronization** can be a solution. Data synchronization copies files locally to mobile computers. Then, users can work with the files whether they are connected to a network or not. At some point, the changed files are copied back (uploaded) to the server. The timing of the synchronization varies depending on the technology used for data synchronization.

One key consideration for data synchronization is shared application data. Users cannot access shared app data by using data synchronization unless the app performs its own offline data synchronization process. So, generally, data synchronization is good for personal files but not as useful for shared data.

NOTE 9

For more information about Always On VPN, see Remote Access Always On VPN at https://docs.microsoft.com/en-us/windows-server/remote/remote-access/vpn/always-on-vpn/.

OneDrive

OneDrive is an example of how file synchronization can be used. Multiple computers can access the same OneDrive account, and all the computers can synchronize the files locally. For example, you can use the same OneDrive account on your desktop computer at the office, a laptop, and a desktop computer at home.

By default, OneDrive uses File On-Demand, which does not synchronize files locally until you open them. If you are on a mobile device and expect to be without network connectivity, you should force the files to sync locally. When you choose the Always keep on this device option for a file or folder, changes are automatically synced locally as soon as possible. This is important to be aware of when you are using multiple devices.

When you edit files, it is from a local copy, which is faster than accessing the file remotely. When you modify a file, the changes are synchronized back up to OneDrive. If you are offline when you modify a file, the changes are synchronized the next time you have an Internet connection.

In addition to the consumer version of OneDrive, OneDrive for Business also is included as part of Microsoft 365 and Office 365 cloud services. OneDrive for Business has approximately the same functionality as the consumer version, but it is part of SharePoint Online. You can also synchronize files from libraries in SharePoint Online. The default storage limit in OneDrive for Business is 1 terabyte (TB).

Offline Files

Offline files is a Windows 10 feature that synchronizes files from a shared folder to a Windows 10 computer. Synchronization happens when the computer has connectivity to the server sharing the files. So, files are typically synchronized while in the office, used and modified offline while on the road, and then synchronized again when the computer is back in the office.

Offline files need to be enabled on both the Windows 10 computer and on the file share. If offline files are enabled in both locations, the default behavior is for the user to manually select any files or folders that will be cached (available offline). It is possible to configure a share to automatically make files available offline, but that is not recommended, so as to avoid synchronization errors on clients.

After files have been cached, they are available even when not connected to a network. Users access offline files using the exact same path as was used when the files were cached. If a user enables a folder on a mapped drive letter, such as H:\Important, to be offline, the files are accessible through H:\Important when disconnected from the network.

Typically, the offline files feature is not used for shared data, only personal data (such as a home folder). This minimizes the risk of conflicts where a cached copy of the file has been modified and the original source also has been modified. No automated mechanism exists to resolve such conflicts; the user needs to look at both files and merge the changes together if necessary. Some apps provide functionality to merge changes between two files, but sometimes it must be done manually.

To review any synchronization errors, you can use Sync Center, as shown in Figure 11-14. Sync Center shows any replication conflicts. Sync Center lists the locations being synchronized.

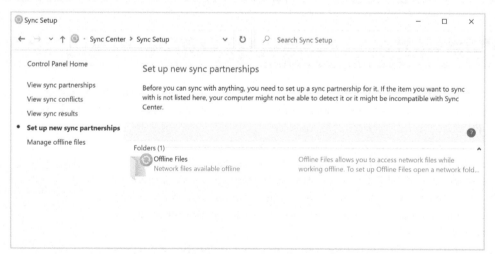

Figure 11-14 Sync Center

Activity 11-13: Enabling Offline Files

Time Required: 5 minutes

Objective: Enable offline files

Description: You want to use offline files to store the contents of your home folder on your laptop. In this activity, you enable offline files on your computer.

1. If necessary, start your computer and sign in.
2. Click the **Start** button, type **Control**, and then click **Control Panel**.
3. In the Control Panel window, in the **Search Control Panel** box, type **sync** and then click **Sync Center**.
4. In Sync Center, click **Manage offline files**.
5. In the Offline Files dialog box, click **Enable offline files** and then click **OK**.
6. Click **Yes** to restart your computer.
7. Close all open windows.

Work Folders

When you implement **Work Folders**, each user is given a unique folder for file storage that can be synchronized across multiple devices. The folder for each user is stored on a file server. So, it is possible to access the folder through a file share and also to synchronize the folder contents by using the Work Folders client. The Work Folders client is available for Windows 7 and newer client operating systems. You can also obtain a Work Folders client for iOS and Android devices.

 TIP   Work Folders is similar to running a private version of OneDrive.

When Work Folders is configured on the server(s), a URL is identified for accessing Work Folders. Clients need to be configured to use that URL. Several methods can be used to configure the clients, but automatic discovery is preferred because it supports devices that are not domain joined.

Automatic discovery of the Work Folders URL is based on the email address of the user. If the user's email address is susan@giganticlife.com, the Work Folders client attempts to connect to https://workfolders.giganticlife.com. In a single-server deployment of Work Folders, this directs all users directly to the server hosting their Work Folder.

If multiple Work Folder servers exist, you can still use automatic discovery, but you also need to configure each user object in Active Directory with the appropriate Work Folders URL. When susan@giganticlife.com contacts https://workfolders.giganticlife.com, she is redirected to the Work Folders URL configured in her user object. The URL is stored in the msDS-SyncServerUrl attribute of the user object.

Another simple method that works when devices are not domain joined is manually entering the Work Folders URL. This is provided as an option in the Work Folders configuration screen, as shown in Figure 11-15. When allowing users to enter the URL, there is always a risk of the URL being incorrectly entered.

For domain-joined computers, you can use Group Policy to configure the Work Folders URL. You can also use Group Policy to force the Work Folders client to be enabled instead of waiting for the user to start configuration.

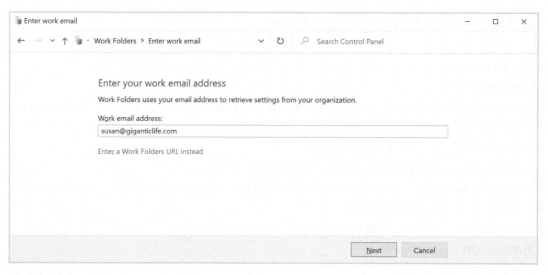

Figure 11-15   Work Folders configuration

SUMMARY

- In enterprise environments you need to use remote connectivity to manage and troubleshoot Windows 10 clients. You can use Remote Desktop, Remote Assistance, and Quick Assist to remote control clients. You can use MMC snap-ins, the registry editor, and Windows PowerShell remoting to remotely configure clients.
- To provide a consistent user environment for roaming users, you can use tools that store data in a central location. Mapped drive letters and folder redirection can be used to centralize data storage. Credential roaming, UE-V, and profile synchronization can be used to store settings centrally.
- VPNs provide secure remote access to network resources over the Internet. A VPN connection can use various protocols such as PPTP, L2TP, SSTP, or IKEv2. Always On VPN and DirectAccess provide automatic connectivity for remote users.
- Data synchronization is an important consideration for mobile clients to retain access to data when they don't have network connectivity. OneDrive can synchronize data between a client and a cloud service. Offline files and Work Folders can synchronize data with a file server.

Key Terms

Always On VPN	Point-to-Point Tunneling	User Experience Virtualization
data synchronization	Protocol (PPTP)	(UE-V)
DirectAccess	Protected EAP	virtual private network (VPN)
Extensible Authentication	Quick Assist	VPN Reconnect
Protocol (EAP)	Remote Assistance	Windows PowerShell remoting
folder redirection	Remote Desktop	Windows Remote Management
Internet Key Exchange v2	Remote Desktop Connection	(WinRM)
Tunneling Protocol (IKEv2)	remote procedure calls (RPC)	Work Folders
Layer 2 Tunneling Protocol (L2TP)	Secure Socket Tunneling	
offline files	Protocol (SSTP)	

Review Questions

1. You want to connect to a user desktop to review Windows 10 configuration settings when the user is not present. Which technology should you use?
   a. VPN
   b. Remote Desktop
   c. Windows PowerShell remoting
   d. Remote Assistance
   e. Quick Assist

2. Which of the following technologies allows you to access files from a Windows 10 computer that is not currently connected to a network (wired or wireless)? (Choose all that apply.)
   a. VPN
   b. Work Folders
   c. OneDrive
   d. Remote Desktop
   e. offline files

3. PPTP is the preferred VPN protocol. True or False?

4. Which of the following are authentication methods that can be used by IPSec? (Choose all that apply.)
   a. pre-shared key
   b. hash value
   c. certificates
   d. Kerberos
   e. NTLM

5. Which port numbers and packet types are relevant for allowing L2TP/IPSec through a firewall? (Choose all that apply.)
   a. TCP port 1723
   b. UDP port 4500
   c. TCP port 443
   d. IP protocol type 47 (GRE)
   e. IP protocol type 50 (ESP)

6. Which port numbers and packet types are relevant for allowing SSTP through a firewall?
   a. TCP port 1723
   b. UDP port 4500
   c. TCP port 443
   d. IP protocol type 47 (GRE)
   e. IP protocol type 50 (ESP)

7. Which VPN protocol supports the VPN Reconnect feature?
   a. PPTP
   b. L2TP/IPSec
   c. SSTP
   d. IKEv2
   e. DirectAccess

8. Which remote connectivity type automatically connects clients to the main office when they are roaming? (Choose all that apply.)
   a. PPTP
   b. Always On VPN
   c. SSTP
   d. IKEv2
   e. DirectAccess

9. Selecting a VPN type of Automatic is suitable for most VPN deployments. True or False?

10. Which automated method for VPN connection deployment would work best in combination with Microsoft Intune or Microsoft Endpoint Configuration Manager?
    a. CMAK
    b. Group Policy Preferences
    c. Windows Configuration Designer
    d. Windows PowerShell

11. EAP is a framework for implementing authentication protocols rather than an actual authentication protocol. True or False?

12. Which VPN authentication protocol uses SSL?
    a. PAP
    b. CHAP
    c. MS-CHAP v2
    d. EAP
    e. Protected EAP

13. When you configure a VPN connection, the VPN must be used as the default gateway. True or False?

14. Which technology, based on templates, allows you to synchronize application settings across multiple computers for domain users?
    a. mapped drive letters
    b. folder redirection
    c. credential roaming
    d. UE-V
    e. profile synchronization by using a Microsoft account

15. Which option for mstsc.exe prevents connection information from being cached on the local computer?
    a. /admin
    b. /shadow
    c. /restrictedAdmin
    d. /remoteGuard
    e. /public

16. Remote Desktop in Windows 10 allows multiple users to connect to one computer at the same time. True or False?

17. Which technology allows you to store user profile data, including documents, on a central file server instead of on the local disk?
   a. mapped drive letters
   b. folder redirection
   c. credential roaming
   d. UE-V
   e. profile synchronization by using a Microsoft account

18. Automatic configuration for Work Folders is based on the email address of the user. True or False?

19. Which command can you use to configure Windows PowerShell remoting on a computer running Windows 10?

   a. winrm quickconfig
   b. Enter-PSSession
   c. Set-WSManQuickConfig
   d. VPN_Profile.ps1
   e. Enable-PSRemoting

20. You want to connect to a user desktop and have the user demonstrate a problem that they are having. Which technology should you use?
   a. VPN
   b. Remote Desktop
   c. Windows PowerShell remoting
   d. Remote Assistance
   e. Quick Assist

Case Projects

Case Project 11-1: Data for Traveling Users

Hyperactive Media Sales needs to provide a remote access solution for its traveling salespeople. They have a server running Windows Server 2019 that can be configured as a remote access server for VPN connectivity. You have been reviewing the VPN protocols that are available and need to decide on the best protocol. The traveling salespeople often stay in hotels, so firewall compatibility is a serious concern. Which VPN protocol has the best compatibility with firewalls

Case Project 11-2: Managing Mobile Computers

Big Bob's Construction has many construction sites where computers running Windows 10 Pro are located. At the remote sites, Internet connectivity can be of poor quality and intermittent. Because the computers are onsite and have poor connectivity to the main office, they are not currently domain joined, although they could be if required.

   You want to be able to manage the computers at the construction sites. Which technology can allow you to do this and not force users to reconnect constantly?

Case Project 11-3: Managing Enterprise Clients

Gigantic Life Insurance has a centralized help desk that supports users in multiple physical locations. The computers in company-owned buildings are domain joined and are running Windows 10. Sales agents are also in independent offices with computers running Windows 10 that are not domain joined. The independent offices don't have direct connectivity to the Gigantic Life Insurance network.

   When users call in to the help desk with problems, they often have trouble describing the issue accurately. You need the ability to view the user desktop as the user demonstrates the problem. You'd like to standardize on a single tool for this purpose. Which tool should you select, and why?

AUTOMATING WINDOWS 10 DEPLOYMENT

After reading this chapter and completing the exercises, you will be able to:

1. Choose a method for installation
2. Choose a type of installation
3. Describe tools in the Windows 10 Assessment and Deployment Kit
4. Perform an unattended installation of Windows 10
5. Prepare Windows 10 for imaging
6. Use DISM for imaging
7. Use provisioning to customize Windows 10 installations
8. Describe enterprise deployment tools for Windows 10

For end users, operating system deployment is a rare event that doesn't need to be optimized. For professionals in the computer industry, optimizing deployment is a critical process that can save many hours of work and reduce support calls. You need to be aware of the various installation methods so that you can choose one that is appropriate for your organization.

Most organizations have developed some variety of automated deployment process. In this module, you will learn how to perform an unattended installation by using answer files. You will also learn how to use Sysprep and the Deployment Imaging Servicing and Management (DISM) tool to perform image-based installations. To configure already deployed instances of Windows 10, you will learn how to create and apply provisioning packages. Finally, you will learn about using enterprise deployment tools to further automate the deployment of Windows 10.

WINDOWS 10 INSTALLATION METHODS

Windows 10 supports several different installation methods. Which method you choose will vary depending on the number of computers in your organization, the speed of your network, and the level of customization that is required.

OEM Installation

When you purchase a new computer from a hardware vendor, it contains a preinstalled copy of Windows 10. This Original Equipment Manufacturer (OEM) installation of Windows 10 is a standard configuration used by the vendor for that specific model of computer. This is a fully functional version of Windows 10 that you can use. An OEM installation of Windows 10 will include all the manufacturer-specific hardware drivers that are required for that model. Some vendors also include additional utility software that is useful beyond the basic drivers. Using the OEM installation is a large time savings because Windows 10 is ready to go when you receive the computer.

The only drawback to using the OEM installation of Windows 10 is the potential for extra unwanted software. Some hardware vendors receive money from software vendors to include their software. Sometimes, the software slows down the system or just confuses users. Removing the included software can be time consuming. This is more of a problem with lower-end consumer systems with slim profit margins than business systems.

Removable Media Installation

The removable media installation method is the least-suitable method for a large volume of computers. It requires you to visit each computer with removable media containing the Windows 10 installation files and leave the removable media in the computer during the installation process. This method is suitable for small organizations that only occasionally install Windows 10.

 TIP The speed of removable media has a large impact on installation speed. Using a USB drive with Windows 10 installation files is typically much faster than using a DVD.

If you are using Windows 10 installation files from volume licensing, it might not include the manufacturer-specific hardware drivers for your computer. This is most likely on newer computer systems. You will need to download additional hardware drivers for installation during or after installing Windows 10. If you use Windows 10 media from your hardware manufacturer, it usually includes the necessary hardware drivers, but not the most up-to-date version.

When you install from removable media, Windows updates apps are not included. If you are using older media, you need to apply updates immediately after the installation. This can be time consuming if many updates are required. Apps are also not included and need to be installed.

Installing from removable media is typically a manual process that is not automated. You need to manually select all the necessary configurations during the installation process. It is possible to automate the installation process by using an answer file that contains installation settings, but it is not common to do so because smaller organizations don't find it worth the effort to automate a task that is rarely done.

Distribution Share Installation

A distribution share installation requires computers to be booted into Windows Preinstallation Environment (Windows PE) from removable storage and then run the Windows 10 installation from a distribution share on a server. You need to configure Windows PE on the removable storage to allow network connectivity. The Windows 10 installation files on the distribution share are configured by Windows System Image Manager (SIM).

The speed of a distribution share installation varies because the files must be transferred across the network. Over a 1 Gbps (gigabits per second) network, a distribution share installation is typically faster than a DVD boot installation. On a wireless network, installation speed will vary with the strength of the network signal.

The level of customization for a distribution share installation is higher than a DVD boot installation because you can include additional files, such as updates or drivers, as part of the installation process.

Image-Based Installation

An image is a copy of a previously prepared operating system that has been copied to a file. Image-based installation requires you to create a customized image that you apply to each computer. After the customized image is created, it is placed on a distribution share by using Windows SIM. This installation type requires computers to be booted into Windows PE from removable storage and then copy the customized image onto the computer.

An image-based installation is the fastest type of installation because most configuration is already complete; however, you might need several images for different types of users. In larger organizations, it is reasonable to put forth the effort required to develop multiple images.

The highest level of customization is achieved by using image-based installations. Image-based installations can include service packs, updates, additional drivers, and even installed applications. You need to remember, though, that as you perform additional image customization, it becomes more time consuming. For example, if you include applications in the image, you need to consider how you will apply updates to those apps to ensure they're up to date when you deploy them.

WINDOWS 10 INSTALLATION TYPES

When an organization moves to a new desktop operating system, the network administrators must decide whether to upgrade existing systems or perform clean installations. A **clean installation** is an installation of Windows 10 performed on a computer that does not have existing data or applications. If you are deploying to existing computers, a clean installation requires you to wipe the hard drive first. If clean installations are performed, you need to consider whether user settings need to be migrated from the old operating system to the new operating system and how you will do that.

In the past, most organizations chose to perform clean installations when deploying a new operating system because the computers tended to be more stable afterward. Now, however, Microsoft recommends in-place upgrades instead. This is because in-place upgrades to Windows 10 perform a clean installation in the background and then migrate settings.

Upgrade Installations

An **upgrade installation** is also referred to as an in-place upgrade. Upgrade installations automatically migrate the user settings, files, and applications that exist in the previous operating system to the new operating system on the same computer. For example, when you perform an upgrade from Windows 8.1 to Windows 10, the user settings and files are retained. All the compatible applications are retained, as well.

To upgrade to Windows 10, a computer must be running Windows 7 with Service Pack 1 or Windows 8.1. Additionally, upgrades must be to an equivalent version. For example, Windows 8.1 Pro can be upgraded to Windows 10 Pro.

To upgrade to Windows 10, you need to obtain Windows 10 installation media. You cannot use image-based installation when you perform an upgrade to Windows 10. You must run Setup.exe to properly upgrade an existing computer. Only DVD boot installations and distribution share installations use Setup.exe.

Because the Windows 10 installation is image-based, the upgrade process captures settings from the previous operating system and applies them after Windows 10 is installed. You can see this during the upgrade process. A potential downside to this process is that the upgrade may not migrate all settings and applications, because settings stored in a nonstandard way might be missed.

> **NOTE 1**
>
> For a complete list of allowed upgrade paths, see Windows 10 upgrade paths at https://docs.microsoft.com/en-us/windows/deployment/upgrade/windows-10-upgrade-paths.

Most computer hardware and software are compatible with Windows 10. In a business environment, however, you should verify that all important applications are compatible with Windows 10 before upgrading. Check with the application vendor for compatibility information.

Clean Installations

Most Windows 10 installations are clean installations. Home users typically get Windows 10 when they buy a new computer. A new computer always has a clean installation. Even in corporate environments, new operating systems are often implemented when new computers are purchased. Using new computers ensures that they are powerful enough to run the new operating system, and new applications are often introduced at the same time.

When a clean installation is performed on an existing computer, the hard drive of the computer is wiped and reformatted to erase the contents before installation. This raises concerns about losing files stored on the local hard drive of the computer.

In most corporate environments, computer usage rules dictate that users cannot store any files on their local hard drive. In practice, though, many users store important files on the local hard drive despite the usage rules. Network administrators are, therefore, always concerned about locally stored data as part of performing a clean installation on an existing computer.

Even when a clean installation is performed on a new computer, concerns with data migration arise. When a new computer is obtained, users often want to retain files and settings from the old computer.

Clean installations can be performed by any installation method. This includes the DVD boot, distribution share, or image-based installation methods.

Migrating User Settings and Files

Most organizations discourage users from saving documents locally on their computers. If data is stored in a central location, such as a file share or OneDrive, you don't need a process in place to migrate that data when users are given a new computer. The new computer is configured to access that shared data. If data is not stored centrally, you need to copy it from the old computer to the new computer.

Many users want the Windows settings and application settings from their old computer to be migrated to their new computer. This can include personal settings, such as Microsoft Edge favorites, and application specific settings, such as default save locations and document templates. Migration works well for Windows settings and application settings stored in a central location by using services such as folder redirection or User Experience Virtualization (UE-V), or by syncing settings with a Microsoft account. Unfortunately, most organizations do not have roaming configured for Windows settings and application settings.

During an upgrade to Windows 10, profiles are automatically upgraded, and settings within the profile are retained. When a clean installation is performed, many organizations do not migrate settings from the older computer to the new computer. Instead, users need to reconfigure their new computer as desired. Company standard settings can be applied by using Group Policy.

> **TIP** Windows 8.1 included Windows Easy Transfer to migrate user profiles to a new computer. Windows 10 does not include a utility to migrate user profiles. Microsoft has partnered with Laplink to provide PCmover for user profile migration at reduced rates.

Microsoft provides the **User State Migration Tool (USMT)** for migrating user profiles to Windows 10. USMT is a set of command-line tools that are part of the Windows 10 Assessment and Deployment Kit (ADK). Larger organizations create scripts to capture user profile data before operating system deployment and apply user profile data after operating system deployment.

Most small organizations do not use tools for migrating user profile data. Instead, administrators manually copy important profile information, such as favorites and documents. Small organizations typically do not move Windows settings and application settings.

WINDOWS 10 ASSESSMENT AND DEPLOYMENT KIT

In larger organizations, administrators need tools to help automate the installation and configuration of Windows 10. To help network administrators deploy Windows 10, Microsoft provides the **Windows 10 Assessment and Deployment Kit (ADK)**. Windows ADK contains tools to prepare for deployments and automate the deployment process. Figure 12-1 shows the features available in the Windows 10 ADK.

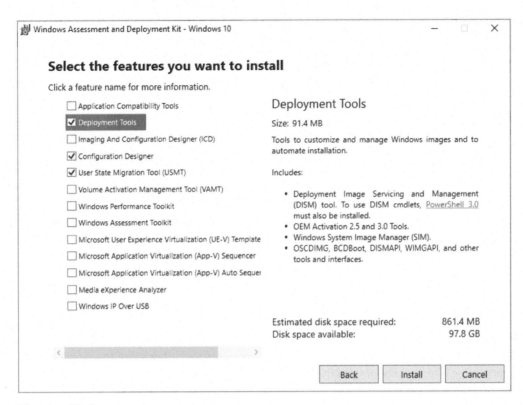

Figure 12-1   Windows 10 ADK features

The Windows 10 ADK includes many tools. You should identify your goals for automating system deployment and then select the appropriate tools. Table 12-1 describes the tools in the Windows 10 ADK.

Table 12-1   Windows ADK Tools

Tool	Description
Application Compatibility Tools	This option includes the Compatibility Administrator and Standard User Analyzer tools. Compatibility Administrator helps you configure older applications to run in Windows 10. Standard User Analyzer helps you to identify why older applications are not compatible with Windows 10.
Deployment Tools	This option includes several command-line tools that can be used to configure Windows 10 and boot images for Windows 10. Deployment Image Servicing and Management (DISM) is used to configure running instances of Windows 10 or offline images. Windows System Image Manager is used to create files that automate unattended installations.
Imaging and Configuration Designer	This is an older tool that has been replaced by Configuration Design as of Windows 10 version 1703.
Configuration Designer	This tool creates provisioning packages that can be applied to running installations of Windows 10 or offline images.
User State Migration Tool (USMT)	This option installs a set of command-line tools that can be used to capture and apply user profile data.
Volume Activation Management Tool (VAMT)	This tool can be used to provide volume activation on the network rather than requiring computers to activate by contacting Microsoft servers.

(continues)

Table 12-1   Windows ADK Tools (*Continued*)

Tool	Description
Windows Performance Toolkit	These tools record detailed system performance data for analysis.
Windows Assessment Toolkit	These tools can be used with the Windows Performance Toolkit to simulate user activity for load testing.
Microsoft User Experience Virtualization (UE-V) Template Generator	This tool generates and edits templates that define which settings are synchronized by UE-V for applications.
Microsoft Application Virtualization (App-V) Sequencer	You can use this tool to convert an app that is installed by Setup.exe or Windows Installer for delivery by App-V. The app installation is recorded to identify the necessary changes.
Microsoft Application Virtualization (App-V) Auto Sequencer	This tool helps to automate sequencing multiple applications as a batch.
Media eXperience Analyzer	These tools analyze media performance (for example, video playback can be analyzed).

Windows PE

Windows PE is a limited and non-graphical version of Windows 10 that can be used for installing, troubleshooting, and repairing Windows 10. Windows PE includes networking components and allows you to use current Windows drivers for network connectivity. When you boot from the Windows 10 installation media, Windows PE is the operating system that controls the installation process.

For Windows installation, you can create customized Windows PE boot media to start the installation process. When you configure the Windows PE boot media with the correct drivers for local storage and network adapters, you can use installation files on a distribution share. You can also use customized Windows PE boot media to apply Windows 10 images.

 TIP   Older versions of Windows 10 ADK included Windows PE, but Windows PE is now a separate download.

Activity 12-1: Downloading Windows 10 ADK and Windows PE for Offline Use

Time Required: 30–60 minutes

Objective: Download the Windows ADK for Windows 10 and Windows PE for offline use

Description: The default installation of the Windows ADK for Windows 10 downloads and installs only the components that you select. Windows PE is a separate add-on for the Windows ADK for Windows 10. You anticipate using the Windows ADK for Windows 10 and Windows PE on several different computers. In this activity, you download the files for offline installation. After the files are downloaded, you can copy the directory to any location and install the features that you select.

NOTE 2

This activity provides detailed steps to download the Windows ADK for Windows 10 version 2004. If you are using a newer version of Windows 10, then download the appropriate version.

NOTE 3

To save time, your instructor might have downloaded these files and made them available to you on a network file share or removable storage. Check with your instructor.

1. If necessary, start your computer and sign in.
2. On the taskbar, click **Microsoft Edge**.

3. In the address bar, type **https://docs.microsoft.com/windows-hardware/get-started/adk-install** and then press **Enter**.
4. On the Download and install the Windows ADK page, scroll down, and then click **Download the Windows ADK for Windows 10, version 2004**.
5. In the pop-up box, click **Run**.
6. In the Windows Assessment and Deployment Kit - Windows 10 window, click **Download the Windows Assessment and Deployment Kit - Windows 10 for installation on a separate computer**.
7. In the Download Path box, type **C:\ADK** and then click **Next**.
8. On the Windows Kits Privacy screen, if necessary, click **Yes** and then click **Next**.
9. On the License Agreement screen, click **Accept**.
10. Wait while the files are downloaded. Because the download is approximately 1 GB, it can take a while for the download to complete.
11. When the download is complete, click **Close**.
12. On the Download and install the Windows ADK page, click **Download the Windows PE add-on for the ADK, version 2004**.
13. In the pop-up box, click **Run**.
14. In the Windows Assessment and Deployment Kit Windows Preinstallation Environment Add-ons - Windows 10 window, click **Download the Windows Assessment and Deployment Kit Windows Preinstallation Environment Add-ons - Windows 10 for installation on a separate computer**.
15. In the Download Path box, type **C:\ADKWinPEAddons** and then click **Next**.
16. On the Windows Kits Privacy screen, if necessary, click **Yes** and then click **Next**.
17. On the License Agreement screen, click **Accept**.
18. Wait while the files are downloaded. Because the download is approximately 2.7 GB, it can take a while for the download to complete.
19. When the download is complete, click **Close**.
20. Exit Microsoft Edge.

Activity 12-2: Installing the Windows ADK for Windows 10 and Windows PE

Time Required: 10 minutes
Objective: Install the Windows ADK for Windows 10 and Windows PE
Description: To begin testing automated deployment for Windows 10, you need to install the Windows ADK for Windows 10 and Windows PE. To minimize the disk space used, you will install only the required tools.

This activity assumes that the Windows ADK files have been downloaded to C:\ADK and the WinPE files have been downloaded to C:\ADKWinPEAddons. If your files are in another location, run adksetup.exe from that location instead.

1. If necessary, start your computer and sign in.
2. On the taskbar, click **File Explorer**.
3. In the navigation pane, click **This PC**, double-click **Local Disk (C:)**, and then double-click **ADK**.
4. Double-click **adksetup**.
5. In the Windows Assessment and Deployment Kit - Windows 10 window, click **Next** to accept the default installation location.
6. On the Windows Kits Privacy screen, if necessary, click **Yes** and then click **Next**.
7. On the License Agreement screen, click **Accept**.
8. On the Select the features you want to install page, select only the following features and then click **Install**:
   - Deployment Tools
   - Configuration Designer
   - User State Migration Tool (USMT)
9. If necessary, in the User Account Control dialog box, click **Yes**.

10. On the Welcome to the Windows Assessment and Deployment Kit - Windows 10! page, click **Close**.
11. In File Explorer, browse to **C:\ADKWinPEAddons** and then double-click **adkwinpesetup**.
12. In the Windows Assessment and Deployment Kit Windows Preinstallation Environment Add-ons - Windows 10 window, click **Next** to accept the default installation location.
13. On the Windows Kits Privacy screen, if necessary, click **Yes** and then click **Next**.
14. On the License Agreement screen, click **Accept**.
15. On the Select the features you want to install screen, click **Install**.
16. Click the **Start** button, click **All apps**, scroll down, and then click **Windows Kits**. You can see that the new tools are located here.
17. Close the Start menu.

UNATTENDED INSTALLATION

An **unattended installation** does not require administrator intervention. The entire process can be automated using an answer file. An **answer file** is an XML file that contains settings used during the Windows installation process. Installation settings are read from the answer file instead of requiring administrator input during installation. Unattended installations are faster than attended installations and can be more consistent when the same answer file is used each time.

Using an unattended installation gives you a wider range of configuration options than can be performed during an attended installation. For example, an attended installation does not allow you to configure network settings. An unattended installation allows you to configure network settings and many other settings by putting the necessary information in the answer file.

Configuration Passes

Windows 10 has multiple phases of setup that are named configuration passes. The answer file used for configuration settings has a different section for each configuration pass. Some settings can be configured in multiple configuration passes; however, only the last applied setting is effective. Figure 12-2 shows the configuration passes used by a simple unattended installation.

Figure 12-2   Simple unattended configuration passes

The overall process for a simple unattended installation, booting from Windows 10, uses configuration passes in the following steps:

1. Windows PE starts from the installation boot media.
2. Setup.exe starts and reads the answer file (autounattend.xml).
3. The windowsPE configuration pass is performed.
4. The Windows image is copied to the local hard drive.
5. The offlineServicing configuration pass is performed.
6. The computer reboots.
7. Windows 10 starts.
8. Basic system configuration is performed.

9. Specific configuration is performed, including security ID (SID) generation and Plug and Play components.

10. The specialize configuration pass is performed.

11. The computer reboots.

12. Windows 10 starts.

13. The oobeSystem configuration pass is performed.

14. Windows Welcome is displayed.

The windowsPE Configuration Pass

You can manually perform tasks like disk partitioning before running an automated install. With Windows PE, however, you can automate this early portion of the installation process, just as you can automate the installation and configuration of Windows 10 components.

The **windowsPE configuration pass** is used at the start of the installation to accomplish the following:

- Partition and format the hard disk before installing Windows 10. Including this information ensures that you do not need to manually partition and format the hard disk before installing Windows 10.
- Identify a specific Windows image to install; for example, from a network location.
- Specify credentials for accessing the Windows image. This is useful when accessing the Windows image from a network share.
- Specify the local partition on which to install Windows 10.
- Specify a product key, computer name, and administrator account name.
- Run specific commands during Windows Setup.

The offlineServicing Configuration Pass

The **offlineServicing configuration pass** is used to apply packages to a Windows 10 image after it is copied to the computer hard drive, but before it is running. The packages can include language packs, device drivers, and security updates.

The benefits of applying packages to a Windows image offline are:

- *Faster installation*—It is faster to install multiple packages offline than after installation is complete. This is particularly true if some packages require system reboots when performed online.
- *Enhanced security*—Applying security updates after the system is up and running leaves the system vulnerable until the updates are applied. Applying security updates offline ensures that the system is never vulnerable to the exploits fixed by the update.

The Specialize Configuration Pass

A wide variety of settings related to the Windows interface, network configuration, and other Windows components can be applied during the **specialize configuration pass**. This is the most common configuration pass to implement settings. The settings in the specialize configuration pass are applied after the SID (security ID) is generated for the local computer and hardware is detected by using Plug and Play.

The oobesystem Configuration Pass

The **oobeSystem configuration pass** is applied during the user out-of-box experience (OOBE). The user out-of-box experience is the portion of the installation where users are asked for information after the second reboot. Information requested includes time zone, administrator name, and the administrator password.

Many of the settings you can apply during the oobeSystem configuration pass are the same as the settings you can apply during the specialize configuration pass. When a setting appears in both locations, Microsoft recommends configuring the setting during the specialize configuration pass.

Answer File Names and Locations

When you perform a basic unattended installation, you can specify the name of the answer file or allow Setup to find the answer file automatically. You specify the name of the answer file by using the /unattend switch when you run Setup. If you don't specify the name of an answer file, Setup searches for an answer file. This allows you to perform unattended installations by putting an answer file on removable media and then booting from Windows media.

The name of the answer file searched for varies depending on the configuration pass being performed. The windowsPE and offlineServicing configuration passes use **autounattend.xml**. After the windowsPE and offlineServicing configuration passes are complete, the file is cached on the local disk as **unattend.xml** in the %WINDIR%\Panther folder. Later configuration passes look for only the unattend.xml file.

Setup looks in multiple locations for an answer file. The most commonly used locations are removable storage or the \sources folder in the Windows 10 distribution directory. The setup process uses the first file it finds. Table 12-2 shows the order in which locations are searched for answer files.

Table 12-2 Answer File Search Locations in Order

Location	Notes
Registry key HKLM\System\UnattendFile	The registry key points to the location of the answer file. This is suitable for upgrade installations or when using Sysprep. You specify the name of the answer file.
%WINDIR%\Panther\unattend	This location is not searched when Windows PE is used to perform the installation.
%WINDIR%\Panther	Answer files are cached here during installation for use during multiple configuration passes.
Removable read/write media in order of drive letter	The answer file must be located in the root of the drive. Subfolders are not searched.
Removable read-only media	The answer file must be located in the root of the drive. Subfolders are not searched.
\sources directory in a Windows distribution folder	Valid only for the Windows PE and offlineServicing passes. The file must be named autounattend.xml.
%WINDIR%\system32\sysprep	Valid for all configuration passes except the windowsPE and offlineServicing passes. The answer file must be named unattend.xml.
%SYSTEMDRIVE%	Typically not used.

It is important to realize that answer files are cached in the %WINDIR%\Panther directory and are reused during later actions that look for an answer file. For example, if an answer file is specified during the initial Windows 10 installation, it is cached to %WINDIR%\Panther. Later, if Sysprep is run, the cached unattend.xml is reused before searching removable media or the sysprep folder. To resolve this problem, you can specify an answer file when running Sysprep, remove the unwanted unattend.xml file from %WINDIR%\Panther, or place the new unattend.xml file in a location that is higher in the search order. The variable %WINDIR% represents the installation directory for Windows 10, which is C:\Windows.

Windows System Image Manager

Windows System Image Manager (SIM) is the utility that allows you to create and modify answer files that are used for unattended installations. You can also use Windows SIM to create a distribution share that's used for installing Windows 10 over the network.

Creating or Updating an Answer File

To create an answer file, Windows SIM needs a list of the configurable settings. The list of configurable settings can be read directly from a Windows image or from a catalog file.

A catalog file lists all settings and packages included in an image. The states of all the settings are also included in the catalog file. For example, if the image has configured the screen saver to lock the system after 10 minutes, this will be reflected in the catalog file created by scanning that image. Using a catalog file is faster than scanning the image directly; however, catalog files are not updated automatically. You must manually update the catalog file for an image after you update the image.

 **CAUTION** Some versions of the Windows ADK include catalog files for Windows 10. If you use the included catalog files, ensure that you use a version that matches your edition of Windows 10.

After you create an answer file, you can easily update it by opening the existing answer file with Windows SIM and modifying it. When you modify the existing answer file, Windows SIM ensures that all the settings are still valid based on the catalog file or the image. Some of the answer file settings you may want to include for an unattended installation are listed in Table 12-3.

Table 12-3   Answer File Settings

Configuration Pass	Setting	Description
windowsPE	Microsoft-Windows-International-Core-WinPE | UILanguage	The default language used for the installed operating system
windowsPE	Microsoft-Windows-International-Core-WinPE | SetupUILanguage | UILanguage	The default language used during Windows setup
windowsPE	Microsoft-Windows-Setup | UserData | AcceptEula	The option to accept the license agreement
windowsPE	Microsoft-Windows-Setup | UserData | ProductKey | Key	The Windows 10 product key used to identify the edition of Windows 10 in the WIM (Windows image) file
windowsPE	Microsoft-Windows-Setup | ImageInstall | OSImage | InstallToAvailablePartition	The option to specify that Windows is installed to the first available partition; alternatively, you can specify the disk and partition to install by using other settings
specialize	Microsoft-Windows-Shell-Setup | ProductKey	The product key used for activation
specialize	Microsoft-Windows-Shell-Setup | ComputerName	The computer name for the Windows installation; to generate a random name, use * (asterisk)
oobeSystem	Microsoft-Windows-International-Core | InputLocale	The default input locale for the Windows installation
oobeSystem	Microsoft-Windows-International-Core | SystemLocale	The default system locale for the Windows installation
oobeSystem	Microsoft-Windows-International-Core | UILanguage	The default UI language for the Windows installation
oobeSystem	Microsoft-Windows-International-Core | UserLocale	The default user locale for the Windows installation
oobeSystem	Microsoft-Windows-Shell-Setup | OOBE | HideEULAPage	The option to avoid displaying the license agreement
oobeSystem	Microsoft-Windows-Shell-Setup | UserAccounts	The user accounts that are created during installation
oobeSystem	Microsoft-Windows-Shell-Setup | UserAccounts | AdministratorPassword	The password for the local Administrator account
oobeSystem	Microsoft-Windows-Shell-Setup | TimeZone	The time zone of the Windows installation

Adding Device Drivers or Applications

Windows 10 ships with many device drivers that support most hardware available at the time of release. As new types of hardware are released, however, there is a need to install additional drivers or updated versions of drivers. To include device drivers as part of an unattended installation, you must create a distribution share to store the device drivers you are installing.

A distribution share contains the following two folders for updating drivers:

- *OEM*—The drivers located in this folder are used during the initial setup of Windows 10 when Setup.exe is run from installation media or a distribution share. These drivers are available for Windows when Plug and Play hardware is detected.
- *Out-of-Box Drivers*—The drivers located in this folder can be used either during the windowsPE configuration pass or the auditSystem configuration pass. The windowsPE configuration pass is performed for all unattended installations where Windows PE is used to run Setup.exe. The auditSystem configuration pass is performed only when the Sysprep utility is used to prepare images. Adding drivers during the auditSystem configuration pass allows you to add drivers to an existing Windows image without running Setup.exe from the installation media or a distribution share.

Windows SIM allows you to create a distribution share and then specify applications and device drivers from the distribution share that are to be installed during an unattended installation. The path to the distribution share should always be referred to by the Universal Naming Convention (UNC) path to ensure that it can be accessed over the network during unattended installations. For example, a distribution share on a server should always be referred to by a path such as \\servername\sharename.

Creating a Configuration Set

A distribution share typically has device drivers and packages that are used by multiple answer files. For example, a company might have only a single distribution share for all its Windows 10 installations, but the various answer files are used to build workstations for different user types. Each answer file uses only some of the files on the distribution share.

A configuration set is the subset of files in a distribution share that are required for a particular answer file. For example, a retail store might have an answer file that includes a special scanner driver for the computers running the cash registers. A configuration set for that answer file would include the special scanner driver, but not any of the other drivers and packages in the distribution share that are not referenced by the answer file.

It is best to use a configuration set when workstations cannot access the distribution share. A configuration set allows you to minimize the amount of data that is placed on removable media or copied to a remote location. The answer file created when you create a configuration set uses relative paths so that the configuration set can be moved without introducing errors in the answer file.

Applying Offline Updates to a Windows Image

Offline updates are software packages containing device drivers or security updates that are applied to an image during the offlineServicing configuration pass of the installation. If offline updates are included as part of the installation process, they are installed before Windows is functional.

Installing software updates before Windows 10 is running ensures that problems are fixed before the system is functional. This is particularly important for security updates that could be exploited between the time of system installation and installing the security updates.

 TIP   Software packages used for offline updates are included in a configuration set.

Activity 12-3: Creating an Answer File

Time Required: 30 minutes

Objective: Create an answer file that can be used for an unattended installation

Description: You would like to streamline the process you use for installing new Windows 10 workstations. The biggest problem you run into when deploying new installations of Windows 10 is finding the proper product key. In this activity, you create an answer file that automatically enters the product key for you during configuration.

> **⚠ CAUTION** This activity assumes that you are using a 64-bit evaluation copy of Windows 10 Enterprise edition. There may be slight variations in these steps if you are using another edition of Windows 10.

1. If necessary, place the Windows 10 DVD in your computer.
2. Right-click the **Start** button and then click **Windows PowerShell**.
3. At the Windows PowerShell prompt, type **md c:\wininstall** and then press **Enter.**
4. Type **Copy-Item -Path D:* -Destination C:\wininstall -Recurse -Force** and then press **Enter**. This command assumes that the DVD drive on your computer is assigned the drive letter D:. If the DVD drive letter is different, replace D: with the appropriate letter. This copies the contents of the Windows 10 DVD to your hard drive. This step will take some time to complete depending on the speed of your storage.
5. When copying is complete, close the Windows PowerShell prompt window.
6. On the taskbar, click **File Explorer**, browse to C:\, right-click **wininstall**, and then click **Properties**.
7. In the wininstall Properties dialog box, on the General tab, clear the **Read-only (Only applies to file in folder)** checkbox and then click **OK**.
8. In the Confirm Attribute Changes dialog box, if necessary, select **Apply changes to this folder, subfolders and files** and then click **OK**.
9. Close the File Explorer window.
10. Click the **Start** button, type **windows system**, and then click **Windows System Image Manager**.
11. In the Windows Image pane, right-click **Select a Windows image or catalog file** and then click **Select Windows Image**.
12. Browse to **C:\wininstall\sources**, click **install.wim**, and then click **Open**.
13. In the Select an image dialog box, select **Windows 10 Enterprise** and then click **OK**.
14. In the Windows System Image Manager dialog box, click **Yes** to create a catalog file.
15. In the User Account Control dialog box, click **Yes**. This process may take up to 15 minutes.
16. Click **File** on the menu bar and then click **New Answer File**. A new untitled answer file has been created in the Answer File pane. Notice that it lists the configuration passes in the components folder and also lists packages.
17. In the Windows Image pane, if necessary, expand **Windows 10 Enterprise** and then expand **Components**. This lists the categories of settings that you can configure in the answer file.
18. Expand **amd64_Microsoft-Windows-Setup_10.0.xxxx.xxxxx_neutral (.xxxx.xxxxx** represents a subversion number that changes depending on the revision version of Windows 10) and then expand **UserData**.
19. Click **ProductKey**. Notice that the upper-right pane is now labeled ProductKey Properties and shows information about the ProductKey setting. You can see that the only configuration pass that this setting can be used in is the windowsPE configuration pass.
20. In the Windows Image pane, right-click **ProductKey** and then click **Add Setting to Pass 1 windowsPE**. This adds the setting to the currently opened answer file and selects it in the Answer File pane.
21. In the ProductKey Properties pane, double-click **Key**. This allows you to edit the product key.
22. Type the product key for Windows 10 Enterprise, including the dashes (-), and then press **Enter**. If you do not have a product key for Windows 10 Enterprise, type NPPR9-FWDCX-D2C8J-H872K-2YT43 (a generic key provided by Microsoft for trial installations).
23. Click **WillShowUI**, click the arrow, and then click **OnError**, as shown in Figure 12-3. This configures the product key entry screen to be displayed only if an error is encountered with the product key in the answer file.

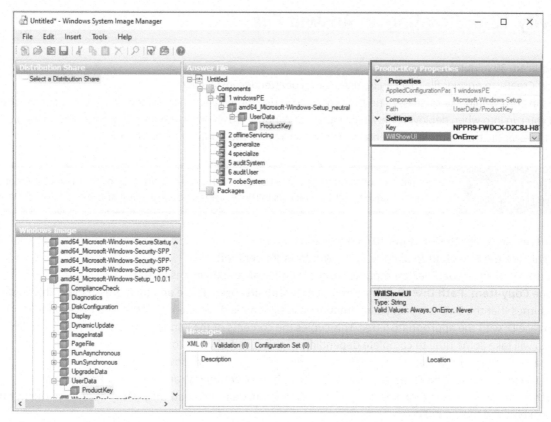

Figure 12-3   Windows SIM settings

24. Browse through some of the other settings available in the Windows Image pane. Take note of which configuration passes the different settings can be configured in.
25. Click **File** on the menu bar and then click **Save Answer File As**.
26. In the File name text box, type **autounattend** and then click **Save**. This file can be copied to removable storage or another appropriate location for use during an unattended installation.
27. Close Windows System Image Manager.
28. Click **Microsoft Edge** on the taskbar.
29. In the address bar, type **C:\wininstall\sources\autounattend.xml** and then press **Enter**.
30. You can now see the structure of the XML file you created with Windows System Image Manager. It shows the product key you entered and the OnError choice for showing the user interface.
31. Exit Microsoft Edge.

Activity 12-4: Creating a Distribution Share

Time Required: 5 minutes
Objective: Create a distribution share that can be used for installing Windows 10
Description: After receiving some new computers, you find that they are able to display a resolution of only 1024 × 768 with 256 colors when Windows 10 is installed from DVD. After doing some research, you realize that Windows 10 does not include the correct video driver for the new computers. To avoid manually updating the video driver after installation, you decide to create a distribution share that you can place the appropriate video drivers in. In this activity, you create a distribution share.

 **CAUTION** This activity creates a distribution share on the local C: drive of the computer running Windows 10. The distribution share is normally located on a server and accessible over the network.

1. Click the **Start** button, type **windows system**, and then click **Windows System Image Manager**.
2. In the Distribution Share pane, right-click **Select a Distribution Share** and then click **Create Distribution Share**.
3. Select the **C:\wininstall\sources** folder and then click **Open**.
4. In the Distribution Share pane, expand **C:\wininstall\sources**. Notice that three folders are listed, as shown in Figure 12-4. These folders are used to store device drivers and packages that can be added to the Windows 10 installation. You must copy any device drivers and packages into these folders to make them available.
5. Close the Windows System Image Manager window.

Figure 12-4   Distribution share folders

PREPARING WINDOWS 10 FOR IMAGING

In a corporate environment, you need a quick and easy way to deploy workstations. Attended installations take too much time to be practical. Unattended installations are better suited to deploying multiple computers, but after installation, you still need to install additional applications and customize them to meet corporate standards. An image-based installation allows you to quickly deploy Windows 10 to computers, complete with applications and customizations.

The overall imaging process is as follows:

1. Install and configure Windows 10 and applications on a source workstation.
2. Use Sysprep to generalize the source workstation for imaging.
3. Boot the source workstation using Windows PE.
4. Use DISM to capture the image from the source workstation and store it in a distribution share or external storage.
5. On the destination workstation, use Windows PE to connect to the distribution share or external storage.
6. Use DISM to apply the image to the destination workstation.

Windows 10 includes the Sysprep utility to prepare workstations for imaging. This process is known as generalization. Generalization removes system-specific data from Windows. System-specific data includes the computer name, computer SID, and hardware information. After generalization is complete, the workstation image is captured and placed on a distribution share.

When a generalized image is applied to a computer, that computer generates all of the system-specific data that is required, including the computer name and computer SID. It also detects the Plug and Play hardware and loads drivers for the detected hardware. After the system-specific information is generated, the computer is either put into audit mode or Windows Welcome is run.

Configuration Passes for Image-Based Installation

When you use Sysprep to prepare a system for imaging, you can use an answer file to automate configuration. This process has unique configuration passes that are not used during an unattended installation. Figure 12-5 shows the configuration passes used for imaging.

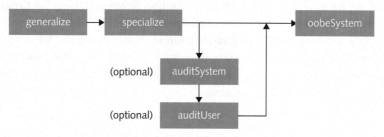

Figure 12-5   Sysprep configuration passes

The configuration passes that can be triggered by Sysprep are:

- The **generalize configuration pass** is performed when you run Sysprep and select the Generalize option that removes computer specific information. If you generalize an image, the next time the image starts, the specialize configuration pass is performed, and hardware is detected to load drivers.
- The **auditSystem configuration pass** and **auditUser configuration pass** are used when you run Sysprep and select the Enter System Audit Mode option. Audit mode is entered the next time the image is started. The auditSystem settings apply before user sign-in, and the auditUser settings apply after user sign-in.
- The oobeSystem configuration pass is used when you run Sysprep and select the Enter System Out-Of-Box Experience (OOBE) Mode option. This option is used when a computer is ready for delivery to a client.

You can specify an answer file when you run Sysprep. If you do not specify an answer file, Sysprep searches for unattend.xml to use as an answer file. If an unattend.xml file was used during the initial Windows 10 setup, it is cached to the local hard drive and will be detected when Sysprep is run.

Sysprep System Cleanup Actions

When you run Sysprep to generalize an image, you must also select a system cleanup action, as shown in Figure 12-6. The system cleanup action determines the behavior of Windows 10 on the next restart.

Figure 12-6   Sysprep cleanup actions

In most cases, you will choose the **System Out-of-Box Experience (OOBE) cleanup action** when generalizing an image. This configures the image so that on first boot, Windows Welcome is launched to collect any necessary information from the user before the configuration is finalized.

The oobeSystem configuration pass is performed when Windows Welcome is launched and uses an unattend.xml answer file if one is available. If the answer file is properly configured, the entire Windows Welcome can be automated.

Audit mode is used by organizations that want to perform additional modifications to an image before distributing it to users. In audit mode, you can install additional drivers or applications for users and then use Sysprep to trigger Windows Welcome on the next boot. You can also use audit mode to verify that the workstation is properly configured before delivery to the end user. To enter audit mode, select the **System Audit Mode cleanup action**.

Using audit mode is also helpful when you want to use the same base image for many different varieties of hardware and end users. A single base image is applied to the computers, and then audit mode is used to add any specific drivers required by that model of computer and any specific applications required by the end user. Using audit mode prevents the OOBE from running. The process for using audit mode involves the following steps:

1. Perform initial installation and configuration of the operating system.
2. Run Sysprep and select audit mode.
3. Take an image of the prepared operating system. This is the base image.
4. Apply the base image to a computer and sign in to add drivers or applications.
5. Run Sysprep and select OOBE.
6. Take an image of the updated operating system.
7. Deploy the updated operating system to computers.
8. Have the users start the system and run OOBE.

The capability to continue using the same base image is particularly important for organizations that must perform significant testing on workstations to ensure quality. When a consistent base image is used, the testing for the functionality in the base image needs to be performed only once. Only the additional modifications need to be tested.

Sysprep Limitations

Sysprep is a very useful tool and is a requirement for deploying Windows 10 by imaging; however, like any tool, Sysprep has a few limitations you should be aware of, particularly those restrictions related to hardware.

Sysprep limitations include the following:

- Drivers must be available to support Plug and Play hardware of the destination computer. This ensures that drivers are properly loaded when the image is applied to new hardware. However, the hardware does not need to be identical.
- Sysprep generalization resets the activation clock a maximum of eight times (rearms). This limits the number of times Sysprep can be used on derivative images before activation is forced. For example, a computer manufacturer may make multiple modifications to an image and run Sysprep with the Generalize option after each modification to prepare the workstation for imaging. Activation is cleared from the computer only eight times. On the ninth time, an error is generated.
- If a computer is a member of a domain, running Sysprep removes the computer from the domain. Newly imaged computers must be added to the domain.
- Sysprep does not run on upgraded computers. To prepare Windows 10 for imaging you need to perform a clean installation of Windows 10 and configure it.
- After running Sysprep, encrypted files and folders are unreadable because the encryption certificates are lost when user profiles are removed.

Sysprep Command-Line Options

Sysprep has both a command-line interface and a graphical interface. In most cases, system administrators prefer to use the graphical interface because it is more intuitive. To run Sysprep in graphical mode, run C:\Windows\System32\Sysprep\Sysprep.exe without specifying any options. In high-volume situations, you might prefer to use Sysprep in scripts. Running Sysprep in scripts requires you to use command-line options. The command-line options for Sysprep are listed in Table 12-4.

Table 12-4 Command-Line Options for Sysprep

Option	Description
/audit	Starts the computer in audit mode on reboot. Cannot be used with /oobe.
/generalize	Removes system-specific information from the computer, such as computer SID.
/mode:vm	Optimizes the functionality of /generalize for virtualized environments. Hardware settings are not generalized and redetected. Must be used with /generalize and /oobe.
/oobe	Starts Windows Welcome on reboot. Cannot be used with /audit.
/reboot	Reboots the computer after Sysprep completes. This is useful for immediately testing the post boot experience. Cannot be used with /shutdown or /quit.
/shutdown	Shuts down the computer after Sysprep completes. This is useful to prepare for imaging. Cannot be used with /reboot or /quit.
/quiet	Prevents Sysprep from displaying dialog boxes. This is useful when Sysprep is used in batch files.
/quit	Allows the computer to continue running when Sysprep completes. Cannot be used with /reboot or /shutdown.
/unattend:answerfile	Specifies an answer file to use for unattended setup.

Activity 12-5: Generalizing Windows 10 by Using Sysprep

Time Required: 30 minutes

Objective: Use Sysprep to generalize Windows 10 for imaging

Description: After using unattended installations for a period of time, you decide that you would like to include applications automatically as part of the Windows 10 installation to new workstations. You have not used Sysprep before, and you want to see what the user experience is like after Sysprep is performed to ready a workstation for image capture. In this activity, you use Sysprep to generalize Windows 10 for imaging, then you restart Windows 10 to see the user interface that is presented when the image is applied to new workstations.

1. Sign in to your computer as **User*x***.
2. Click **File Explorer** on the taskbar.
3. In the Address bar, type **C:\Windows\System32\sysprep** and then press **Enter**.
4. Double-click **sysprep**.
5. In the System Cleanup Action box, select **Enter System Out-of-Box Experience (OOBE)**. This option is used to prepare a computer for delivery to an end user.
6. Check the **Generalize** check box. This option removes computer-specific information, such as SID and computer name.
7. In the Shutdown Options box, select **Shutdown**. This turns off the computer after Sysprep is complete so that an image can be captured from it.
8. Click **OK**. Sysprep looks for an unattend.xml file to process during the generalize configuration pass, generalizes Windows 10, and shuts down Windows 10. After Windows 10 is shut down, it is ready for an image to be captured. To capture an operating system image, you would boot Windows PE from removable storage and run DISM to place the image on external storage or a network share.
9. If you get the error 'Sysprep was not able to validate your Windows installation,' use the following steps to resolve the error:
   a. Click **OK** to close the error dialog box.
   b. In File Explorer, double-click **Panther** and then double-click **setupact**.
   c. In Notepad, scroll down to the bottom of the file and a line stating that 'Package *PackageName* was installed for a user, but not provisioned for all users. This package will not function properly in the sysprep image.' Make note of the package name.
   d. Click the **Start** button, type **powershell**, right-click **Windows PowerShell**, and then click **Run as administrator**.

    e. In the User Account Control dialog box, click **Yes**.

    f. In the Windows PowerShell window, type **Get-AppxPackage** *PackageName* **| Remove-AppxPackage** and then press **Enter.** You can use wildcards in the package name.

    g. After this is complete, run Sysprep again. If the error is generated again, review **setupact** for additional packages that are blocking Sysprep and repeat these steps until Sysprep runs successfully.

10. Start your computer. Notice that the startup screen is the same as that seen during installation. Windows 10 now detects Plug and Play hardware, reboots, and then starts the out-of-box experience. If an unattend.xml file is found, the settings for the oobeSystem configuration pass are applied.

11. Click **Yes** to accept the default setting for region.

12. Click **Yes** to accept the default setting for keyboard layout.

13. Click **Skip** to avoid adding a second keyboard layout.

14. Click **Accept** on the page with the license agreement.

15. On the Sign in with Microsoft screen, click **Domain join instead**.

16. In the Who's going to use this PC box, type **Userx** and then click **Next.** Notice that you cannot reuse the same local user name because Sysprep did not remove the existing user account. You need to enter a new user account to continue. You can avoid being forced to create a new user account by using an answer file.

17. In the Who's going to use this PC box, type **NewUserx** and then click **Next**.

18. In the Password box, type **Pa55word!** and then click **Next**.

19. In the Confirm password box, type **Pa55word!** and then click **Next**.

20. In the Security question (1 of 3) box, select **What was your first pet's name?**.

21. In the Your answer box, type **Fluffy** and then click **Next**.

22. In the Security question (2 of 3) box, select **What's the first name of your oldest cousin?**.

23. In the Your answer box, type **Jeff** and then click **Next**.

24. In the Security question (3 of 3) box, select **What was your childhood nickname?**.

25. In the Your answer box, type **The dude** and then click **Next**.

26. On the Choose privacy settings for your device screen, click **Accept**.

27. On the Do more across devices with activity history screen, click **No**.

28. On the Let Cortana help you get things done screen, click **Not now**.

29. Notice that you are automatically signed in as NewUserx. If necessary, in the Networks dialog box, click **Yes**.

USING DISM FOR IMAGING

In Module 2, Using the System Utilities, you saw that the DISM utility included in Windows 10 can be used to modify a running instance of Windows 10 to enable and disable features. DISM can also be used to capture and apply images used for installing Windows 10. You can also use DISM to mount and modify images that are offline.

Image File Formats

DISM can capture images and store them in a Windows image (WIM) file, virtual hard disk (VHD) file, or full flash update (FFU) file. Each option for image storage has specific advantages and disadvantages that make them best suited to specific scenarios.

The WIM format for image storage is the most flexible and best suited to ongoing image storage and maintenance. When using WIM files for imaging, the images are file-based rather than sector-based. This means that individual files are copied from a specified volume and there are no dependencies on hard drive configuration. For example, when an image is taken of the C: drive, it can be applied to another hard drive that is larger or smaller than the source as long as the new target hard drive contains a volume that is large enough to hold the imaged data.

A single WIM file can store multiple images. To reduce the storage space required for images, single instance storage is used within the WIM file. If the same file is included in multiple images, then the file is stored only once in the

WIM file. If you add a second image of Windows 10 to the same WIM file, only the differences are added to the size. For example, a WIM file holding a single image of Windows 10 is about 4.5 GB. If a second image includes new software that is 200 MB, then adding the second image increases the WIM file to 4.7 GB.

 TIP   Images in a WIM file can be any set of files specified during imaging, but for operating system deployment, an image is the entire C: drive.

NOTE 6

For detailed steps on how to boot from VHD, see the Boot to a virtual hard disk: Add a VHDX or VHD to the boot menu page at https://docs.microsoft.com/en-us/windows-hardware/manufacture/desktop/boot-to-vhd--native-boot--add-a-virtual-hard-disk-to-the-boot-menu.

NOTE 7

For more information about image file formats, see the WIM vs. VHD vs. FFU: comparing image file formats page at https://docs.microsoft.com/en-us/windows-hardware/manufacture/desktop/wim-vs-ffu-image-file-formats.

NOTE 8

For detailed information about creating bootable Windows PE media, see the Windows PE (WinPE) page at https://docs.microsoft.com/en-us/windows-hardware/manufacture/desktop/winpe-intro.

An FFU file is a sector-based format that stores hard drive information rather than copying individual files. This captures all the data on the hard drive, including partitions. Applying an image from an FFU file is faster than applying an image from a WIM file but is less flexible. An image from an FFU file must be applied to a hard drive that is the same size as the source hard drive or larger. Also, an FFU file can store only one image. So, it is less efficient when you need to store multiple images.

A VHD file is typically used by virtual machines. When you use DISM to create a VHD file with an image of Windows 10, that VHD file can be used by Hyper-V to boot a virtual machine. This is commonly used by administrators for computers to test software updates. The VHD file can also be used for virtual desktops that are provided and managed by Remote Desktop Services (RDS). It is also possible to configure a physical computer to boot from a VHD file, but this is rarely done.

Windows PE Boot Media Creation

The operating system on a hard drive can't be running while an image is being taken or applied. You need an alternative way to get access to the data on the hard drive and run DISM. Windows PE, a small version of Windows that can be installed on removable boot media, can be used as part of the imaging process. Windows PE is an add-on for Windows 10 ADK.

The Windows PE files are in the boot.wim file. You can customize Windows PE to include additional drivers or tools that you want to use. You can use DISM to add drivers to Windows PE. To create Windows PE boot media that you can use for imaging, complete the following steps:

1. Run copype.cmd to create the folder structure with the necessary files.
2. Mount ISO\Sources\boot.wim to a folder.
3. Copy any desired files into boot.wim or use DISM to add device drivers.
4. Commit the changes to boot.wim.
5. Use MakeWinPEMedia.cmd to create a bootable USB drive or .iso file.

Activity 12-6: Creating Windows PE Boot Media

Time Required: 10 minutes
Objective: Create Windows PE boot media
Description: To enable imaging, you need to have a portable operating system with the ability to run DISM. In this activity, you create an .iso file that can be burned to a CD and used for imaging operations.

1. Click the **Start** button, type **deploy**, right-click **Deployment and Imaging Tools Environment**, and then click **Run as administrator**.
2. In the User Account Control dialog box, click **Yes**.

3. Type **cd ..\Windows Preinstallation Environment** and then press **Enter**.

4. Type **copype.cmd amd64 C:\bootiso** and then press **Enter**. This command creates the necessary folder structure for the 64-bit version of Windows PE in the C:\bootiso folder. For a 32-bit version of Windows PE, use the option x86 instead of amd64.

5. Type **dism /mount-image /imagefile:C:\bootiso\media\sources\boot.wim /mountdir:C:\bootiso\mount /index:1** and then press **Enter**. This command mounts boot.wim to C:\bootiso\mount, where you can browse and modify the contents.

6. Type **dir C:\bootiso\mount** and then press **Enter**. This is the content of boot.wim.

7. Type **dir C:\bootiso\mount\dism.exe /s** and then press **Enter**. This command searches through the mount folder to find instances of dism.exe. You can see from the results that it is already in boot.wim and boot.wim does not need to be modified.

8. Type **dism /unmount-image /mountdir:C:\bootiso\mount /discard** and then press **Enter**.

9. Type **MakeWinPEMedia.cmd /iso C:\bootiso C:\winpe.iso** and then press **Enter**. This command creates a bootable .iso file based on the content in C:\bootiso. You can use the .iso file to create removable boot media.

10. Close the Deployment and Imaging Tools Environment window.

Capturing and Applying WIM Images

After a workstation is prepared for image capture, you must shut down the computer before imaging. Shutting down the computer ensures that no files are open when imaging is performed. Then, you can boot the computer using Windows PE to perform the imaging operation. Table 12-5 describes the important DISM options for capturing a WIM image.

The syntax for capturing an image is:

DISM /Capture-Image /ImageFile:*imagefile.wim* /CaptureDir:*path* /Name:*imagename*

Table 12-5   DISM Options for Capturing a WIM Image

Option	Description
/Capture-Image	Specifies that an image is being copied from disk to a WIM file. This option assumes that no WIM file already exists. To add an image to an existing WIM file, use the /Append-Image option instead.
/ImageFile:*imagefile.wim*	Defines the .wim file that will hold the image. If you specify only the name of the .wim file, it is created in the current directory.
/CaptureDir:*path*	Defines the source files that are to be captured as part of the image. To capture an entire volume, specify the root of the volume. For example, specifying C:\ captures the entire C: drive.
/Name:*imagename*	Specifies a unique name for an image that can be referenced as an alternative to an index number.

Activity 12-7: Capturing a WIM Image

Time Required: 10 minutes

Objective: Create a WIM image using DISM

Description: After confirming how Sysprep is used to generalize Windows 10 for imaging, you want to try capturing an image. To keep your test manageable in scope, you are imaging only part of the file system rather than the entire C: drive. In this activity, you image the C:\Program Files (x86)\Windows Kits\10 folder.

NOTE 9

When imaging the entire C: drive, including the operating system, you must boot from Windows PE to ensure that all files are closed. When imaging data files, DISM can be run from Windows 10. This activity allows you to perform the basics of imaging without using Windows PE.

1. Click the **Start** button, type **deploy**, right-click **Deployment and Imaging Tools Environment**, and then click **Run as administrator**. DISM must be run using administrator privileges and does not automatically elevate privileges by using UAC.
2. In the User Account Control dialog box, click **Yes**.
3. Type **md \images** and then press **Enter**. In a production environment, you would typically store images on a network server rather than a client computer.
4. Type **dism /capture-image /capturedir:"C:\Program Files (x86)\Windows Kits\10" /imagefile:C:\images\Win10ADK.wim /name:Win10ADK** and then press **Enter**. This takes an image of the Windows 10 ADK folder and creates the Win10ADK.wim image file. The image is given the description Win10ADK. Any options with spaces must have quotes around them.
5. Type **dir \images** and then press **Enter**. The file WIN10ADK.wim is approximately 3.0 GB.
6. Type **dism /append-image /capturedir:"C:\Program Files (x86)\Windows Kits\10\Assessment and Deployment Kit\Windows Preinstallation Environment" /imagefile:C:\images\Win10ADK.wim /name:WinPE** and then press **Enter**, as shown in Figure 12-7. This command images the Windows Preinstallation Environment folder and places it in the same Win10ADK.wim image file. The image is given the description WinPE.

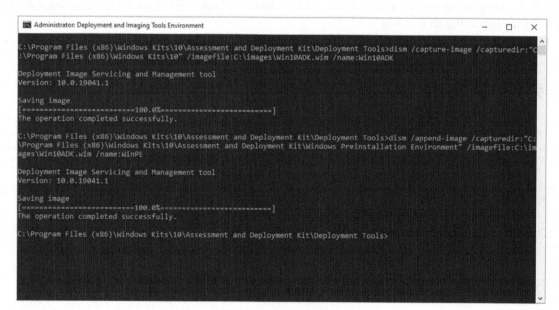

Figure 12-7   Using DISM to append an image

7. Type **dir \images** and then press **Enter**. Notice that the file Win10ADK.wim is still approximately 3.0 GB because of the single-instance file storage used by WIM files. The Windows Preinstallation Environment folder contains about 2.8 GB of data.
8. Close the Deployment and Imaging Tools Environment window.

Similar to when you capture an image, to deploy images with operating systems and applications, you must boot using Windows PE and connect to the distribution share holding the image file. After you are connected to the share, you can use DISM to apply an image to the local workstation.

The syntax for applying a WIM image is:

DISM /Apply-Image /ImageFile:*imagefile.wim* [/Index:*imageindex* | /Name:*imagename*] /ApplyDir:*destinationpath*

The /Apply-Image option indicates that an image is going to be placed on a local hard drive from the imagefile. wim. The imageindex or imagename is used to specify which image from imagefile.wim is applied. The /ApplyDir option specifies the location on the local drive where the image will be placed. For example, C:\ indicates that the image will be placed at the root of the C: drive.

> **(!) CAUTION** DISM does not create volumes on a hard drive. You need to create the necessary volumes, by using a utility such as diskpart before applying the image.

Activity 12-8: Applying an Image

Time Required: 10 minutes

Objective: Apply a WIM image to a computer

Description: One of the unique benefits of the WIM format is the ability to add files to an existing computer when an image is applied. Applying an image does not remove the existing files on a partition. You want to test this functionality. In this activity, you apply the WinPE image to restore missing files.

1. Click the **Start** button, type **deploy**, right-click **Deployment Imaging and Tools Environment**, and then click **Run as administrator**.
2. In the User Account Control dialog box, click **Yes**.
3. Type **dism /get-imageinfo /imagefile:C:\images\Win10ADK.wim** and then press **Enter**. This displays information about the images included in Win10ADK.wim. Notice that image number 2 is named WinPE. You can refer to images by their name or index number.
4. Type **rd "C:\Program Files (x86)\Windows Kits\10\Assessment and Deployment Kit\Windows Preinstallation Environment" /s /q** and then press **Enter**.
5. Type **dir "C:\Program Files (x86)\Windows Kits\10\Assessment and Deployment Kit"** and then press **Enter**. You can see that the Windows Preinstallation Environment folder is not there.
6. Type **md "\Program Files (x86)\Windows Kits\10\Assessment and Deployment Kit\Windows Preinstallation Environment"** and then press **Enter**. This re-creates the Windows Preinstallation Environment folder so that the WinPE image can be placed in it.
7. Type **dism /apply-image /imagefile:C:\images\Win10ADK.wim /name:WinPE /applydir:"C:\Program Files (x86)\Windows Kits\10\Assessment and Deployment Kit\Windows Preinstallation Environment"** and then press **Enter.**
8. Type **dir "C:\Program Files (x86)\Windows Kits\10\Assessment and Deployment Kit\Windows Preinstallation Environment"** and then press **Enter**. You can see that the files have been restored to the Windows Preinstallation Environment folder.
9. Close the Deployment and Imaging Tools Environment window.

Capturing and Applying FFU Images

When you capture and apply FFU images, you are capturing and applying copies of an entire hard drive. Before you can perform an imaging operation, you need to accurately identify the disk number of the physical disk. You can use the list disk command in diskpart as shown in Figure 12-8.

Figure 12-8   List disks by using
diskpart

 TIP   The free space identified by the list disk command is unpartitioned space on the disk, not free space in volumes.

In most cases, a desktop computer has only one hard drive, which is disk 0, but if you connect a USB drive, it will also be listed. To ensure that you select the correct disk for imaging, verify the size of the disk that you want to image before booting into Windows PE. If you use a mapped drive letter to connect to a network share, the mapped drive letter is not displayed by the list disk command.

Capturing and applying an FFU image is done by using DISM, but with different options than when working with WIM images. The common options for capturing and applying an FFU image are listed in Table 12-6.

Table 12-6   DISM Options for Capturing and Applying FFU Images

Option	Description
/capture-ffu	Indicates that an FFU image is being created.
/apply-ffu	Indicates that an FFU image is being applied.
/imagefile	Specifies the name of an FFU file that is being used for the operation. You should include the full path to the image file, such as Z:\Win10.ffu.
/capturedrive	Identifies the physical drive that is being imaged, based on the drive number that can be identified with the list disk command in diskpart. For drive number 0, the option would be /capturedrive=\\.\PhysicalDisk0.
/applydrive	Identifies the physical drive that an image is being applied to, based on the drive number that can be identified with the list disk command in diskpart. For drive number 0, the option would be /applydrive=\\.\PhysicalDisk0.
/name	Provides a name for the image in the FFU file. This name is displayed by the /get-imageinfo option. Providing a meaningful name can make it easier to identify the purpose of an image.
/description	Provides a description for the image in the FFU file. This description is displayed by the /get-imageinfo option. Providing a meaningful description can make it easier to identify the purpose of the image.

The syntax for capturing an FFU image is:

DISM /capture-ffu /imagefile=*imagefile*.ffu /capturedrive=\\.\PhysicalDrive*X* /name:*imagename*
/description:*imagedescription*

The syntax for applying an FFU image is:

DISM /apply-ffu /imagefile=*imagefile*.ffu /ApplyDrive:\\.\PhysicalDrive*X*

When you apply an FFU image, it creates volumes on the hard drive that are the same size as the original source. If you apply the FFU image to a larger hard drive, you can expand the C: drive and use all the available hard drive space after the image is applied. Applying an FFU image removes any existing data on the hard drive.

Image Maintenance

When you use images to deploy Windows 10, you can include a preconfigured installation of Windows 10 and applications. When you build the image, you include any necessary applications and updates that are available at that time. Maintaining images requires you to apply software updates to those images and possibly modify Windows 10 features that are enabled in the image. You can maintain an image by using DISM or Sysprep with audit mode.

DISM allows you to perform a wide variety of maintenance tasks on a Windows 10 image while it is offline. An offline image is still stored in a WIM file or FFU file and not applied to a computer. Maintaining an image offline simplifies maintenance, but you are limited in the tasks you can perform.

Some common scenarios for using DISM for offline maintenance include:

- *Add device drivers*—As your organization purchases new computers that require new drivers, you can add those drivers to an existing image. This ensures that all hardware is properly detected when the image is applied.
- *Apply Windows updates*—Over time, additional updates for Windows 10 are released that are not included in the image. Deploying Windows 10 without the latest updates is a security risk because some malware takes advantage of computers without security updates. Applying updates before an image is applied reduces the security risk. Windows updates must have an .msu or .cab extension.
- *Enable Windows features*—After initial development of an image, you may find that a specific feature that is needed for users has not been enabled. Rather than modifying the configuration of each computer after an image is applied, you can use DISM to enable the feature.
- *Identify the need for application updates*—To determine whether applications in an image need to be updated with a specific application update, you can use DISM to query whether a specific .msp file is applicable. However, application updates cannot be applied by using DISM. Application updates must be delivered after the image is applied to a hard drive.

If you are using DISM to add multiple device drivers and install multiple Windows updates, performing the maintenance at a command line can be quite time consuming. Each driver and Windows update requires a command to be entered separately. As an alternative, you can use an answer file with DISM. First, you build an answer file by using Windows SIM that includes the necessary drivers and Windows updates in the offlineServicing portion of the answer file. Then, run DISM and specify the answer file. DISM uses only the offlineServicing portion of the answer file.

The only way to have complete control over the update of an image is to apply that image to a computer, make any necessary modifications, and then capture the image again. This is time consuming, but it allows you to apply any type of software updates, including applications and service packs.

Typically, you run Sysprep to generalize an image just before capturing it. Each time you run Sysprep to generalize an image, however, it requires reactivation. Windows 10 can be reactivated only eight times, and then Sysprep will cease to function. You must carefully consider this as you update images.

 TIP   Well-designed and automated Windows update and application update processes mitigate the need for frequent image updates.

PROVISIONING

Using **provisioning** speeds up the deployment process for new computers and mobile devices. In the past, computers were reimaged with a new operating system to meet the configuration standards of the organization. With provisioning, one or more provisioning packages are deployed to the operating system installation already in place. The provisioning packages configure Windows 10. It is much faster to apply a provisioning package than to reimage an entire operating system.

Provisioning packages support the following scenarios:

- *New computers from a manufacturer*—When your organization purchases new computers, an operating system typically is already installed. Most of the time, this operating system is Windows 10 Pro; however, many large organizations use Windows 10 Enterprise. In addition to applying configuration settings and joining the domains, a provisioning package can be used to update the operating system from Windows 10 Pro to Windows 10 Enterprise.
- *Bring your own devices (BYOD)*—Some organizations have moved to a model where employees select and purchase their own devices that are used on the company network. A provisioning package is a quick way to make various devices meet organizational standards and deploy universal applications. Universal applications are obtained from the Windows Store.

You create provisioning packages by using Windows Configuration Designer. The provisioning packages are stored in .ppkg files that you need to apply to computers or devices. The permissions required to deploy a provisioning package vary depending on what is being configured. For a provisioning package that performs administrative functions, such as creating local user accounts, an administrator account must be used.

The items you can configure by using a provisioning package include:

- Assign device name
- Configure product key
- Join Active Directory or Azure AD
- Configure Wi-Fi and VPN connections
- Install software or remove preinstalled software
- Create local administrative account
- Configure certificates

When you create a provisioning package, you are given the option to encrypt the package. Encrypting the package ensures that any sensitive information in the package, such as passwords, cannot be accessed without the encryption key. However, you also need the encryption key to deploy the package, which makes it more difficult to deploy. After encrypting a package, you should document the encryption key and keep it in a safe place.

 TIP You can use provisioning in combination with images you create and maintain, but the greatest benefit is typically derived from using the base operating system installation provided by your hardware vendor and avoiding the effort of maintaining your own customized image.

Provisioning packages can be deployed manually on computers by end users. When you provide users with the .ppkg file, they can double-click the file to initiate installation. Alternatively, users can use the Add or remove a provisioning package option that is available in Settings > Accounts > Access work or school.

For automated deployment of provisioning packages, as part of operating system deployment, you can place the .ppkg files in C:\Recovery\Customizations. During the OOBE phase of setup, provisioning packages in C:\Recovery\Customizations are copied to %ProgramData%\Microsoft\Provisioning and applied. Some customizations, such as software installation, may be completed after the OOBE setup phase is complete.

 TIP C:\Recovery is a hidden folder that remains after you perform a reset of Windows 10. After a reset, the provisioning packages in C:\Recovery\Customizations are reapplied.

Activity 12-9: Creating and Applying a Provisioning Package

Time Required: 10 minutes

Objective: Create and apply a provisioning package to an already deployed Windows 10 computer

Description: Your company has many remote workers with computers that are not domain joined. To simplify management, you want a consistent local administrator account on all the computers. You've decided to create a provisioning package that creates a local administrator account and have all of the remote workers run it on their computer.

1. Click the **Start** button, type **windows imaging**, and then click **Windows Imaging and Configuration Designer**.
2. In the User Account Control dialog box, click **Yes**.
3. In the Windows Imaging and Configuration Designer window, click **Advanced provisioning**.
4. In the New project dialog box, in the Name box, type **SetLocalAdmin** and then click **Next**.
5. On the Choose which settings to view and configure page, click **All Windows desktop editions** and then click **Next**.

6. On the Import a provisioning package (optional) page, click **Finish**.

7. In the Available customization pane, expand **Runtime settings** and read the list of categories. You can add universal applications, drivers, and Windows updates here.

8. Expand **Accounts** and then click **Users**.

9. In the Users pane, type **DesktopAdmin** and then click **Add**.

10. In the Available customizations pane, click **UserName: DesktopAdmin**. Notice that the Password field is marked as a validation error because no password has been defined.

11. In the Password box, type **Pa55word!**. Notice that the validation error is gone.

12. In the UserGroup box, select **Administrators**, as shown in Figure 12-9.

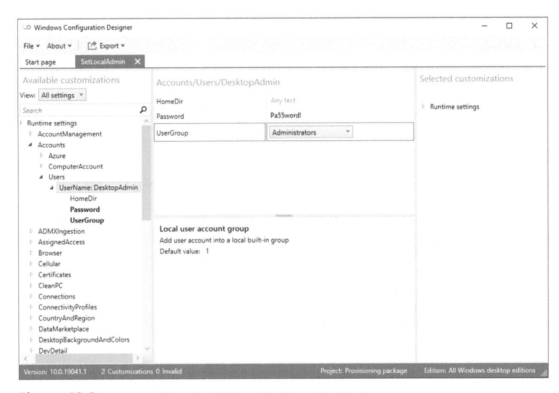

Figure 12-9   User settings in Windows Configuration Designer

13. Click **Export** on the menu bar and then click **Provisioning package**.

14. In the Build dialog box, click **Next** to accept the default settings.

15. On the Select security details for the provisioning package screen, select the **Encrypt package** check box.

16. In the Encryption password box, type **secret99** and then click **Next**.

17. On the Select where to save the provisioning package screen, click **Next** to accept the default location in your user profile.

18. On the Build the provisioning package screen, click **Build**.

19. On the All done screen, click **Finish**.

20. Close the Windows Configuration Designer window.

21. On the taskbar, click **File Explorer** and browse to **Documents\Windows Imaging and Configuration Designer (Windows ICD)\SetLocalAdmin**.

22. Read the list of files and identify the RunTime Provisioning Tool.

23. Double-click the **SetLocalAdmin** file of type RunTime Provisioning Tool, as shown in Figure 12-10. This is the .ppkg file that you run to apply the package.

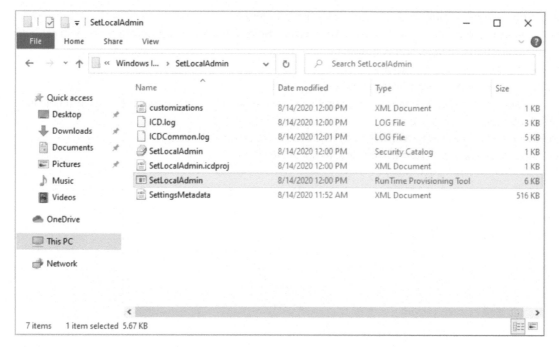

Figure 12-10   Windows Configuration Designer project and provisioning package files

24. In the User Account Control dialog box, click **Yes**.
25. In the Enter the package password dialog box, type **Secret99** and then click **OK**.
26. In the Is this package from a source you trust dialog box, click **Yes, add it**.
27. Right-click the **Start** button and then click **Windows PowerShell (Admin)**.
28. In the User Account Control dialog box, click **Yes**.
29. At the Windows PowerShell prompt, type **Get-LocalUser** and then press **Enter**.
30. Read the list of users and verify that DesktopAdmin exists.
31. Close all open windows.

ENTERPRISE DEPLOYMENT TOOLS

In large organizations, there is a need to automate as much of the deployment process as possible. Simple unattended installations and basic imaging are too cumbersome for an enterprise. As part of a large-scale deployment, you want tools to move user profiles from an old computer to a new computer. You also want to initiate deployment without carrying boot media to each computer.

User State Migration Tool

When you provide users with new computers, you can use USMT to migrate user profiles. USMT can copy Windows settings, application settings, and documents. This allows users to keep a consistent work environment from the old computer to the new computer.

 **CAUTION**   Before using USMT to migrate user profiles, consider whether user profile migration is necessary. Implementing USMT is complex, and you might be able to centralize profile information by using technologies such as folder redirection instead.

USMT has only a command-line interface and is designed for scripting. All configuration for USMT is done by using .xml files with the necessary information. The .xml files used to control USMT are as follows:

- *MigApp.xml*—Used to include or exclude the setting for specific applications.
- *MigUser.xml*—Used to control which file types, user folders, and desktop settings are included in the migration.
- *Config.xml*—Used to allow you to control the migration process in detail. For example, this custom configuration file can control which operating system component settings or which specific applications settings are migrated.

USMT Migration Process

USMT includes ScanState.exe and LoadState.exe to migrate user profiles. ScanState.exe is executed on the old computer to collect the user profile. LoadState.exe is executed on the new computer to deploy the user profile. Figure 12-11 shows the USMT migration process.

ScanState.exe   LoadState.exe

Source computer   **File Share**   Destination computer

Figure 12-11   USMT migration process

When ScanState is used to collect settings and files, they are stored in an intermediate location, such as a network file share. The settings and files cannot be transferred directly to an existing Windows 10 computer.

All applications should be installed on the destination computer before LoadState is used. This ensures that the installation of the application does not overwrite any of the imported configuration settings. Using LoadState before the necessary applications are installed can have unpredictable results.

Using Config.xml

Config.xml does not exist by default. It is generated by running ScanState.exe with the /genconfig option. This option captures all of the settings that are being migrated. You can then edit this file to control which of the settings are actually migrated when ScanState.exe is run.

To create a single Config.xml file that includes all possible application settings, install a workstation explicitly for this purpose. On this workstation, install each application used in your organization for which you want to migrate the settings. Then, after all applications are installed, you can create the Config.xml file based on this workstation. This single Config.xml file can be used to migrate settings and applications for all computers in the organization, rather than maintaining separate Config.xml files for computers with a specific set of applications.

You can use multiple Config.xml files to control the migration process in different ways for users with different needs. For each component listed in the Config.xml file, you can specify yes or no to migrating the component.

Windows Deployment Services

Windows Deployment Services (WDS) is a server role included with Windows Server that you can use to deploy images over the network. With a gigabit network, this means you can deploy an image in only a few minutes. WDS can be managed by using the Windows Deployment Services administrative tool or the wdsutil.exe command-line tool.

The following are required for successful installation and use of WDS:

- *Active Directory*—The WDS server must be a member server or domain controller in an Active Directory domain.
- *DHCP*—DHCP is used by client computers to obtain an IP address and communicate with the WDS server.
- *DNS*—DNS is used by client computers to resolve the host name of the WDS server.
- *An NTFS partition on the WDS server*—The images must be stored on an NTFS-formatted volume on the WDS server.

WDS Images

WDS uses different image types to accomplish different tasks in the deployment process. The four types of images are:

- *Install image*—These are WIM images that are deployed to workstations. They include the operating system and may include applications. You can use an unattend.xml file to modify the operating system as part of the deployment process.

- *Boot image*—These are WIM images that include Windows PE. They are used to deploy install images. The default boot image (boot.wim) displays a menu that allows you to select which install image to deploy.
- *Capture image*—These images are used to automate the collection of an install image from a computer that has been configured as a reference image. Sysprep is run on the computer before the image is captured. The capture image uses Windows PE as an operating system and runs imaging software to collect the image.
- *Discover image*—These images are used to deploy the install images on computers that do not support booting directly from the network. Discover images are ISO files that can be stored on removable media, such as a DVD or USB drive. At the client, you can boot from removable media to connect to the WDS server and download images.

WDS Deployment Process

WDS uses the Preboot Execution Environment (PXE) functionality in a network card to start the imaging process. PXE allows a computer to start and then retrieve an operating system from a source on the network. That operating system can then be used for tasks such as imaging. WDS on Windows Server functions as a PXE server in this process. DHCP is used to provide configuration information to the PXE client. Figure 12-12 shows the WDS deployment process.

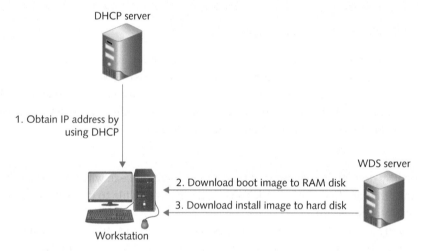

Figure 12-12 WDS deployment process

When deploying an image by using WDS, the following process is used:

1. Enable PXE in the client computer and configure it to boot from the network first.
2. Reboot the workstation and then press **F12** to perform a PXE boot.
3. The workstation obtains an IP address from a DHCP server and contacts the WDS server.
4. Select a PXE boot image if required. You may create additional boot images to support network drivers not available in the default Windows PE configuration.
5. The boot image is downloaded to a RAM disk on the client computer and Windows PE is booted.
6. Select an install image to deploy from the menu.
7. The install image is copied to the computer.

Microsoft Deployment Toolkit

The **Microsoft Deployment Toolkit (MDT)** is a solution that helps you configure automated installations of Windows 10 and applications. You can use MDT with Endpoint Configuration Manager and WDS or on its own. If you use MDT with Configuration Manager, you can perform zero-touch installations that are completely automated. If you use only WDS, MDT can configure lite-touch installations.

A lite-touch installation requires someone to start the remote computer from a boot image. After the boot image is started, though, the entire installation process for the operating system and applications can be automated.

In addition to tools that configure scripted installations of Windows 10 and applications, the MDT includes a wide range of documentation about the deployment of Windows 10. This guidance on best practices for deployment is as valuable as the scripted installations.

NOTE 10

The documentation for MDT can be found at https://docs .microsoft.com/en-us/mem/ configmgr/mdt/.

Windows AutoPilot

Windows AutoPilot uses several cloud services to simplify the deployment of new computers. Instead of maintaining images with installed applications, a computer with Windows 10 installed by the vendor is provisioned by using Windows AutoPilot. The setup process is triggered based on the computer being registered with the Windows AutoPilot service.

TIP   Windows AutoPilot registration can be performed by the computer vendor or system administrators. Having the computer vendor perform registration is preferred because it allows computers to be shipped directly to the end user.

When the computer is delivered and started for the first time, it contacts the Windows AutoPilot service for configuration information. The configuration information is contained in an AutoPilot profile that is assigned to the device. These settings identify a limited set of items, including the following:

- Deployment mode
- Join Azure AD, Active Directory, or hybrid Azure AD join
- Device name template
- User account type

To deploy additional settings and applications, Microsoft Intune is required. Microsoft Intune is included with a number of Microsoft cloud service licensing options.

TIP   It is possible to use a mobile device management (MDM) platform other than Microsoft Intune, but Microsoft Intune is the best supported.

The deployment mode that you configure in the AutoPilot profile defines what the user experience looks like when a new device is configured. The three most commonly used deployment modes are described in Table 12-7.

Table 12-7   Windows AutoPilot Deployment Modes

Deployment Mode	Description
User-driven	User-driven mode prompts the user for sign-in information on first startup. The device then joins Azure AD or Active Directory. Microsoft Intune applies all the specified configuration settings and installs applications.
White glove	While glove deployment speeds up the user experience by allowing a technician to perform the time-consuming steps where configuration settings are applied and applications are installed. Otherwise, the process is similar to user-driven mode.
Self-deploying	Self-deploying mode is used for devices configured to use kiosk mode. No user account is associated with the device.

NOTE 11

For detailed information about Windows AutoPilot, see Windows AutoPilot documentation at https://docs.microsoft .com/en-us/mem/autopilot/.

SUMMARY

- New computers include an OEM installation of Windows 10. You perform a customized installation of Windows 10 by performing a removable media installation, a distribution share installation, or by imaging. Removable media installations have low customization and are suitable only for infrequent installations. Distribution share installations allow you to add extra drivers and packages. Image-based installations can include installed and configured applications along with the operating system.
- Clean installations require user settings and data to be migrated from the old computer to the new computer. Upgrades are simpler when deploying a new operating system because the process automatically migrates user settings and data.
- The Windows 10 ADK provides tools such as ACT, Windows PE, Windows SIM, and Windows ICD to help you migrate to Windows 10 and automate deployment.
- An unattended installation uses an answer file to pass configuration to Setup, with a network administrator answering questions. During a basic installation, the windowsPE, offlineServicing, specialize, and oobeSystem configuration passes are performed. Windows SIM is used to create answer files, add device drivers or packages to an answer file, create a configuration set, or apply offline updates to a Windows 10 image.
- Sysprep is used to prepare computers for imaging. After Sysprep is run, Windows 10 can be configured to enter audit mode or start the out-of-box experience.
- DISM is used to capture, modify, and apply images. WIM is file-based imaging and allows you to store multiple images in a single image file. FFU is a sector-based imaging format that is faster to capture and apply.
- Windows Configuration Designer is used to create provisioning packages that are applied to Windows 10 computers that are already deployed. Provisioning avoids the need to reimage new computers and BYOD devices.
- You can use enterprise deployment tools to provide a high level of automation for deployment. USMT automates copying of user profiles. WDS deploys images by booting client computers over the network. MDT is a suite of tools that allow you to configure lite-touch and zero-touch deployments. Windows AutoPilot is used to automate provisioning.

Key Terms

answer file
auditSystem configuration pass
auditUser configuration pass
autounattend.xml
catalog file
clean installation
configuration set
distribution share
distribution share installation
full flash update (FFU)
generalization
generalize configuration pass
image
image-based installation
Microsoft Deployment Toolkit (MDT)

offline update
offlineServicing configuration pass
oobeSystem configuration pass
original equipment manufacturer (OEM) installation
provisioning
removable media installation
specialize configuration pass
Sysprep
System Audit Mode cleanup action
System Out-of-Box Experience (OOBE) cleanup action
unattend.xml
unattended installation
upgrade installation
User State Migration Tool (USMT)

Windows 10 Assessment and Deployment Kit (ADK)
Windows AutoPilot
Windows Configuration Designer
Windows Deployment Services (WDS)
Windows image (WIM)
Windows PE
Windows System Image Manager (SIM)
windowsPE configuration pass

Review Questions

1. Which task cannot be performed by using DISM?
   a. Create an image.
   b. Add files to an image.
   c. Apply application updates to an offline image.
   d. Apply Windows updates to an offline image.
   e. Apply an image.

2. Which utility is used to create answer files for unattended installations?
   a. DISM
   b. Windows PE
   c. Windows SIM
   d. Windows Configuration Designer
   e. Sysprep

3. Which utility is used to prepare computers for imaging by removing specific information, such as the computer name and computer SID?
   a. DISM
   b. Windows PE
   c. Windows SIM
   d. Windows Deployment Services
   e. Sysprep

4. Which installation methods require booting into Windows PE before Windows 10 starts? (Choose all that apply.)
   a. removable media installation
   b. distribution share installation
   c. upgrade installation
   d. image-based installation
   e. Windows AutoPilot

5. Which installation method can be used to distribute Windows 10 with applications already installed?
   a. removable media installation
   b. distribution share installation
   c. unattended installation
   d. image-based installation
   e. clean installation

6. Which methods can you use to migrate user settings from Windows 8.1 to Windows 10? (Choose all that apply.)
   a. Copy the user profile from the old computer to the new computer.
   b. Perform an upgrade over the top of the old operating system.
   c. Use Windows Easy Transfer.
   d. Use the User State Migration Tool.
   e. Use Remote Desktop to copy to files.

7. Which methods can you use to place applications from a previous operating system on Windows 10? (Choose all that apply.)
   a. Copy the applications from the previous computer to the new computer.
   b. Perform an upgrade over the top of the previous operating system.
   c. Use Windows Easy Transfer.
   d. Use the User State Migration Tool.
   e. Reinstall the applications on the new computer.

8. Which utility can be used to update drivers in an existing Windows 10 image?
   a. Windows SIM
   b. Windows Configuration Designer
   c. DISM
   d. Sysprep
   e. Windows Update

9. Which configuration passes automatically search for an autounattend.xml file, if an answer file is not specified? (Choose all that apply.)
   a. windowsPE
   b. offlineServicing
   c. specialize
   d. generalize
   e. oobeSystem

10. Which configuration pass can be used to perform disk partitioning operations?
    a. windowsPE
    b. offlineServicing
    c. specialize
    d. generalize
    e. oobeSystem

11. Which configuration pass is performed only by Sysprep?
    a. windowsPE
    b. offlineServicing
    c. specialize
    d. generalize
    e. oobeSystem

12. Windows Configuration Designer can be used to completely automate the deployment of Windows 10. True or False?

13. A WIM image file containing two Windows 10 images will be approximately twice as big as a WIM image file containing one Windows 10 image. True or False?

14. Which of the following are scenarios where you could use provisioning? (Choose all that apply.)
   a. deploying Microsoft 365 Apps
   b. updating Windows 10 Pro to Window 10 Enterprise
   c. upgrading Windows 8.1 to Windows 10
   d. deploying new Windows Store applications
   e. performing a clean installation of Windows 10

15. Which tool is used to create provisioning packages?
   a. Windows PE
   b. Windows Configuration Designer
   c. Windows SIM
   d. ACT
   e. PCmover Express

16. Which two files are included in USMT to copy user profiles?
   a. loadstate.exe
   b. sysprep.exe
   c. dism.exe
   d. setup.exe
   e. scanstate.exe

17. Which image type in WDS is used to start Windows PE and apply an image?
   a. Install image
   b. Boot image
   c. AutoUnattend.xml
   d. Capture image
   e. Discover image

18. The zero-touch installation option in MDT requires the use of Microsoft Endpoint Configuration Manager. True or False?

19. How many times can you use the generalize option in sysprep on a single image?
   a. 3
   b. 5
   c. 8
   d. 12
   e. Unlimited

20. The user-driven mode for Windows AutoPilot can join the computer to Azure AD or Active Directory. True or False?

Case Projects

Case Project 12-1: Installation for a Small Organization

Buddy's Machine Shop has 30 computers running a mix of Windows 8.1 and Windows 10. Computers are replaced only as required by hardware failure or new software requirements. Jeff performs system administration tasks for Buddy's 25 percent of the time and spends 75 percent of his time doing computer automated design work. For a small environment like Buddy's Machine Shop, how do you think they should deploy new computers?

Case Project 12-2: Using Image-Based Installation

Superduper Lightspeed Computers builds over 100 computers per week for customers. The computers use a wide range of hardware depending on whether they are built for gaming, home use, or office use. Create a plan for Superduper Lightspeed Computers to start using imaging, including audit mode, to install Windows 10 on their new computers.

Case Project 12-3: Installation for a Large Organization

Gigantic Life Insurance has 4000 users spread over 5 locations in North America. They have hired you as a consultant to provide a solution for standardizing Windows 10 configuration. There is a mix of desktop computers and tablets running Windows 10. The computers and tablets come from a variety of vendors because Gigantic Life Insurance allows agents to purchase their own computers and devices. How do you recommend they standardize their Windows 10 installations?

MICROSOFT WINDOWS EXAM MD-100 OBJECTIVES

MD-100

Exam Objectives	Notes
1.0 Deploy Windows (15–25%)	
1.1 Deploy Windows 10	
• Configure language packs	Module 2, Settings Overview
• Perform a clean installation	Module 1, Installing Windows 10
	Module 12, Windows 10 Installation Methods
	Module 12, Windows 10 Installation Types
	Module 12, Windows 10 Assessment and Deployment Kit
	Module 12, Unattended Installation
	Module 12, Preparing Windows 10 for Imaging
	Module 12, Using DISM for Imaging
	Module 12, Enterprise Deployment Tools
• Migrate user data	Module 12, Windows 10 Installation Types
	Module 12, Windows 10 Assessment and Deployment Kit
	Module 12, Enterprise Deployment Tools
• Perform an in-place upgrade (using tools such as MDT, WDS, and ADK.)	Module 1, Installing Windows 10
	Module 12, Windows 10 Installation Types
	Module 12, Windows 10 Assessment and Deployment Kit
	Module 12, Enterprise Deployment Tools
• Select the appropriate Windows edition	Module 1, Windows 10 Editions
• Troubleshoot activation issues	Module 1, Activating Windows 10

Exam Objectives	Notes
1.2 Perform post-installation configuration	
• Configure Edge and Internet Explorer	Module 7, Browsers
• Configure mobility settings	Module 12, Synchronizing Data for Mobile Clients
• Configure sign-in options	Module 3, User Accounts
	Module 3, Creating and Managing User Accounts
	Module 3, Advanced Authentication Methods
• Customize the Windows desktop	Module 2, Settings Overview
	Module 2, Display
	Module 3, Start Menu and Taskbar Customization
	Module 7, Accessories and Shortcuts
2.0 Manage devices and data (35–40%)	
2.1 Manage local users, local groups, and devices	
• Manage devices in directories	Module 10, Active Directory
	Module 10, Group Policy
	Module 10, Microsoft Cloud Services
• Manage local groups	Module 3, User Accounts
	Module 3, Creating and Managing User Accounts
• Manage local users	Module 3, User Accounts
	Module 3, Creating and Managing User Accounts
2.2 Configure data access and protection	
• Configure NTFS permissions	Module 5, File and Folder Permissions
• Configure share permissions	Module 5, File Sharing
2.3 Configure devices by using local policies	
• Configure local registry	Module 8, The Registry
• Implement local policy	Module 6, Windows 10 Security Policies
	Module 6, Auditing
• Troubleshoot group policies	Module 10, Group Policy
2.4 Manage Windows security	
• Configure User Account Control (UAC)	Module 6, User Account Control
• Configure Windows Defender Firewall	Module 4, Windows Defender Firewall
• Implement encryption	Module 6, Data Security
3.0 Configure connectivity (15–20%)	
3.1 Configure networking	
• Configure client IP settings	Module 4, Networking Overview
	Module 4, IP Version 4
• Configure mobile networking	Module 4, Networking Overview
	Module 4, Wireless Networking
• Configure VPN client	Module 11, Using a VPN for Remote Access
• Troubleshoot networking	Module 4, IP Version 4
• Configure Wi-Fi profiles	Module 4, Wireless Networking

Exam Objectives	Notes
3.2 Configure remote connectivity	
• Configure remote management	Module 11, Troubleshooting and Managing Enterprise Clients
• Enable PowerShell Remoting	Module 11, Troubleshooting and Managing Enterprise Clients
• Configure remote desktop access	Module 11, Troubleshooting and Managing Enterprise Clients
4.0 Maintain Windows (25–30%)	
4.1 Configure system and data recovery	
• Perform file recovery (including OneDrive)	Module 7, OneDrive
	Module 9, Local File Recovery and Backup
• Recovery Windows 10	Module 9, System Recovery
• Troubleshoot startup/boot process	Module 9, System Recovery
4.2 Manage updates	
• Check for updates	Module 6, Windows Update
• Troubleshoot updates	Module 6, Windows Update
• Validate and test updates	Module 6, Windows Update
• Select the appropriate servicing channel	Module 6, Windows Update
• Configure Windows update options	Module 6, Windows Update
4.3 Monitor and manage Windows	
• Configure and analyze event logs	Module 9, Troubleshooting Windows 10 Errors
• Manage performance	Module 9, Performance Tuning Overview
	Module 9, Performance Monitoring Tools
	Module 9, Performance Options
• Manage Windows 10 environment	Module 2, Settings Overview
	Module 2, Administrative Tools
	Module 2, Command-Line Administration Tools
	Module 2, Managing Optional Features
	Module 2, Hardware Management
	Module 2, Power Management
	Module 2, Task Scheduler
	Module 9, Controlling Application Startup

PREPARING FOR CERTIFICATION EXAMS

This book and the course provided by your instructor are excellent resources to begin preparing for the MD-100: Windows 10 exam that is part of the Microsoft 365 Certified: Modern Desktop Administrator Associate certification. However, most students (the authors of this book included) need to go beyond any one book or course to be successful in passing certification exams.

STUDYING FOR THE EXAM

The questions for Microsoft certification exams are generated by a team of subject matter experts using the same exam objectives listed in this book. Review the exam objectives (listed in Appendix A) and make sure that you understand each one. If you are not sure you understand an objective, put a little more time into studying that area.

The activities in this book are a good start for learning to use Windows 10 and becoming comfortable with its features, but you should do more. Create some activities of your own to try out different features. The process of creating the activities helps you understand how they could be used.

Use additional resources for learning. Microsoft provides extensive documentation for its products at https://docs.microsoft.com. If you want to learn more about how share permissions work, go read about it. Even though the MD-100 exam is testing on Windows 10 features and configuration, sometimes understanding the server part of the configuration helps you to understand the entire process better.

TAKING THE EXAM

The questions on certification exams are not designed to be tricky. The developers of the exam questions put a lot of time into trying to create questions that have only a single correct answer. If you think that you have found a tricky question, take another look; you might be overthinking it.

For some questions, being able to identify incorrect options is as important as identifying the correct options. When you can identify incorrect options quickly, it reduces the amount of information you need to consider in order to determine the correct answer.

There will be some questions that you do not know the answer to. It's important that you do not dwell for an extended period of time on a single question. Answer the questions you know and mark some for later review if you would like to spend more time on them. And if you truly do not know the answer to a question, eliminate the obviously incorrect options and make a guess. You might get lucky!

Your exam might include hands-on questions. These questions test your ability to perform a configuration task by using virtual machines running Windows 10 and possibly Windows Server. Scoring for these questions verifies the result requested and not the method used to achieve it. Use the method you are most familiar with that meets the requirements. Hands-on practice is essential to successful completion of these questions.

GLOSSARY

.NET Framework   A commonly required application environment, available in multiple versions, for Windows apps.

802.11   A group of IEEE standards that define how to transfer data over wireless networks.

802.1x   An IEEE standard designed to enhance security of wireless networks by authenticating a user to a central authority.

A

access control entry (ACE)   A specific entry in a file or folder's ACL that uniquely identifies a user or group by its security identifier and the action it is allowed or denied to take on that file or folder.

access control list (ACL)   A collection of ACE items that explicitly defines what actions are allowed to be taken on the file or folder to which it is attached.

Account Lockout Policy   A collection of settings, such as lockout duration, that control account lockouts.

Action Center   A list of operating system and application notifications in addition to buttons that enable and disable some common options.

Active Directory   A centralized directory used for domain-based networking that contains user and computer accounts.

Active Directory site   A set of IP subnets representing a physical location that is used by Active Directory to control replication.

Active Directory-based activation   A method for activating software internally without needing to implement a KMS server.

address prefix   The network portion of an IPv6 address.

Administrative Tools   A group of MMC consoles that are used to manage Windows 10. Computer Management, Event Viewer, and Services are the more commonly used.

Administrator   The built-in Windows 10 account that is created during installation and has full rights to the system. This account cannot be deleted or removed by the Administrators group.

administrator account   The type of user account that is made a member of the Administrators local group and has full rights to the system.

Advanced Configuration and Power Interface (ACPI)   The current standard for power management that is implemented in Windows 10 and by computer manufacturers.

Alert   An event that is triggered when a count value is above or below the specified threshold value.

alternate IP configuration   A set of static IP configuration information that is used instead of APIPA when a computer is unable to contact a DHCP server.

Always On VPN   A VPN configuration for Windows 10 that can automatically connect when users are outside of the office.

answer file   An XML file used during an unattended setup to provide configuration to Setup.exe. Windows 10 answer files are created by using Windows (SIM).

application environment subsystem   A software layer that exists between apps and the operating system to simplify app development.

application programmer interfaces (APIs)   Methods for application developers to make requests to an operating system to perform tasks.

application programming interface (API)   The interface used by a program to request services from the application environment, which in turn interfaces with the operating system to provide those services.

Application Virtualization (App-V)   A technology that deploys applications by streaming and isolates them in a virtual environment.

applications   Software used to perform tasks, generate data, and manipulate data. Microsoft word is an example of an application.

AppLocker   A feature in Windows 10 that is used to define which programs are allowed to run. This is a replacement for the software restriction policies found in Windows XP and Windows Vista, but it is not available in Windows 10 Pro.

APPX file   A file for installing a UWP app.

assigned access   A sign-in option that you can configure for a single local user account that restricts the user to using only an assigned Windows Store app; often used to configure Windows 10 as a kiosk.

asymmetric encryption algorithm   An encryption algorithm that uses two keys to encrypt and decrypt data where data encrypted with one key is decrypted by the other key.

attrib   A command-line utility to manage attributes for files and folders.

audit policy   The settings that define which operating system events are audited.

auditing   The security process that records the occurrence of specific operating system events in the Security log.

auditSystem configuration pass   The configuration pass that is performed *before* user sign-in when Sysprep triggers Windows 10 into audit mode.

auditUser configuration pass   The configuration pass that is performed *after* user sign-in when Sysprep triggers Windows 10 into audit mode.

Automatic Private IP Addressing (APIPA)   A system used to automatically assign an IP address on the 169.254.x.x network to a computer that is unable to communicate with a DHCP server.

autonegotiation   A signaling mechanism used by two network connected devices to choose common transmission parameters such as speed and flow control.

autounattend.xml   An answer file that is automatically searched for during the windowsPE and offlineServicing configuration passes.

Away Mode   An instant-on power-saving mode that keeps the system in the S0 state.

Azure AD   A cloud-based directory service hosted by Microsoft.

Azure AD join   A process to register Windows 10 in Azure AD to allow for centralized management.

B

Backup and Restore (Windows 7)   The legacy backup utility that is included to provide access to backups from Windows 7.

baseline   A set of performance indicators gathered when system performance is acceptable.

basic disk   A storage type that supports dividing a hard disk into multiple partitions, but doesn't support advanced features such as fault tolerance.

biometric authentication   Authentication method that is based on physical characteristics of the user, such as a fingerprint or facial recognition.

BitLocker Drive Encryption   A feature in Windows 10 that can encrypt the operating system partition of a hard drive and protect system files from modification. Other partitions can also be encrypted.

BitLocker Network Unlock   A system that allows the Windows 10 boot process to bypass the requirement startup PIN when performing system maintenance.

BitLocker To Go   A new feature in Windows 10 that allows you to encrypt removable storage.

bottleneck   The component in a process that prevents the overall process from completing faster.

Branch Office Direct Printing   A feature that allows Windows 10 computers to print directly to a printer shared from a print server rather than sending the print job through the print server.

BranchCache   A feature in Windows 10 that speeds up access to files over slow connections by caching files. It operates in distributed cache mode or hosted cache mode.

broadcast address   An address that indicates that the destination for a particular packet should be all available computers.

built-in local groups   Groups that are automatically created for each Windows 10 computer and stored in the SAM database.

C

cached credentials   Credentials that are stored in Windows 10 after a user has signed in to a domain or Microsoft account and can be used to sign in when a domain controller cannot be contacted or when no network connectivity is detected.

catalog file   A file used by Windows SIM to read the configurable settings and their current status for a WIM image.

cipher   A command-line utility to manage encryption attributes for files and folders in the NTFS file system.

classless interdomain routing (CIDR)   A notation technique that summarizes the number of binary bits in an IP address that identify the network an IP address belongs to, counted starting from the left side of the IP address as written in binary form. The number of bits is written at the end of the IP address with a slash (/) symbol separating the two values (e.g., 192.168.1.0/24 or FE80::/64).

clean installation   An installation that is performed on a new computer, or does not retain the user settings or applications of an existing computer.

Click-to-Run   A new streaming installation technology that is used to deploy Office 365 ProPlus.

Client for Microsoft Networks   The client that allows Windows 10 to access files and printers shared on other Windows computers by using the SMB protocol.

Client Hyper-V   A feature in Windows 10 that allows you to create and run virtual machines.

client   A client allows you to communicate with a particular service running on a remote computer.

Clipboard history   A new feature in Windows 10 that allows you to copy multiple items to the clipboard at the same time.

cloud licensing   Licenses that are available only when upgrading Windows 10 Pro to Windows 10 Enterprise. The licenses are enabled when users sign in to Azure AD.

cloud services   Services or apps, such as Microsoft 365, Azure AD, or Microsoft Intune, that are available over the Internet.

cmdlet   A Windows PowerShell command in verb-noun format. Most cmdlets have parameters that can be used to pass options to the cmdlet.

compact   A command-line utility to manage compression attributes for files and folders in the NTFS file system.

Compatibility Administrator   A tool included in the Windows 10 ADK that includes a database of compatibility fixes for older apps.

computer hardware   The physical components of a computer, such as memory, hard drive, and peripherals.

Computer Management   One of the more commonly used administrative tools. This MMC console contains the snap-ins to manage most Windows 10 components.

configuration partition   The Active Directory partition that holds general information about the Active Directory forest and application configuration information. It is replicated to all domain controllers in the Active Directory forest.

configuration set   The subset of files from a distribution share that are required for a particular answer file. A configuration set is more compact than a distribution share.

Control Panel   An alternative location to configure Windows 10 settings. Used when advanced settings are not available in Settings.

controlled folder access   An anti-malware feature that limits the ability of programs to access specified folders.

counters   The performance indicators that can be recorded in Performance Monitor.

D

Data Collector Set   A grouping of counters that you can use to log system data and generate reports.

Data Execution Prevention (DEP)   A feature designed to prevent the installation of malware by monitoring processes to ensure that they do not access unauthorized memory spaces.

Data Manager   The Performance Monitor component that is used to automatically manage performance logs.

data synchronization   A system that synchronizes files between multiple devices. This allows data to be accessed when offline.

default gateway   A router on the local network that is used to deliver packets to remote networks.

default profile   The profile that is copied when new user profiles are created.

Desktop Analytics   A cloud-based solution for monitoring and reporting on app compatibility.

device driver signing   A system that ensures that a device driver is from a known publisher and that the device driver has not been modified since it was signed.

device drivers   Software that manages the communication between Windows 10 and a particular hardware component.

device identification string   One or more identifiers included in a hardware device that is used by Windows 10 to locate and install an appropriate driver for a hardware device.

Device Manager   An MMC snap-in that is used to manage hardware components and their device drivers.

device setup class   An identifier included with a hardware device driver that describes how the device driver is to be installed.

DirectAccess   A technology similar to Always On VPN but is compatible with Windows 8.1 and Windows 10.

Disk Management console An MMC console snap-in used to administer hard disks in Windows 10.

disk quotas A system of tracking owners for file data within an NTFS-formatted partition or volume and the total disk space consumed by each owner. Limits or warnings can be established to restrict disk space usage.

DiskPart A command-line tool for managing disks that allows you to perform advanced operations that are not available in Disk Management.

display resolution The number of pixels that your display can show.

Distributed File System (DFS) A server role in Windows Server that includes replication of shared folders and virtualization of paths providing access to the shared folders.

distribution share installation An installation of Windows 10 that is started by running Setup. exe over the network from a distribution share.

distribution share A share configured through Windows SIM to hold drivers and packages that can be added to Windows 10 during installation.

domain A networking model that centralizes authentication and management. The list of users and computers is contained in a domain database.

domain controller A server that holds a copy of Active Directory information.

Domain Name System (DNS) A system for converting computer host names to IP addresses.

domain network The location type that is used when a computer joined to a domain is on the domain network, for example, a corporate office.

domain partition The Active Directory partition that holds domain-specific information, such as user and computer accounts, that is replicated only among domain controllers within the domain.

domain A logical grouping of computers and users in Active Directory.

domain-based network A network where security information is stored centrally in Active Directory.

driver store A central location in Windows 10 where drivers are located before they are installed. A large set of drivers is included with Windows 10.

DVD boot installation The installation option for Windows 10 that requires you to boot from a DVD to perform an installation; uses the same process, but is faster when booting from USB media.

dynamic disks A method for organizing disks that was introduced in Windows 2000 as a replacement for basic disks but was never very popular. Dynamic disks can have a large number of volumes and also support some fault-tolerant disk configurations.

Dynamic Host Configuration Protocol (DHCP) An automated mechanism to assign IP addresses and IP configuration information over the network.

dynamic lock A security feature that locks Windows 10 when a paired Bluetooth device moves out of range.

E

Encrypting File System (EFS) A feature of the NTFS file system that allows users to encrypt files and folders for additional security.

Encrypting File System (EFS) An encryption technology for individual files and folders that can be enabled by users.

eSIM An embedded, nonremovable SIM in a device.

Event Viewer An MMC console that is used to view messages generated and logged by Windows 10, applications, and services.

Extensible Authentication Protocol (EAP) A framework that allows multiple authentication protocols to be integrated with the VPN sign-in process.

F

Fast Startup A system that speeds up the shutdown and startup process of Windows 10 by using hibernate for the core operating system functionality.

fast user switching A sign-in method that allows multiple users to have applications running at the same time but allows only one user to use the console at a time.

feature updates Windows 10 updates, released semiannually, that include new features.

File Allocation Table (FAT) A file system used to organize files and folders in a partition or volume. FAT doesn't include security permissions.

File and Printer Sharing for Microsoft Networks The service that allows Windows 10 to share files and printers by using the SMB protocol.

File History A feature that is used to back up user files to an external hard drive or file share.

File Signature Verification utility   A utility (sigverif.exe) that verifies the digital signature on operating system files and device drivers.

folder redirection   A feature that redirects profile folders from the local computer to a network location.

folder redirection   A system that allows some user profile data to be stored on file shares instead of the local hard drive.

Foreign Disk   A dynamic disk moved to another computer is flagged as a foreign disk in Disk Management.

forest   Multiple Active Directory domains with automatic trust relationships among them.

fsutil   A command-line utility to perform tasks related to managing FAT and NTFS file systems.

full flash update (FFU)   A sector-based image format developed by Microsoft that contains only a single image per file.

full packaged product (FPP) license   A license for Windows 10 that you purchase from a retailer.

Full Volume Encryption Key (FVEK)   The key used to encrypt the Volume Master Key (VMK) when BitLocker Drive Encryption is enabled.

fully qualified domain name (FQDN)   The full name of a host on the network, including its host and domain name. For example, the FQDN www .microsoft.com includes the host name www and the domain name microsoft.com.

G

generalization   A process performed by Sysprep to prepare a computer running Windows 10 for imaging. The computer SID, computer name, and hardware information are removed during generalization.

generalize configuration pass   The configuration pass that is performed when Sysprep is run to generalize Windows 10.

generic volume license key (GVLK)   A generic product key that needs to be entered in Windows 10 when using KMS or Active Directory-based activation.

global catalog server   A domain controller that holds a subset of the information in all domain partitions for the entire Active Directory forest.

Group Policy   A feature that allows administrators to configure settings on Windows client computers.

Group Policy object (GPO)   A collection of Group Policy settings that can be applied to client computers.

Group Policy Preferences   Part of a Group Policy object that is typically used to configure the user environment. Preferences can be changed by the user but are reset again at next sign-in.

Group Policy   A feature integrated with Active Directory that can be used to centrally manage the configuration of Windows 2000 and newer Windows computers, including Windows 10.

Guest   A built-in Windows 10 account, initially disabled by default, that provides minimal privileges intended to give very limited access to Windows 10.

GUID Partition Table (GPT)   A partition style that supports up to 128 partitions on a disk in Windows 10. Windows 10 can boot from GPT disks when using UEFI firmware.

H

hard link   A directory entry that associates with a different file on a file system, in addition to the file's original directory entry.

hardware drivers   Small pieces of software used by an operating system to manage specific types of hardware.

hashing algorithms   One-way encryption algorithms that create unique identifiers that can be used to determine whether data has been changed.

hibernate   An ACPI power state that saves the contents of RAM to disk and then disables power to all devices including RAM; also referred to as S4 state.

hive   A discrete body of registry keys and values stored in files as part of the operating system.

hostname   A command-line utility that can be used to identify the name of the computer.

Hotspot 2.0   A standard for public-access Wi-Fi.

hybrid sleep   The sleep method used by Windows 10 that combines the S3 state and S4 state. When the computer moves to the S3 state, it also saves the memory file required for the S4 state.

I

icacls   A command-line utility capable of displaying and updating NTFS permissions for files and folders.

IE Mode   A feature in Microsoft Edge that automatically configures various compatibility modes for websites.

image A collection of files captured using DISM and stored in an image file.

image-based installation An installation that uses DISM to apply an image of an operating system to a computer. The image can include applications as well as the operating system.

initial account The account with administrative privileges created during the installation of Windows 10.

initialize A process that prepares a new disk for use with Windows by configuring the MBR or GPT partition style. If the disk is already initialized, initializing it again will erase all previous partitions and their data.

Institute of Electrical and Electronics Engineers (IEEE) A professional society that promotes and nurtures the development of standards used in the application of electronic technology.

Internet Connection Sharing (ICS) A Windows 10 feature that allows multiple computers to share an Internet connection by performing NAT.

Internet Key Exchange v2 Tunneling Protocol (IKEv2) A VPN protocol that uses IPSec to secure data but can authenticate by using a user name and password. This protocol supports VPN Reconnect.

Internet Protocol Version 4 (TCP/IPv4) The standard protocol used on corporate networks and the Internet.

Internet Protocol Version 6 (TCP/IPv6) An updated version of TCP/IPv4 with a much larger address space.

IP address The unique address used by computers on an IPv4 or IPv6 network. An IPv4 address is commonly displayed in dotted decimal notation, for example, 10.10.0.50.

ipconfig A command-line utility that can be used to display and manage IP address settings for network interfaces on a computer.

IPSec A protocol that is used to secure and authenticate an IPv4 connection.

ISP An Internet Service Provider supplies services for connecting to, and using, the Internet.

J

junction point A special type of symbolic link that points to another directory in the NTFS file system.

K

Key Management Service (KMS) An internal activation service that organizations can use if they purchase volume licensing.

kiosk A computer in a public space that is dedicated for a single purpose.

L

Layer 2 Tunneling Protocol (L2TP) An authentication-only VPN protocol that is combined with IPSec to provide data encryption. It is seldom used because it is difficult to configure.

libraries Virtual folders in File Explorer that combine content from multiple locations to simplify file access.

Link-Local Multicast Name Resolution (LLMNR) A protocol that defines methods for name resolution of local neighboring computers without using DNS, WINS, or NetBIOS name resolution services. LLMNR can operate on IPv4 and IPv6 networks with the use of specially crafted multicast addresses to query client names on other computers.

Local Security Policy A set of security configuration options in Windows 10 that are used to control user rights, auditing, password settings, and more.

local user account A user account, valid only for the local computer, that is defined in the SAM database of a Windows 10 computer.

Local Users and Groups MMC snap-in An MMC snap-in that is used to manage users and groups.

location type The type of network: public, private, or domain. Different configuration settings are applied based on the location type.

loopback address The IPv4 address 127.0.0.1 or IPv6 address ::1, which are used to represent the local computer itself on the network. Traffic sent to the loopback address does not get passed over an actual network; it is processed within the operating system without using an actual network connection.

M

malware Malicious software, including viruses, worms, and spyware, designed to perform unauthorized acts on your computer.

mandatory profile A profile that cannot be changed by users. Ntuser.dat is renamed to Ntuser.man.

Master Boot Record (MBR) The legacy partition style required to start Windows 10 when using BIOS firmware. Disk size is limited to 2 TB with a maximum of four partitions.

MBR2GPT A utility to convert a disk from Master Boot Record (MBR) to the GUID Partition Table (GPT) partition style without modifying or deleting data on the disk.

metadata Information or properties for a file or other object. Windows 10 allows you to include tags as additional metadata for files.

Microsoft account An account, stored online by Microsoft, that you can use to authenticate to multiple Microsoft cloud services and Windows 10.

Microsoft BitLocker Administration and Monitoring (MBAM) A tool included in the Microsoft Desktop Optimization Pack that is used to centrally deploy, manage, and monitor BitLocker.

Microsoft Deployment Toolkit (MDT) A set of software tools that you can use to configure lite-touch or zero-touch deployment of Windows 10.

Microsoft Edge The more recent browser in Windows 10 that has better support for web standards, such as HTML5, than Internet Explorer.

Microsoft Endpoint Configuration Manager A software package that can perform inventory, implement a standardized configuration, deploy software, deploy operating systems, and deploy software updates.

Microsoft Intune A cloud service that can be used to manage computers running Windows 10 that are not joined to a domain.

Microsoft Management Console (MMC) A graphical interface shell that provides a structured environment to build management utilities.

Microsoft Store for Business A customizable online store for businesses to organize UWP and MSIX apps for their users.

mklink A command-line utility to create symbolic links or hard links for files and folders in the NTFS file system.

MMC snap-ins Small software components that can be added to an MMC console to provide functionality. An MMC snap-in typically manages some part of Windows.

Mobile Device Management (MDM) A system used to manage mobile devices. This can be used when Windows 10 is joined to Azure AD.

Modern Standby A new "instant-on" sleep mode in Windows 10. The computer remains in the S0 state but powers down as much hardware as possible.

MSI file An app packaged for installation by the Windows Installer service.

MSIX A new app packaging option that supports Win32 apps, .NET Framework apps, and UWP apps.

multicast A type of address that is shared by multiple computers or devices. All hosts in the multicast group listen for communication on the shared address and all can respond.

Multiple Activation Key (MAK) A product key available through volume licensing that can be used for multiple instances of Windows 10.

multiple monitors Attaching two or more displays to a single computer. The information can be exactly the same on each display, or each display can be used independently by using extended mode.

N

nbtstat A command-line utility that can be used to display protocol statistics and current TCP/IP connections using NetBIOS over TCP/IP.

net command-line utility A legacy command-line utility used to manage a variety of network settings, including network shares, printers, and users.

NetBIOS A specification, originally created by IBM in 1983 and later enhanced and evolved by Microsoft, that allows access to shared services and data over a local area network. This is considered a deprecated protocol, but many components of the specification are still in use within a Windows client or server environment.

netsh A command-line utility that can be used to display, change, add, and delete network configuration settings on a computer, including basic and advanced settings.

netstat A command-line utility that can be used to display protocol statistics and current TCP/IP network connections.

Network Address Translation (NAT) A system that allows multiple computers to share a single IP address when connecting to the Internet.

Network and Internet Settings A central location to view network status and configure network settings, part of the Settings app. The preferred interface for updating network-related settings.

Network and Sharing Center A central location to view network status and configure network settings, part of Control Panel. Although a deprecated interface, it still provides some advanced settings and controls.

network discovery A setting that controls how your computer views other computers on the network and advertises its presence on the network.

network driver The software responsible for enabling communication between Windows 10 and the network device in your computer.

network location awareness The capability of Windows 10 to detect when it is connected to a different network and perform actions based on the change.

New Technology File System (NTFS) The most commonly used file system for Windows 10. NTFS supports advanced features to add reliability, security, and flexibility that file systems such as FAT do not have.

notification area The area on the taskbar that is used by applications to display notifications; this area also contains the system time and Action Center.

nslookup A command-line utility that can be used to view or debug the data returned from a DNS server in response to a DNS name resolution query.

Ntuser.dat The file containing user-specific registry entries in a user profile.

O

octet A unit of information, 1 octet = 8 binary bits = 1 byte.

offline files A feature that Windows 10 clients can use to synchronize files from a file share to the local computer for offline use.

offline update An update that is applied to Windows 10 during installation before Windows 10 is started. The packages used for offline updates are supplied by Microsoft.

offlineServicing configuration pass The second configuration pass that is performed after the Windows image has been copied to the local hard drive. This configuration pass applies packages, such as security updates, language packs, and device drivers, before Windows 10 is started.

OneDrive for Business The version of OneDrive that is included with an Office 365 or Microsoft 365 subscription.

OneDrive Cloud-based storage that is provided when you create a Microsoft account. You can access files in OneDrive through File Explorer or a browser.

Online Sign-Up A secure sign up service for Hotspot 2.0 services.

oobeSystem configuration pass The final configuration pass before installation is complete, applied during the user out-of-box experience (OOBE). This configuration pass is typically used in conjunction with Sysprep and DISM.

Open Database Connectivity (ODBC) A standard mechanism for applications to access databases.

operating system Software that manages the hardware and applications running on a computer.

organizational units (OUs) Containers within a domain that are used to create a hierarchy that can be used to organize user and computer accounts and apply group policies.

original equipment manufacturer (OEM) installation The installation of Windows 10 that is performed by the computer vendor before shipping to a customer.

original equipment manufacturer (OEM) license A license for Windows 10 that is provided by a computer manufacturer. This license cannot be transferred to another computer.

P

page description language A language that defines the layout of content for a print job.

partition table The data structure on a basic disk that contains information about where partitions are located.

Passpoint A designation applied to certified Hotspot 2.0 compatible devices.

pass-through authentication Automatic authentication to a remote resource when the local computer passes the local credentials to the remote computer.

password policy A collection of settings to control password characteristics, such as length and complexity.

pathping A command-line utility that can be used to test IP communications between the computer running the utility and a remote target. In addition to the basic IP communication test, the pathping utility traces the routers involved in establishing the IP communication path.

peer-to-peer network A network where all computers store their own security information and share data.

Performance Monitor An MMC console used to monitor and troubleshoot the performance of your computer.

Performance Monitor A tool within the Microsoft Management Console (MMC) that allows you to visually display the data generated by counters.

performance tuning   The process for collecting system performance data, analyzing system performance data, and implementing system performance improvements.

Personal Area Network (PAN)   A computer network for connecting electronic devices to an individual's personal computer environment, typically implemented with infrared, ultrasonic, and wireless Bluetooth and Wi-Fi technologies.

Personal Vault   A feature in OneDrive that allows you to store encrypted data that requires a second level of authentication to unlock.

picture password authentication   An authentication method in which you use gestures on a picture.

PIN authentication   An authentication method in which you enter a device-specific PIN rather than a user name and password.

ping   A command-line utility that can be used to test IP communications between the computer running the utility and a remote target.

pixel   A single dot on a display.

Point-to-Point Protocol over Ethernet (PPPoE)   A protocol used to secure connections over most DSL lines.

Point-to-Point Tunneling Protocol (PPTP)   An older VPN protocol that authenticates based on user name and password. It is generally considered insecure, but it is easy to configure.

Portable Document Format (PDF)   A popular document format that is also supported as a page description language by some printers.

PostScript   A common page description language used by printers to describe how a page is printed.

power plans   A set of configuration options for power management.

powercfg.exe   A command-line utility for configuring power management and generating power management reports.

Previous Versions   The tab in the Properties dialog box that is available to restore files and folders that have been backed up by File History or Backup and Restore (Windows 7).

Print Management snap-in   A printer management tool in Windows 10 that allows you to manage local and remote printers.

Printer Command Language (PCL)   A common language used by printers to describe how a page is printed.

printer driver packages   Enhanced printer drivers that can contain additional software.

printer driver store   A location in Windows 10 that caches printer drivers and is capable of storing multiple versions of a printer driver.

printer driver   Software used by Windows 10 to properly communicate with a specific make and model of printer.

private network   The location type that is used for trusted networks where limited security is required, such as a small office.

product activation   A license verification process that Microsoft instituted to reduce piracy.

Protected EAP   An enhanced variation of EAP that secures authentication by using TLS. For PPTP VPN connections, it can secure MS-CHAP v2 authentication.

protocol   A standard set of rules that defines how different components of a system operate together.

provisioning   A configuration process for Windows 10 that modifies the configuration of an already installed Windows 10 operating system to match corporate standards. Windows Configuration Designer creates provisioning packages that perform that configuration.

public network   The location type that is used for untrusted networks where high security is required, such as a public wireless hotspot.

public profile   A profile that is merged with all other user profiles. The public profile does not contain an Ntuser.dat file.

Q

Quality of Service (QoS)   A process of measuring and managing the effective delivery of network traffic by devices involved in the timely delivery of data that is sensitive to delays, packet retry or loss, inefficient paths, and bottlenecks (e.g., digital video).

Quick Assist   A remote control tool for Windows 10 that works well over the Internet and through firewalls.

R

RADIUS server   A server that operates according to the Remote Authentication Dial-In User Service protocol defined as an Internet Engineering Task Force (IETF) standard that provides authentication, authorization, and accounting for users who connect to use a network service. In a Windows environment RADIUS typically operates as a service using user data and certificate services related to Active Directory data and supporting services.

recovery drive   An external drive, which can include Windows installation files, that is configured with WinRE as bootable media for repairing and troubleshooting Windows 10.

Registry Editor   The graphical tool, commonly known as regedit, included in Windows 10 to edit the registry.

registry key   A section within a hive that can contain other registry keys and values; it appears similar to a folder in the Registry Editor.

registry   A central store for application and operating system configuration information in Windows 10.

Reliability Monitor   A utility that rates the system stability of Windows 10 over time and correlates system events with changes in system stability.

Remote Assistance   A feature in Windows 10 that allows a helper to connect to a Windows 10 computer and view the screen or to remotely control the computer.

Remote Desktop Connection   The client software included in Windows 10 that uses RDP to connect to Remote Desktop and RDS. It can be started at a command line with additional options by running mstsc.exe.

Remote Desktop Services   A server role for Windows Server that is used to provide virtual desktops and RemoteApp programs to users.

Remote Desktop   The feature in Windows 10 that you can enable to allow remote control of the computer by using RDP on port 3389.

remote procedure calls (RPC)   An older network communication protocol that uses randomized port numbers.

RemoteApp   A feature in Remote Desktop Services that presents clients with a single app in a window.

removable media installation   An installation of Windows 10 that is started by booting from removable media, such as a DVD or USB drive, to run Setup.exe.

Reset this PC   A recovery option for Windows 10 that removes apps and puts settings back at their default values; also provides an option to retain user data.

Resilient File System (ReFS)   A file system that supports basic NTFS-like features but is optimized for very large volumes. Windows 10 supports ReFS only with Storage Spaces technology.

Resource Monitor   A utility that provides real-time monitoring of the most common system performance indicators.

restore point   A snapshot of operating system and program files at a specific point in time that can be restored to roll back to a point in time when the operating system or apps were stable.

roaming profile   A user profile, which moves with a user from computer to computer, that is stored in a network location and is accessible from multiple computers.

route   A command-line utility that can be used to display and manage the routing table.

routing table   A data table that is used by Windows 10 to select the next IP address data must be delivered to, to ultimately deliver data to a given target address.

S

S0 state   The ACPI power state used when a computer is fully functioning. Power can be disabled to specific devices as requested by the operating system, but keeps the overall system running.

S3 state   An ACPI power state that disables power to all devices except RAM.

S4 state   An ACPI power state that saves the contents of RAM to disk and then disables power to all devices including RAM; also referred to as the hibernate state.

schema partition   The Active Directory partition that holds the definition of all Active Directory objects and their attributes. It is replicated to all domain controllers in the Active Directory forest.

secure sign-in   A sign-in method that adds the requirement to press Ctrl+Alt+Delete before signing in.

Secure Socket Tunneling Protocol (SSTP)   A VPN protocol that uses SSL to secure authentication credentials and data.

Security Accounts Manager (SAM) database   The database used by Windows 10 to store local user and group information.

security identifier (SID)   A user- or group-specific number that is added to the access control list of a resource when a user or group is assigned access.

security key   A hardware device that uniquely identifies a user, requiring a PIN or biometric information to unlock the security key.

Security Set Identifier (SSID) A unique ID that identifies a wireless access point to the wireless networking clients that send data to it.

Server Message Block (SMB) A network sharing protocol implemented in Windows to share resources between a client and server.

Server Message Block (SMB) The protocol used for Windows-based file and printer sharing.

service A Windows application that runs in the background without user interaction.

Services An MMC console used to manage Windows services.

Settings A central interface for managing common Windows 10 settings. It is available on the Start menu.

SIM A subscriber identity module, typically a small removeable card, used to securely identify a device (e.g., cell phone) to a telephone carrier and associate the device to a paid cellular subscription.

smart card A physical card containing a certificate that can be used as an authentication method.

Software Restriction Policies An older technology that is used to control which programs can run in Windows 10.

specialize configuration pass The configuration pass that is performed after hardware has been detected. This is the most common configuration pass to apply settings.

standard user account A type of user account that does not have privileges to modify settings for other users. This type of account is a member of the Users local group.

Standard User Analyzer (SUA) A tool included as part of the Windows 10 ADK that can be used to monitor apps, identify why they are not compatible with Windows 10, and provide fixes.

Start menu A menu in Windows 10 that allows users to access applications installed on their computer.

stateful automatic address configuration In IPv6, this is automatic address configuration by using DHCPv6.

stateless automatic address configuration In IPv6, this is automatic address configuration obtained from the network routers.

Steps Recorder A tool that can be used to record the steps required to generate a problem and store the steps and screenshots in a file.

storage pool A logical collection of disks that have been allocated to Storage Spaces. Disks must be assigned to a storage pool before Storage Spaces can use them.

Storage Spaces volume A virtual disk created from the space made available by a storage pool in Storage Spaces. Also referred to as a storage space.

Storage Spaces A Microsoft software-based disk pooling technology that allows for different levels of resiliency to disk failure and provides virtualized volume storage within the disk pool.

subnet mask A number that defines which part of an IP address is the network ID and which part is the host ID.

symbolic link A file that contains a reference to another file in the file system, using an absolute or relative path as a shortcut.

symmetric encryption algorithm An encryption algorithm that uses the same key to encrypt and decrypt data.

Sysprep A tool that is used to generalize Windows 10 and prepare computers for imaging.

System Audit Mode cleanup action An option in Sysprep that triggers the computer to enter audit mode and run the auditSystem and auditUser configuration passes on reboot.

System Configuration The administrative tool that gives you access to control the boot configuration, service startup, application startup, and system tools.

System Information A tool that provides detailed information about Windows 10 hardware and software configuration.

System Out-of-Box Experience (OOBE) cleanup action An option in Sysprep that triggers the computer to run the oobeSystem configuration pass and start Windows Welcome on reboot.

T

takeown A legacy command-line utility that allows the administrator to take over ownership of a file by making the administrator the owner of the file.

Task Manager A utility that allows you to view a summary of current system performance information and manage processes.

Task Scheduler A utility that allows you to schedule tasks to run at a particular time or based on the occurrence of specific events.

Task View A display that shows currently running applications and provides the capability to switch between virtual desktops.

taskbar A horizontal bar at the bottom of the desktop that contains the Start menu, search area, running application icons, and the notification area.

Time To Live (TTL) The time a piece of data is allowed to exist before it is considered obsolete and replaceable.

tracert A command-line utility that can be used to trace the routers involved in establishing an IP communication path between the computer running the command and a target address.

U

unattend.xml An answer file that is automatically searched for during the generalize, specialize, auditSystem, auditUser, and oobeSystem configuration passes.

unattended installation An installation that does not require any user input because all necessary configuration information is provided by an answer file.

unicast A type of network address that is assigned to a single computer or device.

Universal Naming Convention (UNC) path A UNC path specifies how to locate a resource, such as a shared folder, on a network.

Universal Windows Platform (UWP) An application environment subsystem that is designed to make development easier across multiple device form factors.

upgrade installation An installation that migrates all of the settings from a preexisting Windows operating system to Windows 10.

user account Required account used for authentication to prove the identity of a person signing in to Windows 10.

User Account Control (UAC) A feature in Windows 10 that elevates user privileges only when required.

User Accounts applet A legacy interface for user management in Control Panel.

User Experience Virtualization (UE-V) A system that provides advanced options for synchronizing profile settings for roaming users.

user profile A collection of desktop and environment configurations for a specific user or group of users. By default, each user has a separate profile stored in C:\Users.

User State Migration Tool (USMT) A set of scriptable command-line utilities that are used to migrate user settings and files from a source computer to a destination computer.

V

Virtual Desktop A new feature that allow you to create virtual desktops with unique sets of running applications.

virtual hard disk (VHD) A file that is internally structured to store data like a file system. You attach a VHD file in Windows 10 to access its contents.

virtual memory A paging file on disk that is used to simulate physical memory.

virtual private network (VPN) An encrypted connection from a client to a remote access server over a public network.

virtual smart card An authentication method similar to a smart card, but the certificate is stored in a TPM on the motherboard rather than on a physical card.

Volume Activation Management Tool (VAMT) A tool included as part of the Windows ADT that allows you to configure a computer as an activation proxy or KMS host.

volume licensing A license agreement that an organization enters into with Microsoft that provides licenses for Windows 10. Software is downloadable from a website.

Volume Master Key (VMK) The key used to encrypt hard drive data when BitLocker Drive Encryption is enabled.

volume mount points Empty folders in an NTFS-formatted file system that are used to point to other FAT, FAT32, or NTFS partitions.

volumes Regions of disk space reserved to store file data. The term is used to generically refer to both dynamic disk volumes and basic disk partitions.

VPN Reconnect A feature of IKEv2 VPN connections that automatically reconnects after a network interruption.

W

Wi-Fi Direct A specification developed by the Wi-Fi Alliance as a peer-to-peer wireless connection technology that allows devices to securely discover, connect, and transfer information among one another without setting up and attaching each device to a WAP first.

Windows 10 Assessment and Deployment Kit (ADK)   A collection of utilities and documentation for automating the deployment of Windows 10.

Windows 10 Education   The edition of Windows 10 that is oriented to educational institutions. The feature set is equivalent to Windows 10 Enterprise.

Windows 10 Enterprise   This edition of Windows 10 is oriented to larger organizations. The feature set contains additional options for manageability and security.

Windows 10 Enterprise Long Term Servicing Channel (LTSC)   The variation of Windows 10 Enterprise that is optimized to reduce updates in specialized environments. Some features of Windows 10 Enterprise are removed.

Windows 10 Home   The edition of Windows 10 that is oriented to home users.

Windows 10 in S mode   A mode that limits Windows 10 to running only applications from the Microsoft store.

Windows 10 Pro   The edition of Windows 10 that is oriented to small and mid-sized organizations. A key feature in this edition is the ability to join a domain.

Windows 10 Pro Education   The edition of Windows 10 that is oriented to educational institutions that do not need the full features of Windows 10 Education. The feature set is equivalent to Windows 10 Pro.

Windows 10 Pro for Workstations   The edition of Windows 10 that is oriented to data analysts and engineers that need a higher level of processing power and more memory.

Windows API   An application environment subsystem, available as Win32 and Win 64, that is used by Windows programmers.

Windows AutoPilot   A cloud-based service that is used to automate the provisioning of computers running Windows 10.

Windows Configuration Designer   A tool in the Windows 10 ADK that is used to create provisioning packages.

Windows Defender Antivirus   Anti-malware software included with Windows 10 that scans memory and the file system.

Windows Defender Application Guard   A feature that mitigates risk when browsing websites by isolating Microsoft Edge in memory.

Windows Defender Firewall and Advanced Security utility   A utility that is used to configure Windows Defender Firewall and IPSec rules.

Windows Defender Firewall   A host-based firewall included with Windows 10 that can perform inbound and outbound packet filtering. In previous editions of Windows, this was referred to as Windows Firewall.

Windows Defender Smartscreen   Anti-malware software included with Windows 10 that monitors downloads from the Internet and malicious websites.

Windows Deployment Services (WDS)   A role in Windows Server that you can use to deploy images over the network.

Windows Hello   Infrastructure in Windows 10 that supports passwordless authentication.

Windows Hello for Business   An enhanced passwordless authentication system that uses certificates to uniquely identify each user.

Windows image (WIM)   A file-based image format developed by Microsoft to store multiple images in a single file.

Windows Internet Naming Service (WINS)   A system used to resolve computer NetBIOS names to IP addresses.

Windows Memory Diagnostics Tool   A utility used to perform tests on the physical memory of a computer.

Windows on Windows 64 (WOW64)   A system in Windows that allows 32-bit Windows apps to run on a 64-bit operating system.

Windows PE   A limited version of Windows that can be used to perform recovery tasks and install Windows 10.

Windows PowerShell   An enhanced command-line interface that can be used to perform administrative tasks.

Windows PowerShell ISE   An integrated scripting environment for Windows PowerShell that includes color coding as you type, along with debugging functionality.

Windows PowerShell remoting   A method that you can use to run Windows PowerShell cmdlets and scripts on a remote computer over the network.

Windows Recovery Environment (WinRE)   A small instance of Windows 10 with options for troubleshooting and repairing Windows 10.

Windows Remote Management (WinRM)   A web-based remote management protocol that is used by PowerShell remoting and contains some administration tools.

Windows Server Update Services (WSUS)   A Windows Server application that is used to control the process of downloading and applying updates to Windows servers and Windows clients.

Windows System Image Manager (SIM)   A utility that is used to create answer files for Windows 10 unattended installations. Windows SIM can also create distribution shares and configuration sets.

Windows Update for Business   Settings that allow you to delay the installation of feature updates and quality updates for up to one year.

Windows Update   A feature in Windows 10 that automatically downloads and installs updates.

Windows Virtual Desktop   A cloud-based service hosted in Windows Azure that provides access to remote desktops or RemoteApp programs.

windowsPE configuration pass   The first configuration pass performed during Setup, which can be used to perform tasks such as disk partitioning and entering the product key.

wireless access point (WAP)   A device that allows wireless devices to connect through it to a wired network.

Wireless Ad Hoc   A standard allowing computers to communicate with one another dynamically without centralized administration.

Wireless Fidelity (Wi-Fi) Alliance   A nonprofit organization that promotes Wi-Fi technology and certifies products to its standards.

Wireless Hosted network   A form of wireless ad hoc networking introduced as a feature by Microsoft with Windows 7.

Work Folders   A system that allows users to synchronize a single folder on a file server between multiple devices. The Work Folders client is included in Windows 10.

workgroup   A networking model that organizes computers for browsing but does not centralize authentication or management.

WPA2-Enterprise   A modern security type for wireless networks that uses 802.1x authentication.

WPA2-Personal   A modern security type for wireless networks that uses a pre-shared key for authentication.

WPA3-Personal   Stronger encryption and attack protection than WPA2-Personal.

X

x64 architecture   The processor architecture that is required to support the 64-bit version of Windows 10.

XML Paper Specification (XPS)   A document format, similar to Adobe Portable Document Format (PDF), that describes how a page should be displayed.

INDEX

16-bit software, 6
32-bit versions, 6
802.1x protocol, 137
802.11 mode, 135

A

access control assistance operators, 74
access control entry (ACE), 188
access control list (ACL), 188
accessories and shortcuts
    graphics editing, 293
    text editing, 292–93
account lockout policy, 215–16
account policies, 214–16
    account lockout policy, 215–16
    password policy, 214–15
accounts settings, 26
ACT (Application Compatibility Toolkit), 228, 288. *See also* app compatibility
Action Center, 17
Active Directory (AD), 2, 11
    DNS, 363–64
    domain, 365–66
    domain controller, 359
    offline domain join process, 366–67
    organizational units (OUs), 360
    partitions, 363
    server roles, 361–62
    site, 363
    sites and replication, 363
    time synchronization, 366
    trees and forests, 360–62
address prefix, 123–24
administrative tools
    command-line administration tools (*See* command-line administration tools)
    computer management, 32–33
    Microsoft Management Console (MMC), 29, 31–32
    services, 33–36
administrator, 72–73
advanced auditing, 225
advanced audit policy settings, 224–25
advanced authentication methods
    dynamic lock, 93
    personal identification number (PIN) authentication, 90
    picture password authentication, 90
    security key, 92–93
    smart cards, 93
    Windows Hello Biometric Authentication, 91–92
    Windows Hello for Business, 92
    Windows Hello PIN, 90–91
advanced Configuration and Power Interface (ACPI), 53–54
Advanced Encryption Standard (AES), 137
advanced network settings, 102
advanced window management, 18–19
airplane mode, 138–39
alerts, 333–34
alternate IP configuration, 114
Android, 3
answer file, 422
    creating, 424–45
    locations, 424
    names, 424
    updating, 424–45
app compatibility, 228, 288. *See also* ACT (Application Compatibility Toolkit)
    Application Virtualization (App-V), 315
    Client Hyper-V, 314
    Desktop Analytics, 314
    RemoteApp, 314–15
    settings for executables, 311–12
    virtual desktop infrastructure, 314–15
    Windows ADK tools, 312–14
App history tab, 327
Application Compatibility Toolkit (ACT), 228, 288. *See also* app compatibility
application environments
    legacy applications, 300
    .NET Framework, 299
    subsystem, 297
    Universal Windows Platform (UWP), 299
    Windows API, 298
application programmer interfaces (APIs), 2, 297
Application Virtualization (App-V), 4, 315
AppLocker
    auditing, 218
    configuring, 222–23
    definition, 217
    rule collections, 218–19
    rule conditions, 220–21
    rule exceptions, 221
    rule permissions, 219–20
apps settings, 26

Assessment and Deployment Kit (ADK)
    downloading, 420–21
    installing, 421–22
    tools, 419
    Windows PE, 420
assigned access, 70–71
asymmetric encryption, 240–41
attrib, 187
auditing
    Advanced auditing, 225
    Advanced Audit Policy Settings, 224–25
    Auditing File Access, 226–27
    Basic auditing, 225
    file access, 226–27
Auditing File Access, 226–27
auditSystem configuration pass, 430
auditUser configuration pass, 430
authentication protocols, 406–7
automated deployment, 404–6
Automatic Private IP Addressing (APIPA), 113, 124
automatic sample submission, 234
automatic sign-in, 70
automating MSI installation, 305–7
autounattend.xml, 424
Away Mode, 55
Azure AD, 380
    account, 400
    Join, 21, 96, 380–81

B

Background Intelligent Transfer Service (BITS),
    378
backup. *See* file recovery and backup
Backup and Restore (Windows 7), 347
backup operators, 74
baseline, 322
basic auditing, 225
basic disks, 165
BitLocker Drive Encryption, 246–51
    BitLocker Encryption Keys, 247
    BitLocker Hard Drive Configuration, 247
    BitLocker Network Unlock, 249
    BitLocker To Go, 251
    disabling, 250
    enabling, 248–49
    recovering, 250–51
    Recovering BitLocker-Encrypted Data, 249–50
BitLocker Encryption Keys, 247
BitLocker Hard Drive Configuration, 247
BitLocker Network Unlock, 249
BitLocker To Go, 251
boot image, 444

bottleneck
    disk bottlenecks, 322–23
    memory bottlenecks, 323
    network bottlenecks, 324
    processor bottlenecks, 323
BranchCache, 378–79
branch office direct printing, 283–84
bring your own devices (BYOD), 439
browsers
    group policy settings, 288
    IE Mode, 289–91
    Microsoft Edge, 285–88
    security zones, 287–88
built-in local groups, 74–75

C

cable, 129
cached credentials, 95–96
capture image, 444
catalog file, 425
cellular, 130
Chromium-based Microsoft Edge, 286
cipher, 187
clean installation, 417
cleanup actions, 430–31
Click-to-Run, 310
Client Hyper-V, 314, 361
cloud-based protection, 234
command-line administration tools
    command prompt, 36–37
    Windows PowerShell (*See* Windows PowerShell)
command-line interface (CLI), 36
command-line options, 431–33
command prompt, 36–37
component services, 30
compressed files, copying and moving, 188
computer hardware, 2
computer management, 30, 32–33
configuration options, 281–82
configuration partition, 363
configuration passes, 430
configuration set, 425, 426
configuration settings, 286–87
configuring Windows, 266–67
Config.xml, 443
confirm current settings
    IP version 4, 120
    IP version 6, 128
connections
    clients, 107
    network drivers, 107
    protocols, 107

Quality of Service (QoS), 107
Server Message Block (SMB), 107
services, 107
viewing, 108
controlling application startup
managing application startup, 336–38
startup methods, 338–39
Control Panel, 27
Cortana settings, 27
counters, 330–31
CPU tab, 328
Create A Shared Folder Wizard, 202–3
credential roaming, 399
cryptographic operators, 74

D

data collector sets, 332–33
data connections
IP version 6, 129
Data Execution Prevention (DEP), 237, 336
data manager, 334
data security
BitLocker Drive Encryption, 246–51
encrypting file system (EFS), 242–46
encryption algorithms, 240–41
data synchronization, 409–12
definition, 409
offline files, 410–11
OneDrive, 410
work folders, 411–12
default folder permissions, 188–89
default gateways, 112
default groups, 74–75
default profile, 85–86
default user accounts
administrator, 72–73
guest account, 73
initial account, 74
other accounts, 74
Deployment Imaging Servicing and Management
(DISM), 415
full flash update (FFU), 437
image file formats, 433–34
image maintenance, 438–39
provisioning, 439–42
Windows image (WIM), 434–37
Windows PE Boot Media Creation, 434–35
Desktop Analytics, 314
desktop backgrounds, 44
device drivers, 48–49, 425
compatibility, 49
signing, 51–52

device identification string, 372
device installation
controlling, 374
Group Policy settings, 373
identifying devices, 372
removable storage Group Policy settings, 373–74
device manager, 32, 49–51
device owners, 74
device security, 238–39
device setup class, 372
devices settings, 25
DHCP Unique Identifier (DUID), 127
dial-up, 130
digital subscriber line (DSL), 129
direct access, 409
DirectX 9, 41
discover image, 444
disk bottlenecks, 322–23
disk management, 32
Disk Management console, 167
DiskPart, 167–69
disk partition styles, 165
disk quotas, 180–82
disk systems
basic disks, 165
disk partition styles, 165
disk technology, 164
dynamic disks, 165–66
external disk, 164
file and folder attributes, 185–88
file and folder permissions, 188–96
file sharing (See file sharing)
file system (See file system)
internal disk, 164
management tools, 167–70
physical disks, 170–71
storage spaces, 166–67, 174–78
types, 165–67
virtual disk management tasks, 171–74
virtual hard disk (VHD), 164
Disk tab, 328–29
disk technology, 164
display
desktop backgrounds, 44
multiple monitors, 45–46
screen savers, 44–45
settings, 41–43
visual effects, 43–44
display resolution, 41
distributed cache mode, 379
Distributed File System (DFS), 377–78
distribution share installation, 416

domain, 365–66
domain-based network, 95. *See also*
      Active Directory (AD)
domain controllers (DCs), 20, 359
DomainKeys Identified Email (DKIM), 119
domain model, 20–21
Domain Name System (DNS), 21, 112
domain network, 104
domain partition, 363
drive letters, changing, 184
DVD boot installation, 7
dynamic disks, 165–66
Dynamic Host Configuration Protocol (DHCP), 113
dynamic link library (DLL), 218
dynamic lock, 93

E

ease of access
    features, 28
    settings, 26
Encapsulating Security Payload (ESP), 402
Encrypting File System (EFS), 79, 224, 242–46
    lost encryption keys, 243–44
    moving and copying encrypted files, 244
    recovering lost encryption keys, 245–46
    sharing encrypted files, 244
    using, 244–45
encryption algorithms, 240–41
    asymmetric encryption, 240–41
    hashing, 241
    symmetric encryption, 240
enhanced search, 264
enterprise clients
    Remote Desktop, 386–87
    troubleshooting, 385–86
enterprise deployment tools
    Microsoft Deployment Toolkit (MDT), 444–45
    User State Migration Tool (USMT), 442–43
    Windows AutoPilot, 445
    Windows Deployment Services (WDS), 443–44
enterprise file services
    BranchCache, 378–79
    distributed file system (DFS), 377–78
enterprise management tools
    Microsoft BitLocker Administration and Monitoring
      (MBAM), 376
    Microsoft Endpoint Configuration Manager, 376
    Windows Server Update Services (WSUS), 374–76
event logs, 342
    forwarding, 343
Event Viewer, 30, 32, 341
    event log forwarding, 343

event logs, 342
    finding events, 341–42
    scheduled tasks, 342
    using, 343–44
    Windows PowerShell, 344
exclusions, 234
Extensible Authentication Protocol (EAP), 407
external disk, 164

F

family settings integration, 68
Fast Startup, 57
fast user switching, 70
file access, 226–27
File Allocation Table (FAT), 178–79
File Explorer, 186
    configuring, 263
    libraries, 263–64
    ribbon tabs, 262–63
    search, 264–67
file/folder attributes
    compressed files, copying and moving, 188
    File Explorer, 186
    managing attributes, 187–88
file/folder permission
    advanced NTFS permissions, 190
    basic NTFS permissions, 190
    content, 194
    default folder permissions, 188–89
    effective permissions, 193
    managing, 195–96
    ownership, 193–94
    permission inheritance, 192
    permission scope, 190–92
    strategy considerations, 195
file history, 345–6
file recovery and backup
    Backup and Restore (Windows 7), 347
    configuring, 347
    file history, 345–46
    previous versions of files and folders, 347–49
file sharing
    creating, 198–205
    individual files, 196–97
    managing, 198–205
    monitoring, 205–07
    public folder, 197–98
file system. *See also* shared folders
    converting, 184–85
    File Allocation Table (FAT), 178–79
    New Technology File System (NTFS), 179–83
    Resilient File System (ReFS), 183–84

tasks, 184–85
    Universal Disk Format (UDF), 184
files migrating, 418
finding events, 341–42
folder attributes. *See* file/folder attributes
folder permission. *See* file/folder permission
folder redirection, 87, 399
Foreign Disk, 171
forest, 360
forget wireless networks, 138
fsutil, 188
full flash update (FFU), 437–38
full packaged product (FPP) license, 10
Full Volume Encryption Key (FVEK), 247
fully qualified domain name (FQDN), 112

G

gaming settings, 26
generalize configuration pass, 430
Generic Routing Encapsulation (GRE), 402
generic volume license key (GVLK), 12
global catalog server, 363
globally unique identifier (GUID), 372
graphics editing, 293
group policy, 2, 147
    configuring preferences, 370–71
    controlling device installation, 372–74
    inheritance, 368–69
    multiple local policies, 371
    preferences, 369–71
Group Policy object (GPO), 7
Group Policy Settings, 288, 373
Guaranteed unique identifier (GUID), 68
guest account, 73
GUID Partition Table (GPT), 165

H

hard disks. *See* disk systems
hard link, 183
hardware component installation, 52
hardware drivers, 2
hardware management
    device driver compatibility, 49
    device drivers, 48–49
    device driver signing, 51–52
    device manager, 49–51
    hardware component installation, 52
hardware requirements, 6–7
hashing algorithms, 241
HKEY_LOCAL_MACHINE, 301–02
HKEY_USERS, 301
hosted cache mode, 379

Hotspot 2.0 networks, 139–40
Hybrid sleep, 55
Hyper-V administrators, 75

I

icacls, 188
IEEE 802.11 Wireless, 134
IE Mode, 289–291
image-based installation, 416–17
image file formats, 433–34
image maintenance, 438–39
imaging
    auditSystem configuration pass, 430
    auditUser configuration pass, 430
    configuration passes, 430
    DISM (*See* Deployment Imaging Servicing and
        Management (DISM))
    generalize configuration pass, 430
    Sysprep (*See* Sysprep)
inbound rule, 151
Indexing Options dialog box, 265
inheritance, 368–69
initial account, 74
installation
    clean, 417–18
    distribution share installation, 416
    files, 418
    image, 416–17
    migrating user settings, 418
    Original Equipment Manufacturer (OEM) installation,
        416
    removable media installation, 416
    types, 417–18
    unattended installation, 422–29
    upgrade, 417
install image, 443
installing apps
    automating MSI installation, 305–07
    Microsoft 365 Apps, 310–11
    MSI file, 305
    MSIX deployment, 309–10
    UWP apps, 307–9
    Windows 10 in S mode, 310
Institute of Electrical and Electronics Engineers (IEEE), 132
Integrated Scripting Environment (ISE), 39
interactive logon, 217
internal disk, 164
Internet, 287
Internet Connection Sharing (ICS), 130, 131
Internet connectivity
    shared Internet connectivity, 130–33
    single-computer Internet connectivity, 129–30

Internet Key Exchange v2 Tunneling Protocol (IKEv2), 402

Internet Protocol version 4 (TCP/IPv4), 107. *See also* IP version 4

Internet Protocol version 6 (TCP/IPv6), 107. *See also* IP version 6

Internet settings, 26, 102

Internet settings categories, 102

Intune/Endpoint Configuration Manager, 147

iOS, 3

iPadOS, 3

ipconfig, 117–18

IPSec settings, 149–50

IP version 4

    addresses, 109–10

    configuring methods, 113–16

    confirm current settings, 120

    data connections, 121

    default gateways, 112

    domain name system (DNS), 112, 120

    ipconfig, 117–18

    IPv6, 125

    netstat command, 118

    nslookup command, 118–19

    PowerShell cmdlets, 119

    subnet masks, 110–11

    troubleshooting, 120–22

    validate connectivity, 120

    Windows Internet Naming Service (WINS), 112–13

IP version 6

    address notation, 123

    address types, 123–24

    automatic configuration, 127

    configuration commands, 127–28

    configuring methods, 125

    confirm current settings, 128

    data connections, 129

    DNS name resolution, 128–29

    global unicast, 124

    link-local unicast, 124

    multicast, 125

    special addresses, 125

    static configuration, 126–27

    troubleshooting, 128–29

    tunneling through IPv4, 125

    unique local unicast, 125

    validate connectivity, 128

isolation, 154

J

junction point, 183

K

Kerberos, 402

Key Management Service (KMS), 11

L

language settings, 26

Layer 2 Tunneling Protocol (L2TP), 402

legacy power management, 55

libraries, 263–64

    file management issues, 263

    using, 264

Link-Layer Topology Discovery Mapper I/O Driver, 107

Link-Layer Topology Discovery Responder, 107

Linux, 3

Local area network (LAN), 401

local intranet, 287

local printing, 273

Local Users and Groups, 32

Local Users and Groups MMC snap-in, 79–83

location type, 103–04

lock screen, 14–15

Long Term Servicing Branch, 252

lost encryption keys, 243–44

M

MacOS, 3

malicious software. *See* malware

malware

    app & browser control, 237–38

    device security, 238–39

    virus and threat protection, 232–36

    Windows Defender Advanced Threat Protection (ATP), 231

mandatory profiles, 86

mapped drive letters, 398–99

Master Boot Record (MBR), 165

MBR2GPT, 165

memory bottlenecks, 323

Memory tab, 328

Microsoft 365 Apps, 310–11

Microsoft Account, 400

Microsoft apps integration, 68

Microsoft BitLocker Administration and Monitoring (MBAM), 376

Microsoft cloud services, 379–80

    Azure AD, 380

    Azure AD Join, 380–81

    Microsoft Intune, 381

Microsoft Deployment Toolkit (MDT), 444–45

Microsoft Edge, 288

    Chromium-based Microsoft Edge, 286

configuration settings, 286–87
configure, 286–87
group policy settings, 288
Microsoft endpoint configuration manager, 376
Microsoft Intune, 381
Microsoft LLDP Protocol Driver, 107
Microsoft Management Console (MMC), 29, 31–32, 302
Microsoft Store for Business, 308
migrating user settings, 418
migration process, 443
mklink, 183
MMC snap-in. *See* snap-in
Mobile Device Management (MDM), 21
mobile hotspot, 130–31
Modern Standby, 54–55
MSI file, 305
MSIX deployment, 309–10
Multiple Activation Key (MAK), 11
multiple disks, 164
multiple local policies, 371
multiple monitors, 45–46

N

naming conventions, 72
NetBIOS, 112
net command-line utility, 204
Net Commands, 204
.NET Framework, 299
netsh, 114, 147
netstat command, 118
Network Address Translation (NAT), 130
network bottlenecks, 324
network configuration operators, 75
networking
connections, 106–8
Internet settings, 102
remembered networks, 103–6
sharing center, 102–3
tools, 116–19
network integration
Azure AD join, 96
cached credentials, 95–96
domain-based network, 95
peer-to-peer network, 94
network printer, 274
networks. *See also* wireless networking
discovery, 104–6
driver, 107
location awareness, 103
name, 103
settings, 26, 407–8

settings categories, 102
status, 102
Network tab, 329
network time protocol (NTP), 366
new computer-connection security rules creating, 154
New Technology File System (NTFS)
disk quotas, 180–82
symbolic link, 183
volume mount points, 182–83
notification area, 17–18
nslookup command, 118–19

O

offline domain join process, 366–67
offline files, 410–11
offlineServicing Configuration Pass, 423
offline updates, 426–29
OneDrive, 410
client, 267–68
controlling network utilization, 270–71
managing files, 270
managing synchronization, 270
OneDrive for Business, 271
Personal Vault, 271
sharing files, 270
sharing folders, 270
using, 271–72
web interface, 268–70
OneDrive data synchronization, 410
OneDrive for Business, 271
oobeSystem configuration pass, 423
Open Database Connectivity (ODBC), 30
operating systems
alternative, 3
applications, 1
architecture, 2
Windows 10 Extras, 2
optional features, 46–48
organizational units (OUs), 360
original equipment manufacturer (OEM)
installation, 416
license, 10
Outbound rule, 152
ownership, 193

P

packaged app, 218
page description languages, 275
partitions, 363
partition table, 165
Passpoint, 135
pass-through authentication, 94

Password Authentication Protocol (PAP), 407
password policy, 214–15
password protected sharing, 198
password reset capability, 68
peer-to-peer network, 94
performance, 32
    log users, 75
performance monitoring, 30
    alerts, 333–34
    counters, 330–31
    data collector sets, 332–33
    data manager, 334
    definition, 329–30
    reports, 334–35
    resource monitor, tools, 327–29
    task manager, tools, 324–25
    users, 75
    using, 331–32
performance options, 335–36
Performance tab, 326
performance tuning
    baseline, 322
    bottleneck (*See* bottleneck)
    overview, 321–22
    tuning performance, 324
personal area network (PAN), 132
personal identification number (PIN)
            authentication, 90
personalization settings, 26
Personal Vault, 271
phone settings, 26
physical disks, 170–71
    moving drives, 171
    new drive adding, 170–71
picture password authentication, 90
ping command, 118
pixel, 41
Point-to-Point Protocol over Ethernet (PPPoE), 129
Point-to-Point Tunneling Protocol (PPTP), 402
Portable Document Format (PDF), 275
PostScript, 275
power button options, 57–58
powercfg.exe., 58–59
power management
    Advanced Configuration and Power Interface (ACPI),
            53–54
    Fast Startup, 57
    legacy power management, 55
    Modern Standby, 54–55
    power button options, 57–58
    power plans, 55–57
    troubleshooting power management, 58–60

power plans, 55–57
PowerShell cmdlets, 119, 154
power users, 75
Printer Command Language (PCL), 275
printer configuration, 281–85
    branch office direct printing, 283–84
    configuration options, 281–82
    managing print jobs, 284–85
    printer sharing, 283
    security, 283
printer drivers
    packages, 274
    page description languages, 275
    printer driver store, 275–76
    staging, 276
    store, 275–76
printer management tools, 277–80
    devices, 278–79
    printers, 277, 278–79
    print management snap-in, 277, 279–80
    scanners, 277–78
printer sharing, 283
printing
    drivers, 274–76
    local printing, 273
    network printer, 274
    printer configuration, 281–85
    printer management tools, 277–80
    scenarios, 273–74
    shared printer, 274
print management, 30
print management snap-in, 277, 279–80
privacy settings, 27
private network, 104
Processes tab, 325–26
processor bottlenecks, 323
product activation, 10
profile information synchronization, 68
profile synchronization, 400
protocols, 401–3
public folder, 197–98
public network, 104
public profile, 87–90

Q

Quick Assist, 393–94

R

RADIUS server, 137
random access memory (RAM), 6
real-time protection, 234
Recovering BitLocker-Encrypted Data, 249–50

recovery drive, 30, 355
reg.exe, 303–4
registry
  definition, 300
  editing tools, 302–5
  structure, 300–2
registry editing tools
  backup restoring, 303
  Registry Editor, 302
  Windows PowerShell, 304–5
Registry Editor, 30, 302, 396–97
registry key, 301
reliability monitor, 340
remembered networks, 103–6
remote access, 400–1
RemoteApp, 314–16
remote assistance, 391–93
remote desktop, 386–91
  connection, 388–391
  enabling, 387–88
  settings, 387
Remote Desktop Connection, 388–91
Remote Desktop Protocol (RDP), 315, 388
Remote Desktop Services
  RemoteApp, 315–16
  remote desktop protocol (RDP), 315
  session-based virtual desktops, 315
  virtual desktops, 316–17
  virtual machine-based virtual desktops, 315
  Windows virtual desktop, 317
remote desktop users, 75
remote management users, 75
remote procedure calls (RPC), 394
removable media installation, 416
replicator, 75
reports, 334–35
Reset this PC, 350
Resilient File System (ReFS), 183–84
Resource Monitor, 30, 327–29
  CPU tab, 328
  Disk tab, 328–29
  Memory tab, 328
  Network tab, 329
  using, 329
restore points, 353–55
restricted sites, 288
ribbon tabs
  File, 262
  Home, 262
  Share, 262
  View, 262
roaming profile, 86–87

roaming user
  credential roaming, 399
  folder redirection, 399
  mapped drive letters, 398–99
  profile synchronization, 400
  user experience virtualization (UE-V), 399
router connection sharing, 130
routing table, 112
rule collection, 219
rule conditions, 220–21
rule exceptions, 221
rule permissions, 219–220

S

scanners, 277–78
scheduled tasks, 342
schema partition, 363
screen savers, 44–45
script, 218
search, 264–67
  configuring Windows, 266–67
  enhanced search, 264
  Indexing Options dialog box, 265
  settings, 265
Search interface, 16
search settings, 26
Secure boot, 239
secure sign-in, 68–70
Secure Sockets Layer (SSL), 402
Secure Socket Tunneling Protocol
      (SSTP), 402
security, 283
security key, 92–93
security policies
  account policies, 214–16
  Advanced Audit Policy Configuration, 224
  AppLocker, 217–23
  IP Security Policies, 224
  local policies, 216–17
  Local Security Policy, 213–14
  Network List Manager Policies, 224
  Public Key Policies, 224
  Software Restriction Policies, 223
  Windows Defender Firewall with Advanced
      Security, 223
Security Set Identifier (SSID), 135
security settings, 27
Security zones, 287–88
Semi-Annual Channel, 252
Sender Policy Framework (SPF), 119
Server Message Block (SMB), 203
server roles, 361–62

service, 33–36
Services tab, 327
session-based virtual desktops, 315
settings, 265
    access features, 28–29
    categories, 25–27
    display, 41–43
    ease of access, 26
    exploring, 28
    gaming, 26
    Internet, 26
    language, 26
    network, 26
    personalization, 26
    phone, 26
    search, 26
    security, 27
    system, 25
    time, 26
    update, 27
Shake feature, 18
shared folders, 32
    advanced folder sharing, 200–2
    Create A Shared Folder Wizard, 202–3
    creating, 198–99
    managing, 198–99
    monitoring, 205–7
    Net Commands, 204
    PowerShell, 203
    simplified folder sharing, 199–200
shared Internet connectivity
    Internet Connection Sharing (ICS), 130, 131
    mobile hotspot, 130–31
    Network Address Translation (NAT), 130
    router connection sharing, 130
    Wi-Fi Direct, 132–33
    Wireless Ad Hoc, 132
    wireless hosted network, 132
shared printer, 274
sharing center, 102–3
sharing encrypted files, 244
sharing files, 270
sharing folders, 270
shortcuts, 292
sign-in methods
    assigned access, 70–71
    automatic sign-in, 70
    fast user switching, 70
    secure sign-in, 68–70
    Windows sign-in screen, 68
SIM card, 130
Simple Mail Transfer Protocol (SMTP), 121

simplified folder sharing, 199–200
single-computer Internet connectivity
    cable, 129
    cellular, 130
    dial-up, 130
    digital subscriber line (DSL), 129
single set of credentials across devices, 57
smart cards, 93
snap-ins, 31
solid-state drives (SSDs), 322
specialize configuration pass, 423
staging, 276
standard user account, 75
Start menu, 15–16
startup methods, 338–39
Startup tab, 327
stateful automatic address configuration, 127
Steps Recorder, 339–340
storage cmdlets, 169
storage pool, 166–67
storage spaces, 166–67, 174–78
    fault tolerance, 177–78
    initial storage pool, 174–76
    storage pools, 176–77
subnet masks, 110–11
symbolic link, 183
symmetric encryption algorithm, 240
Sysprep
    cleanup actions, 430–31
    command-line options, 431–33
    definition, 429
    limitations, 431
System Audit Mode cleanup action, 431
System Configuration, 30
System Information, 30
system managed accounts group, 75
System Out-of-Box Experience (OOBE) cleanup action, 430
system recovery
    options, 349
    recovery drive, 355
    Reset this PC, 350
    restore points, 353–55
    system reset, 351
    Windows Recovery Environment (WinRE), 351–53
system reset, 351
system restore points, 354
system settings, 25

T

tamper protection, 234
taskbar, 16–17

477

.b, 326
es tab, 325–26
ervices tab, 327
Startup tab, 327
Users tab, 327
using, 327
tasks, 184–85
Task Scheduler, 30, 32
creating, 62–63
features, 61
network administrators, 60
using, 62
Task View, 18
TCP/IP network protocols, 107
TCP/IP version 4. *See* IP version 4
TCP/IP version 6. *See* IP version 6
Test-ComputerSecureChannel cmdlet, 365
text editing, 292
time settings, 26
time synchronization, 366
troubleshooting
enterprise clients, 385–86
Event Viewer, 341
IP version 4, 120–22
IP version 6, 128–89
MMC Snap-Ins, 394–96
power management, 58–60
Quick Assist, 393–94
Registry Editor, 396–97
reliability monitor, 340
Remote Assistance, 391–93
Remote Desktop, 386–91
steps recorder, 339–340
Windows PowerShell Remoting, 397–98
trusted sites, 287
tuning performance, 324

U

unattended installation, 422–29
answer file names, 424
answer file search locations, 424
configuration passes, 422–23
Windows System Image Manager (SIM), 424–29
unattend.xml, 424
Universal Disk Format (UDF), 184
Universal Naming Convention (UNC) path, 199
Universal Windows Platform (UWP), 299
apps, 307–9
unlocking removable storage, 251
update settings, 27

upgrading
Edition, 9
installation, 417
Windows 10, 9
User Account Control (UAC), 78
application manifest, 228
configuration, 228–30
options, 229–30
User accounts
administrator account, 76
advanced authentication methods, 90–93
command-line user management, 83–84
creating and managing, 75–84
default groups, 74–75
default user accounts, 72–74
local user account, 77
Local Users, 79–83
Microsoft account, 77–78
naming conventions, 72
network integration, 94–96
sign-in methods, 68–71
standard user account, 75
Start menu, 88–90
taskbar customization, 88–90
User Accounts applet, 78–79
user profile, 85–88
User Accounts applet, 78–79
User Environment Virtualization (UE-V),
4, 399, 418
user interface, 18
user profile
default profile, 85–86
folder redirection, 87
mandatory profiles, 86
public profile, 87–90
roaming profile, 86–87
users, 75, 327
User State Migration Tool (USMT), 418, 442–43
Config.xml, 443
migration process, 443
.xml files, 443

V

VHD. *See* virtual hard disk
virtual desktops, 18, 316–17
infrastructure, 314–15
virtual disk management tasks, 171–74
attaching, 173–74
creating, 172–73
detaching, 173–74
virtual hard disk (VHD), 164
boot image, 444
Client Hyper-V, 314
virtual machine-based virtual desktops, 315

virtual memory, 336
virtual private network (VPN)
    always On VPN, 408–9
    authentication protocols, 406–7
    automated deployment, 404–6
    clients, 401
    connection, 403–4
    data synchronization, 409–12
    direct access, 409
    network settings, 407–8
    protocols, 401–3
    remote access, 400–1
virus and threat protection, 232–36
    definitions, 233
    group policy configuration, 234
    protection history, 233–34
    ransomware protection, 234
    scanning, 232–33
    settings, 234
    Windows Defender Antivirus, 232, 236
    Windows PowerShell configuration, 235
visual effects, 43–44
Volume Activation Management Tool (VAMT), 12
volume licensing, 10
Volume Master Key (VMK), 247
volume mount points, 182–83
volumes, 165
VPN clients, 401
VPN connection
    authentication protocols, 406–7
    creating, 403–4
    deployment, 404–5
    network settings, 407
    Windows PowerShell, 406
VPN protocols
    Internet Key Exchange v2 Tunneling Protocol
        (IKEv2), 402
    Layer 2 Tunneling Protocol (L2TP), 402
    Point-to-Point Tunneling Protocol (PPTP), 402
    Secure Socket Tunneling Protocol (SSTP), 402

W

web interface, 268–70
Wi-Fi Direct, 132–33
Win32 apps, 298
Win64 apps, 298
Windows 10
    activating, 10–14
    editions, 3–6
    installing, 6–9
    licensing, 10
    networking models, 19–21

security policies, 213–24
S mode, 310
upgrading, 9
using, 14–19
Windows 10 Education, 5
Windows 10 Enterprise, 4
Windows 10 Enterprise Long Term Servicing Channel
    (LTSC), 4
Windows 10 Home, 3–4
Windows 10 N & KN editions, 5–6
Windows 10 Pro, 4
Windows 10 Pro Education, 5
Windows 10 Pro for Workstations, 4
Windows 64 (WOW64), 298
Windows ADK tools, 312–14
Windows API, 298
Windows AutoPilot, 445
Windows Defender Advanced Threat Protection (ATP),
    231
Windows Defender Antivirus, 232
Windows Defender Application Guard, 237
Windows Defender Firewall
    advanced configuration, 146–47
    basic configuration, 144–46
    configuring, 156–57
    configuring firewall properties, 148–49
    IPSec settings, 149–50
    monitoring, 154–56
    new computer-connection security rules creating,
        154
    new firewall rules creating, 152–53
    PowerShell Cmdlets, 154
    viewing and editing firewall rules, 150–51
Windows Defender Firewall with Advanced
        Security, 31
Windows Defender Smartscreen, 237
Windows Deployment Services (WDS), 443–44
    deployment process, 444
    images, 443–44
Windows Display Driver Model (WDDM), 41
Windows Hello Biometric Authentication, 91–92
Windows Hello for Business, 92
Windows Hello PIN, 90–91
Windows image (WIM), 434–37
Windows Insider Preview Branch, 252
Windows Installer, 218
Windows Internet Naming Service (WINS), 112–13
Windows Management Instrumentation (WMI), 33
Windows Memory Diagnostics Tool, 31
Windows PE, 420
Windows PE boot media creation, 434–35
windowsPE configuration pass, 423

147, 169–70, 344, 406
, 40–41

, 39
noting, 397–98
scripts, 39–40
Windows Recovery Environment (WinRE),
    351–53
Windows Remote Management (WinRM), 395
Windows Server Update Services (WSUS), 374–76
Windows sign-in screen, 68
Windows System Image Manager (SIM), 424–29
    answer file, 424–25
    configuration set, 425
    device drivers, 425
    offline updates, 426–29
Windows updates
    computer protecting, 256
    controlling, 252–55
    delivery optimization, 255
    Microsoft Store Apps, 256–57
    removing, 255–56
    servicing branches, 252
    Windows Updates for Business, 254–55
Windows virtual desktop, 317
Wired Equivalent Privacy (WEP), 137
wireless access point (WAP), 134
Wireless Ad Hoc, 132
wireless connections
    creating, 135–37
    managing, 137–40
    troubleshooting, 140–43

Wireless Fidelity (Wi-Fi) Alliance, 134
wireless hosted network, 132
wireless networking
    802.1x protocol, 137
    802.11 mode, 135
    airplane mode, 138–39
    connection
        creating, 135–37
        managing, 137–40
        troubleshooting, 140–43
    forget wireless networks, 138
    Hotspot 2.0 networks, 139–40
    IEEE 802.11 Wireless, 134
    properties, 136–37
    security, 135, 137
    Security Set Identifier (SSID), 135
    wireless access point (WAP), 134
    Wireless Fidelity (Wi-Fi) Alliance, 134
    WPA2-Enterprise, 137
    WPA2-Personal, 137
    WPA3-Personal, 137
WlanReport.html file, 142
work folders, 411–12
workgroup model, 20
WPA2-Enterprise, 137
WPA2-Personal, 137
WPA3-Personal, 137

X

x64 architecture, 6
.xml files, 443
XML Paper Specification (XPS), 275